W9-AXS-898

FROM "TWO GUYS WHO ARE ALWAYS GOOD"*

Jack W. Germond & Jules Witcover

An Eye-Opening, Challenging, And Important Book

★

WHOSE BROAD STRIPES AND BRIGHT STARS?

★

"FRESH AND SOMETIMES POLITICALLY EXPLOSIVE MATERIAL. . . . The showdown in Los Angeles is only one of the many memorable episodes that appear in Jack W. Germond and Jules Witcover's excellent book."
—*Washington Post Book World*

★

"SUSTENANCE FOR POLITICAL JUNKIES. . . . Valuable lessons for reporters and their bosses, who are faulted for giving the last campaign unusually shallow coverage."
—*New York Times Book Review*

★

"DETAILED, SOLID . . . good reporting . . . a fresh view."
—*San Jose Mercury-News*

★

"A WELL-RESEARCHED AND BEAUTIFULLY CRAFTED ACCOUNT. . . . As one would expect from these authors, it's all here."

—*Library Journal*

★

"THERE ISN'T A DULL PAGE . . . IT JUST BRISTLES ALONG."
—Larry King, *USA Today*

★

*David Brinkley

Also by Jack W. Germond and Jules Witcover
Blue Smoke and Mirrors: How Reagan Won and Why Carter Lost
    the Election of 1980
Wake Us When It's Over: Presidential Politics of 1984

Also by Jules Witcover
85 Days: The Last Campaign of Robert Kennedy
The Resurrection of Richard Nixon
White Knight: The Rise of Spiro Agnew
A Heartbeat Away: The Investigation and Resignation of
    Vice President Spiro T. Agnew (with Richard M. Cohen)
Marathon: The Pursuit of the Presidency, 1972–1976
The Main Chance (A Novel)
Sabotage at Black Tom: Imperial Germany's Secret War
    in America, 1914–1917

WHOSE BROAD STRIPES AND BRIGHT STARS?

The Trivial Pursuit of the Presidency 1988

Jack W. Germond & Jules Witcover

WARNER BOOKS

A Time Warner Company

Printed in the United States of America
First Trade Printing: November 1990
10 9 8 7 6 5 4 3 2 1

Library of Congress Cataloging-in-Publication Data

Germond, Jack.
  Whose broad stripes and bright stars? the trivial pursuit of the
presidency, 1988 / by Jack W. Germond and Jules Witcover.
      p.   cm.
  ISBN 0-446-39187-5
    1. Presidents—United States—Election, 1988.   2. United States—
Politics and government—1981-1989.   I. Witcover, Jules
II. Title.
E880.G47   1989
324.973′0927—dc20   88-40566
                                                                  CIP

Book design: H. Roberts
Cover design: Mike Stromberg
G. Bush photograph: Diana Walker/Time Magazine
M. Dukakis photograph: Frank Micelotta/Time Magazine

For Tom Ottenad, greatly missed on the campaign trail
by his old friends—and by the proprietors of
countless Italian restaurants.

"The whole aim of practical politics is to keep the populace alarmed (and hence clamorous to be led to safety) by menacing it with an endless series of hobgoblins, all of them imaginary."

H.L. Mencken

Acknowledgments

In chronicling the presidential campaign of 1988, we drew on the assistance of many individuals encountered at every level of the long experience, from the candidates and their strategists to campaign foot soldiers in the field, reporters who covered them and voters who decided their fates. After the verdict was in, we conducted nearly one hundred interviews to supplement and expand on our own observations. Among those who were generous with their time and insights during the campaign and afterward were these leading players in the drama:

Governor Michael S. Dukakis; Senators Lloyd Bentsen, Joseph Biden, Robert Dole, Albert Gore Jr., and Paul Simon; Representatives Richard Gephardt and Jack Kemp; former Governor Bruce Babbitt, former Senator Gary Hart, the Reverend Marion G. (Pat) Robertson and the Reverend Jesse L. Jackson. President George Bush would not consent to an interview but did answer written questions submitted by the authors. Vice President J. Danforth Quayle did not respond to repeated requests for an interview.

Others to whom we are particularly grateful for their assistance include:

In the Republican ranks: E. Spencer Abraham, Roger Ailes, Saul Anuzis, Lee Atwater, James A. Baker III, Charles Black, Rich Bond, Bill Brock, Joseph Canzeri, Richard Darman, John Engler, Robert Goodwin, David Keene, James Lake, Mary Matalin, Marc Nuttle, James Pinkerton, Tom Rath, Edward Rollins, Stuart Spencer, Roger Stone, Peter Teeley, Robert Teeter, Richard Wirthlin.

Among the Democrats: Gerald Austin, Charles Baker, Robert Borosage, Paul Brountas, Bonnie and Ed Campbell, Charles Campion, Bill Carrick, Jack Corrigan, Natalie Davis, Tad Devine, William Dixon, Tom Donilon, John Emerson, Susan Estrich, Bob Farmer, Tubby Harrison, Lanny Johnson, Ted Kaufman, Brian Lunde, Nick Mitropoulos, Richard Moe, Kirk O'Donnell, Tony Podesta, Larry Rasky, Will Robinson, John Sasso, Alice Travis, Joe Trippi, Paul Tully, Teresa Vilmain, John White.

And among our colleagues in the news media: Tom Bettag, Ken Bode, Ann Compton, Tom Fiedler, Susan Forrest, Ed Fouhy, David Hoffman, John

Mashek, Andrea Mitchell, Bernard Shaw, Margaret Warner, Paul West, David Yepsen.

We also appreciate the special help we received from Toni Grucninger and Richard E. Noyes of the Center for Media and Public Affairs of the American Enterprise Institute and from Alexander O'Meara and Ariane DeVogue of the Baltimore Sun Washington bureau library, and we thank Paul Witcover for his collaboration on the title. For Chapters 12 and 13, we drew particularly on the extensive reporting of the Miami Herald.

To all these, and to the many others who helped us in ways large and small along the way, we are indebted.

Jack W. Germond
Jules Witcover
Washington, D.C.

Contents

Introduction

In the spring of 1988, when the identities of the Democratic and Republican presidential nominees became clear, Democrat Michael S. Dukakis took to comparing the approaching election with that of 1960. Then as now, he repeatedly reminded his audiences, an extremely popular Republican president (Dwight D. Eisenhower in 1960, Ronald Reagan in 1988) was ineligible to seek another term and his vice president (Richard M. Nixon in 1960, George Bush in 1988) would be running against "a son of Massachusetts" (John F. Kennedy in 1960, Dukakis in 1988). And when Dukakis selected Senator Lloyd Bentsen to be his running mate, he was able to add to the parallel, noting that Kennedy had chosen another Texan (Senator Lyndon B. Johnson) to run with him, forming the "Boston-Austin Axis." It won in 1960 and, Dukakis suggested, it would win again in 1988.

He was wrong. The differences between these two presidential campaigns and elections twenty-eight years apart were great, and an examination of them charts a sea change in the country, in its politics and in how candidates and elections are observed and reported to the American electorate.

In 1960, Eisenhower was completing eight years of essentially caretaker government. He had spoken in opposition to the then-entrenched New Dealism of his immediate Democratic predecessors, Franklin D. Roosevelt and Harry S Truman, but had done little to root it out. Hard-line conservatism was then regarded as a fringe faction in the Republican Party and Senator Barry Goldwater, its emerging icon, as a somewhat daffy Neanderthal. Vice President Nixon seemed so centrist that one of Kennedy's prominent supporters, Harvard historian Arthur Schlesinger, Jr., felt compelled to write a campaign tome entitled "Kennedy or Nixon: Does It Make Any Difference?"

In 1988, in sharp contrast to Eisenhower, Reagan was winding up eight years of change in what was widely billed as "the Reagan Revolution." He was credited with burying the last vestiges of the New Deal in a relentless assault, rhetorically at least, on welfare government. Conservatism supposedly had not only come of age but had rooted itself in the national mainstream as firmly as had the New Deal. Vice President Bush embraced it, and Reagan, pledging to continue that "revolution." But George Bush was not Ronald Reagan. A central question to be resolved by the 1988 election was whether that revolution was genuine and lasting, or merely an aberration based on the extraordinary popularity of one man passing through the political scene.

That another revolution had occurred between 1960 and 1988 could not, however, be reasonably disputed. The political process for selecting the American president had undergone a fundamental transformation over this period, both structural and attitudinal. In 1960, the process began as it had since the end of World War II with primaries in both major parties in New Hampshire, where Kennedy and Nixon won without serious opposition, and ended in California with only a few stops between. By 1988, there were thirty-five state primaries, twenty of them by the Democrats and seventeen by the Republicans on a single "Super Tuesday."

The decisions to hold more primaries, to hold them earlier and to bunch them together as in the southern regional grouping had critical ramifications for the whole electoral process. The proliferation of early contests required a proliferation of professional consultants, pollsters and media experts—"hired guns" in the trade—to plan strategy and deploy resources, and of professional fundraisers to bankroll the expanded effort. Candidates' time, money and energy were stretched to a breaking point by the frenzied schedule that resulted, ultimately warping the nature of presidential campaigning and the reporting of it to the American voters. Candidates, like prizefighters herded into a Las Vegas casino for a televised bout, campaigned from television studios over satellite hookups and made quickie "media hits" from airport runways as they dashed by jet plane from one Super Tuesday state to several others in the course of a single day.

In 1960, when John Fitzgerald Kennedy declared his candidacy for the presidency, those of us who accompanied him were in the truest sense his traveling companions. Although from the start he was considered a major candidate and even, by some, the front-runner for the Democratic Party nomination, reporters were able to stroll the streets of small-town New Hampshire, Wisconsin or West Virginia at his side. You could chat and joke with him between handshaking excursions into neighborhood barber and butcher shops, cigar stores and groceries, many now gone from the Main Streets of America.

In a private car or on a campaign bus, the relatively few members of the press who were chronicling Kennedy's odyssey in those earliest days were able to observe and get to know him up close, in a manner unimaginable to most campaign reporters who took to the trail for the first time in 1988. There was relatively little buildup, either, for the campaign of 1960. Kennedy and one aide, usually Theodore Sorensen, unobtrusively visited party leaders in key states throughout 1959, quietly apprising them of Kennedy's plans to seek the Democratic nomination the following year. He did not declare his candidacy until early January of 1960, and only then did the national press corps pay much attention to him. There were no press planes or "zoo planes" carrying the "animals" of the press corps—the television cameramen, technicians and still photographers that would become standard in later election years. If you were very lucky, you might cadge a seat on the Kennedy family plane, the *Caroline*, named for Jack and Jackie's baby daughter.

The process was so intimate and relatively obscure to the public, in fact, that when author Theodore S. White produced his classic account of that campaign, *The Making of the President 1960*, it became an instant and overwhelming best-seller. The 1960 campaign on one level had taken place in full view, but not until after White in his dramatic fashion had told what it was like inside the Kennedy operation did American journalism really begin to lift the flap and peer into the tent of presidential elections and presidential candidates. Even at that, the country was to learn much later, matters of a personal nature went on that might have denied Kennedy the presidency had they been reported at the time.

Seven presidential elections and twenty-eight years later, as we set out to cover yet another campaign for the White House in 1988, the sort of intimate look at a man destined to be president of the United States that was possible in the election of 1960 was infinitely less feasible. For one thing, as a result of the mindless violence that visited President Kennedy in 1963, his brother Robert and the Reverend Martin Luther King, Jr., in 1968 and Alabama's Governor George Wallace in 1972, security for presidential candidates had become much more severe and restrictive. Secret Service agents, tell-tale wires plugged into their ears and their eyes endlessly scanning the crowds for suspicious characters, kept members of the press corps at bay. In 1988, long-shot candidates such as former Governors Pete duPont of Delaware and Bruce Babbitt of Arizona were as accessible as Kennedy had been in 1960, but those who were anointed by the polls or press opinion as serious contenders were effectively insulated from the rabble. It was still possible to gain access, for reporters of favored or influential publications, or those with personal or regional connections with a front-running candidate, but such access was hardly as commonplace as it was in 1960.

Importantly, too, the notion of presidential campaign as no-holds-barred battleground had entrenched itself between 1960 and 1988. Politics had always been extremely competitive, but the scale on which it was contested—in terms of money, manpower and mass-media persuasion—had raised the stakes and the willingness to pull out all the stops. The cliché of politics as the ultimate sports event continued but was increasingly replaced with the metaphor of politics as warfare. Platoons of campaign troops had become armies, and their generals—and sometimes unsupervised lieutenants—did what they had to do to win, skirting campaign finance and other laws on occasions, violating ethics on others. While the operative slogan was not yet "All's fair in politics and war," campaign conduct had often come perilously close to that. Dukakis, clinging to the sports analogy, called it a marathon, but it was more like running an obstacle course over marathon distance wearing full battle gear.

It was no surprise then, given the tone of the 1988 campaign, that about as many Americans eligible to vote turned their backs on the political process on Election Day as went to the polls and cast their ballots. In 1960, more than 60 percent of the voting-age population cast ballots in the Kennedy-Nixon contest. In 1988, that figure dropped below 50 percent, to the lowest level, in fact, since 1924. And even that comparison probably underestimates the decline. In 1960, five years before passage of the landmark Voting Rights Act, 60 percent was artificially low because the number of eligible voters included millions of blacks kept from the ballot box by racial intimidation.

Any reasonable analysis of how American society changed in those twenty-eight years would suggest that higher voting participation should have been expected. Americans were far better educated in 1988 than in 1960. They were being offered far more information from many more sources than in 1960. And political campaigns had become vastly more sophisticated in communication skills, with much more money to spend reaching the electorate. Moreover, although political parties had lost much of their relevance to the daily lives of Americans, some process changes clearly argued for higher party participation than in the days of clubhouse politics. Decisions on presidential nominees were no longer made in smoke-filled rooms; they were made in primaries and caucuses open to tens of millions of voters.

But something had gone terribly wrong. In one campaign after another, the familiar complaint was that the choice was between the lesser of two evils. Technique had reached new levels of sophistication, and professional hands were ever willing to use it to its maximum. But in 1988 political technique was no substitute for the kind of political leadership that could really motivate Americans to take part, with pride and enthusiasm, in this fundamental exercise of individual rights.

Presidential elections, after all, finally come down to the voters; to the quality and accuracy of the information they receive; to their ability—and willingness—to separate fact from fiction and reality from perception, and to cast their ballots based on rational judgment. Regrettably, they do not always do so. But unless the candidates, directly and through the news media, give them the raw material on which to base such a decision, the process by which a president is elected is irrelevant. And the voters themselves are prey to manipulation on the single most important political act most of them are called upon to perform.

WHOSE BROAD STRIPES AND BRIGHT STARS?

PART I

Picking The Forty-first President

1

A Killer Question

Once again, as in the three previous presidential elections, the two major candidates—this time Republican George Herbert Walker Bush, vice president of the United States, and Democrat Michael Stanley Dukakis, governor of Massachusetts—were standing intently at lecterns across from each other awaiting the opening of debate.

Several thousand invited guests seated in the Pauley Pavilion on the UCLA campus and an estimated television audience of more than 70 million Americans in living rooms, bedrooms, hotel rooms and barrooms across the United States waited with them in anticipation, curiosity and, for the partisans, hope. The campaign of 1988 had gone on, up to this moment, for three years and more, through a seemingly endless ordeal of party dinners, forums, caucuses, primaries, national conventions and then months of nonstop, jet-propelled stumping. Now, for most yet-undecided voters, the choice was probably coming down to the next ninety minutes in the television era's version of political hand-to-hand combat.

For the two combatants, Bush and Dukakis, it was their second visit to the debate pressure cooker in eighteen days. The first had been at Wake Forest University in Winston-Salem, North Carolina, and by the reckoning of most observers and the public-opinion polls, Dukakis had been the winner. He was crisper, cooler, in better control of the facts—and of himself—against a rattled and on occasion even incoherent Bush.

So it might have been expected, on this tense night in Los Angeles, that the greater pressure to recover would be on the vice president. Instead, though, the heat was on Dukakis. In spite of his superior performance in that first debate, he still bore the scars of a relentlessly negative campaign against him by Bush, and continued to trail the vice president in the polls. Indeed, Dukakis appeared to be falling farther behind. One television network, ABC, on the previous night had reported the findings of state-by-state polls—some of them woefully out-of-date—indicating that Bush had already built up an insurmountable majority of electoral votes.

On three negative issues dealing, incredibly for a critical presidential campaign, with the pledge of allegiance to the flag, prisoner furloughs and the death penalty, Bush had painted Dukakis as unpatriotic, soft on crime and, by implication at least, soft on national defense. The campaign, in fact, had been reduced in a sense to a tug-of-war over the American flag, and Dukakis was losing it.

The two men who stood before moderator Bernard Shaw of the Cable News Network and panelists Ann Compton of ABC News, Margaret Warner of *Newsweek* and Andrea Mitchell of NBC News were contrasting enigmas. George Bush seemed a relaxed and comfortable man, given to easy if awkward, lopsided grins, but curiously inarticulate at times for a person of such long experience in public life. Michael Dukakis, on the other hand, had the poise of a trial lawyer. It was offset, however, by an aloof, even grim, impersonal aspect, punctuated often by an unattractive smirk and seldom relieved by a warm smile. For many, it was hard to take George Bush seriously; for many, it was even harder to take Mike Dukakis any other way.

Yet in the campaign leading up to this second debate, Bush had put aside his easygoing manner in favor of a slashing, dead-serious effort to undermine public confidence in Dukakis. Unable into the summer of 1988 to do much to make voters feel more favorably toward himself, Bush followed the advice of his experienced strategists to cut Dukakis down to size—and had succeeded.

When two presidential candidates meet face-to-face on any occasion, there is certain to be electricity in the air. But because presidential campaigns for so many Americans have come to be encapsulated into these highly charged ninety-minute confrontations, the stakes for the contestants are immense. And it is not so much that one of them will far outdistance the other in the brilliance of his expositions as that one will commit a gaffe so glaring that it will doom his chances. That is what makes the presidential debates such gripping theater to those who watch them with more than idle curiosity. At any moment, something can be said or done that will make or—more dramatically—break a bid for the presidency.

Such, indeed, was the hope of the strategists who had brought Michael Dukakis this far. They were convinced, from his performance as campaigner all year and in that first debate at Wake Forest, that he was the superior candidate, in both substance and style. He had not risen in the polls thereafter, they firmly believed, because George Bush's strategy—waging that brutally negative campaign that questioned Dukakis' patriotism and his toughness against crime—had forced him onto the defensive and kept him there. But if Dukakis could only hit back hard enough in this second debate, his advisers felt, and in the process demonstrate some passion that would counter that cold and aloof image, he might yet turn the tables on Bush. In the first debate, Bush perhaps unwittingly had put his finger on one of Dukakis' problems. Rattled himself by a question, a confused Bush blurted: "Wouldn't it be nice to be the iceman so you never make a mistake?" That was Michael Dukakis, all right—the iceman.

The first question of the second debate went to the moderator, Bernard Shaw In a pleasant, even voice, he welcomed the audience, introduced his fellow panelists and the two candidates and briefly stated the ground rules. Then, without further ado, he addressed the Democratic presidential nominee.

"Governor," Shaw inquired, "if Kitty Dukakis were raped and murdered, would you favor an irrevocable death penalty for the killer?"

The question came matter-of-factly, almost conversationally, but it made a whole nation suck in its breath. A whole nation, that is, except Michael Dukakis, who without indication of surprise or dismay proceeded to answer it calmly, concisely, unemotionally. Shaw might have asked Dukakis how he would feel if a man were caught jaywalking, for all the sense of outrage the question seemed to generate in the governor of Massachusetts.

"No, I don't, Bernard," Dukakis said, as the audience in Pauley Pavilion and in living rooms across the country listened in shock. "And I think you know I've opposed the death penalty during all of my life. I don't see any evidence that it's a deterrent, and I think there are better and more effective ways to deal with violent crime. We've done so in my own state. And that's one of the reasons why we have had the biggest drop in crime of any industrial state in America; why we have the lowest murder rate of any industrial state in America."

Dukakis went on like that, segueing inexplicably into an exposition on how as president he would wage the war on drugs as a means to reduce violence. If the answer was not quite as shocking as the question, it nonetheless triggered murmurs of disbelief through the arena—and loud observations of incredulity in the adjoining hall where hundreds of reporters monitored the exchange on television. How could Shaw have asked that question? More astonishingly, how could Dukakis have failed to explode at it?

None were more baffled at the Democratic nominee's flat, bloodless response than the members of the team that had prepared Dukakis for the debate. In a holding room elsewhere in the hall, they watched and listened with a mixture of bewilderment and chagrin. In rehearsals for both the first and the second debates, Dukakis had been drilled in a reply that was geared to shatter his image as a cold automaton and convey once and for all that he was a man of deep compassion and understanding for the victims of crime. No fewer than thirteen times, according to one of the debate preparation team, Dukakis went through the answer and heard it played back on tape in advance of the second debate, and it went something like this:

"Let me tell you two stories. The first is about a seventy-year-old doctor in his office one night, bound, gagged, robbed by an intruder looking for drugs. The second is about a guy in his forties cut down in the prime of life by a driver on drugs or drinking. The first was my father, the second was my brother. I don't need any lectures from George Bush or anybody else about crime or its victims or its cost. And I stand second to no one in my commitment to crime-fighting."

But instead of giving this very personal reply, he answered Shaw's hypothetical question about the rape and murder of the one person who clearly was most important to him in the world as if he were reading from a briefing book and had turned to the wrong page.

The performance was all the more baffling because Dukakis was not always such an iceman. During the New York primary the previous April, one of us was traveling with him on the night his cousin, Olympia Dukakis, was favored to win an Academy Award for the best performance by a supporting actress in 1987. Dukakis had been scheduled to watch the telecast of the Oscar presentations in a Greenwich Village restaurant while news cameras watched him. But a rally at the Shalimar banquet hall in the far reaches of Staten Island ran late, so he watched in the manager's office there.

Dukakis, a few staff members, Staten Island Borough President Ralph Lamberti and his family crowded in and took seats arranged in a semicircle around the television set. Dukakis, in an upright office armchair, watched the screen intently as the envelope was opened. The winner, for her performance in *Moonstruck*, was—Olympia Dukakis!

The room erupted in cheers—from everyone but Dukakis. He sat rigidly staring at the screen, gripping the arms of his chair until his knuckles showed white, while streams of tears rolled down both cheeks. A moment later, accepting the award, Olympia Dukakis looked into the camera and shouted: "Let's go, Michael!" Again, the office in Staten Island shook with cheers and applause—and again Dukakis sat there gripping the arms of his chair as more tears ran down his cheeks.

A few minutes later, settling into his car for the long ride into Manhattan, the emotion poured out—this time in words rather than tears. No one could imagine, he said over and over, how long and how hard his cousin had labored for this moment; all those years of acting in obscure theaters without any recognition until now. It was a moment of high triumph and intense feeling from a candidate who six months later would confound the nation with his failure to react emotionally to Bernard Shaw's question.

George Bush, standing opposite Dukakis on the stage at UCLA, didn't need to say anything to be the winner on that first question. But he made sure by pointing out that he and Dukakis were in total disagreement on capital punishment. "I do believe," he said, "that some crimes are so heinous, so brutal, so outrageous, and I'd say particularly those that result in the death of a police officer, for those real brutal crimes I do believe in the death penalty. And I think it is a deterrent, and I believe we need it."

The debate went on, for the full ninety minutes, but Dukakis never seemed to recover from that unaccountable first catastrophe. When it was over, and he finally walked off the stage, his chief political adviser, John Sasso, came up to him. "I blew it," Dukakis said.

Aides reported much later that he was ill all that day, that he had canceled a final morning of debate preparation and slept all afternoon. But they did not offer that fact as an excuse immediately afterward because they wanted as usual to give the impression that they believed he had done well. But even being out of sorts that day did not seem to account adequately for Dukakis' inability to rise to the occasion.

Shaw's shocking question, as a matter of fact, had provided Dukakis with a golden opportunity to deal with both soft spots in his campaign style—his failure to counter Bush's "soft on crime" attacks frontally and effectively and his inability to show a human side of himself to the voters. Had he lashed out in anger at the question, he could have demonstrated the passion his critics said he lacked. And at the same time he could have capitalized on the public's general hostility toward the news media and the particular outrage predictably generated by Shaw's question.

Bush's media adviser, Roger Ailes, for one, said later that while he thought the question might have been "not very tastefully presented and therefore it bordered on unfair," that "my conservative mind has the feeling that Bernie obviously wanted Dukakis to win, not George Bush, and he saw this as a way of giving one right over the plate. Here's Dukakis' chance to knock it out of the park. I think Bernie thought he was serving up a softball." Shaw emphatically denied the suggestion.

Dukakis' answer, Ailes said, "collapsed his internal support" within his campaign when he failed to deliver in the second debate. Instead, in Ailes' words, "in effect he became the defense attorney for the murderer and rapist of his wife, as opposed to the outraged husband." Like Dukakis' fellow Massachusetts Democrat, Ted Kennedy, when he muffed a question from Roger Mudd in the 1980 campaign on why he wanted to be president, Dukakis saw his dwindling chances to be elected smolder in the ashes of a single answer to a single question. The odds were that he would not have won in any event, but this one snapshot in a marathon campaign captured the candidate's most glaring vulnerabilities, and was remembered.

That so much should have been riding on this one debate, and on Dukakis' response to that one opening bombshell directed at his political weak spots, was a commentary on the trivialization of presidential politics in 1988. Was a candidate's position for or against capital punishment the acid test for the presidency? Or in a more general sense, was his attitude toward the perpetrators and victims of violent crime such a test? Could anyone believe that any individual who had become his party's presidential nominee could be truly "soft on crime," even assuming that dealing with crime was a prime function of the presidency? If reducing the national crime rate had been the measurement of an effective president, get-tough Ronald Reagan himself would have failed.

The same kinds of questions could have been asked about the other principal scare issue in the Bush campaign arsenal—that Dukakis had vetoed a state bill requiring teachers to lead the pledge of allegiance to the flag in their classrooms. Dukakis in his stiff, legalistic approach to things had relied on a state supreme court panel's advisory opinion that the law was an unconstitutional abridgment of the First Amendment right of freedom of speech. Was a presidential candidate's position on this question, right or wrong, a litmus test for the presidency? Did his position mean he was unpatriotic, that he had insufficient love of flag and country? More important, did issues like the flag pledge, prison furloughs and the death penalty warrant crowding out such ostensibly transcendent issues of national importance as the stability of the economy, homelessness, the global trade imbalance and relations with the Soviet Union?

Increasingly, since presidential debates first were held in the post–World War II era, they had become burial grounds of candidates who misspoke, didn't look quite right or simply failed to grasp a fleeting moment of opportunity when an apathetic electorate had them briefly tuned in. The first one of this era, between Democratic nominee John F. Kennedy and Republican candidate Richard M. Nixon in 1960, was an example. While no single gaffe did Nixon in, Kennedy's visual force and aggressiveness against a wan, sick-looking and defensively patronizing opponent enabled the Democrat to establish himself as more than a match for the older, supposedly more experienced Nixon. In the process, Kennedy disposed of the major criticism that he was too young and inexperienced to be president, and in three later debates he avoided the kind of mistake that had to happen if Nixon were to overcome that first, politically fatal debate performance.

As George Bush and Michael Dukakis stood at their lecterns at UCLA, the parallels with the Nixon-Kennedy debates were obvious. An incumbent vice president with strong foreign-policy credentials found himself face-to-face with a son of Massachusetts whose own experience was the subject of doubt. There was much riding on the outcome of the ninety-minute exchange about to begin, just as there proved to be in that first Nixon-Kennedy debate, and Dukakis hoped the confrontation would yet work the same magic for him that it had for Kennedy twenty-eight years earlier.

The memorable experience of the first Nixon-Kennedy encounter had not been lost on presidential nominees of both parties in the intervening years. Nixon had fared much better in the next three, but few remembered them; it was that first impression that counted. At first, the memory of the first Nixon-Kennedy encounter chilled the institutionalizing of the televised presidential debate. The high price of Nixon's debate shortcomings dwelled prominently in the minds of campaign strategists over the next twelve years. In the 1964, 1968 and 1972 elections, the front-runners in the public-opinion polls each time— Lyndon B. Johnson in the first and Nixon in the next two—refused to debate, lest their underdog opponents—Barry Goldwater in 1964, Hubert H. Humphrey in 1968 and George McGovern in 1972—emulate the Kennedy turnaround.

In 1976, however, unelected incumbent President Gerald R. Ford, trailing challenger Jimmy Carter in most surveys, agreed to debate—to his eventual chagrin. His debate observation that Eastern Europe was not under Soviet domination stalled his comeback campaign for more than a week and may have cost him the election. In 1980, Carter, now the incumbent but now also trailing in the polls, also agreed to debate his Republican challenger, Ronald Reagan —to Carter's ultimate disappointment, when Reagan with a smooth performance quelled fears that he was too old to be president.

In 1984, Reagan was so far ahead of his Democratic challenger, Walter F. Mondale, that he could have declined to debate and still been reelected with ease. Indeed, Carter predicted that the man who had bested him in 1980 would duck debates against Mondale. But by now the voters had come to depend on presidential debates as a prime source of their decision-making on the election. Moreover, there was growing academic and news media pressure for locking the debates in as a standard part of the election process. Reagan, a proven television performer, in June of 1984 replied at a news conference to Carter's jibe by using the line that had undone Carter in their 1980 confrontation. "There he goes again," Reagan said. "I would look forward to a debate." The tradition had finally taken hold.

In 1988, the absence of an incumbent president seeking reelection, the large field of presidential contenders in each party and the expectation of a very close election dictated that the eventual Republican and Democratic nominees would debate. When Bush overcame an early summer Dukakis lead in the polls and established a comfortable lead of his own, his managers made it clear they wouldn't hesitate to walk away if most of the debate conditions they wanted were not met by Dukakis. By now the underdog Dukakis could not afford to lose the debate opportunity, and so his negotiators acceded to Bush's insistence on only two presidential-nominee encounters, neither of which was to take place in the last three weeks of the campaign.

Bush's campaign chairman and longtime friend, James A. Baker III, wanted to make sure there was plenty of time for his candidate to recover if he fared poorly in both debates. After the first debate, Bush had one strike against him, but that fact didn't seem to affect the polls. Back-to-back debate failures, however, might have been something else. As for Dukakis, he would have preferred a later second debate, but he had to play the cards dealt by master negotiator Baker. And so on the night in Los Angeles, October 13, 1988, Michael Dukakis met his moment of truth, and in his own first words afterward, he blew it—and probably his last chance to upset George Bush.

The undoing of Michael Dukakis in the UCLA debate had its genesis in a sense back in April of the election year. Then the Bush campaign conducted a private roundtable discussion, called a focus group in the trade, among Democrats in Paramus, New Jersey, who had voted for Reagan but were leaning to Dukakis. The session established that these voters could be turned against Dukakis by acquainting them with certain information about his record as governor. With voters having negative feelings about both candidates, Bush media expert Roger Ailes said later, the Bush campaign had to define Dukakis in the worst possible terms by trumpeting his "negatives" before the Dukakis campaign effectively did the same to Bush. "It was all a matter of who hit first," Ailes said, "and who made it stick."

At the Republican National Convention in New Orleans in August, Bush promised that he and his controversial choice for vice president, Senator Dan Quayle, would go after Dukakis like "a couple of pit bulls," and Bush was true to his word. He and Quayle, using the political intelligence culled from the New Jersey focus group, painted the Democratic nominee as soft on patriotism, soft on criminals, soft on defense. As the centerpiece of his own campaign, Bush used criticism of those Dukakis actions as governor that had struck the most responsive chords with the focus group. They soon had become familiar to anyone who watched the evening news on television: Dukakis' veto of the Massachusetts flag-pledge bill; a Massachusetts prison furlough program in which a convicted murderer named Willie Horton, released for a weekend during Dukakis' tenure, fled and later committed rape; and Dukakis' opposition to imposition of the death penalty.

In the face of all these attacks, Dukakis had for the most part coolly turned the other cheek, preferring to concentrate on his own proposals for action rather than defending himself against what he saw as diversionary issues and tactics by Bush. But with the dismal polling figures on where the race stood, a debate had been going on within the Dukakis campaign over how the Democratic candidate should comport himself in his second and last face-to-face debate against the front-running Bush. Going in, there were two major criticisms of Dukakis' style inside and outside his campaign, and both had to be confronted.

The first was that he was letting Bush get away with murder and he simply had to respond more forcefully to the attacks. The second was, in a sense, contradictory to the first—that Dukakis was coming across as too harsh and cold, that he needed to project more personal warmth, more "likability," to smile more and open himself more to voters. But the overriding consensus of those who were preparing Dukakis for the second debate was that being tough and responding had to take preference. Nick Mitropoulos, Dukakis' campaign aide-de-camp and confidant, told him he had to be like a "mongoose" (described in the *New Webster's Encyclopedic Dictionary* as a "a quick-eyed and agile" mammal that stalks and strikes swiftly at rats and snakes) ready to pounce on his quarry. Tom Donilon, who had helped prepare Mondale for his debates with Reagan in 1984 and headed Dukakis' debate preparation team, agreed. "If he could be nice, okay," Donilon said later, but the first priority had to be defending himself against the attacks that were destroying his credibility. "To the degree that we had to sacrifice likability for that, we did," he said of the debate strategy.

In the first debate, Dukakis followed his advisers' counsel to be, in Donilon's words, "the appropriate aggressor . . . who dominates the dialogue, who crowds his opponent, not let him off the hook . . . get in his face." But it all had to be done, Donilon advised Dukakis, in a confident, not prosecutorial or whining manner, because he was dealing with the vice president and he was in effect the challenger.

Dukakis at one point in that first debate went right at Bush, expressing indignation at the implication that his veto of the mandatory flag-pledge bill meant he lacked patriotism. When Bush denied that he was making that allegation, Dukakis snapped: "Well, I hope this is the first and last time I have to say this. Of course the vice president is questioning my patriotism. I don't think there's any question about that, and I resent it. I resent it."

But Bush, Quayle and their surrogates on the stump had continued to nourish the implication, as if they had some exclusive claim to the Stars and Stripes as the symbol of their campaign. Dukakis at first resorted to a legalistic defense of his flag-pledge veto, citing the state supreme court panel's opinion that the law was unconstitutional. But soon he was engaging Bush in a competition over which of them could produce more Star-Spangled Banners at his rallies.

Even more damaging to Dukakis, however, was Bush's soft-on-crime charge. He used as his most effective weapon the prisoner-furlough program. The furlough law had been enacted under a Republican governor, Frank Sargent, and was similar in some ways to other laws in forty-five states and another covering federal prisoners. But these facts did not in the least deter the Bush campaign. In only four other states would an individual with Horton's sentence of life imprisonment without possibility of parole have been eligible for furlough.

A Bush television commercial by Ailes showed prisoners leaving a jail through a revolving gate while a narrator told of the Massachusetts furlough experience. "Governor Michael Dukakis vetoed mandatory sentences for drug dealers," he said. "He vetoed the death penalty. His revolving-door prison policy gave weekend furloughs to first-degree murderers not eligible for parole. While out, many committed other crimes like kidnapping and rape and many are still at large. Now Michael Dukakis says he wants to do for America what he has done for Massachusetts. America can't afford that risk." The national Bush campaign did not use a photo of Horton in its television ad, but at least one Bush state committee, in Illinois, circulated fliers bearing his picture that said Dukakis' election would set murderers and rapists free across the country. An independent group calling itself the National Security Political Action Committee also briefly ran a television spot containing a picture of Horton, but it was repudiated by the formal Bush campaign.

Dukakis also responded to this attack reluctantly and again legalistically, noting that the bill had been passed under a Republican governor and that he, Dukakis, had seen to it after the Willie Horton episode that the policy was changed to exclude convicted murderers. Dukakis seemed not to appreciate the damage this assault was inflicting on his candidacy, or the need for a more forceful and direct reply to the soft-on-crime implication. The prison-furlough matter actually had first come up in the campaign back in January and February during the New Hampshire primary, but didn't prevent him from winning the impressive victory he needed to counter his third-place finish in the Iowa caucuses eight days earlier.

During that primary, reporters from the *Lawrence Eagle-Tribune*, just south of the state line in Massachusetts, pressed him repeatedly on the murderer-release aspect of the law, still on the books at the time. An *Eagle-Tribune* reporter, Susan Forrest, and others on the staff had written stories establishing that Dukakis had never apologized to the Maryland rape victim, Angela Barnes, and her husband, Clifford, who was severely beaten at gunpoint by Horton, or even talked to them when they tried to protest the Massachusetts policy that had so tragically affected their lives.

Charlie Baker, a young Dukakis aide who ran the New Hampshire primary campaign for him, reasoned later that the furlough issue didn't affect the outcome then because the voters in New England had a rounded picture of the familiar Massachusetts governor. "We were inoculated for it because it could be put in perspective of his [complete] Massachusetts record," Baker said. Later, though, "We didn't have the base nationally," he said, to prevent the issue from being blown out of proportion.

The newspaper, incidentally, shortly thereafter won a Pulitzer Prize for its relentless pursuit of the Willie Horton story. It ran more than 175 articles that helped stimulate a statewide petition drive for a law change finally enacted and signed by Dukakis. This newspaper crusade, and the potential for using the issue against him, surprisingly was lost for several months on the usually alert Bush campaign. It was not until Bush had wrapped up the Republican nomination and Jim Pinkerton, the Bush campaign's "opposition research" chief, had turned his attention to Dukakis as the likely Democratic nominee, that the Horton case came to his attention. Pinkerton was reading a transcript of a Democratic candidates' debate held during the New York primary in April when he came across an inquiry by Senator Albert Gore to Dukakis about Massachusetts' program of "weekend passes for convicted criminals." Dukakis had lamely discussed the program and reported it had been canceled for murderers not under life sentences.

Pinkerton immediately tracked down Andy Card, a Massachusetts native who was a key Bush operative in New England, and asked him what he knew about it. Card filled him in and when Pinkerton expressed astonishment, Card said to him: "If you think that's weird, wait'll you hear this." And he proceeded to tell Pinkerton about Dukakis' veto of the flag-pledge bill. Pinkerton took both stories, the prisoner furlough and the pledge veto, to Lee Atwater, Bush's national campaign manager and a master of negative-attack politics, who knew what to do with them.

When the focus group was assembled in New Jersey shortly afterward, its participants were asked what they thought about a governor who let murderers out on furlough to rape innocent victims, and who would oppose the pledge of allegiance in the schools. The Bush strategists got the answers they had expected, and from then on Dukakis was plagued by Bush's constant pounding on this case history of "softness on crime" as well as on a lack of patriotism.

With these matters in mind, the moderator of the second debate, Bernard Shaw, had thought long and hard about how he could use the question to Dukakis allotted to him to discover what manner of man he was dealing with. He also would be asking one question of Bush, but by prearrangement, his first would go to the governor. "I wanted to ask him a question that related to some of the basic charges that Bush had leveled against him," Shaw explained later. "I wanted to ask him a question that dealt with crime, a question that dealt with emotion, his alleged lack of emotion. I wanted to see, if I could, to what extent did emotion influence his decision-making. And I sensed the question had to be as personal in nature as possible, to get his attention."

In interviewing candidates all year, and in moderating a debate during the New York primary back in April, Shaw recalled, he had been struck with— and frustrated by—the candidates' artful dodging. "Time and time again, what was notable to me was that these guys did not answer questions directly," he said. "They chose whatever question asked them as a springboard to say whatever they chose. You know how it is asking politicians questions. It's a cat-and-mouse game in the formulation of the very words of the question." So Shaw decided he would have to be very precise and direct in his leadoff question to Dukakis.

After just a few words on the ground rules, Shaw asked it. To millions of Americans watching on television, he was like a prizefight referee charging out of a neutral corner at the opening bell and landing a haymaker on Dukakis' chin before he could get his guard up.

Shaw said after the election that his question provided Dukakis with a chance to shore up his image by demonstrating both backbone and ire, and then launching into the standard liberal reply that in a government of law the responsible citizen does not take justice into his own hands. But that certainly was not his intent in asking it, he said. "This debate was the important last outing for both candidates," he explained later, "so that means that you come to the arena prepared. I asked that question to probe, to see what was there. . . . My intent was not rolling a grenade across the stage."

The three panelists did not see it that way. On the morning of the debate, they had met with Shaw in Ann Compton's room at the Westwood Marquis Hotel a few blocks from the UCLA campus to discuss their roles and make sure all important areas were covered in their questions. Inasmuch as the debate format called for Shaw to pose the first two questions, the panelists asked him what they were going to be. He knew full well that the actual wording of the Dukakis question, as he had turned it over in his mind repeatedly in his hotel room late into the previous night, was in for severe criticism. But he was determined not to be deterred, and so he was, he said later, "intentionally cagey. I said, 'I'm going to ask Dukakis about crime and Bush about Quayle,' and I was hoping that would be enough. But it wasn't."

Well, the question came back, specifically what was he going to ask? Shaw ducked. He told the three women he didn't like the idea of reporters sharing questions, or for that matter the idea of reporters sitting around in a room talking about what they were going to ask.

Well, one of the others said, they had to have some idea because they didn't want to step on each other's questions. Shaw was unmoved. The solution to that, he said, was for each panelist to come to the debate with a sufficient number of questions to deal with that possibility. But the panelists pressed him. Finally, Shaw remembers, "Well, I said, this is what I'm going to ask Governor Dukakis"—and he let them have it just as he delivered it later that night. Their reaction also was just as it was later among the viewing audience—one of utter shock and disbelief.

"They said, 'That's a tough question, that's a very tough question,' " Shaw recalled, "and they looked at me and they looked at one another, and the look was, 'He's really going to ask that question!' " Little more was said right then, but the three women were obviously chagrined. Shortly afterward, when the group went to Pauley Pavilion for light and sound checks on the set, Shaw spied the three of them huddled together in the debate staff office. He walked over and joined them, whereupon Andrea Mitchell turned and mildly asked him whether he couldn't ask his question without mentioning Kitty Dukakis by name, and instead just say "your wife."

Shaw recalled her saying: "Bernie, it's clear your question has shock value. You saw the way we reacted. And I know you can take the heat you're obviously going to get." Margaret Warner and Ann Compton then each took a crack at him, but to no avail. "I'm not changing my question," Shaw said, now angry at the pressure but keeping it to himself in the interest of an effective debate. "They spoke to me professionally," he recalled, "and I listened to them professionally." He listened, but he wasn't budging.

Ironically, neither Shaw's controversial question nor any other would have been asked had Dukakis had his way about the debate format. He wanted a face-to-face encounter in the Lincoln-Douglas tradition, but the Bush side would not even entertain that idea. Bush's handlers, however, thought right into the second debate that Dukakis might yet try to pull it off, by suddenly challenging Bush to ignore the panel and engage him directly.

Robert Goodwin, a Washington executive who assisted Ailes in the debate negotiations and then handled the technical side of the debate staging, said later that during the day of the debate "a member of the technical crew said he had heard Dukakis was going to break out of the format sometime that night, in a way that might be perceived as taking charge." Goodwin called Ailes and told him. Ailes, Goodwin recalled, "thought Dukakis might say, 'Wait a minute. Let's talk about real issues. These questions are not what the voters want to hear.' " So a counterstrategy had to be devised.

With its accustomed thoroughness in anticipating all possibilities and preparing for them, the Bush team worked out a gambit for the vice president that could turn Dukakis' gesture to his own advantage. It was decided that Bush would promptly step out from behind his lectern and say something like, "Okay, Mike, you want to talk about issues. Come down from behind that podium and talk man-to-man."

The caper had a built-in advantage for the much taller Bush. The Dukakis campaign was so concerned about the fact Dukakis was short in stature that one of the points insisted on in the debate negotiations had been that Dukakis be permitted to stand on a riser behind his lectern. The Bush side after some negotiation finally agreed. And so in the first debate the Dukakis technicians brought in a tapered mound that fit around the bottom of the lectern and permitted Dukakis to walk up onto it without taking a step up.

The special riser became the subject of a running gag among Bush aides. They referred to it as Dukakis' "pitching mound," and during the sound and light checks before the second debate, Atwater made a beeline for the riser and began jumping up and down on it. One of the Bush advance men, Frank Lilly, bought a softball to put on the lectern just before Dukakis arrived, but the curtain was open when Lilly got there, so he couldn't do it without the audience seeing him.

During Bush's rehearsal for the second debate, Dick Darman, playing Dukakis, suddenly challenged Bush to debate man-to-man. Bush according to an eyewitness stepped right out and shot back: "I agree, Governor. But if we're going to throw the rules away let's get from behind these podiums and get right out here. Get off your pitcher's mound and get out here!"*

Ailes instructed Goodwin to ask the officials running the debate whether a hand microphone could be placed behind Bush's lectern in case he needed it. Ed Fouhy, the former CBS producer who was running the debates, decided that the agreed-upon format should be honored, so Goodwin came up with another idea. He noted that the stationary mike taped to the lectern could be swung around toward the front if the tape were removed, so that it could pick up the voice of a speaker standing in front of it. During the sound and light test that afternoon, he untaped the mike on Bush's lectern and turned it around just to make sure Bush could so adjust it if necessary.

Dukakis aides in the hall saw Goodwin playing with Bush's microphone and immediately surmised that it was Bush who had some caper up his sleeve to break the stationary format. Donilon informed Dukakis and warned him point-blank to expect the worst—such as the Bush team bringing Angela and Clifford Barnes, Willie Horton's victims in Maryland after he jumped his furlough, into the hall and confronting Dukakis with them.

"They're out there practicing," Donilon says he told his candidate. "What we suspect it could be, if Bush could turn around and look at you and say, 'The Barneses are here in the second row. What do you have to say to them? . . . You didn't apologize to them when this happened. You wouldn't see them afterward when you were considering the legislation [to bar furloughs for convicted murderers]. What do you have to say to them?' We expected a Bush grandstand on that."

In the end, it was probably fear that any such gambits would backfire that deterred their use, rather than any sudden rush of conscience or fair play. Donilon

---

*Just before Bush actually went out onto the stage at UCLA for the debate, according to Goodwin, Ailes—ever the confidence-booster—said to him: "Remember, you're the president [sic] of the United States. Shorty's just the governor of a state."

acknowledged afterward that challenging Bush to a third debate was considered and might have been used if it was thought advantageous, regardless of the fact that the memorandum of understanding between the two debating candidates specifically stated that "they will not issue any challenge for additional debates during the broadcast of any of the . . . debates." So important had the presidential debates become, and so critical had this second one become for the slipping Dukakis, that the campaign was reduced to such gamesmanship, with an anything-goes mentality on both sides.

Bernard Shaw triggered a great deal of criticism with his startling opening question. In an election year in which the search for, and investigations into, the "character" of political candidates had gone beyond all previous bounds, probing for the depths of a presidential nominee's emotions by suggesting to him the hypothetical rape and murder of his wife seemed to some the lowest blow. But the question found its inspiration in the campaign itself. It never would have been asked had not Bush's hired guns orchestrated their ruthless campaign to make voters believe Dukakis was a softheaded, cold-hearted bureaucrat who would be more protective of criminals than of their victims.

There was no doubt that the Republican candidate and his managers had succeeded in elevating such matters to the forefront of the nation's examination of Michael Dukakis. It could be argued that Shaw's question unintentionally gave Dukakis the opportunity to neutralize the issue against him and persuade the voters to move on to other yardsticks for evaluating his candidacy. But because Dukakis failed to take advantage of the dramatic question, a consensus developed almost at once that the second debate, and that first question and answer particularly, had sealed his fate.

Whether that was so or not, such a perception certainly took hold. A late conversion by Dukakis to a more aggressive, even outraged, campaign style in a populist mode improved his standing in the polls for a time; there was even talk of an eleventh-hour "surge" of Democrats returning to the fold. But it proved to be too little and too late.

Twenty-five days after that dismal night for Dukakis at UCLA, the voters gave George Bush a victory of near-landslide proportions. In winning forty states with 426 electoral votes he did not equal Ronald Reagan's landslides of 1980 and 1984. But the Reagan legacy of peace and prosperity, together with the severe doubts sewn about Dukakis, did put Bush in the White House—and gave the Reagan Revolution another four-year lease on life; that is, if Bush so decided to continue it, as he had indicated throughout the campaign he would do.

The future of the Reagan Revolution had not been at all certain heading into the election of 1988. After a rocky second term and with Reagan barred constitutionally from seeking a third, there seemed to be a legitimate question whether the voters would choose to continue Reaganism without him. The conservative movement that now bore his name and his indelible ideological imprint faced the test of staying afloat on its own. And the Democrats saw the challenge as their opportunity to regain national power after eight years of frustration at Reagan's special magic.

On the eve of the presidential campaign of 1988, therefore, a central question was whether the Reagan Revolution would prove to be an aberration fashioned on the tremendous popularity of one man or an enduring landmark in the political history of the country. The 1988 campaign promised, in fact, to be basically a contest between those who hoped to sustain that revolution in some form and those who wanted to see it depart, along with its amiable yet maddening namesake.

PART II

Approaching 1988

2

A Revolution
Under Siege

After Ronald Reagan's second landslide victory in the presidential election of 1984, the concept of a Reagan Revolution took on much greater plausibility. The American voters had, after all, overwhelmingly endorsed a first term marked by a determined Reagan effort to roll back the social-welfare philosophy that had reigned for more than half a century in the United States. A Republican president seemed finally to have driven a stake into the heart of the New Deal and successor policies that had endured in Democratic and Republican presidencies alike throughout the post–Franklin Roosevelt years.

This conservative revolution had been a long time coming. On the other two occasions since World War II when a Republican had been elected to a second term—Dwight D. Eisenhower in 1956 and Richard M. Nixon in 1972—there was little sense in the country that any era of drastic philosophical or ideological swing to the right was being ushered in.

Eisenhower was the candidate of the eastern-oriented moderate wing of the party in 1952, turning aside the challenge of the conservative favorite, Senator Robert A. Taft. His eight-year tenure was regarded generally as a caretaker regime, returning the country to middle-road normalcy after the upheaval of World War II and Harry Truman's Fair Deal. When Nixon in 1960 sought to succeed Eisenhower, the Republican mainstream flowed down the center of the party; there was no talk of an Eisenhower Revolution.

That year the eastern moderates, and some liberals, who had brought Eisenhower into politics threw in with Nixon rather joylessly against the conservatives, led this time by Senator Barry Goldwater. Goldwater was no match in 1960 for the party establishment, but his supporters on the right died hard, placing his name in nomination against his explicit wishes. Goldwater thereupon took to the convention floor, asked that his name be withdrawn and sounded what proved to be the rallying cry for what ultimately became the Reagan Revolution.

Warning his ideological associates that they would have to get out of the debating forums and into the political trenches if they ever hoped to seize party and national power, Goldwater exclaimed:

"We have lost election after election in this country in the last several years because conservative Republicans get mad and stay home. Now I implore you—forget it! . . . We've had our chance. We've fought our battle. Now let's put our shoulders to the wheels of Dick Nixon and push him across the line. . . . This country in its majesty is too great for any man, be he conservative or liberal, to stay home and not work just because he doesn't agree. Let's grow up, conservatives! Let's, if we want to, take this party back. And I think we can someday. Let's get to work!"

In the fall campaign, Nixon's message of continuity could not drown out the urgent call of young John Kennedy to "get this country moving again" after eight years of Eisenhower drift. The result was a bitterly narrow Republican defeat, but it spurred the conservatives to respond to Goldwater's command with energy and determination. Over the next four years they organized diligently in regions of the country, the South and West particularly, where their message of less intrusive government and free enterprise found particularly receptive ears. They appealed to the old pioneer spirit of the Southwest and West to build a new base in what came to be called the Sun Belt, and four years later they succeeded in nominating Goldwater.

But still their time had not come; they staged a revolution, but it failed. The nominating convention in San Francisco was rancorous and so divisive that it destroyed any chance of Goldwater's election. Few who witnessed the scene on the floor of the 1964 convention at the Cow Palace—when Governor Nelson A. Rockefeller of New York, the unabashed liberal defeated by Goldwater, rose to challenge the triumphant conservatives—are likely ever to forget it. Defending a platform resolution that called on the party to repudiate "irresponsible" extremist groups specifically including the ultra-right-wing John Birch Society, Rockefeller was repeatedly drowned out with booing, hooting, catcalls and demands that he abandon the rostrum.

Goldwater's acceptance speech amounted to a declaration of war against any middle course, openly inviting his foes within the Republican Party to take a walk. "Anyone who joins us in all sincerity we welcome," he intoned. "Those who do not care for our cause, we don't expect to enter our ranks in any case. And let our Republicanism, so focused and so dedicated, not be made fuzzy and futile by unthinking and stupid labels." And then came the most memorable words of Goldwater's career. "Extremism in the defense of liberty is no vice," he thundered. "Moderation in the pursuit of justice is no virtue."

At this, a collective frenzy seized the vast hall, and the convention press corps—assumed by the conservative delegates to be liberal nay-sayers—took more than its share of the wrath. As Goldwater's words rang out across the Cow Palace, delegates turned to the press sections just off the floor, shaking their fists and shouting epithets. For those of us in the press seats that memorable night, there was a distinct sense of imminent mayhem as police in the hall closed in—whether to protect us or join in the assault, we could not be certain. It was at this convention that John Chancellor, then an NBC News reporter, was arrested on the floor and escorted off by local police as network cameras recorded the scene, with Chancellor signing off by identifying himself as being "somewhere in custody." If you were not with these emotionally fired-up conservatives, you were against them. Their opponents within the GOP openly predicted that the price of putting Goldwater at the head of the ticket was certain defeat, and they were right. Goldwater's overwhelming loss to President Lyndon B. Johnson in the fall reflected a rejection of both the man and his conservative tenets, or so it seemed then.

Thus crushed, the Republican right regrouped and awaited another chance behind another leader. Ironically, he surfaced in that same 1964 Goldwater debacle, although few recognized the fact at the time. A popular Hollywood actor and television-drama host named Ronald Reagan, making a televised fund-raising speech for Goldwater, told his fellow Americans:

"You and I have a rendezvous with destiny. We can preserve for our children this last best hope of man on earth, or we can sentence them to take the first step into a thousand years of darkness. If we fail, at least let our children and our children's children say of us, we justified our brief moment here. We did all that could be done."

The speech was pure schmaltz and political sophisticates laughed. But they would learn in time that the appeal of Ronald Reagan was no laughing matter. Two years later, Reagan established a major conservative beachhead in American politics by sweeping to the governorship of California. And two years after that, in 1968, he carried the conservative banner briefly onto the national scene with a tentative challenge to the reviving Nixon for the Republican presidential nomination. Reagan's marching song, like Goldwater's, excoriated a government that was too big and too intrusive, but he sang it less threateningly and more convincingly, and many true believers of the right began to listen. But again the revolution failed.

The challenge started as a draft-Reagan effort with four television showings of a biographical documentary during the Wisconsin primary, in which Reagan mustered only 11 percent of the vote to nearly 80 percent for Nixon. The documentary was shown again during the Nebraska and Oregon primaries and Reagan's vote doubled to nearly 23 percent in each state, but still he trailed Nixon badly.

Reagan went to the party convention in Miami Beach as California's favorite son. But the reluctance of conservative delegates, in the South particularly, to abandon Nixon for less than a full-fledged candidate persuaded Reagan in the end to "bow" to the draft that his own operatives had been pushing all spring and into the summer. The effort proved too little and too late to stop Nixon, and it was generally forgotten thereafter. But it did serve notice to the political community that conservatism was already rising from the ashes of Goldwater's overwhelming defeat, and would be heard from henceforth in the

Republican Party. The year 1968 witnessed the resurrection of Richard Nixon, but it also marked the recovery of the conservatives so emphatically scolded by Goldwater at the convention only eight years earlier.

Nixon's celebrated political comeback, therefore, was not seen as any signal of a conservative revolution in the making. What brought Nixon into office, more than any ideological tide, was disaffection with retiring President Lyndon Johnson, dissatisfaction with Hubert Humphrey as his anointed heir and disillusionment over the military stalemate in Vietnam. And Nixon's tenure in the White House in a way masked the growth of the conservative movement. He proved to be a pragmatic centrist who mouthed the conservative rhetoric essentially to keep his party's right wing happy. He did little to roll back the New Deal or Johnson's Great Society, and in fact he expanded some very expensive social-welfare programs in education, housing and nutrition for the needy.

When in 1974 the Watergate affair drove Nixon from office, and Vice President Gerald Ford succeeded him with a very shaky political base beneath him, Reagan at last had his opening. He brought conservatism back full swing in 1976 with a very credible though eventually losing effort against an incumbent president for the Republican nomination. In the fall campaign against Jimmy Carter, Ford's pardon of Nixon made him particularly vulnerable, and Carter's narrow victory over him helped clear the Republican landscape for Reagan and his growing conservative army.

Carter's election tended to obscure a central political fact of the period—that the social revolution created by Franklin Roosevelt and sustained over the next forty-odd years had been eroded by its own success, and excess. That revolution had been a key factor in the wide expansion of the American middle class, reducing at the same time the legitimate recipients of the revolution's various welfare programs. Millions of have-nots became haves, and those left behind became targets of criticism about their indolence, their life-style and, deplorably, their race. The myriad welfare schemes that had become government policy increasingly seemed unproductive or wildly extravagant to taxpayers who were no longer beneficiaries, and in many cases by the 1970s they were just that. Carter himself, though a Democrat, campaigned against the Washington bureaucracy that had mushroomed in response to the relentless growth of the liberal social revolution. And together with public dismay over Watergate and the Nixon pardon, Carter was able to use taxpayer disfavor toward "Washington" to fashion his own election.

But the lament against big government was more naturally a theme of the conservative Republicans, one they had been developing and refining ever since Goldwater's heyday. Now Reagan the Great Communicator, who had been sounding this complaint for years, was ideally suited to exploit it. Firmly in control of the party's heart and mind by 1980, he led conservatism into the White House and launched the Reagan Revolution. What twenty-eight years earlier had been a frustrated fringe philosophy in the party had now become its mainstream force.

Reagan's 1980 victory over Carter, however, was probably as much or more the product of the voters' disappointment with the Democratic incumbent than a belief that Reagan would really, as he promised in his presidential campaign that year, "get the government off your backs." But when he sailed into his first term by pushing a 25 percent tax cut through a mesmerized Congress, the public began to believe. Further cutbacks in social-welfare programs that put teeth into his persuasive conservative oratory recruited millions of foot soldiers in this burgeoning Reagan Revolution. They seemed all too willing to believe that Reagan was waging war in their behalf on the government he was in fact running, a government that was getting larger and more costly with every passing day.

No one was a more fervent disciple now than George Bush, who had lost the Republican nomination to Reagan in 1980 but then became his running mate, after a bizarre flirtation over the position between Reagan and former President Ford at the party convention in Detroit. Reagan saved Bush from political oblivion by selecting him—with some reservations—to be on the ticket, and after their election Reagan became Bush's meal ticket for the next four years and beyond.

It was clear from the start of the Reagan administration that Bush's presidential ambitions for 1988 would hinge on the fortunes of his benefactor. As vice president, Bush marched so closely in lockstep with Reagan that he seemed not to cast his own shadow, while basking in the sun of public approbation that shone on the new and popular president.

Bush embraced even Reagan's ludicrous formula for balancing the federal budget—by cutting taxes while increasing military spending, which in 1980 candidate Bush had accurately dubbed "voodoo economics." But now, indisputably, he was putting himself under its spell, and if there was a revolution in the making, he intended to inherit it. Bush's slavish acceptance of Reaganomics drew wide ridicule, but he steadfastly toed the line. That was how George Bush was. All during the first Reagan term, while Democrats, the press and other critics snapped at Reagan's heels, the voters gave him high approval ratings. And as long as things went well for Reagan, Bush's knee-jerk fealty was politically advantageous to him.

Ironically, one of the main reasons things went well in that first term was the fact that Reagan had chosen as his White House chief of staff the man who had run Bush's 1980 campaign against him—James A. Baker III, Bush's politically closest Texas friend. Baker provided a steady hand and a moderating influence on Reagan. Paranoiacs in the Republican right wing saw Baker as the linchpin in a Bush "conspiracy" to infect the Reagan administration with the virus of moderation, but Reagan came to trust Baker implicitly.

Reagan, and Bush with him, traveled a relatively smooth course right through the election of 1984, in which the Republican team won another landslide victory, this time over the Democratic ticket of Walter Mondale and Geraldine Ferraro. Bush's campaign performance against the first woman named to a major-party ticket left much to be desired; he looked weak and patronizing in debating her and was gaffe-prone on the stump. But Reagan's great popularity again carried Bush along.

The second Reagan-Bush term, however, was destined to be another matter. There were political storm clouds ahead, clouds that would darken the political horizon of the Reagan Revolution and of George Bush, just as the sun that had shone on Reagan in the first term had warmed his future then. The clouds were largely man-made, and their seeding may well have begun in a seemingly casual conversation that reportedly took place about a month before the 1984 election. An event followed that revealed to a startling degree the hands-off nature of the Reagan presidency and created a new White House chemistry threatening to Reagan's popularity—and to Bush's crowning ambition, tied to that popularity as it was.

One day in mid-October, according to Richard Darman, Jim Baker's chief deputy and confidant, Secretary of the Treasury Donald Regan invited him to his Treasury office for lunch. As Darman recalled the meeting later, it was ostensibly a social get-together, with a general conversation that touched upon the expectable—the anticipated second Reagan term and their roles in it. At one point, Darman remembered, Regan inquired casually about his and Baker's plans. Darman told him they were indefinite, and little more was said on the subject.

Darman, recounting the story afterward, said he recognized that perhaps there was more to Regan's inquisitiveness than idle curiosity and promptly informed Baker of the inquiry and his reply. It was common knowledge in and out of the Reagan administration that Baker was worn out in the chief of staff job and wanted a department of his own in the second term. He, along with Darman, had used up a considerable amount of their goodwill with the president. They had constantly, as one insider put it, "gone against the grain with him" to save him, in their view anyway, from legislative or political defeat or embarrassment—and, at times, from himself. They had talked him out of things he had been persuaded by his right-wing ideology, or by its high priests, should be done. And they had talked him into things he first viewed as violations of the true conservative faith, such as an unprecedented $99-billion tax increase in 1982 required to help undo the fiscal damage of his 1981 tax cuts. Insiders said Baker and Darman realized that to some degree they had worn out their welcome with Reagan and it was the prudent time to move a bit farther out of his orbit.

Regan on the other hand had been obliged to spend relatively little political capital with Reagan while over at Treasury, and as a former corporate executive he might want to get closer to the real seat of national power.

To the outside world and within strict bureaucratic protocol, Regan's cabinet position clearly outranked Baker's staff job. But that wasn't necessarily so to the corporate mind of Don Regan, former chief executive officer of Merrill Lynch. "From his perspective," one insider said later, "being chief of staff at the White House would be the top of the heap." The strong hand that Baker had exerted in the first term in keeping cabinet members in line also was persuasive that here was where the power was. "It was natural that Regan would wish to move up the equivalent of the corporate pecking order," this observer said. Considering all this, could Regan have a deal in mind? According to Darman, Baker waited for the first opportunity, in a casual way, to find out.

Shortly afterward, Regan had what another Reaganite described later as "one of his temper tantrums" on a policy matter concerning Treasury. In his own book, *For the Record*, Regan wrote that a Treasury report about to be presented to the president was leaked immediately after a cabinet meeting at which he had made "a strong case to the president for discipline in relations with the press—and for strong disciplinary action against leakers, particularly White House staffers." Regan wrote: "I was infuriated by this treacherous insult to the president and to me and . . . I called Jim Baker and gave him the full benefit of my reaction in Marine Corps terminology . . . [ending by] slamming down the receiver." Then, Regan wrote, he dictated a letter of resignation to Reagan, only to be called by the president and told the letter was refused because "you're the only friend I have around here. If you go, I'll have to get my hat and go with you."

One of Baker's jobs was to stroke cabinet members on such occasions. A few minutes after Reagan's call, Regan wrote, "Jim Baker called to ask if he could drop in 'just for a chat.' It was obvious that he wanted to explain the leak and smooth things over. I asked him to stay for lunch. My anger cooled, and I was glad enough to have the opportunity of talking to Baker. He seemed tired, distracted. He dropped into a chair, sighed loudly, shook his head, gave a wry smile. I asked him what was bothering him."

Baker's recollection of the conversation was slightly different. After he had disposed of the subject of Regan's immediate irritation, Baker recalled, the treasury secretary himself brought up the question of the future.

"I read in the paper where you'd like to consider doing something else," Baker remembered Regan saying to him.

"Yeah," Baker replied, "this is really an interesting job, but after a while you get a little bit of burnout, and frankly I'd like to get into something where you could deal in a little more depth with substance." As a practicing lawyer for twenty-two years, he said, he was used to dealing directly with problems. In the White House job, he went on, "it's a very powerful job, you deal with all the major issues affecting the world, but you just hit 'em a glancing blow on their way into the president. It's primarily a purely political job, and I'd like to do something where maybe I can get a little more involved in substance."

"Well," Baker remembered Regan telling him, "I want to make you an offer you can't refuse."

Baker willingly swallowed the hook. "I said, 'What do you mean?' " Baker recalled. "He said, 'Why don't you and I swap jobs?' I said, after a minute, 'You're serious, aren't you?' And he said, 'I damn sure am.' "

Just like that. Never mind that it was the prerogative of the president of the United States to appoint both the secretary of treasury and the White House chief of staff. Don Regan was blithely taking it on himself to hand over to Jim Baker the job Ronald Reagan had given him, and take his place at the White House. To be sure, the idea would have to be run by the president for his okay, but Regan didn't seem to consider that technicality a problem. He knew Ronald Reagan, after all, as did Baker.

Baker in collusion with Regan brought Reagan's most trusted White House aide, Michael Deaver, into the conspiracy, knowing that Nancy Reagan would also have to approve and that she relied heavily on Deaver on matters affecting her husband's best interests. For tactical reasons Deaver decided it was best to wait until after the Christmas holidays to approach the president. When he finally did, Reagan didn't hesitate. "Sounds like a good idea to me," he said, according to an insider. He liked both Baker and Regan and didn't want to lose either one. If this switch was a way to keep both of them, why not?

After overnight clearance with the first lady, Baker and Regan were called into the Oval Office and the deed was done. No discussion whatever took place about how Regan would run the White House or what Baker's posture and activities would be at Treasury. The news was a bombshell, but Baker, who had won strong support on Capitol Hill as a deft and diplomatic legislative negotiator in the first term, got swift and enthusiastic confirmation by the Senate. Regan did not need Senate confirmation for his new job, so in short order the White House operation was in new hands for the second term. Reagan, asked about the Baker-Regan switch at a news conference, said "they're just changing chairs at the cabinet table. . . . They'll still be around. I don't care what side of the table they're talking from, I'll be listening."

It did not take long, however, for the significance of this casually made change to surface, in destructive ways for the president. Shortly after his second inauguration, plans were disclosed for a state visit to West Germany in conjunction with a Western Powers' economic summit conference and the fortieth anniversary of the end of World War II. In deference to U.S.–West German relations, the White House decided in February that Reagan would not take part in ceremonies in West Germany to mark the Nazi surrender on V-E (Victory in Europe) Day, May 8, but instead would address the European Parliament at Strasbourg.

As the itinerary was being drawn, American Jewish leaders urged that Reagan visit one of the most hated symbols of Nazi terror, the extermination camp at Dachau. The idea was quickly rejected, Reagan explaining in his weekly radio talk that he was interested in "reconciliation," not in "recalling . . . the hatred that went on at the time."

Through February and March, amid increasing complaints from the American Jewish community, the president stuck to his guns. In a March 21 news conference he argued that "instead of reawakening the memories and so forth, and the passions of the time, that maybe we should observe this day as the day when, forty years ago, peace began, and friendship" with the defeated German people. Reagan, to the astonishment of those who heard him, offered that "the German people have very few alive that remember even the war, and certainly none of them were adults and participating in any way."

Even in terms of Reagan's celebrated talent for verbal boners, this one was a mind-boggler. The controversy mushroomed in early April with word that the president's itinerary in West Germany, coordinated by his new White House chief of staff and advanced by Deaver, would include a visit to a German military cemetery, where Reagan would lay a wreath at a memorial honoring German soldiers who fought in World War II against the Allies. The cemetery was in the town of Bitburg, not far from the border with Luxembourg, and the protests mounted to an uproar with the discovery that among those buried there were members of the Waffen SS, Hitler's elite perpetrators of mass terror, brutality and execution.

The graves contained the bodies, the *New York Times* duly reported, of soldiers of the Second Waffen Panzer Division, a unit held to have massacred more than six hundred inhabitants of the French village of Oradour-sur-Glane in 1944. Expressions of outrage blossomed everywhere: among Republicans and Democrats alike in Congress; from American veterans' associations, Jewish and other religious groups and foreign governments subjected to Nazi horrors in World War II, including the Soviet Union. Embarrassed by the controversy, West German Chancellor Helmut Kohl wrote Reagan urging him to visit a concentration camp, synagogue or some other monument to "victims of fascist terror." He pointedly observed that "that was why I suggested that you visit the Dachau memorial." That observation only compounded the anger, particularly among Jewish groups that earlier had pressed the president to visit a concentration camp to emphasize American memories of the Holocaust.

Reagan finally yielded on that point, agreeing to go to the Bergen-Belsen death camp, where Anne Frank perished, before proceeding to the Bitburg cemetery. But the controversy raged on. When Holocaust survivor and author Elie Wiesel was honored by the president in a White House ceremony, he made an emotional plea to Reagan to call off the trip, but without success.

Appeals to Kohl to call off the Bitburg wreath-laying ceremony fell on deaf ears. The West German government made it clear it would consider cancellation an insult. So Reagan, insisting that he was "morally right" in proceeding, and comparing the critical press to "a dog worrying a bone," went first to Bergen-Belsen and then to Bitburg. Many foreign officials, and some German, boycotted the visit, but television cameras and a large press contingent duly recorded the somber event. To the dismay of the Reagan image-shapers, the cemetery visit completely overshadowed the economic conference and the rest of the president's European trip. It was precisely this kind of major judgmental error and public-relations fiasco that Baker and Darman had short-circuited repeatedly when they ran the White House operation.

Shortly after the Bitburg fiasco, upon Deaver's departure to private life, Regan assumed personal control of the president's daily schedule. In the process, he made himself the subordinate closest not only to Reagan but to the first lady, who concerned herself constantly with her husband's work load. When the president underwent surgery for intestinal cancer in July, Regan set up shop near his room, and when Reagan returned to the White House, Regan and his circle of sycophants were in unchallenged command. Baker in his best days never enjoyed such preeminence.

Baker, reflecting later on the job swap with Regan, confessed: "He had never given us cause for heartburn [at Treasury]. . . . What I misread was his inordinate desire to be seen to be in control of everything all the time. He made the mistake of trying to cut off all access to the president. I misread his unwillingness to surround himself with capable people. He ran anybody capable off, like Rollins. . . . If you're so insecure that you're unwilling to surround yourself with good people, you'll fail. The idea that one person can run the White House [is wrong]. . . ." The job of White House chief of staff, Baker said, "is a great big catcher's mitt" for problems tossed in the president's direction. Consequently, having good political operatives like Deaver, political director Edward Rollins, Darman and legislative aide Ken Duberstein was an immense help, he said. Even Ed Meese, who held the title of counselor and with whom Baker often was rumored to be feuding, was a help, Baker said, because "he was a pretty good fall guy for mistakes made."

Whether Baker's departure was the prime cause of the president's problems or not, they were only beginning in the Bitburg affair. Two days before that much-deplored visit, as Reagan attended the sessions of the economic summit in Bonn, a meeting took place in the office of Israeli Prime Minister Shimon Peres that was in time to have an infinitely more destructive impact on the Reagan presidency. In this matter, too, the political antenna of Jim Baker, removed to the Treasury Department and attuned to other concerns, was sorely missed, replaced as it was by Regan's accommodating attitude toward Reagan's every wish.

Peres' visitor was Michael Ledeen, a consultant to the National Security Council dispatched to Israel by President Reagan's national security adviser, Robert McFarlane, to explore closer U.S.-Israeli cooperation on matters dealing with Iran. Among other things, according to Ledeen later, Peres asked him to tell McFarlane that, in the words of the later congressional report on the whole affair, "Israel wanted to sell artillery shells or pieces to Iran but would do so only if it received U.S. approval." The United States had been insisting that all of its allies honor an arms embargo against all countries practicing or abetting international terrorism, specifically including the Khomeini regime in Iran.

As the scheme developed into an arms-for-hostages swap, the president was informed of the negotiations and eventually agreed, all the while rationalizing that it was no such thing. The plot thickened and the transaction went forward, in spite of a written internal warning from Secretary of Defense Caspar Weinberger that the idea was "almost too absurd to comment on." Secretary of State George Shultz was similarly negative. But in the environment for free-lance policy-making that now existed in the Reagan White House, the snowball was rolling downhill. Unimpeded by presidential restraint or any presidential assistant willing and politically sensitive enough to see the immense danger ahead, that snowball would from then on get bigger by the day.

Under the devious direction of Lieutenant Colonel Oliver North of the National Security Council staff, proceeds from the arms sales were secretly diverted to the contra rebels in Nicaragua, an action that ultimately exploded into the Iran-contra fiasco that shook the Reagan administration—and threatened an abrupt end to the Reagan Revolution. In all this, Bush's role was cloudy, but his political dependence on Reagan's success meant that his future, too, might be imperiled by the scandal.

Other foreign-policy missteps also plagued the second Reagan term. When disclosure that the United States had mined Nicaraguan harbors led the Sandinista regime to turn to the World Court for redress, the administration early in 1985 declared it did not recognize the Court's jurisdiction, creating an uproar on Capitol Hill. In a subsequent speech, Reagan fueled the fire by comparing the contras to the American Founding Fathers and in May by declaring an emergency in Central America and imposing an embargo on air and sea shipments into Nicaragua.

Through all this, according to later testimony, Regan played the loyal yet cautious Oval Office doorkeeper. He protected the president from undue pressures from subordinates, determined what the president wanted done, then saw that it got done while, importantly, keeping his own nose clean.

On the domestic-policy front, too, the second Reagan term suffered from the Baker-Regan job swap. In 1982, when the wages of the Reaganomics folly of the previous year came due in a mushrooming budget deficit, Baker had joined forces with then Senate Majority Leader Howard Baker and then Senate Finance Committee Chairman Bob Dole in an unspoken cabal to bail Reagan out. They negotiated and then talked Reagan into accepting a record $99-billion tax increase as the only way to get Senate support for other important matters on the Reagan agenda. The deal didn't stop Reagan from continuing his appealing rhetoric against new taxes, and his deficit-inducing military and other spending policies. But when the same problem of deficit reduction came around again in 1985, Baker was gone, Regan had taken over from him and no similar cabal was possible. Regan replaced Jim Baker's conciliatory and personable style with a cold arrogance that many members of Congress in both parties read as outright contempt toward them and their constitutional powers.

Where Baker had let Reagan's rantings about profligate Democrats in Congress go in one ear and out the other, working with that Congress for a solution, Regan took up the battle cry. When Senate Republicans, now led by Dole as majority leader and believing they had White House acquiescence, agreed to a Social Security cost-of-living rollback to ease the deficit nightmare, the Reagan/Regan White House pulled the rug out from under them. It sided instead with House Republicans who balked at the deal, leaving the forty-nine

Republican senators who voted for it hanging out to dry. Of these, twenty-two held seats up for reelection in 1986 and did not appreciate the conspicuous isolation. Eventually, six of them lost, and in the process the Republicans lost control of the Senate.

Their anger grew, and focused specifically on Regan, when only a few days later he publicly denounced the inability of Congress to agree on a budget. "Every municipality in this country," he stormed, "has a budget. Every state in the Union has a budget. The federal government, the world's largest economy, the strength of the free world, is about to go into its new fiscal year. How ridiculous can you be? . . . They cannot come to grips with the fact that we're overspending . . . they are afraid to come to grips with it and I challenge them to do it."

Dole for one did not take the criticism lying down. "I think he better come to the Hill and get acquainted with some of the senators who made the hard choices," he said. "We want to work with the president. We can't do it without Ronald Reagan." And then he added, pointedly: "We could probably do it without Don Regan."

Regan eventually made a conciliatory gesture to Dole, calling on him with a two-foot ceremonial peace pipe from the Pipestone National Monument in Minnesota. "I just wanted Senate Republicans to know I'm at peace with them," he said. Dole, in accepting the pipe, characteristically wisecracked: "Is there anything ticking?"

A few months later, Regan got himself in hot water with American women's groups. In advance of Reagan's initial summit meeting with Soviet leader Mikhail Gorbachev, Regan dismissed the failure to include a woman in the American delegation and American women's interest in the summit by observing: "They're not going to understand throw-weights or what is happening in Afghanistan or in human rights. Some women will, but most women . . . would rather read the human-interest stuff of what happened."

Eight months after that, in July 1986, Regan appeared not to have learned anything from the uproar this putdown had created. In an interview in which he sought to explain the Reagan administration's opposition to economic sanctions against South Africa, Regan asked: "Are the women of America prepared to give up all their jewelry? Are the Israelis, the Belgians, the Netherlands' people prepared not to engage in any more diamond trade? Are we telling ourselves that industrial diamonds—things that we need for etching, cutting, shaping of tools and so forth—that we now have to go, if anywhere, to the Soviet Union?" Regan's image as an insensitive and arrogant lout continued to grow.

There were other more serious second-term woes. In addition to the continuing battle with Congress over contra aid, an American air strike at Libya in April 1986, in retaliation for suspected terrorist bombings in Europe that killed American troops, renewed liberal concerns about saber-rattling. Those concerns grew with the subsequent disclosure that the administration had floated a "disinformation" program through the American news media, planting the idea that the Qaddafi regime was on the verge of crumbling and that Libyan terrorists were believed to be plotting Reagan's assassination. And at home, investigations into alleged conflicts of interest and breaches of government ethics laws against Meese and former White House aides Deaver and Lyn Nofziger sustained the parade of Reagan intimates and associates accused of improprieties. The sleaze factor, the Democrats called it, with an eye on its prospective use in the 1988 presidential campaign.

Starting in October 1986, the Reagan administration, with Don Regan in an increasingly conspicuous leadership role, hit its stormiest days. A U.S.-Soviet summit conference at Reykjavik ended in failure after Reagan appeared to be on the verge of accepting Soviet leader Gorbachev's dramatic, surprise proposal for the mutual scrapping of all nuclear weapons. American military and strategic experts were appalled at the notion of leaving Europe naked to the Soviet Union's vastly superior conventional forces—and at the spectacle of the American president apparently considering an ad hoc decision on a matter of such earthshaking significance about which he was abysmally uninformed. On this occasion, too, Regan came in for his share of criticism for his insistence on being—and being photographed—at the president's elbow at nearly every possible moment, including camera sessions with Gorbachev.

On top of this diplomatic fiasco came a severe political setback. Reagan put his personal prestige on the line in an intensive campaign effort to retain Republican control of the Senate in the November off-year elections, making them a referendum on his leadership. The voters soundly rejected the plea, and the Democrats scored a sweeping upset that gave them a decisive ten-seat Senate majority. One critical window on the Reagan Revolution was abruptly slammed shut.

But all these events were eclipsed by the fire storm that now engulfed the Reagan administration, with the revelation in a Lebanese newspaper that the United States had been selling arms to Iran. The disclosure shortly afterward that some of the profits had been diverted to the contras in Nicaragua at once immersed the White House, and the president personally, in a scandal of immense proportions.

The national security adviser under whose knowledge the diversion went forward, Admiral John Poindexter, was immediately fired and the scheme's chief implementer, Poindexter's deputy North, was transferred back to Marine Corps duty. But also among the victims was Regan. A man who went out of his way to declare his tight control over the White House operation, he took much of the heat for having failed to blow the whistle on what soon came to be called the Iran-Contra Affair, and for the White House's failure to deal expeditiously and effectively with the disaster once it occurred. In short order there was a clamor for Regan's head. Describing the task of damage control the crisis had imposed on him, Regan compared himself and White House subordinates to "a shovel brigade that follow[s] a parade down Main Street."

For more than two months Regan tenaciously held his job, but when the review board on the affair chaired by former Texas Senator John Tower criticized him sharply, the president in late February—prodded by his wife, Nancy—finally dumped him, replacing him with former Senate Majority Leader Howard Baker. All through 1987, Baker like Regan before him was occupied with damage control as the Iran-Contra Affair smothered everything else on the Washington agenda. The joint House-Senate hearings that stretched from spring into the fall, culminating in a devastating majority report in November, preoccupied the administration, stifled its meager legislative agenda and compounded the inherent weaknesses of a lame-duck presidency.

The majority report—signed by all the Democratic committee members and three Senate Republicans—laid the responsibility squarely at the president's feet. Although Reagan insisted throughout that he had never considered the arms sales a swap for hostages and had never been told about the diversion of profits to the contras, the report said, "nevertheless the ultimate responsibility for the events in the Iran-Contra Affair must rest with the president. If the president did not know what his national security advisers were doing, he should have." Although subordinates "lied, shredded documents and covered up their actions," the report noted, "the president has yet to condemn their conduct." And whether he knew of the diversion or not, it said, "the president created or at least tolerated an environment where those who did know of the diversion believed with certainty that they were carrying out the president's policies."

Somewhat miraculously, Reagan's personal popularity remained high throughout all this, but the corrosive effects of the ordeal took their toll on his support in Congress, along with the devastating impact of the Democratic takeover of the Senate. The latter factor was emphatically demonstrated in the summer of 1987 when Supreme Court Associate Justice Lewis Powell announced his retirement and Reagan nominated a strong conservative, federal appellate court judge Robert Bork, to succeed him. Senate Democrats, bolstered by southern members of the freshman class of 1986 whose victories depended heavily on the support of black voters, attacked the nomination on a range of grounds, including Bork decisions on civil rights cases that they argued painted him as a man who might try to roll back the civil rights gains of the previous decades.

In the fierce debate that ensued, and in Senate Judiciary Committee hearings televised to the nation, Bork's credibility crumbled and his nomination was rejected by the Senate. Reagan's replacement, a young federal judge, Douglas Ginsberg, also drew Senate Democratic criticism. He was forced to withdraw his name when it was disclosed that he had smoked marijuana, a federal law violation, not only when he was in college but as a professor of law at Harvard.

These setbacks underscored Reagan's waning influence and appeared to diminish the value of the political legacy he was leaving to the Republican candidates already lined up to seek the party presidential nomination to succeed him. Even when, late in 1987, a historic breakthrough in nuclear arms-control negotiations was achieved with the Soviet Union, culminating in the signing at a Washington Reagan-Gorbachev summit of a treaty to eliminate certain small and medium-range nuclear missiles in Europe, the political blessings seemed mixed. The six Republican candidates remaining in the field at that time fell to squabbling over the treaty, with only the front-runner, Vice-President Bush, categorically embracing it from the outset.

The Reagan administration thus embarked on its final year in a knot of contradictions and ironies. The president who had entered the White House seven years earlier to "drain the swamp" of New Deal debris at home, with a new economic gospel that would simultaneously slash taxes, vastly increase military spending, wipe out the federal deficit and balance the annual budget, instead had plunged the nation into a fiscal morass.

Yet at the same time a general prosperity seemed to have taken hold. Unemployment, inflation and interest rates were dramatically down, and most Americans—though certainly not all—could honestly answer "yes" to Reagan's favorite question to the voters: Are you better off today than you were four (or eight) years ago?

In foreign policy, the president who had promised to replace Democratic softheadedness toward the communist menace abroad with an unyielding posture of distrust, and had vowed to retaliate against international terrorism, had wound up doing major business with both menaces, to the consternation of most of the right wing. But he had achieved that arms-control breakthrough with the Soviet Union, something neither his ardent foes on the left nor ardent supporters on the right could ever have imagined.

Thus, together with the economic recovery at home, Ronald Reagan provided his eventual successor as the Republican standard-bearer in 1988 persuasive grounds to seek the White House on the always alluring and positive slogan of peace and prosperity.

Still, the future of the much-ballyhooed Reagan Revolution, and all the earlier assumptions that it had fathered in pursuit of a long-sought basic realignment of the major political parties, did not now seem all that assured. Reagan's personal popularity was proving to be a deceptive veneer over discontent with his policies in many quarters, among fellow conservatives as well as expected Democratic critics. As a result, the election year began with the outgoing president's relevance uncertain. The Democratic candidates felt free to assail the Reagan policies while taking care to avoid criticisms of the man himself; the Republicans could not depend on any transfer of his personal appeal, while having to bear the burden of the conspicuous fiascos of his second term.

On the eve of the 1988 presidential election year, then, the prospects for the two major parties appeared to be much more even than might have been anticipated in a contest following the White House tenure of one of the most personally popular presidents ever. Instead of a platoon of Republican candidates marching united behind this popular leader, only one of those who approached the starting gate—the ever-loyal Vice President Bush—professed to swallow whole all aspects of the Reagan Revolution. Even Jack Kemp, the New York congressman who considered himself the rightful philosophical heir to that revolution, had had his fallings-out over the 1982 tax increase and other fiscal and monetary matters. And for the competing Democrats, the phenomenon of Republican uncertainty presented a much more tempting political target than might have been imagined after Reagan's triumphal first term and his resounding reelection in 1984. The Democrats believed, at the end, that in 1988 they would be doing battle against the eventual Republican nominee on a level playing field.

Whether the Reagan Revolution would prove to be genuine and enduring, or merely a feel-good interlude, would depend in great measure on the outcome of the 1988 election. That Reagan had been extremely successful in selling himself as the voters' shining-armored knight against the excesses of the federal bureaucracy could hardly be questioned. The fact that the electorate saw him thus, in the face of that bureaucracy's growth and a wildly spiraling federal debt under his stewardship, only made his particular political magic seem all the more awesome, if unfathomable. Could Reaganism endure without that magic, in the hands of Bush, the man who served so unquestioningly at the foot of the master, or some other Republican? That was the central question the presidential election of 1988 would answer.

3

The Democratic Search for Identity

Different Democrats drew different lessons from the debacle the party suffered at the hands of Ronald Reagan in 1984—lessons that reflected the basic ideological fault line that had developed within the party since 1972.

The dimensions of the defeat were so imposing—Reagan won 59 percent of the popular vote and 525 electoral votes—that it was easy for party activists, most of them liberal, to find excuses or at least rationalizations. Reagan's personal popularity, they said, was an extraordinary, one-time-only phenomenon not matched by popular support for his policies. Because he had been Jimmy Carter's vice president, Walter F. Mondale had been precisely the "wrong" candidate for 1984, they said; the one choice that allowed the Republicans to make the election a referendum on the past rather than on the future.

And Mondale had made such a hash of things anyway. He had allowed the perception to develop, accurately or not, that he was a prisoner of the Democratic Party constituency groups the Republicans so successfully labeled "special interests"—the AFL-CIO, the women's movement as represented by the National Organization for Women (NOW), blacks as represented by Jesse Jackson. Mondale's choice of Geraldine Ferraro as his nominee for vice president had proven to be a disaster because she was such a quintessential northeastern liberal and because she had been obliged to spend so much of her political capital explaining her husband John Zaccaro's convoluted and questionable business practices. Finally, Mondale had compounded the felony by declaring at San Francisco that as president he would indeed raise taxes.

Democrats seeking a silver lining also could point to the lack of a Reagan mandate from a 1984 campaign that consisted largely of mindless braying about "walking tall" and "going for the gold" and the United States being "number one." Despite the Reagan landslide, the Republicans had lost two seats in the Senate and regained only seventeen House seats, too few to reconstitute the de facto conservative majority that had served him so well in the first year of his first term. "I don't think there was any mandate whatsoever," said the speaker of the House of Representatives, Thomas P. ("Tip") O'Neil, Jr. Many politicians, including some Republicans, agreed.

These rationalizations, although different in specifics, were not dissimilar to those the Democrats had found for other political failures in the recent past. It had become part of the accepted wisdom of American politics, for example, that Humphrey would have defeated Nixon in 1968 if that campaign had lasted another week or ten days. That judgment may have been correct, but it avoided facing such questions as how someone so personally and politically flawed as Tricky Dick Nixon could win an election, or what in the world was going on in the South? Even the disaster that befell the Democrats in 1972 could be attributed to the crazy rules that produced a George McGovern, the chaos at the convention in Miami Beach and the bizarre episode of Tom Eagleton and his electric-shock treatments.

The understandable reluctance to look too closely was equally apparent after Jimmy Carter won the presidency in 1976. Few were inclined to wonder very much about how he managed to win only by a whisker against such a badly compromised—by the pardon of Nixon—and inept opponent as Gerald Ford. Democrats chose to ignore the warning sign in the fact that even Georgian Carter failed to capture a majority of the white vote in the South.

But for every liberal Democrat willing to explain away the disaster of 1984, there seemed to be a conservative Democrat willing to go to the other extreme; to distance himself from, if not totally abandon, the positions on social and economic justice the party had represented from the days of Franklin Delano Roosevelt through Truman, Kennedy, Johnson and Carter. Southerners in particular seemed convinced that any identification with the "national party," as they chose to call it, would be political poison.

But the self-questioning went beyond the most conservative Democrats. It was probably no accident that in the weeks just after the election white liberals were conspicuously silent in the embryonic movement to impose economic sanctions against South Africa. It seemed to be a sign of the times—or at least the moment—when the liberal hero of San Francisco, Governor Mario Cuomo of New York, took pains to complain when his "state of the state" message to the legislature in Albany was described as a throwback to the New Deal.

The distance of the southern white Democrats was not hard to explain. Over the twenty years since the Voting Rights Act had been passed, a symbiosis had developed between black and white politicians in the South. Within the Democratic Party, these politicians understood that they needed one another and found, sometimes to their great surprise, that they could work together amicably and effectively on many state and local issues. On some occasions militant blacks and white good ole boys were able to find enough different but definite virtues in progressive candidates to elect such governors as Richard Riley of South Carolina, Bill Clinton of Arkansas and William Winter of Mississippi.

But these arrangements were more difficult to maintain at the federal level, where the Republicans had gained so many Senate seats in the South over the last few years, and particularly in presidential elections. The relationship where the national party was concerned was more one-sided. At the state level, blacks usually would end up supporting relatively conservative white candidates because they preferred them to the Republican alternatives. At the presidential level, white voters were not at all hesitant to cross the party line if the Democratic candidate was too liberal for their tastes.

Southern white voters had split essentially even for Adlai E. Stevenson in his two campaigns against Dwight D. Eisenhower in 1952 and 1956, and again for Kennedy against Nixon in 1960. And they had cast 58 percent of their votes for Johnson against Barry Goldwater in 1964. But in 1968 Humphrey and George C. Wallace, running as a third-party nominee, managed to win only 56 percent of the southern white vote combined against Nixon. From that point forward the split had been all bad news—23 percent of southern whites for McGovern, 46 for Carter, only 35 for Carter the second time and a dismal 28 percent for Mondale in 1984.

For southern Democratic politicians, the menacing questions were obvious: At what point would these presidential-year behavioral Republicans begin to vote Republican in state and local elections? At what point would the movement toward the Republicans in party registration and self-identification by voters reach a tipping point? In 1984, there had been a particularly instructive lesson in the registration pattern in Louisiana: Over the course of the year, there were 100,000 voter registrations—60 percent Republican, 21 percent Democratic, just under 20 percent independent. The new Democratic registration gain came entirely among black voters inspired by Jesse Jackson; the number of white Democrats actually declined by 2,175 registrants.

But if the whites were alarmed, the blacks in the South were not satisfied with the arrangement, either. Mayor Richard Arrington of Birmingham complained acerbically late in the 1984 campaign about white politicians who had urged black leaders to go along with unpopular choices—George Wallace, most notably—in the interests of party unity at the state level, but who then had themselves walked away from Fritz Mondale, a candidate about whom blacks could be enthusiastic.

In the aftermath of the 1984 election, the tensions between the two groups of Democrats first manifested itself in the selection of a new chairman of the Democratic National Committee—and specifically in the resistance to the leading candidate for the post, Paul G. Kirk, Jr., a Washington lawyer and longtime political adviser to Senator Edward M. Kennedy.

In the great scheme of things, the question of who serves as national chairman of either party is not of cosmic significance. The chairman may be seen speaking for the party on *Meet the Press* and he or she can have a significant influence on internal party decisions on matters such as delegate selection and the choice of a convention site. But not many voters' perceptions of the two parties, let alone their votes, are likely to be shaped by the personalities of their functionaries. But Democrats love to argue over how many nuances you can stuff onto the head of a pin. So the contest over Kirk was far more intense than it might have been had the Republicans been choosing their chairman—particularly in the draw-the-wagons-in-a-circle Democratic atmosphere after the 1984 defeat.

The opposition to Kirk never had a satisfactory and obvious "southern" alternative. On the contrary, his most prominent rival at the outset was Nancy Pelosi, a liberal former state chair from California later elected to Congress. Eventually the determination to block Kirk centered around the candidacy of Terry Sanford, the former governor of North Carolina subsequently elected to the Senate, despite the fact that Sanford himself was probably far more liberal than most of his backers. Kirk, with solid backing from organized labor and most black and liberal committee members, won easily. But the simple fact of the contest was revealing. Kirk, then forty-six, was an articulate, intelligent and sophisticated operative with far more national political experience than many of his predecessors. And, among those who knew him, it was clear that Kirk had no intention of taking the chairmanship as some kind of surrogate for Ted Kennedy. But in the political climate of 1985, anything or anyone identified with liberalism or the "national party" was automatically suspect in the South.

That same attitude was reflected in the spring with the formation of the Democratic Leadership Council (DLC), an organization of moderate to conservative Democratic officeholders, most of them from the South and the West, making a point of setting themselves apart from the Democratic National Committee. The prime movers in the DLC included Governor Charles Robb of Virginia, the son-in-law of Lyndon Johnson already being touted as hot property for a future national ticket, and Senator Sam Nunn of Georgia, whose expertise on defense matters had given him a special stature in a party for which the defense issue was such a continuing and vexing problem. The first chairman of the DLC was Representative Richard Gephardt of Missouri, the chairman of the House Democratic Conference and a politician already being widely advanced as a potential presidential nominee on the strength of his demonstrated skills as an inside player in the House.

Athough its leaders issued pro forma denials, the DLC was intended to be a counterweight not only to the DNC itself but to a Democratic Policy Commission Kirk was establishing under the leadership of a highly regarded former governor of Utah, Scott Matheson. The DLC would make its own studies of the issues, publish its own reports and—most of all—provide a haven for Democrats not wanting to be tarred with the "national party." Kirk was not happy about it. "The last thing the party needs is a separate entity," he said at one point. But there was simply nothing he could do about it.

The DLC did not get off to a flying start. The original forty-one members consisted of ten governors, fourteen senators and seventeen members of the House. Unfortunately from a public-relations standpoint those numbers included no women at all and only two blacks, Representatives William H. Gray III of Pennsylvania and Alan Wheat of Missouri. Unsurprisingly, the DLC quickly became known by its critics as "the white boys' caucus," a label that clearly irked the ambitious Robb and embarrassed several others involved in the early stages. To its credit, the DLC began taking steps to become more representative, but given the attitude toward it on the part of most liberal Democrats, the going was heavy. By the time the DLC had eighty members, there were still only four women, three blacks and two Hispanic-Americans. By contrast, the DNC's rival Democratic Policy Commission had a membership of eighty-seven, including thirty-five women, thirteen blacks, six Hispanics, one Native American and one Asian-American. It was a quintessential example of the Democrats' devotion to the balancing-act guidelines the white country-club Republicans ridiculed with such relish.

However, although he played the conventional game on the policy commission, Kirk took several steps in the next few months to help the Democratic Party shed its image as a collection of special interests trying to cut up the national pie. He set up a "fairness commission" to study Jesse Jackson's leftover complaints about the delegate-selection rules of 1984. But he made it clear the group was to make its changes at the margins rather than providing for still another overhaul of party rules. The new chairman also scuttled the midterm party conferences of the sort the Democrats had held in 1974 at Kansas City, 1978 at Memphis and 1982 at Philadelphia. He argued that they most often became occasions for rubbing raw internal party differences and presenting to the television-viewing public a picture of full-grown party activists fighting fiercely over the wording of meaningless resolutions. And Kirk quickly took away the special status of such subgroups of the DNC as the Asian-Pacific,

Liberal-Progressive, Lesbian and Gay, and Business and Professionals caucuses. There was some gnashing of teeth but the party survived.

Meanwhile, on an entirely separate track a movement began with far greater implications for the future of the party than anything done by either Paul Kirk or the DLC.

Southern Democratic politicians had been talking among themselves for years—as far back as the early 1970s—about a southern regional primary. With the party staggering from the McGovern debacle, the idea was seriously discussed by Tom Murphy, speaker of the House in Georgia, and Ned Ray McWherter, his opposite number in Tennessee (and later its governor). But that early momentum lost its steam when Jimmy Carter broke the long-standing taboo against southerners and was elected to the White House in 1976. In 1982 the idea was revived when the Southern Legislative Conference (SLC), an organization of mostly Democratic legislative leaders from across the region, passed a resolution calling for such a primary in 1984. But, since some southern legislatures don't meet every year, that action came too late to be implemented for 1984. So it was not surprising the idea was revived again in 1985 after Mondale led the Democrats to the kind of defeat that could only be compared to their experience with McGovern.

The prime mover this time was Governor Bob Graham of Florida, the chairman of the Southern Governors' Association. He raised the idea with his fellow governors, and several of them, including Dick Riley of South Carolina and Mark White of Texas, agreed. But the governors had no mechanism for pursuing their goal, so the first real steps toward achieving the primary were taken at an SLC meeting in Biloxi, Mississippi, late that summer. That group passed another resolution and, more to the point, devised a strategy for taking the plan back to their own states while there was still time to implement it.

The goals of the southerners were no mystery. The underlying purpose was to produce a presidential candidate who, although not necessarily southern himself, would be broadly acceptable to southern voters in the general election. The SLC delegates talked hopefully among themselves about Nunn or perhaps Robb, but they were less focused on an individual than on the idea of a candidate who would address the "special concerns" of southern voters, not just those of the liberal activists who were so influential in the Iowa precinct caucuses and the New Hampshire primary. They theorized that the candidate obliged to come South and win southern primary votes would be forced to take issue positions that would make him marketable in the November election—or at least marketable enough to get more than 28 percent of the white vote in the South.

There was also a certain amount of lingering resentment among the southern politicians about being treated as minor players in the presidential nomination process by the candidates and the national press. If all these southern delegates could be put up for grabs the same day, they reasoned, then the candidates and network television cameras would follow as night follows the day. There were, to be sure, some questions raised about whether the plan would work as advertised. If primaries were being held in Texas and Florida the same day, would the small states win any of that attention? What was the potential for white candidates splitting the vote and allowing Jesse Jackson to win the regional primary, an eventuality clearly in conflict with the sponsors' goals? Could a candidate campaign effectively in the southern regional primary without becoming cast as a parochial ''southern candidate'' and thus rendered unacceptable elsewhere? Other than national defense, what were these ''special concerns'' of southern voters the candidates would be required to address? What about the possibility of an all-liberal Democratic field that would encourage conservative Democrats to vote in the Republican primaries where the choices were more palatable?

But for most of the legislators who gathered at Biloxi, these questions were nit-picking. They had all been through the experience of being given little or no voice in the selection of the Democratic presidential nominee and then being forced to swallow—or desert—a liberal candidate chosen elsewhere. The Super Tuesday regional primary concept might be a mistake. But they were as entitled to make their mistakes just as the liberal activists had been doing in screwing around with the rules every four years since 1968. It was full speed ahead.

Three states—Alabama, Florida and Georgia—had held their primaries on the same date in 1984 and already were scheduled to do so again in 1988. As legislatures met in 1986, nine other states joined in scheduling primaries for March 8, 1988—Kentucky, Louisiana, Maryland, Mississippi, Missouri, North Carolina, Oklahoma, Tennessee and Texas. The following year Arkansas and Virginia also went along.

The southern politicians were bullish. By the time the SLC met again at Fort Worth in the late summer of 1986 it was apparent the Super Tuesday regional primary was going to be held and play an important, perhaps even decisive, role in the politics of 1988. The delegates cheered when Tom Murphy, with perhaps more prescience than he would have claimed, declared: ''The southern primary is going to elect the next president of the United States.''

Meanwhile, there were other political events that gave the Democrats some reason to believe there could be life after Ronald Reagan, even in the South. One was a special congressional election in the First District of Texas that was called after the conservative Democratic congressman, Sam B. Hall, Jr., was named a federal judge.

In ordinary circumstances, a special election to fill a House seat can be expected to attract little, if any, national attention. Who cares who represents a rural district whose principal urban center is Texarkana, a city of 35,000 that sits squarely astride the Texas-Arkansas border? But the district is demographically and culturally far more representative of the Deep South than of Texas or the West. Such Republicans as Senator Phil Gramm quickly saw the special election as an opportunity to demonstrate that ''yellow-dog Democrats''—who ostensibly will vote for any old yellow dog so long as he's a Democrat—could be persuaded to vote Republican in something other than a presidential election The district had given 61 percent of its vote to Reagan and 56 percent to Gramm in 1984, but Sam Hall hadn't even had a Republican opponent.

The Republicans recruited a more-than-presentable candidate in Edd Hargett, a pleasant and attractive political neophyte who had become a local legend as the quarterback almost twenty years earlier on the last Texas A&M football team to win the Southwest Conference championship and the Cotton Bowl. In rural Texas, the support of the Aggies is worth something, and old grads were conspicuous in their maroon hats and sweaters at Hargett rallies. By contrast, the putatively strongest Democratic candidates chose not to run, and they were left with Jim Chapman, a colorless lawyer and former prosecutor from Sulphur Springs. Republican optimism grew as such leading consultants as Lee Atwater, who had been the deputy manager of President Reagan's reelection campaign, arrived in Texarkana to help them decide how to use most effectively the more than $500,000 that poured into the Hargett campaign.

As it turned out, the First District campaign was something less than a valid test of whether Republicans could convert yellow-dog Democrats. Chapman proved to be a better campaigner than expected, carefully positioning himself on the conservative side of the social issues that seemed to have the most salience in East Texas. At a debate between Chapman and Hargett about three weeks before the election, we were taken aback to realize it was the Democrat who was so vehement in his support of the school prayer and balanced-budget amendments and in his hostility to gun control.

But Hargett's inexperience as a candidate also helped the Democrats considerably. At one point, he mused aloud that "I don't know what trade policies have to do with bringing jobs to East Texas"—a classic blunder in a district in which a Lone Star Steel Co. plant had just closed because of Japanese competition. Chapman won by fewer than 2,000 votes in an election in which more than 100,000 were cast. And nationally Democrats breathed a sigh of relief. They could still win in the Deep South—and they had even found an issue, trade, that had some legs and could be used in the future. If they had been more realistic, the Democrats would have been asking themselves why they had squeaked by with 51 percent in such a district. But in the climate of August 1985, they were not disposed to look too closely.

The first stirrings of the potential presidential candidates for 1988 also had become apparent. Dick Gephardt and Senator Joe Biden of Delaware were particularly active on the party speaking circuit. Reports filtered back to Washington that, as expected, Biden was winning the oratorical prizes but Gephardt was making a strong impression as determined and knowledgeable. But the candidate already anointed as the early front-runner and thus the recipient, if not necessarily the beneficiary, of the greatest attention was Gary Hart. Indeed, the Colorado Democrat had come out of the gate early in 1985 with a speech at Boston on what he called the "true patriotism." The speech had two obvious objectives: first, to juxtapose his own views against the "new patriotism" Ronald Reagan was being credited with having engendered; second, to begin defining himself and his views before his critics were able to do so. Hart had learned a hard lesson in 1984 when he allowed Mondale to project a damaging picture of him before he had time to project his own. Hart also had moved quickly to embrace segments of the Democratic Party—including blacks and officeholders—who had supported Mondale in the 1984 contest for the nomination but now would be available.

In May of 1985, on a brief trip with Hart to Atlanta and Talladega, Alabama, where he delivered a commencement address at Talladega College, we found signs of far greater receptivity to Hart than had been there four years earlier. To some extent, this may simply have been a function of his new stature as the early leader for 1988. But it was also apparent that Hart was getting credit, if belatedly, for having been right in 1984 when he argued that the Democratic Party needed to turn toward a new generation and away from the past to compete with Ronald Reagan.

The other leading figure still on the stage from 1984 was Jesse Jackson, now the subject of intense, hand-wringing speculation among Democrats who knew he intended to run for president again but still had found no successful formula for dealing with him. It was easy to say, as many Democrats were saying, that the next nominee must avoid at all costs appearing, as Mondale did, to have caved in to Jackson. And it was easy to suggest that the white candidates might be wise to take on Jackson directly at some point to establish their own independence in the minds of the press and voters. But just how this was going to be accomplished without great political risk was not so easy. Joe Biden made a tentative step in that direction in 1986—far enough to trigger a demonstration of the alacrity with which Jackson could be expected to respond.

In a speech in Baltimore to a national convention of the National Association for the Advancement of Colored People, Biden—then the ranking Democrat on the Senate Judiciary Committee—made an oblique criticism of Jackson's support of a black primary challenger to Representative Peter Rodino of New Jersey, the chairman of the House Judiciary Committee and a longtime champion of civil rights. The NAACP, said Biden, should "reject the voices in the movement who tell black Americans to go it alone . . . and that only blacks should represent blacks."

A few days later Jackson turned up in Wilmington, Biden's hometown, with a few observations of his own to make, somewhat less obliquely. In a speech there and another in Washington, Jackson described the members of the DLC, which Biden had now joined, as "Democratic centrists" who were "riding with the Kennedy credentials on the coattails of Reaganite reaction." Those who, like Joe Biden, had voted for the Gramm-Rudman-Hollings deficit-reduction bill, were "combing their hair to the left like Kennedy," Jackson said, "and moving their policies to the right like Reagan." In a particularly stinging passage, Jackson called the DLC "Democrats for the Leisure Class . . . who didn't march in the sixties and won't stand up in the eighties." When a reporter in Wilmington asked Jackson if he was making a "thinly veiled" attack on Biden, Jackson replied that there was nothing "thinly veiled" about what he had to say. Then he told us: "I did not go up there and attack him, but I did make a clear distinction on what constitutes the progressive direction the party should take."

The exchange between Jackson and Biden was not overlooked by the other potential candidates or the community of political professionals. It was fresh evidence of the problem Jackson could pose for the Democrats by acting as the goad from the far left and using his solid black support as a club. If there had ever been any realistic prospect that differences in the party could be swept under the rug for the next election, the presence of Jackson was a reminder that such notions were pure folly.

These potential problems seemed distant, however, in the fall of 1986, when the Democrats, exceeding their own wildest dreams, scored a net gain of eight seats and recaptured the control of the Senate they had lost in 1980. It was a success made all the sweeter because Reagan campaigned for his party's candidates more extensively than any other president in history, making a particular point of telling voters that these elections were a referendum on his own performance. And it was a success made all the more reassuring because it included triumphs in five Senate elections in southern states in which the party and Fritz Mondale had fared so poorly only two years earlier—Florida, Alabama, Louisiana, Georgia and North Carolina. The lesson seemed to be that the right candidate could indeed hold together the black-white coalition essential for success in those states.

There was no better example than in Louisiana, where the veteran Democratic Senator Russell Long was retiring and the seat seemed ripe for a Republican, after Ronald Reagan had polled 61 percent of the Louisiana vote in 1984. The Republicans had an impressive candidate in Representative W. Henson Moore, a young and articulate Baton Rouge lawyer who could be counted upon to defend the oil industry as Louisiana's only member of the House Ways and Means Committee. The Republicans also seemed to have a favorable context from the investigations of political corruption that were just then bringing that insouciant Democratic rogue, Governor Edwin Edwards, to trial. But the Republicans were also suffering a hubris problem that led them to two destructive mistakes.

In Louisiana, all candidates of both parties run against one another in what is known as the "first primary." If no one manages 50 percent of the vote, the two with the most votes are matched in a runoff. The Moore campaign, with help from national Republican consultants, made the mistake of raising the expectation that Moore would win the necessary 50 percent in that first primary in September. Then, when he got "only" 44 percent of the vote in a five-candidate field, this showing was seen as a sign of weakness compared to the

37 percent for his principal Democratic opponent, Representative John Breaux, a street-smart Cajun and onetime aide to Edwards who had been in Congress since 1972.

The second mistake was a clumsy "ballot security" program cooked up by the Republican National Committee in an obvious attempt to intimidate black voters. Registered letters were sent to confirm the validity of voter registrations—but only to precincts that went heavily for Mondale, meaning only black precincts. The plan energized the black vote and dismayed even many of the conservative whites whose support Moore was seeking. On a visit to North Louisiana late in that campaign, we were struck by the feeling among whites that, as one put it, "we don't want to drag up all that stuff again."

The Republican blunders were not the whole story of the campaign. Breaux put heavy emphasis on traditional Democratic economic themes, a message for which there was a ready market in the state after the collapse of the oil industry a year earlier. The result was a Democratic coalition of blacks, Cajuns and blue-collar voters that gave Breaux a six-point victory in the runoff—and cheered the Democrats far out of proportion to its real meaning.

In fact, the inferences drawn by national Democrats from these Senate elections clearly were not justified in several cases—or at least to the degree that they were applied to the national political equation.

In Florida, for example, Governor Bob Graham's ten-point triumph over Republican Senator Paula Hawkins was more a testimonial to Graham's personal strength after eight years as governor than to his credentials as a Democrat. Although he came from a wealthy family and was a graduate of Harvard, Graham had achieved a populist image by continuing through his eight years in Tallahassee a practice he had initiated as an unknown candidate for governor in 1978. Every month he set aside a "work day" on which he took over the job of some ordinary worker—plucking chickens, to cite an example we observed firsthand—as a means of keeping in touch with his constituents' lives. And although he took conventionally liberal positions on some issues, such as environmental protection, Graham enjoyed the fundamental conservative credential by consistently supporting the death penalty and signing warrants to see that it was carried out.

Hawkins meanwhile had gained a reputation in Washington as a bit of a political flake by concentrating—with assiduous campaigning for media credit—on issues that were considered tangential inside the Beltway. She also had some renown as a dangerous politician to cross in public. The late John Lindsay of *Newsweek*—known to his friends as "the real John Lindsay" to distinguish him from the former mayor of New York—once observed Hawkins snapping at a colleague during a Senate committee hearing and remarked to a fellow reporter: "In India they'd keep *her* in a wicker basket." And if Hawkins had any chance against Graham, she lost it with a disastrous performance in a televised debate.

Nor could the Democrats draw too much encouragement from the contest in Alabama in which Representative Richard Shelby, a conservative Democrat from the Black Belt, upset Republican Senator Jeremiah Denton, the former admiral who had been elected in 1980 largely on the strength of his record as a heroic prisoner of war in Vietnam; he had blinked the word "torture" in Morse code when his captors allowed him to be filmed for propaganda purposes. Shelby beat Denton by seven thousand votes after a campaign in which he criticized the Republican heavily for supporting a congressional pay raise and voting to freeze Social Security cost-of-living increases. The real killer in this case, however, was the reputation Denton had acquired for ignoring the home folks once he had been elected—a reputation he solidified by declaring at one point: "I can't be down there patting babies on the butt and get things done in Washington."

There was somewhat more validity in the encouragement the Democrats drew from two other Senate successes in the South—the elections of Terry Sanford in North Carolina and Wyche Fowler in Georgia.

Sanford had been a progressive governor of North Carolina in the early 1960s but essentially out of active politics since then as president of Duke University, except for a halting stab at the Democratic presidential nomination in 1976. He was challenging Republican James Broyhill, a veteran congressman who had been appointed to the seat a few months earlier when Senator John East committed suicide. Although Broyhill was the favorite in a state in which Jesse Helms had beaten popular Democratic Governor Jim Hunt only two years earlier, Sanford put together what national Democrats hoped might be a prototypical new southern coalition. It included blacks, blue-collar workers, traditionally Democratic farmers and just enough suburban white-collar voters to make a majority—in his case, voters attracted by his record on education. But whether a candidate without Sanford's history could have succeeded was open to question.

For the Democrats the election of Wyche Fowler over Republican Senator Mack Mattingly in Georgia was the one that seemed to offer the most hope for the future. Fowler was a five-term congressman who represented the majority black Atlanta district that Andrew Young had served before Jimmy Carter appointed him ambassador to the United Nations. Unsurprisingly, Fowler had a voting record more liberal than that of any of his colleagues from Georgia. And that record, plus his position as "the Atlanta candidate," made him a bad bet; it was an axiom that Atlanta candidates couldn't even win Democratic nominations. But Fowler won the primary without a runoff over Hamilton Jordan, Carter's former chief of staff, then slipped by Mattingly by two percentage points in the general election. What made Fowler's success so impressive was the fact that he captured almost 40 percent of the white vote despite that liberal record and identification with Atlanta.

One of the reasons, clearly, was that conservative Georgia Democratic leaders, including even Governor Joe Frank Harris and Speaker Tom Murphy, were willing to throw in with Fowler just two years after walking so briskly away from Mondale. They had learned the lesson, it appeared, that solidarity behind a too-liberal Democrat is still preferable to election of a Republican, particularly when legislative seats may be in peril.

In Buchanan, Georgia, late that summer at Murphy's regular election-year barbecue at City Park, the speakers included not only Murphy but also Harris, Senator Sam Nunn and Lieutenant Governor Zell Miller, all lined up on the platform preaching the virtues of Fowler. The congressman, Murphy explained, had just been "voting his constituency" in the same way that he, Murphy, voted his constituency from time to time, not always enthusiastically. Now that Fowler had a statewide constituency, the speaker suggested, his votes would reflect its attitudes. Asked whether he had ever given a similar barbecue blessing to such a candidate, Murphy replied: "We didn't know we had a problem 'til we got our butts kicked. . . . We just never had to do anything like this before."

But the national Democrats probably read too much into Fowler's success. Mattingly, after all, was a weak candidate who was no match for Fowler on television. And Fowler, even as an urban candidate wearing a polo shirt with an embroidered alligator over the pocket, had a rare ability to show a hint of good ole boy when he campaigned. And it was clearly much easier to use television to sell a carefully packaged Fowler as a prospective senator than it would be to sell a presidential candidate. Most voters know far less about Senate candidates than they do about presidential nominees. Many of them obviously understand that there's little a senator can do on his own to change voters' lives one way or the other, compared to a president. Their perception often is that a legislator's solution to any problem is to hold a public hearing.

That indeed was the lesson of this strange dichotomy that had developed, in which the Democrats continued to overwhelm the Republicans at the congressional, state and local levels while losing the White House in one election after another. Voters saw presidential elections in terms quite different from those they applied to other political decisions.

But the Democrats were looking for those little signs of fresh political growth after the political holocaust of 1984, and Wyche Fowler's victory and the return to Democratic control of the Senate were definitely good news. Even better news was the realization that Ronald Reagan was on the way out and, if the Democrats were lucky, they would get a chance to run against George Bush.

Happy days were here again.

4

A Changed Political Environment

The political culture in which the Republicans and Democrats would compete for their parties' 1988 presidential nominations was vastly changed from the one in which John F. Kennedy and Richard M. Nixon waged their memorable campaign in 1960.

The choice of the nominees would still be made officially at party conventions in July and August—the party out of power always goes first—that would be superficially quite similar to those of 1960. There would be festivals of banners and flags, funny hats and windy speeches, demonstrations both scripted and spontaneous and, of course, the requisite on-camera bickering over the language of meaningless party platform planks. But the process of making the decision on the nominees had been so radically altered as to be almost unrecognizable.

In 1960 Jack Kennedy won the Democratic nomination after defeating Hubert Horatio Humphrey in only two primaries. His triumphs in Wisconsin and West Virginia were trivial in terms of delegates—far less important than a nod from, for example, Governor David Lawrence of Pennsylvania or Mayor Richard J. Daley of Chicago. But the primary successes were essential not only to demonstrate popular appeal but also to prove points symbolically. Thus, Kennedy's victory in West Virginia "proved" that a Roman Catholic candidate could win Protestant votes. Once that point was made, the Lawrences and Daleys could do the rest.

Nixon's capture of the Republican nomination had even less to do with primaries, in none of which he was directly challenged. The only remote threat to his success was represented by Governor Nelson A. Rockefeller of New York, a political star who had burst onto the national stage two years earlier by defeating the Democratic incumbent in Albany, W. Averell Harriman. Rockefeller tested the waters extensively late in 1959 and evoked a popular response to his celebrity and personal style that suggested serious political potential. But the icy response he received from party leaders deterred him from making a challenge he later regretted he had passed.

So the pivotal event of the Nixon prenomination period was not a primary, but a meeting on the eve of the Chicago convention in Rockefeller's New York apartment in which an agreement was reached on the language of the platform. Quickly labeled "the Compact of Fifth Avenue," it was signed by Nixon as the choice of the dominant Republican regulars and Rockefeller as the standard-bearer of the party's Eastern Establishment, and Nixon flew back to Chicago, where he claimed the nomination.

Now, seven presidential campaign cycles later, the candidates would be obliged to win the delegates needed for the nomination in primaries and caucuses in all fifty states. Changes in the rules, largely driven by the Democrats, had democratized the process or at least broadened the opportunity for rank-and-file participation. Conventions had become no more than ratification ceremonies.

As significant as these changes may have been, however, they paled in comparison to more fundamental changes in the game itself. Politics had become mechanized and, inevitably, dehumanized. The paradox was striking: Although millions of voters were now involved in choosing their parties' nominees, the number of people steering the process was as small as or smaller than it was in the days when party leaders made decisions in smoke-filled rooms. The difference now was that professional manipulation of public opinion had been substituted for leadership and advocacy.

Except for the role they played in writing delegate-selection rules, the Republican and Democratic party structures had become much less important. The members of the two national party committees had little influence beyond the votes they could cast as delegates to the conventions. State party chairmen and county chairmen might be solicited for their support, but they no longer had any substantial voice in the choice of candidates or the direction of campaigns. With a few conspicuous exceptions, there were no governors or senators, big-city mayors or congressmen who could deliver much more to a candidate than their own endorsements—and those were often good for no more than a picture on an inside page and a brief mention on the six o'clock news. These onetime party heavyweights often were no longer the people "in the room" when the critical decisions were made.

Instead, the campaigns were being run largely by professional political operatives—"hired guns," as they were inevitably, if sometimes unfairly, characterized. They showed up every four years in presidential campaigns and spent the interim running Senate or gubernatorial campaigns, working in Capitol Hill offices, sometimes lobbying for corporations or foreign governments, perhaps practicing law. This arrangement for preserving political campaign talent, known as "warehousing," was a particular strength of the Republicans, who seemed to have more available resting places for their troops.

The consultants had become the wizards of the business. Some conducted public-opinion polls and convened "focus groups" to find out where the voters wanted their politicians to lead them. Using "tracking polls," they could take the public temperature daily and sometimes even more often. Others were expert at translating those poll findings into television and radio advertising and then getting the spots on the air at the right time. There were still other specialists in direct-mail advertising, scheduling candidates' personal appearances, raising money, running field operations and designing telephone canvasses of voters that would identify potential supporters and get them registered and then to the polls. There were specialists in "politics"—in dealing with other groups of politicians. And others were particularly adept at reaching organized labor (in the case of the Democrats) or conservative-cause groups (in the case of the Republicans) or blocs of voters from particular ethnic groups (both). And they were, finally, specialists in manipulating the news media.

Beyond all the tasks these political technocrats performed to enhance the image of their candidate/employer and advise him on critical decisions, they increasingly filled the void as surrogates for the candidate in dealing with the press. By 1988 they had moved in en masse as filters between candidate and reporter. The "spin patrol"—the dispatching of campaign operatives to put the most self-serving interpretation on a candidate's words and actions—had become a standard phenomenon on the campaign trail, especially after candidate debates. The desire of some reporters to cut through all this flak—and the "flacks" who sought to substitute it for direct access to the candidate and independent analysis—further encouraged the journalistic concentration on "character."

The consultants were often a target for political scientists and editorialists who pictured them as unprincipled mercenaries who moved from one camp to another following the dollar or the prospect of power or both. That was true of some of the people who made their living as consultants—a title anyone could claim, by the way—but by no means all of them. Many were lured by the politics of their candidate as well as his purse. If you were a Democrat, for example, you knew you could expect Paul Tully to turn up in the campaign of the most liberal candidate with a genuine prospect of winning. Similarly, if you were a Republican, you knew that Charlie Black would be working for a true-blue conservative.

Critics of the system also questioned the symbiotic relationship that had developed over the years between the consultants and political reporters. But it was one that served both groups well. Reporters and consultants alike recognized that they would be dealing with each other not just in this one campaign but in many others two or four or even ten years later. The reporters understood that the consultants' first obligation would be to their candidates, and that they would put the best face possible on these clients' campaigns. But the reporters also knew that there were limits beyond which the wise consultant would not go in misleading reporters because he—or, more commonly of late, she— understood that he or she needed to preserve his credibility for those other campaigns in the years ahead. The result was often more accurate reporting of what was going on in politics than had been the case when reporters were more dependent on state and county party chairmen and other amateur or semiprofessional political leaders who would vanish from the screen the morning after the election.

Some of the relationships have endured for years. For example, we have dealt with Stuart Spencer, a Republican professional with a special knack for instant understanding of the permutations of any political development, since Nelson Rockefeller's 1964 primary campaign in California—through the first Reagan gubernatorial campaign of 1966 on to the Gerald Ford campaign of 1976 and the Reagan presidential campaigns of 1980 and 1984. There are a dozen others—in both parties—with whom we have had similar histories for almost as many years.

But whatever their virtues or their failings, much of the criticism of the political consultants has missed the point. They have been only as important in American politics as the candidates let them become. The willingness of candidates to allow themselves to be molded, packaged and merchandised has varied significantly from one to another.

What had made these consultants increasingly important in the last few elections was the fact that campaigns had become far more contests of technique and mechanics than of issues and ideas. In the 1980s there were few issues that qualified as truly legitimate measuring sticks for politicians. In the late 1950s and the 1960s, the civil rights question was a critical issue on which candidates were sorted out. In the late 1960s and early 1970s, it was the war in Vietnam. But by the mid-1980s, there were few such great questions of national policy and conscience to be settled; instead, the basic arguments within each party and between the two parties were increasingly over methodology rather than absolute goals. Candidates were defined as ''liberal'' or ''conservative'' on the basis of domestic social issues such as abortion, gun control, the death penalty and prayer in the public schools—issues on which a president could have minimal influence.

Small pockets of left-wing ideologues in the Democratic Party and right-wing ideologues in the Republican sought to move their party's agenda to the extremes. But they did not occupy the mainstream of thought and action in either party.

There were still legitimate arguments over priorities—how much to spend on the MX missile or the Strategic Defense Initiative, whether to fund the contra rebels against the Sandinistas in Nicaragua, the size and shape of tax cuts, if any. But the disagreements were at the margins. Who was against an adequate national defense, getting the communists out of Central America, tax reduction if possible? The issue was how to get such things done.

There were, in short, few questions on which a candidate might offer a unique—or even distinctive—vision of the kind of world he would like to see, thus setting himself truly apart from his rivals and perhaps stirring the imagination of the electorate.

The emphasis on mechanics that grew out of the paucity and blandness of issues brought with it a corollary emphasis on political money that had not been seen in presidential campaigns since Watergate—the scandal that moved Congress to reform the process by passing a public financing law in 1974. By the time the 1988 campaign began, the problems with that law had become evident to nearly everyone in the business.

The financing of the nomination campaigns worked this way: A candidate qualified for federal matching money by raising at least $5,000 in amounts of $250 or less in each of twenty states, starting in the calendar year before the presidential election. Once that requirement was met, the candidate would receive federal matching for every contribution up to $250 he received. The ceiling on individual contributions to any candidate was $1,000; on political action committee contributions, $5,000. In exchange, a candidate was forced to accept limits on the amount he could spend in any one state primary or caucus and an overall ceiling on spending for the entire prenomination period.

On its face, the arrangement sounded reasonable enough. Certainly it was no longer much of a problem for a candidate to qualify, as it had been for some the first time the system was applied in 1976. But the contribution limits had remained static while the spending ceilings, keyed to inflation, had risen dramatically along with the costs of running a campaign. Although it was a relatively simple matter to raise $100,000 to qualify, it was extremely difficult—given those contribution ceilings—to raise the $8 or $10 million that seemed to be the minimum a candidate would need to become a serious player in the campaign.

As a result, money now dictated the political schedule as it had never done even in those days of crude influence-buying by a few fat cats. First, although they might delay the formal declarations of their intentions, candidates had to open their campaigns early in 1987 to attract as much of that matchable money as quickly as possible. Second, they had to spend an inordinate amount of time—usually some every single day—raising money. Rather than listening to voters talk about their concerns, the candidates were either on the telephone soliciting contributions from big hitters or having drinks or dinner with gatherings of people who already supported them but had to be asked for their money. At a maximum of $1,000 a pop, this could be time-consuming work.

It was also a throwback. We can remember Hubert Humphrey coming out of a Los Angeles hotel room late one afternoon during the California primary campaign of 1972 and cursing vehemently because he had just been forced to spend two hours on the telephone to raise the cash he needed the next morning to buy radio and television time. "It's cash and carry," he said, "and it's making us all beggars. I hate it worse than anything I have to do."

He was not alone. Earlier that same year several campaign managers complained bitterly about being summoned to a vegetarian dinner and an evening of unsolicited advice from an heir to a General Motors fortune who fancied himself a political sage. It was the price they felt they had to pay to remain on good terms with someone who could write a $250,000 check at the stroke of a whim.

The 1974 law was supposed to have changed all that, but by 1988 the system was clearly out of whack. And the candidates were making the same complaint Humphrey had made sixteen years earlier. (Indeed, the system was so noxious that former Governor Reubin Askew of Florida, operating under the same contribution limits, quit his 1988 Senate race in midcampaign because, he said, he could not abide the daily fund-raising.)

The most significant changes in the political culture, nonetheless, had little or nothing to do with money or consultants or the primary-caucus system. Instead, the most significant was the transformation in the communications between candidates and voters—including the relationship between the news media and the campaigns and between print and broadcast journalism.

Entering the 1988 campaign, it was already a cliché to say that television had become the dominant force in American politics. That had been true for at least two or three campaigns. The voters were getting the meat and potatoes of their political nourishment from television. Smart campaign reporters had long since learned that the most important part of their day was likely to be the hour spent in their hotel rooms watching network and local news reports on the campaign.

The newspapers remained a primary source for an elite of the most politically aware elements of the electorate—activists, political junkies, serious voters who understood a campaign was more than fleeting glimpses of the candidates and a couple of ninety-minute debates that were supposed to provide penetrating insight into the candidates. But those of us who wrote for newspapers—now derided by our colleagues from television as "printheads"—no longer enjoyed the influence we had taken for granted two or three campaigns earlier.

Even before television's preeminence had been fully recognized, the special reach of the medium had become clear to those who ran campaigns. The legend of the 1960 debate between Kennedy and Nixon was well fixed in political lore: The polls showed Nixon won the debate among those who heard it on radio, but lost it among those who could see him perspiring and uncomfortable on the screen.

The willingness to alter campaign practices for television exposure was apparent even in 1964. That year the devoted conservatives—not consultants —running the Barry Goldwater campaign recognized that the widespread use of chartered jets, and the new Boeing 727s that could land in smaller cities, offered them a chance to reach more "media markets" every day. They would schedule Goldwater with a breakfast rally on the East Coast, then follow the sun and the time zones to the Midwest for lunch and the Mountain States or West Coast for dinner or a night rally. This cruel and unusual scheduling was not done exclusively for television, of course, but the Goldwater managers understood that they could get widespread and generally uncritical exposure on local television stations simply by getting their candidate into the range of those stations' cameras.

Four years later Richard Nixon refined the technique of manipulating television about as far as it ever seemed likely to go. Throughout most of the campaign the Nixon managers limited him to a single carefully staged event each day to show him in his best light. The events were held relatively early in the day and, as often as possible, near an airport with frequent service to New York, because in those days before satellites network reporters had to ship their film to headquarters to get it on the air. Producers in the home office might have two or three possible pieces of film to use on Hubert Humphrey, but the one piece they had on Nixon was nearly always the one his campaign arranged for them to have. At the time this exercise seemed to be the height of sophisticated political technique, a laughable notion now.

The one thing that had become clear in the politicians' increasingly successful manipulation of television over those twenty years was their understanding that the "visual" was dominant. First, a good piece of film would be shown apparently without a great deal of questioning by either network producers or local news directors of its news value or the merits of the story. Second, a good piece of film would have far more impact on viewers—and voters—than the words that were being spoken while it was being shown.

Television is not always surefooted in using this power, but the networks have become increasingly assertive about making their own judgments. In the 1976 and even the 1980 campaigns, you could see political stories that appeared in major newspapers ripple through the three networks' coverage over the next several days. That phenomenon was particularly apparent in cases in which those newspaper stories detected a new trend in a campaign or defined a new conventional wisdom about one of the candidates.

By 1984, in contrast, the networks were quite prepared to make their own political judgments, sophisticated or otherwise, and set the agenda for the newspapers and the political community. There was no better example than what happened on the night of March 8, 1984, the Super Tuesday of that campaign. There had been nine primaries and caucuses that day and Gary Hart had won seven of them, Walter Mondale only two—the primaries in Alabama and Georgia, the latter quite narrowly. By any reasonable standard, the most that could be said for Mondale was that his campaign was hanging by a thread, as many print reporters duly noted. But the networks had been conditioned by a carefully orchestrated Mondale strategy to accept the proposition that the standard for success was winning two of the three southern states—the third was Florida, which Hart won—whose votes were being counted that night. So all three networks treated the results for the day as no worse than a wash for Mondale. And, tellingly, that judgment—or misjudgment—became the conventional wisdom in the political community and most newspapers, too, within a few days. The big guys on the block were now Brokaw and Jennings and Rather.

The growing power and assertiveness of the television networks has not been the only important change in the political press over the last few campaigns.

In several ways the press had become increasingly an active player in campaigns, not just a chronicler of them.

The most obvious example of press participation has been in the epidemic of opinion polls sponsored by news organizations. It sometimes seemed that no newspaper or broadcast station of even the most modest pretensions could survive without conducting its own opinion surveys or hiring someone to do so for it. By the beginning of the 1988 campaign, several imposing combinations were becoming institutionalized—the CBS–*New York Times* poll, the ABC–*Washington Post* poll, the NBC–*Wall Street Journal* poll, the CNN–*USA Today* poll. But these were only the most visible; there were literally scores of others conducted by individual newspapers or local broadcast outlets or combinations —plus the national polls for which Gallup has been the prototype. By one count, there were during the general election campaign 124 national polls compared to 40 only four years earlier.

This poll mania has been made all the more threatening by an accompanying suspension of standards in judging the quality of the polls and what they really measure. As in the case of political fund-raising, this trend represented a throwback to a darker era more than twenty years earlier. Facing the prospect of a potentially difficult campaign for election in 1968, President Lyndon Johnson began dropping selected items of poll data into the outstretched palms of willing reporters, few of whom in those days understood either opinion sampling or statistical method very well. ''Selected'' was the key word here. At one point, Johnson showed reporters a survey of voters from Republican New Hampshire that showed him with a huge lead. Only after closer inquiry was it discovered that the poll had been taken in the single most Democratic county in the state.

That episode and others involving other politicians misusing polling data were so grossly misleading that the polling experts themselves became alarmed at the potential long-term threat to their credibility. In 1967, George Gallup invited a dozen political reporters to Princeton, New Jersey, to spend a day being briefed on Gallup poll methodology and how to judge polls in general. A few weeks later his prime competitor in the published poll business at the time, Lou Harris, held a similar session for the same reporters at the National Press Club in Washington. In fact, those sessions accomplished their purpose. Leading political reporters wrote about polls with more sophistication, and later other reporters followed—to the point that con jobs by candidates were much harder to pull off.

But by the time the 1988 campaign opened, those lessons were all too often ignored. Even the best newspapers, including those with their own polls for points of reference, routinely reported uncritically on opinion surveys their own reporters recognized were questionable at best, garbage at worst. In so doing, the press had become unwitting accomplices of political consultants who used poll results to mislead the unwary or unsophisticated. It had become routine, for example, for campaign managers to buy advertising time on television in advance of newspaper polls or their own, thus ''driving up the numbers" in such polls. Then they would use the artificially inflated poll figures to encourage contributors to give more money—with which the managers would buy more advertising that would drive up the numbers once again.

A more serious complaint could have been made, however, about the way newspapers and broadcast outlets alike allowed their sponsorship of opinion polls to shape their own coverage. Once a newspaper or network reported a poll finding, there was an inevitable inclination to see campaign developments through the prism of those findings. Thus, you had the spectacle of a network reporting that Candidate A was leading Candidate B by ten percentage points in its latest poll, then reporting that Candidate B was "bringing his struggling campaign" to the Middle West or wherever. Following that network report, some twinkie, male or female, doing a tease for the local news might add: "It's all uphill for Candidate B. Details at eleven."

In fact, the poll findings might not necessarily mean that a trailing candidate was struggling uphill at all. But even if that were the case, it would be hard to justify framing all of his actions in terms of poll results. Candidates do react to polls, but polls are not the only thing to which they react during the course of a campaign.

There has always been a valid argument for what is known as "horse-race journalism" in covering campaigns, as long as it is not the only aspect of a campaign reported. The first thing readers usually want to know about any election contest is who's ahead, and the reporter who doesn't answer readers' first questions should go into proctology or the ministry. But there is a difference between reporting on opinion-poll findings as an indicator of who's ahead, and allowing those poll findings to become the shaping element of the coverage. The latter clearly has happened with increasing frequency as more news organizations have become more deeply involved—in terms of money and their corporate psyches—in the polling business. Anytime a newspaper spends the money for an opinion poll—a minimum of $20,000 for a worthwhile survey —the editors of that newspaper are not likely to be shy about exploiting the results as fully as possible.

Polls aside, the press had become more of a participant in the political process because it had changed its rules about what was legitimate news, particularly but not exclusively in reporting on the private lives of politicians.

The changes were not dissimilar from the ones that had taken place throughout our society in the discussion of supposedly taboo subjects. In 1960, there was an unspoken understanding that personal privacy was to be respected. Newspapers were considered daring if they referred to a politician who was a heavy drinker as having a reputation for "conviviality" or, in the case of a notorious lush, "excessive conviviality." Elected officials who were conspicuous womanizers were described then as possessing "an eye for a well-turned ankle." But by 1988, many newspapers felt free to describe oral sex techniques, and in political reporting, too, there was a new "freedom"—for the press, not for the candidates.

The old guideline, seldom discussed, was that if personal conduct didn't affect the candidate's performance on the stump and wasn't a detriment to his conduct of the office he was seeking, it was his business. Now everything, in the view of a new generation of reporters schooled during or after a dark period of betrayal by politicians at the highest levels, was fair game.

This development should not have been surprising after the epidemic of political scandals of the early 1970s—the deception that forced Eagleton from the Democratic ticket in 1972, the Watergate affair, the revealed corruption that drove Vice President Spiro T. Agnew from office, the resignation in disgrace of President Nixon. In the wake of all this, the press had become much more alert to its watchdog role. No longer could that responsibility be fulfilled only by reporting what the candidate said, or even by what he was like with his hair down. The dominant issue had now become whether the candidate had the moral fiber, on and off stage, to be president.

That question, to be sure, had always been important in assessing the candidate, but now it drove the news media more than any other. It would come to be known as "the character issue," and even before the election year of 1988 had begun, it would turn politics, and the reporting of it, on its head. Issues of domestic and foreign policy, which, it seemed, always had to be spoon-fed to a resisting electorate, would be shoved even farther than usual to the background as the candidates in both major parties underwent much closer personal scrutiny. Amateur psychoanalysis was being practiced by a new crop of journalistic Sigmund Freuds, driven by a legitimate compulsion to discover the "real" candidates.

This press interest in the private lives of high-office seekers may also have been a reaction to its failings in the past. Some well-paid national reporters in Washington were never comfortable with the fact that the story of the Watergate scandal had been broken by two young reporters from the metropolitan staff of the *Washington Post*. And veteran White House and political reporters alike were defensive about their inability or failure to tell the world contemporaneously about the Jack Kennedy womanizing stories that came to light only long after his time. Everyone was now on the alert.

This change in the role the press saw for itself also came at a time of geometric increases every four years in the number of reporters covering campaigns from newspapers, magazines, television and radio. The biggest increase had come in the number of local television stations from major cities that, thanks to satellite technology, could now assign their own reporters and camera crews rather than leaving campaigns entirely to the networks. But there were also more newspapers and magazines that had become persuaded they needed their own reporters on the scene even if, as was often the case, those reporters had no primary sources of information whatsoever and were essentially doing no more than covering the spectacle of the campaign. The sheer numbers in the press mob changed the game.

Campaign managers found the horde overwhelming at times. And that applied even to such seasoned professionals as Paul Tully, a Democrat with experience in five presidential campaigns and many long-established relationships with reporters.

"Quantity changes quality," he said one day after the campaign. "There are now so many outlets, so much coverage and so much inquiry . . . you are doing your work around the beast. . . . The problem used to be how to feed it and feed it in a way that's conveying information that you want—your message, right? It's a delivery mechanism, got a big mouth and power, but how to feed it? . . . Well, now it's developed taste and standards and spits stuff back at you. It's not just the size of the thing. It's a new player that's got a very specific kind of appetite. It's got even more demands. And it's got its new evolved, self-defined role. 'We got the standards and [if] that little asshole Quayle don't make the standards, we're going to rip his head off.' "

If an attitude like that reached a Paul Tully, who had worked for years with reporters, had confided regularly in them and numbered many as friends, it should have been no surprise that it had spread to political operatives with less basis for trust and confidence in them, and infected the candidates for whom they worked. That, too, was part of the new culture of the politics of 1988— a far more distant, official and often wary relationship between politicians and reporters. It was one for which both sides paid a price.

There are memories of easier days. It was possible in 1960 to sit in the back of a half empty campaign bus with Jack Kennedy, drinking a beer and exchanging political yarns while lurching through the hilly West Virginia countryside, and then end the day soaking up his impressions along with a scotch or two. Four years later it was possible to play "Albany rummy"—a card game peculiar to the Capitol pressroom in that city—with Nelson Rockefeller while he flew around California and speculated about what Barry Goldwater's next move might be in the contest for the Republican nomination. Or you could find yourself in 1968 in the bar of the Holiday Inn at the Weir-Cook Airport in Indianapolis, drinking after hours and needling Robert Kennedy about a speech in Evansville in which he had appeared to be pandering to conservative Democrats.

Such occasions were "off the record" or, more accurately, "on background," although neither the candidate, campaign press secretary nor reporter usually felt it necessary to spell out the rules. The understanding was that you wouldn't quote the candidate's speculations about the relationship between, let's say, his opponent and a sheep. But reporters learned a lot about the candidates and their attitudes and thinking that eventually would find its way into better reporting on the candidates.

We can remember, for example, riding with Robert Kennedy in the rear of a chartered plane flying from Omaha back to Washington late one night and spending the entire time sipping whiskey and talking about the difference between the lives of the black children we had seen in Omaha that day and the lives of our children and Kennedy's. There was no design in this on either side.

It was not a case of a reporter interviewing a candidate, or a candidate trying to peddle a story about how much he loved children. Instead, it was a natural reflection of what both had seen that rainy Saturday in Omaha. There was no story in it but it wouldn't be forgotten that those kids had interested him enough to occupy more than two hours of conversation. It was something for a reporter to file away against the day that candidate or President Kennedy had to make decisions on programs for children of the ghettoes.

One reason this sort of hair-down access was possible was that the great technological improvements in communications, such as the hand-carried television camera and the boom microphone, were not yet in commonplace use, or at least not used in the totally intrusive way they were by 1988. The simple tape recorder, not yet a reporter's staple in the pencil-and-notepad days of 1960, inspired a new level of caution by candidates in what they said in the course of a Main Street stroll or late-night bull session aboard the campaign bus.

In 1972, George McGovern on a flight from South Dakota to Washington sat down next to one of us to discuss the Eagleton controversy. The candidate had gotten only a few words out of his mouth in what was intended as a private conversation when we looked up and saw tape recorders being thrust in our faces. That ended the conversation.

This kind of relationship between reporters and politicians didn't suddenly end sixteen years ago. On the contrary, there are still occasions when candidates are willing to have a few drinks with reporters they trust not to blow them out of the water with an exclusive story the following day about how Candidate A really feels about Candidate B. Many of the candidates in the last two or three campaigns have been remarkably accessible most of the time—especially the long shots, starved for press coverage. But the game has changed.

The numbers alone make it more difficult. The candidate who invites a reporter for a drink has to realize that there are legions of disappointed and resentful suitors complaining in the bar of the campaign hotel about "special treatment" being accorded one of their number.

But what has been perhaps most responsible for the change is the growth of the feeling among the politicians—candidates and managers alike—that the press these days is so judgmental reporters cannot be trusted. Many senior political operatives, according to Paul Tully, now say that if they don't know a reporter "for *x* number of years over time, there's no off-the-record whatsoever. It does not exist. If a reporter comes as a stranger, it's all on the record, no matter what they say or what they do. . . . There are few and far-between exceptions. . . . Now the beast has this very strange sense of standards—uphold this and uphold that, and whack! . . . You can't trust the word. There's no word that's given. And the person you're dealing with may be perfectly fine," Tully said, but he may have an editor who won't honor an off-the-record or background interview. "There's no source protection that's bankable," he said.

So the political culture of 1988 was, in fact, not only vastly different from what it had been in 1960 but much harsher. The campaigns would be run by hired guns rather than old friends in the party, financed by contributions doggedly extracted, measured by bloodless opinion polls, decided on the basis of technique rather than issues—and then reported by people who had to be kept at arm's length. It was not a pretty picture, but those were the rules of the rocky road as a full field of political marathon runners lined up in each party for the 1988 race for the White House.

PART III

The Republican Nomination

5

George Bush Against the Field

Throughout his political career, George Bush and the Republican Party's most conservative elements had a mutual feeling toward each other. If it was not quite contempt, it was certainly akin to the way the late Democratic Senator Robert S. Kerr of Oklahoma once said he regarded Republican Senator Homer Capehart of Indiana. Kerr observed, in keeping with the Senate's honored tradition of collegial courtesy, that he held Capehart "in minimum high regard."*

The genesis of this mutual lack of admiration was partly Bush's suspect Eastern Establishment background. His father, Senator Prescott Bush of Connecticut, came out of the Wall Street banking-investment wing that dominated the Republican Party before and immediately after World War II. That wing nominated Wendell L. Willkie and Thomas E. Dewey, twice, in futile attempts to defeat the great liberal, Franklin Delano Roosevelt, and his seemingly vulnerable heir, Harry S Truman, before nominating Dwight D. Eisenhower over the beloved Mr. Republican of the 1950s, Robert A. Taft, Jr. Prescott Bush was an ardent supporter and frequent golf partner of Eisenhower during his White House tenure.

Beyond that family history, George Bush as a freshman congressman from Houston had displayed the temerity to support an open-housing bill in the House in 1968. And although he was a Goldwater delegate to the party's national convention in 1964, the suspicion clung that Bush's voluntary Texas transplant never really took. In style and manner—proper and deferential to a fault—he was a sitting duck for the label of "preppy," and it stuck like flypaper.

Bush's loss to Democrat Lloyd Bentsen in a Senate election in 1970, a race he made at the urging of Richard Nixon, led to a series of high appointive jobs and ultimately his first shot at the Republican presidential nomination in

---

*Kerr's exact description, uttered on the Senate floor, was that Capehart was "a rancid tub of ignorance whom I hold in minimum high regard."

1980. That effort didn't endear him to conservatives, either, inasmuch as he was the principal challenger to their hero, Ronald Reagan. For a time, indeed, it appeared that Bush might derail Reagan's march to the White House, beating him in the Iowa precinct caucuses, only to fall to Reagan's strong and determined comeback in the New Hampshire primary—and his own inept performance in the most memorable political theater of the nomination fight. He was reduced by Reagan to a straight man at a Republican debate in Nashua, New Hampshire, at which he woodenly played the heavy as Reagan magnanimously sought to open the scheduled two-man confrontation to the full field of Republican candidates. It took Reagan, and the others, too, a long time to forgive and forget, and some never did.

Then there was that not-to-be-forgotten Bush description of the conservative, supply-side solution to the federal deficit—balancing the budget by cutting taxes while increasing military spending—as "voodoo economics." Bush was right, but even conservatives who agreed with him wished he hadn't hung that quotable tag on one of their party's major embarrassments.

When later at the 1980 Republican convention Reagan escaped from his flirtation with a Gerald Ford "co-presidency" and fell back on the safe choice of Bush as his running mate, many in the party's right wing were dismayed. They had hoped that one of the conservative true believers like Jack Kemp or Paul Laxalt would be anointed, but Reagan didn't need any help on the right so he selected in Bush a man perceived then to have some appeal to moderates and even Democrats. At the very least, he would not hurt the ticket, and didn't.

As Reagan's vice president, Bush proved to be all that was expected of him, which was hardly anything of substance at all. His immediate predecessor as vice president, Democrat Walter F. Mondale, had been somewhat of a pioneer, in that President Jimmy Carter had elected to elevate the office above the brunt of jokes it had become over the years. He gave Mondale an office in the White House proper, brought him into important executive decision-making and gave him access to most Oval Office meetings. In return, Mondale displayed constant public loyalty to Carter and all his decisions. But as a Washington insider wise to the ways of the town, Mondale knew how to get his true feelings out on those rare occasions when he had basic disagreements, such as when Carter in 1979 retreated to Camp David for thirteen days to reassess his presidency and came away blaming the American people for losing faith. Afterward, Mondale simply leaked his dissent to a reporter on a no-attribution basis. Bush, however, never yielded to that temptation. From the moment he joined the Reagan team, he was its most faithful supporter and cheerleader.

This posture, one might have thought, would have at last earned Bush the support of all elements in his party. Instead, the suspicion of him on the right continued, and in some quarters even grew. Philosophers and self-appointed spokesmen of the New Right such as direct-mail guru Richard Viguerie talked darkly of a Bush "conspiracy" to infiltrate and moderate what already was being referred to on the right as the Reagan Revolution. Reagan's selection of

Bush's buddy James Baker to be his White House chief of staff only heightened the suspicion. It grew during the first term as Baker and his chief deputy, Richard Darman, repeatedly acted as a buffer between the president and the true believers of the right. Darman was another Republican of suspect moderation. As a former sidekick of onetime Nixon Attorney General Elliot Richardson of Massachusetts, he helped bring another New Right icon, Spiro T. Agnew, to justice.

Through all this, however, George Bush hewed to the Reagan line and kept his mouth shut. Reagan, who had expressed strong reservations about Bush to political associates after the Nashua debate fiasco, came to like and trust his vice president, who studiously gave him no cause to do otherwise. Rumblings against Bush on the right got nowhere as Reagan prepared to seek a second term, apparently with no thought of doing so without Bush at his side. And when the Reagan-Bush team was resoundingly reelected in 1984, what little doubt there might have been that Bush would seek the presidency himself in 1988 vanished.

This was so in spite of the fact that his 1984 campaign performance against the Democratic vice presidential nominee, Geraldine Ferraro, bordered at times on ineptitude and served to compound the sense of weakness about him fanned by the Democrats and his critics on the Republican right. As part of the Reagan team he was snug in his leader's political embrace; on his own he was the subject of relentless ridicule—as a preppy, as a toady, yes, as a wimp. He gave the latter word a special prominence in American politics and it was all his, never mind that he had been a star baseball player in college and a combat navy pilot shot down in the Pacific in World War II.

From the outset, Bush's presidential hopes rested on the goodwill, good performance and good fortune of Ronald Reagan. The Republican Party under Reagan had indisputably become the party of conservatism, and Ronald Reagan was George Bush's ticket into the fraternity. If he had been a doubter and even a critic in some regards earlier, he was now an unswerving loyalist not only to the man but to his cause.

Reagan in obvious gratitude said of Bush in March, 1985: "I don't think there's ever been a vice president that has been as much involved at the highest level in our policy-making and our decisions than George, or that has been a better vice president than he has. He's been the best." Yet after the 1984 election and for a considerable time thereafter, his potential rivals for the 1988 Republican nomination did not see him or accept him as the certain or even logical heir to the Reagan Revolution.

On purely ideological grounds, supporters of Jack Kemp believed stoutly that their man was the rightful inheritor. He had been the most strenuous advocate of the deep tax cuts and unregulated economy that guided the rhetoric if not always the actions of that revolution. When it came to the conservative orthodoxy, indeed, many on the New Right saw Kemp as more Catholic than the ideological Pope who spoke ex cathedra from the Oval Office on all such matters. And he worked—like no one else in the party. He made 269 speeches in 1984, raising $1.6 million, and 60 in the first quarter of 1985, racing through airports every weekend peddling the conservative message—and his own availability for higher challenge.

Kemp's main rival on the far right appeared at this stage to be Paul Laxalt, acknowledged to be Reagan's best friend and closest political confidant in the Senate. If Laxalt were to run, the expectation was that he would make a very large dent in the most conservative wing in the party. It was often said, with considerable confidence, that the man Reagan would really like to be his successor was Laxalt, even if he would never say so publicly. And those close enough to know had few doubts that Laxalt would have been the choice of Nancy Reagan.

A third potential threat to Bush on the far right, not yet being considered seriously as a candidate, was Pat Robertson. But he had few credentials within the party, and there were doubts about how much political activity he could stir among the religious fundamentalists to whom he catered, to make him anything approaching a formidable candidate. For the rest, his confessions about getting personal instructions from God about his political future, about faith healing (including hemorrhoids) and about how he once successfully commanded a hurricane to bypass his Virginia Beach home base and move harmlessly to sea were a bit too much even for many of the most starry-eyed conservative faithful.

Then there was Bob Dole, who as the Senate majority leader had had his differences with the programs of the Reagan Revolution but more times than not had been leading the charge for them in the Senate. He would be laying claim, too, among party conservatives as the man to carry the revolution forward, and as the one best able to do so, because polls suggested he had more appeal than the others among Democrats and independents. But Dole's sharp edge, demonstrated so destructively in his 1976 debate with Walter Mondale when he ranted on about "Democrat wars," still gave many party leaders pause about his self-discipline in a crunch. Not even a definite softening of his bite —attributed, many said, to the influence of his popular wife, former Secretary of Transportation Elizabeth Dole—could erase the earlier memories.

Dole, in fact, had learned to turn his humor from others onto himself. He liked now to tell audiences that the biography in his campaign literature that said he volunteered for the Army in World War II, the scars and handicaps of which he still conspicuously bore, were "technically correct." What happened, he would say, was that "the draft board called me up and I said I'd be right down." On his return, he would say, a local Republican leader asked him to run for the state legislature "because he thought people would vote for me because I got shot." Undecided between the parties, he would relate, he learned there were five times as many Republicans in his county than Democrats, so "I made a philosophical decision and ran as a Republican." Such stories warmed audiences, but they failed to shake the concern of some in the party that under severe pressure Dr. Jekyll might turn into Mr. Hyde.

Lesser figures in the competition, at this juncture or later, included former Governor Pierre S. ("Pete") duPont IV of Delaware, former General and Secretary of State Alexander Haig, former Secretary of Defense Donald Rumsfeld and former Senate Majority Leader Howard Baker. While none of these was seen as a serious contender for the mantle of Ronald Reagan, all but Baker had the potential of draining off some support on the far right from conservatives who had feelings of apathy, doubt or suspicion about Bush.

One of duPont's main problems, though, was that he had no history of fighting in the political trenches with far-right foot soldiers for their most cherished causes. And his most newsworthy proposals—such as phasing out all farm subsidies in five years and requiring drug testing of any teenager seeking a driver's license—generated more controversy than support.

As for Haig, the public's clearest picture of him, as disclosed in polls and focus groups, was as the bug-eyed secretary of state in the White House briefing room shortly after Reagan was shot in 1981 declaring—incorrectly according to the constitutional line of succession—that "as of now, I am in control here." In one later focus group, a participant compared him to Rambo, and another, asked his impression of Haig, simply held up his hands, wiggled two fingers on each to signify quotation marks and said: "I'm in charge."

Rumsfeld, for his part, concentrated on building a base of business entrepreneurs like himself, and in the process demonstrated more than anything else his political naïveté. Of all the prospective 1988 candidates at this stage, only former Senate Majority Leader Howard Baker could not hope to tap into the far-right constituency at all.

When all was said and done, George Bush was the vice president in the Reagan administration and the boss after some early reservations had come to like him. That was more than the others could say. Moreover, there were certain things that could be done by Bush to capitalize on his special position, looking to 1988. Among those who also were looking, with a possible Bush presidential candidacy in mind, was Lee Atwater, at age twenty-nine deputy political director in the Reagan White House by way of South Carolina Republican politics. Very early, as far back as 1982, Atwater began to think about what was going to happen in the Republican Party after the Reagan years. He concluded, not surprisingly considering his background, that the candidate who could get a lock on the South well in advance of 1988 would have a strong leg up on the party's next presidential nomination. He had worked with Bush and saw in him a potential that eluded many other political professionals in and out of Republican ranks. In scheduling White House political events, Atwater made sure that Bush got his share of assignments and that he met the key political players in all the southern states.

After the reelection of the Reagan-Bush team in 1984, Atwater left the White House and joined the burgeoning Republican political consulting firm of three of the party's most aggressive and effective pros, Charlie Black, Paul Manafort and Roger Stone. He had been working there as a partner only a short time when George Bush asked him to run the political action committee he was establishing as the first, only thinly veiled, step toward a 1988 presidential candidacy. The recruitment in itself was a signal to the party's most conservative elements that Bush had found a home on the right, although Atwater in reality, though unquestionably conservative in his views, was first and foremost a pragmatic political operative.

Atwater proceeded to sow Bush seeds across Dixie, in state after state where he had been involved as a consultant or campaign manager in Republican primary elections. Atwater knew most of the hundred or so individuals who constituted the party's activist core in each state and he set about bringing them aboard the embryo Bush campaign.

In late 1985, Atwater undertook a deliberate campaign to position Bush on the party's right, particularly to eat into Kemp's base and make it difficult if not impossible for any candidate to run to Bush's right. He believed that for all the noise emanating from the far right, it had lost its clout as the nominating wing of the party, which it was with Goldwater in 1964 when there was a vanishing moderate wing. By the Reagan years, Atwater reasoned, the mainstream of the party had shifted toward a more centrist conservatism, leaving the far right with no more than 30 percent of the GOP base. So if Bush could collar only a fair portion of it, he could effectively neutralize Kemp as a threat, as well as any other candidates depending heavily on the far-right constituency.

"At the beginning of the process," Atwater said much later, "Kemp was the one I worried about. Dole didn't have a base and wasn't going to get a base. Kemp had the potential of having a base, and what I had to do early was keep Kemp destabilized. . . . I knew that if Bush made an incursion in there on the right, he could grab twenty-five percent of it. And more importantly, I felt like as an early front-runner we could fool the whole field into going over to the [far] right." If Bush moved in that direction, he said, "as if it were still the nominating wing of the party," some of the other candidates might be suckered into doing the same. "The key was to get everybody over there thinking that wing of the party was the dominant wing," Atwater said, "so you could move back" once Bush had siphoned off enough of the right-wing support to render that bloc nonthreatening to him.

The first major gesture in this effort came in December of 1985. Atwater decided to have Bush attend a dinner in honor of the memory of William Loeb, the ultraconservative publisher of the *Manchester* (N.H.) *Union Leader*, for years the scourge of liberals in both parties and, indeed, any Republican who even flirted with the political center. Loeb in his lifetime had taken particular relish in excoriating Republican moderates in as vile terms as he crucified liberal Democrats.

He called President Dwight D. Eisenhower "Dopey Dwight" and "a stinking hypocrite"; Henry Kissinger "Kissinger the Kike"; Gerald Ford "Jerry the Jerk"; Eugene McCarthy a "skunk's skunk's skunk"; Edmund Muskie "Moscow Muskie"; Nelson Rockefeller a "wife-swapper"; and Ted Kennedy a "coward." And all this before breakfast, usually on the front page of the *Union Leader*.

In the 1980 campaign in which Bush lost his "Big Mo"—momentum—in New Hampshire, Loeb chose a different primary target—conservative Republican Representative Phil Crane of Illinois. Presumably Loeb saw Crane as more of a threat to Reagan's grip on the right-wing vote than was Bush, whom he clearly regarded as a closet moderate. The publisher accused Crane, with no proof, of being a reckless womanizer and boozer—to the degree that Reagan felt compelled to phone Crane and tell him his staff had nothing to do with the Loeb smear.

But the publisher did have a few rounds in his shotgun for Bush. He accused him, among other things, of being the perpetrator of "Bushgate," the alleged acceptance of tainted money in his failed 1970 campaign for the Senate against Lloyd Bentsen. So eyebrows were raised when it was announced that Bush would be the main speaker at the dinner, at the request of Nackey Loeb, the publisher's widow and successor at the newspaper, who sought to carry on in her husband's sleazy tradition. Those eyebrows shot up even higher when Bush spoke about the man who had sought to crucify him in 1980.

To show he was a good sport and it was all in fun, Bush started out by recalling some of the softer Loebisms about him, such as "hypocrite . . . [guilty of] double-standard morality, involved up to his neck in Watergate . . . unfit to be the Republican nominee." He never mentioned a word about the much more serious if outdated "Bushgate" charges.

But Bush had come to praise his old pal Bill, not dredge up old slights. He lauded Loeb as "part of a great newspaper tradition of outspoken publishers" and even compared him to H. L. Mencken. "No one can doubt," Bush gushed, "that Bill Loeb always spoke the truth as he saw it." So, one could speculate, did Adolf Hitler—as he saw it.

In defense of Bush's appearance, Atwater tried to sell the notion that it really was an act of political courage, considering the abuse the vice president would take from the news media for showing up and saying nice things about the man who so often had savaged him. The spin was audacious, even for a campaign manager fighting "the wimp factor," but it didn't take with political reporters who knew Loeb and his venom. They wrote stories castigating Bush for caving in—while conservatives in the audience applauded him and others who weren't there heard about it and took a second look at this supposed closet moderate.

"Bush," an insider said later, "was not at all pleased about going to the Loeb dinner. He felt he had been treated not only unfairly but rather brutally by Bill Loeb in the 1980 campaign. . . . But there was a good deal of support for it and he acquiesced in the major opinions at that time and said, 'Fine, okay, I'll do it.' "

Predictably, Bush brought down on himself a flood of editorial criticism for such transparent pandering to the right in the state that held the nation's first presidential primary. A few weeks later, in January 1986, Bush addressed the Conservative Party of New York and then spoke to a conference of the Reverend Jerry Falwell's Liberty Federation in Washington, proclaiming to his host that ''America is in crying need of the moral vision you have brought to our political life.'' He urged the group to plunge ahead in its plans to get more deeply involved in politics. And around this time he met privately with television evangelist Jim Bakker, long before the sex scandal that devalued Bakker's political support.

Bush also made an appearance at the Conservative Political Action Conference, leading one anti-Bush wag to observe, recalling Walter Mondale's courting of Democratic special-interest groups in 1984, ''At least Mondale pandered to his friends.'' Another who said he hadn't forgotten how Bush had ignored the far right for so long asked rhetorically, ''Where was he when he didn't need us?'' Among the harder raps in print for Bush's courtship of the ultraconservative wing was one from columnist George Will dubbing him a ''lapdog,'' a somewhat ironic label coming from one of the right's prime bootlickers.

At the same time, some of the other prospective 1988 candidates did indeed attempt to follow Bush's rush to the right. The most notable was duPont, who during his career in the House of Representatives and as governor of Delaware had been regarded as one of the party's most prominent moderates, and was a political ally of Nelson Rockefeller.

In April 1986, a new organization of the dying breed of Republican moderates, calling itself the Republican Mainstream Committee, held a meeting in Chicago to consider ways to move the party back toward the center. DuPont was the featured speaker, and Atwater, concerned that Bush's move to the right had been overdone, dispatched an agent, Ron Kaufman, to observe the proceedings and report whether the vice president's recent activities were backfiring.

''Kaufman called me the night before,'' Atwater recalled, ''and said, 'I'm a little worried. All these moderates—duPont is looking awfully good to them. I'm afraid we're gonna get a terrible story that all the moderates are now glomming onto duPont.'' The next morning, after duPont had spoken, Kaufman called Atwater again. ''He said, 'You ain't gonna believe what happened. DuPont gave a speech kicking the shit out of the moderate wing of the party!' And I said to myself, 'Good God! Eureka! You talk about something working.' ''

Soon Dole and others were making obvious gestures to the right, to Atwater's satisfaction. ''The point is, everybody went over there, we got our chunk of it, and we moved on along,'' he said buoyantly later.

Kemp after the election gave Atwater credit for the strategy ''to make Bush the heir to Reagan, knowing full well that I would campaign as the heir to Reagan or the heir to the Reagan Revolution. If you look at what Bush did,'' he said, ''he very early came out and advocated a cut in the capital-gains tax, he stuck very close to the Reagan agenda and to Reagan himself. . . . His strategy in retrospect was to cut me off from what would have been, at least in our perspective, a natural constituency for Kemp—the Reagan wing of the party. . . . The fault line in the party turned out not to be a conservative-versus-moderate fault line as much as it turned out to be a Reagan wing of the party, which was more optimistic about the future and what we had done . . . [against those who said] that we were in deep trouble. Bush and I were trying to make the case that Reagan was right, that we were on the upswing. I was going after the optimistic wing of the party, and I think Bush cut me off. He preempted it, he got that vote. . . .''

Although Atwater expressed some wariness about Bush appearing to go too far in courting the far right, his candidate had little to fear as long as in doing so he remained Reagan's loyal servant. Anytime there was the slightest public perception that Bush might be getting out of step with his benefactor, the vice president quickly rectified or blurred it. For example, in September 1984, speaking in Charleston, South Carolina, Bush indicated he favored abortion in the case of a rape victim. When it was pointed out that Reagan's only stated exception to a total opposition to abortion was when the life of the mother was imperiled, Bush the next day in Savannah, Georgia, was asked whether he had a credibility problem on the matter. "I don't think so," he said. "There are an awful lot of things I don't remember." It was a line that would come in handy for Bush as time went on.

One thing George Bush always did remember, and that was his place. He was the classic number two man—deferential almost to the point of obsequiousness. It probably never occurred to him to utter Nelson Rockefeller's memorable disavowal of interest in the vice presidency (before accepting it): "I was not made to be standby material." Bush, it seemed, was custom-made for the job. And never was his suitability clearer than in his conduct in July 1985 when Reagan underwent surgery for intestinal cancer. Reagan on advice of counsel signed a temporary transfer of the duties of the presidency to Bush for the period the president would be under anesthesia. Bush, at his summer home in Kennebunkport, Maine, at the time, leisurely returned to Washington, where he stayed—not at the White House, but at his own official residence at the old Naval Observatory—maintaining a low profile until Reagan returned home a week later. Then Bush went back to Maine.

At the same time, however, he and his growing presidential campaign staff were busy lining up most of the prominent establishment Republicans in nearly every state and building up an unprecedented campaign war chest. His political action committee raised $3.9 million in 1985, of which only $150,000 was disbursed to help other candidates get elected. Kemp raised only $1.2 million in the same period, and the others less. By October of 1986, the Bush campaign bankroll was up to $12.6 million. Only Robertson was close, having raised $11.7 million but having spent all but $300,000, much of it in trying to generate the 3 million petition signatures Robertson said he would need to persuade him to run.

By the end of 1985, the Bush PAC had nine paid political consultants and a staff of twenty-four, including four regional directors and state directors in the first three delegate-selecting states on the Republican side—Michigan, Iowa and New Hampshire. And the Bush campaign hierarchy was taking shape. In addition to Atwater, it eventually included former New Jersey Senator Nicholas Brady, an old Bush friend, as campaign chairman; Detroit pollster-strategist Robert Teeter; New York media specialist Roger Ailes; fellow Texan Robert Mosbacher as finance chairman; and Craig Fuller, the vice president's chief of staff. The group came to be known as "the Gang of Six," or "G-6" for short. Not included, but always waiting in the wings to move to the top at the appropriate time, was Bush's Texas buddy and closest political friend, Secretary of the Treasury Jim Baker. It was a formidable high command.

Still, the perception continued that Bush was too weak, too namby-pamby, to win his party's presidential nomination, for all his obvious advantages of position and money. For this reason, the other hopefuls were not deterred from making their own plans and moves. With Reagan ineligible to run again, at least eight other Republicans—Dole, Kemp, Laxalt, Howard Baker, Robertson, duPont, Haig, Rumsfeld—expressed interest in one degree or another. Many of their supporters assured themselves that once Bush had to step out from the shadow of Ronald Reagan, he would melt into political nothingness.

In November 1986, two events of great political implications reinforced this impression of Bush's vulnerability. The first was the Republican loss of a Senate majority, in spite of President Reagan's energetic, personal campaigning in behalf of Republican incumbents who fell. The result cast doubts on the transferability of Reagan's political magic, of which Bush clearly hoped and figured to be the chief beneficiary in 1988. The second event was of even greater potential peril to Bush's White House aspirations—the Iran-Contra Affair.

One of the vice president's principal credentials in seeking the presidential nomination was his claim to a degree of foreign-policy experience that no other candidate could match. His claim went far beyond the ceremonial function of attending the inaugurations and funerals of world leaders. He was a member of the National Security Council and the head of special presidential task forces to fight terrorism and the international drug trade. Earlier, he had been ambassador to the United Nations, special U.S. representative to the Republic of China and director of the Central Intelligence Agency. If ever there was a public official trained to recognize what was going on in the sale of arms to Iran, described as a terrorist-aiding state in the report of his own task force, it was George Bush.

For six years, Bush had been telling audiences about his insider role in the Reagan administration; how he had been brought in on major decisions with special, direct access to the president at weekly lunches with just the two of them in the room. While he made it a cardinal principle never to criticize or differ with Reagan in public, he said, these lunches gave him the opportunity to express private disagreements and offer private counsel to his leader. The critical questions now emerged: If Bush was so deeply in the White House loop of decision-making, how could he not know what was going on? And if he did know, what did he say and do to save the president and the administration from this incredibly foolish and disastrous policy?

On top of all this, Bush was well positioned to be aware of the facts and political implications of the second half of the bizarre deal, the diversion of profits from the arms sale to the Nicaraguan guerrillas—the contras—seeking to overthrow the left-wing Sandinista regime in Managua. Bush's own national security adviser, Donald Gregg, had been informed the previous summer of Oliver North's resupply operation to the contras. When in October a CIA-underwritten plane carrying arms, uniforms and medicine to the contras was shot down and crew member Eugene Hasenfus was captured, the first word of the event came in a telephone call to Gregg in Bush's office. It also came to light that Bush had met in his office with Felix Rodriguez, also known as Max Gomez, a former CIA agent deeply involved in shipping arms to the contras.

Bush's dilemma was compounded three months after the Iran-contra story broke with the disclosure of a memorandum written by Craig Fuller, his chief of staff, summarizing a meeting he and Bush attended the previous July in the Jerusalem office of Amiram Nir, an Israeli official. Fuller wrote of Nir:

"He described the details of their [the Israelis'] efforts from last year through the current period to gain the release of the U.S. hostages. He reviewed what had been learned, which was essentially that the radical group was the group that could deliver. He reviewed the issues to be considered—namely that there needed to be a decision as to whether the items [arms] requested would be delivered in separate shipments or whether we would continue to press for release of the hostages prior to delivering the items in an amount agreed to previously."

Fuller also wrote specifically that Nir had told Bush: "We are dealing with the most radical elements. . . . They can deliver . . . that's for sure. . . . This is good because we've learned they can deliver and the moderates can't."

Fuller's memo contradicted the administration's stated view that those dealing in the arms sales believed they were doing business with moderates inside Iran who might gain the hostages' release and bring about a change of attitude eventually as successors to the Ayatollah Khomeini. The memo also made clear that Bush at the very least knew what was going on long before the scandal became public. His advisers responded that the Fuller memo had been turned over to North and that Bush subsequently was told by NSC officials that Nir was wrong in saying the negotiations on the hostages were being conducted with radicals. So Bush simply continued to contend that the Reagan administration was merely seeking contacts with more moderate elements in Iran who someday might restore the old American-Iranian relationship.

In all this, Bush was careful not to say that he personally believed that there was no arms-for-hostages swap with terrorists of the sort his own task force report on terrorism had only recently condemned. Instead, he simply said he believed Reagan believed it. "The problem on all this, of course," he said in a *Time* magazine interview, "is the perception that arms were traded for hostages. The president is absolutely, totally convinced in his mind that that isn't what happened. I know him, I know what his feeling is on this. I have heard what he said, and I accept it.'' But what did Bush himself believe? And did he inform Reagan? Hiding behind his convenient policy of not disclosing what he discussed privately with the president, he wouldn't say.

In a very telling interview with David Broder of the *Washington Post*, Bush said he was not present when Secretary of State Shultz and Secretary of Defense Weinberger expressed strong opposition to the arms sales. But had he been, he added, ''maybe I would have had a strong view''—not exactly a ringing tribute to his independence of thought and conviction. Not impressive, either, was his explanation to Broder for not having been at the meeting in question—that he was ''off at the Army-Navy football game'' that day.

One effect of Bush's Iran-contra problem was a growing conviction among the party's New Right stalwarts that Bush could not be elected—and that a stronger right-wing challenger to him had to be found. They still admired Jack Kemp and his doctrines. Almost alone he had stood at the ramparts of the far right on basic positions on the economy, national defense and foreign policy. But they increasingly doubted that he could stop Bush.

This attitude clearly manifested itself in the search for some alternative. Bob Dole was too much of a pragmatic operator for them, suspect particularly on holding the line against more tax increases. Pat Robertson was an unpredictable, undependable figure with his own agenda and his own special constituency. Pete duPont was too recent a convert to the faith, with an alien Eastern Establishment background and style. And Al Haig was regarded by just about everyone in the party as a loose cannon more driven by ego than ideology of any stripe.

For a time in early 1987, the far right in its throes even inspired one of its most prominent verbal bomb throwers, Patrick Buchanan, then director of communications in the Reagan White House, to mull over a candidacy. An enthusiastic but hopeless draft effort surfaced briefly for former United Nations Ambassador Jeane Kirkpatrick, the self-important formerly Democratic academic who had found a new home among adoring hard-liners of the right. But even the heavies of the far right were not ready to go that far.

At the annual Conservative Political Action Conference in February, Kemp made a determined effort to hold on to his base. He pulled out all the stops, calling for the resignation of the far right's pet hate, George Shultz, making a stout defense of Reagan's space-defense ''Star Wars'' scheme and strumming the tightest strings in the antiabortion harp. ''Isn't it true,'' he intoned, ''that the same liberal leadership which cries on cue for compassion and human rights utters not one word of concern over the loss of inalienable rights of four thousand unborn children every day?'' And on the Iran-contra mess: ''The very people who see the smoking gun of scandal in Washington over Iran still remain blind to the real smoking gun of communist expansionism in Central America.''

In the wake of this kind of raw-meat rhetoric and Bush's conspicuous absence from the conference, Kemp easily won the straw poll of 813 conference attendees, with 68 percent of the vote to 9 percent on write-ins for Buchanan, who by now had taken himself out of consideration, and small change for the others. Only one third of those present voted, however, and Dole supporters complained vigorously that the vote had been rigged. At any rate, Kemp's showing at the conference had little impact nationally and the yearning for another far-right candidate continued. Shortly afterward, in New Hampshire, Kemp challenged Bush to join him in pledging the deployment of Reagan's Strategic Defense Initiative (SDI)—in the face of overwhelming evidence that any meaningful deployment was years off. Clearly, the old professional quarterback was throwing the long bomb to hold on to his base and convince the conservative wing of the party that he remained the logical alternative to the front-running Bush.

In March, however, Paul Laxalt answered the call—sort of. He was believed to have reservations about Bush's abilities as a candidate and as a president, but he also had doubts about his own chances of election. He had agonized long over the feasibility of a strategy that would depend on his survival through the early 1988 contests in Iowa, New Hampshire and the South and then emergence from a muddled field in his own Far West. Now, amid much fanfare, he announced the creation of a committee to "explore" his candidacy. Many of the old Reagan hands were in conspicuous evidence at his press conference at the National Press Club. And none was more so than Lyn Nofziger, the former Reagan White House political director then under investigation by a special prosecutor for alleged violations of a federal ethics law involving lobbying. Nofziger, who presided at the conference, was later convicted, but Laxalt said at the time: "I adhere to the presumption of innocence, especially where it involves my friends." The far right seemed to have found its new champion—at Kemp's expense.

Undeterred, Kemp in early April formally declared his candidacy. In introducing him, House Republican Whip Trent Lott referred to him as "our spiritual leader" who would "continue the Reagan Revolution." Kemp again served up the conservative agenda undiluted, complete with a call to make the 1988 election "a national referendum" on early deployment of SDI. By this time, though, the reality of Kemp's political situation was no match for his seemingly bottomless enthusiasm. The most recent NBC News–*Wall Street Journal* poll, for instance, had him running at only 8 percent among Republican and Republican-leaning independent voters, far behind Bush at 28 percent and Dole at 23 percent. And Laxalt, who was not mentioned in the poll, was poised to jump in, further undercutting Kemp on the right, not to mention Pat Robertson. And on top of everything else, Kemp's campaign was already in the red and obliged to borrow against the federal matching funds that he would get at the start of 1988. Money, in politics as in life, was not everything, but it did make things easier. Kemp needed all the help he could get and he just wasn't getting it. DuPont's campaign coordinator in New Hampshire, Fred

Maas, may have summed up Kemp's appeal when he remarked one day that "Kemp's kind of like a hot pipe. It keeps you warm, but don't touch it."

Kemp did get a bit of good fortune in August when Laxalt after further agonizing decided not to run, thus joining Rumsfeld and Baker as early dropouts. He cited the difficulty of raising the kind of money needed to make a successful race, and indeed by this time he was far behind the others, and especially Bush. Friends said he never did realize the time, effort and commitment it would take to win the nomination and he was just settling into a lucrative law practice in Washington after a lifetime of public service. Kemp again became the obvious alternative to Bush for the support of the far right, but by now Bush had already siphoned off enough of that support, and Robertson was showing enough strength, to reduce Kemp to the status of a fringe candidate.

Dole, meanwhile, had not given up in the fight for right-wing support. In August he journeyed to Central America and a much-publicized, much-photographed meeting with Nicaraguan President Daniel Ortega. It turned out to be a heated exchange after which Dole complained that his host had "attempted to use us as props in a circus atmosphere." But Dole's lament was undercut by the fact that he had his own camera crew along to capture the scene for possible use in campaign commercials later on. In pitching to the far right, Dole like duPont was playing into Atwater's strategy of "suckering" the opposition into competition for a segment of the party that was no longer dominant, and splintered at that.

Dole's Central American trip was, however, little more than a detour on his main campaign itinerary throughout 1987. Taking a pass in the early competition in Michigan, where the first national convention delegates of 1988 would be chosen, Dole concentrated on making up for a slow start in Iowa, the first broadly competitive caucus state where he hoped to establish himself clearly as Bush's chief challenger.

The reality of the Republican pecking order became clear in late October in the first joint appearance of the six surviving candidates—Bush, Dole, Kemp, Robertson, duPont and Haig—in Houston. With columnist William F. Buckley and former Democratic National Chairman Robert Strauss as moderators, the format was a loose version of Buckley's syndicated television show, *Firing Line*, and Bush was squarely on that line. He had declared in his formal announcement of candidacy a couple of weeks earlier that although he had kept his own ideas to himself as a loyal vice president, "you're going to see a tiger unleashed" henceforth. It hadn't happened yet. The other candidates had waited for months for a crack at the insulated vice president and they took advantage of this forum to try to cut him down to size.

But Bush was equal to the task. Coolly and firmly, he defended his refusal to differ with Reagan in public, making a virtue of his loyalty without sounding like the sycophant he so often resembled in the past.

At the same time, efforts of the long-shot candidates, Haig and duPont, to use Bush as a punching bag, and thus elevate their standing or at least their visibility at his expense, fell flat and even helped him. At one point, after Bush had defended Reagan's recent nuclear arms reduction with the Soviet Union, Haig cracked that when he had spoken against such reductions in Europe, "I never heard a wimp out of you, George." The audience groaned.

At another point, when duPont criticized Bush for not demonstrating compassion for the plight of the poor, implying that Bush was an aloof elitist, and talked about a need to overhaul Social Security, Bush shot back: "Pierre, I think it's a nutty idea to fool around with the Social Security system." The use of "Pierre" instead of "Pete" had its desired effect with the audience, and was no coincidence. Ailes, in briefing Bush for the debate, warned him that duPont, trailing badly in all the polls, might try to confront the front-running vice president as a way to get attention, and might try to put the elitist tag on him. "If he starts this crap—George Herbert Walker Bush," Ailes told him, "you should say, 'Look, Pierre. . . .' " Bush replied, according to Ailes, "I can't say that." But Ailes told him he couldn't just sit back when there was going to be "a firing squad" against him and that, "make no mistake it will be 'Get Bush.' " When duPont did try that number on him, Ailes said later, he got under Bush's skin and the vice president slapped back.

In this and later debates and confrontations, Ailes and Atwater insisted after the election, Bush's strong dislike to attack was always a problem for his handlers. Only when he was convinced that he was being assaulted, they said, could he be persuaded to strike back. For this reason, Atwater said later, a basic "counterpunch strategy" evolved that guided Bush throughout the 1988 campaign. It came to be a major element later, he said, in dispensing the image of personal weakness that haunted Bush's candidacy and for a long time threatened to do it in.

But counterpunching wasn't always sufficient, as Bush learned in the final debate of the preelection period, at the Kennedy Center in December 1987. This time it was Haig who bored in on Bush. As head of the president's task force on antiterrorism that recommended that the United States "never engage in paying blackmail to terrorists," Haig asked, "where were you when the administration made a decision to do precisely that?" Bush replied weakly that "I wrote the antiterror report. It is the best antiterror report that any country has ever had." Haig, with his fiercest, most indignant look, shot back: "You're running for president, and I think the American people want to know the position you took."

Just as important as Haig's question, however, was the inherent recognition in it that George Bush, after all the preliminaries, remained on the eve of the 1988 presidential election year the candidate to beat for the Republican nomination. And although it was Haig who posed the question that now loomed as a major pothole on Bush's road to the nomination, it was equally clear to Atwater that Dole was the prime Republican beneficiary of the circumstances that gave rise to Haig's question. Only Dole, as the Senate minority leader, had the recognized stature to go up against the vice president of the United States on the critical Iran-Contra Affair.

"The Iran-contra controversy was a royal pain in the ass," Atwater conceded later, "but that finished off Kemp more than anything else. It made it a two-man race between Bush and Dole. The veep went down during that time, Dole had a meteoric rise and in effect everybody else was shut out of the race." Because of his position, Atwater said, "Dole was on television literally every night" saying the administration and Bush should make a clean breast of things. "It made Bob Dole," Atwater said. "There's no [other] way Dole would have risen up and made this a two-man race a year out."

Although the Iran-contra controversy caused the Bush campaign much grief, Atwater in retrospect claimed to be grateful for it because, in his view at least, it shut out the one candidate, Kemp, who had the kind of potential base that could sustain him—and served up in relative isolation the one major opponent who lacked just such a base. On matters of age, generation, ideological base and issue constituencies, Atwater argued, Kemp offered a much sharper contrast to Bush and potential for growth than did Dole.

At any rate, Bush headed into the presidential election year of 1988 still at the head of the pack. He stood there in spite of the foreign-policy scandal within the Reagan administration that threatened to destroy his candidacy—and in the face of developments already taking place in the GOP delegate-selecting process that were casting severe doubts on Bush's front-runner status. While the rest of the nation was still engaged in political dress rehearsals, the real thing was not only well under way but at a fever pitch among the Republicans in Michigan—with the clear potential of disaster for the vice president of the United States.

6

Michigan: Dodging the Bullet

It was like the rain: Everybody complained about it but nobody ever did anything about it. For years, ever since New Hampshire with its kickoff presidential primary and then Iowa with its even earlier precinct caucuses launched the selection of delegates to the two national party conventions, politicians elsewhere grumbled. Why should these two pip-squeak states have such inordinate say in deciding who would be the presidential nominees?

The lament came particularly from politicians in larger states that held their primaries and caucuses later in the preconvention season. By the time the candidates got to the larger states, the chances were that the nomination would be decided or that a number of the presidential hopefuls would have dropped out. Whatever luster they had would have been rubbed off by defeat and further dulled by a consequent inability to raise the campaign funds needed to persevere.

In Michigan in 1980, the state's moderate Republican wing had felt especially frustrated. Under the leadership of then Governor William Milliken, the moderates lined up behind presidential candidate George Bush against the candidate of the conservatives, Ronald Reagan, and beat him soundly in the GOP primary in May. But as the Bush campaign in the state was wildly celebrating that victory that night, the television networks were reporting that elsewhere Reagan had accumulated enough delegates to clinch the party's nomination. Bush's Michigan primary triumph had been rendered meaningless even before it could be properly savored. If only the Michigan voting had come earlier in the process, the Bush supporters reasoned, the whole outcome of the 1980 race for the presidential nomination might have been different.

The state's Democrats weren't happy about their 1980 delegate-selection process, either. National party reforms had forced them to abandon the primary because it was open—that is, Republicans and independents were eligible to vote in it. So the Michigan Democrats had turned to the caucus system, producing a contorted process unfamiliar to the voters and largely ignored by them. Only about sixteen thousand cast ballots in the 1980 statewide caucuses in which challenger Edward M. Kennedy narrowly edged President Jimmy Carter. That result didn't mean much, either.

Aware that the Michigan Republicans in 1980 had attracted a much larger turnout with their primary, the Democrats in 1983, having won control of both houses of the state legislature, outlawed the primary altogether. It was a move that, unwittingly, gave the Republicans in the state an opening to move ahead of all the other states in the GOP delegate-selecting process. With the primary dropped, the Republicans were left with an old system on the books whereby presidential delegates were to be chosen at a state convention on an undetermined date. Furthermore, the old system provided that delegates to this convention were to be picked in precinct elections held about two years in advance of the GOP's national nominating convention. In other words, individuals elected then would have critical roles in deciding which presidential candidate would control the Michigan delegation to the national party convention two years later.

The national Democratic Party had a rule stipulating that no aspect of its delegate-selection process could begin before the start of the presidential election year, but the Republicans had no such prohibition. A handful of leading Michigan Republicans saw in the forced switch away from the presidential primary the opening they needed to move to the head of the process in future presidential elections. New Hampshire had a state law requiring that its own presidential primary be the first in the nation, but it did not stipulate that the primary be held ahead of any state precinct caucus or election of the sort Michigan would now be holding. As for Iowa, then the first caucus state, it was concerned only with conducting precinct caucuses before the New Hampshire primary, and its state elections law so specified.

For the 1984 presidential cycle, the Michigan Republicans routinely selected their national convention delegation at their state convention, attended by individuals elected at the precinct level in August of 1982. Because there was no contest impending for the presidency in the Republican Party in 1984 —Reagan was certain to be renominated unopposed—the process attracted little attention even in Michigan. But after the reelection of Reagan and Bush, a light bulb went on over the heads of state party leaders and other activists. Why not schedule the 1988 Republican state convention before the Iowa caucuses and the New Hampshire primary? That simple move would in turn assure that the routine Michigan precinct-delegate elections of 1986 would become the first battleground of the 1988 campaign for the Republican presidential nomination.

At first blush at least, the notion of moving Michigan to the head of the Republican delegate-selection process for 1988 seemed a surefire boost for the presidential aspirations of Bush, victor over Reagan in the state only four years earlier. Controlling such a large bloc of national convention delegates (seventy-seven) at the very start of the process figured to get the Bush campaign off flying, heading into Iowa and New Hampshire.

Iowa particularly was recognized from the start by Bush strategists as a potential pitfall. In 1984, the state was one of the weakest for the Reagan-Bush ticket, largely because Iowa's farm-oriented economy remained mired in recession—long after the Reagan recovery had lifted most other states out. Reagan, remembered fondly in Iowa before 1980 as the onetime re-creator of Chicago Cubs baseball games for listeners of WHO radio in Des Moines, alienated many Iowa farmers with seeming indifference or even callousness toward their plight. They particularly weren't amused by his crack, concerning the grain embargo against the Soviet Union, that maybe the country should keep the grain and ship the farmers there. So it wouldn't hurt Bush to come into the Iowa precinct caucuses in early 1988 with Michigan's hefty delegation already aboard his campaign.

Bush supporters in Michigan weren't the only ones, though, to see the potential in the new situation. After Milliken left the governor's office in 1982, the moderate Republican wing of the state party that had dominated for twenty years—six under Governor George Romney and fourteen under Milliken— began to give way to a much more conservative faction. This circumstance gave two other 1988 Republican aspirants cause to believe that Bush might well be ambushed in Michigan.

The first was Jack Kemp, the new-generation hope of the right. He was particularly popular with Republicans of very conservative bent who had survived as part of the party establishment in the state legislature after Milliken's departure and who identified themselves as the real Reaganites, as opposed to the old Bush backers who got aboard the Reagan bandwagon after the 1980 GOP convention. Kemp's allies in Michigan operated openly and with dispatch, forming a Michigan Opportunity Society under Detroit lawyer W. Clark Durant III and State Senator Dick Posthumus to advance the Kemp ideology and candidacy.

"I had to establish some quick credibility that I was a legitimate candidate," Kemp said after the election. "Frankly, it got started in Michigan earlier than I would have chosen. Some conservatives and others who were interested in my candidacy kind of took off before I was even ready. They went off on their own to a certain degree. My campaign in Michigan got mixed up in some other agendas, one of which was who would lead the so-called conservative movement in Michigan for the future."

Charlie Black, looking back later, said he thought in 1986 that "we had a great opportunity, maybe not to beat Bush in Michigan, but to finish a strong second and get a lot of delegates and get some attention out of it." But that thinking was based on the notion, or the hope, that Kemp would get a clean shot at the front-running Bush. That did not prove to be the case. Another presidential prospect was also alert to the political possibilities in Michigan— Pat Robertson. But unlike Kemp, who launched an obvious presidential effort in the state, Robertson infiltrated, almost surreptitiously. He created political cells masquerading as mere voter-education brigades that would have been the envy of the godless communists he so conspicuously despised.

Robertson established a Freedom Council with branches in Michigan and other key primary and caucus states. He vowed at first to be interested only in encouraging God-fearing Christian Americans to take part in the political process, to protect their values against the threats of liberals and other atheistic radicals. But he, too, saw the potential for using the new, earlier Michigan schedule to give Bush a political black eye and burst onto the national political scene himself.

Robertson recruited a crafty young veteran of right-wing Republican politics, Marc Nuttle, to run his campaign. A basic assumption from the start, Nuttle said later, was that "George Bush would dominate the party and the party structure with an iron fist," and that the theory that he would collapse if he tripped in just one state was fallacious. Therefore, Nuttle went on, Robertson would have to demonstrate his strength outside the party establishment, especially because "no matter what success Pat Robertson had he would never be perceived by the press or the public as a candidate who could win the nomination, or if he did, could win the election." In order to make believers of the party regulars, Nuttle said, Robertson had to run well in states with processes of relatively low turnout, such as caucuses, and in low-turnout congressional districts and a few small states. Michigan with its relatively obscure precinct elections was just such a state, and Robertson set out to win it.

But it was Bob Dole, not Kemp or Robertson, who was the perceived chief threat to a Bush nomination, and Dole saw Michigan differently. He sent one of his chief political agents, Don Devine, to reconnoiter the state, and Devine reported back that Bush already had a lock on it. Dole made some trips there, too, and concluded the same. "Everywhere I went, I was too late," he said after the election. "It was going to be a tough state where Bush had all the party apparatus wrapped up. The party controlled the process. I might have picked up a few delegates, a few districts, but Secchia was playing hardball. If you weren't for Bush you weren't going to get speakers for your district. We just decided it wasn't worth it."*

Dole said he had to win the first state in which he competed "and couldn't do it in Michigan. It seemed all along that if I was going to have any success against Bush it would have to be very early, but we didn't think people focused very much on Michigan." The caucuses in Iowa, a farm state like his own Kansas, looked like a much better bet for him, so he took a pass on Michigan.

By the late spring of 1985, the battle lines between Bush and Kemp in the state were already emerging, with little thought of Robertson as a serious contender there. Bush and Kemp attended a Midwestern Republican Leadership Conference in Grand Rapids and in September, when the state party held its annual conference on Mackinac Island, again the national party heavy hitters descended.

Jim Baker, then secretary of the treasury, was the main speaker, and although he vowed that he was wearing only his cabinet hat, he met privately with the Bush leaders in the state to discuss the presidential political situation. Among other things, he told them that Bush as the front-runner had to compete against all comers for the Michigan delegation, beginning with the precinct-delegate elections now slated for August 1986.

In the late spring of 1986, as the Bush and Kemp forces continued to recruit support from the essentially limited universe of state Republican activists who traditionally voted in the precinct elections, they got their first real clue that Robertson meant business in Michigan. A suburban Detroit housewife named Marlene Elwell surfaced as the prime Robertson organizer. A deceptively ingenuous middle-aged woman, Elwell was known within Michigan Republican politics as a relentless, crackerjack practitioner of grass-roots recruiting from the antiabortion movement. She and associates set out to recruit into activist Republican ranks the large community of religious evangelicals to whom Robertson was a revered public figure and guiding light.

At this point, both the Bush and Kemp forces saw the Michigan contest as a two-man race between their candidates. Kemp strategists in the state and at the national campaign headquarters adopted a posture of friendly insouciance toward Robertson. They figured that he was not going anywhere politically and that once he recognized that fact Kemp would be the natural, ideological heir to whatever voting strength the Robertson effort had been able to mount in Michigan. Bush's brain trust, meanwhile, calculated that any support for Robertson would take away from Kemp on the party's right, helping Bush. So the

*Peter Secchia was Kent County (Grand Rapids) Republican chairman, national committeeman from Michigan and a leader of the Bush campaign forces in the state. Bush later made him Ambassador to Italy.

Bush and Kemp camps concentrated on the party establishment and didn't worry about Robertson. That was fine with the cable television preacher from Virginia. He went about his business of collecting 3 million signatures petitioning him to run—at a cost, he said later, of $10 million, a burden that severely handicapped his campaign thereafter.*

Even before Robertson proved that his opponents' attitude of ignoring him was an imprudent one, however, the new Michigan process and prominence were creating legal and money headaches for the Bush campaign. None of the candidates had as yet formally declared for the presidential nomination, for good reason. Once you became a declared candidate, a condition of receiving the federal campaign subsidy was acceptance of spending limits applied for the entire period in advance of the national convention. With the presidential election more than two years away, Bush's undeclared candidacy did not want to be pouring money into Michigan that it would need later. And once you started spending money earmarked for your candidacy, the Federal Election Commission overseeing campaign spending could consider you a formal candidate. So to head off the Kemp threat in Michigan, the Bush campaign used a separate political action committee called the Fund for America's Future to underwrite its effort, contending that money spent was not for Bush, but was merely to encourage greater participation in the precinct elections as a party-building enterprise. This premise was a transparent subterfuge from the start, but the Bush campaign was able, with a sympathetic FEC, to get away with it for valuable months in early 1986.

In March of that year, the legal staff of the FEC wrote a draft opinion arguing that the election of precinct delegates in Michigan was indisputably "the first level in the Michigan process of selecting delegates to the 1988 Republican National Convention." Therefore, the legal staff advised, any money spent by a presidential candidate, declared or undeclared, to aid in the election of such precinct delegates constituted action beneficial to his own candidacy. It should be charged, the staff said, against the legal limit he could spend in that state and nationally in pursuit of the nomination.

But the Republican-controlled FEC, never known for having a backbone, rejected the draft and gave Bush and the other candidates a green light to continue the subterfuge in Michigan. The day after the opinion came out, Bush took off for his ninth trip to the state in little more than a year to engage in more "party building." Thomas E. Harris, a dissenting Democrat on the commission, said that "only someone just alighting from a UFO" could fail to see that Bush was running for president and financing the effort through the back door of his political action committee. Bush's PAC by this time had raised nearly $4 million, far more than any other candidate. If the Bush campaign had hoped at one time to pick up the Michigan delegation on the cheap and without a very major,

*Robertson delayed declaring his candidacy, he said, because "I wanted to make sure I was doing God's will." Since he responded to the petitions, we asked him later, wasn't the catalyst the will of 3 million people? "Well," he said, "God works through people."

wrenching effort, that hope had long been shattered by now. With Bush pumping so much money into the state, Robertson's manager, Marc Nuttle, said later, Michigan "became a true championship game" that the front-runner could ill afford to lose.

The Bush campaign took pains, however, to perpetuate the dodge. A memorandum to members of the PAC's national steering committee from Ede Holiday, the Fund's special counsel, provided guidelines on what and what not to say. "The Vice President has made no decision as to his political future and has not authorized anyone to promote any future candidacy," it said. "DON'T refer to Vice President Bush as a candidate for President. He is not. DO identify Vice President Bush as the Founder and Honorary Chairman of The Fund. DO promote the goals of The Fund which are to support the Republican Party and Republican candidates in 1986. DON'T 'handicap' the 1988 presidential 'horse race.' Avoid associating The Fund with any elections after 1986. . . . DON'T state or imply that a contribution to The Fund is a contribution to any future candidacy of the Vice President. . . . DON'T state or imply that The Fund is a campaign committee. DO say that The Fund is a multicandidate committee formed to assist Republicans in 1986. . . . While we cannot control speculation by others, we must not add fuel to any premature talk about 1988. Let's keep our eye on the 1986 elections."

The Kemp and Robertson campaigns in varying degrees also played fast and loose in Michigan with the federal campaign spending laws. The Michigan Opportunity Society functioned as the prime front for Kemp's undeclared candidacy in the state and was the mildest of the dodges. The worst was Robertson's scheme for bankrolling his ambitious political operation in Michigan.

Robertson's campaign operated behind his multistate cover for building a political organization, the Freedom Council, until the Internal Revenue Service began to investigate its tax-exempt status, which barred support of federal candidates. The writer of a syndicated religious news column, Michael McManus, obtained past tax returns of Robertson's Christian Broadcasting Network under the Freedom of Information Act and reported that CBN had given or loaned more than $8 million to the Freedom Council between 1984 and 1986. When asked about the report, Robertson called it "irresponsible, outrageous and totally unsubstantiated"—but he never provided any serious rebuttal.

When the IRS turned the heat on, Robertson shut the council down and replaced it with a political action committee called the Michigan Committee for Freedom to carry on the recruitment of the religious right into Republican politics in Michigan. A flier distributed at a Committee for Freedom dinner in suburban Detroit specifically listed among its functions providing "the organizational catalyst to control the presidential delegate selection process" in Michigan. It also invited corporate contributions to the committee's "Civic League"—contributions barred by law for the purpose of influencing a federal election. "Unlike political committees," the flier said, "there is no limit on how much an individual or corporation can contribute."

The Civic League did not endorse candidates, but a Michigan Committee for Freedom Political Fund, which didn't take corporate funds, did on a local and state basis. The separation provided legal protection for the Robertson operation, but for all practical purposes all these elements were part of its effort to project Robertson onto the national political stage.

The flier provided the flavor of the Robertson campaign's appeal. It asked: "If principled citizens were in positions of governmental authority, would we have pornography running unchecked in our communities? Would God be banned from our public schools? Would Secular Humanism continue its cancerous growth in the sciences, in our schools, in the media, in our legal system, and in the fields of entertainment? Would abortions be paid for by our tax dollars? Would criminals appear to have more rights than their victims? Would homosexuality be applauded as a viable alternative lifestyle and its expression taught to our children and protected by law? Would the traditional Judeo-Christian view of the Family be subjected to ridicule and attack?"

From the start, the delegate-selection process put a premium on organization, which in turn required money. For years, the Republican precinct elections had been routine affairs in which only a relative handful of party activists participated. With about 12,700 precinct-delegate slots available to attend county and district conventions in the state's eighty-three counties, about 4,000 in the past had gone begging for individuals interested enough to file for them. But now the stakes were much higher.

A precinct delegate could be elected to his county or congressional district convention and then to the state convention where he could cast his vote for, or become part of, the Michigan delegation to the national convention nominating the Republican presidential candidate. The campaign that could mobilize the most candidates for precinct delegate around the state, and get them elected, would be best positioned to reap the benefit at the state convention. And because in many, many precincts historically there had never been enough delegate candidates to fill available slots, simply getting someone to file was often tantamount to election.

The filing deadline for precinct delegate was May 27, 1986, with the precinct elections scheduled for August 5. Suddenly, all three competing hopefuls—Bush, Kemp and Robertson—began to show an inordinate interest in the health and welfare of the Michigan Republican Party. Labeling the precinct filings and elections as essential party-building events, they set about recruiting and supporting precinct-delegate candidates across the state, all with the prime objective—they insisted—of making the Michigan GOP all that it could be.

Before long, charges and countercharges were flying over who was spending how much for what. Were the Michigan precinct elections purely local affairs outside the purview of the Federal Election Commission? Or were they the first official step in the state's national convention delegate-selection process, and hence subject to federal limits on money spent and national candidate behavior?

"All of them lied so much," state party chairman E. Spencer Abraham said long afterward of the spending. "They put spins on what they were spending and made accusations about what the others were doing."

On May 27, the filing deadline, county clerks across Michigan were astounded at the turnout. In all, more than 9,000 Republicans filed for precinct delegate, or an increase of about 300 percent over any previous filing. Immediately, the three rival camps began to claim victory. The Bush and Robertson campaigns each said about 4,800 of their people had filed, and the Kemp forces said neary 3,700 of the total was theirs. Obviously, there was some heavy exaggerating going on. But one thing was clear from reports around the state: There were a great many folks showing up whom county clerks—party regulars—hadn't seen before. Many said they had been recruited by the Freedom Council and were getting involved in politics for the first time at the urging of Robertson, to do their part to restore religious and family values to a process he told them was devoid of both.

The Robertson filings jolted the Bush and Kemp camps. The precinct elections were only ten weeks away, and the door was now closed to further recruitment of candidates for delegate. The name of the game now was making sure the Bush and Kemp delegate candidates got elected. But Robertson had recruited candidates in many precincts previously uncontested where filing was tantamount to election. Suddenly the vice president of the United States, for all his prestige, organization and money, was facing the prospect of a major political defeat. Rich Bond, Bush's national political director, was rushed into the state.

"I'd just as soon not have had Michigan," Lee Atwater, Bush's young campaign manager, said after the election, reviewing the high and low marks, "but I don't think we could have avoided it, was the point. And the one mistake I assume responsibility for, that I made in the whole thing, was I might have insisted and fought to put about two hundred grand more in Michigan in the first stage." Had that been done, Atwater said, the Bush campaign could have filed 8,000 delegates and won the state easily, without all the grief and wrenching political work that was eventually required. "That's what made it such a Vietnam for us," he said. In the end, he said, the Michigan fight provided a lot of drama for those watching and Bush was able to show his tenacity by surviving there, "but Michigan was a giant pain in the ass for the most part."

As for Kemp, his own numbers were vastly inflated. He was staring at the distinct possibility of being a distant also-ran in this first test for 1988, which he had hoped would propel him into the picture as a major contender, and just possibly be the beginning of the end for the Bush candidacy.

A full two years before the 1988 Republican National Convention, Michigan became an all-out presidential campaign battleground. First Bush, and then Robertson, decided that it was no longer feasible to maintain the fiction that party building in Michigan was all that was at stake in the precinct elections. "It got to the point where, frankly, I sat down with [the Bush campaign's lawyers] and we just couldn't stretch it," Atwater recalled. "It didn't make sense. We were doing stuff that you couldn't say was party building. We were doing stuff that I felt like the only reason you could justify doing it was to help George Bush get elected president.''

So, in early July, Bush dropped the pretense and filed a presidential exploratory committee with the FEC, acknowledging that he was "testing the waters" for a 1988 candidacy. This step enabled him to advocate openly the election of delegate candidates pledged to him. At the same time, it limited contributions to the exploratory committee to $1,000 from an individual and, if Bush became a declared candidate, would place such funds under the federal spending limits for the preconvention period. Ten days later, Robertson did the same, forming an Americans for Freedom exploratory committee. But Bush continued his regular PAC as a way to solicit additional funds that could be funneled into Michigan without counting against the federal limit. And Robertson continued to build a network of interlocking political committees, leading to allegations of illegality that plagued his candidacy through 1988.

Nuttle said after the election that critics found it "hard to understand that you can actually motivate people for a cause or an issue, and that's what the Freedom Council was about." Such people were often politically unsophisticated, he said, and did not understand the legal distinctions on what could and couldn't be done under the law by the different Robertson-backed committees.

Others less sympathetic to the Robertson operation in Michigan, however, questioned that it was all that innocent. They suggested that Robertson deliberately and repeatedly tried to skirt the spending limitations in the state and to avoid close scrutiny by the FEC by having various committees established.*

Bush, in a style becoming the vice president of the United States, campaigned in Michigan in carefully programmed, antiseptic circumstances, like a potentate among his subjects. The extravaganza of *Air Force Two* setting down at medium-sized city airports around the state, with Secret Service agents keeping the subjects at bay, gave Bush's campaigning a regal air. Delegate candidates received gilt-edged invitations to meet him at limited-access meetings in which they were able to shake his hand and maybe have a picture taken with him. These were the party faithful, some who were with him in 1980, others who had backed Reagan but now accepted Bush as his converted surrogate. He made a point of telling them he wasn't yet a candidate, but he left no doubt that he was on his way.

Robertson, by contrast, was the political chautauqua itinerant, preaching

---

*Not until the end of December 1988 did the FEC formally charge the Robertson campaign with violating the federal election law, and then the commission administered a mere slap on the wrist. It fined his campaign a piddling $25,000 for continuing the pretext that Robertson was not a presidential candidate for a year longer than the facts and his actions warranted. The FEC ruling noted that when Robertson held a mass rally at Constitution Hall in Washington in September 1986, with satellite feeds around the country, and added a direct-mail appeal for support, he "went beyond the testing of the feasibility of a campaign" and as a formal candidate should have started filing reports on all campaign spending. Instead, he didn't do so until thirteen months later. The inability of the FEC to act during the Michigan campaign enabled Robertson to make a mockery of the law.

God, family and America. Typical of his road show was a stop in the Detroit suburb of Sterling Heights a few days before the August 5 precinct elections. The crowd gathered early at a public park in a distinctly family-picnic atmosphere. A local Robertson organizer named Foster Brown, a red, white and blue boater perched saucily on his head, climbed a wooden platform, grabbed a microphone and proceeded to warm up the audience awaiting Robertson's arrival.

"How many of you remember the pledge of allegiance?" he asked. "There are many places where it isn't even said anymore because it mentions God." (Some hisses and boos from the crowd.) Not surprisingly, nearly everybody in the audience did remember, and with the warm-up man leading the way, the crowd dutifully recited the pledge, right hands over hearts.

Next, Brown asked all those present who were running to become precinct delegates to raise their hands. What seemed to be a majority of the audience did so. One by one, Brown called up selected witnesses to give testimony of their new interest in politics, and to explain it, just as if this were an old-time revival meeting. One of the delegate candidates, Theresa DeGrand, spoke optimistically of the effort to make Pat Robertson president. "If God is for us," she asked, "who can be against us?"

The rally went on like that until a motorcade came up a dirt road leading into the park, causing an excited stir. Out of one of the limousines climbed a beaming Robertson, shaking hands and waving as he made his way to the platform. He felt, he told his already entranced listeners, like the early colonist Captain John Smith when he proclaimed: "I would rather be a settler in America than the good Queen Bess sitting on the throne of England." Robertson said it with that breathless wonder that characterized his speech. "We love America," he intoned. "Don't you love America?"

As the Chief Patriot went on in this vein, men, women and children in the crowd, armed with small American flags provided by Robertson volunteers, cheered and waved them happily as he got down to the business at hand. "You can get involved in the process," he told them. "You can become a leader. You can help keep America free. This nation needs people like you who love God, who love this country and who love freedom."

And as voters in Michigan, Robertson said, they could send the whole country a message in the approaching precinct elections. "You here in Michigan have a privilege that no other state has," he said. In voting for pro-Robertson delegates, he said, they would be like the Royal Air Force pilots who held off Hitler's Luftwaffe in World War II's aerial Battle of Britain, of whom Winston Churchill said: "Never have so many owed so much to so few."

As for Kemp, it was becoming clear already that his own organizing was falling short and that Robertson was moving in on him on the right. Even before the August 5 precinct elections, Kemp strategists in Michigan and Washington began to discuss the possibility of forming a conservative coalition with Robertson to stop Bush in the state. "The Kemp national strategy was to stop Bush and then emerge as the most acceptable conservative alternative," Abraham said later. "The Kemp people felt that Robertson was just a flash in the pan."

On August 5, as the precinct elections took place across the state, the Michigan Republican Party found that it had given birth to a monster it could not keep tabs on. For one thing, all precinct delegates were elected unpledged to any presidential candidate. For another, reporting procedures from the precincts to the counties and on up to the state committee proved haphazard and totally inadequate in trying to gauge which presidential hopeful had fared best. In the absence of reliable figures from the state committee, the three rival campaigns rushed in with their own reports and calculations to lay claim to victory or, in Kemp's case, at least a respectable showing.

The Bush campaign, having taken a psychological beating from the Robertson camp in the late May reports on numbers of delegate candidates who had filed, was prepared this time. "We decided to set up our own de facto board of elections for the state of Michigan," Rich Bond said later. He enlisted Bill Canary, a friend from the Suffolk County, Long Island, Board of Elections, to oversee the operation, which included hundreds of volunteers phoning precinct results that went into computers and were analyzed by the Bush pollster, Bob Teeter. Not surprisingly, these sophisticated-looking statistics showed Bush clearly ahead.

The Robertson campaign's state political director, David Walters, offered a separate set of less sophisticated-looking figures indicating Robertson had won, but the lists did not seem to be as comprehensive as Bush's. And Bond and Teeter were two veterans with established credibility with the political writers who flocked to Lansing to report on the results. Nuttle contended long afterward that Bond and Teeter had snookered the press with a masterful job of "spin control" on the precinct election results, especially because Teeter came from Michigan and knew many members of the local as well as national news media.

Whether that indeed was what happened or not, most stories the next day did indicate that Bush had come out on top, with as much as half of all the precinct delegates elected in the three-man field. This reading later proved to be wrong, when the Robertson forces were able to substantiate that they had at least held their own with Bush, with Kemp getting a small share. But the first widespread impression was that Bush had beaten back both Robertson and Kemp.

The cost, however, was already high. Two full years before the next Republican National Convention, the Bush campaign had pumped at least a million dollars into this one state. And because Bush was the front-runner, there was no climbing out of this political black hole now.

As for Kemp, his Michigan showing by all yardsticks was anemic; from this point on his role in the Michigan battle changed drastically, in ways that now compounded Bush's problems in the state. If Kemp was not going to be the odd man out, it was now clear that his agents would have to persuade

Robertson that the Kemp support in Michigan was needed, in a right-wing coalition, if Bush was going to be denied the Michigan delegation. After the August 1986 precinct elections, Black said later, "you didn't have to be a strategic genius to see that Bush was way below fifty percent. And if he was the front-runner, then what we really needed was a Kemp-Robertson coalition to puncture the front-runner, and worry about Robertson later on down the line."

Although Robertson had been able to turn out many more troops than Kemp did at the precinct elections, Kemp still had most of the politically experienced conservatives in his camp. The Kemp strategists in Michigan, with Posthumus' legislative aide, Saul Anuzis, as the chief architect, proposed to the Robertson leaders that they pool their resources to deal with first things first—beating Bush—and address their own ambitions later. "Each side felt it could control the other side," Anuzis said later. "Robertson had the grass-roots strength; the Kemp strength was that we were the margin needed to beat Bush. Our national strategy was that Robertson would not be there in the long run and his people eventually would fall Kemp's way. It was all a marriage of convenience." The Robertson camp, obviously, believed it would be Kemp who fell, with Robertson the ultimate beneficiary.

Some in the Bush national headquarters may have believed at this point that the worst was over for their side in Michigan. But if so they were very wrong. The battle was only starting in what eventually would be the most hard-fought and complex sideshow of the entire 1988 presidential election cycle. The Robertson forces in the state, having tasted the fruits of their rather incredible organizational diligence, were not about to beat a retreat. With their new accomplices in what Clark Durant of the Kemp camp openly called the "Anybody But Bush" effort, they sought a way to convert their combined strength into control of the state party itself.

Although the Michigan fight seemed to outsiders to focus on the rival presidential ambitions of Bush, Robertson and Kemp, insiders recognized that for Michigan Republican activists it was just as much a struggle for the direction of the GOP within the state. Bush's Michigan chairman, John Engler, had ambitions to be governor. His state Senate colleague, Dick Posthumus, co-chairman of the Kemp campaign in Michigan, had worked closely with Engler in the Senate and was equally ambitious. The other Kemp cochairman, Durant, represented the more conservative wing. When the Kemp camp after its disastrous showing in August decided to throw in with Robertson to stop Bush, Kemp activists like Posthumus did so with much less enthusiasm and comfort than did Durant and his more right-wing colleagues in the Kemp camp. In time the behavior of Robertson and some of his most zealous supporters would cause severe strains within the coalition, but at first it functioned effectively.

The Bush campaign in the state, believing that it had turned back the Robertson challenge, sought to reach out to this potentially valuable new constituency in the party. At county and district conventions in February 1987, the

Bush forces agreed to proportional representation with the Robertson-Kemp coalition in sending delegates to the party's county and district conventions, which in turn sent delegates to the state convention. The Robertson forces, however, in counties where they had elected a majority of precinct delegates the previous August, changed the rules and adopted a winner-take-all approach, shutting out the Bush side.

As a result, the Bush campaign, relying on intelligence from local supporters that matters were well in hand and not believing the old party regulars in the Kemp camp would put presidential politics above state party harmony, got blindsided by the coalition at the ensuing state convention. The Robertson Kemp alliance, in a shocking coup, took over the Republican state central committee. Such control gave the coalition an important piece of machinery for mischief-making, through party rules changes, as the Bush forces were soon to learn. Suddenly George Bush was in the fight of his life in the state where he had bested Ronald Reagan seven years earlier, the victim of high expectations. "It was totally a two-by-four upside the head," said one of the Bush operatives later. "No one could believe what had happened. No one expected they [the Kempites in league with Robertson] would tear the party apart over a national election two years hence."

According to Spencer Abraham later, "the Bush people relaxed and never saw the implications of the state committee being elected on the basis of presidential preference. They never dreamed they would change the rules." But that was precisely what happened; the political newcomers, the Robertson amateurs, were suddenly playing hardball, with the experience in party affairs of their new Kemp allies calling many of the shots. The fat was in the fire, with not only the ambitions of the presidential candidates at stake now, but also Michigan Republican Party harmony, which state party chairman Abraham saw crumbling before his very eyes.

In April 1987, Abraham stepped in and negotiated an agreement among the three presidential campaigns on the rules for selecting the national convention delegates. All sides agreed that there would be no more rewriting of rules, but with one open question: Who could be a precinct delegate to the county and district conventions leading up to the state convention? This one question could not be resolved because the Bush campaign had found a vehicle in the existing rules that could salvage a majority of the Michigan delegation for Bush, and the anti-Bush coalition was determined to block it.

The coalition argued that only those individuals elected as precinct delegates in August were entitled to participate. The Bush campaign cited a state law stipulating that all local and state nominees for office in the previous year's elections were to become automatic delegates. There were approximately twelve hundred such former party nominees and most of them were establishment Republicans very likely to be for Bush. The Bush campaign pointed out that many of these GOP standard-bearers did not run for delegate in the precinct elections because they were told that the state law and party rules already made them delegates to the county and district conventions. Many were urged not to run, the Bush campaign said, so that others could be elected. This block of delegates, the Bush lawyers contended, could be critical in any chance for a Bush comeback victory at the county and district conventions in mid-January, and then at the state convention. As a practical matter, one Bush insider acknowledged later, the twelve hundred number was "a red herring," because as many as nine hundred of these party candidates had actually run and were elected as precinct delegates.

The Robertson-Kemp coalition's control of the state committee hung ominously over the Bush campaign's efforts to recover. There were severe doubts at the national headquarters in Washington that the whole mess was salvageable. "When they thought they could win, they tried," said one Michigan Republican veteran later. "When they thought they couldn't, they started writing it off."

A key Bond deputy, Mary Matalin, moved into the state in the spring and hung on tenaciously for the rest of the Michigan delegate fight, refusing to be beaten. A savvy political operative of thirty-five with a street politician's grit and a vocabulary to match, Matalin—in league with Engler, Bush lawyer David McKeague and other Michigan campaign leaders—undertook an extensive and shrewd program of what she called "creative apportionment."

Going county by county and congressional district by congressional district where Bush forces had a majority, they engineered some fancy, old-fashioned gerrymandering to maximize Bush strength, looking to a showdown at the next state convention. Set for January 29 and 30, 1988, this convention would select the first delegates anywhere in the country to go to the Republican National Convention, and hence would draw considerable national attention. It loomed as a must for Bush now that he was committed so deeply to the Michigan fight, although the Washington headquarters, not believing in miracles, continued to low-ball expectations and denigrate the importance of the contest. By the time it was over, however, the Bush campaign, according to Bond, had sunk more than $2 million into the state, and Bush had reason to suspect he would spend the rest of his career in Michigan. "Why am I here?" he would vexatiously ask his agents in the state on each visit.

The Robertson-Kemp coalition's next major move came in September 1987 when its ruling majority on the state committee called a special meeting and changed the party rules to bar the twelve hundred party nominees from the delegate-selection process—in spite of the April agreement among the three presidential camps. The Bush campaign was back on its heels again. Engler, Bond, Matalin and McKeague held what Bond called a series of "doomsday meetings" to anticipate what other schemes the coalition might attempt, and plot what legal recourses would be available.

Convinced that the state committee's action had violated the law, Bush lawyers sought relief in state court. The judge ruled in their favor, but the coalition wasn't finished yet. It called on Abraham to convene still another special state party committee meeting to consider another party rules change barring county and district conventions from writing their own plans for delegate selection. This move was a direct assault on Bush-dominated counties and districts in which Bush operatives, in the words of a Kemp campaign memo at the time, were "roaring around the state gerrymandering apportionment lines like a bunch of Democrats."

As all this maneuvering was going on, uneasiness grew in the Kemp camp with the "marriage of convenience" with Robertson. Leading Kempites such as Posthumus, Saul Anuzis and his brother Andy had longtime ties with Engler and other Bush leaders in the state Republican establishment, and they were chagrined at how the state party—and their own personal relationships—were being torn apart by the infighting.

Party regulars in the Kemp faction also were disturbed by the attitude of many of the grass-roots troops being mobilized by Robertson—a concern observed with growing interest by the Bush operatives in the state. "The leaders on the ground would come to these political meetings," Mary Matalin recalled later, "and say things like, 'We don't really care if Republicans or Democrats are in there. What we care about is advancement of Christian philosophy.'" While the party regulars for the most part shared that philosophy, she said, "and had all the right values, they were Republicans first and foremost. And politics at that level is a neighborhood kind of thing." The newcomers were not interested in the social side of politics that nurtured the regulars' participation, nor were there political "war stories" to share of the sort that made for harmony and enthusiasm at the local level. "They were for another agenda, and the fragile coalition started to fall apart," said Matalin, and she and her Bush sidekicks were more than willing to encourage the disintegration.

Moreover, some in the Kemp camp grew very suspicious that Robertson in the end would renege on a deal to throw enough delegates to Kemp at the state convention to enable him to finish second to Robertson, and beat Bush. At a party conference on Mackinac Island in September, Robertson had behaved with unusual arrogance, even for him. He declared that he intended to depose Secchia as a Michigan national committeeman, get rid of Abraham as state chairman and said Kemp had approached him about being his running mate. All this made many Kempites wonder about the strange bedfellow with whom they had climbed under the sheets.

Here was a crack in the coalition wall, and the Bush operatives in Michigan leaped at the chance to widen it. One day in November, the Bush campaign set up a conference phone call in Engler's office at the state capitol in Lansing involving Atwater, Bond, Engler, Matalin, Posthumus and Saul Anuzis. The subject was yet another deal, with former Governor Romney as an intermediary between Engler and Posthumus. To many in the Kemp camp, Robertson had become a pariah, and more to be feared, both in the short term and the long, in the interests of both the Kemp candidacy and the future of the party in Michigan, than Bush. Knowing this, the Bush brain trust proposed the same deal to the Kempites that they had with Robertson—with confidence, engendered by their longtime relationship, that the agreement would be kept.

Posthumus, the Anuzis brothers and as many other Kemp supporters as

could be brought aboard would quit what the Bush campaign called "the Robertson-Kemp axis" but would remain Kemp backers, while throwing in with
Bush against the proposed rules change. In return, Bush would help elect enough
Kemp delegates to give him second place in Michigan ahead of Robertson—
the same basic deal Robertson had cut with Kemp earlier. Posthumus at first
balked because the Bush operatives declined to accept his condition that all
lawsuits by the Bush campaign against the coalition-controlled state committee
be dropped—literally, its court of last resort. But he finally agreed.

Andy Anuzis, who was 17th Congressional District Republican chairman,
wrote a long letter of explanation to rank-and-file Robertson supporters explaining that his gripe was not with them, but with their leadership. He said
Robertson and his lieutenants had slighted the Kemp campaign in Michigan,
acting as if the coalition could succeed without it. He called Robertson's contention that Kemp had asked to be his running mate "a lie and a slap in the
face to all of us who have worked tremendously hard on Jack Kemp's presidential
campaign." And he noted that a recent claim by Robertson that he would take
forty to forty-four national convention delegates out of Michigan suggested he
would welsh on the deal with Kemp, because if Robertson kept that many, it
would leave Kemp in third place behind Bush.

"The Kemp people in Michigan suddenly realized," Saul Anuzis said
later, "that Robertson was not going to go away. Robertson was becoming as
much of a threat to Kemp as Bush was." So, he said, it made more sense to
thrown in with Bush, in the long-term interests of the state party as well as in
Kemp's short-term interest.

For yet another time, it appeared as if Bush was back from the political
dead in Michigan. The diligent and alert Bush team in the state had kept tabs
on the disintegrating situation within the Robertson-Kemp coalition and moved
in deftly to exploit it at just the right time.

In Washington, however, the Kemp campaign was dismayed. Kemp had
given his word to Robertson on the original deal, and his prime goal in Michigan
continued to be to stop Bush. Kemp phoned Posthumus urging him not to jump
ship, but when Posthumus refused, Kemp removed him as cochairman of his
Michigan campaign. Kemp flew into the state and made personal appeals to his
precinct delegates to stay in the coalition with Robertson. By now all was total
chaos in Michigan Republican politics, with the Bush campaign still scrambling
to avert disaster.

On December 12, at the showdown state committee meeting in Lansing,
the Bush forces, with this urgent transfusion from the Kemp camp and help
from Abraham as a defender of the April agreement he had forged, nevertheless
fell short. Into the early morning before the vote, Kemp worked the phones
diligently, urging his supporters on the state committee to stay with the old
coalition. He succeeded in turning two votes, breaking a 50–50 tie and producing
a 52–48 vote victory for the original coalition against Bush and the Kemp
defectors from the "axis" to throw out the elaborate gerrymandering dreamed

up by the Bush camp. Bush's Michigan managers began to talk of the possibility of holding rump conventions at the county, district and state levels and sending a disputed delegation to the national convention, meanwhile struggling to keep aboard their new allies from the Kemp camp, especially a now thoroughly demoralized Posthumus. Chaos reigned.

Former Governor Romney, warning that the party was being torn apart, told the state committee members: "You can kiss goodbye to Republican victories in 1988 in Michigan." One Kemp leader, Paul Welday, expressed a general mood about the whole process aimed at putting Michigan at the head of the delegate-selection calendar. "It's been called Byzantine, it's been called crazy, it's been called a Rube Goldberg contraption and some have even called it a monstrosity of infinite proportions," he said. "As someone who works in this process day in and day out, I'll tell you—it stinks. But unfortunately it's the only one we've got."

Again the Bush lawyers went back to court. In early January another judge again upheld them, ruling that the state committee had again acted illegally in changing the rules to take away the counties' right to set their own voting boundaries. The Robertson-Kemp coalition appealed in both the state and federal courts but was turned down—one day before the county and district conventions were to meet to elect 1,805 delegates to the state convention two weeks later.

Still the "axis" would not quit. With Robertson going about the state charging that Bush was "stealing" the Michigan delegation from him, his coalition on the night of the conventions, January 14, set out to blur its numerical weakness by simply muddying the waters. Of 124 county and congressional district conventions held across the state to choose fifty-four of Michigan's seventy-seven delegates, 33 were rump sessions—28 by the coalition and 5 by the Bush forces—in each case where each was in the minority.

None of the conventions was more chaotic and bitter than the one for the 16th Congressional District, held in a small, one-room catering restaurant called Elmer's Steak Pit Hall in the downriver Detroit blue-collar suburb of Wyandotte. The district machinery was in control of the original "axis" and the chairman, a Kemp backer named Perry Christy, set the stage for bedlam early. He announced in advance that any members of the news media who wanted to attend the meeting, supposedly an open and democratic affair, would have to pay as much as $850. Christy said special assessments for camera equipment would be made.

The night of the conventions was bitter cold, with temperatures near zero. The Robertson-Kemp forces issued special credentials to their own people and kept the legitimate Bush and defecting Kemp supporters standing outside. The single front door was guarded by several gents who could have played linebacker for the Detroit Lions. One by one, elected Bush precinct delegates had their credentials checked at the door, at about the pace that blacks were registered to vote in the 1960s at the local courthouse in the Mississippi Delta, and with approximately the same enthusiasm. Old women were among those kept waiting, as was one of Bush's sons, Marvin. The Bush campaign had brought its delegates in a fleet of eight small vans, and drivers kept their motors running so that Bush delegates—and reporters also banned—could get in from time to time to warm themselves.

After establishing clearly that they were being forcibly kept from the meeting, the Bush delegates on signal from their local leader, William Runco, stormed the door, brushing past the "axis" gorillas into the small hall, with reporters and television cameramen pressing in close behind. Christy ordered that the media intruders be thrown out by the sergeants at arms, and most of them with much complaining retreated back into the frigid night. One of us, however, hunkered down on the floor at the rear of the hall, amid some credentialed delegates, and witnessed what happened next.

Bush supporters sprinkled through the assemblage began to protest: "Where's the press? . . . Let 'em in!" The din got so great that Christy in desperation called for the singing of "God Bless America." The crowd rose and complied, some in it placing hand over heart. After one chorus, somebody yelled out, as if it were Saturday night at the frat house, "One more time!" Obediently, the delegates belted it out again. Only then could the meeting be called to order. More wrangling ensued, all to the purpose of disenfranchising enough of the Bush delegates who had forced their way in, to maintain "axis" control.

Runco, inside, had a walkie-talkie through which he was keeping Rich Bond, outside, apprised of developments. When it was established beyond doubt that the Bush forces were not going to be given their due, Bond ordered them out.

As the Bush delegates exited the hall, they boarded the eight vans and were driven to the nearby Downriver Italian-American Club, where a Bush rump convention promptly elected sixty-six Bush rump delegates to the state convention, on grounds their treatment at Elmer's Steak Pit Hall had nullified the district convention there. Meanwhile, back at Elmer's, the "axis" split the sixty-six delegate slots between Robertson and Kemp backers, setting the stage for still another showdown at the state convention in Grand Rapids.

The scene at Elmer's was so outrageous that Kemp's Michigan campaign manager, Dick Minard, sent a letter of apology to Bush that indicated the "axis" had unraveled beyond repair. "It was appalling and totally unrepresentative of Jack Kemp," Minard wrote. "We apologize to the vice president, his son and to the hundreds of people who got stuck out in the snow." L. Brooks Patterson, a Bush cochairman known for his acid tongue, was more direct. "Perry Christy is an only child," he said, "which goes to show that his parents learned from experience."

Across the state that night, Bush won 910 of the 1,805 state convention delegates elected at the recognized county and district conventions, or more than 50 percent, to 22 percent for Robertson and 17 for Kemp, but with the certainty that the opposition would challenge many of them as a result of the rump convention results and rival credentials claims. The Robertson camp, feeding in its rump results, claimed to have won 47 percent to 26 percent for Kemp and 25 for Bush. But the Robertsons were whistling in the dark. The outcome translated, with the help of the Kemp defectors, into a majority for Bush of the fifty-four national convention delegates effectively selected that night—three in each of the eighteen congressional districts. This result in turn assured that the Bush campaign would be able to claim all twenty-three at-large delegates to be elected at the state convention—and hand over enough to Kemp to enable him to finish second.

The next morning, Bond opened a joyous press conference at the Detroit Press Club by exclaiming: ''Good morning, Vietnam!'' The reference was to the Robin Williams movie just out—and in recognition that the Bush campaign at last could see the light at the end of the tunnel in this political quagmire.

The sniping from the Robertson bunkers continued, however, through the state convention two weeks later, with the old ''axis'' issuing its own credentials to a state rump convention in the same hall in Grand Rapids. But Kemp informed his supporters that he wanted no part of a rump challenge to any of the court rulings or the results of the county and district conventions. The embattled Abraham came out of hiding in time to preside over the roll call, tightly controlled by the disciplined new Bush-Kemp alliance. Bush finally got thirty-seven delegates of the seventy-seven, to thirty-two for Kemp and eight for Robertson.

Robertson paid a surprise visit to his rump convention on a lower floor, proclaiming it ''the duly authorized'' session and himself the winner. The other convention, he intoned, was ''an attempt by a few to mislead a vast number to maintain control of their petty little political fiefdoms.'' His people elected a rump slate to the national convention of forty-three delegates for Robertson, twenty-one for Kemp and, somehow, twelve for Bush. He vowed to go on to the national convention in New Orleans in support of this slate but, as often seemed the case, he was functioning in his own special dream world.

The fervor of his troops remained undiminished to the bitter end. Clara Giordano, a longtime Reagan supporter from Perry Christy's district in Wyandotte, screamed into television cameras on the rump convention floor: ''We conservatives will come back! Look around you! The conservative movement is alive and well in Michigan. We will get the White House again.'' Warning that Bush ''has lost an army,'' she predicted his loss to the Democrats in the fall. ''They'll send out a Mario Cuomo,'' she said, ''and he'll chew us up and spit us out.''

That prognostication was neither the first nor the last misguided vision into the future from the Robertson camp and its candidate with an alleged special pipeline to Higher Authority. After all the teeth-gnashing, eye-gouging and groin-kicking of the previous stormy two years in Michigan, George Bush had finally emerged victorious. But in the process, the fight for the first official delegates of 1988 had become so convoluted, so confusing, so muddied that about the most that could be said for the vice president was that he had escaped in one piece. He had been given one hell of a scare by a neophyte in politics, a television preacher/con man, in a state where he had beaten the mighty Ronald Reagan eight years earlier. He had poured a small fortune down this particular black hole while his principal rival, Bob Dole, stayed out and busied himself building an impressive lead in the polls in Iowa, where most political observers—and more important, the voters of the state—considered that the "real" race for the Republican nomination would begin.

While Bush was scrambling to avert disaster in Michigan all through 1987, Dole was concentrating on Iowa's precinct caucuses, to be held only nine days after the Michigan state convention. There, too, Robertson had become, in the truest sense of the words, a wild card, so Bush had no time to savor his Michigan "victory." He could expect little boost from it in Iowa, where the campaign had already been going on for more than two years, and where another Bush victory over Reagan in 1980 had built in high expectations. Much had happened there since then, however, to lower them—and compound Bush's problems going into Iowa.

Charlie Black, reflecting later on about Michigan, mused that had Bush lost there, with Iowa coming up next, "I've got to think it would have taken the wind out of his sails," and then, with a loss in Iowa, it could have meant a third straight loss in New Hampshire a week after that. "I've got to believe, the way the news would have played that," Black said, "you lose Michigan and then you lose Iowa . . . I just think the guy would have been out of it by New Hampshire."*

But politics, like life, is full of what-ifs that don't matter. Michigan was hardly a resounding triumph for Bush, especially considering the exorbitant price in time, money and exasperation that competing there had cost him. But it was better than losing, and if Black's assessment had any validity at all, the effort made in Bush's behalf in Michigan managed to keep him on the track to the White House. And in terms of battle-testing the Bush operation, Bond said later, it was "a training exercise with real bullets" that paid off down the campaign trail.

As for Michigan's Republicans whose ambitions to play a larger role on the national political stage had been responsible for the whole nasty ordeal, they had had enough. Engler and Posthumus quickly helped push through legislation in the 1988 session of the Michigan legislature repealing the nightmare process and, with the agreement of the state's Democrats, reviving the presidential primary in Michigan for 1992. No tears were reported shed by anybody. In retrospect the Republican delegate fight in 1988 had been one to remember—and then, for almost everyone involved, quickly to forget.

---

*After the election, Robertson told us he believed that Black and Lee Atwater, partners in the same consulting firm before the campaign, "probably" were in collusion all along to make sure Bush won in Michigan. "At the national level, somewhere along the way there was a deal made, no question about it," he said.

7

Iowa: Bush's Worst Moment

Ever since the 1980 Iowa precinct caucuses, George Wittgraf, George Bush's campaign manager in the state, had been keeping the Bush loyalists together. Remaining fresh in their minds was that wonderful night in January 1980 when Bush, flushed to the point of giddiness with his upset over heavily favored Ronald Reagan, stood before a battery of television cameras and microphones in the Fort Des Moines Hotel and gushed that he had "the Big Mo" (for momentum). If he could win the approaching New Hampshire primary, Bush proclaimed to the glee of his cheering supporters—and the chagrin of his more cautious advisers—then "there'll be absolutely no stopping me."

Well, he couldn't, and there was. Reagan's swift comeback in New Hampshire, and Bush's fall from his self-deceptive euphoria, disappointed Bush's Iowa enthusiasts. But some of them continued to harbor thoughts that there would be another night like that glorious one at the Fort Des Moines in 1980, and another day for George Bush's presidential ambitions. After Bush's election as vice president, Wittgraf began mailing newsletters to these Iowa loyalists at regular intervals, keeping them posted on the activities of their favorite Republican. In addition, he held periodic gatherings for them looking to the time Bush would need Iowa again to set him on course to the Oval Office.

In 1980, 33,530 Iowans had turned out on caucus night for Bush—2,182 more than Reagan managed—catapulting Bush into the headlines as a political giant-killer heading toward New Hampshire. Generating those 33,530 Bush supporters hadn't been easy. Rich Bond, a young New Yorker who really ran Bush's Iowa operation, had devised a shrewd grass-roots approach that succeeded in breaking down the resistance of voters who had never attended a caucus and may have been intimidated by the very open process. In a primary or general election, the voter walked into a polling booth, cast his ballot in privacy and went home. The Iowa caucus process, though, required that the voter attend an open meeting of an hour or more in a public hall or private home and declare his or her presidential preference. Shortly before caucus night, Bond mailed postcards to individuals earlier identified as leaning to Bush, advising them of the names of their neighbors who would be there.

These and other innovations boosted turnout beyond the expectations of the Reagan managers, who had figured 30,000 votes would be adequate to carry the state. This miscalculation, coupled with a decision in the Reagan camp to hold the front-running Reagan out of a candidates' debate televised statewide, a decision that offended many Republican voters, left Reagan on the short end on caucus night, and Bush an overnight flash.

Afterward, Wittgraf, a lawyer from the small western Iowa town of Cherokee, reasoned that by maintaining a sense of identity with Bush among a nucleus of Iowa Republican activists, they could be held in readiness for 1988. Several critical things had occurred in the meantime, however, that worked against this easy strategy. Some of these 1980 supporters of Bush were with him then because they wanted a more moderate alternative to Reagan, and now Bush was his thoroughly obedient courtier. They were already looking elsewhere, particularly to Bob Dole from their near-neighbor farm state of Kansas.

Furthermore, many 1980 Reagan backers in Iowa—Governor Terry Branstad and Senator Charles Grassley among them—had cooled to Reagan, believing he had been insufficiently sensitive to Iowa's condition of near depression, prolonged by the farm economy's failure to achieve the recovery enjoyed elsewhere under Reagan. At a National Governors' Conference in February 1986, Branstad complained: "I don't think his advisers are even keeping him informed on the extent of the farm crisis. We've got a crisis in agriculture and no one is in charge."

The Iowa Poll by the *Des Moines Register* charted Reagan's fall from grace in a state that earlier, based on his radio-announcing days, had claimed him proudly as a transplanted native son. By April 1985, only a bare 51 percent of Iowans surveyed approved of the job he was doing and only 42 percent of farmers. By November, his approval rating fell to 43 percent overall; 77 percent disapproved of his handling of farm issues to only 16 percent who approved, and 69 percent disapproved of how he was dealing with the federal deficit.

Erosion on the right from the Reagan base to Jack Kemp and Pat Robertson seemed inevitable. Kemp started campaigning in Iowa as early as July 1985, along with duPont, but Bush did not make an appearance until November, when at Branstad's insistence he met with a group of disgruntled farmers. Afterward, Bush called the session "a listening thing," because he didn't "come out here with a lot of new programs or easy answers." Branstad put the best face on the matter by saying Bush had "a much better fix" on the farm problem as a result, but the farmers were not assuaged.

In April of 1986 in Des Moines, Robertson supporters came out of nowhere to win control of the Polk County Republican Committee. They were making quiet inroads into the party apparatus elsewhere as well.

But Robertson's credibility problem grew along with these first signs, in Iowa as well as in Michigan, of his newfound political heft. In June 1986, he said in an interview with the *Washington Post* that "a Supreme Court ruling is not the law of the United States," and that the Founding Fathers had never intended it to be "paramount over the other two branches." As a private citizen, he said, he did not feel "bound by any case or any court to which I myself am not a party." These views from a graduate of the Yale Law School caused eyebrows to raise throughout the political community.

On top of this development, former Republican Congressman and presidential candidate Paul N. ("Pete") McCloskey of California, a decorated Korean War veteran, charged that Robertson on a troopship taking both of them to the Pacific in 1951 had talked openly about asking his father, then Senator A. Willis Robertson of Virginia, to intercede to keep him out of the battle zone. Shortly afterward, McCloskey charged, Robertson was taken off the ship and sent to a supply base in Japan. Robertson stoutly denied the charges and sued for libel. But again he found himself on the defensive just as he was giving up his role as host of *The 700 Club*, his religious talk show, to inject himself more aggressively into the presidential competition. (The suit eventually was thrown out of court and Robertson was ordered to pay McCloskey's court costs.)

Meanwhile, Wittgraf in Iowa proceeded on the smug assumption that the Bush cadre from 1980 remained a vital force that would carry the day for him in 1988. At a news conference in Des Moines in May 1987, Wittgraf claimed to have Bush chairmen in all ninety-nine Iowa counties and five thousand Iowans firmly committed to work for the vice president. He said he had thousands more names of Bush backers on the dotted line with more being added, anticipating an even larger turnout at the Republican caucuses in 1988 than had occurred in 1980. Bush strategists in Washington took Wittgraf's word and went along assuming he was doing what he could to deal with the adverse conditions that had developed since 1980.

But when Atwater made an inspection trip to Iowa in March of 1987, he came away with a realistic view. "The thing had atrophied," he acknowledged later. "It had gotten to be a little bit of a social club," he said. "It was one little group. There's a mythical thing about keeping an organization together for seven years. What they had kept together had become almost a social club coffee klatch. Every time I'd go out there, I'd see the same clique of people." He touched all the political bases in the state and on his own visited three shopping malls just to talk to Iowans and walk behind them listening in on their casual conversations. What he heard was not good.

"I was just convinced that we couldn't win Iowa," he said later. "I never really told anybody that [in the state], because, number one, it really wouldn't do any good, it wouldn't help the organization, and number two, you never say never. But I was convinced enough to where, when I got back on Friday, I picked up the phone and called John Sununu and set up a dinner at his house in New Hampshire the following Monday, because I knew then we had to have a campaign in New Hampshire that could withstand a loss in Iowa."

Atwater spent more than five hours with the feisty Republican governor and his wife "and didn't leave until he agreed to set up the Bush campaign for us." Sununu had not before this meeting committed himself to Bush. That was

why, Atwater recalled, "the most important conclusion I came to in terms of
my three-day trip into Iowa was not particularly anything we ought to do in
Iowa. It was, 'I better get my ass up to New Hampshire and get Sununu signed
up *muy pronto*,' which I did, two days later."

Atwater also conveyed his pessimistic reading on Iowa to Bush—that in
his judgment, largely because of Reagan's tarnished image in the state and
because he no longer had a real base of his own there, he could not win the
state. "When you're a doctor," Atwater said later, "and you go in and look
at a patient, and he's got a bad liver, you say, 'Well, that's bad.' Then you
look at his lungs and one of them's gone, you look at his heart and three of
those arteries are gone, then you look at his intestine and he's got gangrene in
it, before long you say, 'This guy ain't gonna make it.' "

Nevertheless, because Bush had won the Iowa caucuses in 1980, much
would be expected of him in the state, especially from the national press corps
that descended on it early in the post-1984 period. The delegate fight in Michigan, because of its unfamiliarity, its complexity and its confusing and volatile
picture, got short shrift from most of the national news media. That fact originally seemed a blessing for Bush but it later proved to be a disappointment
because his ultimate victory in Michigan was so muddied. And going into Iowa
this time around, he needed all the help that even a blurred success in Michigan
could bring. Iowa Republicans, for their part, never seemed to take the Michigan
delegate contest seriously. As far as they were concerned, the presidential
campaign was starting in Iowa in 1988 as it had for years, no matter what
Michigan decided to do to try to steal Iowa's political thunder.

The politically aware in Iowa, as in New Hampshire, took great and jealous
pride in their special function as the early arbiters of presidential hopefuls'
claims for their parties' nominations. While the significance of the Iowa precinct
caucuses on the Republican side was not as demonstrably important as Jimmy
Carter's Iowa victory in 1976 had been for the Democratic caucuses, the Republican participants did play a role. In 1980, that upset victory they gave Bush
over Reagan did not bring him the nomination, but it did shake up the shocked
Reagan operation and set it on its winning course in the New Hampshire primary
and thereafter. And Iowa effectively "winnowed out" Howard Baker, Bob
Dole and the rest of the 1980 Republican field.

In the early years of the Iowa caucuses, covering them constituted hardship
duty for the relatively few reporters who ventured to Des Moines. The capital
city's central location in the state seemed just about its only virtue. It lacked
first-class hotels and decent restaurants and the winters were bitter cold, as icy
blasts whistled down its wide and barren streets. An unprepossessing downtown
restaurant, Babe's, was the principal hangout, and its biggest attraction was the
clientele—warm and friendly midwesterners who couldn't quite believe that
newsmen would come "all the way" from Washington, D.C., to find out how
they felt about the few presidential candidates who also were just discovering
Iowa's early caucuses.

The growing prominence of the caucuses, however, and an enterprising business community, in time made Des Moines much more attractive. The old Fort Des Moines Hotel, sanctuary of the Republicans, and the even older Savery Hotel, refuge of the Democrats, were remodeled, and some of the larger chains built new hotels downtown or on the fringes. The Savery gave birth to the first decent downtown restaurant, Guido's, run by an Italian immigrant of the same name who delighted in the arrival of television luminaries during the caucus season. The city fathers built an elaborate indoor skywalk system linking most of the major downtown buildings that made the fierce winters more bearable. Covering the Iowa caucuses became more civilized, and just in time as they overtook the New Hampshire primary in 1980 and later as the prime campsite for early White House dreamers, and the growing corps of news gatherers who became their political camp followers.

In advance of the 1988 caucuses, it appeared for a long time that Iowa would again be a launching pad for Bush and a political burial ground for other Republican hopefuls. Bush's celebrity and a slow-starting Dole campaign in Iowa kept the vice president's numbers up in the Iowa Poll among the 1988 presidential aspirants. In May of 1986, at about the time Bush was being ambushed by the flood of Robertson filings for the early precinct elections in Michigan, he led Dole by 34 percent to 16 in the poll, taken by the *Des Moines Register*.

Dole as usual was having trouble getting his campaign act together. His first campaign chairman, Robert Ellsworth, an old Nixon hand, and David Keene, chairman of the American Conservative Union serving as a key political adviser, had a falling-out. Dole also seemed unable to make up his mind whether he wanted another veteran adviser, John Sears, who had run Reagan's campaign in 1976 and in early 1980, to take over for him. Apparently unwilling to give Sears the completely free hand he demanded, Dole finally signed on Bill Brock, the former Tennessee senator and Republican national chairman, to run the campaign, but not until late 1987.

Dole himself, however, had made one important decision and he acted on it diligently in 1986. He concluded that he had to win somewhere in his first outing to demonstrate that he was a major contender. And the ideal place for a candidate from a plains state with a strong record in support of farmers was, obviously, Iowa. He began to work the state religiously, eventually making more than fifty visits before the 1988 caucuses, with his popular and personable wife, Elizabeth, pitching in, with him or on her own.

Still lacking much of an organization in the state, Dole jolted the Bush camp in December 1986 by moving ahead of the vice president in the Iowa Poll, 28 percent to 25. The sample was small, only 205 Republicans, and the statistical margin of error of 7 percent meant the contest really was even, but it nevertheless sent Bush a message that confirmed Atwater's earlier on-the-ground fears. The Iran-contra scandal had just broken and it appeared that Bush's slippage had resulted from doubts about his involvement. The poll found that

41 percent of all Iowans surveyed believed he knew money had been diverted to the contras and that only a third were satisfied with his handling of the controversy.

But less than half were satisfied with how Bush was doing his job generally, and knowledgeable Republicans like GOP state chairman Michael Mahaffey credited Dole with closing the gap through his own efforts. "Vice President Bush still has the best organization," he said at the time, "but Bob Dole is on a political roll here in Iowa. He's a midwesterner and he plays well in rural Iowa. People say, 'Bob Dole knows agriculture.' And they like it when he pokes fun at himself and the system."

It was, indeed, a more self-deprecating Dole who was campaigning in Iowa. In contrast to the slashing, bitter veteran and critic of "Democrat wars" of the 1976 campaign, Dole told a meeting of the Associated General Contractors of Iowa in Des Moines that he had just been to South Dakota, which also would be holding an early delegate contest in 1988. "I went up to Mount Rushmore for a fitting," he cracked. When the laughter had died down, he added: "I had to stand in line because Bush and Kemp had beat me there." And he confided the advice his strategists had given him: "Now, Bob, don't be too funny. They don't want any Jack Bennys in the White House."

But as responsible for Dole's rise in Iowa as his humor was the Reagan straitjacket that Bush was wearing, on Iran-contra and other administration troubles. Mary Louise Smith, a former Republican national chairman from Iowa and a longtime Bush supporter, said at the time that "George Bush is a victim of events beyond his control, and Bob Dole has been the beneficiary." Bush had to "show what a Bush administration would look like," she said, but she acknowledged that it wasn't likely yet because "loyalty is a hallmark of his whole public service."

That the Bush campaign was deeply concerned over Dole in Iowa was evident in April in an internal memorandum written, according to inside sources, by Bond and released by Wittgraf, the designated hitter of the Bush operation. Dole had played a leadership role in the enactment of the 1985 farm bill that ultimately would mean about $2 billion in subsidies to Iowa farmers. The Wittgraf memo called the bill a "disaster" in which Iowa's interests were largely ignored and "Iowa corn farmers were rolled." The memo suggested that Dole was more interested in protecting the interests of wheat, cotton, rice and sugar producers and had been guilty of "pandering to North Carolina tobacco interests to take farm assistance away from the corn and soybean farmers of Iowa."

Taking Dole on over farm issues was not wise, because they were among his strongest suits in the Farm Belt—and the subsidy benefits of the farm bill were beginning to reach Iowa farmers. Dole deftly put the blame for the memo on "Vice President Bush's lawyers" who didn't understand agriculture problems. "If they have a better idea," he said, "I'd like to hear it."

Delegating the hardball tactics to subordinates was part of the Bush strategy to run as if he were the incumbent. It was, ironically, very similar to the above-it-all attitude that dictated Reagan's own strategy in Iowa in 1980 in his loss to Bush. Then, Reagan as the acknowledged front-runner had ducked a critical debate with his challengers and pretty much left his Iowa campaign to his subordinates. Now Bush as vice president was playing the Imperial Candidate, seemingly oblivious to the comparison. At a Midwest Republican Leadership Conference in Des Moines, Bush insisted that he be the sole speaker at lunch while six other presidential hopefuls were relegated to assembly-line remarks. Among them was Dole, who was one of those shut out in Nashua in 1980 when Bush balked at Reagan's invitation to them to join their scheduled two-man debate. Neither he nor the others were amused.

DuPont, striving to get some news media attention, led the way in chiding the vice president for, as duPont said, staying in a "cocoon" aboard *Air Force Two* with Secret Service protection while he and the others were out pressing the flesh with the voters. Or, as Alexander Haig put it, refusing to "come out of the cattle chute for fifteen minutes apiece" as the others were obliged to do at the party conference.

"I thought to myself," duPont said then, "how does George Bush get the sort of wisdom that can be found only in the coffee shops and living rooms and the county courthouses, talking to the American people? One way he might do that is to become a candidate and come debate with us the future of this country, exchange thoughts with us, the other candidates, on where America ought to be going and how it ought to get there."

Robertson added his two cents, saying he was beginning to "get the feeling that he's afraid to get on the same platform with us." He suggested that Bush was employing "a Rose Garden strategy without the Rose Garden." There was, however, enough pomp and ceremony attached to the vice presidency that it was easy for Bush, in effect, to borrow Ronald Reagan's Rose Garden, and he did so.

In mid-September, however, Bush's Imperial Candidacy in Iowa began to crack, in ways more dramatic than his slippage in the Iowa Poll. The state party held a glorified pep rally on the Iowa State University campus at Ames, just north of Des Moines, in the Hilton Coliseum, a large, modern indoor arena. The prime lure was a presidential straw poll that the Iowa Republican Party hoped would bring a record turnout—and national exposure for the party. Five of the six Republican candidates still in the race attended—Bush, Dole, Robertson, Kemp and duPont. (Haig had decided not to compete in the Iowa caucuses.)

The arena in Ames was the same place where Jimmy Carter in 1975 scored a surprise victory in a similar straw poll by packing the hall, and in the process ignited his eventual presidential nomination and election. The Republicans created a carnival atmosphere for the event, with each of the candidates setting up a tent in the sprawling parking lot outside the Coliseum. Holders of the twenty-five-dollar tickets to the rally—the only ones who could vote in the straw poll—were lured in with free beer and a chance to meet and listen to the candidate.

In Bush's tent, however, the trappings of the vice presidency minimized his contact with them. Secret Service agents stood attentively scanning the crowd as he spoke, and when he finished he climbed into the rear seat of his awaiting White House limousine airlifted in from Washington. As he settled in, he picked up a hand microphone wired into the car, and as the limousine slowly moved out he spoke into the mike through the closed window to the people gawking and waving at him outside. "Thank you, thank you very much," he said as the black limousine inched along. "Thank you, the guy in the green shirt. . . ." The Imperial Candidate was exposing himself to the hoi polloi— in his fashion—and they seemed suitably impressed.

But inside the hall, Bush and Dole, who was now running slightly ahead in the Iowa Poll, were in for a shock. The ticket holders cast their straw ballots on the way in, and Iowans sporting Robertson T-shirts, straw boaters, signs and balloons packed the house. Each of the candidates spoke, and it was clear from all the Robertson cheering, well before any results of the poll were announced, that the political newcomer from the world of television evangelism was going to win in a walk.

The vice president, speaking after Robertson and for the first time as part of the pack of hopefuls, obviously was embarrassed by being upstaged by this upstart neophyte. He said his piece quickly and cleared out, with many of his college-student volunteers heading out, too, once their obligatory attendance had been fulfilled. The depth of their commitment was expressed by one chagrined Joe College who mumbled: "No beer, no booze, no broads. Some campaign."*

Dole, sitting in a holding room while Robertson spoke, heard the crowd's roars and got the picture. When his turn came, he made a point of welcoming the new people into the party. He thanked Robertson for recruiting them into the Republican ranks, and, he said, because the newcomers "don't have the foggiest notion who we [the other candidates] are," he told them who Bob Dole was. He emphasized his small-town childhood in a working-class home and his war record and long hospitalization that, he said, made him sensitive to people's pains and needs. And he told them something had to be done to break the party's country-club image, of which the newcomers clearly were not part. Like Kemp in Michigan, Dole figured that Robertson sooner or later would fold, and he wanted to keep his lines open to the Robertson army.

In the straw poll, Robertson won handily with 1,293 votes, or 34 percent of the total, to 958, or 25 percent, for Dole and only 864, or 22 percent, for Bush and the rest trailing badly. The first question was: Where were even a decent number of the 5,000 Bush loyalists from 1980 that Wittgraf claimed as firmly involved in his campaign, and the thousands of others signed on, now that Bush needed them? The answer was that the Bush list was Swiss cheese;

---

*Bush, suffering at the time from what was called "the wimp factor," had in his text the following line: "For the last seven years I've stood side by side with one of the greatest presidents this country has had—and I'm damn proud of it." When he delivered the line, he changed the end to "and I'm very, very proud of it"—setting off loud guffaws in the press section.

although Wittgraf had been promised whatever money he needed to make sure Bush won the Ames straw poll, the bodies could not be produced.

The second question was: Is Pat Robertson for real? The Ames straw poll, remember, occurred while he was still flying high in Michigan, before Bush's late comeback there. The answer was self-evident, although some strategists for other candidates, such as former state chairman Steve Roberts, working for Dole, said Robertson was able to win because there was a heavy fundamentalist population in that immediate central Iowa area. The fact was, however, that busloads of Robertson enthusiasts came in from every quarter of the state.

That night, as *Air Force Two* flew back to Washington, Rich Bond was summoned up front by Barbara Bush. She wanted to know point-blank why her husband had lost in a state where he had beaten Ronald Reagan seven years earlier. She told Bond that she expected him to get back to Iowa and park there from then until the caucuses were over. For the next five months, he did just that, with only occasional trips home or to see what was going on in pesky Michigan.*

Atwater, who after his March inspection visit to the state had no illusions about Bush's chances there, nevertheless acknowledged later that he and Bond had been "asleep at the switch doing other things" when the campaign was jolted by the Ames straw vote. The event should have been a pushover for the vice president of the United States with all his resources, but it wasn't. "Our strategy was for them to turn out 2,500 votes in Ames," Atwater said, "and if they turned out 2,500 votes in Ames there was no way we could get beat. 'How much money you need, we'll give you whatever you need to turn out 2,500 people.' " There was nothing wrong with Atwater's arithmetic, but the Bush organization in the state was such jelly by that time, and the enthusiasm for the candidate so lukewarm, that fewer than 900 showed up.

Of Robertson's showing, Wittgraf told the *Des Moines Register* in the understatement of the season: "I guess we should have been taking him seriously ever since last February and April and June, as we went through the convention process." In explaining the failure to Bush, Wittgraf told him the Ames event had occurred on the one Saturday in the fall when neither Iowa nor Iowa State had a home football game, so numerous social and community events were held all over the state. Other Bush aides later blamed this bit of intelligence on Iowa social habits for Bush's own explanation of his setback, which became the subject of widespread ridicule: "A lot of the people that support me, they were off at the air show, they were at their daughters' coming-out parties, or teeing up at the golf course for that all-important last round."

The Robertson operation indeed had zeroed in on Ames as a special op-

*Bond was also required to spend every fourth night outside Iowa as a result of a regulation in the federal campaign finance law. It stipulated that expenses incurred by a campaign aide beyond three days in any state had to be charged against the federal spending limit in that state. Aides in the various campaigns struggling to stay within the Iowa limit often overnighted in places just across the Iowa border like Omaha, Nebraska, and Moline, Illinois, to comply with the "three-day rule."

portunity to give its candidate much-needed political credibility. The Jimmy Carter exploitation of the event in 1975 was not lost on either the candidates or the news media. Marc Nuttle, the Robertson national campaign manager, said later that he believed at the outset that "the press was going to make up its mind about what was important and what wasn't, and you had to be there, particularly when you're an unknown or not credible, like we were. . . . We didn't think we were going to win it. We thought we'd come in second, again just trying to maintain credibility and progress. Because other candidates made it an event, we were there to play. We were going to do whatever it took."

As for Dole, by this time he had the nucleus of an organization in the state and, more important, the endorsement of Senator Grassley. The senator, a country-bumpkin type who had a lock on the trust and affection of Iowans, earlier in the day of the Ames event announced his support for Dole as a Kansan well versed in farm problems who was "one of us" and could win. It was a phrase that became the centerpiece of Dole's appeal in the state and he was soon incorporating it in his stump speeches and television ads. Grassley had already brought an extremely tangible benefit to Dole in the person of Tom Synhorst, a young Senate staff aide whose parents still ran an Iowa farm and who was a crackerjack organizer. He bought up enough tickets for the Ames affair to give Dole a very respectable second place in the straw poll, thus making Bush's showing all the more damaging in the eyes of the news media that flocked to the event. But Synhorst made no effort to match the cavalcade of church and chartered buses that streamed onto the Iowa State campus from all corners of the state, bringing hundreds of political neophytes revved up to give their all for Pat Robertson.

Neither did Kemp. While his agents in Michigan were valiantly attempting to salvage something for him from very little there, he was being blotted off the political radar screen in Iowa—by the Robertson grass-roots effort among conservatives who shared his general philosophy, by the "one of us" appeal of Dole and by the celebrity of the vice president. "We were going through the valley of the shadow of death with the farm problem," Kemp said later, "and Reagan appeared not to be as popular as he was in some other states. I was running as a Reaganite, for the Reagan wing of the Republican Party. . . . Listening to my speeches, I was celebrating the Reagan years and what we had to do next. We had come a long way, we had a long way to go. I was unabashedly, unambiguously going to the Reagan wing of the party, and I didn't realize how small it was in Iowa."

Obviously, Bush was having the same problem in the state, and supporters such as Mary Louise Smith were urging him to demonstrate in various ways that he did, indeed, cast a shadow of his own outside of Reagan's. The opportunity seemed to present itself in mid-October, when Bush formally declared his candidacy and plunged back into Iowa. Speaking at Linn-Mar High School in the Cedar Rapids suburb of Marion, Bush made a declaration of independence of sorts.

"For nearly seven years I have been vice president," he said. "This week I begin a new challenge—running for the biggest job in America. Now it's time to define my own agenda." At last, George Bush was going to stand up and be "his own man." But his formal speech was a sweeping endorsement of Reagan foreign and domestic policies, and when a student asked him to name the issues on which he disagreed with Reagan, he balked. "I'm not going to start now pointing out differences with the president or other Republicans," he said.

What he would do, Bush went on, was discuss "unfulfilled objectives" in such areas as education, the environment and arms control, "but leave it there. I am not going to go back and criticize a president that I have served loyally through thick and through thin, in good times, and didn't jump away from him in bad times . . . and thus play into the hands of those six Democratic candidates that are running all over Iowa." Having said that, he cloaked himself in generalities about all issues raised in the questions. The George Bush declared and thus liberated candidate sounded remarkably like George Bush the strait-jacketed vice president.

There was, however, considerably more than timidity in Bush's unwillingness to move away from Reagan. Atwater's strategy from the start was anchored in the South, where Bush's closeness and loyalty to the president would be his best credential and selling point in the Super Tuesday cluster of primaries and caucuses in March. "I always knew that no matter what happened, Reagan would be a giant plus for Bush on Super Tuesday," he said later. "So our strategy was never to do any distancing or anything in Iowa that would hurt, because the Reagan association would pay off rich dividends on Super Tuesday."

That decision contributed to some of Bush's roughest sledding in Iowa as the election year began. Questions on what he knew about the arms sales to Iran for hostages, and when he knew it, clung to him. In an appearance at the National Press Club on January 5, he turned away such questions, saying only that "I stood with the president" and refusing to divulge what he had said to him on the subject because "I'm not a kiss-and-teller."

Two days later, the *Washington Post* ran a page-one story saying that Bush had "watched the secret arms sales to Iran unfold step by step and was more informed of details than he has acknowledged because of his regular attendance at President Reagan's morning national-security briefings and other meetings." The story, based on Bush's statements to the Tower Commission investigating the scandal, other documents and interviews with former administration officials, went on to quote an unnamed participant at the national-security sessions who said that Bush attended "several dozen such meetings that touched on the Iran initiative." From them, the source said, Bush "knew basically as much as the president" and had "never voiced reservations. He was not pro. He was not con. . . . Bush kind of echoed the president."

The *Post* story was picked up by the *Des Moines Register* and given lead play, and Dole immediately jumped on it. Noting an approaching Republican candidates' debate in Des Moines, Dole said he thought it would be "in his [Bush's] interest and in the interest of all Republicans to tell us precisely what he knows. . . . I think now is the time to lay it out. The American voters will continue to ask questions." But Bush, campaigning in Iowa, insisted irritably there was nothing new in the *Post* story, that he had already told all he knew and he wasn't going to reveal what he had said to Reagan.

The next night, in the debate staged by the *Des Moines Register* and moderated by its editor, James P. Gannon, Bush came out swinging—at Gannon and the newspaper. Before the debate began, Roger Ailes went into Bush's hotel suite and found him steaming over a long article in the *Register* of that day by veteran Washington correspondent John Hyde. The article provided a detailed chronology of events in the Iran-Contra Affair with the public information available on Bush's role. Hyde prefaced the piece with questions about what Bush knew concerning the arms-for-hostages swap and the diversion of its profits to the contras that he said the vice president hadn't answered.

Unlike the situation before the Houston debate, when Ailes suggested that he meet any attack from duPont by calling him "Pierre," Ailes insisted later he didn't have to prompt Bush this time. As soon as Gannon asked in his opening question why he hadn't answered all questions about the Iran-Contra Affair, Bush lashed out at him.

"Contrary to the hypothesis of your question," he said, "I have answered every question save one. The one question is what did you tell the president of the United States, and I shouldn't do that. Al [Haig] didn't go out talking about what he told the president in the depths of Watergate. Bob [Dole] didn't do it when he was national [party] chairman. I didn't do it and I'm not going to do it."

Then Bush turned the issue onto Gannon and the *Register*. "I've answered every question and I'll continue to," he snapped. "What I'd like to do tonight, since your paper had a full page on this suggesting that I didn't answer questions about diversion, is to ask you now, each one of you that's shooting at me, to ask the question and let me answer it. Save the one. You asked about diversion. I didn't know about the diversion of funds to the contras. The Congress had an eight-to-ten-million-dollar hearing; they never suggested that I did. The Tower report said that I didn't and you, your paper today, had that question raised as if I hadn't answered it. And I resent it, frankly, and I think you owe me now . . . to ask me the question I haven't answered. You owe me in fairness."

But Gannon wasn't about to turn the debate into a one-sided forum for Bush. Instead, he noted that Secretary of State George Shultz and Secretary of Defense Caspar Weinberger both had told Congress what advice they had given Reagan. "They aren't disloyal to the president," he said. Why couldn't Bush do the same? The vice president replied that he supported Reagan's attempts to find a way to improve relations with Iran through "something better than dealing with this madman Ayatollah Khomeini.'' There had been reports of the torture of William Buckley, the captured CIA station chief, he said, "and if we erred, and I think we did in retrospect looking back, a deal that wasn't supposed to be arms for hostages proved to be that; if we erred it was on the side of trying to free Americans held by terrorists.''

Thus, Bush met the demand for more specifics with the same denials and generalities, capped by a defense that he and Reagan had acted with the most humane motives.

It fell to Haig shortly afterward to blow the whistle on the vice president. Deriding his attack on Gannon and the *Register* as "a little political terrorism," Haig put it directly to Bush: "George, as vice president you do have a right to protect your advice to the president and you should do so with whatever fervor you can muster. But you are now seeking the office of the president. Two young men [Poindexter and North] are facing trial and possibly imprisonment for doing the policies of this administration, and I do think the American people want to know what you said, and sooner or later you're going to have to do it. If you can't answer your friends, what in heaven's name is going to happen if you are our standard-bearer and these Democrats get after you on this subject?"

Bush tried to turn the issue back on Haig, asking him what as Richard Nixon's White House chief of staff he had told the president during Watergate. "Or did it take you fifteen years?" he asked. Haig replied: "George, I wasn't asking the Republican Party to support me as a candidate. You have an obligation.''

Dole had little to say on the matter that night, preferring to play the cool-headed front-runner. But the next morning he observed of Bush's confrontation with Gannon: "It may be kind of the ghost of Spiro Agnew coming in and taking on the press.'' Bush declined to rise to the bait. Asked about Dole's remark at the Adel-DeSoto High School outside Des Moines, Bush waved off the query, saying only "Next question, next question.''

At the same event, in a makeshift press conference at which reporters were herded behind a rope, Bush went into his routine of being completely open on Iran-contra, in his fashion. Turning away from David Hoffman of the *Washington Post*, who had been among his most persistent and informed press interrogators for weeks, Bush badgered a young reporter unprepared for a confrontation with the vice president for a question: "Fire one you need to know right now because I'd like to try to get a chance to respond. What question is plaguing you on this? Which one would you like to ask? Go ahead.'' When the flustered reporter could not come up with one, Bush said: "Oh, you don't have any questions.'' And he moved on.

A few days later, in written response to written questions from columnist Mary McGrory, Bush said he had voiced "reservations'' about the Iran arms sales that "turned out to be well founded.'' But he failed to say when he had done so or to whom, except to claim they were made in a "setting with others present.'' And he said he didn't remember "any strenuous objection'' expressed by Shultz or Weinberger at the January 1986 meeting at which they said they had come down hard on the arms sale scheme. Bush said he "probably" took part in that meeting.

In response to one pointed question on how he could "brag about" his antiterrorism report "when you were secretly subverting it," Bush replied that he "was not subverting it because I do not believe in trading arms for hostages. I simply refer you to the president's many comments on this." This answer seemed to use the same ploy he had tried earlier—to suggest that because Reagan didn't *believe* he was trading arms for hostages, it was somehow excusable, and that because he, Bush, believed that Reagan believed, that fact somehow relieved him of responsibility.

At the time, the way the Iran-contra questions hung on was a source of irritation to the Bush camp. But in retrospect, Bush strategist Lee Atwater insisted later, the issue served in effect to clear out the underbrush and make the fight for the Republican nomination a two-man race between Bush and Dole, the two most credible candidates with the greatest ability to command television news time.

"I don't want you to be fooled," Atwater said after the election, "that I woke up during Iran every day and said, 'Boy, this is great.' It was the old making chicken salad out of chickenshit. But it was also a very realistic thing that I saw happening."

He acknowledged afterward that Bush's willingness to field questions on Iran-contra, even in his evasive way, was "media-driven"—that is, determined by how much heat was generated. It was coldly calculated that voters had made an early assessment of the affair, he said, "that it was wrong, that they didn't like it, but they got tired of the media hammering on it over and over and over again. They kind of felt like, 'this is wrong, we don't like it, but we're sick of the media beating it to death.' . . . No one was trying to get rich off this; their motives were good—to try to get these hostages out. So I felt like the Iran thing would burn out by the summer. . . . So I was not worried about it after a point, unless I saw some new legs or new story line develop, which it never did."

Accordingly, Bush dodged when he could get away with it, understanding that probably just as many voters were sympathetic toward him having to undergo the pounding of the irreverent newshounds as were looking for the press to pressure him for more explicit information about his role. "That was ad hoc," one of the strategists admitted afterward. "You had to do what the traffic would bear. That was all based on the media. The media drove our strategy on that. What you wanted to do was minimize his visibility during that period up to a point, and when the media got too much of a hard-on about it, then you had to get him out and answer questions and be forthcoming about it. But that was all media-driven. . . . It was a media issue, not a public issue."

This frank and revealing response by a Bush insider was the best justification for a diligent and tenacious press corps, undeterred by public expressions of disfavor toward that very diligence and tenacity. Here was a major campaign strategist acknowledging that all that mattered was how the public was reacting, and whether the candidate could play on public weariness toward the issue and public irritability toward the probing news media to extricate himself from a sticky situation.*

Further shaping the campaign as a Bush-Dole contest now were stories about Dole's finances, and those of his wife. The *Hutchinson* (Kans.) *Daily News* reported that a blind trust owned by Elizabeth Dole had bought an office building in Overland Park, Kansas, in January 1986 in a deal negotiated by a man named David Owen, who later became her husband's national campaign finance chairman. A middleman in the complex transaction, a former Dole aide named John Palmer, as a black man had earlier received a $26-million army contract under the Small Business Administration's program to help minority enterprises, on Dole's acknowledged recommendation.

The newspaper did not allege any impropriety about the deal, but photocopies of the article were soon making their way into the hands of reporters covering the presidential campaign in Des Moines. The Dole camp immediately pointed an accusing finger at Bush, who was pressing Dole to release his income tax returns in an obvious effort to undercut Dole's effective pitch to Iowans that he was "one of you." Such returns, the Bush campaign clearly hoped, would reveal that the Doles actually were wealthier than the Bushes. And that fact might counter Dole's constant comparison of himself as the poor country boy with the rich blue-blood from New England.

With refreshing candor, Bush's press secretary, Pete Teeley, 'fessed up: "Did we put it out? Sure, with a lot of other clips. The article is in the public domain." Teeley's admission was in sharp contrast with the earlier clandestine disclosure of damaging material to Democratic candidate Joseph Biden by aides of rival Michael Dukakis, the ramifications of which are discussed in a later chapter. Dole compared the Bush campaign's conduct with that of the Dukakis aides in the Biden affair, but the press made little of it, in large part because Teeley acted openly and admitted that he was merely giving wider circulation to information already made public. It was a distinction that most reporters covering the campaign seemed to understand and appreciate.

At any rate, a contest of rather ludicrous poor-mouthing by two well-cushioned candidates now ensued between Bush and Dole, with Bush releasing fourteen years of income tax returns, including his 1986 return showing that he and his wife had paid $115,000 on an adjusted gross income of $346,000.

---

*The callous wisdom of this calculation would in time be emphatically confirmed, in the post-election trial of Oliver North for various offenses in the Iran-contra affair. The government was obliged to reveal a deeper Bush involvement in covert aid to the contras through Honduras in contravention of Congress' prohibition. It became abundantly clear that Bush had not been "forthcoming" about his role. But by then he was safely ensconced in the Oval Office, where he continued to stonewall on the whole matter, this time pleading the conduct of the North trial as requiring his silence. Afterward, he resumed his flat denials of involvement.

Dole's financial filing required by the Senate and his wife's as Reagan's transportation secretary in the same year, both less specific, indicated they made close to $500,000. (Shortly afterward, Dole released his 1986 joint return showing that the Doles had earned $508,000 that year.) But Dole counterattacked that he had risen from humble beginnings and "I've given about $500,000 to charity over the last several years. I'd like to see the Bushes match that." And so it went—as the other candidates grimly watched the publicity for the two poor-mouthers leave them in the shadows.

One of the others, however, didn't seem to mind. All this time, Pat Robertson continued his courtship of Iowa voters awakened to his invitation to put Christianity into practical politics. In late January he conducted a two-day, twenty-seven-town bus caravan across the state that was geared to win local press coverage and flush out the true believers.

The Robertson road show had all the trappings of a traveling carnival, with the now "retired" television preacher cast as chief pitchman. He rode in a specially modified bus with a veritable sound studio in its luggage compartment below the seating area. As the bus approached each stop with loudspeakers blaring patriotic songs, young men in Robertson sweatshirts would hop out, open the luggage space and start assembling a speaker's platform complete with lectern, attached microphones and portable stereo speakers on poles jutting out from either side. Then they would unfurl large American and Iowa state flags and fit them into stands at the rear corners of the portable platform.

Then some local dignitary—it was the mayor in Marshalltown northeast of Des Moines—would introduce the great man, who would descend from the bus grinning broadly and looking astonished that all these wonderful people had turned out just for him. "Gee, what a wonderful crowd!" he gushed at Marshalltown—although the bulk of it had climbed out of other buses and cars in the caravan and gathered around the platform, just as at previous stops. The faithful never seemed to tire of hearing Robertson say the same things over and over—and always with the same sense of wonder that folks would stand out in the cold to hear them.

"What I'm running as," he said in Marshalltown with that wavering pulpit voice of his, "is a conservative who cares about people and wants to speak out for all the people, not some narrow segment, not some special-interest groups. I am for the farmers, I am for the workers, I am for the business people, I'm for the people in rural America, I'm for the people in the cities, I'm for the people in the West and the East and the North and the South and the great heartland of America. I'm for the senior citizens and I'm for the unborn children."

Robertson did not seem to miss anyone, and the crowd cheered as he went on: "The reason I'm running is very simple. I love God, I love America, I love families, I love my children and I love my grandchildren, and I want to make this a better place for you to live and a better place for your children and grandchildren. . . . I am absolutely going to make a commitment that no child in America who has the mental capacity to learn would be denied the ability to read and write in the schools of America.''

Who could be against all that? Nobody in this crowd, certainly, judging from the shrieks of support Robertson's motherhood-and-apple-pie litany brought forth. Had he said mandatory prayer had been put back in the schools or abortion outlawed, he couldn't have generated a much more ecstatic response. In his administration, he said, ''we will stand for freedom—not only the freedom of every one of you to determine what you should do as God gives you life to do it . . . but I want to make sure that America is on the side of freedom. I am against slavery, I am against coercion and I am against communism, and I think we should stand as Americans against communism throughout the world. . . . My platform, if you can call it a platform, is to restore America through moral strength.''

And when he finally leaves the White House, Robertson intoned, he wanted to be able to tell America's children that ''we didn't fail you. When we had our chance, we let the torch of freedom burn as brightly as ever, and we give you the United States of America, strong—free—proud—the strongest nation on the face of the earth . . . a beam of righteousness for all of the nations of the earth to come to. And for our children and grandchildren, we proudly give you—America, one nation, under God.''

Robertson had a way of saying ''America'' that made it sound like ''Heaven''—and that he was, if anybody doubted, the man to lead his rapt listeners to the promised land. When he had finished his political sermon without saying one thing specific about a program or policy, he would step down from the platform and shake eagerly extended hands, his beatific face beaming down on the modest multitudes, many of whom had reached for his grasp at the previous stops. As he did so, his young stagehands would quickly disassemble the props and stuff them back into the bowels of the bus. Orders would be shouted for all to reboard their buses and cars and off would go the Robertson political magic show to the next town.

To those uninspired by all this, Robertson seemed a very crude peddler of political snake oil. But in Michigan he had demonstrated his ability to make the sale, so he could not be dismissed out of hand. The Dole and Bush camps were reassured about Robertson, however, in the next Iowa Poll by the *Des Moines Register*, published three weeks before the caucuses. It showed the political pitchman running a distant third, with only 11 percent of 409 ''likely'' Republican voters surveyed, to 41 percent for the front-running Dole and 26 percent for Bush, with Kemp at 8 percent, duPont at 4 and Haig at 1. These figures were hardly good news for the vice president, but at least Robertson seemed to be no threat to embarrass him.

Bush's main problem in Iowa continued to be Dole, and Dole—and the news media—continued to press the matter of the vice president's role in the Iran-Contra Affair. In this context, there now occurred an event that Atwater later said "helped more than any single other event in the campaign . . . the best moment in the whole campaign, for either candidate in either party."

8

"Tension City": the Bush-Rather "Debate"

George Bush's "best moment" in Lee Atwater's eyes began with a decision by CBS News to do profiles on each of the Republican and Democratic presidential candidates. Richard Cohen, the senior political producer for the *CBS Evening News*, in early January sent Bush a letter advising him of this fact and informing him that anchorman Dan Rather "is very interested in your profile and has decided to do it himself."

Cohen, according to Pete Teeley, representing Bush, proposed that Rather interview Bush on tape for an hour. The tape then, according to Teeley, was going to be edited down to a seven-minute segment for use in a one-hour campaign profile on the vice president. The Bush campaign balked, not wanting to give the network a mandate to take the hour interview and extract whatever seven minutes its producers wanted. The campaign made a countersuggestion that Bush go on live for the seven minutes, thus giving Bush some control in the situation.

Cohen consulted with Tom Bettag, executive producer of *CBS Evening News*, and they agreed. The CBS people, Teeley said later, told him Rather would be asking Bush about the Iran-Contra Affair but the profile would not be exclusively on that subject. Bettag, for his part, recalled afterward that he told Teeley it was CBS policy not to restrict questions in any interview to specific areas but that the "prime focus" of the interview would be "the vice president's role in Iran-contra." Furthermore, Bettag said, he told Teeley that if Bush "tries to wander off the subject we would have to bring him back," because the network was not providing time for a live interview to the other candidates and was sensitive to the charge that Bush would be getting special treatment. If Bush tried to filibuster, Bettag said he told Teeley, "you're liable to get a very tough Dan Rather."

Atwater, for one, was against putting Bush on live. "I thought it was a setup," he said later. "My point to him was Rather was some middle-aged guy with a sagging career and he was trying to take Bush out, a la the Roger Mudd–Ted Kennedy interview." Atwater's reference was to the interview

Mudd, then with CBS News, held with Kennedy in the early fall of 1979, in which Kennedy stumbled badly in responding to a question about why he wanted to be president, and to others about his personal life.

Atwater went on: "The veep got a little upset with me. He said, 'Dan Rather's a nice man. I've known the guy twenty-five years and he's a fair man. He wouldn't do this to me.' I said, 'Well, I've just got a hunch.' " Rather had covered Bush's early adventures in politics as a television reporter in Houston and later had done what the Bush insiders felt was a very flattering segment on him on CBS' *60 Minutes*.

On the weekend before the interview was to take place, CBS News began to run promotional ads that said Rather would be conducting, according to Teeley, "an exclusive interview with Bush on Iran-contra." These ads, he said, made the Bush strategists "a bit mystified." Why they should have been, Bettag said, was a mystery to him, because his conversations with Teeley and the promotions, including one after *60 Minutes* on Sunday night asking "What did George Bush know?" couldn't have been "more straightforward."

That night, Roger Ailes received a phone call at his home in New York from Bob Teeter, the campaign pollster and brainstormer. "He said, 'You're aware Bush is going on Rather. . . . It's live.' " Ailes said that was exactly what he wanted, because he didn't want CBS editing down a canned interview. But Teeter told him, Ailes recalled, "Okay, I've just been getting rumblings that there's more here than we know. Maybe you'd better get down and get with him."

Bush was out on the road and Ailes made plans to meet him at Andrews Air Force Base just outside Washington late the next afternoon, just before the television appearance. "So I started calling around to some friends," Ailes said later, "and asking them, 'What do you hear about this?' And then I heard they were going to cancel over half the news, which was unprecedented, because they couldn't get him taped and edited. . . . And we knew it would be Iran. So I called a friend inside CBS and he went outside to a pay phone. . . . He said, 'Ailes, I'll get fired if anybody knows I've told you this, but they're running around the newsroom saying, 'We're taking Bush out of the race tonight.' . . . They've cut a five-minute piece which basically indicts him, and Dan's job is to execute him on the air.' "

Ailes said he was told CBS had brought in Tom Donilon, the Democratic political consultant importantly involved in the Joe Biden campaign until Biden's early withdrawal, "to coach Rather over the weekend on how to engage Bush." Donilon was serving as a CBS News consultant at the time in one of an increasing number of arrangements that blurred the line between the practitioners of politics and those supposedly reporting on it from an unbiased perspective. If Ailes and the other Bush operatives had qualms about the interview, Donilon's involvement certainly gave them understandable reason.*

---

*Later in the campaign, Donilon played the lead role in preparing Michael Dukakis for his debates against Bush.

Ailes recalled thinking, "This doesn't sound like normal news coverage to me."

Teeley, too, began to get bad vibes. On Monday morning he got several phone calls from reporters covering the campaign "who said they had received calls from the CBS publicity department stating that Bush and Rather were going to have this interview tonight exclusively on Iran-contra. There were some overtones to the conversations. One reporter said to me, 'Teeley, what the hell's going on here? I mean, it sounds like it's going to be a big confrontation.' "

About two hours later, Teeley got a phone call from a friend who used to work at CBS. "He said," Teeley recalled, " 'Pete, are you aware of what's going on tonight on this Rather interview? . . . Well, let me tell you. I've just had lunch with a guy at CBS who started describing how this thing's going to be set up.' And his words to me were, 'This interview is designed so that one of these guys is gonna crack. And we want to see if Rather still has it.' We had alarm bells that were going off earlier than that, but that was pretty startling.' "

The CBS staff did indeed make rather elaborate preparations for the Bush interview, Bettag said later, but the notion that it was planned as some kind of vendetta or *High Noon* shoot-out was flat wrong. Instead, he said, the CBS producers reasoned that if Bush was willing to go on the air live, "he must be ready to break news." Bettag said Rather was indeed taken through a briefing on what Bush was likely to say, and where Rather should try to take him to develop the story. One of the staff even played Bush, Bettag said, as in a mock debate preparation that the candidates routinely conducted, with Rather throwing questions at him. Donilon sat in on part of the session, Bettag said, but played a minor role in preparing Rather for the interview.

Ailes flew to Washington and drove out to Andrews, where he met Bush's plane. It was getting late, so they went in Bush's limousine directly to his office as president of the Senate on Capitol Hill. En route, Ailes filled Bush in on what he had heard. "He said, 'No, they won't do that,' " Ailes recalled Bush saying. " 'I know Dan. They're going to ask me questions about Iran. I've answered all the questions. I've told them everything I know. How can it be any different?' "

Ailes told him it just didn't feel right. But considering Bush's trusting attitude, Ailes said, he proposed that Bush "have a game plan, A and B. If it goes your way, answer the same old questions. But if it doesn't, you've got to engage him. And you've got to say, 'This is outrageous.' " Ailes recalls telling Bush: "I've seen those pieces. They'll put two or three guys on the screen who've been indicted, and then they'll put your picture up there with them. It's the old guilt-by-association trick and the public will think you're guilty of something. If they start that crap, you'd better fight back." This approach dovetailed with the basic "counterpunch" strategy Ailes and Atwater had devised for Bush in all his debates, taking into consideration what they said was Bush's reluctance to start a fight but his willingness to strike back if attacked.

As Bush's limousine headed toward Capitol Hill, Ailes started getting his tiger prepped for battle. He conducted what he called a "mini pepper drill" on Iran-contra questions Rather might pose, but Bush felt he'd heard them all before and didn't need to go over them again. More important, Ailes well understood that television news celebrities, and Rather particularly, aroused negative feelings among many viewers, especially conservatives to whom Bush continued to play as a candidate. He intended to play on those feelings if the opportunity presented itself. So he reminded Bush of something: when Rather the previous September walked off the CBS set for six minutes, leaving dead airtime, in a dispute over delaying the evening news because of a late-running tennis match. Ailes mentioned the incident to Bush, he said later, "in terms of getting him cranked up on Rather a little bit. . . . I said, 'This guy's not exactly a hero, even to broadcasters. I've been in broadcasting enough to know the one thing you never do is let dead air go, or let a station go dark, and this guy walked off the air.' "

When they got to Bush's Senate office, the vice president called Atwater. After they had discussed some campaign matters, Atwater reminded him of his reservations about the interview. "I sure hope you don't get bushwhacked," Atwater told his boss. But Bush seemed unconcerned. "I'm telling you," he said of Rather, "this guy's a straight shooter."

Ailes meanwhile was talking to Mary Martin, the CBS deputy bureau chief in Washington. He said he understood the show was to be a political profile, was that right? She replied, Ailes said later, that the show was going to lean more heavily on one subject. Then he knew "they had sucked us in and sandbagged us," he said. So he went to Bush and said to him, as he recalled, "You've either got to go in there and go toe-to-toe with this guy, or you're going back to Kennebunkport. This is a tough night here."

The show began with Rather at his anchor's desk in the CBS studios in New York and Bush wired for sound in his Senate office in Washington, with a television monitor showing him what was on the air at the time. The show opened with a recapitulation of nearly five minutes in which the major questions about which Bush had been evasive were reviewed, including what Donald Gregg, his national security adviser, and Felix Rodriguez, Bush's former CIA associate, knew about American efforts to supply arms to the contras in Nicaragua, efforts about which Bush himself pleaded ignorance.

As Bush watched on the monitor in his office, he grew visibly angry, especially as the screen flashed a promotion spot about the approaching interview, the subject of which was billed as the Iran-Contra Affair. "That's not what I'm here for," Bush snapped, off the air but over an open microphone in his office. He complained about another grilling on the scandal, warning that if it took place, CBS was going to see "a seven-minute walkout here"—an obvious reference to Rather's earlier walkout, planted in Bush's mind just a short while earlier by Ailes. When a CBS technician advised Bush that his mike was open, the vice president was heard to reply: "That's fine. I want him to hear what I'm saying."

In New York, Bettag, in the studio's control room, picked up Bush's remarks and conveyed them to Rather, with whom he was in continuing communication through a wire plugged into the anchorman's ear. But Rather proceeded as planned with his opening question: "Donald Gregg still serves as your trusted adviser. He was deeply involved in running arms for the contras and he didn't inform you. Now, when President Reagan's trusted adviser, Admiral Poindexter, failed to inform him, the president fired him. Why is Mr. Gregg still inside the White House and still a trusted adviser?"

Bush replied that he had confidence in Gregg and that the whole matter had been thoroughly investigated by the House-Senate committee and the Tower Commission. Then he lit into Rather, charging that it was "outrageous" to suggest in the introductory report that he had learned of the aid to the contras from Rodriguez when he had testified that the subject was never discussed between the two of them. Then he accused CBS of "misrepresentation" in telling him the show was going to be "a political profile . . . and then you come up with something that had been exhaustively looked into."

Clearly, Ailes' Plan B was going into effect. Rather and Bush went back and forth over what was and wasn't said, in the Iran-contra matter and in negotiations for Bush's interview, voices and temperatures rising with each passing minute. When Rather cited a poll indicating one fourth of those surveyed "believe you're hiding something," Bush shot back: "I am hiding something. . . . You know what I'm hiding? What I told the president, that's the only thing, and I've answered every question put before me." Then he went into his taunting drill. "Now, if you have a question . . ."

Rather: "I do have one."

Bush: "Please."

Rather: "I have one."

Bush: "Please, fire away."

Rather: "You have said if you had known, you said if you had known this was an arms-for-hostages swap . . . that you would have opposed it."

Bush: "Exactly."

Rather: "You also said that you did not know . . ."

Bush: "May I answer that?"

Rather: "That wasn't a question, it was a statement."

Bush: "It was a statement and I'll answer it."

Rather: "Let me ask the question if I may, first."

Bush: "The president created this program . . . he did not think it was arms for hostages."

Rather: "That's the president, Mr. Vice President."

Bush: "And that's me. Because I went along with it, because, you know why, Dan? Because . . ."

Rather: "That wasn't a question, Mr. Vice President."

And so it went. Rather pressed Bush on a few specific matters on which the vice president had been evasive. He asked about Bush's July 1986 conversation in Israel in which antiterrorism specialist Amiram Nir indicated that arms were being traded for hostages, and about the meeting at which Shultz strenuously opposed the arms sales. Finally, Bush had enough.

"I don't think it's fair to judge a whole career, it's not fair to judge my whole career by a rehash on Iran," he said. "How would you like it if I judged your career by those seven minutes when you walked off the set in New York? Would you like that?"

Rather looked as if he had been dashed in the face with cold water. "Mr. Vice President," he said when he recovered. But Bush pushed on.

"I have respect for you," he said, "but I don't have respect for what you're doing here tonight."

Rather tried to recover. "Mr. Vice President," he said, "I think you'll agree that your qualifications for president and what kind of leadership you'd bring the country, what kind of government you'd have . . . what kind of people you'd have around is much more important than what you just referred to. . . ." And he tried to get the exchange back onto Bush's role in the arms deal.

Both men were talking animatedly at the same time now, breaking in on each other. Finally, Rather demanded: "Mr. Vice President, you've made us hypocrites in the face of the world. How could you, how could you sign on to such a policy? And what does this tell us about your record?"

Bush said for the second time in the exchange that he was motivated by a desire to see Buckley, the captured CIA station chief allegedly being tortured, released, and "maybe you err on the side of a human life." Then he tried to change the subject again, charging that "there's nothing new here. I thought this was a news program."

In the control booth in New York, Bettag, Cohen and the other producers were getting apoplectic. They had planned for the interview to run anywhere from three to seven minutes, and it was already over that time. Other news segments had been summarily killed, and Bettag was now screaming into Rather's ear piece: "Cut! Cut! Cut! You gotta cut!" A harried Rather made one more pitch:

"Mr. Vice President, I appreciate your joining us tonight. I appreciate the straightforward way in which you've engaged in this exchange. There are clearly some unanswered questions. Are you willing to go to a news conference before the Iowa caucuses, answer questions from all . . ."

Again Bush broke in: "I've been to eighty-six news conferences since March, eighty-six of 'em since March . . ."

Now Rather broke in: "I gather that the answer is no. Thank you very much for being with us, Mr. Vice President. We'll be back with more news in a moment."

Now it was Bush who looked stunned, at the abrupt way Rather had ended the interview. Apparently believing his microphone was off or forgetting about it, he snapped to some of the CBS staff in his office: "The bastard didn't lay a glove on me. . . . Tell your goddamned network that if they want to talk to me, to raise their hands at a press conference. No more Mr. Inside stuff after that.'' And he said of Rather: "That guy makes [CBS correspondent] Lesley Stahl look like a pussy.''

Ailes, hearing Bush behind him making the remark, turned to grab the small snap-on mike still pinned to his candidate. "I think he was saying that to me as a joke, not realizing the mike was on,'' Ailes said later. "It was not said in anger, because when I looked at him he was smiling.''

The public reaction was almost immediate—and one-sided against Rather. Phone calls flooded the CBS switchboards in New York and Washington and at the CBS affiliate in Des Moines. Dave Busiek of KCCI there reported more than two hundred callers, many of them "cussing and yelling.'' The next night, Rather defended his conduct on the air, saying Bush had not been misled by CBS on the subject of the interview. "Trying to ask honest questions and trying to be persistent about answers is part of a reporter's job,'' he said, "and however it may seem at any given time, the intention of even persistent questions in a spirited interview is to do an honest, honorable job. The fact that more attention is sometimes given to the heat than the light is regrettable, but it goes with the territory.''

As for the abrupt ending, Rather observed: "Ending live television interviews under time pressures sometimes isn't done as gracefully as we hope or intend, and last night was one of those times.'' But the decision to attempt so important a live interview in such a short period of time, and to subject it to the constraints of a commercial business, which is what television is, was inviting trouble. The way Rather was obliged to end the interview may well have generated as much or more public hostility toward the man and his network than did any of the questions asked or the manner of their asking. This was fast-food journalism at its worst, and CBS got a big bellyache out of it. But the fact was that Bush, for all his taunting of reporters to ask him about the Iran-Contra Affair, would never agree to a full-dressed, sit-down news conference at which he would answer all questions put to him on the subject. It was easier to throw out the taunt on the run, and then escape, making it appear that he was being forthcoming.

At CBS, an immediate postmortem was undertaken, Bettag said, to discover whether Bush indeed had been misled in any way about the nature of the interview, or why he thought he had. Ailes and others in the campaign pointed to Cohen's early January letter requesting an interview for a "profile'' as clear evidence that Bush had been sandbagged. Bettag said later that Cohen's request was for a separate interview that was dropped in favor of the live interview on the Iran-Contra Affair and in retrospect Bush should have been so informed. But he insisted that Bush had not been misled. Well, we asked him, was it possible that Ailes had sandbagged CBS by saying Bush had been unfairly treated, thus setting the stage for the vice president to attack the controversial Rather? Bettag declined to speculate, but only would say: "I know we didn't sandbag them. We didn't mislead them for a second.''

The way Bush pounced on Rather, however, was reminiscent of his behavior earlier in the month at the *Des Moines Register* debate, when he sought immediately to put the moderator, editor James Gannon, on the defensive over an article in the paper raising questions about the vice president's role in the Iran-Contra Affair. On that occasion, Bush's attack drew largely favorable reactions. So it was not out of the realm of possibility that the deft Ailes would see the opportunity of an even more effective assault on everybody's favorite whipping boy, the news media, in Bush's interview with Rather, who himself raised many viewers' hackles with his sometimes superior airs.

Bush, for his part, reveled in the aftermath of the Rather interview. The next day, campaigning in Cody, Wyoming, he told one audience: "I need combat pay for last night. . . . It's tension city when you're in there." But he said he had "no hard feelings. I did what I know is right. I don't want a big running fight with Dan Rather or anyone else." In Pierre, South Dakota, Bush expressed regret for some of his language. "If I had known the microphone was on I would not have taken the Lord's name in vain, and I apologize for that," he said. "I was not amused and I'm afraid I said something that was not appropriate. . . . I didn't know I was being taped or I wouldn't have done it. You didn't hear me talk that way on the show."

Bush made no mention of his remark about Lesley Stahl, but Teeley said he meant that Stahl, herself a very persistent interrogator as moderator of the CBS News show *Face the Nation*, was a "pussycat" compared to Rather, and Bush's comment was not "a sexist remark."

In Iowa, Bush's man Rich Bond said that Rather "tried to bully the vice president" and that "I don't think it can possibly hurt in Iowa." Indeed, Bush did move up somewhat in his campaign's tracking of Iowa voter sentiment for a few days, but he fell right back again, according to Atwater later, because "Iowa was just dead-ass locked" for Dole with his "one of you" appeal to that heavily farm-oriented state.

Nevertheless, Atwater stuck to his assessment of the Bush-Rather confrontation as the best moment of the whole campaign for the vice president. It was, he said, "a defining event" that in a few brief moments shattered Bush's previous image as a weak, cowed figure, so often characterized as "the wimp factor." From then on, Atwater said later, the voters began to see Bush in a different, much more positive light.

"In presidential politics," Atwater said, "each candidate ends up having two or three defining events, events that are so big that they actually transcend the political echo chambers universe, meaning reporters, political operatives and political people who sit around and talk about this stuff, and actually melt down to the public." This happens, he said, "to such an extent that the next day after any defining event, if you go to any bar in America, or ride in any taxi, or go to a laundromat or the YMCA, and stand around for a few moments, that's the event people are going to be talking about. The trick in the defining-event business is to know there's going to be two or three one way or the other, and they either work against you or for you. You want to make sure that defining events are not negative defining events."

Such a negative defining event, he recalled, happened to Bush in the 1980 campaign in Nashua, New Hampshire, when Reagan used him as a pawn in his "fight" to open their two-man debate to the other Republican candidates called into the hall at the last minute. "That also turned out to be a positive defining event for Ronald Reagan," Atwater noted. "The optimum defining event for George Bush, I felt at the outset, would be one that would enforce the notion of strength and the notion that he could engage with someone and come out on top."

To do so was important "particularly in the South," this drawling son of South Carolina said. "People in the South love someone who can kick somebody's ass. And the optimum defining-event situation is when somebody else throws the first punch. That's an American tradition; it's a southern tradition. That's why we like John Wayne so much; that's why we like Clint Eastwood; that's why we like Gary Cooper. They never throw the first punch, but when the other guy starts something, they finish it. I think that's popular all over the country, but it's particularly popular in the South, where Super Tuesday was going to be."

The Rather interview was just such a defining event, Atwater said, because it "totally demolished any notion of the so-called wimp factor. It never resurrected its head after that." Secondly, he said, it was impossible to calculate "how much it reinforced his base in the South. I remember thinking at the time that that strengthened him so much in the South, in South Carolina and Super Tuesday, that we would be able to overcome even a defeat in New Hampshire."

All this was not clear to everyone at the time, however. A *USA Today/Cable News Network* poll of 373 registered Iowa Republicans found about two-thirds saying Rather had been out of line and that Bush was justified in how he handled himself. But only 16 percent said they would be more likely to vote for Bush as a result. Many reporters in Iowa (us included) wrote that the picture of the vice president of the United States complaining about the terms of an interview in which he was being asked pointed questions about his conduct regarding the Iran-Contra Affair was a defensive and even demeaning one. But in so saying we did not adequately gauge the television-viewing public's hostility toward the news media, especially one of its "stars."

Mary McGrory in the *Washington Post* had it right when she wrote that "the screening of America is now complete. Dan Rather has probably nominated the Republican candidate and may even have elected the next president. What Bush actually said seems of little consequence. What matters is the reaction. Thousands of viewers who got through on the network's jammed lines have recorded their passionate conviction that Rather is a boor and a bully. Actually, he was asking questions and the vice president was ducking them. . . . Rather's prosecutorial, pneumatic-drill interviewing style brought to roaring flames the ever-smoldering resentment of the news media, which is particularly strong on the right flank of the GOP."

The notion that a television reporter's interview with the vice president of the United States and front-runner for the Republican presidential nomination would be a "defining event" in a national campaign was a remarkable commentary on the role television had assumed by 1988. Even more so was the observation by that candidate afterward that he should have received "combat pay" for enduring "tension city" in the presence of that reporter. But the television news business itself had come to see its role, and that of its featured performers, as larger than life. Richard Cohen's letter to Bush read as if the candidate was being offered a precious stone of incalculable value in an interview with none other than the jewel of *CBS Evening News*.

"Dan Rather is very interested in your profile and has decided to do it himself," Cohen wrote. Himself! "Mr. Rather feels," the letter went on, "that because you are the incumbent Vice President and a front-runner, that your candidacy deserves special attention." Cohen wrote that he was "officially requesting an interview for Mr. Rather" and that "he would be happy to travel to Washington at your earliest convenience." In other words, Rather was even willing to come to the vice president! How could Bush possibly say no?

The Bush-Rather confrontation that resulted was not exactly in the league of the first Kennedy-Nixon debate of 1960, or even the Nixon–Nikita Khrushchev "kitchen debate" of 1959 in Moscow. But the attention it drew and, if Atwater was right, the way it changed the public perception of Bush, were astonishing nonetheless. The episode cried out for a greater sense of perspective by the viewing public, but it was a cry that was not being heard in the era of the Almighty Tube and its High Priests.

Atwater unquestionably was correct in his observations about "defining events" in politics that either confirm or shatter preconceptions about the weaknesses of public figures. There are many previous examples: Gerald Ford's gaffe on the absence of Soviet domination in Eastern Europe in his 1976 debate with Jimmy Carter, mentioned earlier; George Romney's observation in 1967 that he had undergone a "brainwashing" in Vietnam; George McGovern's statement that he was "a thousand percent" behind Thomas Eagleton as his running mate in 1972, before dropping him from the ticket; Edmund Muskie appearing to cry while excoriating a publisher for attacking his wife in print during the 1972 New Hampshire primary; Carter reportedly being attacked by a rabbit while boating in a Georgia pond in 1979.

Bush's "victory" over a controversial television anchorman was another such episode. And Atwater's—and no doubt Ailes'—clear understanding of the nature and political potential in a "defining event" fed the inevitable speculation, in the news business at least, that it was CBS News that got "sandbagged," not the other way around. After his election victory in November, Bush found himself able to take a more positive view of "tension city." Defending the format, he told us: "We insisted on live coverage because we believed the voters should see the candidates as they are. Live interviews offer full discussion. If one or both of the interlocutors gets animated with the spirit of the exchange, that is no indictment of this type of TV news format. Politics can be rough, but I like to think there are no hard feelings at the end of a campaign.''

Bush could afford by then to look back benignly at the episode. Beyond the manner in which the Rather interview served to diminish the ''wimp factor,'' the CBS anchorman's intemperate style enabled Bush to play the wronged victim of the bullying news media, and thus once again avoid answering on his role in the Iran-Contra Affair. He could now point to Rather's grilling to contend that he had faced the roughest of inquisitions, when in fact what he had done was reduce Rather's tough questions to a personal catfight in which he offered only the same old dodges. Increasingly thereafter, Bush would simply stonewall further questions on the matter, saying he had answered all the legitimate inquiries.

In Iowa the incident as noted provided Bush with only a temporary lifeline. The public pulse-taking of his own staff found Bush in the long run to be a hopeless case in the state that believed Ronald Reagan had forgotten it and that one of its own, Bob Dole, had not and would not. But as caucus night approached, Bush's ground troops were not giving up. All along, they nourished the idea that Dole's celebrated short fuse would be his undoing, and to give him reason to blow up, Bush's ever-ready hit man, George Wittgraf, in collusion with Rich Bond, put out a stingingly personal press-release blast. It said that ''Iowa Republicans must weigh Bob Dole's record of cronyism and his history of mean-spiritedness carefully before they decide whom to support as our party's nominee for president.'' Wittgraf wrote that Dole ''showed his mean-spirited nature in 1976, when he nearly single-handedly brought the Republican national ticket down to defeat.'' And while Dole talked of his poor childhood in Kansas, Wittgraf wrote, ''he fails . . . to mention that he and his wife are now millionaires and had an income of $2.19 million from 1982 through 1986. Dole and his wife also live in Washington's posh Watergate apartment complex and vacation regularly at a Florida condominium purchased by them'' with the help of a wealthy agribusinessman.

Dole was, or at least appeared to be, furious at this eleventh-hour assault, calling it vindictive and personal. But he didn't self-destruct in response. Instead, he soberly demanded that Bush fire Wittgraf as his state campaign manager, that he say whether or not he authorized the press release and that he apologize to his wife, Elizabeth, for suggestions by Wittgraf that her blind trust had acted illegally in the matter of the Kansas building purchase.

Bush, campaigning in Clinton, Iowa, when asked about the press release, said: ''I don't endorse it, but I don't reject it.'' Dole thereupon decided to exploit the charges for all they were worth. When he and Bush both had to fly back to Washington for a critical vote on contra aid, Dole confronted the vice president as he presided in the Senate chamber. Dole strode angrily to the podium where Bush sat, waved the Wittgraf press release at him and apparently chewed him out in tones that could not be made out in the press gallery above. Bush did not apologize then, but on a nationally televised interview show the final weekend, he said that he saw nothing in the Wittgraf statement "that I thought was a criticism of Elizabeth, but if so, I would totally apologize to her. She's a friend." But he declined to apologize to Dole for the press release, which he said Wittgraf put out on his own because he was tired of hearing Bush "pounded and pounded" by the Dole campaign.

This late flurry did nothing to change the Iowa outlook. On the day before the precinct caucuses, Dole still led in the Iowa Poll, with 37 percent of 660 likely Republican caucus-goers, to 23 percent for Bush, 13 for Robertson, 11 for Kemp, 7 for duPont and 1 for Haig. By this time, the Bush forces in Iowa were resigned to a defeat at Dole's hands, but the development that they now feared more, and began to recognize could happen, fell on them the next night.

Dole won the Iowa caucuses handily, with about 37 percent of the vote, just as the *Des Moines Register*'s final poll had indicated. But in precinct gatherings across the state, thousands of new faces appeared, answering the call of the political pitchman, Pat Robertson. These newcomers to political action gave him 25 percent of the vote, nearly twice what the Iowa Poll had indicated he would get, leaving the vice president of the United States running a poor third, with 19 percent, in the state where he had beaten Ronald Reagan eight years before. Brock, Dole's national campaign manager, crowed that Bush "has taken a direct hit," and suddenly his status as the front-runner was severely shaken. His team had diligently identified 38,000 supporters, five times the number of hard committeds signed on in 1980, but nearly half failed to turn out.

Rich Bond, a master at making silk purses out of sow's ears, recalled Reagan's comeback in 1980 after his defeat by Bush in Iowa. "A loss in Iowa for George Bush in 1988 is the same as a loss for Ronald Reagan in 1980," he said wishfully. "We're going to win in New Hampshire." But Richard Wirthlin, the veteran Reagan pollster of the 1980 campaign who was now with Dole, predicted that Dole would pick up at least 10 percent in the polls in New Hampshire as a result of his two-to-one victory over Bush in Iowa, making the first primary of 1988 a horse race.

As for Robertson, he claimed that the result proved he had expanded his base beyond the Christian Right church network to Roman Catholics, students and regular-party Republicans. But Wirthlin scoffed at the contention, suggesting instead that "Robertson probably has the most politically formidable organization to turn out one of the smallest constituencies that exists." He predicted that in the more open primary process in New Hampshire, Robertson would be buried.

The other Republican candidates didn't have to wait. They had already had plenty of dirt thrown on them in Iowa. Kemp got only 11 percent of the vote, duPont 7 and Haig less than 1.

Already, after only one contest involving most of the Republican presidential hopefuls, the field was narrowing. As the campaign moved quickly into New Hampshire, where the primary would be held in only eight more days, two questions begged for answers: Was George Bush finished? And, once again, was Pat Robertson for real? In the very asking, the victory of Bob Dole seemed somehow overshadowed. But he was the winner, and if Wirthlin was correct in how large a "bump" he would get out of his Iowa success in New Hampshire, the Republican presidential nomination of 1988 might well be decided right then and there.

On the Bush entourage's gloomy flight to New Hampshire, Atwater recalled later, "it was the single most depressing event of my life, not because we lost, but because we got waxed." He had reason to recall a conversation with Bush supporter Governor John Sununu before the Republican candidates' debate in Houston in mid-October. The two of them were having dinner at the Houstonian Hotel and Atwater confided to him: "John, let me tell you something. I don't think we can win Iowa. Do you think we can win New Hampshire, no matter what?" Sununu replied: "You're damn right we can. I figure we're gonna lose Iowa, too." He said he planned to stump in every New Hampshire county personally. "I'm going to run New Hampshire as if we are going to lose Iowa."

Now Iowa was lost, and as Bush's plane landed in Manchester, Sununu walked up to Atwater. "Don't worry about it," he said. "I'm going to give you a nine-point win here." Atwater confessed later: "I felt he was out of his damned mind." If most of the other "experts" now flocking to New Hampshire had heard Sununu, too, they doubtless would have felt the same.

9

New Hampshire: the Resurrection of George Bush

At seven o'clock the morning after the Iowa caucuses, George Bush, in his pajamas and bathrobe, met with his principal advisers—campaign chairman Nick Brady, campaign manager Lee Atwater, chief of staff Craig Fuller and polling expert/strategist Bob Teeter—in his suite at the Clarion Hotel in Nashua. The defeat had been no surprise. Indeed, Bush had fled Iowa for New Hampshire the previous night before the votes were counted so he could avoid having to explain his loss. But finishing behind not only Bob Dole but also Pat Robertson was jarring.

Although he had expected Bush to lose in Iowa, Atwater was shaken and prepared to take the blame. "I had my whole little speech ready," he recalled.

But Bush waved off the question of blame. "We've got eight days," he told his visitors. "Let's sit down here right now and let's don't get up until we figure out how to win this campaign."

Several decisions were obvious. Bush would have to maintain a presence in the state for every news cycle for the next eight days. That meant that, as planned, he could return to Washington the following day for his regular weekly luncheon with President Reagan—and the all-important pictures of that meeting—but then would return to New Hampshire rather than spending the night at home. A scheduled trip to the Southern Regional Republican Conference in New Orleans was quickly scrapped. Bush himself pressed to do more personal campaigning, less waving to the masses through his limousine windows. "You guys," he told his advisers, "have got to let me get out there and get with the people."

None of these decisions required any special political genius. As Atwater said later, "You get a sudden realization the day you get the hell pounded out of you exactly what you need to do." The result was a schedule Bush was to follow the rest of the week. He would rise early, do five or six radio interviews between 6:30 and 7:30, appear at a campaign event early enough in the day for reports on that event to filter through the New Hampshire news media, then spend the rest of the day on intensive personal campaigning at locations chosen principally by Sununu. The state was small enough, Teeter reasoned, "so we can see enough people to make a difference." And, because Bush was always more relaxed campaigning with someone else, attention-getting celebrities— Ted Williams, an icon anywhere in New England, and test pilot Chuck Yeager—were booked to accompany him.*

While there was nothing extraordinary about any of these activities, the professional dispatch with which the Bush campaign laid its plans for survival was a manifestation of one of the lessons of the campaign of 1988: There is no substitute for experience, preferably long experience, in running a campaign for president of the United States.

Unlike Iowa, New Hampshire was supposed to be fertile ground for George Bush. This was, after all, a state in which Ronald Reagan was still an enormously popular president. Bush's organization—run by two capable operatives from Massachusetts, Ron Kaufman and Andy Card—was markedly superior to any other in the Republican competition. And Bush had the active and aggressive support of Governor Sununu. So it was no surprise when a week before the Iowa caucuses several polls showed Bush comfortably ahead, with margins ranging from ten to twenty percentage points over Dole.

But Dole's triumph in Iowa seemed to change the political atmospherics overnight. New polls showed the race tightening, and the political wise guys speculated that New Hampshire might be the place where George Bush would

*At one stop with Ted Williams, Bush remarked on how thrilled youngsters often were to meet baseball stars, then told of asking one of his grandsons what he wanted to be when he grew up. The boy replied, Bush said with a straight face, that he wanted to be "a drug-free rock guitarist."

confirm their long-held suspicions that, once cut, he would be a political hemophiliac. The conventional wisdom held that Bush was teetering on the edge of political oblivion.

Inside the Dole campaign there was heady optimism. Tracking polls by Richard Wirthlin showed the race tightening steadily in the first days after the Iowa results were tabulated. Bush had been leading Dole 41 percent to 24 percent two weeks earlier, but that lead now had dropped to 31–24 in the first two days after Iowa, then to 28–23. Public polls told the same story. A *Boston Globe* survey had the contest in New Hampshire dead even; a week earlier the same poll had shown Bush leading by twenty points. Dole himself, still believing that he was trailing by about eighteen percentage points, encountered Wirthlin shortly after he arrived in New Hampshire.

"He was just smiling from ear to ear," Dole said later. ". . . He was whistling 'Hail to the Chief' and all that stuff. He told me, 'You're going to be the next president.' . . . That's pretty heavy stuff. I don't know what happened to the eighteen-point deficit."

Within the Bush operation, there was a similar recognition that the context of the campaign had changed radically. Although Ron Kaufman had been warning New Hampshire supporters all along of the likelihood that Bush would lose Iowa, the reality took some explaining. But, as they showed in that early morning meeting, Bush's strategists understood that the way to confront a setback was to start looking for ways to overcome it.

New Hampshire offers an almost ideal arena for the kind of intense, personal politics Bush now felt it necessary to practice. The state is small enough for candidates to base themselves in one place, usually in or near Manchester, and not have to drive more than an hour or so in any direction to reach most of the voters. Reporters find it similarly inviting. They can set out to cover the campaign every morning confident they can be back to the warmth of the bar at the Wayfarer in Bedford, the hotel that becomes a de facto press headquarters every four years, by dinnertime. (Unless they have the misfortune to be assigned to a Democrat making the obligatory visit to Berlin, a paper-making heavily Democratic community that lies an often hairy ninety-minute flight over the mountains to the north.)

But the popular picture of the electorate—one encouraged by a new generation of reporters every four years—is far from accurate. The voters are depicted as laconic Yankees waiting at crossroads general stores to shake each candidate's hand for the third time and answering questions with "Ay-yuh." In fact, the state now has a population of more than 1 million, and most of the growth has come in high-tech industries inside southern New Hampshire but less than an hour from Boston's Logan Airport. And although the vote in the primary is small enough to make retail campaigning useful—about 110,000 Democrats and 150,000 Republicans—television has become as much the critical medium there as anywhere in the nation.

Presidential candidates rarely used television advertising in New Hampshire until 1980. The only commercial outlet within the state, Channel 9 in Manchester, had a small audience in those days, and buying time on Boston stations was considered too expensive and wasteful. But in 1978 the late Hugh Gallen, then a Democratic candidate for governor, invested a modest $35,000 in Boston television that was credited with putting him over the top in upsetting the Republican incumbent, Meldrim Thomson. The new conventional wisdom became: Buy Boston TV.

New Hampshire campaigns had changed in many ways. Before the heavy use of television, the candidates put great emphasis on the endorsements of leading political figures. Because the state's governors serve only two-year terms and seem to be a hardy lot, any candidate with any pretensions of seriousness could find a former governor to be chairman of his committee. And the highest priority was given to compiling endless lists of supporters from every crossroads in the state. Lacking television, the candidates relied on word-of-mouth personal testimony in their behalf.

Direct-mail appeals were also used extensively, particularly by the Republicans, whose voter lists were more likely to be up to date. In 1964, two young Republicans from Boston, David Goldberg and Paul Grindle, ran an unauthorized write-in campaign for Ambassador Henry Cabot Lodge, then stationed in Vietnam, that was based principally on mailings of two-part postcards. Voters supporting Lodge were asked to send in to headquarters that part that contained a pledge of that backing. Goldberg and Grindle finally convinced skeptical reporters that their campaign was gaining speed simply by allowing the reporters to open the mailbags of hundreds of pledge cards arriving at their office on Main Street in Concord every morning. The technique, woefully unsophisticated by today's standards, worked, and Lodge defeated both of the active competitors in the Republican primary campaign that year, Senator Barry Goldwater and Governor Nelson A. Rockefeller of New York.

There was, however, another difference in those earlier primary campaigns probably more significant than the absence of television. Prior to 1976, when an obscure Georgian named Jimmy Carter seized national attention overnight by winning the Iowa caucuses, the New Hampshire primary was the scene of the first competition and thus the place where the pecking order of candidates was established. Voters there received them with essentially open minds because they had so little information about most of them. But by 1988, Iowa had usurped that function, and New Hampshire had become something more like the semifinals. The experience since 1976 suggested strongly that any candidate who finished in the "second tier"—meaning not among the recognized leaders—in Iowa could not hope to compete effectively in New Hampshire. As the poet might have said, no primary is an island.

Devising Bush's new schedule, Atwater and Teeter had a clear picture of at least the dimensions of the target group of voters. For three years the vice president had been supported by about 40 percent of New Hampshire Republicans in opinion polls, but now that market share had dropped under 30 percent in the post-Iowa surveys. These were the voters whose support had to be reclaimed. "We had lost a lot of people in a hurry who had to be soft voters or we wouldn't have lost them," Teeter said. "But we also knew that a week before that, they were willing to vote for George Bush. They had some propensity to vote for Bush. And so if you just simply got them back and made them feel comfortable with Bush again after he had lost Iowa, they were there."

Atwater had seen that trick accomplished when he worked in the Ronald Reagan campaign of 1980. Reagan, he remembered, had a consistent base of 45 percent of New Hampshire voters before he was upset by Bush in the Iowa caucuses that year. He quickly lost 20 percent in the first two weeks of what was then a full-month interval before the New Hampshire primary. But Reagan plunged into the campaign and, as Atwater put it, "plugged back into that original base" to pull ahead a week or more before the primary.

There was a curious role reversal between the 1980 and 1988 situations. In that earlier primary Bush had been undone in some measure because he refused, once he had captured the national attention by winning in Iowa, to build on the foundation of his success by spelling out his own vision of the sort of president he would be. Instead, in that campaign, candidate Bush, to the consternation of his managers, kept talking about the "Big Mo"—for momentum—he had achieved in Iowa, and about political mechanics. Now Dole had that same attention focused on him—and he, too, seemed to lack the kind of coherent message to take advantage of the opportunity. Dole stumped the state intensively and made some strong speeches, but neither he nor his advisers had produced a thematic approach that might have had a broader appeal.

The result was a situation in which, as Teeter saw it, the voters "didn't see any significant differences between Bush and Dole." Both were high-ranking Republicans of acceptably conservative views and impressive résumés of political and public service. So the key was which could succeed in setting himself apart. Dole had done it—for the moment, at least—by winning in Iowa. Now it was up to Bush to do the same if he was to reclaim that 13 or 14 percent of the Republican electorate that had drifted away on Monday night.

None of the other Republicans in the field was ever a serious contender. Alexander Haig, the former secretary of state and White House chief of staff under Richard M. Nixon, was carrying a burden of negative perceptions that he never succeeded in overcoming. Pete duPont had captured the endorsement of the *Union Leader*, the bleeding-at-the-throat right-wing Manchester newspaper whose late publisher, William Loeb, had been the subject of George Bush's posthumous obeisance at a Washington dinner. But duPont had been written off by an electorate uncomfortable with proposals for so much radical change from a virtual stranger.

Pat Robertson's position was more difficult to assess, particularly in the light of that second-place finish in Iowa. It wasn't even clear how large a base of fundamentalist Christians there might be in New Hampshire; different experts made estimates ranging from 10,000 to 30,000, and Robertson said it was only

6 percent of the population. But no one seemed very confident of his figures, and new polls showed Robertson evoking negative reactions from almost 60 percent of Republican and independent voters.

Robertson's paper trail of controversial statements—that he would abolish Social Security and end communism inside the Soviet Union, for example—had grown so long it was undermining his credibility. His bizarre claim in a New Hampshire debate that the Russians had installed SS4 and SS5 interme-diate-range nuclear missiles in Cuba was only the last straw. He insisted later that he hadn't said they were there, that he was only asking others in the forum whether the information he had was correct. But it didn't come across that way. And his identification as a minister, he said, was "very hurtful" because of the public's strict adherence to the principle of the separation of church and state. He supported it, too, he said later, and that was the reason he resigned his ministry. But voters still looked at him as a preacher, and looked elsewhere for a candidate.

The one candidate who had seemed to have some potential in New Hampshire all along was Jack Kemp. He had a respectable ground operation and the support of the two most prominent hard-line conservatives in the state, Senator Gordon Humphrey and Representative Robert Smith. And at one point he had lifted his standing in the polls to a respectable third—as high as 18 percent in one survey—with a television advertising attack on Bush and Dole on Social Security. The thirty-second spot showed Dole while an announcer said: "May 10, 1985: Senator Bob Dole proposes that Congress cut future Social Security benefits, but the Senate deadlocks." Then there were pictures of a limousine arriving at the Capitol and Bush presiding in the Senate. Announcer: "Vice President Bush travels to Capitol Hill and casts the deciding vote to cut Social Security." Then there were pictures of Kemp and Reagan together, with this voice-over: "Determined to block this cut, Jack Kemp rushes to the White House and persuades President Reagan to stop this plan to cut Social Security. Social Security is preserved. Jack Kemp. If he wins, we all win."

The ad was, like so many others in the politics of 1988, a gross distortion and oversimplification of what had happened—an attempt to apply a temporary freeze to cost-of-living allowance increases for retirees as part of a major budget-reduction program. But it was effective enough to put Kemp in the picture in a state with a high proportion of aged voters, if only momentarily. The hard truth for Kemp was, nonetheless, that there simply wasn't room for a third person in a political equation in which there were two candidates so well known and highly credentialed.

Kemp originally had seemed to be a candidate of enormous potential if—and it was a big "if"—he could isolate either Bush or Dole as his sole opponent. As the congressional father of supply-side economics, the fifty-year-old New York Republican could make some claim to be the legitimate lineal political descendant of Ronald Reagan, for whom he had worked going back to Reagan's 1966 campaign for governor of California. Kemp was also a candidate of remarkable energy whose personal force evoked enthusiastic receptions from party audiences. More to the point, his prescription for the Republican Party after Reagan seemed to offer his party colleagues a guilt-free rationale for the future. The way Jack Kemp told it, the economic possibilities were bright enough to reach all levels of American society.

This progressive strain in Kemp was not one with which all conservatives were comfortable. Republicans regularly talk about "reaching out" to black voters, but Kemp actually took some steps in that direction. He had joined, for example, with Democrat Walter Fauntroy, the District of Columbia delegate to the House of Representatives, in sponsoring legislation to make it possible for tenants of public housing to buy their apartments. He advocated a federal plan for what he called "enterprise zones"—inner-city districts in which tax concessions and other government inducements would be used to create new businesses and jobs.

Kemp's preoccupation with issues was an obvious asset to him during the debates of 1987 and early 1988, where he consistently earned high marks from most objective analyses—to no avail. "I thought I was doing well in the debates," Kemp said later. "What discouraged me was that no one watched, I mean not many people watched. It had absolutely very little impact."

But the core of Kemp's campaign was his attempt to present himself to conservatives as the logical and even natural successor to Reaganism. "Many of the conservatives were misled by the possibility that after Reagan there was going to be a national referendum on who the next Reagan was going to be," Kemp recalled. That proved to be a mistake, however, because Bush had been so effective in what Kemp called "quietly preempting the conservatives" at the grass-roots level. And this was nowhere more true than with Republicans in New Hampshire. The result was that Kemp's also-ran finish in Iowa effectively scuttled his entire campaign. Bush was the candidate who could legitimately publish a campaign brochure picturing him standing with Reagan and carrying the message: "He's trusted only one man to stand by him—through thick and thin."

Bush had several other advantages as he set out on his campaign to recover those soft voters who had strayed—none perhaps as valuable as John Sununu, the aggressive, sometimes abrasive, always combative governor. Teeter, who had been involved in dozens of Senate and gubernatorial campaigns over the last twenty-five years, was convinced that governors were far more valuable politically than senators. "These guys who get elected governor two or three times successfully know what's going on in their state," he said. Sununu, moreover, was lending more than his name to the campaign. He immersed himself fully in day-to-day, even hour-to-hour scheduling to get the maximum mileage for Bush, calling in political chits from Republicans all across the state. "No politician ever did as much for another politician as Sununu did," Atwater said somewhat extravagantly in retrospect. Dole's chief sponsor in the state, Senator Warren Rudman, who was occupied in Washington through much of the early campaign as a member of the Iran-contra committee, never had a comparable organization. And although he was highly rated by the New Hampshire electorate, Rudman's prickly independence probably meant he was relatively less effective in a Republican primary situation than he would have been in a general election.

What was most striking about the Bush campaign for political resurrection was how insubstantial it really was—a quintessential example of the shallowness of the politics of 1988. Bush did not begin auspiciously on Wednesday, making an awkward joke about how, in New England, he could claim Dole's Iowa slogan of "I'm one of you"—if it hadn't been for Joe Biden and the trouble he encountered using the rhetoric of Neil Kinnock. "I was born in Massachusetts, grew up in Connecticut, live across the way . . . in Maine," he said, "and I understand New Hampshire." He then went on to use the "one of you" formulation several more times, until questioning by reporters persuaded him it was a bad idea.

On Thursday, back in the state after his photo-opportunity luncheon with Reagan, Bush began to score with television coverage. He visited a lumberyard, where he operated a forklift briefly, and then dropped in at Cuzzin Richie's truck stop at Greenland to shake some hands and drive an eighteen-wheeler around the parking lot briefly. The scene was laughable Bush in the cab of the huge truck, Secret Service agents clinging to each side, a black vice presidential limousine inching along right behind, television cameras whirring away. The rank phoniness of this "media event" staged for television seemed to us patently obvious, and we expected the whole scene to be greeted with hoots of derision by viewers who saw it that night. Instead, it apparently was taken as genuine evidence of his interest in the common man. The next day there was a snowstorm bordering on blizzard, and Bush was obliged to limit himself to a short drive on a plow—also acceptable fodder for the television cameras.

The campaign also had brought Peggy Noonan, a gifted speechwriter, to New Hampshire, and she turned out a new text for Bush every day—none particularly noteworthy but all directed at making a point that might reclaim some of those "soft" supporters. Apparently concerned by the political potential in Dole's call for a budget freeze, Bush derided the plan as a "cop-out" and a "decision not to decide" on priorities that would "freeze in stupid and wasteful spending." And he offered his own alternative—a "flexible freeze" vaguely defined as a plan to freeze the overall amount of the budget, then make decisions on individual programs within that limit. But Bush carefully avoided spelling out which programs he might increase or decrease. So long as the television cameras were rolling when he drove a truck around a parking lot, there was no reason to do anything else.

The Bush campaign did not leave everything to the vagaries of television "news" judgments, however. In the final seventy-two hours of the campaign, his managers moved aggressively to reclaim those missing supporters. One key element was a decision to buy a "roadblock" of a half hour of television time

Saturday night on Channel 9 in Manchester, which now had the greatest reach and had become perhaps the single most influential news outlet in the state, plus three Boston stations. The time was used for an "Ask George Bush" program—a staged "town meeting" filmed two days earlier in the Hollis town hall—in which the candidate informally replied to questions from his audience. It was artificial, but Bush's relaxed manner reminded voters why they had once preferred him over Dole by such comfortable margins. The Bush campaign conducted an intense effort to build the audience, distributing more than eighty thousand fliers all over the state, telephoning thousands of undecided Republicans urging them to watch.

Dole, meanwhile, was trying in his own way to establish his differences from Bush. The burden of his case, as it had been all along, was that as the Senate majority and later minority leader he had exercised real rather than ceremonial responsibility in helping, for New Hampshire Republicans, the sainted Reagan carry out his program. On the face of it, this approach was obviously legitimate—even roughly accurate. But Dole neither liked Bush nor thought well of him, and that personal feeling repeatedly came through in the comparisons he made, or implied, between himself and the vice president. Even before Iowa Dole was cutting Bush frequently.

Dole was clearly sensitive to the differences in the backgrounds of the two men. Speaking at a Chamber of Commerce breakfast in Salem one day, for example, he put it this way: "I know a little about real people and real problems. I know precisely where I'm from, precisely how I got where I am and I know how to get back [to] where I'm from. I think I have been tested in my lifetime. I think I made it the hard way." And Dole was just a shade short of contemptuous of Bush's claims to have been an influential player in the Reagan administration. During a debate at Dartmouth in mid-January, for instance, Dole cited Bush's claim to have been involved in a "rescue" of Social Security in 1983. "I thought I fixed it," he said, "but George Bush says he fixed it, too. And I don't recall George being in the loop then, too. He takes credit for a lot of things." A few days later, asked whether Bush could handle the pressures of the presidency, Dole replied: "If you can't stand up to Dan Rather, you're going to have [problems] with Gorbachev and a few other people."

The hazard for Dole in discussing his opponent was his own history as a sharp-tongued candidate and political leader. The conventional wisdom was that Dole had mellowed over the years, and there seemed to be truth in that theory. But he was still a politician with an acerbic wit, at best, and one sometimes given to cutting and bitter sarcasm. The question was always whether he had his tongue under control or whether he was still one of those loose-cannon candidates who may self-destruct at any moment.

Dole also—perhaps inevitably—fell into a trap that is set for all front-runners by spending too much time talking about the politics of the campaign rather than what he would do for the voters. He liked to remind audiences that in his one previous run in a New Hampshire primary, in 1980, he had polled

592 votes. But just look at him now, he implied; how times had changed. "If Bob Dole can win in this state," he told an audience at Peterborough, "I can be president. That's how important it is."

The high point of Dole's week in New Hampshire came during the snow-storm on Friday, when Alexander Haig decided to withdraw and endorse Dole over Bush. The notion that Haig's endorsement was significant was probably farfetched; the opinion polls showed him with less than 5 percent of the vote and continuing high negative ratings. But the weather had shut down most of the campaigning that day, so when Haig arrived in the ballroom of The Center of New Hampshire—a fancy Holiday Inn in downtown Manchester—there were more than 250 reporters and hangers-on to hear him, and thirty-nine—count 'em, thirty-nine—television cameras to record the event. Haig had been even more disparaging of Bush privately, so it was no surprise when he unloaded on the vice president in Dole's behalf. Dole, said Haig, was "head and shoul-ders" above Bush as a potential president because he was a leader who had "made a difference rather than just being there." As for Bush: "I think he's been there—period."

The Bush managers scoffed at the Haig endorsement. The former White House chief of staff had far more negatives than positives and apparently no more than 5 percent of the vote. But the weather made the event "the only game in town," Wirthlin recalled, and "we saw those new numbers really bounce."

For the Dole campaign, the Haig endorsement was just another reason for optimism. Publicly, Dick Wirthlin had told reporters on Wednesday: "It's quite clear that this is a very winnable race." And privately some of the Dole agents were giddy with euphoria. Dole himself was finding audiences substantial and receptive. But the optimism was also leading to caution and robbing the cam-paign of the aggressiveness required to keep control of the political agenda. Nowhere was this more apparent than in the critical matter of the tax issue.

Dole's key adviser in the state was Tom Rath, a Concord lawyer, longtime ally of Warren Rudman and—more to the point—a man who understood how New Hampshire campaigns could turn on the state's obsession with taxes. There was no state income tax or sales tax, and woe betide the politician who even hinted that he might change that state of affairs. One of the features of any campaign in New Hampshire was the candidate taking "the pledge" to fight taxation to the death. So it was no surprise when, on the night of the Iowa caucuses, Rath asked himself, "What are they going to do to us?" and then answered himself: "It's gotta be taxes."

Rath decided that the first imperative would be a commercial that would "inoculate" Dole against the charge he was sure would come from the Bush campaign—that he was plotting tax increases. So the moment the candidate arrived from Des Moines, Rath pressed him to "take the pledge" in a com-mercial. Dole balked at a blanket promise that would cover all taxes, but he did agree he could make the pledge on income tax rates, which Rath figured would do the trick. Plans were made to film Dole at a candidate forum at a party dinner Wednesday night in Nashua, where he was supposed to say: "I pledge to veto any attempt by the Democrats to increase the new lower tax rates." Unhappily for Rath, however, Dole stumbled over the language and the tape couldn't be used for the commercial.

But Rath pursued the inoculating ad. He had set up a podium at the Hilton in Merrimack after the Nashua meeting in the hope of filming Dole there, but the program ran late and Dole didn't get back in time or humor to do it then. Rath then suggested that Dole try the line again in a speech at the University of New Hampshire the following day—again with a camera crew on hand to tape it for a commercial. That one was filmed, but Dole's media advisers weren't satisfied with the result. "It was a terrible spot," campaign chairman Bill Brock said later. "It wasn't believable." And anyway, Rath said later, the chief Dole strategists all seemed to question the urgency because Wirthlin was telling them the tax issue "was not cutting" with the electorate. And by week's end, Wirthlin's tracking—limited to 150 interviews a day by campaign budget constraints—was showing Dole now leading Bush, 27 to 21 percent. Besides, by now it was Friday and everyone "knew" how impossible it would be to get a new commercial not yet made on television over a weekend. "Sometimes things just don't work and this was one of those times," Brock said.

In fact, the campaign already had used one tough commercial—a spot showing a picture of Bush fading from the screen—that some Dole managers feared might be too harsh. (Within the Dole campaign the spot was labeled "Doonesbury.") And they had another zinger "in the can" that became known as the "footprint ad." It showed boots crossing heavy snow on the ground without leaving a trace and made the argument that George Bush was not a candidate who left any footprints. But, as Dole recalled it, Warren Rudman thought the ad was too negative for New Hampshire sensibilities and would backfire. "That's what I've learned the hard way," Dole said later. "They may not like it but they watch it." (The footprints-in-the-snow ad was finally used, briefly, the following week—in Florida.) The decision was to go ahead instead with a commercial showing Dole discussing the Soviet Union and foreign-policy questions.

The following day, however, there were the first faint stirrings of doubt about the direction of the opinion polls. The most recent public surveys showed the contest dead even, and the movement toward Dole no longer so conspicuous. The candidate remembered his polling director, Wirthlin, telling a new and different story over the weekend. "He was saying, 'The numbers are getting soft,' " Dole recalled. "You know, pollsters never say, 'You're in trouble.' It's 'getting soft.' They're like economists."

In fact, Wirthlin's weekend numbers were essentially the same as those showing up in public polls tracking the race—that is, they showed Bush and Dole essentially even over the final two days. They were also showing, Wirthlin recalled, a worrisome 17 percent still undecided and 3 percent of the voters not very committed to their choices. Even more troubling, Wirthlin said later, were "internals" in the polls—answers indicating why voters felt as they did—giving Bush higher marks than Dole on personal attributes such as "strong leader" and "strength to deal with Gorbachev."

Meanwhile, the Bush campaign was having its own internal debate over a commercial. The vice president's advisers had decided a new ad was needed to make those differences with Dole crystal-clear to the voters they were trying to bring back. And it was obvious, as Teeter observed later, that "the tax issue was the one with the most sting." So Roger Ailes prepared what became known as "the straddle ad," dictating the text to his wife in New York, who arranged to have the commercial cut and shipped to New Hampshire.

The thirty-second spot showed pictures of Bush and Dole while the announcer said: "George Bush and Bob Dole on leadership." Then it showed Bush alone with the words "Led Fight for INF" across the screen, as the voice-over said: "George Bush led the fight on the INF treaty for Ronald Reagan." Next it showed two pictures of Dole, one facing the other with the legend "Straddled" across the screen and the announcer saying: "Bob Dole straddled until Iowans pushed him into supporting INF." The ad then cut back to the Bush picture with the printed message "Against Oil Import Tax" and the oral one: "George Bush is against an oil import tax." Then the two Dole pictures returned with "Straddled" across the screen and the voice saying: "Bob Dole straddled, but now says he's for an oil import fee." Then the Bush picture with the written message "Won't Raise Taxes" and the announcer saying: "George Bush says he won't raise taxes, period." Then, again, the two faces of Dole, the legend "Straddled," which then dissolved to become: "Taxes—He can't say no," while the announcer adds: "Bob Dole straddles, and he just won't promise not to raise taxes. And you know what that means."

The spot was a classic case of seizing on an opening and, with just the right amount of distortion, exploiting it. The notion that Bush "led the fight" for the intermediate-range missile treaty was ludicrous, as was the idea that Dole had been "pushed into" supporting the INF ratification. In his role as the Senate Republican leader, Dole had felt justifiably constrained not to endorse the treaty until it had been reviewed by his colleagues, some of whom had serious doubts about it, and by himself. But there was never any question of Dole's support for the treaty, and the claim that he had "straddled" was far-fetched. But the key element of the ad was the charge on taxes, and here Dole had left himself vulnerable because he had not followed Tom Rath's advice and inoculated himself. The truth was that Dole was not willing to "take the pledge" on all taxes at any time, which is what New Hampshire seemed to require. But even the pledge on income taxes alone might have given him some protection from the charge of straddling.

Bush resisted running the spot, however. On Thursday, Atwater said, "We couldn't sell it to Bush." The same was true the following day. "We went in there Friday and tried to sell it," Atwater recalled, "and he wouldn't do it."

This reluctance, Atwater said, was Bush's typical resistance to "going nega-tive." Campaign managers, as they tell it, always seem to be obliged to over-come the scruples and sensitivities of their candidates. But Ailes suggested there was also a practical calculation in the vice president's mind. "He was under the impression . . . that either we were two points ahead or five points ahead or that things looked all right, and he was less worried about going negative than he was [about] the fact the press was going to say, 'George is desperate coming out of Iowa. He's gone negative.' '"

Bush was particularly sensitive, Ailes told Bob Goodwin, a principal aide, over the reaction of Dole to the Wittgraf letter in Iowa, and was afraid "he'll get the same flak" for using it. Goodwin asked Ailes: "Do you think he'll lose without it?" Ailes said: "Yes, I do." Then Goodwin replied, "It's up to you to take it back and try your best to talk him into using it. After all, he's your client. You owe it to him if you believe the ad is that important to the outcome of the primary."

Atwater and Ailes pressed the case with Bush, vouching for the accuracy of the spot. "I just felt we didn't have it won," Ailes said. "I felt we needed this." The facts, Ailes told Bush Friday, had been checked with Jim Pinkerton, the campaign's research director, then run by its lawyers. "The worst thing Dole could do," Ailes recalled, "is ask for documentation of this ad. That would hurt him more than just letting it air."

But Bush continued to resist, and Atwater decided he would have to enlist Sununu to "come down hard" on the necessity of running the spot. "He'll listen to you if you say this ad is appropriate," he told Sununu. "This can make the difference." Indeed, by this time, the Bush advisers were convinced that winning New Hampshire was essential, that another defeat here could put in jeopardy both the South Carolina primary March 5 and the Super Tuesday primaries March 8 in seventeen states. So early Saturday morning the strategists made one more run at the candidate in his hotel suite. Teeter told Bush, Ailes recalled, that he was now running about two points behind Dole.

"What the hell is going on?" Bush asked. "I thought we were five points up." Then he added: "Well, if we're two points down, that's a different ball game." But still Bush resisted giving the green light. Then, as the meeting was about to break up, Atwater insisted once more that "this thing has to air." Sununu chimed in with a critical point, telling Bush: "I don't think the people of New Hampshire are going to be upset by this ad." Barbara Bush also added a voice: "George, I don't see anything wrong with that ad." Bush finally began to yield. "This is your business, not mine," he told his advisers. With that, Atwater and Sununu quickly fled down the hotel corridor before he could change his mind.

By now it was Saturday morning, ordinarily too late to change plans for weekend commercials. But Sununu had a close relationship with the operators of Channel 9, and they agreed to substitute the straddle ad for others scheduled from Sunday through Tuesday. Ailes had connections that helped get the ad accepted by two of the major Boston television stations—with the help of his previously reluctant candidate. According to Goodwin, one Boston station owner "was originally reluctant to get involved, since the deadline to put ads on had expired. But during the conversation he asked Roger if he had anything to do with 'the Rather interview.' Roger said that yes, he was involved. The station owner said, 'In that case, I'll do what you want.' Roger put the vice president on the phone and he talked briefly with the station owner." The owner lived a fair distance from Boston but he then drove in and personally arranged to have the straddle ad put on the air, Goodwin said.

Atwater ordered a huge buy—"about like 1,800 points"—gross rating points in the television advertising parlance, enough to ensure that the theoretical average viewer would be exposed to the commercial eighteen times over those final three days.

On Sunday the Bush campaign got a little help from the back benches in moving the tax issue to the forefront, in a final televised debate at St. Anselm's College in Goffstown. The two leading candidates spent most of the ninety minutes cautiously circling one another. The only moment even slightly barbed came when Dole, obviously reacting to the new commercial, described his own role in winning ratification of the INF treaty and said pointedly to Bush: "You were for it before you read it. I wanted to read it first." But at another point, Bush was given a helping hand by one of the also-rans. Pete duPont suddenly produced a copy of the standard no-tax "pledge" accepted by so many New Hampshire candidates. He thrust it at Dole, who was sitting immediately to his left.

"Sign it," duPont said.

Dole studied the paper quizzically for a moment, then replied: "Give it to George. I have to read it first."

Few could have imagined that this was one of those key crystallizing moments of American political debates. But the incident called attention to the same tax issue Bush was hammering with commercials over the weekend and could reinforce the doubts about Dole. By this point, Bill Brock said, "The hits that were being made on Bob began to take their toll."

Dole recalled himself as being ambivalent on the "pledge" caper by duPont. "I [thought] I'd just take the thing and sign it," he said, "but then you're in the same class as everybody else. Do anything to get elected. You couldn't even close loopholes under that pledge." After the fact, nonetheless, Dole said, "I wondered about whether I should have signed that thing."

Dole's failure in the debate involved more than the decision against signing the pledge. Perhaps because he had a mistaken notion that Sunday night of what the polls were showing, Dole was determinedly cautious when it might have been wiser to draw sharper distinctions between himself and George Bush, beyond the fact that he was the winner of the Iowa caucuses and thus ostensibly the candidate with the political momentum. Lee Atwater argued that, given his long-established foundation of support in the state and the direction of the tracking polls, Bush was the one free to be cautious in the debate.

"The conventional wisdom would be that Bush would really have to deliver in that debate, do something wild,'' Atwater said. ''My feeling was that Bush could play it very safe, very statesmanlike with that base. . . . He really didn't have to prove anything except that, 'Here's our guy we've been with all this time.' The guy who needed to deliver that night was Dole, because all he had going for him was hype. . . . The conventional wisdom was, 'Dole ought to play it safe and statesmanlike. Bush needs to get up there and do some razzle-dazzle to get the momentum back,' and just the opposite was the case. Dole was the guy that needed to do something.''

Just how much the tax issue and the straddle ad had to do with Bush's final success could not be measured with any precision. Atwater saw it as only one device to ''plug into our own people'' and bring them back. And he figured Bush had other advantages, each worth a few points perhaps—a superior campaign organization, overconfidence in the Dole campaign, the possibility that the interest in the Democratic primary and Michael Dukakis might cut back the number of independents voting for Dole in the Republican primary. Looking back, Wirthlin was convinced the ''roadblock'' on television Saturday night had been more important than the straddle ad. In a postelection survey by Wirthlin with open-ended questions, 59 percent of Bush voters said they had cast their ballots for him either because of loyalty to Ronald Reagan or because of Bush's special experience as vice president. Only 2 percent, Wirthlin said, specifically mentioned taxes.

But the tax issue and the handling of it surely dramatized the differences between the two campaigns in terms of their ability to function effectively under pressure.

On the decision to fight the tax issue with commercials, Dole said later, ''They made the right choice and we made the wrong choice.'' Said Tom Rath: ''We saw it coming, we raised the alarm. It was not a question of your game plan's bad. It's a question that we didn't execute.''

The contrast between the two campaigns was clear on Monday, the final day before the voting. The Bush managers imported the ultimate conservative credential, Barry Goldwater, for a final day of stumping, one last attempt to bring those stray voters back into the fold. Dole toured his headquarters, thanking supporters and giving such a convincing performance as the confident candidate that some of Bush's advisers grew a little nervous; they began to wonder if there were some other poll numbers somewhere they hadn't seen. ''He [Dole] spent the day like a guy who thought he had it in the bag,'' Bob Teeter recalled.

In fact, the opposite was the case. The latest tracking polls showed movement away from Dole and back toward Bush, and the internals of at least one public survey began to show the tax issue was indeed undercutting Dole. That tore it for Tom Rath. ''I turned to Jimmy Murphy [Dole's field director] and I said, 'We're going to lose this election.' '' Dick Wirthlin was now telling him, Dole said wryly later, ''it's going to be close.'' Wirthlin recalled Dole asking him that Monday, ''How much are we going to win by?'' To which Wirthlin replied: ''Two or three points, plus or minus four''—meaning the election could go either way.

On election day the early reports on television network exit polls made it clear Rath was right. Shortly before noon Dole went to Concord to have lunch in Rath's law office with some of his principal supporters. "We're going to lose, Tom, by five to seven points," he told Rath. As it turned out, even that forecast was slightly optimistic. Bush won with 38 percent to 29 for Dole, 13 for Kemp, 10 for duPont, 9 for Robertson. Bob Dole had suffered a crushing defeat, Pat Robertson's bubble had burst and—only eight days after hitting bottom in Iowa—George Bush was back in command of the contest for the Republican presidential nomination.

In retrospect, it became clear that the single most damaging mistake the Dole campaign had made was in allowing the notion to build that he was likely to win. Even three or four weeks earlier a second-place finish within nine percentage points by Dole would have been considered at least a survival in the "expectations game" that is always so important in gauging the effect of the early primary results. But Dole had played the cautious front-runner while Bush was playing the fighting underdog to the hilt—and thus earning political credit he never would have received if his success had been apparent all along.

When Dole returned to Washington, he ran into Speaker Tip O'Neill in the Capitol. "You didn't play that right," O'Neill said.

"It got out of hand," Dole replied. "Every little poll in the country was saying we were ahead."

As for Robertson, he had little money or organization in the state, not enough evangelists as voters, and the primary process, as the other candidates had long suspected, was not nearly as hospitable to him as the more closed caucuses in Michigan and Iowa, which put a premium on the zeal of true believers.

As the votes were being cast in New Hampshire, Dole made a bad situation worse. Visiting a polling place on election day he encountered a hectoring Kemp supporter who, as Dole put it, "got right up in my face" until the candidate told him: "Get back in your cave"—a piece of advice that appeared repeatedly on the evening news.

Then, invited to appear on NBC News from his hotel after the returns had been counted, Dole unexpectedly found himself on television simultaneously with Bush, who was in the studio in Manchester. Anchorman Tom Brokaw asked Bush if he had any message for his rival, and the vice president replied: "No. Just wish him well, and meet in the South."

Then Brokaw asked Dole the same question. His eyes dark with anger, Dole shot back: "Stop lying about my record."

Asked about this remark much later, Dole shrugged. "I obviously didn't feel too good." Then he added: "I said what was on my mind. . . . There ought to be some virtue in telling the truth."

In this case, as Bob Dole soon discovered, telling the truth could be an expensive gesture. His jab at Bush over the straddle ad obviously did not affect the New Hampshire result, coming after the polls had closed. But it did resurrect the image of the bitter, brooding Bob Dole that he had so diligently sought to bury—and that the Bush campaign had labored so hard, and now so successfully, to restore. With the Super Tuesday barrage of primaries now approaching, it was a perception Dole could ill afford.*

10

Super Tuesday: Bush Takes Control

A year after the New Hampshire primary, eating corned-beef hash at the Watergate one morning, Bob Dole could look back and assess the cost of his failure to win the expectations game. "I think in my gut I knew it was over when we lost New Hampshire," he said. "I think it's all New Hampshire. I've been over it five hundred times in my own mind, and it all comes back to what went wrong in New Hampshire."

The price of that moment of anger—the reemergence of the "bad" Bob Dole—with Tom Brokaw was particularly high thereafter. "I think it was so widely covered," Bill Brock recalled, "that it took the heart out of everybody and everything. You know that any manager, any candidate, any worker is going to make a statement that you regret. But with today's ability to communicate and repeat and repeat and repeat, it was like a Coca-Cola ad. You never stopped looking at it for the next two or three days on television, and the sense was that it was going to take the guts out of the campaign." On the candidate's plane, said Brock, there was a "very blue atmosphere."

Viewed from a distance, with any objectivity at all, it was difficult to see why a defeat by only nine percentage points, even if coupled with that televised display of pique, should have taken such a toll. But the problem for Dole was that the anger and, more to the point, bad political judgment of his reaction to defeat crystallized all those questions about him that were already abroad. The man who snapped at George Bush was not just a disappointed candidate, but one with a history of being nasty. The candidate who had just lost the New Hampshire primary after being so widely expected to win it was not just a

---

*Bush, for his part, could afford to be magnanimous and he was—especially after the election, when he told us: "Primaries are always hot and none was hotter than New Hampshire. I stood up foursquare for what I believed in, and the voters chose me. Bob and I had some tense moments during the campaign but we always have been, and always will be, friends. The media overplayed their own view that there was deep hostility between Bob and me. The story was grossly overwritten."

candidate who had made a political miscalculation, but one who had a record of running mismanaged campaigns.

Thus, the specifics of Dole's failings were magnified because of the context—just as Joe Biden's use of Neil Kinnock's rhetoric was magnified because Biden was supposed to be a rhetorician above all else; just as Gary Hart's weekend with Donna Rice was magnified because he had been the subject of so much speculation and rumor about womanizing in the past. Bob Dole was, the story line went, an evil-tempered loose cannon who, on top of that, couldn't organize a two-car funeral.

If there had been significant issue divisions among the Republicans, these judgments might have counted for little. But the time had long since passed for confrontations within the Republican Party over questions of dogma. The Eastern Liberal Establishment so influential in the 1950s and 1960s was now just a memory. The few moderates within the party had been dying off or quitting politics in frustration. The conservative movement was not monolithic, but the Republican Party had become monolithically conservative. As George Wallace always liked to say, there wasn't a dime's worth of difference between George Bush and Bob Dole on the issues. And that meant that a display of anger on national television assumed outsized proportions as a political measuring stick.

The cost of Dole's misstep was made even higher by the political calendar. He had made his mistake at the worst possible time. There were caucuses in Minnesota and a primary in South Dakota the following Tuesday, but Bush had simply walked away from both of them. That strategic withdrawal made it certain that Dole would receive minimal credit for winning, which he did with 55 percent of the vote in South Dakota and a somewhat surprising 43 percent in Minnesota, where Robertson and Kemp had been competing furiously for months for Christian fundamentalist support. Atwater, having neglected South Dakota and Minnesota in favor of Michigan, said later that by "punting" in those two states he was able to "totally decimate the Lesser Antilles," as the minor contests came to be called, as a factor in news media assessments of how the Republican race was going.

As a result, Dole's next real chance to repair the damage of New Hampshire would come two weeks later in the Republican version of Super Tuesday, when seventeen states, fourteen of them southern and border states, would hold primaries and caucuses. That would be tough ground. The Bush campaign had poured money and organizers into the South for months to build what Lee Atwater called "a firewall" against the possibility the vice president might have lost both Iowa and New Hampshire and needed a place to recover his footing.

"I didn't see how we could climb that wall," Brock said. The Dole strategists nourished some hopes the senator from Kansas might win Missouri and Oklahoma and perhaps North Carolina and Arkansas, plus a few congressional districts scattered elsewhere across the region. That might have been enough, coupled with Iowa and the other Farm Belt successes, to provide at least a rationalization for continuing through the primaries in the big industrial states—and for giving Bush more time and opportunity to make a blunder of his own.

But the Super Tuesday picture was not encouraging for Dole. It seemed likely that, at a minimum, Bush would win half the 803 delegates at stake—a giant step toward the 1,139 needed to assure himself of the nomination at the Republican National Convention in New Orleans.

Atwater had recognized the potential importance of the South early in the game. In June of 1987 he invited the press to a meeting of some three hundred prominent southern supporters at the Buckhead Ritz-Carlton in Atlanta—a meeting intended as both a pep rally for the Bush forces and a warning shot across the bows of rival candidates. The political muscle on display there was impressive. The delegations from each state seemed to include most of the leading Republican Party leaders and almost all of the region's most talented campaign operatives. These people—white, middle-class "country club" Republicans— were not enough, in themselves, to assure Bush of a Super Tuesday success; not if he came to the South badly compromised by the earlier primaries or, in particular, by some failure of his own as a candidate. Voters in the South watched the same network television news as those everywhere else. But these Republicans were enough to provide a floor for Bush and assure him of remaining competitive in the region if he had lost New Hampshire but run respectably. "What we've got here," Atwater told reporters who crowded into his suite to drink his whiskey, "is an insurance policy."

The Bush campaign was far enough ahead, in fact, that Atwater was hoping his rivals would be lured into trying to "play catch-up ball" at the expense of their efforts elsewhere. "I had that meeting," he said later, "in the hopes that everybody would see a very high, visible [campaign] and know we were going to spend a bunch of money."

In the aftermath of New Hampshire, Bush's dominance of the states in the southern regional primary was imposing. "We had a choice," said Brock, "between a total disaster and an almost total disaster. That's not much of a choice." The campaign manager and his candidate met in Atlanta, and Brock went through the situation in every state. "I told Bob it was mathematically possible but not politically. . . . There was nowhere to stem the tide." So the decision was made to concentrate on a few states and hope to salvage enough, in Brock's phrase, to "maintain some credibility" with the press as a going concern.

But Dole had compounded the felony of his "stop lying" outburst by deciding two days later that he would not compete in a debate in Dallas, one of two scheduled for the Super Tuesday campaign. He had been irked by what he considered the "hometown rally" atmosphere of the Republican debate in Houston the previous October and now he wasn't about to get in a situation where a "Bush cheering squad" would create a similar atmosphere. The fact was that the sponsors of the debate had agreed to give the campaigns of each candidate an equal number of seats in the auditorium. And the operative political consideration in any debate was what could be conveyed through millions of television sets, not the studio audience reaction. But Dole was in no temper to play in Bush's backyard—or to make a cool political calculation.

The decision was disastrous on more than one level. First, by pulling out, Dole simply abandoned all hope of competing seriously in Texas, a potentially costly move. The rules in the nation's third largest state provided for congressional district delegates to be awarded on a winner-take-all basis by district, which clearly favored the home-state candidate, Bush. But they also provided that the at-large delegates would be divided proportionally unless one candidate received more than 50 percent of the total popular vote. With Pat Robertson competing aggressively in some parts of the state and Jack Kemp still on the ballot, there was some realistic chance of Dole denying Bush that majority. But it was a hope that went up in smoke once Dole thumbed his nose at the Dallas debate.

Texas considerations aside, the decision reinforced damaging perceptions about Dole and his viability. The refusal to appear in one of the two major debates in the southern regional primary campaign was widely seen by the press, and his rivals, as evidence that Dole was not even trying to compete full speed in the South. And, unsurprisingly, it was seen as another example of ill-humored petulance that raised fresh doubts about whether Dole could control his moods enough to be an acceptable presidential candidate. As it turned out, Pat Robertson also dropped out of the debate, which then proved to be a little-noticed tête-à-tête between Bush and Kemp. But the real loser was clearly Bob Dole.

In an attempt to change all those negative perceptions, Dole tried a variety of techniques. Some of his supporters argued, for example, that he was being victimized by a double standard because of the history of that 1976 vice presidential campaign. His colleague from Kansas, Senator Nancy Kassebaum, loyally declared: "The vice president lashes out in sometimes rather crude language and no one says anything." Dole himself first tried to make a joke of the New Hampshire episode. Flying into North Carolina, he told his supporters: "I wanted to get here before the TV ads do and tell you right up front that Bob Dole is not going to raise your taxes."

Dole also tried manfully to equate, by implication at least, his display of anger with the kind of toughness required in a successful president. "I believe I have a certain quality that some may be lacking," he told the Georgia House of Representatives. "I am tough. I understand you have to be tough to make tough choices." But the straddle ad was still sticking in his craw—as when he told a Florida audience one day that the voters deserve "someone who's not out trying to distort someone else's record when he doesn't have one of his own." And he could not hide his resentment of Bush's privileged past, telling those Georgia legislators: "I got here just like you did. I got here the old-fashioned way. I earned it. Nobody gave it to me."

The Dole campaign seemed to go from bad to ridiculous. A few days after the Minnesota and South Dakota primaries, the tensions within the operation erupted when campaign manager Brock joined the traveling party. Over break-fast one morning he abruptly fired the two senior operatives who had been traveling with Dole at the candidate's request—veteran professional David Keene, chairman of the American Conservative Union, and Donald Devine, the former head of the Office of Personnel Management in the Reagan admin-istration. Both were prominent conservatives whom Dole had enlisted partly in the hope they would serve as credentials with the so-called movement Repub-licans of the far right. And Keene, in particular, also had a reputation as a street-smart political operative going back to the Reagan campaign against Gerald Ford in 1976 and the Bush campaign of 1980. But, Brock said later, they were "trying to run the campaign from the plane" and had to go.

The two were ordered off the plane in Jacksonville, which made it con-venient for them to go into the airlines terminal and hold a press conference that assured maximum exposure of still another Dole-in-disarray story. Dole didn't help matters by telling reporters that Keene and Devine were "still friends of mine" but that he necessarily had to support his campaign manager Brock.

Scheduling disasters continued to plague Dole. On the same day Keene and Devine were sent packing, the candidate was taken to the site of a moving-picture production facility then under construction in an open field outside Orlando. There were no voters there, but there were four people costumed as Woody Woodpecker, Mae West, Charlie Chaplin and Frankenstein's monster —dandy subjects for pictures with Dole that surely would impress undecided voters.

A few days later Dole turned up at 5 P.M. rally in an office building plaza in Fort Lauderdale. Although there was a band that could be heard by people pouring out of the nearby buildings, the audience never exceeded three hundred and Dole labored through a twenty-minute speech on the differences between himself and Bush that evoked little response from his listeners. But the operative question was: What was Bob Dole doing here at all? Southeastern Florida was Bush's single strongest area of the state—his son Jeb had been the Dade County party chairman—and delegates were to be awarded winner-take-all by congres-sional district. We asked Brock on the spot which Florida districts looked most promising for Dole, and he cited three possibilities—the thirteenth, the eighth and the ninth.

But those are all on the West Coast, we asked, so why are you here on the East Coast? "Yeah," Brock replied, shaking his head, "crazy scheduling." Much later Brock recalled that Dole had gone to the East Coast rather than the Gulf Coast districts to keep a commitment to some Cuban-American leaders in Miami. But he had wasted half a day, flying over three districts where he might have had a chance so he could give a meaningless speech in a district in which he was out of the picture.

The contrast between the two campaigns was never more apparent than at noon the following day when more than a thousand people, attracted by hot dogs as well as a band, jammed another plaza just a block away from the Dole site for a Bush rally. The vice president rolled up with an escort of eighteen motorcycle cops, rushed through a perfunctory six-minute speech—"I have stood with this president through thick and through thin. I believe loyalty is a strength"—and then, after a brief meeting with his local leaders, quickly roared off down the road. It was not very substantial fare even for the politics of 1988, but it served the Bush purpose of providing a snippet of television film and some personal reinforcement of his base.

Indeed, Bush was able to sail through the South essentially above the fray. The damage to Dole had been so severe, the opinion polls all agreed, that there was no need for heaping any more calumny on his head. The vice president could talk about how he wanted to be "an education president"—whatever that was supposed to mean—and about how he was going to remain loyal to Ronald Reagan despite being urged by some never-identified "they" to break with him. As the New Hampshire story reverberated through the region, Bush delighted in telling everyone that he, like Mark Twain, could say that reports of his death had been greatly exaggerated.

Neither of the other candidates ostensibly still standing was a factor in the Super Tuesday calculus. And if they were, that possibility was eliminated when South Carolina Republicans voted in their own primary March 5, the Saturday before the regional primary.

From the outset Bush had been considered a heavy favorite in this primary being advertised as the "gateway" to Super Tuesday. South Carolina was Lee Atwater's home ground, and the Republican governor, Carroll Campbell, was a friend and client of Atwater's. Bush organizers went into the state early and aggressively, and Bush himself appeared before two dozen evangelical preachers in Greenville and assured them: "Jesus Christ is my personal savior." That declaration may have sounded a little strange coming from an Episcopalian from Connecticut, but it was important here in a state in which half the voters claimed to be "born again" Christians. And the motto for the Bush campaign all through 1988 seemed to be: "Whatever it takes."

Even minimal good sense might have told Bush's rivals that South Carolina was a bad bet. But Pat Robertson announced that, polls to the contrary notwithstanding, he intended to win in South Carolina and would have to do so to continue his campaign. Jack Kemp, already heavily in debt, decided to pour $350,000 into the campaign there. And Dole, after first indicating he would give it a miss, plunged in after Senator Strom Thurmond endorsed him two weeks before the primary. The result was an unalloyed success for the vice president. He captured all thirty-seven delegates and 48 percent of the popular vote to 21 percent for Dole, 19 for Robertson, 11 for Kemp. The Thurmond endorsement had proven to be about as valuable to Dole as it had been eight years earlier to John B. Connally, Jr., who suffered a similar South Carolina trauma at the hands of Ronald Reagan. The high turnout, approaching 200,000, attracted by the noise of the campaign had overwhelmed the disciplined Robertson constituency—demonstrating that even in the Deep South the television evangelist could not reach far beyond his core constituency.

Robertson's failure was a reassuring answer to the central questions about his potential that had been worrying Republicans all through the campaign. He had demonstrated in Michigan and Iowa—and earlier in such forums as a Florida state party convention—that he could turn out enough supporters to be a player in any limited universe of voters. Then the New Hampshire result had suggested the limits to Robertson's drawing power—that it simply wasn't enough to make him a factor in a primary situation. But there were always some lingering doubts about whether that would prove to be as true in the South—on Pat Robertson's home ground—as it had been in New Hampshire. And the answer from South Carolina seemed to be that there were real limits indeed.

Atwater was delighted with the returns. The primary, he said, "was set up with one thing in mind—that you break everybody's back." Now all the Bush pursuers were badly tarnished. "George Bush," Atwater said later, "was running unopposed on Super Tuesday four days later."

When the votes were counted March 8, Bush had a landslide. The vice president won primaries in Florida, Texas, Alabama, Arkansas, Georgia, Kentucky, Louisiana, Mississippi, North Carolina, Oklahoma, Tennessee, Virginia, Missouri and Maryland, plus two others—in Massachusetts and Rhode Island —outside the region.

Robertson said after the election: "I don't think anything that would have been done would have made any difference. When we hit the South, George Bush was so far ahead because of Ronald Reagan. We were not running against Bush, we were running against Reagan. And there was just no way we could beat Ronald Reagan in the South." On top of that, Robertson said, Bush had worked the region long and diligently, and without Dole cutting into Bush's vote anywhere, there was no stopping him.

Bush's only Super Tuesday loss was to Robertson in caucuses in Washington. And although the final figures would not be compiled until Virginia delegates were allocated later, it was clear Bush had captured more than 600 of the 803 available. Atwater's only concern had been that Dole would win a few states and make the case that he was still viable as the candidate of the Midwest. But the results robbed Dole of even that rationale. "There was no way anybody could quibble about anything," Atwater said later.

In fact, Dole did come close enough in three states to provide some measure of the direct cost of the incident in New Hampshire and the ineffectuality of his own campaign. He came within a single percentage point of Bush in Missouri, two points in Oklahoma and six in North Carolina—all margins that might have been overcome if Dole had come South as a serious player rather than a candidate who had just confirmed every reservation about himself.

Among Republicans, the southern regional primary had been seen as principally a kind of happy accident. It had been promulgated by the Democrats who controlled the state legislatures across the region, but Republican governors given the opportunity had been more than willing to sign the legislation. They had visions of an all-liberal contest on the Democratic side that would result in a massive defection of conservative Democrats to vote in the Republican primary in the eight states where such crossovers were permitted—Alabama, Arkansas, Georgia, Mississippi, Missouri, Tennessee, Texas and Virginia. And, they reasoned, once these Democrats voted in a Republican primary, they might get in the habit of doing so.

As it turned out, the Republican turnout far exceeded anything the region had experienced in the past—more than 4.5 million votes. In several states, including Arkansas and Mississippi, dramatic gains were easy to register simply because they had never held a truly competitive Republican presidential primary in the past. In the days of Barry Goldwater and Richard Nixon, the makeup of many southern delegations to nominating conventions had been determined principally by a handful of country-club Republicans. And the key to winning those delegations had been personal connections rather than the ability to enlist popular support in primaries. But the inexorable movement toward broader participation—and decisions handed up rather than down—driven by the Democrats had now reached the Republicans as well.

In several of the larger states—Texas and Florida most obviously—the Republicans had been growing generally more competitive with every election. The turnout in Texas ran over 1 million, twice what it had been in the 1980 Republican primary. In Florida, the Republican vote rose from slightly over 600,000 to 900,000 in 1980. But the high turnout there was predictable even after the most perfunctory campaign, because Florida had been growing increasingly Republican in voter registration all through the Reagan years. The same was true in Georgia, where the growing strength of Republicans at the local level in the Atlanta suburbs was reflected in a primary turnout twice what it had been in 1980.

Defections by Democrats did not match the high Republican hopes, however. Opinion polls indicated the crossover by Democrats was less than 5 percent, perhaps because there were good reasons for Democrats to want to vote in their own primaries. One factor was the perception of a serious contest among Democrats. Another may have been the presence of a southern quasi-conservative candidate, Al Gore, in that Democratic contest. And a third simply may have been that in several of those states, including Texas, there were also Democratic primary contests for other offices. Except in a few isolated areas, the Republicans were still far from competitive in local elections.

But if the Super Tuesday regional primary failed to fulfill the Republicans' most ambitious dreams of success, it did something for the party it surely didn't do for the Democrats—settle the question of the presidential nomination. Dole would stumble on toward the Illinois primary, protesting that the game wasn't over, like the fading baseball star who plays one season too long.

But Dole was just hanging on, and the operative question for the Republican Party was whether George Bush could overcome the doubts about himself.

11

Mopping Up—and Gearing Up

The jolt of George Bush's near sweep on Super Tuesday had immediate ramifications. Jack Kemp bowed out of the race two days later, declaring that
while he had lost, "our principles have not been defeated." At the same time,
Bob Dole began circling the wagons, but without much hope of heading off
his scalping. He moved on to the next primary state, Illinois, insisting at an
American Legion hall in Berwyn that "I'm not a dropout" and that he was
in the campaign "all the way to New Orleans." But his actions suggested
desperation.

Amid much rumor, Dole canceled advertisements in daily newspapers
across the state and instead scheduled a thirty-minute live television broadcast
into Chicago and other major media markets. All he bought for his money,
though, was more woe. Speaking from Knox College in Galesburg, where Dole
had hoped to have a debate with Bush but was ignored, he was only about five
minutes into his speech when the television picture was lost. Dole talked on
but in a few moments the telecast's producers cut his voice off in midsentence
and began to run a segment of his campaign video biography. The end of Dole's
opening remarks and the introduction of the biography by his popular wife,
Elizabeth, were not heard. The broadcast had been anticipated as a dramatic
attempt by Dole to reverse his fortunes, but it turned out to be a flat performance
even discounting the technical troubles.

Right down to primary eve in Chicago, Dole insisted that "whatever
happens, we're going to keep going." Bush, meanwhile, comfortable in his
wide lead, played it cautiously. With President Reagan about to veto a civil
rights bill designed to roll back a Supreme Court rebuff to antidiscrimination
laws in the Grove City College case, Bush declined to say where he stood. But
at this point it didn't matter. He routed Dole in the Illinois primary by more
than three to two. Still, Dole insisted he would carry on in the next primary,
in Wisconsin. In a few days, however, he acknowledged that Bush's nomination
was now "a foregone conclusion" and he pledged his support to him. "We
need a Republican in the White House," he said. "That's where I'm coming
from. And if can't be me, it will be George Bush." A week before the Wisconsin

vote he dropped out, pledging his support to the man who beat him, and toward whom he obviously harbored considerable bitterness.

Bush at last had a clear field to the nomination, although Pat Robertson continued as a formal candidate, obviously looking to his moment in the sun at the New Orleans convention. But the vice president remained in the shadow of his benefactor, President Reagan, and of the Iran-Contra scandal.

By now Reagan had vetoed the Grove City civil rights bill and Bush as always was right there behind him. "I'm not going to start differing with the president after seven and a half years into the vice presidency," he said. "I'm going to stand with the president." Bush supporters who had been waiting for the right opportunity for their candidate to demonstrate that he was his "own man" saw this veto as a golden opportunity, and were chagrined when Bush declined to take it.

The Iran-Contra Affair distressed many Bush backers as well. By this time four of the major figures—Oliver North, John Poindexter, Richard Secord and Albert Hakim—had been indicted. And a January 1986 memorandum by Poindexter was released by the congressional investigating committees bearing a notation that Bush was present when Secretary of State George Shultz and Secretary of Defense Caspar Weinberger expressed their strong opposition to the Iranian arms sales. An ABC News–*Washington Post* poll found that three of every four registered Democrats polled, and one of every three Republicans, believed that Bush was lying about his role in the fiasco. The survey furthermore found that 30 percent of Democrats polled who had voted for Reagan said they were less likely to vote for Bush as a result. Through all this, the Vice President continued to stonewall on his role in the Iran-Contra episode, insisting he had told all.

More than these problems, however, a tactical concern weighed on the calculating mind of Bush campaign manager Lee Atwater: how to keep an inactive candidate from dropping off the public radar screen, from falling into what Roger Ailes called a "black news hole." On the night of the Wisconsin primary, in which Bush ran virtually unchallenged, Atwater had dinner with campaign pollster/strategist Bob Teeter and press spokesman and political adviser Pete Teeley at Karl Ratzsch's. "That was when I first got worried that success could spoil Sammy Glick," said Atwater, who in his own hyperactive way did a fair imitation of the classic Budd Schulberg character. "We were going to have a real problem generating news coverage. . . . Not only were we starved for coverage, but it was clear that Jesse [Jackson] could not win the [Democratic] nomination, but that because of the nature of his base, he was going to stay in, and in effect Dukakis was going to have easy, free coverage every Tuesday to California. . . . The nature of Jesse's base served Dukakis well. . . . Dukakis looked like a moderate with Jesse in the race."

Atwater was right about Bush getting squeezed off the front pages and the evening television news shows. The vice president made sorties into several major states through April and into May but mostly got only local coverage for his trouble, and then only secondary play. And when the Dukakis-Jackson primary contests were not elbowing him out of the limelight, stories were being played that didn't do him much good—on Iran-Contra, the administration's failure to oust Panama's Manuel Noriega, flare-ups involving American forces in the Persian Gulf, Edwin Meese's sleaze problems, even Don Regan's report of how astrology governed Reagan's travel schedule.

Nothing seemed to be going the way it should have for a presidential candidate who had made a runaway of the contest for his party's nomination. Even when President Reagan took the occasion at a very large Republican congressional fund-raising dinner to make his endorsement of Bush, it came out halfhearted and, it seemed to some, almost grudging. At the close of Reagan's speech all he said was that he was breaking his silence on his preference and, after ticking off Bush's résumé as a House member, diplomat, CIA director and party chairman, he promised: "I'm going to work as hard as I can to make Vice President George Bush the next president of the United States." Period. There was no "the man who" lavish preface that usually went with such declarations of support. Then, after exchanging a salute with Bush, Reagan returned to the microphone and added merely: "Now on to New Orleans and on to the White House."

The episode served to underline the long shadow that the popular Reagan still cast over Bush—a continuing problem for a candidate who steadfastly declined to move out of that shadow by delineating any important difference with his leader/benefactor, or even say in specific terms what he would do if elected to succeed him. This kind of news coverage Bush could do without.

So, too, were stories given prominent play about the sudden resignation in late May of his longtime sidekick and press spokesman/schmoozer, Pete Teeley, in an internal dispute with Craig Fuller. Teeley was one who believed that Bush should be more aggressive in asserting his own identity. Others were irritated whenever Teeley, traveling with Bush, would toughen up a speech or beef it up to take advantage of some breaking development. Teeley in time found himself increasingly out of the loop and, frustrated as a press aide who wasn't plugged in, finally quit. His departure marked one of the very few occasions of dissent within the Bush organization that broke into print, but it came at an unpropitious time for a campaign that seemed to be in a funk.

As the Memorial Day weekend approached, an ABC News–*Washington Post* poll of 1,172 registered voters gave Dukakis a 53 percent to 40 lead over Bush, an eight-point increase over the same poll's findings in March. The latest Gallup poll had Dukakis ahead even more, 54–38, and the *Los Angeles Times* survey even more than that in California, 53–36. More significantly, the ABC–*Washington Post* poll found that 57 percent of the Dukakis supporters said they planned to vote for him mainly because they were against Bush. That finding alone suggested that if the Bush campaign couldn't make voters feel better about the vice president, it would have to give them reason to dislike Dukakis even more. Still another poll, for CBS News and the *New York Times*, provided another clue on what needed to be done. It found that two thirds of conservatives polled did not see Dukakis as a liberal, and among them he was running even with Bush. Something surely had to be done about that.

As a way to get Bush back in the news in a more rewarding manner, Atwater began to plan a series of regional conferences of Bush supporters as "a way to keep our troops pepped up and show them we were on top of things." Three were scheduled, preceded by a Bush appearance at the Texas Republican convention in early June, he said later, "realizing that by the end of May we were going to be getting pounded and would be way behind, because Dukakis is getting all this coverage."

Atwater confessed later to this period of inactivity having been "a personally tough time for me as campaign manager, because there was just no way we weren't going to go down in the polls. And there was no way my enemies weren't going to be able to use that to criticize me as being too young and all that." So he was particularly alert to the need for the Bush candidacy to get through the slump.

Having decided on these media-attracting events, the next order of business was the message Bush would convey. Earlier, in April, Atwater had gone to Jim Pinkerton, the campaign's lanky director of research. Pinkerton's job during the first phase of the campaign had been, among other things, to dig out material on the opposing Republican candidates that could be used to good effect against them. Now, with the nomination well in hand, he had turned to the Democratic picture, which by this time—after the New York primary in mid-April—had cleared sufficiently to permit the comfortable prediction that Dukakis would be the Democratic nominee. When Atwater approached Pinkerton, he already had a mountain of research material on Dukakis—so much that Atwater was bowled over.

According to someone present at the time, Atwater handed Pinkerton a small card and told him: "Here's a three-by-five card. We're gonna have to use research to win this campaign. You get me the stuff to beat this little bastard and put it on this three-by-five card. I'm giving you one thing. You can use both sides of the three-by-five card."

Pinkerton took the card and a short time later brought it back to Atwater with both sides filled. Among the seven items included were a paragraph on the Willie Horton prisoner-furlough case that Pinkerton had come across in a question from Al Gore to Dukakis in the Democrats' debate during the New York primary, and another on Dukakis' veto of the mandatory pledge-of-allegiance bill that Andy Card had told him about. Pinkerton also had brief descriptive paragraphs on Dukakis' opposition to the death penalty, the pollution in Boston Harbor, a veto on mandatory drug sentences and his positions on taxes and national defense.

Armed with Pinkerton's three-by-five card and a national poll by the campaign, all members of the Bush "Gang of Six" hierarchy except Mosbacher went to Paramus, New Jersey, on the Thursday before Memorial Day.

There, in an office in a shopping/industrial complex, Market Opinion Research of Detroit, Teeter's old firm, conducted two focus groups, part of a series of eight that week, each of about twenty preselected Democrats who had voted for Ronald Reagan in 1984 and said they were for Dukakis this time. As the Bush strategists watched unseen by the participants from behind a two-way mirror, an MOR moderator held a discussion with each group on a range of subjects.

The participants were asked what they knew about George Bush and Michael Dukakis, and they knew very little, even about the vice president of the United States. In the two groups, Atwater recalled, "one voter thought he might have been a congressman. No other voter could identify any other position [except vice president] he'd ever held. And they knew absolutely nothing about Dukakis." Teeter remembered that one knew Bush had been a war hero and that some thought Dukakis was a governor of some northeastern state but weren't sure which one. And Ailes recalled that "they thought George was weak, a wimp, a follower. They came out pretty lukewarm. One guy sort of summed it up for me when he said, 'You'd think the guy'd been there all those years and we'd know something more about him than this.' That was the down side. To a guy like me, it said we have an opportunity to define both candidates. I felt this whole race would be, who defines themselves and who defines the other person would win."

At one point, Teeter remembered, the moderator asked the participants if they weren't bothered by the fact that they knew so little about the candidates for president, that they hadn't been paying attention. Didn't they feel a little guilty? One woman immediately said no. It was still early, she said. "We're not going to vote until November. When it gets to be September and October we're gonna pay attention, and we'll study them and decide who to vote for." This response, too, encouraged the strategists to get busy defining both candidates.

Questions on what issues were on the participants' minds likewise failed to draw a clear focus on any major one. "It was a blank canvas," Teeter said afterward. "It was all mush, cotton candy." Then the moderator began to talk one at a time about the seven items on Pinkerton's three-by-five card—what Ailes called "the negative cluster"—asking the voters whether they knew this or that about Dukakis, and whether knowing the information would make a difference in how they voted.

"That's when it got very interesting," Atwater recalled. He and the others, he said, learned "that there was not one silver-bullet issue, one issue that would just turn a vote. But after they heard two or three—the best ones, I thought, were furlough and pledge, and then national defense was good—after they heard three or four of 'em they started getting very damn hesitant. . . . They [had] said they were for Dukakis. They were solid, but by the same token obviously they weren't that goddamned solid because they didn't know anything about the guy. . . . In one group forty percent switched from Dukakis to Bush, and in the other, sixty. So it was very obvious to me that what was important was to make sure that people saw those issues."

Ailes said later he agreed that "the cluster of those negatives painted a picture of Michael Dukakis that the public needed to have; in other words, that any one of those alone would not have been enough to do much damage."

The Bush strategists were aware, or at least they had reason to expect, that their counterparts in the Dukakis campaign were going through the same exercise—an impression that washed away any reluctance there might have been to "go negative." Ailes got Atwater in the hallway and said, he remembered, " 'I wonder how their focus group's going tonight. They're over there saying we sold arms to the ayatollah, we are responsible for all the drugs in the country. I wonder if our negatives cut their negatives.' The idea was, we know they've got that; they must know we have this. It's only a matter of who hits first and who makes it stick. . . . My whole fear was that he had bigger negatives on us than we had on him. I said, 'Shit, this looks like sort of penny-ante stuff compared to arms to the ayatollah.' I thought, 'These guys are gonna come in and nuke us someday.' " It was clear from such comments that "going negative" against Dukakis was seen not only as a counter to the Iran-Contra issue, but also as a way to divert attention from it.

The next day, as Bush campaigned in New Jersey, Atwater and Teeter rode together in one of the staff vans and for hours discussed the focus-group results. At one event in Liberty Park across from the Statue of Liberty, they sat on a bench and concluded that the Paramus focus groups had given them the raw material with which to defeat Mike Dukakis. The three main conclusions out of the groups, Atwater and Teeter agreed, were that there was a vacuum of information about both Bush and Dukakis, that no general issue really intruded on this vacuum and that when the vacuum was filled with the information provided from Pinkerton's three-by-five cards—voilà!—support for Dukakis nose-dived.

"I felt more relaxed after those focus groups," Atwater said, "than I had since South Carolina that we could really blow up Dukakis, and we had to do it." Always a bundle of pumped-up energy bursting to get out, Atwater remembered telling his wife, Sally, before getting his marching orders from Bush on using the new material: "I feel like a guy in an operating room knowing exactly what needed to be done but couldn't move his hands or legs."

On Friday afternoon Atwater and Teeter went by plane to Kennebunkport for a planned strategy session with the candidate and others of the G-6 strategy group over the holiday weekend. That night Atwater and Teeter had dinner in a seafood restaurant with other major players in the Bush campaign—Ailes, Fuller and Brady—and their wives and reviewed the bidding. The others, and Ailes particularly, quickly saw the potential in the focus-group findings. And in Atwater's view they had come none too soon.

By this time Bush—relatively idle and still being battered by questions on his Iran-Contra role and what now was routinely called "the wimp factor" —had slipped as much as seventeen percentage points behind Dukakis in the major polls. Atwater figured that Dukakis could be expected to pick up another ten points as a result of favorable exposure during the Democratic National Convention in July.

"If we ended up twenty-seven points behind after their convention," Atwater said later, "we might be in a situation where everything would collapse. Morale would collapse inside the party. I knew that personally I couldn't survive it. There would just be a total mutiny. That's just the nature of the game, the nature of the beast." What he was afraid of, Atwater said, was that the Bush campaign would find itself in the same dilemma that the operatives of the Gerald Ford campaign confronted against Jimmy Carter in 1976—when they ran a superlative comeback campaign that just fell short.

For this reason, Atwater calculated, there was no time to waste cutting into Dukakis' lead before the Democratic convention. If it could be reduced eight or nine points before then, he figured, Bush could absorb the "bump" from the convention and make up the ground with a successful convention of his own in August.

The group agreed that in meeting with Bush the next day it would be recommended that he go on the attack immediately after the last primary in California. It was also decided that in light of the way Bush was being squeezed out of the limelight by the Dukakis-Jackson phony war, it was time to shift from playing to the local and regional news media as dictated by the primary calendar and start zeroing in on the national press. The next day, the national reporters traveling with Bush were invited to a lunch and press conference at Bush's house. And the vice president himself would have to deliver the attack message against Dukakis. Surrogates could draw local news media coverage, but the nationals would ignore them; they wanted and needed the candidate himself to sell the story to their editors and producers.

The next morning, Sunday, the group held a two-hour session with Bush on a porch outside his summer home. Teeter briefed him on what had come out of the Paramus focus groups and, according to Atwater, "he was incredulous over the pledge-of-allegiance thing. He just thought that was outlandish. Bush was not cynical about using that issue at all, and he did not have to be talked into it. The two issues that he just thought were just plain outlandish were the furlough thing and the pledge of allegiance. And we didn't have to cajole him."

Atwater then made the recommendation that the focus-group findings be incorporated in Bush's stump speech. He warned that the conventional wisdom was going to berate the campaign for "going negative before we're going positive." But there was one thing that Atwater knew better than his own name, and that was how to do this kind of attack campaigning, and he didn't care what the conventional wisdom said. "I knew it would work," he said later, "and I knew that if we did it and sustained it for three or four weeks, we could knock down this guy's numbers and cut his lead in half.'' Bush readily agreed to play the role of hit man. The Texas Republican convention on June 9 was targeted as the event at which to kick off the attack, and it would then be sustained at the subsequent regional conferences.

In conversations with fellow strategists inside the campaign, Atwater was even more blunt about what had to be done, and why. ''Our negatives are up to forty-nine or fifty percent. Our positives are down to twenty-three or twenty-four,'' one of those present recalled him saying. ''His positives are up in the fifties, his negatives are down in the twenties. We're really in deep trouble and there's no way we're going to win this election with our negatives up this high. We probably can't do very much to drive our own negatives down. We're inheriting a lot of the negatives that are attendant to the Reagan administration and are being transferred to Bush—Iran-Contra, Noriega. It's all the Democrats been out there beating up on Reagan and Bush for the past nine months. . . . The only thing we can hope to do is build up his negatives. We've got to work at that, and he's given us two great issues—the flag and Willie Horton.''

A few mornings later, Atwater and Jim Lake, the 1984 Reagan press secretary just brought in as Bush's communications director, went over to the Hay-Adams Hotel for a meeting of Washington supporters of Bush—businessmen, political consultants and politicians who regularly had lines out to the press—whom Atwater regularly kept plugged in on strategy so they could reinforce the ''spin.'' He gave them a full rundown on the Paramus focus-group findings and how he was going to use them ''to drive up Dukakis' negatives.'' Such was the extent of the coordination involved in getting the negative message through, and making it stick—an effort deemed imperative because there was not a great deal of hope at the highest levels of Bush's own campaign that the voters could be made to feel much better about him.

Although the attack on Dukakis was scheduled to be launched at the Texas convention on June 9, Bush jumped the gun on the night of June 7 at a raucous victory rally in the California conservative stronghold of Orange County marking the end of the primary election season. In incredulous tones, he told the crowd of Dukakis' veto of the Massachusetts bill requiring teachers to lead their classes daily in the pledge of allegiance to the flag.

''I do not question the family values of Michael Dukakis,'' Bush said. ''I don't question the love of his family, one for the other.'' But, he went on, ''I'll never understand, when it came to his desk, why he vetoed a bill that called for the pledge of allegiance to be said in the schools of Massachusetts. I'll never understand it. We are one nation under God. Our kids should say the pledge of allegiance.''

We were in Los Angeles at the time focusing more on the Democratic primary in which Dukakis expected to win the remaining delegates he needed to lock up the nomination. Watching Bush on television making the reference to the flag pledge, our immediate reaction was how preposterous it was that

Bush thought such a matter could be made into a major issue in a national campaign. So much for how we saw it.

That night, obviously girding for an attack from Bush now that the primaries were over, Dukakis warned his Republican opponent to avoid the "quicksand" of a "mudslinging and name-calling" campaign because the voters "aren't interested in slashing attacks. They want to judge our positive ideas for change," he told his victory rally. "The American people aren't interested in what Mr. Bush thinks of me or what I think of him. They want to know which one of us has the strength and ability and the values to lead our country." So much, too, for how Dukakis saw it.

The Bush brainstormers had their own opinion, and were acting on it. At the Texas Republican convention two days later, Bush on schedule unveiled the attack strategy with a stinging speech in which he castigated Dukakis for permitting "unsupervised weekend furloughs to first-degree murderers," warned he would raise taxes and declared him soft on defense. "Governor Dukakis, his foreign-policy views born in Harvard Yard's boutique, would cut the muscle of our defense," said the Yale alumnus. From now on, it would be bombs away. The Democrats had been dominating the news because of their long-running nomination fight, he said, "but today it's a new ball game. Spring training is over, the season has begun, and there's no reason to wait 'til the World Series to start swinging."

In Denver two days later, at the first of the regional party conferences, Bush repeated the attack, and other leading Republicans, including former challengers Dole, Kemp and Haig, joined in. And shortly afterward, the Bush campaign dispatched a "truth squad" of Republican officeholders led by Senator John McCain of Arizona to tail Dukakis and rap him as a tax-happy liberal soft on crime.

At the same time, Bush became much more accessible to the national press. He held another press conference in Denver and was generally more open—in keeping with the decision to swing away from an emphasis on local coverage now that the primaries were over and onto the broader, national focus. No longer needing to pitch for primary votes, Bush campaigned as if he were in the general election in a relentless effort to reduce Dukakis' lead in the polls and to undermine the Massachusetts governor's generally favorable reputation with the voters.

By the time of the Illinois Republican convention in Springfield in mid-June, Bush had his anti-Dukakis theme going on all engines. Accusing Dukakis of having let "murderers out on vacation to terrorize innocent people," he used the Willie Horton case to argue that "Democrats can't find it in their hearts to get tough on criminals." And he asked: "What did the Democratic governor of Massachusetts think he was doing when he let convicted first-degree murderers out on weekend passes, even after one of them criminally, brutally raped a woman and stabbed her fiancé? Why didn't he admit his mistake? Eight months later, he was still defending his program, and only when the Massachusetts legislature voted by an overwhelming majority to abolish this program did he finally give in. I think Governor Dukakis owes the American people an explanation of why he supports this outrageous program.''

In the face of these charges, Dukakis said nothing. He let his campaign manager, Susan Estrich, argue that the furlough program in Massachusetts ''is not a completely appropriate program for the Republicans to attack'' because it was started by Dukakis' Republican predecessor, Governor Frank Sargent. And besides, she said, about forty states and the federal government had such programs and so did California when Ronald Reagan was governor. That was true, but as the *Lawrence Eagle-Tribune* had pointed out in its Pulitzer Prize-winning series, in forty-five states and the federal government program no individual under sentence of life without possibility of parole, as Horton was, was eligible for furlough. And it was the state legislature, not Dukakis, that moved to toughen the law; he went along reluctantly.

Amid growing press criticism about the attacks, Bush took refuge in self-righteousness. ''I will not be deterred by the age-old ploy of calling it negative campaigning,'' he said. He had ''an obligation,'' he said, to say ''here's where I stand and here's where he stands.'' The political professionals liked to say such campaigning was not negative but rather ''comparative.'' But the ''comparisons'' made were often extremely tenuous, like saying my opponent is a wife-beater and I, on the other hand, am not.

In any event, Bush continued to use the Willie Horton story as a bludgeon against Dukakis. Before the National Sheriffs Association in Louisville, he emphasized that Horton ''was sentenced by a judge—sentenced to life in prison. Before eligibility for parole, Horton applied for a furlough. He was given the furlough. He was released. And he fled—only to terrorize a family and repeatedly rape a woman. So I'm opposed to these unsupervised weekend furloughs for first-degree murderers who are not eligible for parole. Put me down as against that. When a judge says life without parole, it should mean just that.''

While Bush maintained the assault through June, Atwater watched the polling numbers carefully. After three weeks of the attack, he said later, the figures in three separate polls all had Bush down from the deficit that had reached as high as seventeen points to nine in one survey, eight in another and six in the third. The message seemed to be getting through.

Any doubt in Atwater's mind that this was so was dispelled over the Fourth of July weekend when he set out on another of his personal pulse-taking sorties. A staff aide scouted around and discovered that a national motorcycle riders' convention was being held at the Luray Motor Inn in the Shenandoah Mountains at Luray, Virginia, about ninety miles west of Washington. Atwater figured he had struck gold, or at least rhinestone.

With Sally and their two kids, he drove over on Friday, and that night at dinner at Brown's Chinese-American Restaurant there happened to be sitting in the booth to his back two couples of motorcyclists, one white and one black.

"I'm sitting there, somewhat relieved that the numbers had come down," he recalled, "but still somewhat perplexed about not having one silver-bullet issue, and trying to figure out whether the pledge would work better or the furlough. . . . This one woman starts talking to the other woman. . . . And one of them said, 'I just read this thing in *Reader's Digest* that you would not believe.' And the other woman said, 'What?' And she said, 'This criminal furlough thing that Michael Dukakis did is the most amazing thing I've ever seen.' So I just turned around and said, 'My God! What in the world are you-all talking about?' And I threw in a few little things to spice up the cake. I said, 'You've got to be kidding.' One of the guys speaks up and says, 'That's the dumbest shit I've ever heard about in my life. That son of a bitch.' You know, he's really going. So I start talking about it. . . . It was the white guy, but it was the black woman who first brought it up, which was significant to me."

Before long, Atwater remembered, another couple who overheard the conversation had joined them around the table, and—at the invitation of Atwater, who never identified himself—eventually others in the restaurant including the cook and two waitresses. It was not bad for an ad hoc focus group. "I said," Atwater recalled, " 'Eureka!' I don't care what the pundits ever say . . . this thing has got a life of its own. I had never seen such passion evoked." Other issues, including taxes, came up, he said, but "what really struck home was that Willie Horton article [in *Reader's Digest*]." Atwater insisted that race never came up in the discussion and the people who raised the matter didn't know Horton was black, he said, because it was the black woman who first spoke up.

Atwater called Teeter that night and Teeter said the same *Reader's Digest* article had just come up in another Market Opinion Research focus group in Alabama. When one of the participants mentioned it, he said, the whole group turned against Dukakis. The silver bullet, obviously, had been separated out. Atwater said care was taken that it was used henceforth in a "comparative" sense with all the "red language" left out to avoid a backlash on the charge of negative campaigning. But what was the comparison? He turns murderers loose to terrorize women, and I don't? To such was the great debate of the 1988 presidential campaign being reduced.

From all this it was abundantly clear not only that the attack campaign to destroy Dukakis was conceived well before the Democratic National Convention, but also that it had been put into extensive operation out of the mouth of George Bush. When that convention opened in Atlanta in mid-July, Bush was off trout fishing with his pal Jim Baker in Wyoming and he claimed not to have heard the jibes at him there. But later, when the criticism mounted of his use of the furlough, flag and other issues against Dukakis, he and his strategists claimed straight-facedly that all Bush was doing was responding to the Democratic convention "brutalizing" of him. In a campaign in which chutzpah was a common commodity, this one took the grand prize.

At any rate, the strategy that began in April with Atwater handing Jim Pinkerton that three-by-five card on which to list the dirt on Dukakis had, by the time of the Democratic convention, achieved its goal. Bush was now within shooting distance of the front-runner in the polls. He was positioned to take in stride the boost Dukakis would get from a successful convention—if he had one—and to match it with a successful convention of his own—if he had one.

PART IV

The Democratic Nomination

12

The Self-Destruction of Gary Hart

Ever since his 1984 presidential campaign, Gary Hart and members of the national political press corps had been engaged in a running debate. The subject was, as it was broadly categorized at the time, "the character issue." The expression embraced a number of specific matters that had emerged in 1984 raising questions about Hart's identity: What kind of man was he, in the eyes of others and in his own? Why had he changed his name and his signature and why had his true age been misrepresented in his official résumé?

These were superficial matters, but because Hart was a very private man —cold and aloof, some even said—such questions garnished the mysterious air about him. "Who is Gary Hart?" was reduced by Walter Mondale's managers after Hart's jolting successes in the early 1984 caucuses and primaries to the punch line of a television commercial of the time for a fast-food hamburger: "Where's the beef?" The line sought to raise doubts in voters' minds about Hart's political substance, although Hart at the time was advancing many more innovative policy initiatives than was Mondale, the New Deal retread. It worked, far beyond the Mondale campaign's dreams.

Along with the questions about Hart's name, signature and age, however, was an even more personal matter, one that flowed as an undercurrent to his 1984 campaign but did not surface in any threatening way. He had the reputation, within political and journalistic circles, of being a galloping womanizer. Within the close fraternity that makes up the political community during a presidential campaign—the politicians, their friends and hired guns, the news media covering them—rumors multiplied about Hart's extramarital proclivities. But they were rumors, and although they increased in number they remained just that— rumors, second-hand and third-hand gossip. No woman ever came forward with a specific allegation or confession regarding Hart, nor was he ever discovered and revealed in compromising circumstances.

After the 1984 campaign, as Hart took aim on a second bid for the Democratic presidential nomination in 1988, political reporters continued to ponder the mystery of Gary Hart. They found in talking to voters a general discomfort about him, not tied to any specific but rather a continuing puzzlement about who he was. Some voters recalled the age, name and signature questions of 1984; others more often would confess to feeling an uncertainty about the man, about what breed of cat he was, about his "character."

Whenever Hart was confronted with reports of such attitudes, he steadfastly, and sometimes angrily, refused to accept them. At one private dinner with a group of reporters in Washington in late 1985, he complained: "Nobody cares about all that except the press. I go all over the country and nobody ever asks me about those things except you." Those questions had been worked to death in the 1984 campaign, he insisted, and were not going to be a problem for him anymore—unless the press continued to beat a dead horse.

At this same dinner, attended by about ten reporters all of whom Hart knew well, he was also pressed about the state of his marriage, which all those present knew had had its ups and downs. He indicated only that he expected to be married to his wife, Lee, in 1988. It was hardly a vow of eternal bliss, but then Gary Hart was never one to engage in public displays or discussions of affection. Nobody asked about the rumors of womanizing, but everyone at the table had heard the rumors, and the question about Hart's marriage was a more delicate way of raising the issue.

Hart in the next year went about the business of becoming a presidential candidate again. Shortly after this meeting, he announced that he would not be seeking reelection to the Senate, and he began organizing for the 1988 race. As an undeclared candidate, he was the chief beneficiary in the national public-opinion polls when Ted Kennedy disclosed that he would not be seeking the nomination. Suddenly Hart found himself the Democratic front-runner, largely because more voters knew who he was than any of the other prospective candidates with the exception of Jesse Jackson, whose electability remained a debilitating factor in most Democrats' minds.

Hart made effective and politically constructive use of his status as his party's front-runner. During the 1986 congressional campaign, he made position papers available to Democratic candidates, campaigned for some of them and gave a series of thoughtful lectures on foreign policy at such prestigious forums as Georgetown University. He shored up his credentials in that area with a much-publicized trip to the Soviet Union, where he had a three-hour conversation with Soviet leader Mikhail Gorbachev. On return, Hart made the most of this experience as he resumed campaigning in advance of his formal announcement of candidacy.

Inside the embryo campaign, however, more than issues and Hart's foreign-policy expertise were on some minds. Leading political professionals, recruited to join the Hart effort, had heard most of the womanizing rumors. They did not want to sign on without assurances that no personal time bomb was ticking that could blow the whole campaign to pieces, and with it their own serious commitment to electing the next president.

Old Hart hands from his Senate races and his 1984 presidential campaign on several occasions raised the matter with him, as important new recruits asked them about it. "His response," one of the old hands recalled later, "was invariably to say something to the effect of 'Those . . . stories . . . are simply . . . *not* . . . true.' It put you in the position where you almost felt like you were calling the guy a liar if you were to pursue the subject."

What bothered some of these old Hart stalwarts more than the womanizing rumors, which they assumed related to the past, were the nagging questions about his age and signature changes and other incidents that painted him as a mystery man. Back in July of 1987, after they had come up in a conversation one of us had with John Emerson, the young California lawyer who ran the Hart campaign in that state in 1984, Emerson sent a memo to Hart warning him that the "character issue" questions were still alive. Hart's reply, Emerson recalled later, was that "I have answered those questions time and time again, and nobody is ever going to be satisfied on it."

One of the new recruits who addressed the whole general proposition of character questions with Hart and his senior associates was Paul Tully, the highly regarded political director of the 1984 Mondale campaign who was tired of losing and wanted a winner this time around. Tully after the 1984 campaign had been recruited by Ted Kennedy to run his political action committee, which Tully and most others in politics viewed as the precursor of Kennedy's own 1988 presidential campaign. When Kennedy decided he would not run, Tully became a much-sought-after property, with the Hart campaign among the most ardent pursuers.

Paul Tully had the appearance and mannerisms of the political hired gun. A heavyset man of forty-three at the time who looked the part of the football tackle he once was at Yale, he talked in the gruff code words and abbreviations of the political world. Tully was, however, a highly motivated liberal schooled in the Vietnam and civil rights protests of the 1960s. He was an Allard Lowenstein disciple who as a student dropout worked to elect Robert Kennedy to the Senate in New York and in 1968 to dump Lyndon Johnson, first behind Eugene McCarthy and later Kennedy. Issue-oriented and issue-driven, Tully needed to be convinced of two things: what Hart would do in the White House, and what his chances were of getting there.

In late November and December of 1986, Tully had conversations with the prospective candidate himself on the first point and came away satisfied that Hart's agenda squared with his own objectives for social justice at home and a realistic, moral foreign policy. On the second point, Tully had general discussions with Hart and conversations at much greater length with Hart's senior managers. But in both he left no doubt that he felt strongly that for people to vote for Hart's agenda they had to have a sense of where it came from in terms of the man's own value system and experience—his "character." Therefore, he told them, the character issue had to be dealt with frontally and effectively. And he had to be assured there was nothing in Hart's conduct, particularly his current conduct, that would sabotage that effort.

On the question of the electability of Gary Hart, Tully spoke with considerable authority. He had been, after all, part of the Mondale strategy team that had sought, identified and effectively exploited the public doubts about Hart in the 1984 Democratic nomination. He warned candidate and advisers alike now of what they could expect. He told them, as he recalled later: "Let nobody have any confusion about a front-runner campaign in any circumstances, with a history [of rumored misconduct] or without a history, and the demands on . . . a campaign in which there's clearly history, and an accumulated interest, rumor, dislike. There are folks out there who are going to cover this campaign who don't like you, think you're no good."

Hart and his campaign, Tully told them, had better "be prepared for a ferocious assault, a tense experience in which it is scrubbed and sandpapered and whatnot, down to kind of a consensus reality—who you are and what are you up to?" And the bottom line, he said, was the candidate's personality, his personal side. "That's the big leftover question," he recalled reminding them, "not in explicit terms about relationships, but that's the question that beat you, that I was part of a team of people who beat you on that stuff. We didn't have to indict and prove. All we had to accomplish was put doubt and risk [in voters' minds]."

Hart, Tully said, had to take "opportunities to convey what you want to do in a setting that [indicates] you have a set of principles underneath that agenda and values that grew out of your education, or grew out of your family, or grew out of the small town or grew out of Denver . . . a set of principles that came from somewhere, [were] rooted somewhere."

The Mondale campaign's greatest worry in 1984 after Hart had his big surge from Iowa through Maine and New Hampshire into the South, Tully recalled telling them, was that Hart would then go back and establish a sense of his roots, "in settings that said something about where you came from, that you weren't an invention that fell from the sky." Had Hart returned to Kansas then, Tully reflected now, rather than racing across the South from one airport to another as he did as "the phenomenon, not a real person," he would have been tough to stop. In not doing so, Tully said, Hart had invited Mondale to say in effect, "He may not be all that real." The age, name and signature questions were unimportant in themselves, he said, but they helped create doubt on which the Mondale campaign could feed. That doubt had to be dispelled if the 1988 campaign was to succeed where the 1984 version had stumbled, Tully argued.

In the course of his conversations with Hart prior to joining the campaign, Tully said, he did ask the prospective candidate whether there was anything of a personal nature that the campaign had to worry about. Hart assured him there wasn't, he said. So when other new recruits came aboard the Hart campaign, including a number of 1984 Mondale hands, and they asked Tully about the womanizing rumors, he told them he had been assured there was nothing to them. And in the meantime, Hart pressed on in the area most comfortable to him—discussing the cosmic issues that would face him as president.

In February 1987, in the living room of Don and Judy Schultz in the New

Hampshire town of Exeter, Hart reported on his long conversation with Gorbachev to a gathering of some fifty voters. For nearly an hour the Schultzes' neighbors sat mesmerized as Hart gave them an inside account of his one-on-one meeting with the leader of the communist bloc. He recounted how he and Gorbachev had sparred over the central issue of arms control, sharing Gorbachev's incredulity as conveyed to him over President Reagan's inept and uninformed performance at the Reykjavik summit meeting. The crowd was, not to put too fine a point on it, awed.

More than what Hart said on this occasion was the aura that enveloped him. No longer was he the tentative, uncertain newcomer on the national campaign trail that he was at the start of the 1984 campaign. Now he was the man who had nearly upset Fritz Mondale for the Democratic nomination in 1984, the clear Democratic front-runner for 1988 and, most important, the American leader who had confronted Gorbachev in the Kremlin and had given as good as he got. Gary Hart was now a certified political celebrity who might well be the next Democratic presidential nominee and the next president of the United States.

After a few more stops as Hart wended his way south toward Boston, he and aide Billy Shore agreed to have dinner with three reporters at Anthony's Pier 4 restaurant, a favorite Democratic hangout in Boston Harbor. It was to be a sociable evening, and Hart was relaxed, regaling his dinner companions with his recent first encounter with former President Richard Nixon at a memorial service for the late Senator Jacob K. Javits of New York. Hart told of how Nixon, sitting next to him in the church pew, kept tapping him on his knee and making comments about the approaching political campaign. Hart did a passing-fair imitation of the deadly serious Nixon telling a Democratic politician he had never met before how to go about winning his party's nomination.

But after a short while the conversation turned serious. Hart was asked what he intended to do about "the character issue." The question was posed in the general context of the public uneasiness and uncertainty about him, not in terms of any specific matter, and no reference was made at all to the longtime womanizing rumors. Confining himself to the old questions of his age, name and signature changes, he reacted with visible irritation. "You're the only ones who ever ask me about those things," he said again. "I go all over and nobody ever asks me." He had said all he needed to say or intended to say about them, he remarked, making an effort to control his obvious pique.

The discussion went on interminably through dinner, and when dinner was over he and Shore excused themselves from the table and left. Hart previously had said he would have to leave right after dinner, but some at the table interpreted his departure as a clear indication of his displeasure with the long, even relentless discussion of his "character." No mention had been made of alleged womanizing, although some eyebrows were raised around the table when, at one point, Hart emphatically insisted that he had nothing to hide from anybody.

Hart nevertheless demonstrated at the dinner that he was aware of the

political threat to him of "the character issue" and was taking at least some
small steps to cope with it. He produced a rather lengthy biographical article
he had written about his boyhood in Kansas, called "One Man's Luck," that
he said he was trying to get printed somewhere. Several newspapers had turned
it down, he said, proof to him that nobody much cared about his personal
life—nobody, that was, but the one-track-minded political press corps. (The
article was finally printed in the *Boston Globe*.)

The article included a very brief and defensive discussion of past marital
difficulties. "Comment was made of the fact that Lee and I suffered short
separations during those years," Hart wrote. "Coming in an age of divorced
presidents, this seems to deserve no more attention than that. Lee is proud of
reflecting, as she should be, that we were able to resolve those temporary
stresses, where others were not. In 1988, we celebrate our thirtieth wedding
anniversary."

"The character issue" took many forms. Indeed, it seemed that any subject
raised concerning Hart could be, and was, examined through the prism of
"character." One example was the matter of his holdover 1984 presidential
campaign debt. He had whittled it down from $4.7 million after the election
to $1.3 million, but his failure to wipe the whole thing out—a failure he shared
with most other Democratic presidential candidates—inevitably was cast as a
shortcoming of character. Bumper stickers appeared in Denver that read "Honk
If Hart Owes You Money," and reports surfaced of 1984 debtors in Iowa and
New Hampshire. How could he campaign there, the question was, if he had to
worry about somebody coming to one of his rallies or speeches and calling to
him: "Hey, Hart! When are you going to pay me what you owe me from last
time?"

U.S. News & World Report, for example, quoted a Hooksett, New Hampshire, auto dealer, Steve Singer, who said he had to wait two years for payment
on twenty cars he leased to the Hart campaign, and then had to settle for twenty
cents on the dollar. "A campaign reflects the personality of its leader," Singer
told the magazine. "If you can't run a debt-free campaign in a small state like
New Hampshire, how are you going to run the country?"

While such matters nagged at the campaign, Hart continued to address
himself to what he considered more pertinent issues. In late March he spent
four days in Gainesville, Florida, lecturing at the University of Florida College
of Law. From there he took the weekend off to relax on a boat kept in Florida
by a Washington lawyer and backer, Bill Broadhurst, known as "Billy B,"
who often accompanied him on the campaign trail as a kind of man Friday.
But Hart had been working hard, and if he felt he needed a day or two off,
nobody was ready to go to the mat with him over it.

The next week, Hart—after much internal discussion and candidate
resistance—made a high-visibility trip to his boyhood home in Ottawa, Kansas.
It was an attempt to "humanize" him, to reveal more of the man by revealing
more about his roots—a calculated effort to do now what he had neglected to

do in 1984, when his Iowa and New Hampshire successes suddenly hurtled him into the national consciousness.

The importance of the visit to Ottawa, Tully said later, was the role it could play in bringing Hart out of himself somewhat and to provide some personal framework for the value system on which he based his agenda, so that it would have voter appeal beyond its intellectual merits. Tully later put his own thinking as a political handler at the time this way: "I need Ottawa in the words—and in him—much more than I need him in Ottawa."

Hart, Tully said, nevertheless resisted the notion that he involve his family or other personal matters. "He had a fierce sense of privacy: 'There is a part of me that is owned by no one, that no one has rights to.' " It was almost, Tully said, that Hart used his privacy "as a measure of his own selfhood." He argued, Tully said later, that using family members and old acquaintances was "exploitative," and that he didn't want to be like Joe Biden, who in Hart's view used his first wife's tragic death to gain sympathy.

He was finally brought around on the trip to his hometown, Tully said, by persuading him that he could go and talk issues rather than "go and kiss the dog." His scheduler, Sue Casey, buttered Hart up, Tully recalled, by telling him the problem in 1984 was that the campaign never understood how much he had in common with regular people and what a regular guy he was. ("I didn't think he was a regular guy," Tully said afterward. "I just wanted to get him there.")

The Kansas hometown visit was rated a success within the campaign as an effective response to "Who is Gary Hart?" But as this aspect of the character issue was at last being dealt with, the other one—the womanizing whispering campaign—rather than fading away was growing louder. One new recruit concerned about it was Joe Trippi, who had run Iowa for Mondale in 1984 and later became a Tully lieutenant in that campaign. Before taking a job as a Tully deputy in the Hart campaign, Trippi had asked his old boss about the womanizing rumors and had been told they were a thing of the past. So he signed on and was dispatched back to Iowa in February 1987 to start organizing the state for Hart.

Almost at once, Trippi said later, he ran into more such rumors about his new candidate. Old 1984 supporters of Hart, including some who were delegates for him to the national convention, told Trippi they wanted no part of the Hart campaign this time around. At the same time, he said later, he phoned a woman who had worked in the 1984 Mondale campaign, to try to recruit her for the Hart campaign.

"She said, 'I can't work for him. Everybody here knows that he's fooling around with a woman in Florida, and that he came out of a bar a few nights ago with some other guy and two college women. . . . I can't work for him.' " The woman gave Trippi the name of another source, who gave him the same story. Trippi informed Tully, who knew the two sources well, and Tully said he'd check it out.

Walking through the headquarters, Trippi ran into Hart's press secretary, Kevin Sweeney, and asked him whether Hart had been in Florida the previous week. Sweeney, according to Trippi, said he hadn't. Trippi told him what he had heard and advised him to inform the candidate that rumors were going around, and if he was doing anything to feed them, he had to stop. Minutes later, Trippi recalled, a Hart speechwriter and issues director, David Dreyer, told him about the good reaction a Hart speech in Florida the previous week had received. When more, similar reports reached him from the same sources, Trippi went to Bill Dixon, the national campaign manager Emerson and Tully himself. He was told that Hart and Broadhurst had gone into a bar in Gainesville where there were some college girls, but that it was all very innocent.

Still, Trippi was worried. For one thing, a planned weekend visit to Puerto Rico he had organized, at which Hart was to meet the governor in an early courting of the island's large delegation to the Democratic National Convention, had suddenly been canceled because, Trippi was told, Hart wanted to spend the weekend on Broadhurst's boat. Trippi complained to Hal Haddon, Hart's closest friend in the campaign who had a special interest in Puerto Rico, but was told the decision had been made.

About this time a reporter phoned the campaign to warn that his news organization, against his wishes, was considering putting a tail on Hart. This was long before Hart issued his open invitation to the news media to do so. Word of the call got to Trippi, and on an organizing trip to Puerto Rico with Haddon, Trippi told him what he had been hearing. Haddon informed him that a different reporter from another organization had called him to warn him of the same plan to put Hart under surveillance. Haddon agreed to confront Hart on their return to Denver. He did so, telling him of the rumors and of the report that two news organizations were thinking of tailing him.

Hart, insiders said later, angrily cut off the discussion, saying the talk was just more of the same garbage. Haddon, apparently relieved, reported to Trippi, in Trippi's words, that "Gary understood how things appear and he was going to be a monk." And shortly afterward, to Trippi's surprise, one of the days for Puerto Rico was restored. Trippi concluded that Hart had decided after the warning from Haddon about possible surveillance that his days on Billy B's boat would have to end, and that Hart did intend to walk the straight and narrow. In fact, at one point Emerson phoned Broadhurst on the road and told him of the reports that he and Hart had been seen cavorting with co-eds in a Gainesville bar, and that rumors of tails being placed on them had been received. Broadhurst's reply, Emerson said later, was that Hart's schedule was going to be so hectic from then on that there would be no time for such socializing.

It was now only a few days before Hart's announcement of candidacy on April 13, and already the rumors were gaining greater visibility. In a *Newsweek* profile about Hart, John McEvoy, a 1984 Hart campaign insider dropped a bombshell. The article first observed that "the Harts' marriage has been a long but precarious one, and he has been haunted by rumors of womanizing. Friends contend that his dating has been confined to marital separations—he and Lee have had two—nonetheless many political observers expect the rumors to emerge as a campaign issue.'' Then McEvoy was quoted on Hart's prospects. "He's always in jeopardy of having the sex issue raised,'' McEvoy observed, "if he can't keep his pants on."

The Hart campaign managers were furious, and their anger did not subside with McEvoy's later explanation that his observation was made "in a speculative and purely hypothetical context, contrary to the actual facts as I know them.'' The assumption from the start in Hart's campaign, one of its managers said later, was that *Newsweek* as an institution was out to get him—a carryover from a strongly perceived hostility toward him in 1984. "They were close to Mondale and they just hated him [Hart],'' this insider said. "They used twenty-year quotes without giving Hart a chance to respond." As for McEvoy, Tully said later, "that [was] end-of-the-line. . . . McEvoy in my world made himself radioactive. Have a nice life, John.''

Hart's own reaction was predictable. In the course of being interviewed for a host of profiles, the personal questions were always asked. "[It was] irritation to the point of 'Enough of this profile shit,' '' Tully recalled. In this context, Hart at one point cited to aides the dinner at the Pier 4 in Boston, observing that "guys I've known for a long time, even they're in on this.'' Tully described Hart's attitude as an "air of victimhood.''

Although Hart finally did agree to do the hometown visit and to tell a few stories about his childhood, he held stubbornly to the notion that even a presidential candidate had a right to privacy—a lot of privacy. Tully recalled Hart saying that "I always thought that if you conducted yourself [properly] in public and didn't hide anything, you'd be all right.'' That approach by a public figure was, to Tully, incredibly naïve, but that seemed to be Hart's personal guideline.

As the April 13 date of Hart's formal announcement of candidacy approached, what Tully later called "quality rumors" began to reach the Denver campaign headquarters about the candidate in Florida. Tully recalled that some of the longtime Hart insiders would dismiss the rumors as a kind of understandable sowing of wild oats in advance of the formal kickoff of the campaign. He remembered, in fact, one aide wisecracking that "announcement day is like getting married.'' The implication was that if Hart was having a bachelor party or two of his own beforehand, well, boys would be boys. Meanwhile, on the eve of the announcement, reporters who arrived in Denver having read McEvoy's comment in *Newsweek* pressed campaign aides about the "womanizing" rumors. There was much "background buzzing,'' recalled Tom Fiedler, political editor of the *Miami Herald* who was in Denver. "It started as a low murmur and was amplified by the pack [of reporters].''

The announcement itself, on April 13, was a carefully staged affair at which Hart stood on a boulder in Red Rock Park in Denver and set the tone for a high-road presidential campaign. "All of us must try to hold ourselves to the very highest standards of integrity and ethics, and soundness of judgment,'' he intoned. At a news conference in Denver the next morning, Hart reflected on his 1984 stumbles. "We genuinely hope this campaign will be different," he said. "I have this strange notion that people care about ideas." He said he hoped he would be "better prepared for victory and defeat" than he was in 1984.

At the time of Hart's staff preparation for his opening press conference, the campaign was told by a reporter that Bob Shogan of the *Los Angeles Times*, a man of bulldog tenacity given to asking interminable questions, was going to open the interrogation by asking the candidate about "the name and age question." Hart, so informed, decided he would reply: "Your name's Shogan and as far as I can tell, you're fifty-seven years old." But the question never came up.

Neither, to the astonishment and great relief of the Hart strategists, was any "womanizing" question asked. Instead, Emerson recalled later, "it was the first time I ever saw a press conference with a candidate that treated the candidate like he was president of the United States. . . . I said to Hart, 'I think we've crossed the bridge where we're now at the point where they are really looking at you as the possible next president.' " Hart as the Democratic front-runner had an opportunity to frame the whole debate and, Emerson concluded happily, the press at last seemed ready to get past the personal questions and listen to what he had to say on serious issues. "I thought we had crossed the bridge over from the Land of Womanizing and Personal Questions to the Land of Substance and Message," he said.

After the press conference, however, as Hart embarked on his first swing as a declared presidential candidate, the character issue reemerged almost at once, in a bizarrely indirect way. Flying from Denver to Amarillo and on to Des Moines on his chartered campaign plane, Hart was being interviewed by a *Washington Post* reporter, Lois Romano. In the course of the interview, Hart said later, she told him that rumors were being spread about him and women other than his wife. "Finally, I just got irritated," he recalled. "I said, 'Come on, Lois, who? Where does it come from?' She sort of said, 'Well, off the record?' And I said, 'Yeah.' And she said, 'The Biden and the Dukakis campaigns.' "

Afterward, another reporter doing yet another Hart profile, Laurence Barrett of *Time* magazine, sat down next to him, Hart said, and told him he wanted to ask him a last time about the rumors and get on with the campaign. Hart replied, he said, "All I know is what the reporters tell me, and the reporters say it's coming from other campaigns, and that's it." With that, Hart recalled, "the plane went into orbit."

Other reporters who overheard parts of the exchange pressed the *Time* reporter for details at the rear of the plane, where most reporters were sitting. Kevin Sweeney, Hart's press secretary, tried to explain that Hart was merely commenting on what he had been told, but the reporters demanded to talk to the candidate, so he walked back to the rear of the plane to answer their questions. He was angry and defensive—angry that the issue had come up again on his very first day out as a declared candidate, and defensive about the suggestion that he was blaming his opposing candidates for spreading rumors about him. "Anybody want to talk about ideas?" he said as he came up to the reporters.

As for the other candidates engaging in rumormongering, he said, "I was told by a number of reporters that they were, period. It was an off-the-cuff comment, not meant to make news. . . . I hope they are not and I believe they are not. . . . The only thing I was going on were statements by other reporters that this was being done by other Democratic and Republican campaigns." The whole business came up, Hart said, when he was asked whether he was facing an endless stream of personal questions. "I said no for two reasons," he explained to the reporters. "One, we're ending the profile season, which comes around announcement time. And two, if campaigns were spreading gossip or rumors, that those campaigns would not succeed because sooner or later that would become the story. My reason for bringing that up was that other reporters have told me that was the case."

For months, Hart had been laboring diligently to establish himself as the candidate of ideas and issues, and the first postannouncement swing through key early caucus and primary states had been designed to hammer that impression home. But already, right out of the gate, the campaign was veering off onto precisely the path the Hart strategists had plotted to avoid. As the plane sped toward Des Moines, the rear section was abuzz with reporters comparing notes and transcribing taped recordings of Hart's remarks. And when the plane landed at the Des Moines Airport, a mad dash for the phones ensued as the reporters raced to communicate Hart's "accusation" that his foes were already trying to cut him down to size by playing dirty pool.

Had Hart simply dismissed the reports of rumormongering, the matter probably would not have taken on the dimensions it did. But in saying what he did, he made those reports the main story of the day, crowding out everything else he had said and done. "It was dumb on my part," he told us later. "I should have said 'No comment.' " But in the new, more strict adversarial relationship between candidates and the press, and the intensified quest for answers to questions concerning personal conduct, Hart was given no quarter for what he later called "a throwaway" observation.

Back at the Hart headquarters in Denver, a phone call from a staffer in Des Moines broke the news of how the candidate had walked to the back of the plane to discuss—the character issue! The strategists in Denver were aghast. But they did not at first grasp the significance of the flap. "It was not perceived as deep trouble [at the time]," Tully said. "It was perceived as a procedural fuckup. . . . Instead of two days or three days of clean message, you have one day." Traveling aides were chewed out for letting Hart sit back with the reporters and talk to them on the record about the prime forbidden subject of the campaign, but the matter was not seen at the outset as a catastrophe.

"Our feeling was it was a one-day story," Emerson said later. "It knocked the great press conference and the whole message of the announcement out of the papers and, more importantly, it returned us back to that issue. What was so frustrating was when we spent so much time dealing with the specter of the press raising the womanizing issue, and when the press didn't raise it, that the candidate raised it."

As the campaign plane flew on to Pittsburgh, press inquiries began to inundate the Denver headquarters. The first impression that the incident was no more than a procedural misstep soon developed into a realization that it was the kickoff of a diversion that was enveloping the whole campaign.

"This was a big deal," Tully reflected later, "and a lot of it was a story about a story. . . . But in some ways I was thankful for it, because it gave you a real good taste of what the dynamic was out there. If ever there was a learning curve, or should have been, that was real good evidence."

To many of the staffers, the experience was just that, Tully recalled, but not to Hart. "His lesson out of it is that, 'no matter what you do, they got this thing, this club, to club me with.' " That was, Tully said, "exactly the worst lesson—victimhood. [Hart said] 'It's about something else. It's opposition and criticism driven by something else—what I stand for, an intellectual corruption in the press corps or something, leftover anti-McGovernism.' " All this did not come out at once, Tully recalled, but it did spill out during what he called the later "meltdown."

The result was that while the staff became much more alert to the political volatility and threat of the character issue, Hart dug in his heels. If the other candidates continued to spread the rumors, Hart insisted, that would become the story, boomeranging on them.

Aides acknowledged to Hart that some members of the press corps were being more intrusive and less sensitive to his right of privacy than decency dictated. But they argued that as long as public uncertainty about him continued, the issue had to be faced, by providing the best case that Hart himself could make. As Tully explained the dilemma later: "Here's the glass. You're well known, a big high, tall glass—Gary Hart. They know the name, and there's a whole bunch of stuff [to be] filled in. . . . You think it's going to stay empty? Who gets to fill it in? You think we ought to fill it in a little bit here, or do you want Biden and Shrum, do you want them to do it? Or do you want Lee Atwater and Stone and Black? You want them doing a little filling?"*

Hart's attitude was that enough "filling" had been done during what he referred to as "the profile period," and now that he was a declared candidate it was time to move on to the issues. In this connection, he claimed also to see the hands of his opposition in the press's tenacity on the personal stuff. In fact, prior to the flap on the campaign plane, he suggested to the reporters that the

*Bob Shrum is a former Ted Kennedy speechwriter who signed on with Biden. Atwater was George Bush's campaign manager. Roger Stone and Charles Black were managers of Jack Kemp.

matter of his 1984 campaign debt had been raised by his opponents because he had frustrated them on the issues in laying out his positions in such detail and persuasiveness. "I hear from other campaigns," he said, " 'Well, we're not going to compete with Hart on the issues. He's too far ahead of us.' "

In all this, Hart was falling prey to conspiratorial musings. The fact was that the news media needed no prodding from other candidates in their determination as professional fact-seekers to fill in the half-empty glass that was Gary Hart. And in his surmise, or hope, that "the profile period" was over, he was sadly mistaken.

An irony in Hart's travail was that it came at a time he was campaigning with vastly more polish and self-assurance than he had in 1984. Shortly after the flap over "womanizing" on the campaign plane, as Hart and his wife, Lee, undertook a southern swing, the personal questions seemed to John Emerson to be tapering off. He recalled only one question on womanizing, and that was greeted with hissing from some of the other reporters in the entourage. Traveling reporters, however, said later that the issue, once the genie was out of the bottle, never faded thereafter.

At any rate, Hart on this swing exploited his position as front-runner with impressive skill, unveiling a new strategy for dealing with the approaching 1988 southern regional primary. He would use much of his time through the spring and summer of 1987, he said, doing the kind of retail campaigning ordinarily limited to Iowa and New Hampshire and seldom before practiced by presidential candidates in the South. As the front-runner, he theorized, he could campaign effectively in small communities without sacrificing coverage by television and major newspapers.

The theory seemed to hold water on this spring weekend. Hart led a small motorcade that made stops in places as small as Eclectic, Alabama (population 1,124) and at a barbecue contest in Columbus, Georgia, and found camera crews from stations in Birmingham, Montgomery and Atlanta ready to follow. Now that he was the candidate in the lead, it was no longer necessary to tailor his schedule to make it easy for the television stations.

Hart was in good form. He had worked out the language to discuss the issues likely to be at the forefront of the campaign, and he seemed to have outgrown the self-consciousness that earlier had made it hard for him to relax in many situations. Now he could visit a crossroads store in Alabama that had become a shrine to Coach Paul ("Bear") Bryant and the Crimson Tide, and joke easily with several dozen voters about whether he might be a secret fan of hated Auburn. And as was the case with most candidates on the road, he would take advantage of stops along the way to duck into a phone booth to catch up on his calls. People were always trying to reach the candidate. That was routine.

Hart on this swing seemed totally unconcerned about the womanizing question, and was relaxed at dinner in Atlanta one night on that weekend, along with Lee, aide Billy Shore, John Emerson and Bill Broadhurst. While the others chatted at the other end of the table, Hart told how the controversy on the plane had developed. After giving his version, he complained that he was now in a position where he couldn't relax around most reporters. Then, thumping the table, he added: "I don't have to worry about that stuff because there's nothing there"—a declaration his listener took to mean that, whatever might have happened in the past, Gary Hart was not going to risk his chance to be president of the United States.

Still, the specter of a suspicious press grated on him. Hart began telling reporters he had nothing to hide—among them Tom Fiedler of the *Miami Herald* in an interview during a stop in Fort Lauderdale. Shortly afterward, on Friday night, May 1, NBC News ran an interview by correspondent Ken Bode with Hart as his campaign van motored across Iowa. Hart repeated that he had nothing to hide. And in an interview scheduled for publication in the *New York Times Magazine* of the following Sunday, Hart told reporter E. J. Dionne: "Follow me around. I don't care. I'm serious. If anybody wants to put a tail on me, go ahead. They'd be very bored."

The clinging news media focus on Hart's personal life and rumors of marital infidelity concerned others besides Hart and his campaign strategists. Within the national press corps itself, the ethics of the pursuit increasingly generated discussion and debate. Among those who pondered the matter seriously and finally decided to address it in print was the *Miami Herald*'s Tom Fiedler. Back in Miami and reading the press reports on Hart, he wrote a lengthy and thoughtful news analysis that began on page one on April 27.

Fiedler cited the campaign-plane flap over alleged rumormongering by Hart's opponents, including Hart's testy lament: "Anybody want to talk about ideas?" Then he went on: "This vignette may tell us something about Gary Hart, a man with an opaque past. But more instructive is what it says about the nature of the modern campaign in a media-intensive age, where the scrutiny seems less intended to test a candidate's intelligence quotient than to expose his or her private life."

Fiedler suggested that "the Hart case raises real and serious questions about media ethics," and he spelled them out: "Is it responsible for the media to report damaging rumors if they can't be substantiated? Or should the media withhold publication until they have solid evidence of infidelity?" (This question by Fiedler would take on a most ironic weight soon afterward.)

"Even if sexual adventures can be proven, do the media have a legitimate interest in a candidate's private sex life, assuming it doesn't interfere with doing the job? Finally, to go back to Hart's question, can't the media stick to analyzing his ideas?"

In a tone very sympathetic to Hart's dilemma, Fiedler recounted the development of the story, beginning with the *Newsweek* profile and McEvoy's damaging quote. The *Miami Herald* reporter then noted how others in the press had jumped on the story, including the *New York Post*'s super-hyped headline on Hart's denials of misconduct: "Gary: I'm no womanizer."

Fiedler wrote: "From everywhere, questions about 'the rumors' pursued him. From nowhere did anyone come forward with evidence of any infidelity." And he quoted Hart: ". . . It's hard to disprove rumors if you don't know where they come from. And no one who asks me about the rumors ever tells me where they got them. I've been in public life for fifteen years and I think that if there was anything about my background that anybody had any information on, they would bring it forward. But they haven't."

Fiedler went on to discuss the history of the private liaisons of presidential candidates and presidents, from the allegations of Grover Cleveland's paternity of an illegitimate child to the stories of extramarital romances of Franklin D. Roosevelt and John F. Kennedy in the White House. Political scientists were cited observing that as the presidential nomination process had moved out of the parties' smoke-filled rooms, where other politicians decided, to the much more open process of primaries and caucuses in which voters played the key role, a greater public demand for information about the candidates was now sought—and was now justified. "And to whom does the public look for its information?" Fiedler wrote. "Who hears the rumors and does the peer review? The media."

Fiedler came down hard on his own profession. "That, however, doesn't resolve the Hart situation, where there has been no substantiation of the rumors," he wrote. "In a harsh light, the media reports themselves are rumormongering, pure and simple. So why have the media rushed the rumors to print? The answer appears to be that the rumors have achieved a critical mass, sustaining themselves through repetition and Hart's failure to categorically and convincingly deny them."

Professor Bruce J. Swain, a teacher of journalistic ethics at the University of Georgia, was quoted as saying the news media had a duty to investigate the rumors and print the results. "A story dispatching the rumors would be just as interesting as one confirming them," he argued. But Hart told the *Herald*: "No one has suggested what you do about vague, unfounded and unproved rumors. I think people are going to get tired of the question."

Fiedler concluded his analysis with that quote.* But one reader of his story in the Miami area clearly did not agree. She was not tired of the question, and she was annoyed at Fiedler's observations in the story that "from nowhere did anyone come forward with any evidence of infidelity," and that therefore "the media reports themselves are rumormongering, pure and simple." At about eight o'clock on that same night, she phoned Fiedler as he labored at his desk at the *Herald*.

"You know, you said in the paper that there were rumors that Gary Hart is a womanizer," the woman said in an acid tone. "Those aren't rumors. How much do you guys pay for pictures?" She refused to give Fiedler her name,

---

*A few days later, Fiedler received a note from Ginny Terzano, a Hart deputy press secretary, thanking him for the views expressed in the article.

but went on: "Gary Hart is having an affair with a friend of mine. We don't need another president who lies like that."

The woman seemed to be taunting him, mocking him, Fiedler recalled later, and at first he dismissed her as a crank caller. He told her she was making a serious charge and had better consider what she was doing. But the woman persisted. She asked what Hart's chances were of being nominated and elected, and Fiedler told her all he could say was that Hart was far ahead for the Democratic nomination in the early public-opinion polls. She said she had pictures and was willing to back up her allegation provided her name wouldn't be used. Fiedler told her there would be no need to use it if she gave him information that he could confirm to his own satisfaction on his own. He concluded the conversation by advising the woman to sleep on the whole business and call him back the next day if she wanted to proceed on the basis he had outlined.

The next morning about 10:30, Fiedler's phone rang again. It was the same caller, but this time the mocking tone was gone. She seemed nervous but said as a liberal Democrat, according to a later *Herald* account, "she couldn't tolerate someone who would say one thing publicly and do another privately. The nation had just seen that happen with President Reagan and the Iranian arms sales."

For the next hour and a half, the woman told an incredible story as Fiedler listened intently. Several weeks earlier, she told him, Hart and an "older man named Bill who said he was Hart's lawyer" were on a yacht in Miami with as many as fifty men and women, most of them in acting, modeling and the music business. "They weren't the kind of people you would think a presidential candidate would want to be around," the caller offered, acknowledging that she had been there herself. Hart, she said, had first come on to her but she gave him a cold shoulder.

Her friend, however, whom she did not name, was attracted to Hart, she said. "They spent a lot of time together that day and when we left she gave him her phone number," the woman reported. She placed the date of the yacht party by recalling that on the night before she had attended the premier of the movie *Making Mr. Right* on Miami Beach. Soon after, she went on, Hart called her friend and invited her to go on "a cruise." They went, the *Herald* account said later, "somewhere and stopped in a port overnight, but the caller didn't know where. She knew only that her friend was by then enthralled with Hart and in the weeks that followed eagerly displayed pictures of the pair together at that port."

The woman told Fiedler these were the pictures she had proposed the night before to sell to the *Herald*, but Fiedler declined. "Politicians have their pictures taken with strangers all the time," he told her. "It proves nothing."

But the woman told him there was more. Hart had phoned her friend repeatedly from the campaign trail, she said, telling her each time where he was calling from and where he was going next. The calls came from Georgia,

Alabama and Kansas, she said, and she knew the dates on which he had called. In the most recent calls, she said, Hart had invited her friend to spend the coming weekend with him at his town house in Washington. They were to meet in Washington on Friday night, she reported. The woman again insisted that she be kept out of any story but she assured Fiedler that if only he would meet her friend and talk to her for about twenty minutes, she'd tell all.

"She's really outgoing," the *Herald* later reported the woman as saying. "Maybe you could fly to Washington on the plane and get the seat next to her." The caller described her friend as a very good-looking blonde in her late twenties with a rich southern drawl, an actress who had made an appearance on the television show *Miami Vice*, so presumably she wouldn't be hard to spot.

Fiedler asked the woman for the flight information on her friend's alleged trip. "I'll get it and call you back," she said. It was now 12:15 P.M. on Tuesday, April 28. But she didn't call back.* Fiedler's interest was whetted by now. He began to check the woman's statements with Hart's schedule. By finding the date of the movie premier she had mentioned, he was able to establish that Hart had indeed been in Miami that weekend, after a fund-raiser at the home of Joel Karp, a Miami laywer. But he was wary; a dirty tricks artist in a rival campaign could well have obtained Hart's schedule, made up the whole story and fed it to him. And although many of the other details in the woman's story seemed to be accurate, three specific points troubled him.

First, the woman said her friend was to meet Hart at his Washington town house on Friday night. As far as Fiedler recalled, Hart lived in suburban Bethesda, Maryland, not Washington. Second, the Hart campaign schedule Fiedler had seen said the candidate was to be in Iowa on Friday and would attend a Kentucky Derby party in Louisville on Saturday. And third, the woman's description of "Bill" as a "really old-looking" man puzzled Fiedler. He knew that Hart's usual and longtime campaign traveling aide was Billy Shore, a man in his midthirties who looked even younger than that. But Fiedler informed two *Herald* associates of the woman's call and then waited, for the next two days, for her to call again. She didn't.

Fiedler, sitting apprehensively by his desk phone, finally decided on Friday to check out some of his doubts. He phoned the Hart headquarters in Denver and asked for the candidate's weekend schedule, saying he might want to go to Kentucky to cover him. The scheduler told Fiedler the Kentucky event had been canceled.

"Where is he going to be this weekend?" Fiedler asked.

"He's going to take some time off in Washington," the scheduler said.

"Where does he stay in Washington? Does he still have his house in Bethesda?"

---

*Speculation as to the identity of Fiedler's caller centered on Lynn Armandt, soon to enter this narrative, and Hart aides said later they were convinced of it. But Fiedler said later he had learned his caller's identity and she was not Armandt, whom he knew by then and whose voice he could recognize.

"No. They've sold that. They have a town house on Capitol Hill."

Suddenly everything the woman caller had told Fiedler seemed to be slipping into place. He hung up and told James Savage, the *Herald*'s investigative editor, what he had. But what next? They still had no information about which airline and which flight the caller's friend was supposed to be taking to Washington that night. And Fiedler didn't even have Hart's new Washington address. Airline schedules showed there were five flights from Miami to Washington that Friday night. The woman in question could be on any one of them.

Savage pondered the situation for a while. Then, a few minutes before five o'clock on that Friday afternoon, he called Jim McGee, a thirty-four-year-old investigative reporter on his staff, and had Fiedler repeat the substance of the phone calls he had received. McGee checked the plane schedules again. Of the five flights to Washington, two were nonstop and he figured the woman would be on one of them if any. One left Miami in only thirty minutes, the next at 7:40 P.M. He raced for the airport with only a stand-by reservation for the 5:30 flight, Eastern 996, sprinted to the gate and got there just in time to hear the final call for the flight. Luck was with him, and he got a seat.

According to the *Herald* later, "that's when [McGee] first saw the woman with shoulder-length blond hair. She was standing at the ticket counter and she was stunning. Hanging from her arms was a bulky, distinctive purse, with shiny stripes across a dark background. She seemed to be in the company of another young woman, also blond, but not as attractive."

McGee's seat was 19D, across the aisle and a couple of rows behind the first blonde with the large purse. The second blonde sat farther forward. Behind him, the *Herald* reported later, McGee saw a third blond woman, also attractive but younger than the first. He decided either Blonde No. 1 or Blonde No. 3 was the lady in question. As the plane headed for Washington, McGee twice got up and walked up and down the aisle, passing each woman and getting a good look at her face. Blonde No. 1 at one point got up, walked forward and arranged to sit next to Blonde No. 2. They talked animatedly for the rest of the flight.

The plane landed at Washington National Airport at 8:01 P.M. McGee spotted Blonde No. 1 again at the baggage area, where she was greeted by a brunette woman and saw them walk off. Blonde No. 3 was met by a young man in his twenties who embraced her zestfully. McGee dismissed her as his target. But neither Gary Hart nor anyone who looked to McGee like he might be a Hart campaign aide was in sight, making the reporter wonder whether after all he had taken the wrong flight. He decided to check in with the Washington bureau of the Knight-Ridder Newspapers, of which the *Miami Herald* is a member.

While McGee was on his way to Washington, Fiedler in Miami had been trying to get Hart's Washington address. By a stroke of luck, Ken Klein, the press secretary to Florida's Democratic Senator Bob Graham, called Fiedler on an unrelated matter. Fiedler asked him whether he knew where Hart lived. "Sure," Klein said. "Buddy Shorenstein [Graham's Senate chief of staff] rents the basement apartment from him." Klein gave Fiedler the address: 516 Sixth Street Southeast. Fiedler phoned the information to the Knight-Ridder Washington bureau news editor, Douglas Clifton. When McGee called, Clifton gave him the address and said he would join McGee there in a little while.

McGee grabbed a cab to Capitol Hill. He found Hart's town house in the middle of a row of them on a street brightly illuminated by streetlights with frequent pedestrians walking their dogs and a steady flow of cars going by. It was not going to be easy for McGee to keep Hart's house under surveillance without being seen himself. But a block away there were benches in a city park from which McGee could see anybody going in or coming out of Hart's front door.

At about 9:30, as McGee stood across the street and about six houses away, the *Herald* account said, he saw "a trim, well-built man with black hair," wearing "a white long-sleeve dress shirt and dark slacks" come out of Hart's front door—with the same beautiful blonde with the large purse he had spotted on the plane. The man was, no doubt about it, Gary Hart. As they walked off, McGee rushed to a pay phone a block away and called the *Herald*'s executive editor, Heath Meriwether, at home. He told his boss the astonishing news and urged that more reporters and a photographer be sent to Washington. He then called Fiedler, who said he would get the next plane to Washington —not until early the next morning.

McGee went back to Hart's address, where in a few minutes Clifton joined him. Clifton staked out the rear of the town house. After an uneventful hour, the two men decided they were too conspicuous on the street at that time—it was now about eleven o'clock—so Clifton took a cab to National Airport to rent a car. As McGee was talking to Savage in Miami on the outside pay phone, he saw Hart's car driving slowly through the nearest intersection. He hung up quickly and ran back to Hart's street. Hart parked his car around the corner and was walking toward his front door, the same blond woman at his side, still toting the easily recognized purse. McGee saw them go inside together.

Clifton returned with the rental car, and he and McGee continued the stakeout, this time with Clifton in front in the car while McGee watched the back street. They saw no one else go in or come out of Hart's house. At about 3 A.M., they decided—in what turned out to be a lapse of reportorial judgment, in light of later developments—to knock off for something to eat. They resumed their watch about two hours later, and still saw no traffic in or out of the house as dawn broke clear and warm on Saturday.

By this time, Savage, Fiedler and Brian Smith, a *Herald* photographer, were on the first flight from Miami to Washington. En route they discussed their strategy. At one point, Fiedler pulled out a sheaf of newspaper articles and wire reports on Hart that he had collected and began to review them. He came upon a computer printout, an advance copy, of the *New York Times Magazine* article that was not to be published until the next day and that he then read for the first time. When he was finished, he handed it to Savage with the bold "put a tail on me" quote circled. Later, this article was often cited as the specific "invitation" on which the *Herald* had acted, rather than the anonymous phone call that really was the catalyst.

The plane landed at National Airport at 10:05 A.M. The *Herald* team rented three cars and arrived in front of Hart's town house at about eleven o'clock. Smith and Savage parked their cars on opposite corners with a clear view of Hart's car but a partially obstructed view of the front door. Fiedler parked his car on the street behind the house and watched the alley entrance. Crucial to the developing story, the *Herald* team decided, was that someone other than McGee see Hart and the blond woman together and thus verify McGee's story. But all morning and into the afternoon, they saw nothing.

Meanwhile, in Hart's Denver headquarters, key staff aides were now busily at work. The pressing business that Saturday morning was the text of an important speech Hart was scheduled to make the next Tuesday in New York, before the annual convention of the American Newspaper Publishers Association. Hart was in the process of laying out a series of central themes to his campaign, and this speech was planned to present his basic position on the national economy.

At the time, the Hart speechwriting corps was in disarray. His chief speechwriter was not producing to Hart's satisfaction, so the candidate simply was not delivering what had been written for him. The campaign's issues and political people were in conflict over substance and style. There was criticism of speeches written in what some insiders panned as "California techno-babble" that didn't communicate the candidate's ideas clearly or, in this case, address the economic challenge in a practical way. As a result, there was much debate back and forth and the writing and rewriting of drafts on the main economics speech.

One late draft, in fact, was to be sent to Hart on Friday as he was finishing his Iowa trip and heading for Washington for the weekend. The plan was for him to work the draft over himself and send it back to Denver for processing of the final version in time for his ANPA appearance in New York on Tuesday. It so happened that the campaign's Washington headquarters was being moved that weekend to larger quarters. All its equipment was out of operation while it was transported to the new address and installed there. It so happened also that Bill Broadhurst had a telecopier at his house, several blocks away from Hart's on Capitol Hill. The plan was to telecopy the draft there and have it delivered to Hart Friday night on his arrival at the airport in Washington so that he could work on it over the weekend.

On Saturday morning, Hart phoned some editorial fixes on the draft to Tully in Denver that were duly made in the draft, which then was run through a word processor. That version was sent back, again by way of the telecopier at Broadhurst's house, with the understanding that Hart would do additional editing and send the draft back again sometime Saturday night by way of the telecopier. After working at the headquarters all day and the draft not yet having come back, Tully went to dinner. As far as he knew, his candidate had been spending all Saturday laboring over the speech draft.

In the meantime, the *Miami Herald* surveillance continued all day and into the evening outside Hart's house. The members of the stakeout saw nobody come in or go out, but the back entrance wasn't covered at all times and the view of the front door was sometimes blocked. Finally, however, at 8:40 P.M., with streetlights burning at the front of the house but darkness enveloping the rear, McGee walked casually toward the rear alley driveway. As he did, he saw Hart and the blond woman coming out of the alley that led to the entrance to Hart's garage. He quickly turned and walked toward the corner where Hart's car was parked. As he did, Fiedler, in a running outfit, jogged by him.

"He's right behind me," McGee whispered to his colleague. Fiedler at once crossed the street to the park, so that Hart, whose campaign he had been covering, would not recognize him. Hart was wearing a white sweatshirt and slacks and his hands were in his pockets as he looked about him, with the woman holding on to his right arm. They walked a few feet, stopped guardedly, then proceeded to Hart's car. But rather than getting in, they turned and walked down the block and into the front entrance of Hart's house.

A few minutes later, Hart came out alone, walked straight to his car, started it and pulled away. Smith, the *Herald* photographer, watching from his rented car, followed. Hart drove only a few blocks, parked the car and started walking back, but by a circuitous route. He walked by the car in which McGee and Savage now sat. He was, in their view, in an agitated state. Then he went down the alley behind his house.

"I think we should talk to him right now," Savage said to McGee in the car. "It's your call."

"Let's do it," McGee said. They got out of their car and walked up the darkened alley after Hart. They turned a corner and there he was.

"Good evening, Senator," McGee said. "I'm a reporter from the *Miami Herald*. We'd like to talk to you." Savage also introduced himself. Hart just stood there, his arms wrapped in front of him as he leaned against the brick wall behind him. McGee told him they wanted to ask him about the young woman staying in his house.

"No one is staying in my house," Hart replied.

Well, McGee said, he and Savage saw a woman go in at 8:40, right after she and Hart had passed him on the street.

"I may or may not have," Hart said.

They asked him what his relationship was to the woman.

"I'm not involved in any relationship," he said.

Then why did she and Hart just go back into his town house? McGee asked.

"The obvious reason is that I'm being set up," Hart said, his voice shaking.

Is she in your house, Senator? the reporter asked.

"She may or may not be," Hart answered.

Savage asked whether they could go into the house, meet the woman and continue the interview. Hart declined.

Well, if she's not in there, how did she leave, and was she staying with him?

"She's been here in Washington over the weekend," Hart replied.

McGee then confronted Hart with all that the *Herald* team had witnessed from the time Hart was seen leaving his house with the woman Friday night. He asked Hart where he was going with the woman just now.

"I was on my way to take her to a place where she was staying," he said.

McGee and Savage continued to question Hart about the woman. He acknowledged that he had known her for "several months" but he declined to give her name. On Friday night, he said, they had come back to his house so the woman could "pick up some things that she had left." She had stayed only "ten or fifteen minutes," he said, but said he didn't remember how she left. "She is a friend of a friend of mine. . . . A guest of a friend of mine," he said.

Fiedler now walked up and Hart said hello to him. Next McGee asked him about the telephone calls to the woman from campaign stops around the country. What did they talk about?

"Nothing," Hart said. ". . . It was casual, political. General conversation."

Hart, to further questioning, said he couldn't recall when he had first met the woman, what her occupation was, and couldn't remember the yacht encounter in Florida. Fiedler and McGee reminded Hart that after the *Newsweek* article he had said he could only respond to specifics, not rumors. Here were specifics. Fiedler also reminded Hart of his promise in his announcement of candidacy to conduct his campaign on the highest moral plane. He urged Hart to clarify the situation, observing that "you, of all people, know the sensitivity of this." The *Herald* was going to run a story on what its reporters had seen and learned and Fiedler again urged him to be forthcoming.

"I've been very forthcoming," Hart said.

The reporters tried once more. What was his relationship with the blond woman?

"I have no personal relationship with the individual you are following," Hart said stiffly.

Well, was he denying he had met her on the yacht?

"I'm not denying anything," Hart said, with anger.

Hart again turned down the reporters' request to interview the woman, or the friend Hart said she was visiting. "I don't have to produce anyone," he said.

McGee, sensing that Hart was about to cut off the interview, asked the big question. Had he had sex with the woman seen with him on the street?

"The answer is no," Hart snapped. "I'm not going to get into all that." He turned and walked up the alley to his house. As Smith snapped pictures of him, Hart remarked, "We don't need any of that," and went inside.

It was now after ten o'clock. The *Herald*'s first Sunday deadline was past and the deadline for the bulk of the press run was a short time off. The three newsmen drove to Fiedler's room at the Quality Inn off Capitol Hill and began to check notes and put their story together. As McGee transcribed his notes, Fiedler wrote the lead on his portable computer:

"Gary Hart, the Democratic presidential candidate who has dismissed allegations of womanizing, spent Friday night and most of Saturday in his Capitol Hill town house with a young woman who flew from Miami and met him. Hart denied any impropriety. . . ."

Back in Denver, Tully had finished dinner and, having been told the draft of the economics speech wouldn't be telecopied back with Hart's fixes until Sunday morning, called into the headquarters once more before turning in. He got Kevin Sweeney, the press secretary, on the line.

"Kevin, I thought you were going to a dinner party," Tully said. "Anything cooking, anything on the wire, anything going down?"

There was a pause. Then Sweeney told him that Billy Shore had just called after talking to Hart from Washington. An emergency meeting was being called at Bill Dixon's place. A bunch of reporters were at Hart's house and there had been a scene with him.

Tully was staying in the same apartment house as Dixon, a few floors below. He hustled upstairs, where Dixon, Emerson, Shore and other campaign figures were in deep conversation. Dixon and Emerson got on separate phones to Broadhurst, grilling him about all details. Then at Dixon's request he turned the phone over to, as Tully put it later, "a very distraught, crying Donna Rice, who no one knew at this end." She denied any wrongdoing, and after they hung up, Emerson said to Dixon: "This woman is not lying to us. She is an emotional basket case." Between tears, Emerson recalled, she answered all of Dixon's questions, mentioning at one point that they had "gone on a boat ride," but she didn't say where. When she was asked point-blank whether she had spent the previous night with Hart in his town house, Emerson said, she replied flatly, no.

"Have you ever slept with him?"

"No," came her plaintive answer, again according to Emerson. "She was really upset for Gary," he recalled. "She kept saying it was terribly unfair."

The first impression was that the whole business was a setup. Dixon decided to get on a red-eye flight to Washington at once. But as he talked to the others, he several times in passing mentioned the possibility that the campaign might be over in the next twenty-four hours. After he left for the airport, Tully, Emerson and Shore asked each other whether Dixon in his mind had already left the campaign, and hence whether he was going to be in any emotional condition to try to bail Hart out.

Meanwhile, there was the *Herald* story to deal with. What was Hart thinking of, talking to the reporters? And where were they now? They had to be found and talked out of writing the story that night. Broadhurst was told by the Denver operatives to find the *Herald* newsmen and have them talk to the woman. He called the *Herald* Washington bureau and finally located the team in Fiedler's room at the Quality Inn. He phoned the room, got Savage and asked to speak to Fiedler, but was told that the reporter was busy filing the story.

Broadhurst told Savage that the woman was his houseguest, not Hart's, and that she was merely accompanying another Miami woman who was staying at Broadhurst's house while considering his job offer to be a social director for his lobbying and entertaining activities in Washington. But Broadhurst declined to provide any details about the movement of Hart and the blond woman between his house and Hart's. He said only that the woman had left Hart's house Friday night and had spent the night at his own house with her friend. As for Saturday, Broadhurst said, he "had not worn his watch Saturday" so wasn't able to provide details of their comings and goings. Nor would he accede to Savage's request that the two women be put on the phone.

Savage ordered that Broadhurst's version be inserted in the story. It was, and as the finished story was being edited Fiedler took the phone. Broadhurst urged him to come to his town house to discuss the whole matter. If he did, Fiedler said later Broadhurst told him, "the girls" would be there. But Fiedler said he received no assurance that they would talk. Fiedler told Broadhurst he would call him back.

The next deadline was closing in now. Executive Editor Heath Meriwether was now at the paper to oversee the story's publication and he decided to go ahead for the bulk of the Sunday run. The informant's reports had been confirmed and Hart had been given his opportunity to explain and to produce the women, and he had declined. Hart, Meriwether said later, "didn't need twenty-four hours to explain what we'd seen."

With the story transmitted to Miami, Fiedler called Broadhurst back and asked if he could now go over and meet the women. Broadhurst refused. "Your story is already written. I don't see any point in that," he told the reporter. Besides, he said, the women were asleep now. Instead he offered to pick the *Herald* team members up and go to a late dinner with them. He did so and they wound up at an all-night restaurant in Chinatown, not far from the Quality Inn.

Broadhurst admitted that he and Hart had been on the yacht with the two women in Miami. But the blond woman was not invited to Washington by Hart, he insisted, but by the other woman. He denied knowledge of any phone calls Hart may have made from the campaign trail and he contended that the *Herald* surveillance had missed vital details. The blond woman, he said, on Friday night had left Hart's house with the other woman and himself minutes after she and Hart had entered by the front door. They had gone out, he said, through the garage that opened onto the rear alley—at the time that exit was not being watched, Clifton having gone to the airport to rent a car. Broadhurst said he actually had come and gone twice that night through the rear garage, using an electronic key in his car.

Late on Saturday morning, he went on, he asked the blond woman to deliver an envelope to Hart at his house seven blocks away—presumably a draft of the economics speech on which he was working, telecopied from Denver. She did so, he said, and then he and the other woman drove over to Hart's, picked Hart and the blond woman up at Hart's front door and the four of them spent Saturday afternoon touring the Alexandria area looking at apartments. But the *Herald* stakeout had not seen anyone leave all day Saturday.

Broadhurst and the reporters talked until about 5 A.M., then split up and went to bed. Broadhurst still refused to identify either of the women. He said only that he would inform them when they woke up that the *Herald* team wanted to talk to them.

Back in Denver, the campaign strategists had decided that the only option was to produce the women and have them tell their story. But they knew from the phone conversation that Rice was in no condition to face television cameras immediately. When they were informed that the *Herald*'s story had already been filed, the strategists began to get suspicious of a setup. When Broadhurst reported on his early-hours dinner with the team, and indications that the reporters had left gaping holes in their surveillance and weren't aware of the garage exit, the strategists began to consider that they might have a case against the newspaper.

One of them, however, saw the prospective damage at once. When Emerson asked Tully how bad he thought the situation was, Tully told him: Even if the parties were innocent and it proved to be only an isolated incident, given Hart's reputation already, there was "one chance in ten" that the campaign could continue with a reasonable chance of winning the nomination. "That floored them," Tully said later. "They knew it was bad, and big bad, but they didn't have the notion that it was odds-on over." But this confrontation was now playing against a two-week cycle of rumors and had to be viewed in that context—a story that was already rolling and now was given a new, much more vigorous life.

Hart, for his part, was furious—again in the grip of what Tully called "victimhood." In phone calls back to Denver, Hart argued that here was an "assault team" from the press that he had uncovered and confronted. Emerson and Dixon, in the conversation with Donna Rice, now at Broadhurst's house, culled from her that she had met Gary and Lee Hart at a party in Aspen the previous New Year's Eve, and that she had recognized him again on the yacht in Miami. They grilled her on the phone calls Hart had made to her. It was well known among Broadhurst's associates that he was indeed looking for a woman to oversee his Washington social operations, so that part of the story of why Donna Rice was in Washington seemed valid enough.

Maybe the whole thing was a colossal screwup by the newspaper after all.

Maybe Gary Hart was the wronged party, and his campaign wasn't down the tubes. Maybe. So went the wishful thinking among some as the damage control began.

13

Too Much Damage to Control

As soon as Bill Dixon arrived in Washington on the red-eye flight from Denver, he took over and launched a counterattack of denial and accusation. He called the *Herald* account "preposterous and inaccurate. . . . . They have taken a casual acquaintance and simple dinner with three friends and political supporters and attempted to make a story where there is none," he said. He accused the *Herald* of getting the story by "hiding in bushes, peeking in windows and personal harassment" in acts of "character assassinations."

But the story was already spreading like an uncontrollable flame. On the ABC News network Sunday morning show, *This Week With David Brinkley*, the host gave nationwide exposure to the *Herald* story, only hours off the presses. Political commentators on the show immediately weighed in with cataclysmic speculations on Hart's political future.

In Denver, Joe Trippi was in the kitchen of his rented house cooking breakfast for his wife, Katie, and their baby daughter when Katie, watching the Brinkley show in the living room, called to him. "Joe, you better get in here," she said. "It's all over." Trippi ran in, just to hear the last lines of Brinkley's commentary. Within seconds, his phone rang. It was Tully. "Joe, get in here right away," he said. "It's all hands on deck."

At the Hart headquarters, the top strategists were gathered in Dixon's office. As soon as Trippi arrived, he found that he had been elected to the unenviable task of dealing with Lee Hart.

"What does she know?" Trippi asked.

"We don't know."

"What do you mean, you don't know?"

"Well, we think Gary called her last night, but we're not sure."

Armed with this meager intelligence, Trippi drove to the Hart house, in a place appropriately called Troublesome Gulch in the mountains outside Denver. There he found a small army of reporters, photographers and cameramen already camped outside a high gate about three hundred yards down from the house. As he walked in, he heard a correspondent from the Fox Broadcasting Network doing a stand-up.

"Here at the foot of the Rocky Mountains," he intoned, as Trippi recalled it, "the Hart campaign is in trouble, and Lee Hart is lying low. But aides do admit she's talking to her husband on the phone."

Trippi walked over to him. "What's this 'admit' stuff?" he asked the television reporter. "If she were admitting that they aren't talking, that would be news, but I talk to my wife on the phone all the time."

The reporter replied: "Did you ever hear of the show *Current Affair*? . . . We're the *New York Post* of television."

At the house, which is a large one-room log cabin, Trippi found Lee sitting in the kitchen area, her face puffed out with a serious sinus infection, but otherwise calm and collected. She told Trippi that she had talked to her husband on the phone, that he had told her it was all innocent and that she believed him, because she knew him well enough to know that he didn't lie to her. Rather than needing political counsel from Trippi, she had already decided what her position would be. She was not going to talk to the reporters or give any written statement. If she went out before the press with her face looking as it did, she said, the next thing they'd be saying was that her husband was "a wife-beater."

On one other thing, too, she was adamant. She wasn't going to reward the newshounds who had set siege to her house by talking to them now, or anytime later. "I was just amazed at how strong she was," Trippi said later. "In fact, I think the worst thing about how the whole incident came out was how she was portrayed as somebody hiding up in the house." Her sinus infection was real, he said, and was the only reason she did not fly East at once to be with Hart—if that was what he and the campaign wanted.

Also present were the Harts' daughter, Andrea, and Lee's personal aide, Linda Spangler. Andrea like her mother was infuriated at the press but she watched the television reports avidly, to Lee's consternation. Trippi settled in as a kind of political hand-holder, although Lee didn't seem to need one. From time to time Hart would call her and, according to Trippi, who could hear her side of the conversation, she would be the one to give reassurances.

There were other phone calls, too, including repeated ones from actor Warren Beatty, a longtime supporter and friend going back to the McGovern campaign of 1971–72. Beatty was full of advice, including at one point, according to Trippi, the suggestion that Lee should tell the reporters: "If you want a monk for president, you don't get me as first lady." Also, Trippi said, feminist friends would call her castigating Hart and urging her to be tough with him—advice that she turned away with assurances to them that her husband wasn't what they were suggesting he was.

Back in Washington, Hart rather incredibly spent much of Sunday, according to Emerson, working on refinements on Tuesday's economics speech by phone with his speechwriter, David Dreyer. But by nightfall the evening news television shows were smothering the story, with footage of Dixon's irate denials and countercharges against the *Miami Herald*. The Hart campaign headquarters identified the blond mystery woman as Donna Rice, a twenty-nine-year-old part-time model and actress, and the search was on for photographs of her and more personal information. The other woman was identified as Lynn Armandt, also of the Miami area, the applicant for the job Broadhurst was seeking to fill.

The *New York Times*, always remembering its self-assigned role as guardian of journalistic taste and ethics, relegated the story in Monday's editions to page 12 under a safe and innocuous headline: "Hart and Paper in Dispute Over Article." Most of the rest of American journalism, however, saw the story for its news value as an undiluted blockbuster likely to turn the 1988 Democratic presidential nomination race on its ear, and ran it big on page one. The *Times* finally woke up to the dimensions of the story the next day.

Others went overboard in the other direction. "I Didn't Sleep With Gary Hart," proclaimed the *New York Post* page-one headline with a sexy photograph of Rice. "Gary Is Not My Lover," said the *New York Daily News*, also with accompanying cheesecake photo. Also dug up was a picture of Rice in a Miami area bar with a Confederate flag draped over one breast, leaving the other bare—but airbrushed into decency by newspaper art departments using the photo.

By now the strategy in the Hart campaign was clear—go after the *Herald* for publishing with seemingly reckless haste a story that was full of holes. The holes held open the possibility that Hart and Rice could claim they really were innocent of any hanky-panky, and offered the chance, Tully said later, "to start making it a process question, not just a factual question. Once the process is fucked up or unfair or whatnot," he said, "you've got some running room. It's a different subject matter," and people might be brought to focus on a newspaper's desire to increase its circulation with a sensational story such as this one. If this incident proved to be one that stood alone, rather than as part of a pattern, Tully reasoned, there might be a chance to weather it. "We had to come out with guns blazing and attack the process," Emerson said.

By this time, the campaign damage-control operation was in full swing. Haddon directed a fact-finding operation on Donna Rice—her background, her former boyfriends, the whole business. At the same time, Sue Casey, the Hart scheduler and one of the most devoted members of the Hart campaign team, recognized Rice's dilemma. She was a young woman in a strange place at a strange time surrounded by men she didn't really know. Casey volunteered to go to Washington and counsel with the woman, up to now left in the hands of men.

Casey combined political astuteness with fierce loyalty to the candidate. The first she had demonstrated as comanager of his New Hampshire primary upset over Mondale in 1984, and the second in moving her family to Denver to work in the 1988 campaign. She was the ideal choice to go to Washington and hold Donna Rice's hand. She flew into Dulles Airport outside Washington, met Rice there, and the two spent the night at a hotel near the airport. Casey, after hearing Rice's story, reported to Denver that she was either the best actress Casey had ever seen or she was telling the truth that the whole encounter was innocent. She had slept at Broadhurst's on both nights, she insisted to Casey.

But there was one other little fact, Casey reported, that Rice had told her. She and her friend Lynn had gone with Hart and Broadhurst on a cruise to Bimini—and stayed overnight.

The pattern that Tully feared emerged Monday, in a way that jolted the Hart campaign. The Denver people had urged that the two women be trotted out in Washington on Sunday, but Armandt had left the city, telling the Hart people she had to go to New York to meet her mother but would call back with a phone number where she could be reached. She didn't. "We smelled a rat," Emerson recalled later. "We never heard from her again."

Rice, with Casey in tow, returned to Miami Monday, where she held a ninety-minute interview with a small, select group of reporters in the office of a lawyer friend of Hart's. In spite of her flat statement that she was "innocent" of any wrongdoing and that "I never slept with him," she dug Hart into an even deeper hole.

She said that after meeting Hart on the yacht at Turnberry Isle, a Miami area resort, and recalling they had met in Aspen, they talked for a while. When she left she gave him her phone number and a couple of days later he called her at her apartment and "invited me on a boat trip." She accepted, inviting her friend Lynn to go along, too. Hart, Broadhurst and the two women set out from Turnberry Isle with a crew of five on a chartered yacht called *Monkey Business* bound for Bimini, intending to spend only that day there. "We got to Bimini and walked around," she said, "but when we went back to the boat to leave, Customs had closed, so we were stuck."

That night, she said, she and Armandt slept on the chartered yacht, along with the crew, and Broadhurst and Hart slept on Broadhurst's boat (called *The Last Affair*), tied up in Bimini for repairs. "For appearance's sake they felt better, I guess, that way," she told the reporters. They all returned the next day, she said.

Rice said Hart had told her he was married, "but because of the nature of our acquaintance, I was not at all concerned. I just felt here were these two guys working hard and who had come down here to relax. . . . If I'd thought there was something fishy about it, I'd have been sneaking around. But we were up front. With two smart men like these, if these accusations were true, every precaution would have been taken." Once on that Friday night when she, Armandt and Broadhurst were leaving Hart's place by the rear exit, she said, "I did think, 'I wonder what anyone would think of this if they see it?' But I wasn't really concerned because it didn't seem to concern [Hart], and he's the one running for president. . . . If he didn't have a problem with it then, hey, I didn't.''

Calmly, she answered all the tough questions straightforwardly:

"Have you slept with Gary Hart?"

"No."

"Do you want to?"

"No."

"Has he ever asked?"

"No."

Rice confirmed that Hart had phoned her "several times" after the Bimini trip, and when Broadhurst invited Armandt to Washington to discuss the job, she "decided to come along." Armandt flew to Washington earlier that Friday, and she and Broadhurst met Rice when she arrived, she said. "It was a purely innocent visit on both our parts," she said. "I wasn't concerned because it was innocent."

Rather than spending Friday night and most of Saturday in Hart's town house, Rice said, she, Armandt and Broadhurst had gone there for only about an hour Friday night and then had gone over to Broadhurst's, where he, a noted cook, made them all dinner of steak, artichokes and corn. She had then driven back to Hart's house with the senator to retrieve an address book she had left by his phone, with Broadhurst and Armandt following in his car. Broadhurst pulled into the garage and the three of them left Hart alone in his house, exited through the garage and returned in Broadhurst's car to his house. There, she said, she and Armandt shared a bed for the night. Broadhurst's wife was out of town.

On Saturday morning, Rice said, "we all just lazed around—Gary was working on a speech at his house." Later, she said, she walked over to Hart's house to deliver a manila envelope at Broadhurst's request. This detail seemed to square with the speech preparations described later by Tully—drafts being telecopied to Broadhurst's house and then sent to Hart—with Donna Rice the messenger, unknown to the campaign people in Denver.

Shortly afterward, Rice continued, Broadhurst and Armandt again drove over to Hart's, picked up Hart and Rice and set off on a leisurely motor tour of suburban Alexandria and Mount Vernon that afternoon. This departure apparently had been missed by the *Herald* stakeout. The purpose of the tour, Rice went on, "was to show us around Washington and let Lynn get a feel for what those areas are like." At one point, she said, she and Armandt went into a delicatessen and bought sandwiches for lunch. When they got back to Capitol Hill, she said, they watched the Kentucky Derby on television at Broadhurst's and then went to Hart's place for barbecued chicken, parking in the garage at the back.

The Alexandria tour suggested another gaping hole in the *Herald* stakeout. Several days later, the *Herald* ran a story reporting that Brian Smith, the staff photographer, who had followed one car on Saturday afternoon to a church where a man and woman got out and had reported his tail was a "false alarm," appeared to have followed the wrong car. But the admission came well after the political damage to Hart had taken its toll.

During the evening, Rice said, she and Hart stepped outside for a breath of fresh air and Hart spotted a man wearing a parka on the street, a fact that disturbed him because it was not cold out. "He was very concerned," Rice said. "He said he thought he had a tail, that someone was watching him. He started acting very funny. He had said he needed something out of his car. We were not arm in arm. He noticed someone up ahead looking back at us and he pointed him out to me. I saw a man in a dark parka get into a car on the other side of the park. We walked around the block, then we saw the same car. He [Hart] said, 'My God! They're staking me out.' " He hustled her back inside the town house, she said. "He must have grabbed my arm to speed me up. The whole thing was so bizarre. I couldn't believe it was happening."

Inside, she said, Hart was upset. He decided he had to go out and confront the people who were "spying" on him. He went out and came back shaken, she said. He told the others to return to Broadhurst's, which they did by way of the rear exit to Broadhurst's car in the garage. She spent Saturday night at Broadhurst's again and was to fly back to Miami Sunday. Instead, she met Sue Casey at Dulles Airport, returning to Miami with Casey on Monday in time for the interview with the Miami based reporters.

Rice's disclosure of the Bimini trip hit the Hart insiders hard. In all their conversations with Hart since his confrontation with the *Herald* stakeout team, when they were all scrambling to keep him afloat, he had never mentioned it. Dixon particularly was jolted. He told Shore he was quitting the campaign. Emerson, however, knowing that action would further devastate the campaign, persuaded him in effect simply to leave Washington quietly and go into hiding. Dixon agreed, returning to his apartment in Denver and not answering the phone, while Emerson covered for him.

Meanwhile, Hart remained out of sight in Washington on Monday. A campaign event for northern New Jersey was canceled as the candidate was reported to be preparing for his speech the next day before the newspaper publishers. The economics speech that had been in preparation for several days now seemed of little moment, as the evening news shows featured Donna Rice's disclosure of the trip to Bimini and more details about her: a Phi Beta Kappa graduate of the University of South Carolina, a former Ms. South Carolina– World beauty queen and swimsuit and poster model, an aspiring television actress making ends meet by selling baby formula and gynecological products to doctors in South Florida for a pharmaceutical company.

The inadvertent timing of Hart's appearance before the ANPA convention in one way was disastrous. But in another it offered him the ideal forum if he hoped to turn the story back on the American press as a prime example of journalistic excess and character assassination. He decided to seize the opportunity and try to tough out the political crisis. That Hart needed such a diversion to have any chance of survival at all was now abundantly clear to his strategists in Denver, who on Monday were calling supporters around the country to assess the political damage within the Hart camp. The reaction among men, Tully said later, was that Hart had been "stupid"; among women, that the episode disqualified him as far as they were concerned.

This reaction among the women put more pressure on Lee Hart, still at home nursing the sinus infection. The campaign strategists desperately wanted her now to join her husband. On Tuesday the swelling had begun to go down and she told Trippi to advise the campaign strategists at the Denver headquarters that she wanted to go East. But she also called some of her women friends, some of whom argued with her, Trippi said, that she should "make him come to you." It might even help him politically to do so, some of them said, and she told Trippi that they might be right. In the end, however, the campaign heavyweights prevailed and preparations were made for her to make a statement and be interviewed by a limited group of reporters in Denver Wednesday morning and then fly to New Hampshire to join her husband.

In New York, Hart's Tuesday appearance before the newspaper publishers now took on the dimensions of a presidential speech. Television network cameras jammed the back of the Waldorf-Astoria ballroom and a host of political reporters stood behind the sea of lunch tables. More than a thousand publishers of the nation's major and minor newspapers and their wives sat in anticipation of the most important confrontation ever with the candidate of a presidential campaign suddenly forced so prematurely onto the public consciousness.

Hart plunged into the controversy full speed ahead, going onto the attack against the *Herald*:

"Last weekend, a newspaper published a misleading and false story that hurt my family and other innocent people and reflected badly on my own character. This story was written by reporters who, by their own admission, undertook a spotty surveillance, reached inaccurate conclusions based on incomplete facts; who after publishing a false story, now concede they may have gotten it wrong; and who most outrageously refused to interview the very people who could have given them the facts before filing their story, which we asked and urged them to do. It is now nonetheless being repeated by others as if it were true."

This contention that the *Herald* stakeout team had refused to interview the two women involved did not, obviously, square with the reporters' account, in which they repeatedly sought and even pleaded for an opportunity to talk with them.

"For twenty-eight years," Hart went on, "I have been married to my wife, Lee, a woman with an inexhaustible reservoir of affection, caring and patience. We've survived separations, and today our marriage is stronger. We've also experienced a level of examination, scrutiny and testing, including deeply personal questions asked by total strangers, that could only be considered normal in the most public of lives. . . . Did I make a mistake by putting myself in circumstances that could be misconstrued? Of course I did. That goes without saying. But did I do anything immoral? I absolutely did not. . . ."

Hart observed that even the "most commonplace and appropriate conduct can be misconstrued by some to be improper," and accordingly, "that just means I will have to raise my own standard of conduct higher."

In a question-and-answer session after the speech, Hart explained the Bimini excursion as a mere inspection trip of Broadhurst's boat under repair there in which they were joined "by two or three friends of his," though Donna Rice had said in her interview the day before that Hart had called her and invited her, and she then had asked Lynn Armandt to go along. He repeated the defense that the party had to stay overnight in Bimini because the Customs office was closed, although a Customs official had since said no Customs clearance had been necessary.

Asked about the phone conversations with Rice, Hart sought to leave the impression that they concerned ways she could help in fund-raising in the entertainment business and that some of them were return calls in response to some she had made to him.

In the foyer outside the hotel ballroom, an even more intense Q-and-A session got under way as soon as Hart finished. Reporters and cameramen, most of them from the New York press corps famed for an aggressiveness that would make Roman paparazzi look like shrinking violets, crowded around Tom Fiedler, the *Miami Herald* political editor. Relentlessly, they grilled him about the stakeout, vying with each other to see who could be the most obnoxious. Some hammered at him to "admit" that the *Herald* had accused Hart of adultery. Calmly and steadfastly, he denied the allegation and refused to characterize Hart's behavior and his relationship with Rice, other than to answer to repeated harassing that the *Herald*'s investigation showed that it was "not political." Now that Hart had spoken to the publishers, the large press corps that was now on the story pressed for a news conference. At first Kevin Sweeney, Hart's press secretary, said there would be none, but then it was decided to bite the bullet. The strategists agreed, Emerson said later, that Hart would have to hold a "Ferraro-type press conference"—meaning an open-ended session until all questions were asked, as Geraldine Ferraro had done in 1984 on questions of her husband's financial dealings. The Hart press conference was finally scheduled for the next day at Dartmouth College in Hanover, New Hampshire, where he was slated to make a foreign-policy address, and reporters scurried for plane reservations.

That night at the Sheraton Centre Hotel in midtown Manhattan, Hart spoke at an expensive fund-raiser. Out of either loyalty or curiosity, a packed house showed up and heard him make another combative defense of his conduct. In fact, he went far beyond a personal defense, attacking unnamed politicians who, not being able to compete on the issues, go after an opponent on personal grounds.

Describing his campaign as a "crusade," Hart said with some stridency: "It doesn't matter if the leader is struck down in battle or with a knife in the back, because the cause goes on and the crusade continues." He went on to castigate a process that permitted practitioners of "old traditional politics . . .

more interested in playing what we call hardball . . . [who will] assassinate someone's character just so they can get to the top." And, finally, he brought cheers to the crowd by saying defiantly, "I may bend, but I don't break." The clear impression he left was that he was not going to be hounded out of the presidential race.

Despite reports already reaching New York from Denver that the campaign was falling apart, aides at the fund-raiser insisted that the crisis would be contained and Hart would be able to press on. Hart, for his part, said he was not going to bend to the conventional protocols of politics simply for appearances' sake. He was not going to use his wife by having her fly East to be with him, just to quiet his critics, he said. Aides told doubting reporters that Lee Hart really did have a serious sinus infection that was keeping her in Denver.

But as Hart made these remarks, the preparations for Lee's trip East, and a departing press interview, went forward. On Tuesday night at the house, Trippi conducted a rehearsal for the interview, grilling Lee on the gamut of personal questions she was likely to face regarding her relationship with Gary. At first it was considered having the campaign heavyweights—Haddon, Tully and others—go out to the house to put her through the jumps, but she rejected that idea. It would not look good, leaving the impression that a small army of campaign operatives had come in to tell her what to say. She knew what she wanted to say about her husband, she told Trippi—that he had told her the truth.

The other thing that Lee Hart was sure about was that she was not going to give the horde of reporters, cameramen and photographers who had laid siege to her house the satisfaction of having their long encampment yield anything. In an elaborate subterfuge, Trippi arranged for a host of Lee's friends to come out to the house Tuesday night for a pizza dinner. Then they all left, loudly saying goodbye to Lee and Andrea, who in the darkness had climbed into Trippi's van and were whisked off for the airport undetected.

On Wednesday morning, Lee dutifully held the interview with a few selected reporters in a private room at Stapleton Airport. "I know Gary better than anyone else, and when Gary says nothing happened, nothing happened," she said. ". . . One thing I know especially about my husband, he does not lie. . . . In all honesty, if it doesn't bother me, I don't think it should bother anyone else. . . . I do not ask Gary what he is doing every moment of his life, nor does he ask me. . . . My support is as strong today as I have always given to him." But then she added: "If I could have planned his weekend schedule, I think I would have scheduled it differently." And she lambasted the *Miami Herald*. "I think there has been a tremendous breach in journalistic ethics in the way this story was printed in the first place," she said. "That is something that I personally find outrageous. . . ."

After the interview, Lee, Trippi and Linda Spangler boarded a private Lear jet and headed for New Hampshire, arriving at the small airport in Lebanon as Hart was making his Dartmouth foreign-affairs speech. By prearrangement, Lee was taken to a room at the Hanover Inn on the Dartmouth campus, where Hart went immediately after the speech, and moments before the scheduled press conference, for his first face-to-face meeting with his wife since the beginning of the whole fiasco.

En route to Lebanon, Lee told Trippi her own plan of how best to handle her arrival. She proposed that Hart actually go to the press conference but before taking questions tell the assembled reporters that he had just learned she had arrived and was waiting for him upstairs. He would say he wanted to go up to see her for a few minutes before he started the press conference, and would be right back. Then, when Hart went up to the room, she told Trippi, she would take out her makeup kit and paint a big black eye on her husband. Then he would turn around and walk back into the press conference, proclaiming, "She loves me!" And then, on cue, she would run into the press conference and give him a big hug.

Lee, Trippi insisted later, was deadly serious in making this bizarre proposal, and he frankly thought it was "a really neat idea," that it might inject just a touch of levity into what otherwise would be an extremely uptight situation. On arrival at the Lebanon airport, Trippi got on the phone to the resident campaign wise men in Denver with Lee's brainstorm. "The response back was, 'Joe, that's a picture that's going to be around for a long time.' " The remark indicated to Trippi that the folks in Denver were still thinking in terms of the campaign being salvageable.

In any event, Hart went directly to the room where Lee was waiting before he went to the press conference. In the room with her were Trippi and Spangler, and the moment Hart opened the door, they hurried out and closed the door behind them. All Trippi heard him say on the way out was, "Hi, babe." Trippi hadn't had a chance to tell Lee that the reaction at the Denver headquarters to her "black-eye caper" was very negative, so he went down to the press conference not knowing whether or not Hart would come in sporting the phony shiner.

He didn't. Instead, he walked in wearing a serious, even somber expression. Lee was not with him. The site was a lounge on the ground floor of the Hanover Inn. Reporters crowded into chairs arranged in a wide arc in the center of the room, with some sitting on sofas along the side. There then ensued what was probably the most tense and personally inquisitional news conference any presidential candidate in the nation's history had ever faced. Earlier, Sweeney had conducted a brief press conference preparation session with Hart, asking him questions he thought would come up, including whether he had ever had extramarital affairs in the past. Hart said in this rehearsal that he didn't have to answer such a question.

Hart began by saying that he did not mean to impugn the motives of anyone nor did he want to get into a battle with the press, but he would continue to fight for "fairness and . . . accurate disclosure of the facts" in the whole matter. "I have nothing to hide," he repeated. "I made a mistake, I made a serious mistake, in fact," that he regretted. But the *Herald* was wrong in several important aspects, he said. The reporters did not confront him, he said, "I confronted them," and rather than walking aimlessly about the neighborhood, as they had written, "what I was doing was finding them. . . . I knew they were out there, and I had known someone was surveilling me and my home for some time."

Second, he said, he answered all their questions, and third, the stakeout had missed the comings and goings "in broad daylight" of his weekend companions. Finally, he said, Broadhurst had offered the reporters a chance to talk to "his guests" at his home "if they would not publish their story until talking to them . . . and depending on what kinds of questions they wanted to ask. . . ." But for reasons best known to the reporters, he said, they declined.

Asked what his actions said about his judgment, Hart launched into a long answer about judgments all public officials are called upon to make, in both their public and private lives. They should be evaluated on the basis of all those judgments, he said; some make "decisions to go to cemeteries in Germany" —an obvious reference to President Reagan's controversial Bitburg visit. He proceeded to cite his own voting record in the Senate that should be taken into consideration in assessing his judgment.

Asked about the weekend with Donna Rice, Hart said that both he and his wife had many friends of the opposite sex with whom they often had dinner and there was nothing unusual or untoward about it. "If I had intended a relationship with this woman," he said, "believe me, I have written spy novels. I am not stupid. If I had wanted to bring someone into a house, an apartment, meet with a woman in secret, I wouldn't have done it this way."

Hart up to this point gave no indication that he would do anything but hang tough. He answered all the questions directly and in a strong voice. When asked how he could convince political leaders that he would not be guilty of similar mistakes in judgment in the future, he replied flatly: "By not doing it. . . . I'll demonstrate it by appealing to the voters on the issues that they care about. . . . As time goes on, people are going to want to know about your judgment and your character on the issues that affect their lives, their family and their nation. That's what this campaign is going to be about. As we go on and I demonstrate that kind of leadership, and this story gets proper perspective, I'll be able to demonstrate that."

A few minutes later into the news conference, however, came a series of questions that guaranteed that the story, in a historical sense, would never fade. A *Washington Post* reporter, Paul Taylor, had this unprecedentedly personal exchange with a presidential candidate:

Q. Senator, in your remarks yesterday you raised the issue of morality and you raised the issue of truthfulness. Let me ask you what you mean when you talk about morality, and let me be very specific. I have a series of questions about it. When you said you did nothing immoral, did you mean that you had no sexual relationships with Donna Rice last weekend or at any other time you were with her?

A. That is correct, that's correct.

Q. Do you believe that adultery is immoral?

A. Yes.

Q. Have you ever committed adultery?

A. Ahhh . . . I do not think that's a fair question.

Q. Well, it seems to me that the question of morality—

A. You can get into some very fine definitions—

Q. —was introduced by you.

A. That's right. That's right.

Q. And it's incumbent upon us to know what your definition of morality is.

A. Well, it includes adultery.

Q. So that you believe adultery is immoral.

A. Yes, I do.

Q. Have you ever committed adultery?

A. I do not know—I'm not going into a theological definition of what constitutes adultery. In some people's minds it's people being married and having relationships with other people, so . . .

Q. Can I ask you whether you and your wife have an understanding about whether or not you can have relationships, you can have sexual encounters with—

A. My inclination is to say, no, you can't ask me that question, but the answer is no, we don't have any such understanding. We have an understanding of faithfulness, fidelity and loyalty.

Another reporter, Tom Oliphant of the *Boston Globe*, tried another tack:

Q. Except for the times you and your wife were separated, has your marriage been monogamous?

A. I . . . do not need to answer that question.

Until now, Hart had demonstrated remarkable emotional control, considering the aggressiveness and personal nature of the questions. Finally, when asked what specifically had been the mistake to which he admitted, he repeated that he had engaged in activities from which wrong conclusions could be drawn. But he wasn't the only one in the episode to have made mistakes, he said. Then he let his feelings out for the first time:

"Look, folks, there is something called fairness in our society. . . . Now I'm going through this, and I will continue to. I will answer questions. I'm doing my best and I'll continue to do my best. But as I said yesterday, there's a broader issue here than what I did and what I didn't do, and that is whether the system of electing national leaders is fair or not. Now I'm going to insist that this be a fair system. You can ask me about adultery, you can ask me any question you want. And believe me, my wife and I have answered more personal questions than anybody in public life, and we'll probably have to continue to, to my regret. But I am going to demand that the system be fair, and I have a right to demand it. And if somebody's going to follow me around, they better follow me around, and they better print all the facts."

At the end, asked about his remarks about a "knife in the back" and character assassination by old-style politicians at the previous night's fund-raiser, Hart again suggested the broad allegation that had gotten him into trouble in the first place—that his opponents were trying to do him in. While denying he was charging anyone with anything, he said he was talking about the system of selecting leaders. "I said there were those . . . who believe the way you get to the top is to tear down others," he said. ". . . That is not the way you win, and it is not what the American people want. It is old politics, and you don't get to the top by tearing other people down."

Regarding that judgment, the 1988 presidential campaign in time would prove how thoroughly wrong Hart was. He went on:

"I was trying to reflect my own kind of philosophy of politics, which is that old-style politics, which is to destroy your enemy is the best way to win, is not going to work anymore. Because I believe the people working in this campaign are not working for me. They're working for something bigger and more important. Even if I'm not here they're going to continue on, and that's what I encourage them to do."

Well, did he believe somebody was trying to destroy his campaign? "No," he said. But Hart would have a bit more to say on that subject in just a couple of days. With that, the news conference ended and Hart, still grim-faced but in control, walked out and back up to the room where his wife waited.

The interrogation he had just endured would have been unheard-of only a few years earlier. That he was asked point-blank whether he had ever committed adultery was a measure of how important the perception of a candidate's character had become in the press's mind—and how the new breed of political reporter viewed its responsibilities. The fact that Hart had refused to answer on that point did not detract from a remarkably gritty performance by a politician under extreme political pressure. But the overriding question for him was not whether he was tough, but whether he was believable, and whether he could still restore his crippled candidacy.

After a few minutes alone in the room, Gary and Lee Hart came out together, hand in hand, and went downstairs to an awaiting car. He got behind the wheel, she sat next to him, and alone, off they drove the sixty-two miles to the next campaign event, in Littleton, north of Hanover, where the crush of reporters and cameramen created near panic in the crowd, and a young child was nearly trampled. It had already been announced to the traveling press that Hart was cutting short his New Hampshire swing and would be returning to Denver after one more day in the state. Now the futility of attempting to continue on the campaign trail with the focus remaining on the candidate's personal life began to sink in.

Two motels were used to house the traveling party, one for the press in Littleton and another just across the border in Vermont for the Harts and campaign aides, except for Sweeney, who stayed with the press corps. The Harts and the ranking aides sat at two tables in the motel restaurant and had a late—

and surprisingly relaxed—dinner. The Harts obviously had had all the intimate conversation between them required by events and they joined in the general discussion, often lighthearted. Lee regaled her table with accounts of dodging the reporters at Troublesome Gulch and how daughter Andrea nearly punched out a reporter who sought to interrogate her outside one of her college classes in Denver.

Hart, who had been told by Lee earlier that everything was fine in Denver, seemed to Trippi to be startled and unnerved by hearing all this. On top of the chaos of the day he had just endured, Hart was getting an additional message of the price to be paid if he continued. So, at one point, he finally said to those at his table, Trippi recalled, "Maybe we should just all go home." If this was what it was going to be like from now on, he said, it was senseless. He observed that he had spoken to a hundred people at the Littleton event and not one of them asked him a question about his personal situation. They asked him about arms control and other such issues, he said, but he knew without looking that the television news shows would use none of it. If he couldn't get his message across, what was the sense of it?

Hart picked up his schedule for the next day, and he asked no one in particular, why was he doing this event and that event? Sue Casey, the scheduler, tried to reason with him, but he was adamant. He asked for ideas on how he could get the campaign back to the issues. Trippi suggested that the campaign buy half an hour of television time at which he would first explain what had happened and then get on to the issues. It would have a huge audience, Trippi suggested, and thus he could talk directly to the American people without going through the filter of the press. Hart seemed interested, but Casey pointed out that as soon as he went off the air, the network anchormen would be on with their own analysts discussing questions he didn't answer, thus giving the story more life. Hart's enthusiasm seemed to plummet.

Somebody else suggested that the campaign continue, doing only large-crowd events, with Hart speaking on the issues only and then getting into a car and moving on. The news media would have no recourse but to write and air what he had said on the issues. Somebody else knocked that one down. Soon it became even more apparent to Hart that he was at a dead end. He finally got up from the table, and as they all walked out, said: "Let's go home."

Trippi said later it was obvious to him at that moment that the campaign was over. The first time Hart said those words, he recalled, he thought Hart meant only that he and his aides go back to Denver for a few days and regroup. But the second time he said it, Trippi said, "it was clear to me that we were out of the race. To convince him otherwise would mean we would be riding a dead man. It was gone. There was no fire. We might be able to go another three weeks, but he would never be able to get back on the saddle."

The true believers like Shore and Casey refused to hear it that way. Some told Trippi they knew Hart and were sure he only meant going back to Denver, or even going to his motel room for the night. Individuals took Hart's "Let's go home'' as they chose to. In a conference call to Denver shortly afterward, Trippi, Casey and Shore tried in their separate ways to convey the sense of the dinner conversation to Emerson, Tully and others. Emerson at first tried to get into a discussion of the next week's schedule, as Trippi sought to convey that in his view, anyway, there wasn't going to be any next week. Emerson pressed Trippi not to be so negative and tried to continue with the schedule review. In the midst of all this, Emerson's other phone rang. It was Kevin Sweeney calling from the motel where the press was staying. Emerson said he had to deal with another problem and he'd call Trippi and the others back.

What Sweeney was calling about proved to be the last straw. Taylor of the *Post* had contacted him at the motel in Littleton shortly before 11 P.M., New Hampshire time, with yet another account of a Hart liaison with another woman. The *Post* had checked out the information and identified the other woman. The meeting was said to have taken place in a Washington town house on the previous December 20 with a woman with whom Hart had had a long-standing relationship. A man not identified had hired a detective to tail Hart on the suspicion the senator was having an affair with his wife, and Hart was traced to the house of another woman. The *Post* had obtained the name of the woman and pictures of Hart leaving her town house and, through a separate source, had obtained an acknowledgment from her, Sweeney was told. The reporter told Sweeney he wanted an interview with Hart to discuss the new material.

Sweeney's phone call confirmed the worst fears of the Denver brain trust. When the questions about adultery had come at the Hanover news conference from responsible reporters of responsible publications, Tully said later, his immediate concern was that they were in the context of something else, not yet known to the campaign. Now he knew.

"That was all she wrote," Tully said. But even before word of the *Post* story came, he said, he realized the campaign was faced with having to decide whether Hart would get out "with blood in his veins, or out as dogmeat."

The Denver advisers telephoned Shore, the aide closest personally to Hart on the campaign trip, and told him Sweeney had been instructed to tell Taylor that Hart was asleep and would be told in the morning. The *Post* would be given an exclusive interview with him then on the condition that the story not be published until the interview had taken place. Shore hung up and went to Hart's room to break the news. Hart had had enough. It was never going to end, he told Shore; let's go home right away. He was insistent on getting a plane and heading back to Denver. Sweeney was told to get over to Hart's motel, where he found the candidate writing a statement on a yellow legal pad.

Shore, shocked, tried to hold on. He told the other campaign aides on the scene that they all were tired and they could beat the thing. Some of the other longtime Hart aides wanted to believe him, but Hart himself was having no part of it now. The small jet that had brought Lee to New Hampshire was readied and the Harts and top aides were whisked off shortly after daybreak.

Meanwhile, Trippi and Sweeney went ahead with the morning's schedule, not telling the press that the Harts had already left. At about 7:30, Taylor knocked on Trippi's door demanding his interview with Hart. By this time the Denver strategists had obtained Hart's approval to call Ben Bradlee, the executive editor of the *Washington Post*, and Haddon had phoned him to inquire of the *Post*'s plans for a story, and to request that the woman's name not be used. Bradlee told him no story had been prepared and the *Post* had never intended to publish the woman's name. But, Bradlee said later, "there were no ultimatums, no negotiations. We simply asked to talk to Hart about the information we had gathered."

Trippi held Taylor off, and the campaign motorcade swung out from the motel for the first stop as if the candidate were aboard. Not until the party arrived at the appointed plant gate in the town of Groveton, and Sweeney and Trippi climbed up on a park bench and began distributing copies of Hart's statement, did the traveling reporters realize what was going on. Cries of "He's getting out! He's getting out!" filled the crisp early morning air as reporters raced to private homes to commandeer telephones.

Hart's statement, however, suggested he was returning to Denver only until things cooled down. "While running for president is important," it said, "right now my family is more important. Lee and I are returning to Denver, to our home and our family. We are going to take a few days, or a few weeks, to be together. This campaign will continue and our cause will succeed."

Back in Denver, however, the campaign heavyweights knew the ball game was over. Their soundings around the country had already told them as much, and by the time the Harts arrived at the small Jefferson County Airport northwest of Denver at noon, Denver time, and headed for the aptly named Troublesome Gulch, word was already going out to Hart staffers around the country that their candidate would be announcing his withdrawal from the race the next morning.

That night, Gary and Lee Hart motored into Denver to the campaign headquarters for a private meeting with the loyalists. "Even though this is the shortest presidential campaign in history," he told them, "we made an impact that will not be taken lightly or forgotten by the American people. Idealism is a flame that continuously flickers within each one of you. Because you have that within you, you will carry that on and pass it to further generations."

On Friday morning, at the Executive Inn in downtown Denver, Hart brought to an end one of the most tumultuous if brief presidential campaigns in American political history—not with a whimper, but with a bang.

"I intended, quite frankly, to come down here this morning and read a short, carefully worded political statement saying that I was withdrawing from the race, and then quietly disappear from the stage," he began. "And then, after frankly tossing and turning all night, as I have for the last three or four nights, I woke up about four or five this morning with a start. And I said to myself, 'Hell, no!' And I'm not going to do that because it's not my style and because I'm a proud man, and I'm proud of what I've accomplished."

At the words "Hell, no!" young diehard supporters in the audience erupted with cheers, obviously interpreting the remark to mean that he had changed his mind and was not getting out of the race after all. But Hart brusquely silenced them. "Let's hold down the applause, thank you," he said. "I appreciate it, but let's get through this."

He proceeded to talk about anger—his own, his children's and "a lot of angry and confused voters out around the country." He was never very good at talking about himself and about playing the political game, he said, and he never felt that the voters much cared. "They're smart enough to know who you are without you telling them," he said. "You look them in the eye and you talk to them and they decide whether you're telling the truth or not. So I haven't spent a lot of time and effort trying to create an image. I am who I am—take it or leave it."

The bitterness was beginning to leak out now. Hart went on to argue that he wasn't a conventional politician looking for the support of other conventional politicians. Most of them, he said, "wait to see how political events are breaking before risking their political capital." What all this meant, he went on, was "that I guess I've become some kind of a rare bird, some extraordinary creature that has to be dissected by those who analyze politics to find out what makes them tick. Well, I resist that. And so, then, I become cool and aloof or elusive or enigmatic or whatnot. And then the more people want to talk about me, the more I resist it, and so on. And so it gets to be like the cat chasing its tail."

So far, so good. Hart was putting into words publicly what his advisers had often heard as he champed at being put under a microscope by the news media. But he went beyond that. This focus on himself, he said now, was making him the issue "and I cannot be the issue, because that breaks the link between me and the voters. . . . If someone's able to throw up a smoke screen and keep it there long enough, you can't get your message across. You can't raise the money to finance a campaign; there's too much static, and you can't communicate."

Hart seemed to be saying that nothing mattered in the choice of a president other than his position on the issues. And who was the someone who was throwing up a smoke screen? Calling the trouble in which he had found himself a "smoke screen" certainly minimized it and suggested that some kind of false charge had been made against him. As for those allegations of deceit that were at the core of the "womanizing" stories, Hart had nothing to say, other than to declare that "clearly under present circumstances, this campaign cannot go on. I refuse to submit my family and my friends and innocent people and myself to further rumors and gossip," he said. "It's simply an intolerable situation." But more than rumors and gossip were involved, as had already become clear—and would become even clearer soon.

Finally, Hart in his anger sought to lay the blame on the political system of choosing national leaders, and on the news media. ". . . It reduces the press of this nation to hunters and presidential candidates to being hunted," he complained. It is a system, he went on, "that has reporters in bushes; false and inaccurate stories printed; swarms of helicopters hovering over our roof, and my very strong wife close to tears because she can't even get in her own house at night without being harassed. And then after that, ponderous pundits wondering in mock seriousness why some of the best people in this country choose not to run for high office."

Hart, whose own actions had brought disillusionment to so many of his idealistic young followers, called on "those talented people who supported me to insist that this system be changed. Too much of it is just a mockery, and if it continues to destroy people's integrity and honor, then that system will eventually destroy itself." But, he said in closing, "the events of this week should not deter any of you who are idealistic young people from moving on and moving up." To them, he said, "the torch of idealism burns bright in your hearts. It should lead you into public service and national service. It should lead you to want to make this country better. And whoever you are and what you do in that cause, at least in spirit, I will be with you."

The Hart swan song was an incredible exercise in self-justification and self-delusion. According to aides later, his decision to lash out at the press and at the political system itself was sparked, in part at least, by an early morning phone call from his friend Warren Beatty, who urged him not to go out without a blast at all those who had done him in.

Some of those who heard the farewell inevitably recalled Richard Nixon's infamous "last press conference" in Los Angeles in November 1962 after having lost the gubernatorial election to Democrat Pat Brown. In it, he promised the assembled reporters that they wouldn't "have Dick Nixon to kick around anymore"—only one of countless promises Nixon subsequently welshed on. But Hart insisted after the election that he did not intend in his own withdrawal news conference to attack the press or blame others for his problems. "I thought then, and I think just as strongly now," he said, "that if candidates are surveilled by news organizations or anybody else, there'll be a lot of people won't run for office. And I think that's important to America. That's all I was saying."

The political impact of the Hart collapse was predictable. A survey by WBZ-TV of Boston and the *Boston Herald* on the night before the Hanover "adultery" press conference indicated that among four hundred likely Democratic voters in the 1988 New Hampshire primary, he had fallen from a 32 percent tie with Michael Dukakis to 27–17 behind him. Other later polls with Hart out projected Jesse Jackson, as the best known of the remaining candidates, into the lead, and speculation resumed once more that Governor Mario Cuomo or New Jersey's Senator Bill Bradley might get into the race after all.

It remained for the *National Enquirer*, the nation's best known gossip newspaper, to apply the finishing touches. In its June 2 edition it ran a picture on the cover of Donna Rice, glass in hand and arm wrapped around Hart's shoulder, sitting on his lap on a pier, presumably on Bimini. Hart wore a T-shirt that said "Monkey Business Crew"—and a smile. "Gary Hart Asked Me to Marry Him,'' the headline on the cover said. Inside, another color photo showed Hart, Rice, Armandt and Broadhurst clowning on the bandstand of a Bimini nightclub. The source of the photos was not disclosed.*

At last the story of Gary Hart's political fall was over. But in the aftermath a controversy continued over the journalistic ethics involved—in delving into a candidate's personal life, putting him under surveillance, asking him such blunt questions. Columnists and editors at the *New York Times* particularly threw themselves into the debate.

In a May 5 editorial, the *Times* had written that "a candidate's private morality may or may not be fair grounds for judging fitness for office, but a candidate's judgment is surely fair game." This was especially so, the editorial said, when he had invited a tail on himself. "Reporters once treated candidates' 'personal' indiscretions discreetly," it concluded. "No longer, and that's to the good. Beyond the proper, debatable bounds of privacy, the public needs to know as much about a candidate as possible."

On the same day, however, *Times* columnist Anthony Lewis wrote: "When I read about the *Miami Herald* story on Gary Hart, I felt degraded in my profession. Is that what journalism is about, hiding in a van outside a politician's home? Is it 'investigative reporting' to write that a woman may have spent the night there—or may not, since we're not sure we watched all the doors? . . . Are we more hypocritical now than we used to be? Perhaps. But the real difference is that we no longer let politicians have a private life. We insist on knowing all. The loss of respect for privacy has exacted a terrible price in American politics. When anyone who runs for President knows that intimate details of his or her life will be shouted to the world, what sensitive person would run? . . . The way we choose Presidents is a national disgrace and a cause of international concern. That is not the press' fault. But the *Miami Herald* stakeout of Gary Hart shows how the press can make it worse."

The next day, the *Times*, commenting editorially about criticism of the gap in the *Herald*'s surveillance, wrote that "if the execution was less than perfect, the *Herald*'s pursuit of this story was eminently justified. There is a line between reasonable reporting and intrusive invasion of privacy—and it shines brightly here."

The next day, though, *Times* columnist and former executive editor A. M. Rosenthal wrote: "I did not become a newspaperman to hide outside a politician's house trying to find out whether he was in bed with somebody." He criticized the *Miami Herald* for the surveillance and for printing the story so hurriedly against a deadline.

A few days later, *Times* columnist William Safire wrote that if he had been asked the adultery question, his answer would have been "Go to hell." He argued that neither the media nor the government has a right to expect an answer

---

*Speculation again centered on Armandt. Tom Fiedler said he was convinced the source of the photos was not his anonymous caller.

to such personal questions, and he called on other journalists "to blaze away at keyhole journalism." The *Post*'s Taylor, who had asked the adultery question, defended himself in a letter to the editor of the *Times*, saying all he did was "ask Gary Hart the question he asked for."

Meanwhile, as the *Times* seemed to be engaged in an intrafamily argument over the whole ethics question, the newspaper was undertaking to survey all prospective Democratic and Republican presidential candidates on their views about the adultery question. Each was asked whether he considered adultery to be a legitimate campaign issue and one of voter concern and how he thought Hart had handled the situation. Who could argue with those innocuous questions? But then the *Times* posed these twin masterpieces of artfulness: (1) "How should a hypothetical presidential candidate who has not committed adultery answer the question 'Have you ever committed adultery?' " (2) "How should a hypothetical presidential candidate who has committed adultery answer the same question?" Far be it for the *New York Times* to sink so low as to ask the candidates directly. The answers were varied, but most of the candidates in one fashion or another, and to one degree or another, took Safire's advice, though more politely.

The *Times* at the same time sent a request, through Washington editor Craig Whitney, to each candidate to provide material to help *Times* reporters prepare in-depth profiles. Most major newspapers do that, but the *Times* broke new ground by asking for the candidate's birth certificate, marriage and driver's licenses, high school, college and graduate school transcripts, full employment records, all investments, state and federal income tax returns for the last five years, and all civil and criminal court cases in which the candidate was involved. Each was also asked for lists of his "closest friends in high school and college . . . present friends, business associates, chief advisors and major fund-raisers." Finally, each candidate was asked to waive his privacy right to give *Times* reporters access to FBI or any other law-enforcement agency's "investigative files," all military and medical records, and permission to talk to the candidate's doctors about his medical history.

Of all these requests, none was more incredible than the call for the FBI's raw files, notorious as the repository of all manner of rumor, gossip and accusation, without proof. Most candidates took Safire's advice on this request as well, and accompanying criticism from within the press persuaded the *Times* eventually to drop the request.

A few weeks after his withdrawal, Hart wrote a letter mailed to thousands of his campaign staffers in which at last he put the blame on himself. "Through thoughtlessness and misjudgment I've let each of you down," he wrote. He expressed similar sentiments to old campaign associates and friends in phone conversations. Campaign aides said he had come to regret the harsh nature of his withdrawal statement, especially since it had generated comparisons with Nixon's "last press conference" of 1962.

One who did not think Hart had made a mistake in going down in flame, however, was that self-same Richard Nixon. Three days after Hart's pullout, Nixon wrote him: "What you said about the media needed to be said. . . . They demand to ruthlessly question the ethics of anyone else. But when anyone else dares to question their ethics, they hide behind the shield of freedom of speech."

Nixon told Hart that "I thought you handled a very difficult situation uncommonly well. You inspired your friends and gained respect from your critics—except for those who have totally lost their sense of objectivity and fairness. . . . What impressed me most was your refusal to quit fighting for what you believed. In politics and every other walk of life, there are more losers than winners. After all, there can be only one number one; all the rest are losers. Those who don't win must be given not just sympathy, which is in essence a degrading sentiment for whoever is its recipient, but the inspiration to fight on. You did exactly that."

In other words, Nixon was congratulating Hart for behaving exactly as Nixon would have done. For those who knew Hart's dislike of Nixon, to the point of ridicule, this letter seemed likely to have been the most mocking aspect of the whole affair. But Hart replied with appreciation for "your thoughtful letter," adding: "I'm sure we agree that concerned citizens, leaders and opinion-makers must try to focus national attention away from what is temporal, sensational and irrelevant to the real challenges confronting our nation and world."

Temporal, sensational and irrelevant as Gary Hart might have felt was the public clamor over the womanizing issue that brought him down, it had more to do with affecting the race for the 1988 Democratic presidential nomination than anything else that had occurred up to this time. It had brought down a front-runner—and left confusion, and an unforeseen opportunity in its wake for all the other Democratic contenders.

Four months after Hart's withdrawal, he made a one-hour appearance on ABC News' *Nightline*, reiterating that he had made a "very, very bad mistake" but continuing in less emotional terms his complaint against the news media's encroachment on his privacy. He told his interviewer, Ted Koppel, in what probably was an unprecedented confession for a political figure, that during his twenty-nine-year marriage, including the two separations, he had not been "absolutely faithful" to his wife. But he argued that he hadn't been "running for sainthood" and that other public figures had been found to have private lives as vulnerable to criticism as his. And once again he sought to compare his private sins to what he categorized as the public sins of the Reagan administration. "No laws were broken" in his case, he said. "No papers were shredded. No money changed hands. No one lied to Congress, and all of those things have happened in this administration."

Hart denied a rumor, widely circulated by the television networks weeks earlier, that he was contemplating a return to the 1988 race. What he did intend to do, he said, was speak out on the issues, including the one that had grown out of his own derailed campaign—the right of privacy for public figures, and the damage inflicted by the intrusion thereof. Hart repeated his earlier contention that such intrusion would keep the best people from seeking public office—after having praised the Democratic candidates still vying for their party's nomination, none of whom was deterred from continuing his campaign.

Hart, after having defended his right to privacy throughout the hour, concluded by voluntarily surrendering it with a fawning bit of television theater. Looking directly into the camera, he apologized before millions—not to them but to his own son and daughter, saying "how sorry I am for letting them down." One might have thought that this most private of political figures would have had an opportunity in the previous four months to have expressed that sentiment to them privately—especially since he had gone off on vacation in Ireland with his son during that time. Once again, it was shades of Richard Nixon, that other public figure who never hesitated to use his family in public, as in his infamous 1960 "Checkers" speech. Nixon also complained about invasions of his privacy, while yielding it when it served his political purposes. But he never sought to conduct a national crusade against the encroachments, as Hart seemed to be doing.

What Hart failed to realize in this attempt to maintain a voice in national affairs was that, for the 1988 cycle at least, he had lost all credibility. Perhaps time and his own actions might help rebuild it without a completely debilitating scar. But Gary Hart was out of the picture now, whether he liked it or not, and the quest for the Democratic nomination by the remaining candidates would have to go forward without him. Or so it certainly seemed then.

14

Filling the Vacuum

The self-immolation of Gary Hart caused radical dislocations in the early stages of the competition for the Democratic nomination.

Up to that point, the goal for each of the other Democrats, except perhaps Jesse Jackson, had been essentially the same: to create a situation in which he could be juxtaposed against the front-running Hart and, by so doing, become perceived as the leading alternative to him. That candidate could then rally support from party regulars who had resigned themselves to Hart's nomination but had never been comfortable with the loner from Colorado. It was widely acknowledged within the party that Hart was the leading candidate, but he never would have been described as the preferred candidate.

Now, with Hart eliminated, the first imperative was to establish a pecking order among the seven candidates remaining. With one exception—Jesse Jackson—none of them could claim national stature. And Jackson's status was the one probably least affected by Hart's withdrawal.

Jackson was entering the 1988 competition in a far stronger position than he had enjoyed in his first campaign for the Democratic nomination four years earlier. There was some lingering bitterness toward him on the part of white Democrats who had not forgotten the great show of recalcitrance the civil rights leader had made before finally endorsing Fritz Mondale—and by doing so only on Labor Day weekend, several weeks too late by any politically rational timetable. And there was a broad consensus among southern white politicians that the perception of Mondale being jerked around by Jackson had cost heavily in white votes.

But Jackson's position was clearly strengthened in two respects. First, there was no white candidate in the field with connections to the black community that could remotely rival those of Mondale; on the contrary, most of the other candidates were almost entirely unknown among blacks. Second, only in part because of this lack of an obvious option, Jackson could count on almost universal support among black party leaders this time around. The huge black vote he had polled in 1984 had sent them a message written in large letters: Get on board or risk your own future.

Despite this crystallizing of Jackson's support, there was little inclination early in 1987 in the Democratic Party or political community at large to believe he had a realistic chance to be the nominee. He was a special phenomenon, but the party was not yet ready to nominate a black candidate for president. Nor were the voters ready to accept one. It seemed that simple. As a result, when Hart created a vacuum at the top, the focus turned on two or three white candidates rather than the black leading the opinion polls.

At forty-four, Senator Joseph Biden of Delaware was well known to Washington insiders as the chairman of the Senate Judiciary Committee. He had caused a small ripple in the political world four years earlier—when he briefly flirted with becoming a candidate himself—with a fiery speech, delivered to several party audiences, that combined scolding and exhortation of his fellow Democrats.

Moreover, Biden had been one of the two potential 1988 candidates—Richard Gephardt was the other—who had been most visibly active in laying the foundation for a campaign soon after the 1984 election. Significantly, he had delivered the main speech at the Iowa Democratic Party's Jefferson-Jackson Day dinner in the fall of 1985.

There were, however, questions about what Biden had to say beyond "the speech" and whether he was heavy enough to be taken seriously as a candidate. Some professionals viewed him as a creation of the *enfant terrible* of the

Democratic Party, Patrick Caddell, the political theorist/polling expert who had urged Biden to run four years earlier. And the word filtering back to Washington from Biden's initial forays was cautious.

"He gave a hell of a speech, had everybody hooting and hollering," one southern party professional reported, "but after he left the next morning, nobody could remember what he said that was so terrific."

Gephardt, the forty-six-year-old Missouri congressman, had been following a schedule similar to Biden's, frequently showing up in the same state two or three weeks later. When his speeches were compared with those of his rival from the Senate, he generally got lower marks for style but higher marks for content. Gephardt's prime asset, however, was his reputation among fellow politicians, who liked him personally and admired his skills as an insider player of congressional politics.

The enthusiasm Gephardt evoked among his colleagues in the House of Representatives was particularly striking because it went well beyond the institutional pride that members of the "lower body" might feel in the candidacy of one of their own. Tom Foley of Washington, then the House majority whip and later majority leader, once held forth for nearly an hour on Gephardt in a hotel lobby during an AFL-CIO Executive Board meeting in Bal Harbour, Florida. Foley told how Gephardt got things done in the House because of his willingness to seek common ground with his colleagues, even if it took a dozen meetings to do so.

This was a qualitatively different kind of support from what his colleagues had given another Democratic House member, Morris Udall, in his campaign for the presidential nomination in 1976. That backing was a mixture of equal parts affection for Mo Udall, respect for his personal decency and pride that "one of our boys" from the House of Representatives might make it. With Dick Gephardt, the core of the case was the conviction that he could be a hell of a good president.

Gephardt also entered the campaign in a position unmatched in one important respect by any of his potential rivals. His advocacy of a get-tough trade bill had given him an issue identification none of the others enjoyed—and one with obvious special appeal to Big Labor in general and the politically important United Auto Workers in particular.

The Missouri Democrat was not without some baggage, however. Some professionals were convinced that any candidate from the House, as opposed to the Senate or a governorship, was not taken seriously because he lacked a large constituency as a base and was likely to be politically obscure. Gephardt himself thought this disadvantage was more than overcome by the active support he received from those House colleagues in their districts. But that may have been a case of making a virtue of a necessity, which was something politicians did with remarkable frequency.

There were also specific problems for Gephardt on the awkward abortion issue. Right-to-life groups were still seething at his decision in 1985 to abandon his support for a constitutional amendment banning abortion, and pro-choice Democrats were just as suspicious of the politically fortuitous timing of his change of heart. The seeds of a flip-flop problem had already been sewn.

Gephardt was one of the candidates most directly affected by the Hart collapse. As he put it later, "Our clear goal was to try to get around Gary Hart," particularly with Iowa Democrats. But with no Hart to get around, a new opinion poll put Gephardt ahead there. In the fluidity of Iowa caucus campaigns, such polls didn't mean much, but they did change perceptions. "We went from insurgent to front-runner in one day," Gephardt recalled somewhat ruefully. He had been robbed of the opportunity to score against Hart the kind of upset that Hart had achieved against Walter Mondale in New Hampshire four years earlier.

The other leading figure among the surviving Democrats—inevitably, if unfairly, labeled "the seven dwarfs"—was Michael Dukakis, who had been so highly esteemed as governor of Massachusetts that he was Mondale's fallback choice for a Democratic vice presidential nominee in 1984 if he had been unable to settle on a woman candidate. Dukakis' stature as the leading liberal in the field—Jackson excepted—seemed to be confirmed by the movement to him of such liberal Hart advisers as Paul Tully, the Hart political director; Teresa Vilmain, Hart's Iowa coordinator; and Alice Travis, a party activist from California who had been in charge of nailing down so-called superdelegates to the convention.

Like Gephardt, Dukakis had based his original strategy on running against Hart. "The initial assumption," Dukakis campaign manager Susan Estrich recalled, "was that Hart was the front-runner and the question was who was going to emerge as the alternative to Hart." The Massachusetts governor, his advisers believed, was particularly well positioned because, as Estrich put it, "new ideas was the test" and Dukakis could present himself as one "who made them work" as an executive. If he could make a credible showing in Iowa, the scenario went, Dukakis then would wipe out Hart in New Hampshire, the state that had lifted Hart from obscurity four years earlier.

Dukakis himself was always confident he could defeat Hart. In conversations with his staff, he brushed off Hart as a theorist with no demonstrated capacity to function effectively as an executive—and as a political leader who made his own supporters uneasy about his personal qualities.

There were some reservations and unanswered questions about Dukakis himself. He was, after all, not only another northeastern liberal but an ethnic as well. No one could be quite sure how voters would respond to a Greek-American son of immigrants. There was also the question of Dukakis' political persona. In Massachusetts he had become essentially unbeatable by wearing well, by demonstrating over a long period of time that he was a serious, straight and effective politician who could get things done. But he had never been a candidate who could arouse the electorate overnight with the force of an electric public personality. And in multicandidate fields, a little pizzazz could take you a long way.

The other candidates seemed more remote possibilities in the spring and early summer of 1987.

Senator Albert Gore, Jr., of Tennessee originally had decided to remain on the sidelines. But he changed his mind after a meeting with a group of heavyweight Democratic fund-raisers banded together as IMPAC '88 to find a moderately conservative candidate, for whom they would raise extravagant amounts of money. Gore had a reputation in Congress for expertise on a few issues, not all of it positive in the eyes of some Democrats, and he was considered back home to be an exceptionally effective stump campaigner. But he decided not to compete actively in Iowa, and that decision typed him as the "southern candidate" lying in the weeds in the hopes of ambushing his rivals on Super Tuesday. And, at thirty-nine, Gore seemed to be a more realistic possibility for the vice presidential nomination, a notion that reporters heard frequently from Democrats taking their first look at him.

Senator Paul Simon of Illinois, who had won his seat by defeating Republican incumbent Charles H. Percy only three years earlier, was something of a surprise in the field. In his brief time in the Senate and ten years in the House, Simon had been considered a garden-variety good-instincts liberal with a special interest in education but no reputation as either a leader or power broker. At one point, he had run for chairman of the House Budget Committee—Dick Gephardt agreed to nominate him—and finished an embarrassing third, with only a dozen votes. More recently his image as a classic liberal had been clouded by his support for a constitutional amendment to balance the federal budget and the Gramm-Rudman bill to force annual reductions in the deficit.

There was also some reason to believe Simon had become a candidate principally to stop the man who now had stopped himself, Gary Hart. Early in the year Simon was in the forefront of those urging Senator Dale Bumpers of Arkansas to make the race. Asked why he thought it was so important, Simon quickly ticked off a list of five or six issues on which he believed Bumpers should run. But, it was pointed out to him, Hart held the same position as Bumpers on all those issues. To which, after a pause, Simon replied: "We need someone who is reliable."

After the campaign Simon was somewhat less cryptic on his preference for Bumpers over Hart. "Dale has a commitment to using the tools of government to solve our problems, frankly more than Gary does," he said. "Second, he doesn't wait to take a poll to decide what to do." And Simon acknowledged that one of the factors in his own decision to run was a conversation with pollster Louis Harris in which Harris said of Hart: "I never polled where a front-runner had that many negatives."

Simon's principal asset was the way his personal image seemed to fit the demands of the moment. At fifty-eight, he was the old-fashioned square who had been married to the same woman for twenty-seven years, still wore bow ties and a 1930s haircut. In short, he was the little guy with the big ears whom no one could ever accuse of being the candidate of charisma. A man with a deep, resonant voice, Simon was, as the joke had it, a politician "made for radio" in the television era—but perhaps also made for the circumstances. As Brian Lunde, his campaign manager, put it, "We had, in a sense, the perfect personality for a character-based election."

The other active candidate when Hart left the stage was Bruce Babbitt, the forty-nine-year-old former governor of Arizona who kept assuring everyone, with good reason, that "I'm resigned to being an underdog."

Babbitt was an intelligent and engaging man, but it was hard to find a conventional constituency for him in the universe of Democrats who voted most heavily in caucuses and primaries. He was arguing that the liberals were, as he put it, "risking the destruction of the welfare state" by refusing to face up to the need for strong measures to reduce the federal deficit.

The problem was that the measures he was proposing were anathema to conventional Democratic liberals, although they did win him some devoted supporters who admired him for his candor. Babbitt backed a 5 percent "consumption tax," a kind of sales tax that could be considered regressive, and he supported means tests for entitlement programs including that most sacred of political cows, Social Security.

Unsurprisingly, Babbitt found all these proposals to be a hard sell, but he took comfort in small successes. "It's been a little slow, the message still isn't popular," he said at breakfast in New Hampshire one morning. Then he added cheerfully: "They're saying now, 'He's right even if I'm not ready to accept it.' It's no longer, 'Shoot the messenger.' "

Babbitt was the only candidate in the field addressing the central issue of the federal deficit with much candor. And his inability to break through with his harsh-medicine message told a great deal about the feel-good politics of the time. The deficit, he said later, "doesn't seem to have any real-world implications" for voters. "It's a future issue," he said. "It's a question of 'What about tomorrow? We're doing great today.' . . . It's very tough in the absence of a crisis to talk about putting a little more discipline and direction into our politics."

The only other Democratic presidential possibility to arise during the summer of 1987 was Representative Patricia Schroeder of Colorado, then forty-seven, who had been in the House since 1972. According to her friends, she had been angered by Walter Mondale's failure to consider her as his running mate when he chose Geraldine Ferraro in 1984. Schroeder disclosed in June that she intended over the summer to test the prospects of running a campaign based on the thesis that after Ronald Reagan, the nation was ready for "a rendezvous with reality."

"I'm not going to do this just to make a statement," she said. "I can do that right now in the House."

Schroeder's tentative offering found few takers, however, and by September she was obliged to abandon the campaign in a tearful public announcement in Denver that caused no little wincing among feminist colleagues.

The absence of any obvious replacement for Hart produced some entirely predictable speculation about greener grass elsewhere. Much of it centered on Mario Cuomo, the second-term governor of New York who had brought himself so forcefully to national attention with his speech at the 1984 Democratic convention in San Francisco.

But the notion that Cuomo might be induced into the race after what happened to Hart was a misreading of the New Yorker. He was one of those rare politicians who grow increasingly thin-skinned during their careers in public life. And the hounding by the press that finally drove Hart out of the campaign was just the kind of thing Cuomo found most noxious—not because he had anything to hide in his personal or family life but because he couldn't abide the constant nit-picking of reporters.

Indeed, Cuomo was so singularly thin-skinned that those who knew him from something other than that oratorical ten-strike at San Francisco questioned whether he could be an effective candidate in the national arena. He always seemed to be looking for issues on which he could engage someone in a combative dime-store Socratic dialogue. In 1984 he had become involved in a long-running rhubarb with John Cardinal O'Connor over the proper role his Roman Catholic faith should play in his public conduct. Two years later Cuomo got into a bootless argument with reporters when he insisted there was no such thing as the Mafia. Such dustups with reporters were common; anyone guilty, by Cuomo's lights, of failing to grasp the nuances of his positions could expect a long expository telephone call to straighten out his thinking. We got a couple ourselves in the course of the campaign.

Thus, it was no surprise that early in 1987 Cuomo used an appearance on a radio talk show to announce he would not run for the presidency in 1988. It was a forum chosen with the obvious intention of zinging the New York political reporters who had been pursuing him and speculating about his future. And there was little reason to believe he would change his mind three months later. So the question of whether Mario Cuomo could play in the big leagues was never answered in 1988.

In a somewhat different way, the same doubts were raised by another potential candidate seen in some quarters as the savior of the Democratic Party, Senator Sam Nunn of Georgia. In sixteen years in the Senate he had won a deserved reputation for thoughtfulness and expertise on national-defense issues. As a result, conservative Democrats were always putting him forward as the logical successor to the late Henry M. ("Scoop") Jackson as the candidate who could save the Democratic Party from being perceived forever as the party of military weakness. But Nunn's record was pockmarked with votes on social issues that would have been counted as "wrong" by liberal Democratic activists. And the Georgia Democrat, an icon who faced only token opposition at home, had never demonstrated he could play in the high-tension world of presidential politics.

The other member of the triumvirate of might-have-been Democrats in 1987 was Senator Bill Bradley of New Jersey, the onetime professional basketball star and Rhodes scholar who had become a leading expert in Congress on international economic questions and was the prime mover in the tax reform of 1986. The rap on Bradley was supposed to be that he lacked an exciting platform style. But just as valid an argument might have been made that he could offer the charisma of substance—a special quality of weight that might have been particularly attractive as a contrast to eight years of Ronald Reagan in the White House. Bradley had enlisted a substantial following across the country among voters that pollsters call "the elites"—those who pay some attention to what is going on in the world around them.

But Bradley was a politician who marched to his own drummer, and he made clear from the outset that he did not consider himself ready to seek the presidency in 1988. That demurrer did not mean that he wasn't intensely interested in what was going on. One night late in 1987 we encountered him on a plane from Miami to Washington and spent the entire two hours discussing in detail how the campaign was developing, which candidates were doing well or poorly and why.

Lacking a national figure who could occupy center stage convincingly, the Democratic campaign was amorphous. The candidates were abroad every week in Iowa, New Hampshire or the South—raising money, enlisting the occasional locally prominent supporter, meeting with the editorial boards of newspapers and trying to get enough attention from television to "drive up the numbers" in the next round of opinion polls. But they were playing to a small audience of activists, and even they hadn't sorted out the candidates yet.

In an effort to reach a broader audience—and more cameras—the candidates seized on ready-made events. Moving almost as a group, they trouped from the annual meeting of the U.S. Conference of Mayors in Nashville to the convention of the National Association of County Officials in Indianapolis and then to meetings of the Democratic state chairmen in Cleveland and the Democratic Leadership Council in Atlanta. Then it was back to Indianapolis (twice in one year!) for the Conference of State Legislatures, down to Miami for the Communications Workers of America, up to Mackinac Island, Michigan, for the Democratic Governors' Association. Some of the candidates—Dukakis most notably—picked up some endorsements along the way. But if traveling this circuit was having any effect on the voters at large, it escaped the naked eye and the public-opinion polls.

Among the political cognoscenti, however, another standard was at work in deciding the seriousness of these Democrats' candidacies: their ability to raise money. The fact that Dukakis had raised $4.2 million in his first quarter as a candidate was a shocker, particularly when compared to $1.7 million for Biden, $1 million for Gephardt and $800,000 for Babbitt in the same period.

Operatives in rival campaigns tried to discount the Dukakis accomplishment. They pointed out that as a governor he had the special advantage of having many corporation executives in Massachusetts who wanted to keep themselves on all the right lists. They pointed out that as a Greek-American he had the special advantage of having the many Greek-Americans around the country who had been successful in business and could afford to help him now. They pointed out that in Bob Farmer, Dukakis had as a fund-raiser the man becoming acknowledged in the Democratic Party as the champ.

What the political professionals understood, despite all that carping, was that Dukakis was already established as one of the players in the game for the long haul. It was going to take large amounts of money and he apparently could raise it. That point was made with special force when it was disclosed in late fall that Dukakis had continued to raise $1 million or more a month while the other putatively leading candidate at the time, Gephardt, had already borrowed $300,000 against his federal matching money to meet day-to-day operating costs.

But although the money was an important credential to the professionals, it was not a standard that was very helpful in providing a structure for the campaign that would tell them who the likely winners would be.

At the same point in 1984 the Democratic candidates were competing in a series of "straw polls"—most often taken at state party conventions—conducted largely to attract the attention of the national news media. But that system of divining a pecking order had proved to be an expensive, divisive and ultimately meaningless exercise.

As it turned out, not a single one of the straw polls taken in 1983 accurately forecast the result of the primary or caucus held in the same state in 1984. And some of the disparities were bizarre enough to demonstrate the folly of the whole process. In Maine, for example, Walter Mondale spent more than $250,000 and campaigned personally in thirty-odd small communities to win a straw vote in September of 1983 in which Gary Hart did not even compete. Six months later Hart buried Mondale in the Maine precinct caucuses that were the first step in the state's official delegate-selection process.

This time the Democrats were determined to avoid making that same mistake. Paul Kirk, the party's national chairman, publicly pressured the state party leaders to abandon the straw votes. Somewhat surprisingly, the state leaders agreed that the attention the polls received wasn't worth the cost in money or harmony.

As a substitute for the straw poll in 1987, a seemingly endless series of debates—thirteen spread over the summer and fall—were held that eventually did succeed in exposing some issue differences among the candidates. Perhaps more significantly, at the same time they threw some light on their political personalities.

The candidates themselves were ambivalent about these confrontations. Most were televised nationally, but only on public broadcasting or cable networks. Because of this limited exposure, they had far more impact among political activists and junkies than among voters at large. Long after the fact, Dick Gephardt recalled: "We never did see the numbers move, the polls move that much off of any of the debates. The thing that really began to move the numbers was the television advertising, and it was dramatic."

The debates also seemed to have some value in honing the skills of these green candidates. "It gave you some confidence," Gephardt recalled. "It was like going through an obstacle course in the military or something. When you get done with it, you feel better about yourself and better about your ability to handle a situation like that."

There were also small lessons that could be learned from the debates, from which a rough pecking order began to take shape. The one consistent "winner" in the debates was, unsurprisingly, Jesse Jackson. As the only candidate who had previously run for the presidency and been through a similar process, he knew how to exploit the opportunities presented by the debates. He was quick, for example, weighing in with an apt one-liner that would be certain to make the brief network reports that enjoyed a far larger audience than the debates themselves. Jackson postured himself as the relaxed elder statesman preaching amity and goodwill, passing the occasional avuncular comment on his rivals.

Jackson also clearly enjoyed the debates, sometimes exchanging *sotto voce* and off-mike wisecracks with his colleagues. In one debate, when Gephardt was comparing unpleasant political medicine with the castor oil he had been forced to take daily as a child, Gore leaned over and asked Jackson if he, too, had been forced to take castor oil. To which Jackson, speaking behind his hand, replied: "No, but I was never that full of shit either."

Jackson's debate performances were so consistently spectacular that it became commonplace to hear liberals remarking that if Jesse were white, this whole contest would have been over a long time before. Very few pointed out that had he been white, he probably would never have made it to those debate stages at all.

As the only black in the field, Jackson was politically insulated from attacks from these other Democrats who hoped to inherit his base in the general election campaign. And this time Jackson made no misstep that might have compromised his special immunity from criticism by his competitors or, in most cases, the press. There was no "Hymietown" episode, no Louis Farrakhan in his entourage.

But the political axiom about debates is that they will do you harm far more often than they will help. And there was some evidence to support that thesis in the 1987 debates.

Bruce Babbitt suffered a political disaster in the first televised all-candidate debate in Houston on July 1. His prominent eyes bulged, his Adam's apple bounced, his head bobbed—and his replies seemed lost in these aberrations of style. Babbitt himself recognized how badly it had gone. In one focus group in Iowa, seven of the eight people who had arrived as Babbitt supporters abandoned him, and he began to take coaching to see that it never happened again.

In fact, at a meeting of Democratic state chairmen in Cleveland just a few days after the Houston debate, Babbitt was articulate and persuasive. But, because of a strike of NBC technicians, there were no television cameras in the room. At a cocktail party that night, we needled him: "What's this new thing you're doing—screw up on national television, then go gangbusters when the cameras are off?"

"It's a new strategy," Babbitt replied solemnly. "It's going to turn everybody around, just wait."

But Babbitt understood fully how much he had been damaged, particularly because this was his first exposure to most voters. "When it's a first impression," he said later, "you've kind of got to row against it the rest of the way."

The debates were less important in terms of winners and losers, however, than in what they told the press and those party activists who were watching about the candidates' strategies and their assessments of one another.

That first Houston debate was not particularly revealing. All the candidates were clearly less interested in confronting one another than in using the forum for attacks on the controversial nomination by President Reagan of Judge Robert Bork for the Supreme Court. But after the debate, Gephardt hurried into the pressroom to complain that Dukakis' criticism of his trade plan meant Dukakis was advocating a "blame America first" trade policy of his own.

The message was clear. The front-running Gephardt had decided that, for the moment at least, the man to worry about was Michael Dukakis. That assessment became increasingly clear as the Missouri congressman sniped at the Massachusetts governor through the rest of July and well into August.

The most important change in the structure of the campaign came, however, shortly after Sam Nunn announced in August that he definitely intended to remain out of the race. Gore seemed to take that decision as a signal he should establish himself even more firmly as the southern candidate and the one true champion of national defense in this field of liberals.

"As soon as Sam Nunn left the field," Paul Simon said later, "you could see a marked change in Al Gore's whole process."

Gore's strategy manifested itself first at a debate on September 27 in Des Moines sponsored by a group of peace activists, STARPAC, for Stop the Arms Race Political Action Committee. When Simon asked Gore to defend his support for the B-1 bomber, the MX missile, chemical weapons and two new aircraft carriers, Gore essentially laid down the gauntlet for all of his rivals.

"This question itself is part of the problem we face as a Democratic Party," he replied. "The American people have been given the impression over the last several presidential elections that the Democratic Party is against every weapons system that is suggested and is prepared to go into negotiations with the Soviet Union on the basis that we get something for nothing."

Throughout that debate and another sponsored by the Democratic Leadership Council in Miami a few days later, Gore seemed to be making a point of underlining differences, particularly with those opponents who were having the most early success in the opinion polls. Gore managed to cite his own support for the invasion of Grenada, the reflagging of Kuwaiti vessels in the Persian Gulf, flight-testing of ballistic missiles—initiatives on which both Dukakis and Gephardt disagreed—and especially the Reagan administration's request for $3 million in so-called "maintenance" humanitarian aid to the contras in Nicaragua.

Gephardt was particularly prickly in rebutting Gore. He noted that despite Gore's stance now, he had voted against either arms or humanitarian aid for the contras on eighteen or twenty opportunities in the past. And when Gore told Gephardt at Miami that the alternative to reflagging the Kuwaiti ships would be "to turn tail and run" from the Iranians, the Missourian, obviously irked, shot back: "Nobody's talking about turning tail and running. But a bad idea never gets better."

The antipathy toward Gore that developed among the other candidates was based both on what he was saying and on the way he was saying it.

All the candidates understood that they were extremely vulnerable on the national-defense issue simply because they were Democrats, and the liberals particularly. They understood that they carried the burden of the perceptions that had evolved from years of wrangling over national priorities that had come to be seen, too simplistically, as choices between necessary weapons and social programs of at least questionable effectiveness.

That understanding, in turn, had led each of them to formulate positions on defense—including support for selected weapons systems—that might get them through the Democratic nominating process without too much careful examination. In their view, Gore was making that impossible in what they saw as a grandstand play to southern conservatives that didn't accurately reflect his own political essence.

Quite beyond Gore's choice of issues, several other candidates—Simon, Gephardt and Dukakis certainly—were annoyed by his manner. Privately Dukakis complained to advisers that Gore was behaving in a "patronizing" and "condescending" manner that put his teeth on edge. The two other candidates from Congress were struck by the difference between the moderately liberal Gore they had seen in the House and Senate and the Gore who was presenting himself to southern Democrats. At one point, Gephardt remarked with some edge in his voice that "maybe the next debate should be between the old Al Gore and the new Al Gore."

The tensions reached the tinder point after an early October speech at the National Press Club in Washington in which, among other things, Gore said: "The politics of retreat, complacency and doubt may appeal to others, but it will not do for me or for my country."

The following day the Democratic candidates met for still another debate in the Concert Hall of the Kennedy Center for the Performing Arts. It was sponsored by the Democratic National Committee and was intended to show-case a fine field of potential party nominees for President. Instead, the event exposed the divisions developing among the candidates and among Democrats in general.

At one stage in the debate the audience of party activists erupted into prolonged applause and cheering when Simon told Gore: "We should be conducting ourselves in such a way that there is meaning to these debates, not just sound, and we are pulling our party together and not tearing it apart."

There was no similar demonstration when Gore responded: "To pretend there are no differences in our party is completely unrealistic. If we are going to pretend there are no differences and we are all just going to say the same kind of vague, general things, that is not the way to reinvigorate our party."

Simon also zeroed in on Gore's Press Club statement about "retreat, complacency and doubt," words that to political veterans seemed akin to McCarthyist questioning of his opponents' patriotism and nerve.

"I don't think it helps any of us to be knifing each other," Simon told Gore on the Concert Hall stage. "I don't think I fall into that category. . . . I think it would be healthy, if you didn't mean any of us, to say so right now and if you do, I think we ought to be named."

Gore demurred, but when the debate ended officially it continued among the candidates as several dozen reporters and television crews crowded around them on the stage.

"Well, if you can't stand the heat, get out of the kitchen," Gore offered at one point.

"You're doing precisely what the Republicans want us to do," Gephardt told him. "Precisely," Simon echoed.

Asked about the Press Club speech, Gore moved away only marginally "Retreat, complacency and doubt," he said, "is a view in part of the Democratic Party that all five of my opponents have come close to subscribing to. . . ."

Gephardt: "Al, you misrepresent what we say."

Babbitt: "Al, kind of lighten up. You're coming on like the tough kid on the block."

Party functionaries and nervous staff members finally steered the candidates off the stage and ended the bickering, but the divisions were clear and so was the bad feeling.

As Simon put it months later, "If Al Gore says I disagree with you on the MX missile, I can answer that. But he said that the other candidates were guilty of the politics of retreat, complacency and doubt. . . . How do you handle that? There was some resentment."

Gore himself insisted after the fact that the accusation that he was posturing for a conservative audience in the South was unfair. The views he expressed, he said, were consistent with the positions he had taken in Congress, including his controversial backing in the House of the MX missile.

"You emphasize divisions within the Democratic Party anytime you talk about national defense or foreign policy," he said later. "I had a set of positions from the start that was different from the positions of the other candidates." What had happened, he said, was that those differences were "highlighted" by the focus of the press and political community on the campaign.

"What am I going to do?" he asked. "Am I going to fuzz it over? . . . I was surprised at the lack of institutional memory within the press corps and community that focuses on campaigns." Gore had revealed his own "lack of institutional memory," however, in his use of the words "retreat, complacency and doubt," which were reminders to older Democrats of the language of Joe McCarthy in his best Red-baiting days. He professed to be astonished, after the election, when we told him of this reaction.

It would be disingenuous, nonetheless, to ignore the political meaning of the course Gore followed through those debates that summer and fall. Whatever his stated intention, the emphasis he placed on the differences between himself and the others was a well-considered plan to nail down his southern conservative base as a safety net against the defeats he would suffer in Iowa and New Hampshire.

The message he was sending about Iowa, almost in so many words, was that the Democrats who would attend the precinct caucuses there were the kind of liberals who could never accept someone who was strong on national defense when offered the option of "retreat, complacency and doubt." Gore had nothing going in Iowa, very little in New Hampshire, but he knew how to make a virtue of necessity.

Gore had a more legitimate complaint about being depicted as a one-issue candidate—a complaint that touched directly on a fundamental flaw in the nominating game as it was played in 1988. Gore argued that, quite beyond the defense issue, he had tried to emphasize the global environment crisis—the destruction of the ozone layer and the "greenhouse effect." But, he said, he had found the issue "heavily discounted" by the press and political community as simply not the kind of issue on which one runs for president of the United States.

"I made hundreds of speeches about the greenhouse effect, the ozone problem, that were almost never reported at all," he said later. "There were several occasions where I prepared the ground in advance, released advance texts, chose the place for the speech with symbolic care—and then nothing, nothing."

Gore was discovering the hard way that in presidential nominating politics, in either party, issues were important only as shorthand in sorting out the candidates ideologically. Thus, the national-defense issue won attention from the press and political community not so much because of its intrinsic importance as because of its value in categorizing candidates. If Candidate X favored the Strategic Defense Initiative, he was obviously a conservative. Next question.

But little attention was given to issues on which no clear ideological lines could be drawn or no interests of particular constituencies identified. It was fair to assume that everyone was "against" the greenhouse effect, so the argument was just over methods. And the candidate who, like Gore in this case, had recognized a complex problem early got little or no credit for giving it a high priority.

Thus, the debates among the Democrats operating in the post-Hart vacuum were important mainly in what they showed about the participants' strengths and weaknesses as politicians and candidates, rather than what they showed about their intellects or insight. That fact was apparent when, at one of two debates on the environment, Gore gave a technical answer to a question and Jackson scoffed: "There are a lot of chemists who can do that who are not running for president."

Some of the responses on relatively narrow questions were, however, revealing. At a debate on education in Chapel Hill, North Carolina, the Democrats were asked what they would do about a situation in Florida at the time in which the people of a small town were driving away a young family whose three hemophiliac children were carrying the AIDS virus.

Most of them offered the predictable politicians' response—a brief lecture on how leadership and money were needed to provide research to solve the AIDS crisis. But Bruce Babbitt, the former governor, clearly won the audience when he said he would send his secretary of health, education and welfare to that Florida town and straighten those people out on the disease.

Babbitt's acuity was not lost on his rivals. Flying from Raleigh to Atlanta later that same day, Dukakis confided: "Babbitt had the right answer. I wish I'd said that."

But, as Dick Gephardt noted later, the debates apparently were exercises for the insiders and activists that "moved the numbers" in the opinion polls minimally and temporarily, if at all. By September 1, almost four months after Gary Hart had left the field, a national poll commissioned by *Time* magazine found Jesse Jackson with the support of 26 percent of Democrats, Dukakis with 11 percent and none of the others out of single digits.

In this period since Hart had been driven from the race over "the character issue," the surviving candidates had done their best through this grinding series of debates to put the campaign back on more substantive ground. As part of this effort, several of them had taken part in yet another debate at the Iowa State Fairgrounds in late August. And as luck would have it—bad luck for one of them—it became the vehicle for demonstrating once again the special salience of "the character issue" in the politics of 1988.

15

More Questions of Character

Flying a private jet to Des Moines on August 23 for still another debate, this one at the Iowa State Fair, Joe Biden was feeling pretty good about his prospects. As he saw it, Dick Gephardt was fading and Michael Dukakis was "dead in the water" in Iowa. And in New Hampshire, he thought, his campaign was "just where we wanted to be, lying in the weeds" to spring at Dukakis after the Iowa caucuses.

Biden spent the first half of the flight working on material from his prime concern at the moment—the impending hearings by the Senate Judiciary Committee, of which he was chairman, on President Reagan's nomination of Robert Bork for the Supreme Court. The unexpected vacancy, just as he was trying to get his presidential campaign in high gear, was "our worst nightmare come true," Biden said later, because of the pressure the dual responsibility would put on him.

An example of that pressure was already at hand. Putting the Bork hearings material aside about halfway through the flight, Biden spent the rest of the time working on his opening statement for the debate. But when he landed, he still hadn't gotten around to writing his closing remarks.

David Wilhelm, the state director of his Iowa campaign, met the plane and asked him: "How you set?"

"I [still] don't have a close," Biden recalls replying. "Then he said, 'Why don't you use the Kinnock stuff?' and I said to myself, 'Great idea.' "

As it turned out, this "great idea"—or, to be more precise, Joe Biden's execution of it that day—destroyed his campaign in an episode that confirmed beyond any question the primacy of "the character issue" in the early stages of the presidential campaign of 1988.

The "Kinnock stuff" that David Wilhelm recommended was a speech Biden had been giving based on one that Neil Kinnock, the leader of the Labor Party, had used in his unsuccessful campaign against Prime Minister Margaret Thatcher in Great Britain that spring.

In a television commercial that was largely credited with raising his approval rating nineteen percentage points, Kinnock began by asking: "Why am

I the first Kinnock in a thousand generations to be able to get to university?'' Then, pointing to his wife seated in his audience, he went on: "Why is Glenys the first woman in her family in a thousand generations to be able to get to university? Was it because all our predecessors were thick?''

Asking why his ancestors, Welsh coal miners, didn't succeed as he had done, Kinnock continued: "Did they lack talent? Those people who could sing and play and recite and write poetry? Those people who could make wonderful, beautiful things with their hands? Those people who could dream dreams, see visions? Why didn't they get it? Was it because they were weak? Those people who could work eight hours underground and then come up and play football? Weak?

"Does anybody really think that they didn't get what we had because they didn't have the talent or the strength or the endurance to the commitment? Of course not. It was because there was no platform on which they could stand.''

Biden had been given a videotape of the Kinnock speech by William Schneider, a political scientist at the American Enterprise Institute and newspaper columnist. Schneider had gone to London to observe the campaign and had been so impressed by the commercial that he made copies and passed them on to several campaigns at home.* Biden apparently was the most taken with Kinnock's approach and began using a version of it—usually but not always with attribution to Kinnock—in his own speeches.

At the Iowa State Fair debate, as he sat waiting to be introduced, Biden hurriedly scribbled down a close for his speech as Jesse Jackson, sitting next to him, playfully tugged at Biden's papers. When he rose to speak, Biden used the excerpts from the Kinnock speech, but in a way that not only lacked attribution but suggested strongly that it was original.

"I started thinking as I was coming over here," he told the audience, "why is it that Joe Biden is the first in his family ever to go to a university? Why is it that my wife who is sitting out there in the audience is the first in her family to ever go to college? Is it because our fathers and mothers were not bright? Is it because I'm the first Biden in a thousand generations to get a college and a graduate degree that I was smarter than the rest?

"Those same people who read poetry and wrote poetry and taught me how to sing verse? Is it because they didn't work hard? My ancestors, who worked in the coal mines of northeast Pennsylvania and would come up after twelve hours and play football for four hours?

"No, it's not because they weren't as smart. It's not because they didn't work as hard. It's because they didn't have a platform on which to stand.''

Some Biden advisers noticed right away that their candidate had failed to cite Kinnock, and they breathed easier when no one raised the question. "There

*Schneider's role in this episode was another example of how the line between practitioners of politics and journalism is blurred by individuals working both sides of the street. A Biden aide said he first saw the Kinnock tape, shown by Schneider, at a Children's Defense Fund meeting held to consider more effective ways to convey the organization's message.

were a hundred reporters covering that debate," Larry Rasky, the campaign press secretary, recalled. "I figured if there was a problem, somebody would have said something to me about it."

As it turned out, the failure to credit Kinnock wasn't noticed—publicly —for almost three weeks, during which time Biden used the material, with attribution, on several other occasions. In a report from New Hampshire for the *New York Times* on August 29, reporter Robin Toner noted in the thirteenth paragraph of a sixteen-paragraph story that Biden had offered a "paean to the Democratic Party and its commitment to equality of opportunity, improvising on a speech by Neil Kinnock, the British Labor leader."

John Aloysius Farrell, a reporter for the *Boston Globe*, also had heard the Kinnock material in New Hampshire and mentioned it in a story the same day. "I followed him for three days and every time he used it, he gave Kinnock credit," Farrell recalled. Farrell earlier had seen Biden's Iowa State Fair version on television without the attribution, he said later, but he had used it every other time "so it was awful hard for me to criticize him for not using it once in Iowa." In fact, he said, he joked with a Dukakis staff member "that it was much more effective not mentioning Kinnock."

In a television interview with David Frost taped on September 3 but never broadcast, Biden also quoted Kinnock extensively, with appropriate attribution, to support his own argument: "That's what this nation has to do, to build a platform upon which people can stand."

So all Biden had ever had to do to avoid this political disaster was to use that attribution again. "All I had to say was, 'Like Kinnock,' " he said later. "If I'd just said those two words, 'Like Kinnock,' and I didn't. It was my fault, nobody else's fault."

On September 12, however, Biden's failure to mention Kinnock at the state fair caught up with him. Both the *New York Times* and the *Des Moines Register* published detailed accounts of the striking parallels between the rhetoric of Kinnock and the senator from Delaware. Biden and his strategists tried to pass the failure off as much ado about nothing, citing other cases in which he had indeed credited Kinnock, including one occasion at a corn boil near Dubuque only ten days before the fair.

"I've been using it all over," Biden said. "A tempest in a teapot," said Rasky.

Biden thought, he said later, that most of the reporters covering the campaign had already heard him use the Kinnock formulation with proper credit—and that this would soon emerge in the press. "I was stunned," he said. "I was just naïve as hell."

"We thought," Ted Kaufman, one of his closest advisers, recalled later, "that it was a one-day story or a four- or five-day story at most." It was not that simple, however.

First, it was clear in this case that Biden had implied very strongly that the ideas in the speech had simply popped into his head on the way to the debate. Politicians are always introducing their weariest rhetoric to audiences as fresh thoughts brought forth especially for the occasion. Listeners are flattered and the practice is usually harmless enough because most of those listeners probably don't believe all they hear anyway. But in this case, Biden was not taking that license with his own thinking process but with that of Neil Kinnock.

More significantly, Biden seemed to be adopting not just the language of Kinnock but the Welshman's persona and part of his family history. Although there may have been a mining engineer and a football star back there among Biden's ancestors, there were no Biden coal miners coming up out of the shafts to play football. His father was an automobile dealer in Wilmington.

Long after the fact, Kaufman would argue that "any objective analysis" of the Kinnock speech would show that it fit Biden's own history much closer than that of any of the other candidates. Biden's forebears may not have been miners but, Kaufman noted, "Joe comes from Scranton, Pennsylvania, coal-mine country."

Biden's point, as he had expressed it to David Frost, was still a valid one. But the picture he had presented of himself in that Iowa debate closing—and also on a videotape made for the National Education Association—was misleading enough to raise many embarrassing questions.

Taken by itself, the single incident probably wouldn't have been enough to cause Biden serious or lasting political damage. Because he could cite those other occasions on which he had quoted Kinnock by name, it might have been plausible to accept the argument that he had neglected the attribution inadvertently because of, as one adviser put it, "the very strong personal association with the concept." And he could reasonably have argued, as he did after the fact, that the omission was partly a product of his own hubris—his confidence that he could scribble out notes for a two-minute closing statement while the debate was still under way.

But the Kinnock story couldn't be taken by itself. As often happens in such cases, the one case suggested there might be others if reporters simply looked for them. That notion quickly proved to be the fact.

Other reporters—perhaps helped along by partisans of rival candidates—discovered other cases in which Biden had used without credit extensive quotations from such other Democrats as Hubert H. Humphrey and Robert F. Kennedy. One speech Biden delivered to a California state Democratic convention earlier in the year attracted special attention in the aftermath of the state fair debate.

In 1968, in a speech in Des Moines, Robert Kennedy had spoken of the measure of a nation in these terms: "The gross national product does not allow for the health of our children, the quality of their education or the joy of their play. It does not include the beauty of our poetry, or the strength of our marriages, the intelligence of our public debate or the integrity of our public officials.

"It measures neither our wit nor our courage, neither our wisdom nor our devotion to our country. It measures everything, in short, except that which makes life worthwhile, and it can tell us everything about America except why we are proud that we are Americans.''

At Sacramento, Biden, also talking about the folly of using materialistic standards for measuring the condition of the nation, said: "We cannot measure the health of our children, the quality of their education, the joy of their play. . . . It doesn't measure the beauty of our poetry, the strength of our marriages, the intelligence of our public debate, the integrity of our public officials.

"It counts neither our wit nor our wisdom, neither our compassion nor our devotion to our country. The bottom line can tell us everything about our lives except that which makes life worthwhile, and it can tell us everything about America except that which makes us proud to be Americans.''

The similarities were not lost on the *San Jose Mercury News*, which reported them and set off another round of questions. Again, the Biden operatives suggested explanations and mitigating circumstances. Biden never knew he was quoting from a Kennedy speech, they said. The villain in the piece, they indicated, was the author of the speech, political consultant Patrick Caddell, because he should have included the attribution to warn both Biden and his listeners. "In fairness to Pat," Biden said later, "he probably assumed that I knew it was Kennedy's.''

But by this time there was sufficient appearance of a pattern to damage Biden. The story about Kennedy had particular impact, Rasky recalled, "because it was made for TV''—meaning the networks could and did show parallel films on a split screen. "That's when it started to get perverse," he said.

Right on its heels came still another blow, a disclosure that as a first-year law student at Syracuse University Biden had been given a failing grade and forced to repeat a course. He had included five pages from a law review article in a paper of his own without any credit. Biden passed the incident off as a mistake, and pointed out that his law school dean had written a letter attesting to his good character—something he presumably would not have done if Biden had been guilty of deliberate plagiarism.

Indeed, the charge of plagiarism in law school stuck in Biden's craw far more than any other. At one point, he said later, some advisers were urging him to simply confess, do a mea culpa and then wait for the issue to die out. But Biden wouldn't go along. "I'm never going to say I plagiarized because I did not," he said.

Rasky took a realistic view of the situation. "My basic feeling about doing these things," he said later, "was it's important not to make a mountain out of a molehill. But when you see a mountain, don't call it a molehill." Or, as Biden himself put it, "The Kinnock thing was the biggie and everything else then became believable.''

The final blow was a C-Span videotape of an incident in New Hampshire the previous April. Biden, irked by a persistent questioner of his academic credentials, had grossly exaggerated his record. "I think I probably have a much higher IQ than you do, I suspect," Biden was shown telling the voter. "I went to law school on a full academic scholarship, the only one in my class to have an academic scholarship. In the first year in the law, I decided I didn't want to be in law school and ended up the bottom two-thirds of my class and then decided I wanted to stay, went back to law school and ended up in the top half of my class."

He also claimed to have been named the outstanding political science student as an undergraduate at the University of Delaware and to have graduated with three undergraduate degrees. But law school records showed Biden ranked eightieth among one hundred students in his first year, seventy-sixth among eighty-five in the final year. The full academic scholarship proved to be half based on need, and the three degrees turned out to be one degree with a dual major in history and political science.

Looking back later, Biden was rueful about the exchange with the questioner. "Hey, pal, you want to compare IQs?" he said. "What an immature thing to say."

This episode, Biden said later, was the last straw. "We did not have an idea how to react," he said, in another reference to the disarray of his national staff. "And then, by the time we began to generate ideas on how to react, the floodgate had opened. It was like the red tide was rolling. And all the time I was having to get up every morning, bang the gavel, know what I'm talking about with Bork, keep my committee in a posture I thought it should adopt."

And on top of everything, Biden was feeling poorly a good part of the time. "I couldn't figure why I was having headaches," he recalled after the election. "I could not figure out why I was living off of extra-strength Tylenol. I'd never had a headache in my life." At a Rotary Club in Nashua, New Hampshire, earlier, he had delivered the first line of his speech when he felt faint, excused himself, walked off and collapsed on a bench outside the room. After about fifteen minutes, he pulled himself up, walked back in and finished the speech. Aides attributed his sluggishness to the tension of the campaign— a woefully inadequate diagnosis as matters ultimately turned out. (Five months later, Biden suffered two brain aneurysms that nearly cost him his life. After months of hospitalization, he recovered and returned to the Senate in September 1988. The case could be made that had Biden's political misfortunes never occurred, he might not have lived out the campaign.)

By now, it was apparent to political professionals outside the Biden campaign that he was finished, and that realization began to seep into the Biden camp as well. Indeed, as Biden remembered it, doubts began to creep into his own inner circle. "Half the people working for me, the pros, they began to wonder," he recalled. "Did you kill Cock Robin when you were in grade school?"

The whole crisis had been intensified by the fact that the first story had broken on the weekend before Biden was scheduled to preside over the Bork nomination hearings. Indeed, that element raised some dark suspicions among Biden supporters, unfounded as it turned out, that the Republicans might have peddled the Kinnock story to destroy the credibility of the one Democrat who would have the most to say about the confirmation of Bob Bork. Ted Kaufman thought of the plot line in Allen Drury's best-seller of the 1950s, *Advise and Consent*, in which the chairman of a Senate committee reviewing a cabinet nomination comes under fearful pressure and attack.

In fact, Rasky said later, the Biden strategists first tried to turn the story away from Biden's culpability to speculation that undermining of the Bork hearings was the prime objective of the Kinnock disclosure. Others in the Biden camp suspected rival Democrats uneasy about the publicity bonanza Biden could score by deft handling of the hearings, and still others saw vengeance against Pat Caddell by one of his Democratic enemies.

But now the Bork matter was in the way of any full-scale defense. Biden was presiding from 10 A.M. to 6 P.M. and running out at recesses to make telephone calls trying to find evidence to refute even further stories about his past. He was calling a law school classmate to ask him to fly to Syracuse to get his academic records. Or the dean at his undergraduate school, the University of Delaware, to confirm his account of his scholarship. Or a lawyer in Hawaii who had been his partner in a moot-court competition he had won. Or even a restaurant manager named Jimmy Kennedy (known as "Charbelly") to back up his story that as a high school student, Biden had pressured him to begin serving black customers. Here he was, in the middle of the Bork hearings, being, as he put it, "nibbled to death."

One night, he recalled, he was on the telephone with a *New York Times* reporter who was questioning him about that moot-court competition. His sister Valerie suddenly remembered he had a plaque on his wall that would prove his point. She ran upstairs, yanked it off the wall and ran downstairs with it, so that her brother could read the citation to the reporter. "It was like we found gold," Biden said. "It was like, we're safe, we're free."

"It just got to the point that I truly believed I wasn't going to be able to fight for my political life and run the Bork hearings," he said. And given the importance to liberal Democrats of blocking the Bork nomination, the choice was clear.

Nor were the reports from Biden's supporters encouraging. "We knew what we were hearing from the field," Larry Rasky recalled, "and we had no reason to believe this was going to end at this point. We were confronted with the reality that it was over."

Ten days after that first story, a handful of those most involved in the Biden campaign—Kaufman, Rasky, Tom Donilon, Biden's sister Valerie and brother Jimmy—caught the commuter train home to Wilmington with him. And there, in an after-dinner meeting in Biden's home, they agreed he should withdraw from the presidential campaign. There was one dissenter, however. One of those involved in the meeting said Pat Caddell, in California, was so angry at the notion of giving up that he "was calling every fifteen minutes" to protest. At one point, one of those in the room reported later, Caddell told Jimmy Biden that he had "no right to give my candidate advice." At another, he told Rasky: "You people have formed a vigilante party to get my candidate out of the race." Tom Donilon quipped: "I know this is going to be like *Poltergeist II*. Pat's going to get up from behind the bushes—he's back!"

The next day, Biden's performance at his swan-song press conference back in Washington was far more restrained than that of Gary Hart four months earlier. But he too raised questions about the way "the character issue" was being applied in presidential politics—arguing that what he called "the exaggerated shadow" of the mistakes he admitted had begun "to obscure the essence of my candidacy and the essence of Joe Biden."

Unlike Hart, Biden didn't choose to lash out publicly at the press. But the core of his complaint, absent the bitterness, was the same as Hart's argument that he had been ruled out of the game on the basis of the mistakes he made with Donna Rice without consideration of the other qualities he brought to the contest. The incidents of apparent plagiarism raised enough questions about Biden's character to forestall any examination of more positive evidence.

The more striking similarity between the two cases, however, was that in each of them, specific incidents took on far more weight than might have been expected because of amorphous questions about both candidates that were already abroad among politicians and the press. Vague doubts were suddenly crystallized.

Hart had been destroyed by the Donna Rice episode because it was seen as part of a pattern of arrogant defiance of conventional standards that other politicians felt obliged to respect. And it happened so quickly because so many of his fellow politicians had suspected that arrogance all along.

In Biden's case, there was little if any personal hostility in the political community; on the contrary, he was generally a popular figure. But there had been pervasive doubts about Biden's intellectual weight and about whether he had something to offer beyond the oratorical flash of that celebrated speech in 1984. And those doubts may have been nourished by the fact that his campaign had not yet, as he conceded himself, settled on a coherent message but instead was relying heavily on his reputation as an orator. The message they were broadcasting, Biden said, was "Hey, look at Biden, he can move people. Look at Biden, he's passionate. Look at Biden, that's why you should be for Biden. . . . In retrospect we were playing right into every preconceived weakness."

Given that context, it would be hard to imagine an accusation that could reinforce those doubts as much as the charges that he had been guilty of plagiarism and inflating his academic credentials. The obvious inference was that "the speech" was just a case of a slick Irish pol delivering somebody else's words.

Biden and some of his advisers also believed he suffered disproportionately because of his long and close association with the controversial Caddell and because of the social distance he had maintained from the press and political community in Washington by commuting to his home in Wilmington every night. "When the shit hit the fan," Rasky said later, "it was the press corps' lack of familiarity with Joe combined with their contempt of Pat that made people willing to believe the worst."

It seemed more likely, however, that Biden was the victim of the new vigilance in the press, and the fact that another "character" question was being raised while the Gary Hart case was so fresh in the minds of reporters and politicians alike. Once again, it seemed, the facts of the case had demonstrated there was a genuine foundation for doubts about a presidential candidate.

But the business of the press applying "character tests" to politicians can be a tricky one. The standards have never been fixed and thus must be written anew for each case. And that process can cause distortions with the potential for exacting political costs beyond reckoning, as the Dukakis campaign soon discovered.

Even before Biden had decided to fold his campaign, his partisans in Iowa and elsewhere were asking bitter questions about the source of the "attack video"—the term coined by David Yepsen of the *Des Moines Register*—that had first shown the parallels between the language of Neil Kinnock and Joe Biden. Someone was clearly "out to get" Biden, so it was entirely predictable that his supporters would attempt to change the subject from the accuracy of the charges against him to their source and motivation. For a variety of reasons, few of them particularly logical, the original suspicions were directed at the Gephardt campaign. Bob Shrum and David Doak, associates of Caddell who had fallen out with him, were obvious suspects as Gephardt strategists, with revenge the speculated motive.

But the suspicions eventually turned on Dukakis' campaign. Dukakis, denying that any of his advisers was responsible, said he would be "very angry" and "astonished" if anyone on his staff were involved. "Anybody who knows me and knows the kind of campaigns I run," he said, "knows how strongly I feel about negative campaigning."

Advisers John Sasso and Paul Tully had taken different tacks. Tully told groups of contributors and reporters that "it is not our campaign and not our people in Iowa" who had been responsible for distributing the tape. Sasso told an inquiring reporter: "I'm not going to speculate on it." But once Dukakis went out on a limb with his denial, Sasso was convinced he had to set it straight. So he went to Dukakis' office and confessed that he had indeed distributed the tapes.

Sasso offered to resign but Dukakis, faced with the loss of his closest political adviser, was reluctant to go that far. He suggested instead that his campaign manager take a leave of absence. As for himself, Dukakis would have to make a clean breast of the affair and apologize to Biden. But the press and political community were in full cry and by the next day it was apparent that Dukakis' mea culpa would not suffice. Sasso would have to go, and he knew it. He informed Dukakis, then announced to a waiting horde of reporters that he and Tully were leaving the campaign.

The whole controversy had grown out of what might otherwise have been considered an alert piece of political work by the two leading political professionals in the campaign.

Tully had attended the Iowa State Fair debate. He had seen the Kinnock tape but, at the time, he failed to make the connection. Nonetheless, he was impressed by the message Biden used in that closing statement. At that very moment, the Dukakis strategists were trying to find a way to hone their candidate's own message stressing "opportunity" and "hope" for a better life. Now here was Joe Biden crowding into their space with just such a message and a damned effective one at that. "You cannot watch," Tully recalled, "and not notice the impact of what Biden was doing." It was, he said, "a knockdown closer"—much more effective than anything in "the speech" for which Biden had been best known.

The political stakes were high—the possibility that Biden might bite into Dukakis' support enough to push the Massachusetts governor into fourth place in Iowa behind not only Gephardt and Simon but also Biden. And the Dukakis operatives were convinced that at least a third-place finish was essential for him to emerge from Iowa with his national credentials intact for New Hampshire.

But if Tully did not make the Biden-Kinnock connection immediately, Sasso did. He had seen the Kinnock tape, and now he saw a tape of the Biden speech made from a Boston television station that had covered the debate. He quickly assigned an intern working in the campaign to put the two on the same tape. Then he played it for astonished members of the senior staff—and at least one reporter who apparently decided there was no story there.

A few days later Maureen Dowd of the *New York Times* telephoned Sasso on an unrelated errand. She was writing an article about Caddell and had noticed Robin Toner's reference to the use of the Kinnock material in New Hampshire. Dowd said she found it curious that Caddell had begun using an appeal for working-class voters that had been used by a failed British politician. Sasso told her about the tape, and she asked him to send her a copy.

Several days passed, however, and when no story appeared in the *New York Times*, Sasso and Tully decided they had to help the process along a little. So Tully, bound for Iowa, took a copy to David Yepsen, the highly esteemed political writer for the *Des Moines Register*. And that same Friday Jack Corrigan, acting under Sasso's instructions, sent a copy of the tape to a member of the NBC political staff, who—to his subsequent sorrow—dropped it into a desk drawer and went home for the weekend. The following morning the Yepsen and Dowd accounts appeared in their newspapers, apparently published quite by coincidence on the same day. NBC found itself obliged to follow up the story by putting together its own tape of the Kinnock and Biden speeches, which was aired in a report that night.

The resignations of Sasso and Tully set off what politicians, with their penchant for hyperbole, like to call a "fire storm" of criticism. In Boston, newspapers and television reporters swarmed all over the Dukakis campaign demanding details and confirmations or denials of every suspicion and every rumor about the incident. In Iowa, supporters of Biden and other candidates huffed and puffed about how "dirty tricks" were not tolerated in politics there, however acceptable such things might be back East.

Boston reporters quickly recalled that Sasso had been involved in "another" tape episode during Dukakis' campaign to reclaim the governorship from Edward J. King in 1982, the suggestion being that this Biden incident was part of a pattern. In fact, the two cases had little in common except electronics and mistakes in judgment. In that earlier incident, Sasso had played for two reporters, on what he thought was an off-the-record basis, an off-color tape never intended for public airing contrived by editing and splicing an Ed King radio commercial.

The disclosure of the "attack video" put Dukakis in a no-win situation. If he had countenanced the distribution of the tape, it was obviously a blot on his well-established reputation for political probity. If he had not, which was in fact the case, then it seemed legitimate to question his reputation, equally well established, as an executive and manager.

But, in the preoccupation with "the character issue" that dominated the political debate of the moment, the whole uproar was predicated on a faulty premise—that making and giving the videotape to reporters had been a "dirty trick" akin to those played by the legions of Richard Nixon in 1972. In fact, the practice of one campaign passing along to reporters damaging information about a rival campaign was routine and defensible—so long as the material being passed on was accurate. It happened all the time. Someone from George Bush headquarters, for example, would telephone us in Washington and ask if we had seen our copy of the *Milwaukee Sentinel* that morning. When we confessed we had not seen that particular paper that day, the Bush agent would point out that on page 6 there was a story quoting Bob Dole as saying something politically stupid. "Just wanted to be sure you didn't miss it," the Bush agent would say. "Ta, ta."

In the Sasso-Biden episode, the ultimate irony was that we and other political reporters in Washington began receiving, in plain envelopes, batches of clippings from the Boston newspapers from someone who wanted to be sure we didn't miss a single word of what was going on. As it turned out, the material was coming from the Republican State Committee, which was using the same basic technique of spreading the truth for which John Sasso was being pilloried.

There were distinguishing factors in this particular incident. One was the use of videotape rather than simply a copying machine, a method that seemed to some to make the whole exercise more exotic and clandestine. The second, more understandable, was the fact that Sasso had not informed his candidate about what he was doing and had tried to avoid the responsibility when the press was catching wise.

But the only crime Sasso and Tully had been guilty of was in their deception of Dukakis and, in Tully's case, the news media. No truly dirty trick had been played on Joe Biden. They had considered Biden a serious competitor, perhaps one beginning to crowd them a little and, handed an opportunity to sting him, had taken it. Their only culpability was in refusing to acknowledge their role in the videotape and thus allowing the notion to circulate that the Gephardt campaign might be responsible for it. Joe Trippi, who had moved from the collapsed Hart campaign to Gephardt's, said later: "There was a sense on our part that they [the Dukakis operatives] had gone for a twofer"—giving Biden a black eye and getting Gephardt blamed for it. But in the rush to make judgments on the character of political players, the distinctions between the real dirty tricks of the Nixon days and what Sasso and Tully had done were lost.

Looking back, Sasso understood how that happened but was no less regretful for the understanding.

"I wish I didn't do it, obviously. Look what it led to," he told us one morning over a postelection breakfast. "On the other hand, I'm not embarrassed about it because it was the absolute truth, number one, and, two, and this is very important to me, I never denied that I did it. Now I want to reinforce this. You can't find anybody in the press who ever said that I told them . . . that I didn't do it . . . So I never denied it. I didn't feel any obligation to step forward and say it was me. Why would I do that? If that's the standard, then nobody can do business anymore. . . . I regret doing it. I think it was a mistake because look what it cost me. That was a hard year. It was the absolute truth. It was the ultimate truth. It was in video, there it was in black and white."

Sasso said later that the most dangerous aspect of the situation was the fact it had occurred just when Dukakis "was introducing himself to the country" as a presidential candidate. "I was worried," Sasso recalled, "that it had the potential to damage Dukakis because this would be the only thing the country knew about him . . . this one incident, and he was indecisive. And given the nature of today's media, if you don't nip something in the same cycle, the same news cycle, you start getting two or three days [of it] . . . and you can go down so quickly."

Tully thought the damage from the videotape might be particularly serious in the Midwest, and Iowa specifically. "In that part of the country it's clearly outside the bounds of their rules, of their custom," he said. "It's a much gentler, more orderly kind of politics out there. . . ." Thus, by Tully's reckoning, if Dukakis had tried to ride out that particular "fire storm," he might have been risking "an embarrassing finish in Iowa"—meaning fourth place—that could have put at risk his credibility in the New Hampshire primary he absolutely had to win.

Political considerations aside, Dukakis was distraught at what he saw as a violation of his own vision of the way he played politics. He called Biden to apologize and, a few days later, did the same with Gephardt, whom he asked not to make the conversation public. Biden described his call from Dukakis this way:

Dukakis: "Kitty and I feel very badly about this. I know what it's like. I'm sorry this happened, but John's a good man."

Biden: "Governor, thanks for calling."

Biden obviously wasn't placated. Long after the campaign, asked why he thought the Dukakis aides had put out the Kinnock tape, he told us: "I think they knew what I knew—that I'd beat them." He was, Biden contended, the only other candidate raising large amounts of money, building "a superior organization" in Iowa and New Hampshire and, except for Jesse Jackson, able to "get any enthusiastic black support."

However, Biden went on, "I didn't pass a moral judgment on Sasso or Michael Dukakis. What angered me the most was that I thought it was a cheap shot at a time when they were smart enough to know I would not be in a position to really be able to respond. It was obviously extremely well and precisely timed. No one in the world can ever convince me that it just all of a sudden appeared on Friday before the Bork hearings, they put it together Saturday and put it out."

In fact, the timing of the "attack video" seemed to have had little or nothing to do with the Bork hearings and everything to do with when the opportunity presented itself. Moreover, neither Sasso nor Tully ever envisaged the episode reaching the proportions that would drive Biden out of the campaign—because neither of them knew of the other revelations that would follow.

The episode had immediate and long-term consequences for Dukakis. In the first instance, he found himself in a position totally new to him in which he was required to defend himself to a national audience. The pressure was enormous, and Dukakis clearly was feeling the heat as he traveled first to Iowa to face the Biden supporters, then to Miami and Washington for debates with other candidates. Dukakis was noticeably subdued. After the debate in Miami, he remained backstage rather than working the room for the usual postdebate interviews, obviously intimidated by the prospect of facing another barrage of questions from a fresh relay of reporters about whether he would ever allow John Sasso to cross the White House threshold.

A similar reticence showed itself in the next debate in Washington. Dukakis remained silent when Paul Simon scolded Al Gore for using divisive rhetoric in the discussion of national-security policy. And when the debate ended, Dukakis quickly left the stage rather than joining in the collective castigation of Gore by the other candidates that ensued in the presence of the descending press corps. "I think he was concerned," campaign manager Susan Estrich said later, "that he would be seen as somehow dirty, negative, the trickster, too harsh."

Nick Mitropoulos, a longtime adviser in Massachusetts and the man at Dukakis' side through the entire campaign, realized this was a new experience for his tiger. As he said later, "All the campaigns for attorney general, lieutenant governor, governor, don't prepare you for what you go through in this kind of situation."

However great the immediate damage to Dukakis, it paled into insignificance when weighed against the loss of John Sasso in his campaign.

Sasso had always held a special position with Dukakis. He was the one person on whom he relied for political advice, both tactical and strategic, as he made his way back from the depths of his Democratic primary defeat in 1978 to political resurrection in 1982 and now a chance at the ultimate prize for any American politician. Dukakis might listen to the counsel of Paul Brountas, his longtime friend and college classmate, on some questions or to Nick Mitropoulos on others, particularly on personnel. As Jack Corrigan, another veteran Dukakis adviser, put it: "If people know what they're talking about, he'll listen." And, in Dukakis' eyes, Sasso stood alone in knowing what he was talking about on questions of politics.

Even in his few months in the campaign Paul Tully had seen how this relationship operated in cases in which advisers accumulated facts and figures to try to persuade Dukakis to take a particular step. "Evidence here has taken us from zero to 90, now we've got 10 percent more to go, called political judgment," Tully said. "He'd listen. Who could make it stick? One person, one person. No doubts about it. No misunderstanding."

That same assessment was evident in Susan Estrich's efforts after she took over for Sasso to find other operatives who had the status with Dukakis to "deal directly" with him. With Dukakis, she learned, having the expertise "only gets you halfway there" in selling a particular course of action. That was the prime reason, she said later, she pressed Kirk O'Donnell, who had been the chief political adviser to Tip O'Neill for years, to join the campaign for the general election. Dukakis had known O'Donnell long enough and worked with him in enough campaigns that Dukakis didn't see him as just another "hired gun." Selling other professionals to Dukakis could be difficult. On one occasion when Estrich was trying to do just that, Dukakis replied: "John Sasso is worth three of those."

Dukakis might well have been just as concerned about losing Tully as about Sasso. Tully had far more experience at the higher levels of presidential campaigns and a particular ability to foresee the strategies the opposition might use and how a campaign would eventually play out. But Dukakis never got beyond thinking of Tully as one of the "hired guns"—an error in judgment for which he paid dearly later in the campaign.

The immediate problem for Dukakis, however, was to staunch the hemorrhaging and regain his balance in the Iowa campaign. The field of Democratic candidates had now been reduced to six, although a clear pecking order was still elusive. Indeed, the controversies over Joe Biden and then John Sasso, coming on the heels of the Gary Hart episode, had made the Democrats dangerously close to becoming a laughingstock—the gang that couldn't shoot straight. Was the nomination simply going to be awarded to the last survivor? Or would the voters of Iowa and New Hampshire finally give the campaign some rational structure?

16

Iowa: Dick Gephardt's Hour

After President Jimmy Carter's defeat at the hands of Ronald Reagan in 1980, he became a kind of political pariah in the Democratic Party. Orators who sought to evoke the glories of the party, who never failed to mention Franklin Roosevelt, Harry Truman, John Kennedy and even Lyndon Johnson, would nearly always ignore Jimmy Carter. It was as if he were a slow-witted aunt or alcoholic uncle in the family, not to be talked about in polite company. But there was one exception. When it came to running for president, no Democrat after Carter's 1976 election would fail to be guided in his own contemplation of a candidacy, or usually in his implementation, by how Carter had used Iowa as his springboard to the White House.

It was part of presidential campaign folklore; how little-known Jimmy in February 1975, shortly after completion of his single term as governor of Georgia, drove from Nebraska over to Le Mars, Iowa, with his alter ego, Jody Powell, for a testimonial dinner honoring Plymouth County recorder Marie Jahn, retiring after thirty-eight years on the job. For agreeing to be the guest speaker, Carter was named Le Mars Citizen of the Day and presented with a free car wash, a movie pass and a coupon for a free pizza. So impressed with Carter's speech was the political reporter of the *Des Moines Register*, James Flansburg, that he wrote that "seldom has a candidate without a fabled name made such a fast and favorable impression on Iowans." The rest became legend: Carter driving from town to town all over the state, staying in ordinary folks' homes, coming out of nowhere to win the presidential straw poll later that year at the annual Democratic Jefferson-Jackson dinner in Ames, then winning the 1976 Iowa precinct caucuses, the Democratic nomination and the presidency.

From then on, the Jimmy Carter experience became the road map to the White House, with Iowa the first stop. Some candidates actually tried to outdo Carter, starting earlier in the four-year cycle, and while none probably matched his record as an overnight guest, the notion that an individual who hoped to be elected president had to work Iowa like a farmer at planting time became political gospel.

Some who decided not to run, such as Governor Mario Cuomo of New York in 1988, cited the Jimmy Carter example as a rationale for staying out of the race. He theorized that Carter had succeeded in part because he was not in office at the time, and hence was free of the responsibilities of governing that would keep a conscientious officeholder at his desk. Cuomo repeatedly mentioned the impossibility for him to be trying to campaign in Iowa and govern in New York at the same time.

But for others with more presidential ambition or less governing responsibility, the Carter example drew them inevitably to Iowa. And soon after the reelection of Republican Ronald Reagan and the resounding defeat of Democrat Walter Mondale in 1984, none was more strongly and conscientiously lured to the state than Democrat Dick Gephardt from neighboring Missouri. In the first year or so thereafter, he made nine visits to Iowa, speaking knowledgeably as a fellow midwesterner about the plight of the farmer and all those whose livelihood depended on the farm economy. He talked of the need to establish national goals to awaken the country from the hypnosis of the popular Republican in the White House. Playing off Reagan's 1984 reelection campaign ads, Gephardt had a message for him: "Mr. President, it's not morning in America. It's twilight, and the light is fading fast."

Others who were not yet so conspicuously on the presidential track, but were taking soundings, also were lured to Iowa. In November 1985, Joe Biden amid much ballyhoo tested the political climate as the main speaker at the annual Jefferson-Jackson dinner, this time held at the spanking-new convention center in Des Moines. In spite of atrocious acoustics, Biden wowed the assembled party activists with a mixture of self-deprecating wit, audacity and compassion-filled phrase-making, capped by a stirring tugging of their heartstrings. In a blatant grasp for the coattails of Kennedys past, he told the crowd: "Just because our political heroes were murdered does not mean that the dream does not still live, buried in our broken hearts." If Ted Kennedy could not resurrect Camelot, those words seemed to say, Joe Biden could.

Biden was saying at the time that he was not running for president and probably wouldn't, considering his age—only forty-three—and obligations to a young family. But his speech served an important tactical objective. It left these Iowa Democratic activists thinking about him and about the kind of exciting campaign he could run—thinking enough to keep them from committing to somebody else. He was freezing the linebackers, in the parlance of the football season then in full sway. After the 1976 experience of Jimmy Carter, establishing a beachhead in Iowa was essential to anyone even considering a presidential bid. And attempts within the party to take away Iowa's status as the kickoff site for Democratic presidential politics were futile. Iowa was the place.

Some of the early visitors to Iowa, in fact, sought to capitalize on their belief that this was so. Bruce Babbitt flatly told Iowans that he would pin all his hopes on Iowa—and New Hampshire—and if he couldn't make a breakthrough in those two states, he'd quit. When he spoke, he was at 1 percent in the Iowa Poll, far behind the leader, Gary Hart with 56 percent, and the runner-up, Mario Cuomo, with 13. If low expectations were good, as they proved to be for Carter in 1976 and for Hart in his second-place finish in Iowa in 1984, then there was some hope for Babbitt.

When Gephardt made his formal announcement of candidacy in St. Louis in February 1987, he flew directly to Des Moines—his twenty-fifth trip and forty-first day in Iowa in two years—and repeated it. A few weeks later Babbitt announced in New Hampshire and flew straight to Iowa, and about a week after that Jesse Jackson opened his exploratory committee headquarters in the farm town of Greenfield, just southwest of Des Moines.

In another month, Michael Dukakis was in, declaring in New Hampshire, then stopping in Boston and Atlanta on his way to Des Moines. According to a series of memoranda prepared by John Sasso, his campaign manager and alter ego, the early battle plan would be to differentiate himself from the pack by emphasizing his executive experience and successes and survive the Iowa caucuses with a presentable showing against front-running Gary Hart. Then, the Sasso memo said, Dukakis could knock him off in his native New England, becoming the political giant-killer in the New Hampshire primary.

But Dukakis got an uncertain start in Iowa. On an early trip, he suggested that the state's farmers take a tip from Massachusetts' economic success by diversifying. He recommended that corn and soybean farmers try growing apples, blueberries, flowers and—Belgian endive. This last haunted Dukakis for months thereafter. Governor Bill Clinton of Arkansas called the formula "yuppie agriculture" and the other candidates milked it for all the laughs they could get. But Dukakis pressed on.

Biden, while not yet announcing, was working Iowa intensively now, jokingly telling audiences, as chairman of the Senate Judiciary Committee, that "I am one of the most important men in America"—and explaining that he was usually mistaken for a look-alike, Peter Ueberroth, the commissioner of baseball. "Look me over," he would say with his irrepressible confidence. "If you like what you see, I'd like your help. If not, vote for the other guy."

Finally, there was Paul Simon, the last Democrat to get into the race. He offered himself as the political Uncola, an undiluted New Dealer with a special regional tie to Iowa, coming as he did from rural southern Illinois just across the Mississippi and exuding midwestern solidity and openness in a bow tie. On his first day in Des Moines in April, he sat in a committee room in the state capitol and spoke to a sprinkling of Democratic legislators and staff workers brown-bagging their lunch, so low-key you could have mistaken him for a Capitol guide. While others in his party were running from the old liberal traditions, he told the few who were listening that he'd like to resurrect a version of FDR's old WPA, putting welfare recipients and the unemployed to work on community needs. That one would take a lot of selling, but Simon was resolute.

Not all the prospective Democratic candidates for 1988 flocked to the state with hat in hand, however. Conspicuous by his absence was Hart. In the fall of 1986 he committed himself to diligent campaigning for Democratic candidates to the Senate—except in Iowa, where one of his 1984 congressional district chairmen, John Roehrick, was making a futile, long-shot challenge to Chuck Grassley. Hart never campaigned for him, nor did he venture into the state through most of 1987. Old 1984 backers were bitter; Barbara Leach, Hart's 1984 cochair in the state, reported that she had not heard from him since then, "not so much as a single thank-you note." Still, such sentiments didn't seem to hurt him in the Iowa Poll at the time. He was riding high—until that weekend at his town house in Washington and his startling exit from the presidential campaign.

A few hours after Hart had withdrawn with his bitter lashing-out at the news media and unnamed, cutthroat Democratic hacks, one of us sat in the bar of the Savery Hotel in Des Moines with a couple of shell-shocked but newly hopeful Biden supporters. "This is the first day of the campaign," said Bill Daley, son of the late Mayor Richard J. Daley of Chicago. The second Biden man, 1986 Democratic gubernatorial candidate Lowell Junkins, was even more pointed. "Jump ball," he said, in the basketball vernacular.

By the time of Hart's withdrawal, he had become the choice of 65 percent of Iowa Democrats surveyed, to 9 percent for Jackson and 7 for Gephardt. In Iowa, at least, Hart's departure from the race seemed to trigger a letdown among some workers for other candidates. They sensed Hart's weakness in the state, bred in part from his neglect, and each had hoped that his candidate could become a political giant-killer by knocking him off or running an unexpectedly strong second to him in the caucuses, as he had used Mondale as a springboard in 1984.

The Iowa precinct caucuses as a magnet of political opportunity was a relatively recent development. When they first emerged as a factor in presidential nomination politics, in 1972, they were a well-kept secret. Only two national candidates, Senator Edmund Muskie of Maine, the overwhelming early favorite, and long-shot Senator George McGovern of neighboring South Dakota, had a bare handful of operatives working in the state. When one of us arrived in Des Moines about ten days before the caucuses, only one other national reporter was there, and on the final weekend only two or three others showed up, none of them from television. A few union members worked a few phones out of a Ramada Inn to persuade labor caucus-goers to vote for uncommitted precinct delegates, as a holding action for Senator Hubert Humphrey, who had not yet decided whether he would run. And when McGovern finished unexpectedly close to Muskie on caucus night, presaging his later upset of the front-runner for the nomination, few people noticed.

One who did, however, was Hamilton Jordan, Governor Jimmy Carter's executive secretary in Atlanta. But in his early game plan for Carter's guerrilla pursuit of the presidency, even Jordan did not seem to realize the potential of Iowa. He wrote that the New Hampshire primary, much better known, not the

Iowa caucuses, was the event that could be Carter's breakout from obscurity. In a rating of priority states in the Carter strategy, Jordan put New Hampshire, Florida and Illinois at the top, and Iowa well down. But the publicity drawn by the Ames straw poll in 1975, and Carter's success in it (winning only 23 percent, behind "uncommitteds") and in the 1976 caucuses, made Iowa an overnight rival to New Hampshire as the first serious presidential election battleground. On the night of the 1976 caucuses, the Iowa Democratic chairman at the time, Tom Whitney, actually sold tickets to the public to watch the national reporters assembled at the Hilton Hotel in Des Moines as they digested the caucus results and wrote and broadcast them.

Surprise was always the secret ingredient in the appeal of the Iowa caucuses to competing candidates, and to the news media. In 1980, on the Republican side, George Bush blindsided Ronald Reagan there, and in 1984, Gary Hart's unexpected second-place finish to Walter Mondale among the Democrats propelled him into serious contention. This time around, as long as front-running Hart was in the Democratic race, the potential for a big surprise was present in upsetting him. The other Democrats came into Iowa in 1986 and 1987 not so much to sneak up on the unsuspecting news media and public, as Carter had done; it was to capitalize on Iowa's new stature as *the* important first Democratic test, easily eclipsing the New Hampshire primary. And doing so no longer meant a lightning strike or two by the candidate at a major political event, but instead political trench warfare—coming into Iowa early and repeatedly, with platoons of aides and volunteers, and with heavy expenditures, up to $760,000 in 1988, the limit imposed by the federal law for the state.

The night after Hart's dramatic exit in May, Gephardt, Biden, Simon and Dukakis all attended a Polk County Democratic steak fry at the Iowa State Fairgrounds in what was now a new ball game. They all skirted around Hart's fall except Gephardt, who called it "a tragedy for everyone in the family of the Democratic Party." But in their grief, they wasted no time trying to recruit the best of the Hart team in Iowa, led by Teresa Vilmain, a frenetic young Iowan who had run a 1986 Senate campaign. In due time, Vilmain and a number of her associates moved over to the Dukakis campaign, where after another interlude she became the state campaign manager.

With Hart out, Gephardt, who had worked Iowa the earliest and most diligently, took over the lead in the Iowa Poll, moving up from 9 percent to 24, with 13 percent for Jackson and 11 for Dukakis, and the rest trailing. As the new front-runner, Gephardt said, "you had to try to continue doing what you were doing but from a different position, a different vantage point. It didn't really change anything we were trying to do, but I think it took away what a lot of people saw what you were trying to do in Iowa, which was surprise people by your result. . . . So now, instead of being an insurgent, you're trying to protect turf and expand turf and build a stronger organization." The spurt raised the spirits of Gephardt's supporters but it also robbed him of the chance to reap the news media attention that would have gone with such an upset.

Not only that, Gephardt campaign manager Bill Carrick said long afterward, as consequence of becoming the clear Iowa front-runner Gephardt had to win the caucuses in his neighboring state or suffer in the perceptions game. "If the Gephardt campaign was a B movie," he said, "we'd almost be 'The Campaign That Was Eaten by Iowa.' " Gephardt, he said, "never imagined he was going to have to go wire to wire in Iowa as the front-runner. So the whole campaign started to be viewed through the prism of Iowa. . . . And I knew in my heart we were not as organized as the media had given us credit for."

At the same time, Babbitt, in a bold move to get on the Iowa political radar screen, decided to spend $250,000 in early television advertising. It was a tactic he later called "a total waste of money" because even likely caucus attendees were not prepared to consider the candidates so early in the game. Others chose to debate each other, for the same purpose. Babbitt and another asterisk, Republican Pete duPont, squared off and got some press attention in a match that Babbitt defined as "at least . . . a cut above Bartles and Jaymes." Gephardt and Republican Jack Kemp tried it next and then in early August Gephardt and Dukakis went at it as an aftermath to their argument in the Houston debate over trade. The exchange exposed Gephardt's vulnerability to the charge that he had flip-flopped on important issues, that he was, in the phrase of Brian Lunde, Simon's national campaign manager, "the water bug of Democratic politics."

Some serious animosity was building between the Dukakis and Gephardt camps now. The Dukakis strategists considered that they had scored a major tactical coup by getting Gephardt to agree to hold the two-man debate in Iowa, where Gephardt was now the front-runner. "We're in Des Moines," Tully said later, "the major media market, one on one with this dude. We've got a chance to start shaping this race for real, instead of this clutter of midgets." It was for this reason that the Dukakis strategists were so euphoric over the outcome of that debate, which they clearly believed their man had won not only by airing Gephardt's voting flip-flops but also by making the point that as an executive he took action while Gephardt as a legislator merely cast votes, and often contradictory votes at that.

In late August, it was in the context of still another debate in Iowa, as already noted, that Biden adapted without attribution whole segments of a Neil Kinnock speech and, with other allegations of plagiarism, saw his own campaign shattered. For the second time in four months, the Democratic presidential picture in Iowa was scrambled. And this time not only was the principal player damaged but two other candidates as well—one, Dukakis, for the role two of his key strategists played in Biden's demise, and another, Gephardt, for widespread rumors and suspicions that his campaign really had been the culprit.

Once again the Iowa Poll indicated it was, in Lowell Junkins' earlier words, "Jump ball," but this time without his candidate in the lineup. On August 30, a week after Biden's use of Kinnock's words at the Iowa State Fairgrounds debate but before the plagiarism charges broke, Gephardt was now only narrowly ahead in the Iowa Poll with 18 percent of Democrats surveyed, to 14 for Dukakis, 13 for Simon, 10 each for Biden and Jackson, 9 for Babbitt. Ironically, it was Gephardt, not Dukakis, who suffered the most slippage, and his strategists later blamed the false rumors.

Dukakis, although personally crushed by the loss of John Sasso, moved quickly to repair the damage in Iowa. In early October, on the first weekend after the resignations of Sasso and Paul Tully, he went to Iowa for a public mea culpa through the heart of Biden's stronghold in the western part of the state. Riding in his car with him, the impression one got was of a man still stunned and personally aggrieved by what had happened, yet resolute in his determination to confront the consequences directly and press on.

Although he clearly was on a personal political salvage mission, Dukakis talked in that earnestly sorrowful way of his about how the series of mishaps that had afflicted the Democratic field, the last of which his campaign was responsible for, was hurting the party's chances to capitalize on the Reagan administration's own embarrassments—the string of indictments and investigations of high officials and cronies. "We shouldn't be throwing that issue away," he said ruefully. It was no wonder, he said, that the news media were taking such a probing look at the character and ethics of all of the candidates. "After what's gone on there in Washington in the last five or seven years, you should," he said.

But it was important, he went on, "that this nomination count for something." One of the reasons he had challenged Gephardt to the debate on trade policy, he said, was that rather than engage in "name-calling" it was better to debate their honest differences out in the open. Now, after the Biden tape episode that had so wounded him politically and personally, he said, he was determined with this trip to get his campaign back on the high road. And this determination was not without its pragmatic side. "As a practical matter," he said as the car at the head of the motorcade rolled over the Iowa countryside, "in addition to being the right thing to do, if you build a good strong campaign, and you start to do well in those early primaries and other people drop off, you want to be their second choice, don't you?"

It was because his campaign was perceived as strong and positive at the time Gary Hart quit the race, he said, that many key operatives including his Iowa campaign manager, Teresa Vilmain, elected to join his staff. He acknowledged that in light of what had just happened, he wasn't likely to win over disgruntled Biden workers, but he was going to make the effort to show them he was genuinely contrite about his campaign's role in the Biden demise, and committed to restoring his image as a positive campaigner.

Accordingly, it was grit your teeth and bear what was coming. In Sioux City, Biden's strongest town, a Biden supporter named Tim Bottaro said in advance of Dukakis' arrival: "He wants to face the music, and in my opinion the music is 'Taps.' "

Bottaro wasn't far wrong as far as some Biden backers were concerned. They greeted Dukakis with anger and stern lecturing and for once at least the often cocky bantam rooster of a man stood in humility and took it all. "I'm very, very saddened and apologetic for what happened to Senator Biden," he said at a Sioux City high school. At this and other stops, he said he had always insisted on the highest standards from his staff and had always sought to run positive campaigns. And he pledged that he would not tolerate any further negative campaigning by his subordinates. "If I had been a supporter of Joe Biden," he said in Ida Grove, "I would be very angry. Sure I would. I myself am angry."

Many of the old Biden backers were in no mood to accept Dukakis' apology. Cecilia Flanagan of Sioux City demanded to know why it had taken "so long" for him to get rid of Sasso. "Timing it [the videotape leak] to come up during the Bork hearings [chaired by Biden] was a horrible thing to do to the Democrats," she complained. And a man in the audience called out: "Why do you want to hang a man who walked on the wrong side of the street?" Another listener admonished the angry Biden backers that "we came to listen to the governor, not you," but Dukakis patiently disagreed and invited his critics to keep hitting him.

Although what Sasso had done was "incomprehensible" to him, Dukakis said, "I'm the candidate. I've got to take responsibility for what happens in my campaign, whether I know about it or not. I accept that responsibility. I expect to be held accountable, and I'm accountable." The closest he came to an alibi was when he told some senior citizens in the town of Onawa: "You can be the most brilliant quarterback in the world, but unless you have a line that protects you . . . you're gonna be sacked every time."

That football analogy didn't play with everybody. In Council Bluffs, the local Biden cochair, Sheila Amdar, recalled the 1982 making of the tape ridiculing then Governor Ed King in Dukakis' gubernatorial comeback, played for reporters by Sasso. "What bothers me is in 1982 he pulled this same type of deal," she told Dukakis. "To be surrounded with people like that is damaging to the Democratic Party, to Joe Biden and a lot of his supporters. Why did you let a person stay with you when he pulled something like that?"

The question had to be particularly bruising to Dukakis, considering it involved the man he described at an earlier stop as "the closest thing I have to a brother." His response was lame; it was, he said, "inconceivable" to him that another videotape incident could take place after that 1982 episode, and he defended Sasso as "one of the best, one of the most open, one of the most honest and ethical people I've ever worked with. You have to know the man," he said, "and remember none of us in this world are perfect."

But Amdar didn't accept that answer. She told reporters she believed the videotape leak against Biden was done with Dukakis' full intent to destroy Biden's campaign. "I believe he felt Joe Biden was the only man he couldn't beat," she snapped. That, Paul Tully said later, was not quite the case. "We were never afraid of Biden as the winner of Iowa," he said. "We understood that Biden took a chunk out of Dukakis' potential of winning. Biden was not special as a target because he was gonna win. That campaign's got enough problems. . . . He had the best potential to take a chunk out of us, and now he's using our message, or a sizable chunk of our message on economic opportunity. . . . He was going to try to play on our turf."

A state legislator named Tom Bisignano who had supported Biden met privately with Dukakis and said afterward he accepted the governor's "honest explanation of what happened," but had not gotten an answer when he asked whether Dukakis if elected would appoint Sasso to the White House staff. Pressed by reporters, Dukakis said that "John Sasso will have no role, formal or informal, in this campaign," but "will I continue to communicate with him as a friend? Of course." Such remarks fanned speculation that only increased as time went on that Sasso continued to direct the campaign from the wings.

Even at this early stage, the rumors were intensifying among Democratic activists in Iowa that the Gephardt campaign had first leaked the Kinnock videotape. At a coffee in Sioux City, Gephardt political aide Joe Trippi recalled later, "a man stood up and just said, 'I can't support you, not after what you've done to Joe Biden.' It would happen stop after stop, and Dick would have to say, 'I didn't do this.' Even after Dukakis took the heat, we'd still run into people who accused Dick." The accusation also came up in focus groups, Carrick said.

Others in the Gephardt campaign assumed that the Darth Vader of Democratic presidential politics, pollster/conceptualizer Pat Caddell, was stirring up a witches' brew against two of Gephardt's chief strategists, David Doak and Bob Shrum, who had been in a partnership with Caddell that had gone sour. They, and Trippi, began to get a flurry of press inquiries about whether they had made the Kinnock tape. "We all thought at the time," Trippi said, "that the Duke people were pointing at us, saying we did it. In the end, when we found out they were the ones who really did it, that ticked us off even more."

One particular incident that stuck in the minds of Gephardt and many of his aides was a party that Teresa Vilmain as the Iowa manager of the Dukakis campaign was alleged to have held for the Biden staff in Iowa after he withdrew. Some in the Gephardt camp were under the impression that she invited people from every Democratic presidential campaign in Iowa except Gephardt's— which the Gephardt people read as a way to peddle the idea that their campaign had been responsible for the undoing of Biden. Afterward, word came back to Gephardt staffers that there was much joking at this party about how the Gephardt campaign had leaked the tape.

Vilmain, however, swore later that she had never held any such party, let alone excluded members of the Gephardt campaign. What happened, she said, was that after Biden's withdrawal some of the Biden staff repaired to Evy's, a Des Moines bar near the Biden headquarters, and that when she and others in the Dukakis headquarters heard about it, they went by to commiserate.

In any event, the rumors that Gephardt staffers had been the videotape leakers, and that Dukakis aides encouraged them, quickly made their way to Biden territory in the state. "I think Dick Gephardt deserves an apology," one woman in Sioux City told a stone-faced Dukakis on the first day of his mea culpa tour. But he declined to apologize, at least publicly. Privately, however, he did telephone Gephardt sometime later, as Gephardt was at the office of Doak and Shrum preparing for yet another debate in advance of the Iowa caucuses, and expressed his regrets. Dukakis for some reason asked Gephardt to keep his apology private, and Gephardt acceded. But others who were in the room when the call came told us later that Gephardt, after clearing the room to take the call, was visibly upset when they were admitted again. He informed his aides, one of them said, that "he had told Dukakis that he was not happy about the party that got held in Des Moines. I think Dick thought that was a calculated thing."

Dukakis himself was upset and called Vilmain directly to ask whether she was spreading the rumor that Gephardt people had leaked the tape. She assured him she had not. Knowing what a stickler Dukakis was about any kind of negative campaigning, she said later, she already had called Dukakis staffers around the state, telling them to say nothing whatever about the videotape incident.

Many Biden backers who met Dukakis on his mea culpa swing seemed impressed with his straightforward expressions of regret. At the senior citizens' center in Onawa, sixty-six-year-old Isabel Carlson, a retired nurse, defended him. "If he didn't know about it . . . I don't feel he should take complete responsibility," she said. "I don't think the rest of us should crucify somebody for what has happened if it really wasn't his fault. And you know, we have a tendency to do that, and none of us is lily white. I think we should take that under consideration. Otherwise we're not going to have anyone good running."

Tully said later that Dukakis' decision to go hat in hand to the Biden people in Iowa was critical in shoring up his credibility, and had he not gotten rid of Sasso he "would have paid the price" in an embarrassingly poorer finish in the caucuses there. The very fact that Sasso meant so much to him—personally as well as politically—made Dukakis' mea culpa particularly effective, Tully reasoned. "It was credible that there was a severe punishment going on. . . . It was credible that it was a big deal, that it was not for free, that there was cost, that he really meant it." But the price had to be paid, he said, "because it was a club that was going to be left on the table to hit you with every two weeks."

Irwin ("Tubby") Harrison, the Dukakis pollster, said later that Dukakis' quick trip into Biden country in Iowa helped keep his losses to a minimum in the state. In fact, about three weeks after Biden's withdrawal, another Iowa Poll had Dukakis' support rising, from 14 percent to 18. Gephardt, beset by rumors of complicity in the Biden tape affair, slipped to third place, favored by only 14 percent of those surveyed, and was replaced in the lead by Simon, with 24 percent. There was, it seemed to the Gephardt team in Iowa, no justice.

The real beneficiary of the Biden pullout, Trippi said later, was Simon, "the only guy left in the race that the deed hadn't been done to and hadn't done the deed" in voters' minds. Many who had been for Biden, Gephardt said later, "then went to Simon." Of the whole tape episode, Trippi said, "if that hadn't happened, I'm not sure Paul Simon would have existed" as a viable candidate in Iowa.

Simon, for his part, worked the former Biden camp diligently. It was not always an easy sell. One of the factors that made Biden attractive to Iowans was his flash, his jaunty, electric style in both appearance and speech that made Democrats believe he was the "electable" politician for whom they had been looking so long. But Paul Simon was plain vanilla in a bow tie.

Before a gathering of Biden supporters at the home of Peter and Rickie Pasher in Des Moines one morning shortly after Biden dropped out, Simon got the "electability" question straight out. He responded with a low-key monologue on how education was one of his strong suits and was on every voter's mind and how, coming from rural Illinois, he could generate support in the South. The pitch did not exactly get his listeners jumping to their feet, but after the afflictions of Hart, Biden and Dukakis, steady old Paul Simon might be the antidote. Rickie Pasher compared him to the tortoise in the old fable. "At the beginning he was somewhat overlooked," she said, "but his campaign has been consistent—slow but steady."

The same could be said of the other two Democrats competing in Iowa, Babbitt and Jackson. Babbitt after his summer television initiative had strengthened his Iowa organization but had little to show for it in the polls. Jackson, meanwhile, was working hard to put more white into his Rainbow Coalition. He opened his state campaign headquarters in rural Greenfield, where in October his supporters set up a huge tent on a friendly farmer's land and conducted an old-fashioned kickoff rally that was part hoedown and part church revival. A black choir clapped, swayed and sang upbeat hymns as grizzled, red-faced farmers in quilted jackets and plump farm wives in turn testified to Jackson's responses to their calls for help from the travails of the farm depression.

Typical was Chillicothe, Missouri, farmer Bill Smith, who told why he and several carloads of friends had driven up to take part in the rally. Jackson, he said, had persuaded local bankers to restructure their loans. "We weren't gonna continue to farm," he said, "and we couldn't have done it without Jesse." Such testimony was the cement with which Jackson hoped to build his coalition along class rather than racial lines. Giant corporations, he told the assembled farmers, were shifting production overseas, forcing industrial workers into the same box they now found themselves in as a result of the squeeze from big bankers. "It's not enough for you to be right," he shouted. "There are not enough of you to save yourselves." The oppressed on farmland and on the assembly line had to come together. It was a message that Jackson had to sell if he hoped to improve his 1984 showing in a state with a minority population of only 2 percent.

One other Democratic hopeful, meanwhile, was making no appeal to Iowa at all, and instead was using the state as a whipping boy in the hope of capitalizing on the tactic later on. Young Al Gore, as the final speaker at the Democrats' annual Jefferson-Jackson dinner in Des Moines, in the guise of truth-telling launched into a tirade of Iowa-bashing. He attacked "a nominating process that gives one state the loudest voice and then produces candidates who cannot even carry that state." Iowa, he noted, hadn't voted for a Democrat for president since 1964. What he didn't say was that he was running a flat last in the Iowa polls and didn't have a prayer in the approaching caucuses.

In a cavalier manner toward his colleagues that increasingly marked his single-minded, take-no-prisoners lurch toward a Democratic nomination that was always beyond his grasp, Gore proclaimed: "I won't do what the pundits say it takes to win in Iowa—flatter you with promises, change my tune and back down on my convictions"—implying that was what his Democratic brethren were doing. "I won't play that game or abide by those rules. . . . I will not barter my beliefs to win votes here or elsewhere. . . . If that is what it takes to win the Iowa caucuses, I won't do it." Fortunately for Gore, the only folks in the audience who were paying much attention at that late hour were a gaggle of Tennesseans shipped in to cheer him on. As for his contention that he wouldn't "play that game," he had in Iowa at the time a paid staff of twenty-one, including fourteen field organizers, and was busing in members of his Tennessee "Gore Corps" to woo Iowa Democrats.

At the same forum, Gephardt, once characterized as a neo-liberal, had no qualms about playing the game, quoting Robert Kennedy to the mostly moderate to liberal crowds of party activists. But even then he seemed to lack spark. He ticked off the many specific positions he had laid out, on trade, tax reform, defense spending and agriculture, but his passion for specificity did not seem to be lighting many fires.

Still, with his candidacy seemingly in the doldrums, Gephardt continued to work the political vineyards, becoming the first Democratic candidate to have visited all of Iowa's ninety-nine counties. By this time, longtime Gephardt aide Steve Murphy had been moved into Iowa to run the state campaign, and he concluded that for all the specificity, the Gephardt campaign lacked a penetrating theme.

At the same time, Bill Carrick noted later, "parallel with the Biden witch-hunt problem was Simon's rise. . . . He was not a neo-anything. Gephardt started losing older caucus-goers to Simon, and liberals." In the late fall, Simon and Dukakis began running radio and television ads, and Gephardt, who was having money problems and was off the air, slipped even more. In December the *Des Moines Register*'s Iowa Poll had him down to single digits. "I'll never forget," Gephardt said later, "David Yepsen [the *Des Moines Register* political writer] saw me one day, and he said, 'You know, Dick, Iowans have heard your message, and they don't like it.' " Congressman Tony Coelho paid a visit and also came back with the view that Gephardt needed a much sharper focus to his message that Iowa voters could identify with.

Gephardt seemed to be getting desperate. In an NBC News debate among all the candidates at the Kennedy Center in December, he went after Simon's call for a welfare work program and his simultaneous support of a constitutional amendment to balance the budget. When Simon described himself as a "pay-as-you-go Democrat," Gephardt broke in with "you're a promise-as-you-go Democrat," and he charged that "Simonomics is really Reaganomics in a bow tie." There were immediate indications in Iowa that the crack might backfire on him. On the night of the debate, a Seattle pollster named Christopher Wheeler got a hundred Iowans to monitor the exchange and register their reaction electronically on hand-held dials moment by moment. Gephardt's remark, Wheeler reported, got "an extremely negative rating."

At the same time, however, Simon acknowledged later that he didn't do well in the debate. He had just flown in from Chicago where he attended the funeral of Mayor Harold Washington, had had no rest and hadn't prepared adequately for the debate, and especially for questions about how he would pay for the WPA-type work program and others and still balance the budget. "I should have had a succinct one-minute answer," he told us later, "but I didn't. . . . It appeared I was ducking—which in fact I was doing." Simon began to look like just another New Deal big spender, and his campaign started to hemorrhage.

Brian Lunde, Simon's national campaign manager, said later that the "Reaganomics with a bow tie" remark hurt badly. "Our whole platform was credibility," he said. Simon was right culturally for Iowa, Lunde said, but "we were down a slippery slope on economics."

At this juncture, along came the third big political explosion of the year. Out of the blue, Gary Hart, after communing with himself, his wife, children and a few friends, on December 15 flew to New Hampshire, where he paid a thousand-dollar filing fee for the state's February 16 primary just under the deadline at the statehouse in Concord. With a smiling Lee at his side, Hart proclaimed:

"I intend to resume my presidential campaign and let the people decide. . . . This will not be like any campaign you've ever seen, because I'm going directly to the people. I don't have a national headquarters or staff. I don't have any money. I don't have pollsters, or consultants or media advisers or political endorsements. But I have something better. I have the power of ideas and I can govern this country. Let's let the people decide. I'm back in the race."

What was Hart up to? The decision, after he had been so thoroughly discredited and ridiculed by the nature and temper of his May withdrawal, triggered numerous theories. Maybe he was simply trying to qualify for federal matching funds to retire his campaign debt. Maybe he just wanted to have a forum to get all his gripes about the news media off his chest. Maybe he thought he could prod the other candidates into a more substantive issue discussion. Maybe he needed final proof that he had made the right decision in getting out in the first place. Surely he didn't think he could be nominated, not after all that had happened.

"I'm not foolish," Hart said that night on ABC News' *Nightline*. "And I'm not going to perpetuate a campaign that's not going anywhere or doesn't have any popular support, or doesn't have at least the chance to take enough delegates to the convention to condition the platform and the policies of this party into the 1990s. . . . But I must say I also intend to win." Hart said, too, that he was through answering questions about his personal life; from then on he would talk about issues, period.

Simon, campaigning in Texas, was among the more generous in his reaction. "I know Gary feels deeply about the issues," he said, "but I hope he isn't fooling himself. My concern is that we don't trivialize the campaign. We should not have a campaign that focuses on what someone did some weekend somewhere."

Although Hart made his announcement in New Hampshire, it hit Iowa with equal force because that was where his first tangible test as a resurrected candidate would come. The other candidates did not, to say the very least, take kindly to the implied suggestion that none of them was adequately carrying the Democratic banner toward the 1988 fray against the Republicans.

Babbitt, who prided himself in being the straight talker of the bunch, minced no words. He blasted what he called "a disturbing tone of arrogance" in Hart, saying "he got out of the race because of the failures of the media, and that he's getting back into the race because of the failures of the other candidates. Well, he's wrong on both counts."

The next day, Babbitt expanded. "Mr. Hart is going around saying he feels bound to run because nobody else is addressing the vital issues of the day," he said. "I resent that. It seems to me that Gary Hart has a hell of a long way to go before he has anything to teach this candidate about grappling with hard choices and standing up for the truth." Later he added that "I think anyone is entitled to make a comeback." But, he snapped, "I don't know if the appropriate model is Sugar Ray Leonard or Jim and Tammy Bakker."

Gephardt struck the same chord. "Nobody doubts that Gary Hart has ideas, but even Gary can't believe he has a monopoly on good ideas or that he's the only candidate with a substantive agenda for America's future. . . . Frankly, I wonder why Gary has never accomplished many of the things he always talks about . . . we agree on many things, but unlike Gary Hart, I have the trust of my colleagues." Simon said Hart was engaging in "an intellectual exercise involving a set of abstract proposals . . . [and] glib phrases about shiny new ideas."

Paul Maslin, Simon's pollster, observed correctly that "all eyes will be on Iowa. We've got a dragon out there," he said. "The question is who is going to be St. George, who is going to slay the dragon, and the first chance is in Iowa." Chris Hamel, Babbitt's campaign manager in the state, was even more pointed. "We all now have a target," he said. "Not until he gets firmly discredited will we be rid of this guy."

The first public reaction, in Iowa as around the country, was the mindless response to the familiar name. A *Washington Post*–ABC News national poll of a mere 318 Democrats, with a 6 percent margin of error, had Hart jumping to the head of the pack. Thirty percent of those surveyed favored him to 20 percent for Jackson, 15 for Dukakis, 8 for Simon, 5 for Gore and only 2 apiece for Gephardt and Babbitt. But 49 percent of those surveyed said they had an unfavorable opinion of Hart and 40 percent said they would not vote for him under any circumstance.

In Iowa, where he was riding high in the polls when he first quit the race seven months earlier, Hart bounced back up to the top again in the first survey taken after his reentry. Conducted the first weekend of January by the Gallup organization, Hart was cited as the choice of 34 percent of 588 registered Iowa Democrats surveyed, or more than twice the support garnered by the runner-up, Simon, with 16 percent. Gephardt was at 15 and Dukakis at 13.

Hart himself, campaigning in New Hampshire and drawing very large crowds, dismissed such polls as "superficial barometers" especially in a caucus process like the one in Iowa, which he called "an organization-minded state that requires a kind of organizational commitment we simply cannot make compared to the other candidates." Already he seemed to be back into the game of lowering expectations, although it was true that the kind of bare-bones campaign he was saying he would run certainly did not figure to offer much hope for him in Iowa.

Hart's pitch was unambiguously antiestablishment. "If you're fed up with these media-oriented campaigns," he said at one stop in South Dakota, "then come with me. . . . A handful of powerful people in Washington are not going to pick the next president. . . . The people of this country are going to pick the next president." Hart adopted a policy of no press conferences, obviously as a way to avoid interrogation about his personal life. When asked after a lecture on foreign policy at Dover High School whether he thought politicians had a right to mislead the voters, Hart replied that he did not, "but on the other hand, the public does not have a right to know everything about everybody's personal and private life." He was counting on voters agreeing with him on the point, but the polls suggested he was sailing against a hurricane on that one.

With the start of the election year and the Iowa caucuses only five weeks off, all the other campaigns geared up for the final organizational push. Gephardt by now had all but closed down his Washington headquarters and his relatively few outposts in southern Super Tuesday states and drawn most available hands into Iowa. After holding back on radio and television commercials while Simon and Dukakis intensified their media buys, the Gephardt campaign finally made its move on the day after Christmas.

In a conversation with Carrick and Shrum one day, Gephardt was talking about the huge cost of buying an American car in Japan and Korea with the import tariff imposed. The discussion proved to be a turning point in the Gephardt campaign. A researcher found an old column in the *Detroit News* suggesting a Ford Taurus would cost something like $76,000 in Korea. Using the Korean tariff base, the cost of the Hyundai if it were applied to the car's sale in this country was calculated at $48,000. Suddenly, a dynamite television commercial was born. First run on less expensive cable television, it caught on as a crispy and catchy distillation of Gephardt's position on trade. In less than three weeks he rebounded from about 9 percent in the polls to 28—yet another illustration of the volatility of polls and how the numbers could be "driven up" by effective television advertising.

Brian Lunde, Simon's manager, said later the ad made Gephardt "the Howard Beal of American politics"—a reference to the television anchorman in the movie *Network* who declared he was "mad as hell and I'm not going to take it anymore," and aroused a nation to the same sentiment.

The Hyundai ad, appealing to free-trade Iowa farmers, marked a distinct upturn in the Gephardt campaign, and it began to pick up again as Simon's slipped, in part because Hart with his reentry replaced him as, in Steve Murphy's phrase, "the flavor of the month." Beyond that, Lunde said later, Simon was reduced in the last weeks to frenetic traveling around the state, substituting motion for substance, "because we didn't have anything more to say." When staffers urged Simon to run negative television ads against Gephardt for flip-flopping on major issues, Simon declined. Also, Lunde said, Simon's bow tie, which he had worn all his life and continued to wear to show he was not going to change to meet the supposed dictates of modern politics, in the end itself became a gimmick. Instead of conveying a sense of independence it suggested a man "too set in his ways."

At the same time, Dukakis struggled with internal problems. He had laid down orders to his staff to abide by all legal limits on spending in every state, and as the campaign in Iowa got closer to caucus night, the squeeze was on. According to Vilmain later, young staff workers were not getting paid and had to scrounge to eat; printing bills were going unpaid and the campaign owed money to the state party, whose headquarters was on the floor above the Dukakis campaign office. At a tense meeting of about sixty-five Dukakis staffers, it was decided to break off relations with the Boston headquarters. No phone calls from that source were to be returned until money was sent out to pay for an estimated $54,000 in outstanding bills. After a one-day "boycott," Tad Devine was dispatched from Boston and the bills paid. Vilmain, for her mutinous behavior, was not given another state to run, according to Boston campaign sources.

Hart did not return to Iowa until the end of the first week of January. He focused on high school audiences and avoided press conferences. But he and his wife submitted to an extraordinary interview with editors and reporters at the *Des Moines Register*. For nearly an hour and a half, the Harts spoke of their objectives in his return to the race and the candidate subjected himself to some withering observations about his personal life, in the presence of his wife.

After saying he intended to compete in the Iowa caucuses although he knew he didn't have the resources required to make a strong showing, and after denying he ever meant to imply the other candidates were barren of ideas, Hart sat and listened as an editor read excerpts of letters to the editor from Iowans touching on his credibility.

A man from Des Moines wrote that he would not "vote for a man who has the morals of an alley cat. If he can't be true to his family, what reason do we have to think he would use proper judgment about anything else?" And a man in Sioux Center wrote: "Hart is not an electable candidate. He may run for president in a free country, and that's his freedom under our Constitution, but he can never outrun his foul reputation as an adulterer. If he cannot keep his vow to his wife, how can he be trusted to keep his campaign promises?"

Hart responded at length. "I let myself down. I let my family down. I let my supporters down," he began. But he said he had "gone beyond practically any public person, at least in my lifetime, in seeking to make amends for that" in all manner of public forums, including apologizing and asking "for the forgiveness of people who were offended and had a right to be offended." But, he went on, he deserved to have his life put in the perspective of fifteen years in public service, and that "if I were a man of bad character, it seems to me that bad character would have come out over time." His own life, he said, "deserves to be put in perspective of what I would call public morality: arms sales to terrorists, illegal covert wars, lying to Congress, shredding of documents, deceiving of the American people where their business is concerned." In other words, what he had done was not as bad as the behavior of figures in the Reagan administration in the Iran-Contra scandal.

Furthermore, Hart said, "an awful lot of leaders in this country, including some of our finest . . . have not had perfect personal lives." And then he added: "If I'm elected I won't be the first adulterer in the White House. I may be the first one to have publicly confessed to that sin, but I won't be the first. Now we may like to think of ourselves as a nation that would never elect someone like that to the White House, but I think we're all old enough to know that that's not the case." In defending his commitment to his marriage of nearly thirty years, Hart said at one point: "We have been married longer than the president in the White House today. We have kept our marriage together. One could argue—I wouldn't—that Ronald Reagan walked away from a marriage. We didn't."

Hart's first major test of his premise that he had better ideas than the other Democratic candidates came in the *Des Moines Register* debate less than three weeks before the caucuses. It was the first time he had been on a platform with them since his reentry into the race, and they were proper but cool to him. The reception from the audience was much the same. Hart sat tight-lipped and determined as he was introduced; a picture on the front page of the *Register* the next morning conveyed his grim tenseness.

Once again, as in the newspaper's sponsored debate among the Republican candidates, editor James Gannon as the moderator got down immediately to what was on viewers' minds. Referring specifically to Hart's acknowledgement in the long *Register* interview that he would "not be the first adulterer in the White House," Gannon asked whether voters should ignore issues of character and trust. Hart replied: "I probably should have said in that interview that I'm a sinner. My religion tells me all of us are sinners. I think the question is whether our sins prohibit us or prevent us from providing strong leadership." And again he compared his personal foibles to what he considered the more serious faults of the Reagan administration, adding that "I would never condone anyone in my administration who breached the highest standard of the sacred trust of the public duty."

But Hart was not competing against the Reagan adminstration in the debate. Whether he acknowledged the fact or not, his very reentry into the race made the argument that if only personal matters could be set aside and he could be judged on the quality of his ideas on matters of national policy, he would be the voters' choice. But clearly the personal equation clung to his candidacy, and the tepid audience response to his comments on substantive issues suggested he had not convincingly distinguished himself from the pack. The reality was that unless Hart was able to sell himself as indisputably superior to the others in that area, he was going to drop like a rock. That soon happened, although it was hard to be sure at first, because by now he had achieved celebrity status quite apart from his candidacy.

That point was underscored the morning after the debate, when Hart drove south from Des Moines to Indianola and dropped into Crouse's Restaurant at breakfast time for a cup of coffee and some handshaking. Accompanied by Lee and a host of television cameramen, he worked the tables greeting the customers and autographing copies of a ninety-four-page pamphlet of his speeches on major issues, which he constantly referred to as the substance that differentiated his candidacy from others. He looked like he had just stepped out of a Marlboro ad, dressed in brown tweed jacket, slacks and cowboy boots, and the local townspeople crowded around him, the younger ones with that gleam in their eyes usually reserved for a movie star. Gary Hart, no matter what his political outlook, undoubtedly was getting celebrity treatment at Crouse's Restaurant.

But after a while of handshaking, Hart moved into a rear room open onto the eating section, climbed on a chair and proceeded to deliver his campaign pitch. Some of the customers walked over to listen, but most others sat where they were, eating breakfast and drinking coffee. Gary Hart the celebrity was one thing; Gary Hart the viable presidential candidate was someone else altogether.

From Indianola, Hart went on to Ottawa, Kansas, his boyhood home, for a visit that looked much like the kind that any orthodox candidate would un-

262 ☆ THE DEMOCRATIC NOMINATION

dertake to get on the evening television news. He spoke at the local Chamber of Commerce annual dinner, making a serious speech on how the federal deficit could be reduced, and attended two crowded receptions. He noted that the last time he had been to Ottawa, when he was still riding high, the biggest issues then were his name, age and "if I did in fact play football and basketball and, if so, how well." He paused, then added: "Ah, for those good old days." He seemed to be in a very good mood, but if so, he soon had reason to be depressed again.

Three days later, Hart's old nemesis, the *Miami Herald*, broke another Hart story. It said one of his key campaign aides "was secretly subsidized in the inital phases of the current presidential campaign at the direction of a Southern California video producer who also pumped thousands of dollars into Hart's campaign in 1984 when it was desperate for cash." The story said the producer, Stuart Karl, paid a salary of $3,000 a month to Dennis Walto, a Hart aide, and since 1983 "chauffered Hart in Lear jets and helicopters." Such a payment would be in apparent violation of federal campaign finance law prohibiting a candidate from accepting more than $1,000 per election, including in-kind contributions, from any giver. The story ran on page one of the *Des Moines Register*.

Hart, who made a distinct point of not accepting political action committee funds, said he would accept responsibility if any violations had occurred. The story broke as others continued to be written about his unpaid 1984 campaign debt and questions about that debt from voters along the trail. An angered Hart in New Hampshire challenged the *Miami Herald* "to put as much effort into covering my budget and my policies as they do to questions like this. We'll see whether or not they're willing to report to their readers serious issues as well." But a few days later in Iowa, Hart acknowledged that some of the Karl contributions had been made in violation of the law and would be returned. That story, too, was out front in the *Register* the next day.

Much later, after the election, Hart said the money stories killed off whatever chance he had to sustain forward progress in his resurrected campaign. "I got off the ground," he said, noting that the first polls taken after his reentry had him leading the Democratic field again. "That situation prevailed, being that I was a nominal front-runner and drawing huge crowds, mobs if you will, practically everywhere we went." Then the *Miami Herald* story broke, he said, and the questions never stopped coming. "It was one of those situations where a new leak was coming out about something in '84 daily, and every time I'd walk out of the hotel in the morning I'd get questions about it. So that the issue of a new kind of candidacy just melted away. . . . It was a whirlwind for thirty days and then the whole thing fell apart on the issue of '84 campaign finances."

At the same time, however, Hart said he doubted his campaign could have flourishcd had thosc storics not appcarcd. Without a serious national headquarters, and with an unwise strategy of not talking to the press, he said, "I think the chance of me having a plausible opportunity to become one of the two finalists for the nomination was one in a hundred, ever, when I got back in, and I understood that   What I couldn't suffer was another collateral attack. And that, curiously enough, was not my personal life, it was campaign finances, which I've tried to be scrupulous about all my life.''

After the election, Hart reflected with us on his decision to reenter the race. ''I thought the chances of doing well or getting into the finals were very, very slim,'' he said. ''I had no money, no organization, no infrastructure. It was admittedly quixotic, not in the bad sense, but it was against the rules. I'm a realist if nothing else. . . . I understood the odds. Why did I do it? Because I felt strongly in what I believed in, and I didn't think what I believed in was being heard: fundamental reform of our political institutions, and our economic institutions; big, sweeping changes in the way the country is running. And I thought the other candidates were too timid and too marginal in their ideas or had none at all, or were avoiding the basic structural problems. And I thought that the record ought to have another voice on it, at whatever cost.''

Hart said he thought he did manage to inject some constructive ideas into the campaign, especially in the debates. ''In one or two of the debates,'' he said, ''people who were objective thought that I was superior to the other candidates. I clearly had a more coherent, more cohesive, well-thought-out approach to governing America than the other candidates, but I was not electable.''

With Hart now crippled beyond recovery, the Iowa race in its closing days turned back to Gephardt, Simon and Dukakis. The next Iowa Poll reflected a virtual three-way tie, with Gephardt the first choice of 19 percent of likely Democratic caucus-goers, Dukakis of 18 percent and Simon of 17. Hart slipped to 13. Another, and equally valid, barometer was the way all the other candidates took aim at Gephardt in the Iowa campaign's final debate, on farm issues in Ames. Gephardt by now had honed his trade message into more of a populist pitch designed to appeal to the farm-oriented state, telling voters with drumbeat consistency that ''I'm on your side,'' and with the effective Hyundai ad providing the backdrop on television. He was following the renowned formula of former state party chairman Dave Nagle for success in the caucuses: ''Organize, organize, organize and get hot at the end.''

All the candidates except Lone Ranger Hart, to be sure, were attempting to apply that formula. Simon got a lift from the endorsement of the *Des Moines Register*, influential with the sort of political activists who attended the caucuses. And the candidates' barbs at each other got sharper, with Gephardt as the perceived front-runner taking the most hits. At a women's conference in Des Moines, Simon rapped him for voting against extending time to ratify the Equal Rights Amendment and for the 1981 Reagan tax bill that, Simon said, ''helped feminize poverty in America.'' In the farm debate in Ames, Simon pointed out Gephardt's vote for the 1980 grain embargo against the Soviet Union, roundly unpopular with Iowa's hard-pressed farmers, and Hart hit his trade amendment, charging that ''the road backward is a road called protectionism.'' Dukakis said an oil import fee favored by Gephardt would cost farmers $1 billion in fuel and fertilizer costs. But with the inadvertent help of these attacks, Gephardt and his positions for tougher trade policies and support of save-the-family-farm legislation were holding the spotlight in the crucial last days.

Dukakis, meanwhile, focused down the Iowa homestretch on shoring up two perceived soft spots—his lack of foreign-policy experience and his image as a cold technocrat. He chose as the vehicle for addressing both of them American aid to the anti-Sandinista contras in Nicaragua, arguing passionately from the stump that "not one more Nicaraguan child should be killed because we didn't have the courage and the wisdom and the respect for law and life to let the people of Central America determine the future of Central America." The pitch was backed by stark television ads using black-and-white still photographs of dead, wounded and starving men, women and children, and guitar accompaniment, giving the ad the somber tone of a Costa-Gavras movie.

The Dukakis campaign, meanwhile, realized that its man was running the risk of finishing third, so far behind both Gephardt and Simon, Susan Estrich said later, that his hold on New Hampshire could be jeopardized. But Simon seemed to be losing support, she said, and with a little encouragement some of it could come to Dukakis. As a result, she said, "there was a good deal of discussion in Iowa as to how strongly to draw some of the comparative lines between Dukakis and the other candidates." The discussion inevitably encountered the problem that always arose with Dukakis—getting him to go on the attack, even on valid issues based on factual information.

Both Simon and Gephardt were vulnerable to criticism of their acceptance of political action committee money—Simon as the self-proclaimed independent man and Gephardt in his populist pitch to Iowans that his fight on trade was "your fight too." However, Estrich said, "that was an argument that Dukakis was not going to make in Iowa." Most of his advisers felt the PAC issue was a powerful and valid issue to raise against them but, as Estrich said later, "Dukakis was always a strong hands-on candidate. . . . His vote is the one that counts," and his vote was "No." That decision conveyed an attitude that was to give Dukakis' managers much grief later on, when crippling allegations were fired at him, and he could not bring himself to respond in kind, or even, for a long time, defend himself.

Dukakis did permit himself to touch on the PAC money issue in a general speech on campaign reform. But when, at a debate before the Sioux City Press Club, as Dukakis was being made up for the cameras, Estrich asked him point-blank whether he would challenge the others not to take PAC money, he declined. Only later, when provoked by an opponent's television ad that he considered below the belt, did he agree to hit back, but by that time the Iowa caucuses were history.

As for Simon, "the flavor of the month" between the time Biden dropped out and Hart got back in, the exposure worked against him. He had considerable early appeal as a straightforward, unhyphenated Democrat of New Deal traditions layered with fiscal restraint and Harry Truman folksiness. But as the spotlight stayed on him, bringing pressures to spell out the costs of his proposals, he displayed a disappointing shallowness that began to erode his earlier support. In the end, his appeal came down to the old "Trust me" message that failed in 1972 for Edmund Muskie and carried Jimmy Carter into the White House in 1976, only to wither with his performance. But the Hart and Biden embarrassments had given the old pitch appeal again, and Simon leaned on it hard. A late television commercial showed the *Register* endorsement with a voice-over saying: "Seven men, all with something to offer. But who can we trust to lead this nation?"

The others, Jackson and Babbitt, meanwhile labored simply to exceed the very low expectations about their chances. Jackson Iowa manager John Norris expressed his conviction that in Iowa, at least, Jackson's main problem was no longer race, but electability. The candidate himself seemed to be addressing the same notion when in acknowledging strong audience reaction at the farm debate he pleaded: "Today you gave me the most cheers. February eighth give me the most votes and we will win."

Babbitt, who had become sort of the pet rock of the news media for his boldness—always the luxury of a long shot, enjoyed a minor boomlet near the end. For the most part he kept it in perspective and garnished it with his wonderful sense of self-deprecation. To criticisms of his disjointed look and sound on television, he remarked at one point that "if they can teach Mr. Ed [television's loquacious horse] to talk on television, they can teach me." And on another: "There are other Democrats who may still get into this race: Mario Cuomo, Bill Bradley—and me." But as the caucuses approached and the boomlet gave him hope, Babbitt turned a bit sanctimonious, painting himself as the only Democratic candidate being honest with the voters. It was true, as he said, that he was the first to try to confront the budget deficit in specifics, but he was going too far in charging, as he did in the *Des Moines Register* debate, that he was the only candidate giving voters "a program of political courage" based on "truth and honesty." And he got carried away a few days later by declaring to the others: "If you can't stand up now to the deficit, how are you going to stand up to terrorists?" Fortunately, Babbitt cooled down somewhat at the end and resumed running a good-natured campaign that did him credit.

The final Iowa Poll released the day before the caucuses confirmed the readings of the other candidates that Gephardt was the man to beat. He led with 25 percent of 612 likely Democratic caucus-goers, to 19 for Simon, 15 for Dukakis, 9 each for Jackson and Babbitt, 7 for Hart and 1 for absentee Gore. And the next night, as Iowans spent an hour or more at 2,487 caucus sites across the state—in living rooms, church and school basements and elsewhere—the poll results generally held up.

The requirement in the caucuses that a candidate win 15 percent of the attendees to be "viable" for a share of delegates to the next level, the ninety-nine county conventions, caused much debate and even heated argument at many sites. Supporters of candidates who had reached that plateau in a first vote pleaded with those of candidates who had not to join with them in the second and final vote, while backers of nonviable candidates huddled to consider coalitions that would salvage something for their favorites. When the dust had cleared, Gephardt was the clear winner with just over 31 percent of precinct delegates elected, to about 26.7 percent for Simon, 22.1 percent for Dukakis, 8.8 percent for Jackson, 6.1 for Babbitt and a pathetic .3 for Hart and .01 for Gore. A record turnout, approaching 120,000, reflected the heavy organizational effort in the state.

For Gephardt, the result marked a major gamble that had paid off. After all he had put into Iowa, at the expense of organizing everywhere else except New Hampshire, he knew he had to win or fall by the wayside. But his victory was not overwhelming, and instead of heading toward New Hampshire as the clear principal challenger to New England native son Dukakis, Gephardt still had to deal with Simon, vying with him for that posture by virtue of his close second-place finish. For Dukakis, finishing on Simon's heels was a disappointment but he, too, did well enough to go on, particularly because he was now heading into his stronghold.

Among the others, Jackson was able to take the most heart, having more than quadrupled his Iowa showing of four years earlier and providing some support in this state with a sparse black population for his claim that there was indeed another color in his Rainbow Coalition. Babbitt had little to show for his long commitment to Iowa, and Hart had much less for his quixotic reentry. As for Gore, who had thumbed his nose at Iowa, the voters gave him the same demonstration of affection in return.

Furthermore, Bill Carrick, Gephardt's national campaign manager, took the occasion to make some pointed remarks about Gore, who in ducking Iowa obviously was on a collision course with Gephardt for southern support. "I can't wait," Carrick told Tom Edsall of the *Washington Post*. "It's bloodlust. Let me at him, I hate him. I hate all of them. I think they are the phoniest two-bit bastards that ever came down the pike, starting with Al Gore, moving through boy wonder ex-wordsmith, the mosquito that roared [Fred Martin, his campaign manager]."

Gore, for his part, was ducking New Hampshire, too, after having laid considerable groundwork for a campaign there aimed at springing a surprise in the North. But Hart's reentry had scared him off. A Gephardt-Gore confrontation in the South was building, but first Gephardt had to get Simon off his back and establish himself convincingly as the alternative to Dukakis. And New Hampshire was where it had to happen.

17

New Hampshire: Dukakis to the Forefront

In other times Dick Gephardt might have had good reason for optimism as he left Iowa for the final week of the New Hampshire primary campaign. As the winner of that first confrontation involving real voters rather than faceless respondents to opinion polls, he was the focus of the media attention being directed at the Democrats. In Michael Dukakis of Massachusetts he would be facing a front-running candidate with such obvious special advantages of local celebrity and political organization that Gephardt might expect to profit from even a respectable second-place finish. In a New Hampshire primary, as seen from what happened to Bob Dole on the Republican side, the expectations game could be decisive. This was the state in which, in 1968, Senator Eugene McCarthy of Minnesota had mortally wounded President Lyndon B. Johnson by polling 42 percent of the vote against Johnson's 49 percent on write-ins.

There was, moreover, history to suggest that neighboring state politicians did not always prosper in the perversity of New Hampshire primaries. In 1972 Senator Edmund S. Muskie of Maine won with 46 percent of the vote but, in part because his campaign chairman had suggested that he would win at least 50 percent, he left as the perceived "loser" to Senator George McGovern, whose 37 percent so clearly exceeded expectations. And in the 1980 Democratic primary Senator Edward M. Kennedy of Massachusetts was defeated by President Jimmy Carter.

Gephardt also could take some comfort in his organization. Joe Grandmaison, the Democratic state chairman who first came to national attention as the organizer of that McGovern "upset" in 1972, rated Gephardt's operation, run by a young professional named Mark Longabaugh, as second only to that of Dukakis. And in the one early test of organizational reach, an essentially meaningless contest over the selection of delegates for a state convention in the fall of 1987, the Gephardt campaign appeared to have proven Grandmaison's point.

But this time the political rules had been rewritten again, and Gephardt didn't get the "bounce" from his Iowa success that he might have expected. The most obvious reason was that Gephardt's triumph in the precinct caucuses had been so widely foreseen. The press has a bias for surprise endings and the latest fads, and gives little credit to those who simply fulfill predictions. That quirkiness was apparent in all the attention Gary Hart earned from finishing a distant second to Walter F. Mondale in the Iowa caucuses four years earlier. Now it was apparent in the ho-hum that greeted Gephardt's Iowa success. "We were expected to win and were holding on to a lead, so it wasn't much of a story that I won," he said later.

In fact, the big story coming out of the Iowa caucuses had nothing to do with the Democrats at all. It was the story of the defeat of Vice President George Bush by not only Senator Bob Dole but also television evangelist Pat Robertson. The "big" story in New Hampshire clearly would be whether Bush could rebound and whether the Robertson phenomenon was an aberration or something more substantial.

Finally, the press attention Gephardt was receiving was not all favorable, not by any means. Instead, the Missouri Democrat was now undergoing the kind of scrutiny of his record that Gary Hart endured four years earlier after his victory in the New Hampshire primary had lifted him to the full attention of the television networks for the first time. Coming out of Iowa, there were "Who is this guy Dick Gephardt anyway?" stories just as there had been "Who is this guy Gary Hart anyway?" stories a week later in the cycle in 1984. The television networks and many newspapers often ran late in filling in the blanks about politicians.

In Gephardt's case, moreover, there were not only switches of position on touchy issues like abortion but also a basketful of votes in the House that didn't seem to square with the moderately liberal populist image he had presented in Iowa. At one time or another, Gephardt had voted against minimum-wage increases, an independent consumer protection agency, community mental health centers, shelters for battered women and extension of the ratification period for the Equal Rights Amendment. And he had supported tuition tax credits, a constitutional amendment to end school busing and the MX missile and B-1 bomber.

The most significant problem for Gephardt, however, was strategic rather than substantive. Gephardt needed to position himself as the obvious alternative to Dukakis and project the picture, nationally and among New Hampshire Democrats, of a two-man race for the nomination. That kind of perception, once achieved, could have been self-perpetuating by helping to attract support and money. Instead, Gephardt found himself obliged to fend off Paul Simon, who, understanding fully that his only chance for political viability lay in finishing second, had gone quickly on the attack. By Thursday, three days after the Iowa voting, Simon commercials accusing Gephardt of "flip-flops" were on the air. "It was obvious very quickly that we had to deal with Simon," Gephardt said.

The result was what William Carrick, Gephardt's campaign manager, called a "terrible week" of engaging the wrong opponent. "All we did was mud-wrestle with Paul Simon,'' he said. Indeed, Richard Moe, a Washington lawyer and senior adviser to Gephardt, was convinced in retrospect that his campaign would have been in a much better position if Dukakis had finished second in Iowa and nipped the Simon candidacy in the bud.

Simon and Gephardt had been friendly colleagues, if not intimates, in the House for many years, frequently flying back to St. Louis—Simon's district was in southern Illinois—together on weekends. Gephardt, it may be recalled, was the one who sponsored Simon for the House Budget Committee chairmanship although convinced he couldn't win it. But presidential politics is a high-stakes game, and relationships can grow tense and testy even when the rival in the way is an old political friend.

Simon had begun sniping at Gephardt in New Hampshire even before the Iowa results were in. In a debate at the University of New Hampshire on January 24, the Illinois Democrat had criticized Gephardt again for voting in favor of the Reagan tax cuts in 1981 after failing to win approval for a Democratic substitute. "I voted against all three [tax-cut bills] and I'm proud of it,'' Simon declared. "And you were wrong,'' Gephardt replied.

But the issue took on considerably more weight when Simon began to use it, along with Gephardt's positions on nuclear plant safety and an oil import fee, to suggest his rival was tailoring his views for each different constituency. Arriving in Manchester, Simon told reporters that the question voters should ask about a candidate's positions was this one: "Is this just an election-year conversion or is this where the person has been for a long time?'' And he quickly bought $110,000 worth of radio and television advertising to pursue his assault. One radio spot referring to Gephardt argued: "Sometimes a candidate's toughest opponent can be his own record.'' A television commercial showed pictures of both men while an announcer asked: "Who can we trust?''

The tension between the two came to a head on the Thursday night before the primary. Gephardt and his wife, Jane, were in their hotel room dressing for a party dinner at Concord when they saw Simon on television on the attack again. "I got angry,'' Gephardt recalled. "I finally decided if he wants to fight on the tax issue, let's fight on the tax issue. . . . I just got mad and decided I was going to answer it that night.''

So Gephardt quickly changed the line he would take that night in Concord. Joining the fight with Simon would be a diversion from Gephardt's principal goal of engaging Michael Dukakis. But, as he saw it, there wasn't much choice. "When you're getting hit with negative ads, you've got to either answer them or run something back on your opponent,'' Gephardt said. "You can't just let it sit there.''

Gephardt startled the Concord party audience by defending his vote for the 1981 tax bill. "I'm here tonight to say I did it,'' he declared with considerable force. "I really did it.'' He had tried with other Democrats to amend the Reagan bill and only when that effort failed had voted to approve it. Then, leaving the dinner, he told reporters: "Enough is enough and I ask Senator Simon to take those ads off television. And if he doesn't, he ought to take off the bow tie because he's just another politician.''

At one level, the Gephardt response on cutting taxes made some elementary political sense. New Hampshire voters, including moderate and conservative Democrats, are notoriously hostile to taxes, and the liberals in the state already were overwhelmingly committed to Dukakis. But in the long run the Gephardt tactic probably did more harm than good. It reinforced the picture of the Iowa winner still trying to deal with a minor candidate nipping at his heels rather than confronting Dukakis. And it seemed to provide added evidence for the suggestions from the press and his opponents that Gephardt had been trimming on the issues.

As matters turned out, the Gephardt-Simon bickering continued through the final weekend and a final debate, while Dukakis managed to remain above the fray clearly untouched by the mud-wrestling. At one point, when Simon and Gephardt exchanged shots at a candidate forum, Dukakis showed he was enjoying things enough to essay a small joke. ''You fellows getting along?'' he asked. ''Anything I can do to help?''

The one candidate who did seem determined to be ''helpful'' in cutting Gephardt down to size was Al Gore. In the televised debate over the final weekend he announced he had found it ''amusing'' that Gephardt was running against his own record. And at another point, he piled on by telling Gephardt: ''You ought to respond to the substance of the Simon commercials rather than taking it personally.'' It was the kind of ''advice'' that did little to endear the thirty-nine-year-old senator to his fellow candidates.

For his part, Gephardt was never able to deal satisfactorily with the charge that he was tailoring his views. He argued, with some validity, that politicians' opinions are not supposed to be static and, indeed, that the evolution of those opinions can reflect thought and experience. Firing back at Simon in the final New Hampshire debate, Gephardt reminded the Illinois Democrat of his youth as a weekly newspaper publisher: ''Back in 1948 you endorsed Tom Dewey and now you campaign on Harry Truman.'' But in presidential campaigns there is never as much of a market for rational argument as for the quick categorizing definition, and in the politics of 1988 being guilty of ''flip-flops'' was a serious sin.

The picture of New Hampshire as only a Gephardt-Simon fight over second place was justified. By the time the Iowa votes were counted or perhaps even earlier, it was clear that none of the other Democrats in the field was considered a serious player there, although several of them had enjoyed brief vogues over the previous year.

Bruce Babbitt had a well-regarded organization headed by a sharp young professional, Mike Muir, and Susan Calegari, one of the best of the indigenous political operatives. But New Hampshire was not a political island, and Babbitt's failure to achieve credibility nationally made him an also-ran there as well. A victory in Iowa did not always give a candidate the kind of lift he might expect, but the experience of 1976, 1980 and 1984 had shown that the candidate who finished far back in those precinct caucuses could not realistically hope to become a serious player in New Hampshire. By the end of the week Babbitt was tacitly conceding he was near the end of the road. And in the bar at the Wayfarer, his managers were talking about his campaign in the past tense.

The reconstituted Gary Hart campaign was, in the end, a joke. This was the state in which his success in trouncing Fritz Mondale had made him a serious contender for the 1984 nomination, and the news media swarmed all over the "story" of the Hart "comeback"—to the consternation of some of his rivals. "There's no question," Babbitt observed early in January, "he's stolen the show from the rest of us. What can I say?" But Hart's return to the competition had brought back only a few of those New Hampshire Democrats who had supported him so enthusiastically four years earlier—among them Ned Helms of Concord, a longtime activist, and Dan Calegari, another of the on-the-ground operatives who had always played important roles in primaries in New Hampshire. And they seemed to have few illusions. Early in the campaign Helms had defined the problem for Hart in graphic terms: "He has to pass the purple test in New Hampshire. He has to present his case without being so embarrassed that he turns purple." That had not happened, and by the time the primary campaign had reached the final days, it was apparent that Hart was fatally flawed as a candidate, and that his suggestion that he alone could offer thoughtful and provocative answers on the issues was hollow. His standing in the opinion polls plunged from more than 20 percent in December inexorably downward—to single digits by the time of the Iowa caucuses. It was clear few were listening.

In 1984 Jesse Jackson had been beguiled into believing he might strike sparks even in a state with fewer than two thousand blacks. And early in that campaign the civil rights leader had ignited some enthusiasm among young voters and a handful of devout liberals who liked his unalloyed leftist message. But in the end Jackson captured only 5 percent of the primary vote in 1984, and this time around he had chosen to give the state only minimal attention.

The one remaining candidate who might have found a constituency among conservative Democats in New Hampshire, Al Gore, was playing a cute game. Having abandoned Iowa as too liberal, he decided in January that the return of Hart would make it impossible for him to compete effectively in New Hampshire either. This was at a point when the opinion polls, in a stark demonstration of their biases and limits, were showing Hart with more than 20 percent of the Democratic vote, in most cases actually in the lead. The first message here was that most voters weren't paying attention yet. The second was that you can never underestimate the flimsiness of the knowledge base on which most poll respondents are standing. Oh, Gary Hart. I remember that name so put me down for him.

After the fact, Gore said he thought Hart "would have a temporary surge and then fade into insignificance" without becoming a serious competitor. "I did think that while he was declining from those poll numbers to insignificance," said Gore, "that he would retard the ability of other candidates to make a breakthrough in New Hampshire."

So Gore settled on a strategy under which he might have it both ways, a desirable condition for any politician. "The fact is we ran a major campaign in New Hampshire," he said. "At the same time, I low-balled the expectations in New Hampshire because I felt that as an outgrowth of my decision not to contest Iowa I necessarily damaged my prospects in New Hampshire."

Gore was hoping that Dukakis might pull an upset in Iowa, thus cutting the legs from under both of his rivals from the Midwest, Simon and Gephardt, in one clean stroke. In that case, Gore was prepared with enough organization and money to buy Boston television exposure and advance himself as the alternative. But he recognized that if Dukakis failed to win Iowa, the winner there clearly would be the option in New Hampshire. Thus, from Gore's point of view, the Iowa result was "the worst possible outcome" and left him no opening. "The competition in New Hampshire," he said later, "was always for something other than first place."

There were, nonetheless, astute Democrats who believed that Gore had missed an opportunity in New Hampshire to make the kind of showing that would score some points in the expectations game and, perhaps more important, dilute his identification as "the southern candidate" in the field. As it worked out, the course he followed only reinforced the notion he was a regional candidate.

Gore was dead right, however, in his belief that the contest was only for place money. Dukakis and his strategists had always considered the New Hampshire primary one he must win, and they had gone to great lengths to protect his position there. Opinion sampling conducted by Tubby Harrison for the campaign showed consistently that if Dukakis could come through Iowa as a credible national candidate, he would win comfortably in New Hampshire. And, although there were minor and temporary fluctuations, other surveys showed the same thing. Polls consistently found Dukakis with 35 to 45 percent of the Democratic vote and none of his rivals closer than fifteen points behind. A survey conducted immediately after Iowa had Dukakis at 37 percent, Gephardt at 21, Simon at 17.

But nothing was left to chance. Charles Baker, one of Dukakis' most highly regarded young managers, had been sent in to run the campaign several months earlier. Kathi Rogers, an operative with an encyclopedic knowledge of the state's politics, was recruited to help. Charles Campion, an old Dukakis hand who had managed the 1984 Mondale primary operation with much-admired skill, was consulted. The state was flooded with young field workers, and offices were opened in every community that might qualify as a population center. Dukakis himself spent much more time in the state during 1987 than his schedule would suggest. On many of his "statehouse days" he devoted to being governor, Dukakis would drive to New Hampshire after work—it was less than an hour to Manchester, Nashua or Portsmouth—for two or three receptions and perhaps a dinner with a small group of potential supporters.

We encountered him in Manchester one night during the summer of 1987. He had attended two receptions in private homes, one a fund-raiser, and then repaired to the Athens Restaurant for a dinner of Greek food with seventeen people who were already aligned with him or clearly leaning that way. Most striking was that, in that early stage of the campaign, Dukakis felt free to spend almost two hours talking in some detail about issues as obvious as the controversy over the Seabrook nuclear power plant and as arcane as insurance regulation.

It was the kind of campaigning Dukakis most enjoyed and, by happy coincidence, the kind that could be most valuable in the long run in this small state. In one meeting after another Dukakis locked new volunteers into his organization and, perhaps more important, enjoyed the chance to hear what was on the minds of the Democrats to whom he was appealing.

It was also the kind of campaigning that the candidates of 1988 could enjoy only in the two states, Iowa and New Hampshire, in which their time was essentially unlimited. Once those caucuses and that primary were past, so was the luxury of listening as well as talking—and grasping for the sound bite on the television networks. There were complaints of varying degrees of validity against Iowa and New Hampshire as legitimate testing grounds for presidential candidates, but the argument for beginning the campaign in states with a manageable universe of voters was compelling. And New Hampshire obviously offered Dukakis an almost ideal opportunity to test out his campaign.

That Dukakis was serious about his commitment was obvious from an incident even before he announced his candidacy.

Joe Grandmaison, not yet the state party chairman obliged to strict neutrality, was serving as chairman of a dinner for the largest Democratic contributors in the state and decided to use the opportunity to give a final lift to Dukakis. Grandmaison had managed Dukakis' first campaign in Massachusetts in 1974. And, although the two had parted company after that race and had experienced a somewhat uneven relationship, Grandmaison remained enough of a Dukakis admirer to want to give him that forum. But he also had doubts about the kind of speech his old candidate might give—doubts he relayed to the governor's political staff. Michael still keeps waving his arms around when he speaks, he complained. Can't you get him a new speech coach?

Dukakis had never been the kind of politician who took easily to speech coaches but in this case he agreed. And he even adopted a suggestion from his son John that helped with the arm-waving problem. When he rose to speak in Manchester that night, he used a lectern adorned with two strips of tape, sticky side up, to remind him to keep control of his hands. The speech, Grandmaison recalled with satisfaction, was a great success—and Michael Dukakis had demonstrated that he was not above learning some new tricks and making some concessions to political necessity.

Throughout 1987 there was, nonetheless, some predictable muttering about Dukakis' potential vulnerability in the state. All those Democrats newly arrived in the southern part of the state, the doubters in other campaigns argued, were people who had fled "Taxachusetts" and could hardly be expected to welcome the candidacy of the governor of that state. Indeed, it was true that there was always some home-state resentment anytime a politician, a senator as much as a governor, reached for national office. To some voters, that politician was going uptown too fast, and they were quick to tell visiting reporters that if they knew the candidate as well as the local people did, they would have an entirely different view of that candidate. Thus, reporters covering the 1988 campaign were always encountering cabdrivers in Boston who assured them that "this guy Dukakis couldn't get elected dogcatcher in this town, for Christ's sake." Those judgments were identical to those you could hear about Mario Cuomo in New York or, in another time, Jimmy Carter in Georgia or Ronald Reagan in California.

But the fact was that Dukakis had been an able and effective governor of Massachusetts for ten years. Although he was something of an odd duck—he still cut his own grass and rode the "T" to work—he also had convinced a clear majority of his constituents that he was serious and sincere. He was, in short, a political leader who wore well under prolonged exposure.

Dukakis had not always been so successful, however. In his first term as governor, he had been stiff-necked and rigid in dealing with his fellow Democrats and generally had treated politics as something to endure only to get the opportunity to govern. If he enjoyed the process, it was rarely apparent. One of us was in Boston the night he was meeting Governor Francis Sargent, an engaging Yankee Republican, in a debate that, for all practical purposes, would decide the 1974 gubernatorial election. Dukakis was far ahead of Sargent in the polls, to the point that, Sargent told us in advance, the Democratic challenger was assured of the governorship if he could get through the debate unscathed.

The night of the debate Dukakis typically insisted he wanted no entourage at the television studio. So Kitty and actor Leonard Nimoy, who was raising money for Dukakis, went along to Grandmaison's apartment in downtown Boston to watch. Dukakis won easily, thus apparently locking up the election, and Kitty quickly telephoned him at the studio so she and Grandmaison could offer congratulations. The four of us, she told him, were going to the Charles Restaurant to eat some Italian food and drink a little celebratory wine. Why didn't he join us? An hour or so later the triumphant candidate did so—but only to eat a piece of cake, drink a cup of tea and worry about the next day's schedule. We have seen many politicians in private moments good and bad and can remember few who seemed to take so little joy from their success.

But after his Democratic primary loss to Edward J. King in 1978—one he never saw coming—Dukakis began to change. Coached by John Sasso, he paid attention to building his political organization and to personal campaigning. Moreover, by the time he came back to defeat King in 1982, Dukakis had even learned to enjoy the political part. "I've learned," he said then, "that you have to build coalitions and bring people along with you." But what was also clear was that Dukakis had finally discovered that seeking votes could be a pleasant as well as an instructive process.

The "new" Dukakis also was a better politician as governor after 1982, one who paid more attention to making the voters understand what he was doing and why he was doing it. And that ability gave him some insulation when things didn't go well.

One of the potential problems campaign director Charlie Baker saw in New Hampshire, for example, came from the crusade the *Lawrence* (Mass.) *Eagle-Tribune* had been conducting against the state policy on prison furloughs. The dangers in the system had been underlined when convicted murderer Willie Horton fled to Maryland during a weekend furlough, raping a young woman and terrorizing her boyfriend. The furlough program, as noted earlier, had been initiated by Dukakis' Republican predecessor, Sargent, but Dukakis was a strong supporter of the theory. He resisted changing it until forced to do so—only a few weeks before the primary—because of the heat generated by the campaign for which the Lawrence newspaper won a Pulitzer Prize.

Baker was concerned about the fallout because he knew that 11 percent of the Democrats in southern New Hampshire were readers of the *Eagle-Tribune*. So Baker made a point of having the personal canvassing of voters in that part of the state carried out by people identified with law enforcement. And when no other candidate raised the issue, that seemed to be enough to prevent any serious damage.

But the critical point about the lack of steam in the furlough issue was that long familiarity with Dukakis among the voters there. "In New Hampshire," Baker said later, "people had another base of knowledge about Dukakis." They saw the Willie Horton mistake as an aberration rather than part of a pattern.

Dukakis also received extraordinary attention from his hometown newspapers and television and radio stations, all of which had large audiences in New Hampshire. Boston is, in most respects, an extremely sophisticated city, but the news organizations went absolutely wild at the prospect of a local boy—and not "just another Kennedy"—becoming a serious contender for a presidential nomination. When Dukakis first made his candidacy official early in 1987, the *Boston Herald* quickly came out with a long series called "Duke and Kitty: The Untold Story," which told us, among other things, that Kitty used to hide her new dresses in a closet in her father's home so Michael the Cheap wouldn't be aware of her extravagance. The intensive coverage by the newspapers wasn't surprising, but the new element was the omnipresence of reporters and camera crews for all three of the major television stations throughout the campaign. Dukakis couldn't turn around in Iowa without "details live at eleven" back home.

The final days of the New Hampshire Democratic campaign were curiously anticlimactic when you considered the rich history of such contests there. This was the state over which legions of idealistic students—presenting themselves as "clean for Gene"—had swarmed to make the case for McCarthy and against the war in Vietnam in 1968; the state in which McGovern had enlisted new legions four years later; the state in which Ed Muskie had crippled his candidacy by "crying" in an angry outburst against publisher William Loeb; the state in which social activist candidate Ned Coll had enlivened a televised debate by producing and waving a rubber rat to make a point about the lives of the disadvantaged.

But this time Dukakis breezed through the entire campaign without ever being in serious jeopardy. In the final days after the Iowa vote, most of the press attention was turned on the Republicans and the sideshow of Dick Gephardt and Paul Simon scratching for a toehold. The results were entirely predictable: Dukakis 36 percent, Gephardt 20, Simon 17, Jackson 8, Gore 7, Babbitt 5, Hart 4. The Massachusetts governor became the first ever to win a contested New Hampshire Democratic primary by more than ten percentage points. Gephardt survived the Simon threat but not by the kind of margin that would either increase his popular momentum or, more to the point, attract contributors to a campaign now living hand to mouth. On the contrary, Gephardt had suffered damage at the hands of Paul Simon quite similar to what Walter Mondale sustained in the same primary from the depiction of him by John Glenn as a candidate of "the special interests"—an image Mondale never shook.

Long after the campaign Simon agreed there was "some validity" in comparing what he had done to Gephardt to what Glenn had done to Mondale. But he argued that, unlike Glenn, he had enjoyed a realistic chance of winning—a thesis open to challenge. His hope, Simon said, had been to win Iowa, then upset Dukakis in New Hampshire. Simon contended that he was "much better organized in New Hampshire than Gephardt was"—an assessment with which few people knowledgeable about New Hampshire politics would agree. And he said, "Our polling showed . . . support for Dukakis was very thin in New Hampshire"—an assessment that events demonstrated was totally mistaken.

In fact, what happened with Simon was what often happens to presidential candidates. They become drawn further into the campaign because they want to take that one last shot at a political miracle. To do that in New Hampshire, Simon campaign manager Brian Lunde said later, "you do have to take Gephardt out of the loop . . . so we just needed to kind of try to begin to expose him, that it was largely an insincere message, that this was the water boy for the establishment in Washington and the flip-flops." As it turned out, however, both Gephardt and Simon were left badly compromised as they looked ahead to Super Tuesday and primaries and caucuses in twenty states just three weeks away.

But even before Super Tuesday, there were two way stations—precinct caucuses in Minnesota and a primary in South Dakota, both a week away. And, although neither was considered a significant testing ground, one of them would have an important, if indirect, bearing on the shape of the Super Tuesday campaign.

Dukakis held a dominant position in Minnesota, as he had for several months. The liberalism of the state made it fertile ground for the Massachusetts governor, and his campaign had used its financial strength to build an imposing organizational advantage early in the campaign. Simon, similarly attracted by the liberalism of the caucus electorate, also planned to compete in Minnesota and, after a meeting with his advisers in New Hampshire at which he first considered folding his campaign, announced that he would continue through those next two states and withdraw if he didn't win one of them. That threat seemed particularly empty considering the fact that he had fallen short both times out of the barn and was $500,000 in debt. But the following Monday contributors poured $137,000 into the Simon headquarters. "It was," he said later, "the biggest day we had."

Gephardt, despite a first in Iowa and a second in New Hampshire, simply couldn't afford to compete in both states and settled on South Dakota, where he could stretch his dwindling money. "We were always hand to mouth, trying to put it together for the next day," he recalled later. In most campaigns early success will turn on the spigots. In 1984, for example, the Hart campaign was starving until he won in New Hampshire and then money began to flood in— at just the point he least needed it because of his ability to command free television attention. But that never happened to Dick Gephardt. "You've got to hope it comes in over the transom," he said, but it never did.

Gephardt did have enough cash, however, to buy $60,000 worth of television advertising for the final days in South Dakota. A television spot attacked Dukakis as a tax-raiser and recalled an early Dukakis blunder—his suggestion in Iowa that hard-pressed farmers might try such alternative crops as "flowers, blueberries and Belgian endive." The spot ended with the announcer asking in tones of incredulity: "Belgian endive?" As Bill Carrick, Gephardt's chief strategist, saw it, "It was a killer."

In advance of the ad being aired, pollster Ed Reilly had called Gephardt and warned him: "When Mike Dukakis sees this, Dick Gephardt will never be his V.P." Gephardt shot back: "He won't be my V.P. either." One reason Gephardt was willing to "go negative" with the endive ad against Dukakis, Trippi said later, was that "everybody thought they had bagged us on the [Kinnock] tape thing." But Steve Murphy, who had run Iowa for Gephardt, warned that the ad would persuade the straitlaced Dukakis at last to return the fire. He was right.

The Dukakis campaign agreed with Carrick that the ad was "a killer." Will Robinson, a savvy young troubleshooter for the campaign, saw the spot and quickly called headquarters in Boston. "It was devastating," he said later. "You could see the numbers moving right away." Dukakis' "hard" supporters were still with him, but the undecideds were breaking heavily for Gephardt. In Boston campaign manager Susan Estrich told Dukakis, "We've got a situation in South Dakota." And Mark Gearan, a press spokesman, was dispatched to try to combat the endive ad through the free media and some radio advertising.

The Dukakis campaign had two tough television ads aimed at Gephardt "in the can" for use in those final hours. One attacked Gephardt for accepting money from political action committees. The other—one of few memorable commercials ever produced by the Dukakis campaign—showed a red-haired tumbler doing cartwheels and somersaults while the announcer's voice talked about Gephardt's flip-flops on the issues. But Dukakis, ever the stiff-necked straight arrow resisting negative campaigning, wouldn't approve the use of either spot. And the radio ad he did authorize, Estrich recalled, was "the least tough" of those that had been prepared.

The result was a mixed bag going into the final two weeks of the Super Tuesday campaign. Dukakis won in Minnesota with 34 percent to 20 for Jackson, 18 for Simon, 7 for Gephardt. But Gephardt beat him 44 percent to 31 in South Dakota—a defeat virtually everyone in the Dukakis campaign was convinced could be traced to the failure to respond on Belgian endive. Looking back later, Susan Estrich could call the defeat in South Dakota "a real blessing . . . a cheap lesson" about the danger of ignoring negative advertising. "When you're the front-runner or one of the front-runners," she said, "there's no place to be above the fray. It's going to find you."

Dukakis himself seemed to get the message. "I'm sorry," he told the campaign staff when the South Dakota returns came in that night. "I'm never going to let that happen again." That, however, was one promise he failed to keep later on, to his ultimate great regret.

Dick Gephardt had gotten by with an unanswered shot. But Super Tuesday was going to be a different story.

18

Super Tuesday: a Super Fiasco

In the fall of 1987, we drove Interstate 20 from Birmingham east to Atlanta, stopping in small communities along the way to ask several dozen voters encountered at random what they knew of the big Super Tuesday southern regional primary, scheduled the following spring, that was all the rage among the politicians. People in towns like Oxford, Alabama, and Bremen, Georgia, seemed to be likely subjects because they lived within the range of both of those major cities' newspapers and television stations, all of which had published or broadcast a great deal about Super Tuesday.

What we found, unsurprisingly in retrospect, was that only a handful of these voters had ever heard of Super Tuesday and that those few had only the vaguest notion of what was involved. William Feathers, whom we came upon eating catfish in Oxford, was typical of the best informed group. "I see where the politicians keep talking about how great it's going to be," he said, "but I don't know that much about it, to tell you the truth."

These conversations taught a significant lesson about the regional primary. From the very beginning, it was a reform of far greater interest and importance to the politicians of the South than it was to the voters. If the man in the street was missing something, he wasn't aware of it.

There was never any mystery about why the Democratic politicians who arranged the regional primary wanted it. They were sick and tired of being left without a voice in their own party.

John Traeger, a state senator from Texas and one of the leaders of the Southern Legislative Conference most responsible for the primary, was a quintessential example. In 1984 he had supported Senator John H. Glenn of Ohio for the presidential nomination only to find his candidate eliminated before Texas held its precinct caucuses in May. "I was so disgusted by the procedure here in Texas," Traeger recalled after the election. "By the time we voted the issue was completely over."

The result was another liberal Democratic ticket—Walter Mondale and Geraldine Ferraro—that simply wouldn't sell in Texas or anywhere else in the South.

But the medicine John Traeger and others prescribed didn't do the trick. As it turned out, the southern regional primary on Super Tuesday, March 8, instead provided the ultimate political irony of the 1988 nominating campaign. The vote in the fourteen southern and border states—among twenty across the nation holding Democratic primaries and caucuses that day—accomplished the direct opposite of what the authors of Super Tuesday had hoped to achieve.

The sponsors of the plan, almost exclusively those Democratic state legislators, had three distinct but related purposes when they put it together at SLC meetings in Biloxi in 1985 and Fort Worth in 1986.

The first was to play a full role in the choice of the Democratic Party's ticket, by obliging the candidates to come South, debate the issues and hear the views of the voters and politicians there. The second was to force the candidates seeking the delegates of the South into acceptable positions on issues of special concern to southern voters. And the third was to use the huge Super Tuesday delegate prize—1,137 of the 2,082 needed to win the nomination at Atlanta—to leverage the Democratic Party toward a presidential nominee moderate enough to avoid a disaster among white voters in the South in the general election.

None of these goals was achieved. Super Tuesday proved to be one of the shallower exercises in a campaign distinguished by its triviality. And, from the standpoint of the southerners, it couldn't even be said that the end justified the means.

Because Michael Dukakis and Dick Gephardt, the winners of the first two events on the campaign schedule, were otherwise occupied in Minnesota and South Dakota, the Super Tuesday campaign proper lasted only two weeks. The notion of candidates either listening to the voters or engaged in serious debate in twenty states was laughable. Instead, the premium was on money spent on television commercials and the quick hit for the "free media"—meaning television news coverage—and then flying on to the next state, perhaps for a fundraiser to help finance some more commercials.

The smaller states among the fourteen in the southern regional grouping, those with the fewest delegates at stake, were given only brush blocks of attention by any of the candidates—an airport rally or press conference as often as not. But the big states were also neglected because there simply wasn't time for anyone to cover the ground effectively. Texas is a state of twenty-six media markets, staggering proportions—it's 750 miles from Houston to El Paso—and remarkable economic and demographic diversity. A presidential candidate could have spent the entire two weeks in Texas alone and only scratched the surface. So much for serious political debate.

The idea that special concerns of southern voters would be addressed was probably equally naïve. For one thing, the country had become increasingly homogeneous over the previous twenty years. Americans all watched the same television, ate the same fast food, traveled in and out of airports indistinguishable one from the other. There were, to be sure, still some regional differences. Southern whites, as a group, were more conservative culturally and politically than similar voters in the Midwest and on the two coasts. And southern voters seemed to be more concerned with national-defense questions than those elsewhere, perhaps because, as the census statistics showed, southerners had always provided a disproportionate share of the men and women in the armed forces.

But the idea that these special concerns, to whatever degree they existed, could be impressed on the candidates in a helter-skelter two-week campaign was never realistic. When all three networks' cameras were focused on every word, candidates inevitably were going to be forced to at least rough consistency in what they had to say about all the issues everywhere.

The result of all these misjudgments was just what those original sponsors had hoped to avoid. As we shall see, the two long-term winners from Super Tuesday were the two most liberal candidates in the Democratic field, Michael Dukakis and Jesse Jackson. And the candidate who might have fit the southerners' original prescription most closely, Dick Gephardt, was destroyed—largely although not exclusively by the competition from a southerner, Al Gore, who had been drawn into believing the extravagant hopes of those original sponsors of the scheme.

There was no mystery in Jackson's strength on Super Tuesday. In 45 of the 167 congressional districts being contested, blacks made up more than 20 percent of the voting-age population. And this time there was no white candidate to compete for that vote, as Fritz Mondale had done in Alabama and Georgia four years earlier. The black political leaders who had supported Mondale in

1984, such as Mayor Richard Arrington of Birmingham, were now fully in the Jackson camp. The only noteworthy exception was Mayor Andrew Young of Atlanta, never a Jackson enthusiast, and he was able to hide out politically by holding that his role as the host mayor for the coming Democratic convention required his neutrality. From the outset, it was clear the civil rights leader could count on 20 to 25 percent of the popular vote, although perhaps a somewhat smaller share of the delegates because his support was so heavily concentrated in certain congressional districts.

Dukakis was in a strong enough position that Tad Devine, his chief delegate-hunter, had been assuring the campaign's managers as far back as November that the Massachusetts governor would be one of the winners and probably *the* winner Super Tuesday. For one thing, Dukakis began as odds-on to win three nonsouthern states voting that day—Massachusetts, Rhode Island and Washington—with 184 of those 1,137 delegates. And he seemed assured of winning in Maryland (67 delegates) or, at worst, splitting the state with Jackson.

The dimensions of Super Tuesday also enhanced the value of Dukakis' extraordinary ability to raise money. Writing a plan for the campaign almost a year earlier, John Sasso saw the regional primary as a chance, as he said later, "to use our advantage of money," particularly in the two largest states, Texas and Florida. "We could put money and organization in there that nobody else could touch," he said. Thus, by the fall of 1987, the Dukakis campaign had dispatched two of its premier operatives from Massachusetts, Steve Rosenfeld and Paul Pezzella, to set up an organization in Florida and a street-smart Pennsylvanian, Tom Cosgrove, to do the same in Texas. In each of these two target states, Dukakis had several dozen field operatives working even before the Iowa caucuses. And when the campaign entered its final phase, he had $3.5 million on hand and was raising more than $1 million a month.

The target groups were the obvious ones. Michael Dukakis was not going to sell in the Florida Panhandle or Southwest Florida, but he had obvious potential with liberal Democrats and especially among Jewish voters in the Miami area well aware of the fact his wife, Kitty, was Jewish. In Texas the opportunities lay in pockets of liberalism, in Austin, for example, and among Mexican-American voters in the Rio Grande Valley, where his fluent Spanish was a pronounced advantage. The strategy, as Tad Devine described it, was to concentrate heavily in those areas—but also to do enough elsewhere to be "in the mix" in other states, such as Georgia and North Carolina. There, Dukakis might appeal to suburban white-collar voters not totally different from those back home in Brookline. Being "in the mix" meant getting enough votes to exceed the 15 percent threshold required under party rules to win a share of the delegates, even if he was unable to compete statewide.

Several states in which the electorate available to any white candidate was largely conservative—Alabama, for instance—were written off early. And so were parts of Texas and Florida. In the summer of 1987 Dukakis had caused a mild stir among Texas politicians by attracting a huge crowd at a rally in McAllen near the Mexican border. The most astute were not deceived, however. As Joe Christie, a onetime Senate candidate, put it: "The first vote Michael Dukakis gets in East Texas will be about three o'clock in the afternoon."

But Dukakis and Jackson both enjoyed an advantage neither could have anticipated—the prospect that the conservative white vote would be split by Dick Gephardt and Al Gore rather than coalescing behind a single other survivor of New Hampshire.

Super Tuesday should have been a golden opportunity for Gephardt. Indeed, it was fair to say he fit better than any of his rivals the original prescription written by those southern Democrats for their nominee—moderate enough in his views to be marketable in the general election but still clearly a national rather than regional candidate.

But the Missouri congressman had already been badly compromised. Back in the fall, during his darkest period in the Iowa caucus campaign, Gephardt had shut down his operations across the South and moved the people who had staffed them to Iowa. The organization was never either wide or deep in its reach, but it had been enough to enlist at least tentative indications of support from some prominent southern Democrats. And the shutdown received the kind of press attention that made it easy for Gephardt's rivals to paint him as "abandoning" the South. When you telephoned some of his southern offices, professionals in other campaigns noted gleefully, you would get a recording giving you an 800 number to call.

From Gephardt's standpoint, however, there was not much choice. "We never did have, before Iowa or after Iowa, the kind of on-the-ground organization that Dukakis had," he said later. "We felt that whatever we had, we had to concentrate it in Iowa. . . . It didn't make a lot of sense to leave people in Texas while you were going down the drain in Iowa."

Now, with Super Tuesday staring him in the face, it was apparent the price had been high. As Gore put it, "You cannot completely destroy a campaign infrastructure and then rebuild it in two weeks. You cannot do it." And Gephardt, already in debt, didn't have the money to rebuild even if doing so had been feasible.

The Gephardt campaign tried to compensate to some degree by exploiting the widespread support he enjoyed from fellow House members across the region. The backing of allies such as Representatives Martin Frost and Marvin Leath in Texas, Mike Synar in Oklahoma and Claude Pepper in Florida was a valued credential. But this support was never a substitute for the resources to establish a full campaign presence in fourteen southern and border states. In some respects, those endorsements may have been a mixed blessing, anyway, in the sense that they lured the candidate into wasting his time and energy. His campaigning in South Florida, with Pepper at his side, was always a bootless exercise.

Gephardt quickly became aware of his situation when he arrived at a condominium complex in Deerfield Beach, Florida, for a one-on-one debate with Dukakis on health care. "They're all walking in and they've all got Dukakis hats on," Gephardt recalled, "and I said, 'What's going on here? Where are our people?' . . . Then I knew I was in real trouble in South Florida, in those condos."

Dukakis' organizational advantage was the least of Gephardt's problems. A far more serious one was the concerted attack both Gore and Dukakis directed at him, each of them trying to pick away supporters on the edges from a classic candidate in the middle. The attack on Gephardt started only two days after the New Hampshire primary, in a debate in Dallas televised across the region. Gore promptly zinged Gephardt for changing his views on abortion and taxes and, beginning an exchange that would become the sound bite for network television reports, told him: "I'm going to lay it on the line, Dick. The next president has to be someone who the people believe will stay with his convictions."

Obviously irked, Gephardt replied: "Lately you've been sounding more like Al Haig than Al Gore."

Gore shot back: "That line sounds more like Richard Nixon than Dick Gephardt."

Gore also pursued Gephardt on his vote for final passage of the Reagan tax cut bill in 1981. In a debate at Williamsburg, Virginia, ten days before Super Tuesday, the Tennessee senator provoked another confrontation that was a natural for the network television sound bite. He called the 1981 measure the "Reagan-Gephardt tax bill"—a world-class cheap shot—and then pressed his opponent: "Is it fair? Is it fair?"

Gephardt: "Are you finished? Are you finished?"

Gore: "If you'll answer."

Gephardt: "I thought they taught you manners at St. Albans [the prep school in Washington that Gore attended]. . . . You bet it's fair to give two thirds of the cuts to families that earn less than $50,000."

Gore: "But was the bill fair?"

Gephardt: "Can you hear, Al?"

Dukakis also was zeroing in on the inconsistencies in Gephardt's positions that had become widely known as "flip-flops." At that health care discussion in Deerfield Beach, for example, Dukakis was asked whether he had changed his own position on a bill sponsored by Pepper to provide long-term care for the elderly. Pointing to Gephardt, Dukakis replied: "There's a flip-flopper over here. I'm not a flip-flopper or a back-flopper."

Gephardt did not roll over for his rivals, snapping back in debates by describing Dukakis as "the candidate with the most money [and] the least message" and Gore as one whose candidacy "seems to rest principally on an accident of geography." But the perception was clearly that Gephardt was the candidate on the defensive on Super Tuesday.

The most significant damage suffered by Gephardt probably came, however, less from the campaign-trail sniping by Gore and Dukakis than from the advertising Dukakis ran—spots he had refused to run until Gephardt used the Belgian endive ad in South Dakota. One commercial ridiculed Gephardt's populist campaign slogan—"It's your fight, too"—by showing on the screen a list of big corporations from whose political action committees Gephardt's campaign had accepted contributions. "Kinda makes you wonder," said the voice-over. "Is Dick Gephardt really fighting your fight—or theirs?"

Dukakis, whose campaign did not accept—or need—PAC contributions, reinforced the advertising frequently. At one point in the Williamsburg debate, he scoffed: "Don't give us this establishment stuff when you're out there taking their money." At another forum, Dukakis told Gephardt: "People in glass houses shouldn't throw stones. . . . You can't beat up on the establishment and go out and take corporate PAC contributions."

The commercial credited with doing the most to undermine Gephardt, one that Dukakis had refused to use in South Dakota, distilled the case against him on inconsistency. The thirty-second spot showed a tumbler—a man in a suit whose hair had been spray-painted red to approximate Gephardt's coloring—doing flips and jumping through hoops, while captions running across the screen said: "The Gephardt record . . . Reaganomics . . . Minimum wage . . . Social Security . . . Corporate PAC money." Meanwhile, the voice-over delivered this message: "Congressman Dick Gephardt has flip-flopped on a lot of issues. He's been both for and against Reaganomics, for and against raising the minimum wage, for and against freezing Social Security benefits. Congressman Dick Gephardt acts tough toward big corporations but takes their PAC money."

Then the visual shifted to Dukakis talking to voters while the voice-over said, "Mike Dukakis refuses PAC money, opposes Reaganomics and supports a strong minimum wage and Social Security. You know where Michael Dukakis stands."

Finally, cuttingly, the spot returned to the tumbler doing a flip and freezing in midair while the announcer concluded: "But Congressman Dick Gephardt? He's still up in the air."

The advertising was particularly telling because none of the candidates—except Jesse Jackson—had enjoyed the opportunity to build for himself a base of familiarity with this huge Super Tuesday electorate. All of them had made many trips to the South before becoming tied down in Iowa and New Hampshire late in 1987, but most of those visits were devoted to meeting and trying to enlist the political activists. If you visited Birmingham with two or three different candidates, you quickly realized that most of the same people—the activists—were showing up to meet them. Most of the voters, like those along Interstate 20, weren't paying much attention until the survivors of New Hampshire came South for those final two weeks of campaigning.

"I had the feeling traveling around," Gephardt said, "that nobody knew anybody or what was going on." And in situations like that, commercials suddenly became prime sources of "information" that shaped the opinion polls. "The only thing we really saw move the numbers was paid TV," Gephardt said. "People didn't have a lot of information about any of us."

Facing such an intense assault, Gephardt had few weapons at his disposal. He had been campaigning hand to mouth in New Hampshire and South Dakota and now was struggling for money to fight back on television. "We were spending everything we raised," Dick Moe recalled. Moreover, in retrospect at least, the money was not being spent wisely. Gephardt might have done better to concentrate on a few states either close to Missouri, such as Oklahoma and Arkansas, or suffering the kind of economic distress, such as Louisiana, where his populist message might have been expected to have its maximum appeal. But the Gephardt strategists had only $1 million and they chose to spread it over six states, including Texas and Florida, where they could scarcely make themselves heard. "In hindsight," campaign manager Bill Carrick said much later, "we were obviously spread too thin."

Joe Trippi of the Gephardt campaign reflected later on how the demands of running simultaneously in so many states worked a particular hardship on Gephardt. His success in winning in Iowa and South Dakota and finishing second in New Hampshire, Trippi said, was built largely on shoe leather. When Gephardt first won his House seat, Trippi recalled, he did so by "pounding on every single door" in his district. So, at the outset of the presidential race, Trippi said, "I think he thought, I'm going to win this thing because I'm gonna pound on every goddamned door in Iowa, and I'm gonna pound on every goddamned door in New Hampshire." He did the same thing in South Dakota, and was able to pick up a phone and raise the money he needed for one more small state.

But right after that heading into Super Tuesday, Trippi said, "he totally lost stride. . . . Suddenly this immense thing . . . 'I can't knock on this many doors.' Until then he had been personally able to control it. . . . He saw it right off the bat, from the first day we were down there. This wasn't the same thing. It was no longer in his hands. He couldn't pick up enough phones, he couldn't knock on enough doors. . . . He had always done everything on his own personal energy and his own personal ability to fight. And he finally got to the stage of the campaign where the part that made him so invincible wasn't enough artillery, and he hadn't banked four million dollars to replace himself. . . . That was the moment Dick Gephardt understood that he couldn't win the presidency on hard work alone."

Nor did Gephardt have the ability to produce and broadcast any intelligible new commercials to combat the particular charges being leveled at him. In the final days, the campaign did run a ten-second spot aimed at Dukakis with this message: "First the Dukakis campaign smeared Joe Biden with a negative attack video. Then the Dukakis campaign was caught spying on Paul Simon. Now Dukakis is trying to smear Dick Gephardt." But it was farfetched to believe most voters remembered the "attack video" episode or that even a tiny fraction knew of the incident in which a Dukakis field operative, on his own initiative, tried to infiltrate a Simon headquarters in Iowa, was found out and quickly fired.

In the end, the Gephardt campaign's principal tool was a thirty-second version of the sixty-second Hyundai ad used in Iowa—woefully inadequate when measured against several million dollars' worth of anti-Gephardt advertising from the Dukakis and Gore campaigns.

By the final weekend of the campaign, it was becoming apparent that Gephardt was in serious trouble as the first signs of movement toward Gore materialized. Ed Reilly, the pollster for the Gephardt campaign, whose surveys according to Trippi had Gephardt ahead or even in as many as fifteen Super Tuesday states after his South Dakota victory, called the candidate to warn him that "the bottom's falling out."

Tennesseean Gore had paid—and would later pay—a high price by allowing himself to be cast as the "southern" candidate in the Democratic field, a label he insisted was inaccurate but one that stuck nonetheless. In fact, Gore was somewhat justified in denying the southern identification—while milking it for all it was worth in Dixie. As the son of a senator from Tennessee, he had been born and raised in Washington, educated in a private school there and then gone on to Harvard. But even a nominal identification with the South had made Gore the only candidate positioned to enlist the support of southern politicians when, late in 1987, it appeared the Gephardt campaign was foundering. While the other candidates were fighting among themselves in Iowa, Gore was moving around the South gathering endorsements—particularly from prominent state politicians such as Speaker Tom Murphy of Georgia, Speaker Gib Lewis of Texas, Speaker Jon Mills of Florida.

In themselves, the endorsements were less than a ticket to success. But they did send a message to those conservative white Democratic activists who were paying any attention that Al Gore was "their" candidate in the Super Tuesday primaries—the last best hope against the liberal Dukakis and the radical Jackson.

Gore's message was essentially what it had been all along—a political rationale. If you nominate Michael Dukakis, he was telling the southern Democratic voters, you are going to be repeating the mistakes you made with George McGovern and Walter Mondale. Such liberals, the argument went, simply wouldn't sell in the South in a general election, and without the South there was no way for the Democrats to win that election. Period.

The implication was that Gore was the kind of moderately conservative candidate who would sell in the South. And to prove it, he continued to stress the foreign-policy, national-security questions on which he believed he could position himself most effectively as tougher and more experienced than Dukakis.

The role was one not always easy for Gore to fill, however, in light of his moderately liberal voting record in Congress, which included votes against funding for contra aid and the Strategic Defense Initiative. At one point, Gore went to Norfolk, Virginia, to advertise his support for two new aircraft carrier groups whose construction, he said, his rivals would stop. "All the other candidates have said they would cancel contracts on aircraft carriers under way in this harbor," said Gore. "I would stand for a strong America." It was an effective argument for a Norfolk and television audience unaware that, as Gephardt's researchers quickly noted, Gore had voted in committee against $644 million in fiscal 1988 funding for those same carriers.

Gore's attempts to depict Dukakis as too liberal and out of his depth on national-security issues caused some testy moments between the two. In the Dallas debate, Gore accused Dukakis of having said he would be willing to accept a Soviet client state in Central America. "I never said that," Dukakis replied. "Please get your facts straight." When Gore persisted, Dukakis continued: "If you're going to be president of the United States, please get your facts straight."

At the next debate, in Atlanta, a still smarting Dukakis derided Gore's claim of superior credentials on such issues. Gore, he said, had been "taken to the cleaners" by the Reagan administration "the only time he ever conducted a negotiation"—a reference to Gore's role in a 1983 deal between the House and White House on funding for the MX missile. Privately, Dukakis was even more annoyed at Gore for comparing him to McGovern and Mondale. As one Dukakis adviser put it much later, "That's real tough inside a party."

Dukakis, however, was concentrating his fire on Gephardt. In the Atlanta debate, he needled the Missouri congressman for his vote on the 1981 tax bill—"a disgrace and Dick voted for it"—and derided him on the failure of his celebrated amendment to the trade bill. The Gephardt amendment is "dead," Dukakis said quite accurately, although "its burial has been postponed until after Super Tuesday in deference to the next of kin."

While all this three-way bickering was going on, Jesse Jackson was playing the candidate above it all, warning his rivals at Atlanta that the Democratic campaign "could devolve to the level of the Republican debacle." It was easy for Jackson to take that posture. None of the other candidates dared to criticize him for fear of alienating the black vote in November. His own "keep hope alive" message was ringing bells throughout the black community loudly enough so it was already apparent he would walk away as one of the winners.

Beyond that, there was always an element of personal intimidation in Jackson's approach to the others. Before their debates, Jackson campaign manager Jerry Austin recalled, his candidate always demonstrated "a great locker-room mentality." Jackson "was always going to see one of the other candidates" in his holding room, Austin said. "It was a combination of psyching them down or psyching himself up. . . . He'd go by and joke, slap five and wish him good luck." It was Jackson's way, Austin said, "to show the others how loose he was, and how uptight they were." But never at this stage, when there was a multicandidate field, Austin said, did he ever go to see one candidate—Mike Dukakis.

Jackson also had his own approach to maximizing his news coverage. While other candidates spent their money on advertising, Jackson put $330,000 a month into leasing a jet, which Austin calculated could be paid for by twenty-one paying passengers—seven each among the staff, the press and the Secret

Service for its assigned agents. In addition to carting the national press with him, Austin said, "once he got there he would get local press—because he was Jesse Jackson. . . . It wasn't so much that we had to come up with great ideas. What we had to do was get to places. That was the real challenge—to get there. That was our media campaign." The same expenditure on television, the campaign manager said, would hardly have made a dent in the broad Super Tuesday target. And by Super Tuesday, Austin said, the press contingent filled the plane.

Jackson toured the South's media markets preaching the message of the New South, campaigning up to eighteen hours a day. He talked in terms of the South having moved past legal segregation to a time rural and blue-collar whites and blacks ought to join forces to oppose "economic violence." Bob Borosage, his issues director, recalled later a Jackson visit to a Teamsters' hall outside Atlanta, with the audience about 30 percent black and 70 percent white. "Most of the white Teamsters came in with their arms crossed and their legs crossed, and very suspicious looks on their faces," he said. "The blacks were very excited and upbeat. Jackson's theory was that if he could get a white authority figure, a local guy, to introduce him and say, 'Listen to this guy,' so that people would actually give him a hearing, that he could win votes." As he spoke, putting his pitch in the context of the civil rights movement and the Jackson rhetoric, Borosage said, "you'd see people melt. Their arms would loosen up, they'd laugh at his jokes and get into it. He wouldn't win all that audience, and I suspect he won the votes of very few of it, but he won the attention and affection of a good portion of it."

An emotional highlight was Jackson's return to Selma, Alabama, where more than two decades earlier he had taken part in the city's famous and brutal civil rights march. He was met by Mayor Joe Smitherman, who twenty-five years ago had tried to have him arrested. Now he gave Jackson the key to the city. "He understood the new math of the South," Borosage said, referring to heavy black voter registration in Selma, which by this time had put three blacks on the City Council while keeping Smitherman. As Jackson led the press across Edmund Pettus Bridge, scene of much earlier bloodshed, Borosage said, "Over the crest of the bridge comes a pickup truck. And out of the pickup truck on the passenger side, sitting up and looking over the hood to see what was going on, is what you would call your classic cracker—T-shirt, cigarettes rolled up into his arm, beer can in his hand, reddish-blond hair, ruddy face. I thought, 'Uh-oh. Here we go.' And this guy looks around and suddenly he sees Jackson. He lifts his beer can and says: 'Jesseee!' "

Such scenes were hardly endorsements; indeed, Jackson got a paltry share of the white vote on Super Tuesday. But that there had been a world of change in Selma since those earlier days there could be little doubt. Borosage reported that in all the time he traveled through the South with Jackson, they encountered not a single racial incident or even a sign that he saw that could be called a racial slur.

Finally, at work in the Super Tuesday campaign as always, was Jackson's unique political antenna—the ability to see the possibilities in a development and exploit it before the others were even aware of it. He would read the *New York Times* and *USA Today* every morning and then pounce. "The beautiful thing about Jesse Jackson," said Austin, "was we never had a pollster. He was our pollster."

Austin recalled that he was in the Chicago headquarters early one morning, about ten days before Super Tuesday, when Jackson called him from the road. He was supposed to go to Tampa. "He calls me up: 'I don't want to go to Tampa. I want to go to Miami.' Why? 'Because the papers this morning have this article quoting some government figure saying that the amount of cocaine that's come into this country in the last two years has gone down. I know that's not true, and I want to go to Miami and I want to see the commandant of the Coast Guard. He knows.' "

So the Jackson plane flew to Miami, where Jackson got the commandant to take him out into the bay in a cutter. In a press conference, the commandant reported that in the previous three years the Coast Guard had interdicted twice as much cocaine each year as in the previous year and the Coast Guard had just had its budget cut by $100 million. "Jackson comes out with the line," Austin recalled, "that the federal government's way of stopping drugs is to bust the Coast Guard. Just say no to the Coast Guard." In so doing, Austin insisted, Jackson "catapulted the drug issue" to greater national proportions by turning the attention of the network television reporters traveling with him to the situation.

Jackson's likely success on Super Tuesday was so apparent that it may have helped Gore. As one veteran southern professional put it at the time, "Albert's going to get a lot of votes because folks are scared to death thinking about what happens if Jesse just walks away with this thing."

When the votes were counted the night of March 8, the worst fears of the conservative southern Democrats were realized.

There were three winners. Michael Dukakis, the northeastern liberal, won just over 26 percent of the popular vote and eight states—Texas, Florida, Massachusetts, Rhode Island, Maryland, Washington, Idaho and Hawaii—as well as American Samoa. And he captured 356 of the 1,307 delegates at stake.

Similarly fulfilling predictions, Jesse Jackson also captured 26 percent and five states—Georgia, Alabama, Louisiana, Mississippi and Virginia—and 353 delegates. An especially high turnout among black voters lifted Jackson well above expectations.

The one surprise was Al Gore, who won just under 26 percent and six states—Arkansas, Kentucky, North Carolina, Tennessee, Oklahoma and Nevada—and 318 delegates.

Dick Gephardt came away with only his home state of Missouri, 13 percent of the vote and 94 delegates. It was a performance that left his candidacy so compromised he began to consider whether he should withdraw even before the Michigan caucuses that would be the next stop on the campaign trail, and turn his attention to holding his House seat. Finally he decided to give Michigan, as he put it, his "one best shot" before retiring to the sidelines.

The Super Tuesday results caused some immediate revisions and sharpening of perceptions about the shape of the Democratic campaign. Dukakis was now clearly the front-runner, in terms of both the number of delegates he had captured and the strength demonstrated in winning not only in the Northeast but also in the Far West and South.

Even before the campaign opened, John Sasso had seen Super Tuesday as just such an opportunity to change attitudes about his candidate. "The press," he said, "will start feeling Dukakis in the South and say, 'Wait a minute, this guy's not supposed to do anything in the South.' So we'll get a double bang for it."

In fact, that is exactly what happened. Dukakis' success in Dixie was almost entirely misleading. He built his triumph largely on minority-group voters in Texas and liberals in South Florida. He clearly made no breakthrough in the most conservative regions of the Cotton South, capturing less than 10 percent of the vote in Alabama and Mississippi, less than 20 percent in Arkansas, Kentucky, Georgia, Louisiana and Oklahoma. Joe Christie had been right; Dukakis did not play in East Texas.

Jackson's vote was similarly predictable, correlating closely with the black share of the Democratic primary turnout in each state. But the civil rights leader's success was significant for quite a different reason—he had now accumulated enough delegates to be established, at least in the eyes of his supporters, as the leading competitor to Dukakis. Democratic professionals, recognizing that Gephardt was a closed book, were beginning to mutter among themselves about the difficulties ahead in dealing with Jackson and his constituency on issue questions and, quite possibly, the vice presidential nomination.

The one remaining wild card seemed to be Gore, who had run well ahead of expectations in the regional primary but had yet to demonstrate any reach at all elsewhere. Gore's success was overshadowed in the news media by the attention focused on George Bush's de facto elimination of Bob Dole from the Republican contest. But it was clear that the Tennessee Democrat had the paper credentials, at least, to be a factor in the next round of primaries.

The reviews on Super Tuesday as a political innovation were mixed and predictable. The most perceptive Democrats from other parts of the country seemed convinced it had been a political disaster. The results had eliminated the one centrist candidate with potential in the general election, Dick Gephardt, and substituted another who was probably a straw man, Al Gore.

The southerners who had promulgated the plan were understandably defensive. They pointed out that their region had seen far more of the candidates than in any previous campaign—121 campaign days spent in the South by Gore, 75 by Jackson, 52 by Dukakis, 50 by Gephardt and even 32 by Paul Simon.

And they could point to dramatic gains in voter participation all across the region. They noted that in both parties 13.5 million votes were cast in primaries in the fourteen southern and border states, roughly one third of the registered vote and one fourth of the voting-age population. These figures compared reasonably well with the turnout in some northern and western states with longer histories of holding primaries. The turnout ran higher than 40 percent of registered voters in Georgia, even higher than when Jimmy Carter ran in 1976, and in Florida, and more than 35 percent in Louisiana and Texas.

The Democratic turnout represented 17 percent of the voting-age population in the region, compared to just under 10 percent in the caucuses and primaries held by the same states four years earlier. Even the states with the poorest performance, Virginia and Kentucky with 23 and 22 percent of registered voters, were no worse than others elsewhere in the country. And, the Super Tuesday apologists noted, the primaries were clearly superior to the caucuses many of those states had held with participation of 1 percent or less of their electorates.

John Traeger of Texas, now retired from the state Senate, was obviously pleased. "We saw more presidential candidates than we've ever seen," he said. "We got participation that we've never gotten before. It was far superior to any primary that we've ever had before."

But there were valid questions raised about the makeup of the turnout and the lessons that could be drawn from it. An analysis of polling data by the Democratic Leadership Council was particularly telling. It showed the Super Tuesday Democratic primary electorate was made up of 35 percent of voters who identified themselves as liberals, 27 percent as conservatives and 39 percent as moderates. In the general election of 1984, the corresponding figures were 21 percent liberals, 43 percent conservatives and 36 percent moderates.

What those figures suggested, quite plainly, was that it would be impossible to draw dependable inferences about the general election from the results of the primaries. The electorate that gave such a lift to Michael Dukakis and Jesse Jackson was quite different from the one that would be deciding which candidate would win the South's electoral votes in November.

There were also legitimate reasons to question the process as a democratic exercise. Although it may be true that Iowa and New Hampshire carried disproportionate weight in choosing presidential nominees, it was equally true that the Republicans and Democrats who voted in those states were given enough exposure to the candidates to make considered judgments about them.

Surely no one could argue that simultaneous primaries in twenty states offered a similar opportunity. The candidates may have visited the southern states more times than in the past, but most of the visits were on the fly—into a city or town for a media event, often at the local airport, and out. And yet Super Tuesday had proved to be the de facto finals of the Republican competition and probably the equivalent of the semifinals on the Democratic side. The process was as distorted as it had ever been, but now in a different direction.

In the months after the election, politicians in half of the regional primary states—Arkansas, Louisiana, Kentucky, Maryland, Missouri, North Carolina and Virginia—began discussing pulling out for 1992. The experiment had been too expensive for some, disappointing for many in terms of the attention they received from either the candidates or the national press.

There were also embryonic movements under way for regional primaries elsewhere, particularly in the Midwest and Far West. But none of them envisaged a grouping of states as difficult for candidates to cover as Super Tuesday had presented.

The experiment had been an interesting one but a failure, nonetheless. And now, with the campaign returning to the Midwest, the Democrats appeared to be left with a choice of another northeastern liberal, a black or a southerner branded as only a regional candidate—hardly an ideal formula for success in the fall.

19

Illinois and Michigan: Jesse Jackson Peaks

As the Democratic race moved past Super Tuesday into Illinois, the political landscape looked only marginally tidier. Dick Gephardt's disastrous showing in the South, and his financial straits, obliged him to make a basic reassessment. The day after Super Tuesday, Gephardt went on to South Carolina where caucuses were to be held on the next Saturday. Former Governor Dick Riley had endorsed him and he felt obliged to campaign there. That night, he met with most of his major campaign strategists at the home of Tim Driggers, his South Carolina coordinator, outside Columbia, to decide whether to throw in the towel or try to hang on. Bill Carrick, Tony Coelho, Dick Moe, Dave Doak, Bob Shrum, Terry McAuliffe, Joe Trippi and Donna Brazile took part in a late-night skull session, and the consensus was a bleak one.

Illinois had two favorite sons, Paul Simon and Jesse Jackson, running in the primary under a winner-take-all scheme only a week away. That one could be and had to be finessed. Gephardt's only realistic chance of a comeback was in labor-driven Michigan ten days after the Illinois test. But if Gephardt lost there, Carrick informed him, the campaign would be more than a million dollars in debt. Gephardt was told that "the prospects in Michigan were dicey," Trippi recalled, "but we had survey data that showed we had a shot there. With Jackson being strong, the Duke might even take a third place." That was all

Gephardt had to hear. He wanted to press on and nobody argued with him. "Dick was just not comfortable getting his nose bloodied for the first real time and dropping out of the race right after that," Carrick recalled. "He was just not a quitter by nature." So it was on to Michigan, bypassing Illinois.

With Gephardt out of Illinois, the primary there at first blush looked attractive to Dukakis. One of the other Super Tuesday winners, Jackson, would have a lock on the black vote, but his history in the state as a confrontational and flamboyant civil rights leader had hardened white voters against him. He figured to sweep the black congressional districts in Cook County and in the East St. Louis area but get very little support elsewhere. The other Super Tuesday winner, Al Gore, was a question mark, but it would take a fast transformation from southern to northern candidate for him to build on his regional success. With his inimitable chutzpah, however, he became a political version of Clark Kent jumping into a phone booth and emerging as Superman in liberal, populist clothes, now that he was out of his native South. He had never, he said with a straight face, campaigned as a regional candidate.

That left Paul Simon. He had been unable to match even his second-place finish in Iowa, finishing a dismal third in Minnesota and fourth in South Dakota, two backyard states, and he had no money for television advertising. One of the reasons he was staying in the race was that Illinois politicians who were filed as Simon delegates wanted to go to the national convention and he was their ticket of admission if they could get elected. But also he had always been very popular in the state and a Gallup poll for the *Chicago Sun-Times* a few weeks earlier had him far ahead, with 46 percent of those surveyed favoring him, to only 19 for Jackson, 12 for Dukakis, 10 for Gephardt and practically nothing for Gore. Now that Simon clearly was on the ropes, however, the Dukakis strategists had reason to hope he would no longer be regarded a credible national candidate. Dukakis could then slip by him, igniting a political fire storm in Illinois that would sweep East through Michigan and into New York and Pennsylvania, giving him the nomination.

Simon by this time had come up with a cute rationale for Illinoisans to vote for him, beyond provincial pride and loyalty. With Dukakis, Jackson and Gore all able to claim victory on Super Tuesday, slicing up the national convention delegates in all those states among them, Simon made the argument that the party might well be headed for a brokered convention. Simon had even telephoned Gephardt and urged him to remain in the race to improve the chances of that happening. And with a lion's share of Illinois' 173 delegates to Atlanta in his pocket, he would be well positioned to have a major say in the nomination, including the possibility of becoming the compromise nominee himself. Some 113 of the delegates in Illinois were to be elected by congressional district, with the slots going to the highest vote-getters. If six Simon supporters ran in a district that had six slots and the Simon supporters finished one through six, all would be elected.

One key Simon aide said of the Democratic nomination at the start of the one-week Illinois campaign: "This could become like the Bataan death march." The analogy was not the cheeriest one, but therein lay Simon's slim chance of resurrection and survival.

The Dukakis strategists, with ample money and more coming in every day, decided to take dead aim on Illinois. They budgeted up to $500,000 for the brief primary campaign and focused their message on challenging Simon's "brokered convention" pitch. Charlie Baker, the architect of Dukakis' New Hampshire victory, came into Illinois pushing the official line. "People don't want to vote for tactical reasons," he said, "they want to vote for president."

Jackson's national campaign manager, Jerry Austin, meanwhile sought to undermine Simon's credibility, saying he "should have gotten out of the race a long time ago. He's not a player for the nomination." And he ridiculed the notion that Illinois voters would support a favorite son who was not going anywhere. "When was the last time a favorite son won?" he asked, noting that when Senator Adlai E. Stevenson III ran as one against Jimmy Carter in the 1976 Illinois primary, he was buried.

But the polls suggested that Simon, while slipping some, was holding on in his home state. A *Washington Post*–ABC News tracking poll had Simon backed by 38 percent of likely Democratic voters surveyed to 33 for Jackson, 16 for Dukakis, 6 for Gephardt, 3 for Hart and 2 for Gore.

It was not taking long for voters outside the South to decide what they thought of Gore even though he was spending time and money in Illinois, and he wasn't doing so well in Dixie anymore either. On the Saturday before the Illinois primary, he got snowed under by Jackson, 54 percent to 18, in Jackson's native state of South Carolina.

As for Hart, the man who had reentered the race in December to "let the people decide," held a news conference in a Denver restaurant and declared: "I got a fair hearing and the people have decided." He was out, satisfied that he had done the right thing in getting back into the campaign to inject his ideas into the dialogue.

Inside the Dukakis campaign, the candidate was still backing away from negative attacks on his opponents. But he did agree to a television commercial that took Simon's "brokered convention" appeal head-on. That appeal was the subject of full-page ads in the two Chicago dailies bought by a group of Simon supporters to run on the day before the primary. The ads said: "The Democratic Party will have a brokered convention. We want Paul Simon to be our voice. We want Paul Simon to be our candidate. Illinois has always been a major player when it comes to choosing presidents. We can continue that tradition in tomorrow's Democratic primary."

Dukakis' television ad made no mention of Simon. Instead, it showed film clips in black and white of old party conventions as a narrator said: "Some people would like to turn back the clock to go back to the days when you didn't really pick the presidential nominee. They say you must turn over the power to them to use at a brokered convention. But you don't have to do that. On

Tuesday you can pick the next president. Mike Dukakis is running for president in every state in America for a better economic future for every American. You decide. . . ."

Simon accused Dukakis of "a touch of arrogance" for suggesting, he said, that a victory for him in Illinois would avoid a brokered convention. "We are headed for a wide-open convention," he insisted. "No commercial can change that." He trotted out three congressmen, from Indiana, Ohio and New York, all states still to hold primaries, who avowed he was still a contender in their states. And Simon told Illinois voters that if he didn't win their primary, he would fold his tent. "I offer you not a thirty-second commercial," he said. "I offer you thirty years of commitment to the people." Meanwhile, his national campaign manager, Brian Lunde, offered statistics suggesting that even with his big Super Tuesday success Dukakis would have to win three fourths of all delegates yet to be selected in twenty-six remaining state primaries and caucuses to clinch the nomination.

Dukakis had one other immediate hurdle in Illinois. As usual, voters in Chicago seemed to be more interested in the local elections than in picking a presidential nominee. The late Democratic Mayor Richard J. Daley summed up the Chicago attitude in 1968 after Richard Nixon had carried the state against Hubert Humphrey. "This is the greatest night in the history of the Democratic Party in Cook County," Daley proclaimed—because Democrats had swept nearly all the local offices. In 1988, too, the campaign for clerk of the Cook County circuit court among former Mayor Jane Byrne and Aurelia Pucinski, daughter of Alderman and former Congressman Roman Pucinski, the Democrats, and former Cook County Democratic Chairman Edward "Fast Eddie" Vrdolyak, now a Republican, seemed to have the voters more excited than the presidential race and the fortunes of Mike Dukakis.

Finally, the calendar worked against Dukakis. The seven short days between Super Tuesday and the Illinois primary gave him little time to tell the voters of the state what he was all about, running against two Illinoisans about whom they knew a great deal. And instead of spending that brief time on filling that information void, Dukakis ran a television ad that had nothing to do with who Mike Dukakis was, and that itself became the subject of news media attention.

The results reflected these Dukakis problems. Simon, the favorite son who seemed to be going nowhere nationally, won a 10 percent victory over Jackson, the favorite son who polarized the electorate in Illinois along racial lines, winning nearly all of the black vote but only about 8 percent among whites. And a hapless Dukakis finished far back, beating out only the more hapless Gore among the active campaigners. Simon won 136 delegates and Jackson took the other 37, shutting out Dukakis. According to the Associated Press count, Jackson now had 460 delegates pledged to him, only 4 fewer than Dukakis.

What was going on? Whatever happened to "momentum," which was supposed to carry winners forward from one primary to the next? One week after his Super Tuesday success and with plenty of money in hand, Dukakis was stopped cold, losing to one oft-beaten candidate, Simon, who bought no television time, and another, Jackson, who spent peanuts—an estimated $40,000. Dukakis badly needed to recover quickly in the next contest, in Michigan ten days later, where Gephardt had leapfrogged ahead to make what could be his last stand. Simon, still bereft of campaign funds, would skip Michigan and go on to Wisconsin, an Illinois neighbor state with a liberal tradition. But Gore, searching desperately for someplace to demonstrate that he was anything more than a Dixie phenomenon, moved on to Michigan, where his imaginative message was: "I want to put the Democratic Party back on the side of working people."

In no other state, in fact, did organized labor play as central a role in Democratic Party politics as it did in Michigan. Labor officials, and those of the United Auto Workers particularly, were powers in party counsels, including the selection and bankrolling of gubernatorial and senatorial candidates. Early on, Gephardt had hoped to win the endorsement of the AFL-CIO with his concentration on new trade legislation designed to help the auto and other industries cope with foreign competition. But the labor federation could not muster the two-thirds majority for any candidate required under its rules for a presidential endorsement and none was given.

The state's Democratic governor, James Blanchard, had not endorsed any candidate, but many of his people were working for Dukakis, reportedly with an approving nod from Lansing.

Jackson's hopes in the state lay with a large black population in Detroit and several other smaller cities. In 1984, Detroit's longtime black mayor, Coleman Young, went all out for Walter Mondale against Jackson, for whom he had a strong personal antipathy, and salvaged the city for the Minnesotan. But since then Jackson had become so strong that Young declared that his political allies in the city government were free to vote as they wished—a thinly veiled admission that he knew he couldn't hold them from Jackson this time around.

Michigan Democrats, with the state primary outlawed, picked precinct delegates in a complex open caucus process known as a "firehouse primary." The neighborhood meetings usually were held in public places, such as schools, church basements and, theoretically, even firehouses. Voters came in and cast ballots just as if they were voting in a primary. The difference was that the party, not the state, ran the election and voters dropped their ballots in boxes set aside for each candidate in open view of poll watchers. The process put a premium on informing voters where the polling places were and monitoring the voting.

By the time Dukakis and Jackson could focus on Michigan, Gephardt had already moved in for what he knew full well could be his last stand. Under other circumstances, the state conceivably could have been the linchpin in his nomination, but instead it was now a cliff he was clinging to. His strong support of trade legislation that his critics called protectionist should have given him an inside track for organized labor's endorsement, both nationally and in Michigan. The UAW earlier in the year had even run television ads around the country supporting the Gephardt trade amendment. But the AFL-CIO's 1984 experience in endorsing Mondale and then getting rapped as a special-interest constituency had made the union leadership wary. Moreover, unlike 1984 when Mondale's long identification with labor made the endorsement almost automatic, there was no clear-cut consensus for one Democrat.

In 1984, the United Auto Workers, the single most powerful union in Michigan, sent out an extensive mailing to its members telling them where the special polling places were and urging them to vote for Mondale. This time, the mailing went out but with no pitch for any candidate. Some individual union leaders were publicly supporting Gephardt but the AFL-CIO's posture against an endorsement barred the use of funds by the Committee on Political Education (COPE), the national AFL-CIO's political-action arm.

Still, Gephardt worked the union halls diligently, seeking to make a virtue of his underdog status. At UAW Local 569 in Flint, for example, he told the assembled members, most of them decked out in shiny jackets with their union local number on the back, that a *Wall Street Journal* editorial had pronounced him dead after his Super Tuesday debacle. "Let me tell you," he shouted, "Dick Gephardt is not dead. The *Wall Street Journal* is dead—wrong."

Amid cheers and chanting of his name, Gephardt continued that "if those editorial writers would come out of their cushy offices" and visit cities like Flint that had suffered so many job layoffs and plant closings, they would understand why his trade message was a winner. "We can't give up on ourselves," he said. "They counted us out, but they didn't count on me and they didn't count on you." Gephardt concluded with his regular tag line—"It's your fight too"—as a stereo system in the hall belted out the theme from *Rocky*. The surface indications seemed good.

Many workers in the hall said later they intended to stick with Gephardt, but the most knowledgeable labor politician in the state, Michigan AFL-CIO President Frank Garrison, confided that many labor leaders, fearful that Gephardt was a goner, were looking at Dukakis as an acceptable alternative. Garrison noted that Douglas Fraser, the popular and influential former president of the UAW, had endorsed Dukakis, but he added that Dukakis' dismal third-place finish in Illinois didn't help him in Michigan.

In the brief Michigan campaign, Dukakis set his sights on knocking Gephardt out of the race. After a slow start, he moved some national operatives into the state, including Paul Jensen, who was Mondale's liaison with organized labor in 1984. But personally he gave Michigan very short shrift. A few nights before the voting, he made an airport stop in Detroit en route to California for a fund-raiser, and used the occasion to try to undercut Gephardt on two counts. The first was Gephardt's congressional support, which Gephardt had used as a badge of his leadership among his peers, and the second was the trade issue.

Appearing at the press conference were Michigan Senator Don Riegle and three other members of the state's congressional delegation, all endorsing him. But more notable was a Dukakis statement that in accepting Riegle's endorsement he supported restrictive foreign-trade legislation that Riegle had steered through the Senate. The Riegle bill was not identical to the Gephardt trade amendment, but was close enough to it to put Dukakis on the same side of the street with his rival in coping with foreign trade as a major labor concern.

Gephardt, who himself had been under continuing attack as a flip-flop artist on a range of issues, immediately laid the same charge on Dukakis. He quoted Dukakis as saying in their two-man debate in Iowa the previous August: "The president of the United States today has all the authority he needs to do something about those unfair trade practices. We don't need more laws or more amendments."

Dukakis tried to recover by noting that he had said in the same debate that "I feel a lot better about the Senate bill" and that Congress was probably going to "pass something close to that." What he meant by that, he suggested, was that he had been for Riegle's Senate approach all along. Dukakis' embrace of the Riegle bill also went counter to his pitch that the basic difference between himself and Gephardt was that he was an experienced executive and Gephardt was only a legislator. As he had said in another debate, "You want a law, Dick. I want to act." But this was Michigan and the stakes were the votes of working stiffs worried about the competition from Japan and South Korea.

Gephardt also worked the trade issue to the very end, giving a thoughtful and reflective valedictory in a major speech before the prestigious Detroit Economic Club. For months he had been plagued by the label of "protectionist," to the point that on one occasion, in frustration, he blurted out that if being a protectionist meant standing up for American workers against unfair foreign-trade practices, "then I'm a protectionist."

In the Detroit speech, he noted that critics "denounce measures to open foreign market—measures like the Gephardt global market access amendment—as 'protectionist.' They insist that nothing should disturb the system they were raised or trained in, even if it now means one-way free trade, and America is on the wrong end of the exchange. . . . Other countries, which are delighted to deploy the word [protectionism] to influence our domestic debates, are equally determined to practice the policy when it comes to 'protecting' their own domestic industries." And the most-favored-nation arrangement with Korea, Japan and other Asian trading partners was a bad deal for the United States, he said. "When they impose high tariffs on everyone, they can and do impose them on us, on the grounds that they are treating us the same as everyone else. The problem is, since they treat all nations poorly, they treat us poorly. And since we treat all nations well, we treat them well."

The captains of industry who listened, most of them rock-ribbed Republicans, applauded politely, but Gephardt was winning few converts—in that audience or among the blue-collar Michigan Democrats he now desperately needed. It was very late in a campaign in which he was already perceived as a loser, and with the AFL-CIO's nonendorsement position sealing his fate.

Gephardt's dilemma was encapsulated in a single scene in Detroit's Cobo Hall immediately after the Economic Club speech and two days before the caucuses. Gephardt held a press conference attended by Owen Bieber, Fraser's successor as president of the UAW. As Gephardt spoke, Bieber stood off to one side out of camera range and had to be coaxed to stand next to the candidate. Then he would not say flatly even that he was going to vote for Gephardt. Instead, as Gephardt stood by looking dazed and forlorn, Bieber said only that "I came here today because I want to pay my respects to Dick and the union wants to pay its respects to him." And in the caucuses two days later, that was about what Gephardt got from the UAW.

Congressman Sander Levin of Michigan, a Gephardt supporter, said later Bieber was on the spot because there were 30,000 black members of the UAW in the state and he could not appear to be taking a position against their obvious candidate preference.

In all this, that preferred candidate, Jesse Jackson, was as usual a big question mark. The Dukakis camp conceded that Jackson would probably sweep the two heavily black congressional districts in Detroit, especially with Coleman Young "agreeing" to let his supporters vote without direction from him. Young's attitude was in itself a telling commentary on Jackson's greatly increased strength since 1984, when the mayor held predominantly black Wayne County for Mondale against Jackson by a vote of more than two to one. One key Michigan Democratic Party official observed: "He recognizes a parade when he sees one, and he doesn't want to be trampled by it."

Outside of Wayne County, however, the Dukakis campaign failed to see the potential for Jackson in other concentrations of black voters in other Michigan cities. Nor did it see the intensive organizational efforts under way to get out the vote for him in a process that rewarded neighborhood organization of a finite electorate. Under the leadership of Joel Ferguson, an experienced black politician who was a Michigan member of the Democratic National Committee, black church and political leaders all across the state were mobilized to identify and maximize the black vote for Jackson. And wherever there were blacks, there was an overwhelming preference for him. The lack of a union endorsement for anyone else made it much easier than in 1984 to attract an overwhelming number of the 30,000 blacks in the Michigan UAW into the Jackson ranks. The state also had a large Arab-American population that Jackson was able to tap into by virtue of his open support for direct talks with the Palestinian Liberation Organization on the Middle East impasse.

All these points were obvious in retrospect. But the result of the Michigan caucuses, when it came in that Saturday night, was a shocker. Jackson, piling up huge margins of twenty-five to one in the state's First Congressional District and nearly seventeen to one in the Thirteenth, both heavily black, beat Dukakis by nearly two to one statewide, carried ten of the state's eighteen congressional districts with outsized black turnout and captured 74 of 137 delegates elected, to 50 for Dukakis, 11 for Gephardt, 3 uncommitted and none for Gore. We were at a reception at the Gridiron dinner in Washington that Saturday night when word of the Michigan outcome swept the room, leaving hundreds of so-called experts with dropping jaws, ours included. Gephardt was out, to no one's surprise, but suddenly Jesse Jackson was taking on the look of a serious candidate for the nomination itself, and Dukakis the look of a jilted suitor. At the same time, Alice Travis, the Dukakis operative assigned to "spin" the press that night, was selling the campaign line that the real meaning of the results was that Gephardt had been eliminated and it was now a two-man race.

Tubby Harrison, the Dukakis pollster, said later that the Dukakis campaign simply was outfoxed and outgunned by the Jackson forces in Michigan in a process not run or monitored by state or local election officials, but rather mostly by party volunteers in makeshift polling places. As a pollster, he said, "no matter what you had done there, if you had polled the morning of the election, you could not have picked up what was happening. [The Jackson campaign had] sound trucks going through the city and urging people to come out, and they did a great job. And there were no controls on it. There were no controls over people voting numerous times. One of our guys voted five times to show what was happening, and there was no check on it. But they beat the hell out of us." However, Harrison said, "in retrospect it was the best thing, because it sealed it [ultimate defeat] for Jackson." Harrison's polling in Connecticut and Wisconsin, the next two tests, indicated that white voter attitudes hardened against Jackson once he won in Michigan and his candidacy might be emerging as more than symbolic.

Susan Estrich, Dukakis' campaign manager, insisted later that his Michigan loss did not result from her candidate's message, his flip-flop on trade or any other act of Dukakis in the state, but because "a different and skewed universe" voted, ferreted out by the diligent Jackson operation. But the defeat nevertheless encouraged the news media, she acknowledged, to focus on "perceived weaknesses" of Dukakis that the campaign had to address. "The risk for us was that unless we appeared to at least be dealing with some of them," Estrich said, "the party and the party leaders and this whole institutional world in which Dukakis was not their choice candidate, was not going to rally around him as their nominee."

The press, at the same time, "was going wild about Jackson," she said. Another Jackson victory over Dukakis in Wisconsin ten days after the Michigan vote, she conceded later, would have imperiled Dukakis' very candidacy. It was not so much a concern that Jackson would become the Democratic nominee, Estrich said, "but the guy who had let Jackson win Michigan and Wisconsin would not be the choice either. We were under real heat in the sense that people saw the potential of a Jackson victory in Wisconsin,'' meaning that Dukakis would be blamed for precipitating the development of a stop-Jackson effort, behind Gore or someone else, that would tear the party apart.

"We clearly had to win Wisconsin," Susan Estrich said.

20

Wisconsin and New York: Dukakis Bounces Back

For forty years, the Wisconsin primary had been an important stop on the campaign route to the major party presidential nominations. Thomas E. Dewey blunted Wendell L. Willkie's comeback try there in 1944 and took the measure of Harold Stassen, General Douglas MacArthur and Senator Robert A. Taft in the state in 1948. In 1960, John F. Kennedy won his first truly competitive test there over Hubert H. Humphrey from neighboring Minnesota, and in 1968 Lyndon B. Johnson in absentia threw in the towel against Eugene McCarthy two nights before the Wisconsin primary. In 1972, George McGovern broke out of the Democratic pack by whipping Edmund Muskie, Henry M. Jackson, John V. Lindsay and George Wallace there. Jimmy Carter in 1976 won a razor-thin victory over Morris Udall in the state to establish himself as the Democratic front-runner, and Carter used Wisconsin to rebound from an upset in New York at the hands of Senator Edward M. Kennedy in 1980.

Still, for several reasons, Wisconsin over those forty years had been gradually shoved off center stage in the nomination drama. The earlier start of the delegate-selection season, the proliferation of presidential primaries—in thirty states by 1976—and the mushrooming attention focused on the nominating process by television all worked to diminish the role of states like Wisconsin that sent relatively few delegates to the national conventions and held their primaries and caucuses later on the political calendar.

Until the 1972 election, the candidates in both parties competed in only a handful of state contests, spaced out in a way that gave them sufficient time to familiarize voters in those states with their persona and views. One of the pleasures of traveling the campaign trail then was the Wisconsin interlude of a few weeks. After a long day of absorbing campaign speeches in Milwaukee's ethnic wards or surrounding dairyland, one could escape to the comforts of the old Pfister Hotel bar in Milwaukee and then repair the ravages of the day with the hearty German fare at Karl Ratzsch's down the street or Mader's a few blocks away, which offered as a bonus a longer walk back to help the digestion. For the more adventurous, there was Frenchy's a short cab ride away. There you could order all manner of exotic game. Always on the menu were lion and tiger, but as often as not an attempt to order either would bring the waiter's confidential advice that the lion or tiger was a trifle tough that night.

But such leisurely pursuits were inhibited by reforms, inspired by liberal activists within the party and enacted by Democratic-controlled legislatures, aimed at opening the delegate-selection process to more voters. Many states that felt they were losing out in candidate and news media attention to places like Iowa and New Hampshire began moving up their primary and caucus dates—"front-loading" the process, as seen in the creation of the Dixie-dominated Super Tuesday. Wisconsin began to take on the trappings of just another refueling stop on the whirlwind, overloaded trail to the conventions.

In 1988, however, the Wisconsin Democratic primary emerged again as a critical event, although more than half the states had already begun or completed their delegate-selection exercises and there were only ten days for campaigning between the previous crucial contest, Jackson's landslide upset of Dukakis in Michigan, and the voting in Wisconsin.

After that Michigan surprise, Susan Estrich said later, some suggestions came to her from Dukakis supporters that he skip Wisconsin as a way to save money and go right into New York, the next showdown state on the calendar in late April. "What can Wisconsin do for you?" the counseling went. "New York is the big gorilla. Save your money. Save your time." But she felt, Estrich said, "we had to go into New York a winner from Wisconsin. We didn't want to go in flat."

Three days after the Michigan vote, Connecticut was holding its Democratic primary, but the fact it was in Dukakis' backyard diminished interest in that election and forfeited national attention to Wisconsin. Jackson stormed into Connecticut with his special brand of political sermonizing, drawing large and exuberant crowds in New Haven and Hartford. About all he succeeded in doing, however, was driving Gore out and into Wisconsin. There Gore's managers felt he'd have a better chance to post a respectable showing that would make him a competitive candidate in New York. There, he had just signed on David Garth, the resident media expert, to give 1988's chameleon candidate a consistent hue.

On primary day in Connecticut, Jackson did succeed in adding an estimated 22 percent of the white vote to his sweep of the black constituency. But Dukakis still scored a landslide 58 percent to 28 victory over Jackson. Gore polled only 8 percent—a showing that, coming after a similar performance in Illinois, made him ineligible for further federal matching funds. A provision of the law disqualified any candidate receiving less than 10 percent of the vote in two consecutive primaries. The Dukakis strategists breathed a bit easier, while looking ahead to Wisconsin as a more revealing test of the Jackson threat on neutral ground.

"We knew we could explain away Michigan," Estrich said later, "if we turned around and won Wisconsin. . . . We could put Michigan in perspective." That was the advantage of having so many primaries, she said. "There's always another Tuesday and another Tuesday and another Tuesday. Michigan could appear as an aberration," she said, "or a fair sign of Dukakis' weakness, and our failure in Wisconsin could be devastating to us."

Dukakis himself was remarkably unshaken by the Michigan experience and prepared for Wisconsin. When Will Robinson, one of the national campaign operatives who had been working in Michigan, met Dukakis at the airport in Milwaukee, he had his suitcase packed and stowed in the trunk of his rental car, a hedge against the possibility he might be fired. But Dukakis told him: "We're going to keep doing what we've been doing. We're going straight ahead."

The Monday after the Michigan loss, Estrich gave Dukakis a two-page memo recommending only some cosmetic changes in his campaign style, to indicate that at least he was responding to the Michigan defeat and listening to a growing clamor of advice from Democratic kibitzers. The recommendations attempted to humanize Dukakis a bit more by having him dress more informally, mix more informally with voters and free him of the hordes of elected officials usually mobilized for his set-speech appearances.

Estrich also made one other key point. "We cannot let Jesse Jackson be the candidate who connects with the anger of working people in this country," she later recalled telling her candidate. A large part of populism's appeal, she said, was how it played to "a sense of injustice, that the rich are getting richer and meanwhile I'm getting screwed," and Dukakis was "giving that away" to Jackson. That theme indeed was exactly the one Jackson was strumming effectively with voters. Gephardt, she reasoned, had won Iowa on that pitch, it had been a factor in Jackson's victory in Michigan, and she could see him using it again in Wisconsin, where there were areas of high urban unemployment and rural depression vulnerable to that message. "That was his most powerful message from our view, and that we had to engage on," she said.

Tubby Harrison, the Dukakis pollster, agreed. "I had felt since Iowa that he had talked too much about creating jobs, and Gephardt's appeal was in saving jobs, with his trade pitch." In Wisconsin Dukakis switched, Harrison said. "He rolled up his sleeves and started to fight. Maybe he was scared." The public polls at the time gave him a reason, with a *Milwaukee Sentinel* survey showing him only 3 percent ahead of Jackson the Monday after the Michigan fiasco. Harrison's own polls, however, while showing a temporary dip after the Michigan vote, indicated a comfortable lead for Dukakis thereafter.

Dukakis gave a somewhat more vigorous and personal speech a few nights later at a major fund-raiser at Milwaukee's Serb Hall, a traditional site for political rallies among white ethnic voters. Rather than criticizing Jackson, the man he had to beat to reinstate himself as the clear Democratic front-runner, he continued to aim his rhetoric at the Reagan administration, though in somewhat sharper terms. "This administration has mortgaged our future to a bunch of defense contractors and merger maniacs and sharp operators on Wall Street,'' he said. ''They've turned Main Street America into a shopping mall for foreign investors. And now they want a new four-year contract from the American people. Who do they think they are? How dumb do they think we are?''

Still his strategists were not satisfied. Dukakis was saying the right words, but the music wasn't there that conveyed the notion that he was a caring human being. Estrich recalled telling him: ''These people ought to be your constituents. This is after all substantively what you're all about—jobs, growth, et cetera. But you can't be just about it as a positive sort of intellectual exercise of who's going to put together the regional development bank. You've also got to connect with their level of anger and frustration, of feeling like they've been left out of the so-called Reagan recovery. . . . We've got to tap into that.'' The stump speech was worked over again and Dukakis was sent into key labor areas like Kenosha and Racine, where he talked about ''saving jobs'' as well as creating them. He began to hit his stride in what Estrich later said was his best week of the preconvention campaign period. But the problem of ''humanizing'' Mike Dukakis had a long way to go, as subsequent events would prove beyond doubt.

While the Dukakis managers were thus attempting to put more of the Jackson-like fire into their candidate, Jackson was in a sense working Dukakis' side of the street. Two of his most prominent white Democratic friends, former Democratic National Chairman John White and former Carter budget director and Georgia state party chairman Bert Lance, arranged a breakfast meeting for him in Washington with a cast of party elder statesmen led by Clark Clifford, the venerable private adviser to presidents going back to Harry Truman.

''It was strictly a touch-feel meeting,'' White said later, but of considerable symbolic meaning. Jackson, White said, pointed out the irony of the ''role reversal,'' with white political leaders meeting with a black presidential candidate, instead of the customary white politician asking black leaders for their support. More than any commitment coming out of the meeting, however—and from all reports the only one was that the attendees would not engage in any stop-Jackson movement—was the signal sent that Jackson was being taken more seriously by party heavyweights. It was, however, a signal that could have its down side for Jackson among white voters who would consider voting for him as a protest, but might think twice if they thought he really could be nominated.

Jackson was not one, though, to waste time fretting over such things in the middle of a campaign. He plunged into Wisconsin with some reason to hope that in spite of the minimal black population in the state—only 3 percent—he could pull another upset over Dukakis. He was no stranger to the Wisconsin labor community, having rallied to the support of strikers in several contract disputes over the previous several years.

Among the most interesting was the strike of Local P-40 of the United Food and Commercial Workers against the Patrick Cudahy pork-processing plant in the predominantly white Milwaukee suburb of Cudahy. In early 1987, the owners of the plant, Smithfield Foods, imposed a sharp wage cut and rollback of other benefits on the workers, a move the union rejected as an effort to kill it. About 850 strikers, mostly white but with more than a smattering of blacks and Hispanics, set up a picket line. The company then went into black neighborhoods of high unemployment in Milwaukee and hired a host of blacks as scabs. The action produced the unusual spectacle of black picketers shouting racial epithets at their black replacements as they crossed the picket line.

The situation posed an interesting challenge for Jackson, who had long insisted that his Rainbow Coalition was not made up only of blacks and interested only in their problems. That insistence had taken on a hollow ring the previous year when Jackson went into Newark, New Jersey, and campaigned against longtime civil rights champion Peter Rodino, chairman of the House Judiciary Committee, who was white, in behalf of a Democratic primary challenger who was black. The Cudahy strike gave Jackson an opportunity to support a strike of multiracial workers against black scabs, and demonstrate that his Rainbow Coalition was indeed driven by more than the concerns of blacks.

Jackson, when he learned of the unusual strike, immediately with his incomparable political antenna saw the possibilities in the situation. He went to Cudahy on Palm Sunday morning and marched with the strikers from the plant to the Cudahy High School football field. There he proceeded to compare the strike situation to Christ's Palm Sunday walk into Jerusalem, when he berated priests in the temples for cheating the populace. Without quite casting himself as Christ, Jackson pointed out that the plant managers, like the priests, similarly had cheated the strikers by trying to force labor concessions from them and then, when they refused to accept them, replaced them with nonunion workers.

But Jackson being Jackson, he did not attack the black nonunion workers. Rather, he told the strikers that the scabs "should have jobs, but not your jobs." He cast them as economic victims used by the company for its own ends, and he met privately with a group of them. Instead of taking the jobs of their brothers, he told them, they should join with the strikers against the "economic violence" of the bosses. It was a breathtaking performance, and one that won him something approaching adoration among many in Cudahy.

So now, a year later, Jackson had a constituency beyond his black base that he believed would turn out in force for him. When he returned to the town a week before the Wisconsin primary, with the strike then in its fifteenth month, about six hundred people, most of them white, jammed St. Frederick's Catholic Church and responded with lusty cheers to his plea for their votes.

A somewhat similar situation existed in Kenosha, farther south of Milwaukee, where a huge Chrysler Motors plant faced a shutdown that would affect 5,500 workers. Months before the Wisconsin primary, Jackson had answered the call of UAW Local 72 and addressed a protest rally against the plant closure. He wrote a letter to Lee Iacocca, the Chrysler board chairman, asking him to keep the plant open. Here, too, Jackson had reason to be confident that in

Kenosha as in Cudahy he had a considerable white constituency in his corner. Local 72 in fact endorsed him in spite of the international UAW and AFL-CIO policies of nonendorsement. He drew a huge crowd on his return visit, as he did nearly everywhere he went in the state in the final week of the primary race.

In Sheboygan, a city of overwhelmingly white population with an unemployment rate of less than 4 percent, Jackson packed the local armory for a weekday noontime rally. He arrived nearly an hour late but the crowd stayed and gave him a roaring welcome. He walked through the crowd shaking hands in a crush reminiscent of a Robert Kennedy happening in his brief but dramatic presidential bid of twenty years earlier. Jackson's message attacking corporate greed and demanding a fair share for the poor and unemployed generated as enthusiastic a reaction as if he had given the speech to an inner-city rally.

But the question about Jackson remained: Could he be nominated and elected? In the emotionalism that his personal appearances generated, many Wisconsin white voters insisted he could. "I wouldn't tell a soul but you," Mrs. Robert Hansen, wife of a watch repairer, told us in her husband's shop in Waukesha on the Saturday morning before the vote, "but we're thinking about voting for Jesse Jackson because he's the only one who's saying anything. We don't see his color anymore." But Carol Campbell, in her novelty shop down the street, said Jackson's race was unimportant to her, but "I have friends who say, 'Forget it.' "

This issue of electability became a major factor in the Dukakis effort as he campaigned determinedly in Kenosha, neighboring Racine and other industrial towns to contest Jackson for the blue-collar vote with the more emotional appeal Estrich had urged upon him.

State Representative Jeffrey Neubauer, introducing Dukakis at a Racine Labor Center rally the final weekend, claimed that Dukakis "has one attribute no other Democratic candidate can claim. He can beat George Bush," Neubauer said, "and I do not want George Bush to be our president. This is serious business. This is no time to cast a sentimental thank-you for our neighboring senator to the South [Simon]. This is no time to cast a vote for a good-looking southern accent [Gore]. This is no time to cast a symbolic vote for an inspirational speech [Jackson]."

In Racine and other towns, Dukakis dusted off the comparison between his campaign and John Kennedy's in 1960, reminding voters in union halls that they had started another Massachusetts candidate on his way to the White House by giving him a primary victory over Humphrey. And this year as in 1960, he pointed out, the Republican foe would be the incumbent vice president. "I kind of like it," he said at the Racine Labor Center. "What do you think? Can we repeat history again twenty-eight years later?" At the same time, his campaign ran an intensive phone-bank operation around the state and used Dukakis' big money advantage to keep his television ads running heavily. A key message to the voters, unspoken, was that Jesse Jackson was on a roll after his Michigan upset and Wisconsin was the place to stop him. Dukakis stuck to his decision not to attack Jackson, but the electability issue did not have to be spelled out

Neither did a comment to reporters by Wisconsin's Republican governor, Tommy Thompson, that if he were a Democrat he'd vote for Jackson. "He's exciting, a very charismatic individual," Thompson said. "Just because he is a Democrat doesn't mean I can't like him. Jesse has got the 'Big Mo' and unless he stumbles it will continue to build." Because Wisconsin had an "open" primary, there was nothing to stop Republicans from crossing over and voting in the Democratic contest. And it was obvious that the one Democrat the Republicans felt they could most easily beat was Jackson. When Thompson's comment was printed, he called the *Milwaukee Sentinel* and insisted he "never encouraged any Republican to cross over" and that Republicans "should stay in the Republican primary and vote for George Bush." But by this time Bob Dole had quit the race and the Republican primary was meaningless. And Thompson repeated of Jackson that "if I was a Democrat, I'd vote for him."

From another quarter, Jackson got mixed blessings. The *Madison Capital Times*, the state's most liberal daily, endorsed him. But the newspaper also greeted his arrival in the state capital with an eight-column banner over a critical *Washington Post* story reexamining his controversial behavior immediately after the assassination of Dr. Martin Luther King, Jr., in Memphis, where Jackson served as a King lieutenant.

Finally, Jackson chose this politically sensitive time to write a letter to Panamanian leader General Manuel Noriega, whom the Reagan administration was pressuring to step down in the face of drug-dealing and other charges. Jackson's letter also urged him to leave, but it immediately precipitated criticism from the other candidates in Wisconsin as unwarranted meddling in the conduct of foreign affairs. A *Milwaukee Sentinel* editorial called it "a grandstand play" that did not square with Jackson's celebrated toughness on drugs.

The Noriega letter, Jackson campaign manager Jerry Austin said later, apparently was something Jackson did "impetuously," but it gave his opponents "a very legitimate reason to criticize Jackson. . . . So you had two or three days of very negative publicity about the whole Noriega thing." And beyond that, the incident gave voters a cover for the real reason they had for not wanting him to be nominated—race. "You had enough things coming together to raise doubt in people's minds," Austin said, "and you had a safe haven in Dukakis."

Gore, meanwhile, presented still another persona, donning lumberjack shirt, down vest and work boots to pitch hay and milk a cow, and proposing an increase in the government price support for diary farmers that a University of Wisconsin professor of agricultural economics promptly declared would cost milk consumers about forty cents a gallon more.

Gore's campaign also ran a television ad in which he sought to muscle in on the action at the Chrysler plant in Kenosha, where Jackson had been involved months earlier and where Dukakis and Simon also were trying to garner votes. The Gore ad showed Lee Iacocca along with an aerial view of the Kenosha plant and pickets marching outside. The ad reported that Iacocca had made $20 million in 1986 while Chrysler was dodging taxes and shifting operations overseas at the expense of workers such as those threatened with the plant closing in Kenosha. "I'll make these corporations pay their share of taxes," Gore intoned in the commercial, "and create jobs here in America. . . . Let's make them put people over profits."

Once again Gore was pumping gobs of money and time into the effort to shoehorn himself into the picture in a northern state. As part of the drill, he went after Jackson on a lack of experience and his positions on the Middle East. Then he accused Dukakis on the final weekend of being "absurdly timid" about criticizing Jackson and being "just scared to death of saying a single word" against him. But Gore's problem was not what the other candidates were or weren't doing. It was what he was and wasn't doing—rapping his opponents while doing whatever he could think of to ingratiate himself to the voters at hand, without defining himself in a coherent way.

As for Simon, the result in Michigan shaped the Wisconsin primary so clearly as a Dukakis-Jackson rematch that the man in the bow tie from the neighboring state never had a chance to be heard again. He campaigned doggedly in Kenosha and other blue-collar battlegrounds but he was just plain dull. Brian Lunde, his campaign manager, later said his candidate had simply been "written out of the story" and did not know "how to get back in," particularly because he was now disinclined to go negative against his opponents.

On the night before the Wisconsin vote, Dukakis pulled out a closer-than-expected victory over Jackson in Colorado's caucuses and then capped it the next day with a surprisingly large margin over him in Wisconsin, 47 percent to 28, with 17 for Gore and 5 for Simon, who in a short time announced he was "suspending" his campaign. Gore, however, already pointing to New York in two weeks, vowed to press on.

Jackson's bubble of optimism, inflated in Michigan, had suddenly burst. Rather than that big upset victory over Dukakis helping Jackson in Wisconsin, Jerry Austin said later, he lost Wisconsin "because we won Michigan. It was no longer a protest vote." That is, voters were willing to go along with Jackson as long as they believed their vote was making a statement through Jackson's candidacy on a number of positions, or as a way to express dissatisfaction with the front-running Dukakis. Many of Jackson's contributors, Austin said, gave money to fund an effective and serious contender for the nomination, but once he became one, they backed off.

Tubby Harrison said the same. Jackson's Michigan victory threw a scare into white voters in Wisconsin, he said, assuring Dukakis' victory there. This fear appeared to exist even in blue-collar towns like Kenosha and Cudahy, where Jackson had made apparently successful efforts to court the white vote —but where in the end he was beaten clearly by Dukakis. Statewide, ABC News exit polls indicated, Jackson got only 23 percent of the white vote.

Jackson saw the Wisconsin outcome in more conspiratorial terms—what he said came to be referred to in "the code words 'the Jackson factor.' " After the election, he told us: "After Michigan the party leadership panicked and pulled out the stops, overtly and covertly, to stop the campaign. Superdelegates who had been committed not to declare themselves officially until after June 7 [the last primary day], after Michigan began to declare themselves publicly." Jackson insisted that the Michigan Democratic Party chairman and head of the Democratic State Chairs organization, Rick Wiener, had said that Jackson's nomination would be a tragedy for the party as "a signal to other state chairs. They set that apparatus loose."

Wiener, when told of Jackson's allegation, flatly denied that he had ever said any such thing, publicly or privately. He noted that he as a superdelegate did not declare for Dukakis until late in the afternoon of June 7, when it was clear Dukakis had locked up the nomination. Furthermore, there was no perceivable public rush to Dukakis among superdelegates after Jackson's Michigan victory. In fact, some superdelegates such as Senator Alan Cranston and Representative Tony Coelho of California, who were poised to endorse Dukakis at the time of the Michigan vote, held off rather than risk the perception that they were involved in any move to blunt Jackson's effort.

Jackson contended also that a stop-Jackson gambit had occurred in Illinois, where state Democrats had "pulled Simon back in for the express purpose of running a one-state campaign that propped him up for the purpose of sustaining the old party arrangement." But the notion that primary voters in Wisconsin were affected by how superdelegates in that state and others may have conducted themselves after Jackson's Michigan victory was farfetched in the extreme.

Jackson was more realistic when he noted at the same time that "Michigan was the last time you had somebody who was viable, in Dick Gephardt," competing along with himself and Dukakis for votes. "Instead of moving toward a heads-up contest [between the Michigan survivors, Jackson and Dukakis]," he said, "the party infrastructure collapsed toward Dukakis." This analysis, too, credited party professionals with Jackson's failure after the Michigan vote, rather than voter preference for Dukakis for whatever reason—race or defection from Jackson as too liberal or personally intimidating—when the contest narrowed down to the two men.

Jackson was probably closer to the mark when he observed that for all his special efforts with labor in Wisconsin, "I also realized that my campaign was going against the winds of history and culture. It wasn't a state where you had a reasonable cross section of African-Americans and Hispanics as well as whites." He said the warm reception he received in the state, while losing, was "a cultural victory" of the sort that was a critical part of his campaign. "Always in my campaign were two tracks," he said. "The political track was getting delegates and votes. The sociological track was changing people's mental perceptions and options. Some people, their perceptions and feelings changed before their votes changed. So many people [said] 'if you keep working, you'll get there. I'll support you.' "

Even individuals working in other campaigns, including the Dukakis campaign, he insisted, "were pulling for me; working for him and hoping I would keep raising the right issues. . . . They wanted me to be the tugboat and provide the energy and wanted him to be the ship to carry them across." In other words, Jackson said, activist progressives looked to him to press Dukakis to take more aggressive positions on a range of issues of particular interest to them. His lecturing on drug use, teenage sex, the state of the welfare system, sanctions against South Africa, neglect of domestic needs in favor of excessive military spending and burden-sharing among the Western allies, he said, were not "left wing or right wing—they are the moral center." Then, speaking in the present tense, Jackson said: "Mine is both a campaign and a movement." It was an observation that went a long way toward explaining his behavior after his political fortunes began to slip in Wisconsin—and throughout the rest of the 1988 campaign and beyond.

At the same time, the Dukakis strategists well knew after their Michigan defeat and subsequent Wisconsin victory that an election that was reduced to choosing between two candidates on racial lines, unsavory as that might be philosophically, could be the key to the nomination for their man. If Dukakis could get Jackson one-on-one in the remaining primaries, the prize would be his. Here was where Dukakis' huge money advantage was paying off, in the war of attrition. One by one the other contenders were being forced out of the race because they had no money, whereas Dukakis could absorb defeats like the back-to-back losses in Illinois and Michigan, two major states, and continue. But without a bank balance, Brian Lunde said later, "you can't show up the next day for the game."

In Wisconsin, he said, "to watch those Dukakis ads come up the week before was like, 'Here comes the army.' It was tactical, though—overwhelming you with communication. Forget what the message was. It was sheer amount of communication, all tactical. . . . We couldn't keep playing."

With the wooden stakes finally driven through the hearts of the Gephardt and Simon campaigns, Dukakis had only Al Gore to deal with before he could isolate Jackson one-on-one and put an end to speculation about the possibility of a brokered convention at Atlanta. "We had to eliminate these people two or three times all over again," Estrich said. "And we had to get the delegates necessary for the nomination."

The Dukakis campaign now had a big enough delegate lead over Jackson to give his first-ballot nomination a sense of inevitability. That circumstance then would give leading Democrats—especially the so-called superdelegates chosen as officially unaligned—a rationale to fall in behind him that would shield them against charges of racism.

There was no secret about the arithmetic in New York. Jackson had polled 26 percent of the primary vote in 1984, finishing third behind Mondale, who had 45 percent, and Hart, who had 27. The black leader had achieved that level, even with Mondale siphoning off some black votes, on the strength of votes from white liberals, some of whom supported Jackson as a device for "sending a message" of defiance to Mayor Ed Koch. In New York politics, such tortured, two-stage reasoning was a staple.

Now, with blacks expected to cast 30 percent or more of the primary vote and no Mondale in the field, New York professionals were predicting that Jackson might receive as much as 35 to 40 percent of the vote. If he reached 40 percent, and if Gore were able to manage as much as 20 percent, Dukakis could be in trouble.

For Dukakis, there were two strategic keys. The first was to increase the size of the turnout to minimize the share of the vote represented by blacks. New York had only held competitive presidential primaries of this kind on two previous occasions, so there was no well-established tradition of participation. In 1980 the vote barely topped 1 million, well under one third of the enrolled Democrats. In 1984 turnout rose to almost 1.4 million, a marked increase but still short of the participation level in other high-interest primaries.

Dukakis could rely on his ability to win a clear majority among the Roman Catholic voters, including Hispanic-Americans, who would make up the single largest bloc in the primary—close to 40 percent of the total. But he also was under pressure to maximize his support among Jewish voters, who could be expected to cast about one fourth of the primary vote. And it was here that Gore was a potentially complicating factor.

The idea that Gore could suddenly become a player in New York seemed ludicrous at first. Here was this Nobody from Nowheresville who had won nothing except some primaries in the South and a couple of dinky caucuses in the West, and who had never scored higher than 17 percent in any nonsouthern primary. And if he knew anything about New York, he hid it well. In the week before the primary, when the collapse of the Williamsburg Bridge between Brooklyn and Manhattan was the dominant local story, Gore referred to the bridge twice one day—first as the "Westchester Bridge" and then as the "Westmoreland Bridge." Who was this guy, anyway?

But there were reasons Gore could not be simply brushed aside. The first was that David Garth had signed on to handle his media campaign. Garth was a consultant with a reputation of almost mythical proportions in New York campaigns, and he had a particularly well deserved reputation for taking a political unknown and successfully projecting an image that even the candidate's mother might find excessively heroic. If Gore could produce $1 million for advertising on television, Garth said, he could be a player, $1.5 to $2 million and he could be a contender. "He's a hell of a horse, but nobody knows him," Garth said.

A second reason for taking Gore more seriously was his juxtaposition to Jesse Jackson. Although it could hardly be said that Gore had "taken on" Jackson, he had been more direct in criticizing him than any of the others and in Wisconsin he had just chastised Dukakis for being reluctant to join in. And Gore had set off a storm of angry reaction in New York by assailing Jackson on his support for the Palestine Liberation Organization and by noting that "we're not choosing a preacher—we're choosing a president." If anyone could be pigeonholed as the "anti-Jackson candidate" in the party, it was Al Gore.

What made this fact particularly important in the spring of 1988 was the extraordinary polarization between blacks and Jews within the city—and the long memories of those Jewish voters. They remembered well Jesse Jackson's references to "Hymietown" in 1984, and his history with Minister Louis Farrakhan of the Nation of Islam and with Yasser Arafat, leader of the PLO.

If the blacks and Jews had not already been polarized, Ed Koch made sure of it by announcing early in the New York campaign that any Jew "would have to be crazy" to vote for Jackson. The question of anti-Semitism aside, Koch also sailed into Jackson on policy issues. "He wants to demilitarize us," he said. "He's against every single major defense program. I believe that if his programs are put into effect—not that Congress would allow it—we would be defenseless in six weeks."

As always seemed to be the case in New York primaries, the issue of policy toward Israel became the critical one in sorting out the three candidates. And here Dukakis was on tricky ground, despite the assets of a Jewish wife and a personal history as the son of immigrants with which many Jewish voters could easily identify. Dukakis shared the views of most liberal Democrats on most policy questions involving Israel, but he was well aware that the appearance of pandering to the Jewish concerns could be politically fatal. That lesson had been brought home quite vividly by Gary Hart's clumsy attempts in 1984 to "get right with the Jews," as one of his strategists described it, by seeming to change his position on the question of moving the United States embassy from Tel Aviv to Jerusalem.

The litmus-test issue this time was Palestinian statehood. Jesse Jackson favored it, Albert Gore opposed it and Michael Dukakis found himself in the middle by saying it was not a decision the United States could hope to impose on either Israel or the Palestinians. Speaking to the principal umbrella group of influential Jewish groups, the Conference of Presidents of Major American Jewish Organizations, Dukakis said: "It is Israel, Jordan, Egypt and the Palestinian leaders who have to make the decision. It's the parties themselves to negotiations who have to make those judgments."

Dukakis also fell short of meeting the Gore standard on another question of particular importance to the most militant Jewish leaders—a letter signed by thirty members of the Senate criticizing the peremptory rejection by Israeli Premier Yitzhak Shamir of Secretary of State George P. Shultz's attempt to open negotiations in the region. While pointing out that he was "very critical of the Arab nations" on their own recalcitrance, Dukakis endorsed the letter and said he would have signed it had he been serving in the Senate.

But Gore rejected the letter, a move that won quick approval from some hard-line Jewish leaders in New York but one that angered some of his Senate colleagues who had taken the political risk of signing it. The signers, moreover, had included Jewish senators such as Carl Levin of Michigan and Frank Lautenberg of New Jersey, the latter locked at the very moment in what appeared then to be an uphill campaign against retired General Pete Dawkins, the onetime Army football star and Rhodes scholar.*

The lines on the Jewish-black question were drawn most sharply, however, when Ed Koch endorsed Gore five days before the primary, declaring that the Democrat from Tennessee would be, among other things, "like a rock" in supporting Israel as president. The endorsement came as something of a surprise because the assumption in the political community had been that Koch would support Dukakis, if anyone, because he might be expected to be more closely attuned to urban needs. One of those most surprised was Gore himself.

"There was an intense competition between Dukakis and me for his endorsement," Gore recalled. "I fully expected him to endorse Dukakis and I think most people did. Most people thought when he surprisingly endorsed me, it was a coup. For about forty-eight hours there, that was what the general interpretation was and there was a little uncertainty in the air. David Garth's doing my campaign and it's a volatile situation, and there was a respectful amount of suspense coming into that. I mean, it dissipated pretty rapidly but there was a little excitement there."

Indeed there was. The Koch endorsement was enough of a surprise that political professionals began to question the opinion polls showing Gore with only about 10 percent of the vote. "The common view was still there's a down side to this," Gore said, "but the up side is much bigger. It didn't work out that way."

Koch now became the dominant figure in the final weekend of the campaign—flailing away at Jackson. Politics in New York was every bit as provincial as that in Chicago or anywhere else in the nation. And that was reflected in the legions of television camera crews and radio reporters thrusting microphones in the mayor's face at every opportunity on the chance—usually pretty good—that he would say something colorful and controversial.

Practically overnight, Koch made Gore a bit player. On Sunday, two days before the primary, the mayor led the young senator up Fifth Avenue at the head of a parade celebrating the fortieth anniversary of Israel, then accused Jackson of showing "arrogance and contempt" for not joining the parade. The same day, in what Gore later considered "the turning point" in Koch's value as a surrogate, the mayor appeared on the David Brinkley show on ABC News and repeated the charge that Jesse Jackson had exaggerated his role on the scene when Martin Luther King, Jr., was shot down in Memphis in 1968.

Gore protested that Koch was "speaking for himself" but the picture coming through the local television news was one of the green candidate from the boondocks being led around by the tough guy with the big mouth from the city. The pattern continued through the final day of the campaign, when Gore

*Lautenberg was, however, reelected.

and his wife, Tipper, went to the Fulton Fish Market with Koch and, once again, the presidential candidate was pushed into the background. To no one's surprise, the film made all the local television shows repeatedly over the final twenty-four hours of the campaign. If there were questions about whether Gore was ready for prime time in presidential politics, the spectacle of him being used by Ed Koch certainly reinforced them.

Looking back on the episode much later, Gore couldn't see where he ever had much choice. "I had plenty of options," he said. "None of them were very attractive. I felt that was the appropriate response, to make it clear that he was speaking for himself and not me, and that I did not agree with what he was saying but I was grateful for his endorsement of my candidacy. The fact that a particular option doesn't work well doesn't always mean that there's another that'll work a lot better."

In fact, even before those final two days, the reaction against the Koch-Gore axis had seemed to set in with some voters who accepted that a vote for Gore rather than Dukakis was a vote for Jackson. At a Gore rally in downtown Brooklyn right after Koch's endorsement, an elderly Jewish voter offered us this piece of cogent political analysis: "You gotta catch wise. This Gore can only split the [white] vote and help Jackson. He can't help himself. He can only hurt himself. You get my meaning?"

Another who also well understood what Koch was up to was Jerry Austin, Jackson's Bronx-born-and-bred campaign manager. Asked by reporters what he thought of the mayor, Austin said: "Ed Koch is an idiot, even by New York standards." Jackson, when he heard about the comment, began to steam. He was attempting to play the political statesman, staying above gutter politics, and on election eve he first stiffed Austin, then, at the Sheraton Centre, had him summoned to him in the hotel lobby. "When he wants to make you feel like you're not there, he looks at his shoes," Austin recalled. Still not looking at him, Jackson asked his campaign manager: "Did you call Ed Koch a moron?" Austin replied: "No. You've got it wrong . . . I called him an idiot."

Jackson did not see the humor in it. It was wrong and would be counter-productive, he told Austin, to insult Koch. But Austin disagreed. "I'm a New Yorker," he told Jackson. "The things I'd say in Columbus, they'd be outraged, but in New York they understand." Even when he ran Democrat Richard Celeste's campaign against Republican Governor James Rhodes in Ohio, he recalled, and he had called Rhodes "brain dead," his candidate had benefited. Rhodes began attacking him, Austin, rather than Celeste, he told Jackson. He drew the heat from Celeste and onto himself, he said, and Celeste won.

But Jackson still wasn't mollified. "You keep forgetting," he told Austin. "You're the campaign manager. I'm the spokesman." Jackson told him he gave him high marks for his management of the campaign but "an A for arrogance" in dealing with the press. Austin replied that he was "honest." The alienation thus created lingered on, and was fed shortly thereafter as Austin continued to speak his mind.

Jackson did not disagree with Austin's view of Koch, only with expressing it publicly at a time Jackson was attempting to remain above the fray. After the election, he told us: "Koch's behavior and style and substance, using religious and racial bait, of course was one of the ugliest parts of the whole campaign. And the national party didn't seek to censure him. . . . He [Koch] played upon the worst of people's fears. He really hurt the nation. In some sense, I came out of New York victorious, because my mettle under heat was shown. It was shown I had mettle [*sic*] and not alloy. I had the capacity to take a punch without my knees buckling. And had enough strength not to react, to keep my composure. In many ways Koch kicked me and broke his foot. Koch lost New York City. I won New York City. . . . We as a nation cannot run race-centered campaigns." While "the race factor is very much in the bloodstream of our country," he said, the answer is "coalition, not confrontation."

Policy toward Israel was not the only issue in the New York campaign. At one point, Gore tried a generational appeal with a television spot showing him in a green field jacket saying: "I'm a Vietnam veteran. One of the lucky ones. I didn't have to kill or be killed. But some of my friends unfortunately weren't that lucky. Because of them, I've worked hard in Congress for arms control, for peace, for a strong bargaining position with the Russians."

And there were sharp exchanges between Gore and Dukakis in the course of several debates. In one of them at the Felt Forum sponsored by the *Daily News*, Gore mentioned the Massachusetts prison-furlough program—although not the specifics of the Willie Horton case—and asked Dukakis whether he would extend that policy to the federal system. "Al," Dukakis replied, "the difference between you and me is that I have run a criminal justice system. You haven't." But under continued pressing from Gore, Dukakis admitted that the policy allowing furloughs for prisoners under life sentences had been canceled. The exchange was largely ignored by the press—but not by George Bush's "opposition research" director, as we have seen.

In that same debate, the testiness also was demonstrated when Dukakis began talking about how he now intended to compete for delegates formerly committed to Gephardt and Simon, then added, "and maybe for Al Gore delegates" as well. "Don't lick your chops too soon," Gore replied somewhat huffily. "New York is going to have a bigger say than you will."

Most of the exchanges were similarly unedifying. In another debate sponsored by CBS, after bickering over whether Dukakis had been advocating first-use of nuclear weapons in Europe, Dukakis made a point of noting that Gore had referred on a previous occasion to King Khalid of Saudi Arabia as still living, when he had died in 1982. "I am waiting for King Khalid to come back from the dead," he said. "Al shouldn't be running for president. He should be running for something bigger than that."

There were a few telling moments, however. One came in a debate on women's issues late in the campaign. The candidates were asked if they supported the $2.5-billion child-care bill pending in Congress, and all three quickly

endorsed it. But Dukakis then made a point of volunteering that he couldn't
promise to fund the program at the level in the bill. Asked the next day why
he had gone out of his way to raise doubts among these activist women, he
replied: "I have to start thinking about governing. We're going to have real
budget problems." In his own mind, at least, Michael Dukakis was already the
Democratic nominee and likely to be president of the United States.

The topics that received the greatest attention in New York were, predictably, drugs and street crime, health care, housing and the homeless, day
care and education. But these candidates were all Democrats with only differences over emphasis and method to divide them on such questions. The different
element in the New York campaign was the high feeling between blacks and
Jews and its potential for affecting a contest for the presidency.

Even before the Michigan caucuses the Dukakis campaign had received
some early and indirect warnings about the tension between the two groups
from Governor Mario Cuomo.

Cuomo had been playing a cute game all through 1987 and the early months
of 1988. Although he had officially taken himself out of the picture even before
Dukakis announced his candidacy, Cuomo had been studiously ambiguous about
his attitude toward the other candidates. The assumption of most Democratic
professionals had been that the New York governor would finally endorse
Dukakis, the fellow governor from the Northeast with whom he seemed to have
the most in common. But Cuomo sent mixed signals—at one time, for example,
sounding as if Paul Simon were his choice.

Then, in a series of conversations with Susan Estrich, Andrew Cuomo,
the governor's son and closest political adviser, seemed—at least in the eyes
of the Dukakis strategists—to be seeking a basis for the long-awaited endorsement. After the campaign, Cuomo said his role in meeting with Estrich was
"only to ask questions" on his father's behalf and that he did so with all the
campaigns still in the field. But the fact was that Super Tuesday had clarified
the situation to the point that the only realistic question was whether Mario
Cuomo would endorse Dukakis or sit it out. Whatever his purpose, the concerns
raised by Andrew Cuomo were intriguing, both for what they said about the
political climate in the state and for the political advice they seemed to offer.

The younger Cuomo asked Estrich, first, if Dukakis might not be willing
to soften his down-the-line support for the letter written by the thirty senators
on the Shultz plan. Perhaps, Cuomo suggested, Dukakis might say something
to the effect that the letter could have been written better, perhaps with more
moderate language. Secondly, Andrew Cuomo wondered if Dukakis might be
willing to say publicly that he would consider Jesse Jackson as a possibility for
the vice presidential nomination.

What he seemed to be suggesting, clearly, were steps that would, in one
case, make Dukakis more acceptable to the most militant Jewish leaders and,
in the other, would have the precise opposite effect.

But such a suggestion, Dukakis and his managers quickly understood, was political suicide. If Dukakis appeared to be giving ground on the letter, he could be undone by the perception of pandering to the Jewish vote. On the other hand, if he deviated from his policy of refusing to discuss vice presidential possibilities to open the door for Jackson, Dukakis would be inviting mass defections not only among Jewish supporters but also among ethnic blue-collar Democrats who were the core of his support.

Indeed, the formula was politically destructive enough to make cynics wonder if Mario Cuomo was still nourishing dreams of another scenario—a collapse of the front-running Dukakis that could be expected to set off a new round of demands for the governor of New York to rescue his party.

Dukakis quickly rejected both notions, and the defeat he then suffered in Michigan made the issue academic. But the idea that Mario Cuomo would raise such bizarre possibilities, however obliquely, spoke volumes about the preoccupation of New York politicians with the tension between blacks and Jews there.

As matters turned out, Cuomo delivered no endorsement until it was no longer needed. Dukakis won the primary handily as the vote rose to 1.6 million, thanks in part to efforts by such operatives from Massachusetts as Paul Pezzella and Joe Ricca imported specifically to work on turnout in such Dukakis-leaning areas as Queens. He polled 51 percent of the vote to 37 percent for Jackson and only 10 percent for Gore.

For Gore, it was the end of the road. His goal all along had been, he said later, "to score a victory of sufficient importance to get the media focus" somewhere outside of the South. "I really thought that if I could get the spotlight," he said, "I could convince people, in whatever region of the country or whatever age group, that I was a person they wanted to vote for." As it was, when he did get that spotlight, Ed Koch was the one doing the talking.

Gore also had fallen far short of that $2 million David Garth thought necessary to make him a contender, in some measure because his campaign wasted so much money in Illinois and especially Wisconsin. "The simple reason," he said, "is that every adviser with New York expertise I know [told me] in order to have a good chance in New York, you had to come into the state with something under your belt in addition to five southern and two western states. I had carried seven states but I had not won a victory in the North, so I tried to pull it off in Wisconsin."

But others with expertise on New York politics would have argued that the notion of a good showing in Wisconsin meaning much in New York was fanciful. On the contrary, the evidence suggested that New Yorkers were more insulated from and immune to news from the hinterlands than voters anywhere in the country. In 1980, for example, President Jimmy Carter managed only 41 percent against Senator Edward M. Kennedy in the New York primary only two weeks after thrashing Kennedy with 65 percent of the vote in Illinois.

Dukakis had needed Wisconsin to prevent doubts about his reach in industrial states raised by Michigan from becoming epidemic within the national press and political community. His success in Wisconsin accomplished that purpose, but there was never any evidence it was directly related to his strength in New York.

Perhaps the most important aspect of Dukakis' victory in New York, however, was the fact he won 164 of the 255 delegates—bringing his total above 1,100 and putting him more than 200 ahead of Jackson.

Michael Dukakis was now positioned to begin closing the sale. He was, at long last, isolated in a one-on-one confrontation with Jesse Jackson. He was holding a respectable lead that he could be expected to widen in the weeks ahead—thus steadily increasing the pressure on those superdelegates and the uncommitted to rally behind him in the interest of presenting a united party against George Bush.

It was just a case of playing out the string in Pennsylvania, Ohio and California. But Jesse Jackson had other ideas.

21

Pennsylvania to California: Jackson's Phantom Campaign

On the night of Jesse Jackson's sound defeat at the hands of Michael Dukakis in the New York primary, he told his cheering supporters that he would press on with "this campaign of expansion" to the end of the primary road—all the way to California seven weeks later. The phrase was instructive. It underscored how Jackson was moving deftly from his earlier emphasis on winning the Democratic presidential nomination to his employment of the campaign process to enlarge his political constituency, force the door of the Democratic Party open wider to it and oblige the eventual nominee to respond to its concerns.

To millions of American voters who never conceived of the notion that Jackson could win the Democratic presidential nomination, his campaign had always seemed quixotic or egomaniacal. But to other millions, especially in the black community, it was another major step in the advancement of a people. Many of them even harbored the hope, against all odds, that somehow it might happen. Jackson's first bid for the nomination, in 1984, had tapped into that sense of history, and the mere running seemed then to be enough for many blacks. But when, in his second try in 1988, Jackson for a time was the front-runner in the national public-opinion polls, and then in the accumulation of delegates to the Democratic National Convention, the hope flowered.

Many of his supporters wanted to—had to—believe it was true for the sake of their own morale, and that may also have been so for Jackson himself. But on another level he had always seen his candidacy in the historical context, not surprising for a man who had reached maturity as an integral player in the paramount social-justice movement of his time. And so the Jesse Jackson campaign for president always was, beyond the surface bid for political power, an extension of the fight for the civil rights of American blacks. And as he brought a bit more color to the Rainbow Coalition, the fight's objectives expanded until it took on the trappings of class struggle, seeking to wed urban and poor blacks and whites with struggling farmers and unemployed blue-collar workers, and minorities of all stripes.

Although his appeal remained predominantly in the black constituency, Jackson did succeed in attracting pockets of white liberal and white rural support, giving a touch more meaning to his claim to be leading a Rainbow Coalition. But that political strength was distorted by the fact Jackson was running in a multicandidate field, where he could win in primaries with a plurality of the vote, or do well with considerably less. When the field narrowed, however, political reality set in.

Competing against only two other candidates, Michael Dukakis and Al Gore, in New York, with Gore a severely crippled contender, Jackson's inability to attract enough white votes was his undoing. And with Gore dropping out, Jackson was left with having to go one-on-one against Dukakis, effectively sentencing him to weekly defeats from then on. Of the remaining primary states, only New Jersey had a black population as large as New York's 12 percent, and the odds against Jackson somehow mobilizing sufficient white support against a white candidate to overcome that deficiency were patently unrealistic.

The collapses of Dick Gephardt in Michigan, Paul Simon in Wisconsin and Al Gore in New York had scuttled the Jackson political battle plan of the two white men who conceived and developed it, Frank Watkins, Jackson's unobtrusive longtime lieutenant, and Jerry Austin, the brash Ohio media expert hired on as campaign manager. On Memorial Day of 1987, long before Austin joined the Jackson campaign, he was watching the Indianapolis 500 car race on television—a commentary on his standing as a sports fanatic. "Al Unser, Sr., won," he recalled. "He started off in twenty-first place and won. He never left twenty-first place. Twenty guys dropped out ahead of him. And I said, 'That's it. That's the way you run for president. You gotta survive. It's all survival.'"

In late October, Austin sat down with Watkins, a veteran of Jackson's 1984 campaign who had already laid out the political road map for 1988. "It was a very simple plan," Austin recalled later. "You had to do better than expectations in Iowa and New Hampshire, at least meet expectations on Super Tuesday and beat expectations in the industrial states in order to get to a one-on-one showdown in California. And it was based on having a very viable candidate through Ohio [two weeks after the New York primary]." This plan fleshed out Austin's own "survival of the fittest" notion, and once Austin signed on, it became the Jackson formula on the purely presidential nomination track. At the same time, Jackson's own mind functioned on its own track, which embraced not only the campaign for the nomination but the historical aspect of a black candidacy and the prospects for forcing change within the party.

The Watkins-Austin "survival" plan worked until the industrial-state primaries, where the elimination process of the other candidates occurred too soon. With Gephardt, Simon and Gore all out by the end of the New York primary, Jackson had to face Dukakis one-on-one in major industrial states where he had little chance—Pennsylvania a week later, and then Ohio and Indiana a week after that—before reaching the California showdown. What really screwed up the works, Austin theorized later, was that Gore rather than Gephardt had come out of Super Tuesday as one of the three winners. By this time thoroughly identified as "the southern candidate," Gore had no credibility in Illinois, Michigan and Wisconsin and had to withdraw after New York. Had Gephardt been a winner on Super Tuesday, Austin reasoned, he probably would have fared better than Gore did in those states and could have survived as the third candidate along with Dukakis and Jackson in the later industrial states. And there, with Dukakis and Gephardt splitting the white vote, Jackson could have stayed seriously in the running to California.

The Gephardt strategists were aware of the virtue of such a scenario for their own candidate. In fact, according to Austin, he got a phone call from Bill Carrick, the Gephardt campaign manager, on the day before the South Carolina caucuses, which were held four days after Super Tuesday, proposing a collaboration. Carrick said he knew Jackson was going to win in his native state (which he did, overwhelmingly) and asked that Jackson throw some votes to Gephardt to help him survive. Austin told him there was no way he could pull that off. Nevertheless, Carrick called him again the day before the Michigan caucuses, Austin said, with the same proposal, warning that unless Gephardt finished second there, he would have to quit. Austin asked him why he thought he could swing such a vote switch in Michigan when he couldn't do it in South Carolina.

In any event, Austin's "Indianapolis 500" theory ran out of gas after New York. In advance of that primary, Austin had watched with interest as well as amusement Gore's thrashing about to survive himself. When Dukakis' campaign manager in Wisconsin, Pat Foercia, told us that "a vote for Gore is a vote for Jackson"—a comment that got him in hot water in his own campaign—Austin could only silently agree. And after Gore's cow-milking caper in Wisconsin, Austin asked: "What's he going to do in New York, get bar mitzvahed?" But not nearly enough voters in Wisconsin, and then in New York, could swallow Gore to keep the Democratic race three-cornered as the "Indy 500" theory required.

Austin understood the reality when, on the day of the New York primary, we had lunch with him and he began to talk of Jackson as a vice presidential prospect, indicating that in light of Jackson's 1988 performance as a vote-getter he had earned the right to be considered by Dukakis. Such comments were not what were usually expected from the manager of a candidate who was still talking about winning that day's critical primary and going on to be nominated. But Austin was nothing if not candid.

His candor, in fact, extended to the next morning. Outside a postmortem press conference by Jackson, some reporters cornered Austin and asked him whether he thought Jackson deserved the vice presidential nomination. Austin replied, as he had at lunch the day before, that his candidate certainly had earned the right of first refusal. Then and later, Austin also talked about Jackson's role ahead in shaping the Democratic Party's agenda in a way that sounded to some reporters as if he were conceding the nomination.

In the press conference, Jackson conceded he had lost the battle in New York but insisted that the war went on. He accentuated the positive, noting that he had increased his share of the vote from 26 percent in 1984 to 37 percent, and more than doubled his delegates from the state. When he heard about Austin's comments on the vice presidency, however, and similar observations by his national campaign chairman, California Assembly Speaker Willie Brown, Jackson was furious. With twenty more primaries still to be contested, Bob Borosage, Jackson's issues adviser, said later, Austin seemed "to throw in the towel." This would not do for a candidate who intended to stay in the race to apply pressure for change, to obtain a stronger voice in the party and, not incidentally, fulfill the historical aspect of his effort. In other words, Jackson was determined to maintain the fiction that he remained a genuine contender for the nomination, and Austin's remarks undercut that perception.

And why shouldn't Jackson have gone on? He already had more than 800 delegates, only 200 fewer than Dukakis, and in spite of the bleak political calendar ahead, who knew what would happen? Had all of the other candidates been guided by the early expectations, none of them would have entered a race in which Gary Hart in 1987 already had 60 percent in the major polls, with nobody else with more than 10 percent or so.

More realistically, though, Jackson's decision to press on in the trappings of a serious contender marked the evolution of the Jackson adventure from a predominantly electoral exercise to more of a politico-sociological one—from a campaign for the presidential nomination to a crusade to move Dukakis on policy matters important to Jackson and his cohorts, and to make a statement for history. To many, Jackson also seemed by now to be on a power trip, driven by the emotion of his own campaign and by the adulation directed toward him by his followers and even some young reporters in his traveling entourage. As in everything he did, there was no beginning and no end to what he called "Jackson Action," just a continuation of his perpetual motion, with adjustments in rhetoric to accommodate the circumstances.

Because Jackson was a special candidate with a special constituency the party could not afford to offend, he escaped much of the pressure a white also-ran would have encountered at this juncture to abandon his campaign and throw his support to the front-runner. The normal pressure on a loser to drop out—the drying up of financial support—also did not touch Jackson to the degree it would have others who lacked a special base of support akin to Jackson's committed black church network. And so Dukakis was obliged to plod on through the late primaries. In one sense, the exercise benefited him, because he was able to post easy victories each Tuesday and stay in the news with a winner image. But he also lost time that could have been profitably used preparing for the fall campaign against Bush.

To some in the Jackson campaign, like Borosage, the objective shifted to running "a campaign on issues, because now that it had gotten [down to] Jackson and Dukakis, it was very important for people to see how conservative Dukakis was presenting himself. And if we could make it a campaign about issues, in fact we would do very well in Oregon and California, the late states, if we could get that far. And there still was a possibility that you would not have anybody with a majority going in, and that meant a whole different ball game."

Jackson himself, who began telling audiences in the face of a string of primary-election shellackings that "we're winning every day," increasingly sought to set the campaign in the context of a continuing civil rights struggle that had moved from drugstore sit-ins and protest marches to a direct bid for political power at the highest level.

But Austin, the acerbic Ohio campaign consultant by way of the rough-and-tumble Bronx, was 100 percent campaign operative and zero percent crusader. Austin's falling-out with Jackson in New York over the campaign manager's freewheeling comments about Mayor Koch and Jackson's vice presidential prospects was only one aspect of the conflict between the two. "Jerry took a tough assessment, as a guy who counts votes, after New York," Borosage observed, "and said, 'The chances of us winning this now are next to nil.' " In fact, after the campaign, Austin said later, Jackson told him: "You gave up after New York." Austin said he replied: "I didn't give up. I knew you couldn't win, and you were starting to crusade, and I ain't Crusader Rabbit."

Austin nevertheless hung in through the primary season, concentrating on apportioning the money flow that enabled the Jackson campaign to outspend Dukakis in all the major states thereafter, and handling the television and radio advertising, his specialty and prime source of income. In Pennsylvania the next week, Jackson hoped that the support of Philadelphia's black mayor, W. Wilson Goode, would more than make up for the mugging he had taken at the hands of Koch in New York, but it was not nearly enough. With less than 9 percent of the state's voting-age population black, the first clear one-on-one confrontation in a major state turned out as predicted—a Dukakis rout by more than two to one. According to the ABC News exit polls, Jackson won the black vote by a whopping eighteen to one; he lost the much heavier white vote by seven to one. Exit polls indicated that blue-collar voters in western Pennsylvania's steel region went to Dukakis by the same margin, indicating that Jackson's white and black workers' "common ground" message was not making much headway.

In Ohio the next week, the prospects were little better, and Jackson knew it. Yet he persevered, hoping on the one hand to nudge Dukakis to the left on a range of issues and, increasingly, to sustain and expand his special constituency among what he proclaimed to be the disadvantaged, the disregarded and the underrepresented. He claimed success in moving Dukakis and the party, telling the Ohio Broadcasters' Association in Cincinnati that "they've ratified my leadership; they've adopted my agenda."

But when Austin told reporters basically the same thing, Jackson hit the roof again. The campaign manager, while noting that "we're not out of this until that final bell sounds," also observed that his candidate "may not win the most delegates or popular vote, but Jesse Jackson is still the big winner of 1988 because of the way he has brought people into the party." Austin went on: "Even if Jesse Jackson does nothing else this year, and he's done a lot of things this year, he's involved people in the process. . . . Sometimes the biggest challenge is to keep people involved once they know that the standard bearer that they want to be nominated is not going to be the nominee."

Jackson, after a rally at the Canton Civic Center, made clear to reporters that he wanted no such talk from his subordinates. "Those statements are utterly untrue and do not represent the spirit and the thrust of this campaign, nor our work," he told reporters. "We can win Ohio. We're in this campaign through June seventh [the last primary date]. California and New Jersey we can win, intend to win, are working on winning. And I speak for the campaign without fear of contradiction." He told the reporters: "Write that down!" As he spoke, Jackson continued the same admonishment, until the crowd listening turned it into a chant punctuating his remarks: "Write it down! Write it down!"

But the tone of Jackson's message was becoming much more inspirational than political. Before a jam-packed crowd of students in an amphitheater-like auditorium at racially integrated Withrow High School, Jackson seemed almost to be preaching to himself on the need to press on even in the face of seemingly insurmountable odds.

"Everybody has a best," he told the attentive students. "Nobody has the right to do less than their best. Every day I run against the odds, yet I defy the odds, and I will win. . . . I never earned the right to do less than my best. I was born in the slum but the slum was not born in me. . . . When I win, you win. When I become president, there will be no more impossible dream."

To a sea of intense black and white young faces looking up soberly at him, Jackson put his personal struggle in the context of civil rights history. He recounted the slow, painful birth and fruition of the movement for racial justice and told the students: "You represent the fulfillment of many years of struggle." And the struggle, he said, was not over. His was "a campaign of hope," he said, and "winning for us is keeping hope alive." The students stood and applauded long and hard afterward, as he made his way up the aisle shaking black and white hands thrust out at him. It was a message of encouragement to them, but it had all the trappings of self-encouragement as well for a man who was seeing one dream slip away and was determined to focus on another, continuing one. At the same time, however, Jackson resisted the interpretation that he had moved from campaigner to crusader—an interpretation fanned by the remarks of Austin and Willie Brown. "Don't let them tell you that it's all over," he told rallies across Ohio. "If the election's over, you don't count. If the election's over, no one has told *you*."

Also, after weeks of relative kid-gloves handling of Dukakis, Jackson began to needle him for failing to spell out a federal budget and for being a cold bureaucrat, in contrast to his own dynamic style. "Leaders are not managers, they hire them," he said at another stop. "In the critical hours, you need leaders who will set the moral tone for the country. You couldn't manage slavery, you had to end slavery." Such observations distressed party leaders who felt that Jackson, now that the nomination was so clearly beyond his reach, was doing the Democratic cause a disservice, and giving the Republicans ammunition for the fall.

Another Tuesday brought two more Dukakis landslides, in Ohio and Indiana, with Jackson as expected carrying the heavily black District of Columbia. For all of his studied optimism, the reality was beginning to get to him. Noting his increasing gibes at Dukakis, we caught up with him for an interview on his campaign bus. While insisting he was not trying to tear down Dukakis, he complained that the news media was not holding the governor to the same standard to which he was being subjected. By drawing Dukakis out on key issues, he said, he could strengthen him for the fall campaign against Bush. Jackson's lament that his opponent was getting soft treatment from the press was amusing coming from a candidate who customarily got kid-gloves treatment from reporters as well as from his rival candidates.

On one Dukakis specific, saying he would earmark $500 million for economic development projects, Jackson was contemptuous. "Don Trump [the New York developer] says one bridge in New York [the Williamsburg Bridge, then closed for repairs] will cost $250 million," he said. "That's a bridge for Massachusetts and a bridge for where else?" He also champed at Dukakis' frequent stump observation that "after seven years of charisma in the White House, maybe it's time to try a little competence." Jackson said the remark was aimed at himself as well as at President Reagan. "He admires Kennedy's charisma, John and Ted, he admires Roosevelt's charisma," he said. "All of a sudden charisma loses its appeal. . . . It wasn't Reagan's charisma that got him in trouble. It was his disregard for the law, his ideology and his narrow world view." As for himself, Jackson said, he was challenging Dukakis' judgment on his priorities, not on his integrity. He said he would be "careful and sensitive" to keep the exchange off personalities, with an eye to having "a healing convention.'' But that was still more than two months off, and a lot could be said and done to disrupt that outcome in the intervening time.

After months of silence on his complaints about party rules and process that he said worked against his candidacy, Jackson also resumed on that front as well. He resurrected his argument that there should be ''a reasonable correspondence'' between a candidate's popular-vote total in a state and how its ''superdelegates''—the automatic party and elected officials going to the convention officially unpledged—cast their votes. But he wouldn't say whether he would institute credential challenges in Atlanta and he affirmed that he expected to support the eventual nominee. But in so saying, he only raised the old specter of Jackson as fly in the ointment. Aides served notice that they would fight for ''specific pledges'' in the party platform on cutting military spending, increasing social-welfare spending and taxing the wealthy more heavily.

Another Tuesday came and went with two more overwhelming Dukakis victories over Jackson, in West Virginia and Nebraska, both states with relatively few black voters. The perception of Dukakis as a vote-getting powerhouse was growing, and little was being said about how much of his vote was antiblack, or more precisely anti-Jackson. Jackson's jibes at Dukakis, in fact, were serving in many cases to cast Dukakis not as a liberal, as the Republicans were saying, but as a centrist—not a bad posture for a general election nominee.

Now it was on to Oregon, a state that on the surface had nothing whatever to give Jackson hope—except huge crowds with few black faces in them that greeted him at many stops. With Dukakis giving the state short shrift to concentrate on the two major windup primary states on the first Tuesday in June —California and New Jersey—Jackson had Oregon largely to himself. He worked the state diligently, energized by the public outpouring toward him.

Oregon had a long and colorful history as a place where upsets happened. Republican Nelson Rockefeller beat absentee Barry Goldwater there in 1964 because, as his slogan trumpeted around the state proclaimed, ''He Cared Enough to Come.'' In 1968, Democrat Eugene McCarthy handed Robert Kennedy there the first primary defeat ever suffered by his family. In 1976, Senator Frank Church beat Jimmy Carter in Oregon, and in 1984 Gary Hart upset frontrunner Fritz Mondale. But Robert Kennedy's experience particularly suggested the state was all wrong for Jackson.

In 1968, Kennedy came roaring into Oregon after having scored primary victories over McCarthy in Indiana and Nebraska. His campaign, like Jackson's, was drawing huge and wildly enthusiastic crowds as he labored frantically to make up for his late start in the Democratic race. Kennedy had not entered until McCarthy in the New Hampshire primary had run embarrassingly close to President Lyndon Johnson, who shortly afterward jolted the political world by saying he would not seek reelection.

In Indiana and Nebraska, Kennedy had constructed a coalition not unlike the one Jackson was trying to assemble—blacks and white, ethnic, blue-collar and farm workers. But when he got to Oregon he found important segments of the coalition missing. The state had a black population of 1 percent, no major industrial base, well-assimilated ethnics and general prosperity. Life was good in Oregon, then as now. During the 1968 primary, when a late-arriving Kennedy strategist asked Congresswoman Edith Green, the state's most influential woman politician, "Have we got the ghettoes organized?" Mrs. Green replied indignantly: "There are no ghettoes in Oregon." And she wasn't far wrong. Voters Kennedy encountered were polite but for the most part not the frantic, grabbing sort who had greeted him elsewhere. "This state is like one giant suburb," Kennedy remarked at the time, and twenty years later the observation still applied.

After one particularly bland day with Kennedy in Oregon during that earlier primary, the traveling entourage flew by charter to California. Kennedy roamed up and down the aisle lamenting the difference between the typical mayhem he encountered in crowds in California and other industrial states and bland Oregon. "Let's face it," he told our old colleague, Jim Dickenson, then working for the weekly *National Observer* but later for the *Washington Star* and *Washington Post*, "I appeal best to people who have problems." A couple of days later, back in Portland, as we were coming off a sight-seeing boat after a "media event"—a tour of the Willamette River harbor—we asked Kennedy how the campaign was going in Oregon. "I've got a problem here," he said. "You can look around and see what it is." He meant, obviously, Oregon was too well-off to respond to his urgent exhortation, as his brother Jack used to put it, to "get this country moving again."

Now, as Jackson sought to mobilize the same coalition in the same comfortable state, there was one striking difference. In many places the crowds of white faces were larger and notably more enthusiastic for him than for Kennedy in 1968. One reason may have been that Kennedy in that earlier primary was contesting for the liberal and youth vote with McCarthy, who painted Kennedy as a hesitant interloper who hadn't joined the fray until Johnson was wounded by McCarthy. Jackson had an added advantage this time in the fact that Dukakis, relying on polls that indicated he was safely ahead in Oregon, gave the state what amounted to a brush block on his way in and out of California. He did return the final weekend, but he was looking to that last big primary state to wrap up the nomination. Perhaps Jackson could successfully work Rockefeller's "He Cared Enough to Come" pitch.

There was something very ironic in Jackson's intense bid to upset "another son of Massachusetts" in the Oregon primary. In oratory and style, he was probably the most charismatic political campaigner to hit the state since Robert Kennedy twenty years earlier, appealing to the same black-and-blue constituency. But as the underdog challenger to the front-runner, Jackson was more like Eugene McCarthy in 1968. And because Mike Dukakis was no Bob Kennedy on the stump, there seemed at least a chance, to those who saw Jackson's large and enthusiastic crowds across the state, that he could succeed in Oregon where Kennedy had failed.

To Oregon voters who had witnessed and heard Robert Kennedy campaigning exactly twenty years earlier and now saw and listened to Jesse Jackson, the similarities were striking. At the core of each man's message was a plea to individuals to make life better for themselves and for the country. "One man can make a difference," Kennedy would insist, shirt sleeves rolled above his elbows, tie loosened at the neck, open hand chopping the air. And Jackson would command his audiences to repeat after him: "I am somebody. My mind is a pearl. I can do anything in the world."

Both Kennedy and Jackson, unlike so many other politicians, did not hesitate to tell voters what they didn't want to hear. Kennedy, on a college campus, would ask the sea of students before him how many were against the Vietnam War. Nearly always, a huge majority of hands would shoot up. Then he would ask them how many were against the draft. The same hands would go up again. Well, he would scold, was it fair that they got deferments from military service while others, predominantly young black men, were drafted to fight, and sometimes die, in that same war?

Jackson in the same way would berate high school boys and girls for being equally culpable for teenage pregnancies and births. He would tell the boys that "it doesn't take a man to make a baby, it takes a man to take care of a baby." And he would tell the girls they were foolish to "trade a short-term thrill for a long-term chill." And in both cases, the lectures would draw thunderous applause.

In some ways, Jackson for all his oratorical skills had the harder task in reaching the emotions of his audiences. When Kennedy ran in 1968, less than five years had passed since the assassination of his brother the president, and the country still suffered traumatic memories for which Robert Kennedy's frenetic candidacy provided an explosive release. Moreover, the national turmoil of the Vietnam War gave a special urgency to Kennedy's candidacy, as did the extensive public animosity toward Lyndon Johnson for which Kennedy was an eloquent and emotional voice. Furthermore, Kennedy aroused voters with his attacks on civil rights wrongs and the plight of the poor in a national climate much more sympathetic to such concerns, and much more responsive, than in 1988. And finally, Kennedy for all his fire on the stump remained an establishment politician who wanted more wrongs addressed with more zeal, but essentially through the same political structure.

Jackson, however, in Oregon as in all the other primary states, was running as a demanding party outsider knocking on the door to get in, and threatening to break it down if it wasn't opened to him. He was impatient with the established structure and was campaigning to change it, by coalescing the have-nots of the society into a political force that could take over the party and the government. And because he not only was black but also was militant, he aroused passions and invited polarization even more than Kennedy did. In the end, both men failed in Oregon, to some degree at least because, as Kennedy had said twenty years earlier, they appealed best "to people who have problems."

Jackson's loss to Dukakis in Oregon, by 55 percent to 38, left California and New Jersey as the last major chances for him to hold Dukakis short of the majority of delegates he needed for a first-ballot nomination. According to the Associated Press, Dukakis now needed only 198 delegates to go over the top, of the 466 to be elected in those two states plus Montana and New Mexico, 314 of them in California alone. As always, Jackson campaigned in California and New Jersey in the manner of a political guerrilla, living off the opportunities that presented themselves on the ground.

In Los Angeles, racked by bloody drug-financed gang wars in which the young warriors were conducting raids in enemy neighborhoods and blasting opponents with sophisticated and deadly semiautomatic assault weapons, Jackson met with gang members in the Watts section. Afterward he held a televised press conference with some of the toughest-looking musclemen imaginable at his side, some of them self-identified as former drug dealers. "I offer the youth today a partnership," he said. "I will help fight the flow of drugs. They must cut the [demand] for the drugs." And in Woodridge, New Jersey, he held another impromptu press conference on the banks of the heavily polluted Arthur Kill, where hypodermic needles and other debris had washed up from the New York side of the harbor. He castigated the big corporations for their disregard of the environment and the federal government for not doing anything about it. Right to the end of the campaign, Jackson was displaying his unique talent for guerrilla politics—going directly to the site of a community problem and using it as a prop to dramatize his position.

At the same time, he continued to push Dukakis to spell out how he intended to meet social needs and how aggressive he would be dealing with South Africa and other foreign-policy challenges. In one debate in San Francisco that touched on both points, Dukakis as usual finessed all efforts to pin him down. After a private meeting later, Jackson came out and needled Dukakis, telling reporters: "I'm trying to balance my ticket with a conservative."

Even before Dukakis had the nomination officially locked up, however, the matter of a running mate began to intrude in a more serious way. In all the questions over all the months about "what does Jesse want," there loomed the prospect—the fear, to many regular Democrats—that Jackson wanted no less than the vice presidential nomination.

On the final day, Jackson raced around California at his customary frantic rate while Dukakis confidently predicted victory and basked in the glow of that expectation in quick stops in the key California media markets. Jerry Austin, after his difficulties with Jackson in New York and later, continued to run the media campaign and was ensconced in the old art deco Roosevelt Hotel in Hollywood, working the phones. As a finale, he scheduled a thirty-minute live television appearance for Jackson with a multimarket hookup, for which the campaign was paying $135,000. Jackson had a rally in Northern California late in the afternoon and was to fly into Los Angeles for the show. In what was a metaphor for the whole ad hoc nature of the Jackson campaign, he was nowhere to be seen at airtime. In desperation, radio disc jockey Casey Kasem interviewed Jackson's California campaign manager for more than half the time, until Jackson finally arrived—seventeen minutes late. The minute the show was over, Austin fled the control room in anger and dismay. Later that night, he encountered Jackson at another event. Jackson asked him: "Where were you?"

The results on the final primary day also were not surprising. Dukakis swept all four states and claimed the nomination in a raucous victory rally in Los Angeles. Jackson graciously congratulated him and praised his "integrity and intelligence" and said he would work for him in the fall campaign. Those remarks, however, did not mean that the Jackson campaign was over. His strategists had been meeting over the last days not to consider how to fold the tent, but rather how to keep the Jackson drive for change going, with the immediate objective of asserting influence on the party platform and rules reform, as well as the candidate's chances to be on the ticket. In a morning-after press conference in Los Angeles, Jackson proclaimed: "One chapter of the campaign is over. A new chapter begins."

And so, as the political spotlight now swung toward the Democratic National Convention in Atlanta in mid-July, and to the writing of a party platform and rules, it was clear that Michael Dukakis was going to have a special problem in making his decision on a running mate. And that problem, as he had long expected and feared, was named Jesse L. Jackson.

PART V

Atlanta: The Democratic Convention

22

Bentsen Sí, Jackson No

For the Democrats, the process of selecting a vice presidential nominee was defined by the experiences of 1972, 1976 and 1984—all of which were vivid in the mind of Michael Dukakis as he began his own search.

At Miami Beach in 1972, George McGovern followed the traditional practice of presidential nominees in both parties. Once his own nomination had been assured, he gathered with his advisers for hours of sorting through alternatives and weighing the political equities. But in the end, that process produced a disaster the choice of Senator Tom Eagleton of Missouri—followed by the disclosure that he had suffered emotional depression so serious as to require electric-shock treatments. The fiasco that followed—McGovern's declaration that he was "one thousand percent" behind his choice, Eagleton finally being forced to withdraw, an embarrassingly long and public search for options, the eventual selection of Sargent Shriver—destroyed whatever chance McGovern had to run a competitive campaign against President Richard Nixon.

By contrast, four years later, Jimmy Carter followed a process that was widely praised as a model, particularly for a candidate from outside Washington lacking long-standing personal relationships with the leading prospects. Carter assigned a senior adviser, Atlanta attorney Charles Kirbo, to canvass senators, congressmen, governors, party leaders and even a few reporters on the potential strengths and weaknesses of a list of possible running mates. Then Carter interviewed the most likely candidates before settling on a choice, then Senator Walter F. Mondale of Minnesota, who made sense both politically and substantively.

In 1984 Mondale himself was in a somewhat different position, in that he already knew the most obvious possibilities and didn't need a Charlie Kirbo to sort them out for him. But the plan Mondale finally followed was almost as politically damaging as McGovern's process—a series of interviews at his home outside St. Paul that included only one white Anglo-Saxon male, Senator Lloyd Bentsen of Texas. The list of ostensibly serious possibilities—the black mayors of Los Angeles and Philadelphia, Tom Bradley and Wilson Goode; Mayor Dianne Feinstein of San Francisco and Mayor Henry Cisneros of San Antonio—seemed to confirm the suspicious that Mondale was more interested in appcaling to Democratic constituency groups, the "special interests" in the Republican lexicon, than in finding the most able person to be a heartbeat from the presidency.

With this history very much in mind, Dukakis waited until he had clinched the nomination in California to name Paul Brountas, his Harvard Law School classmate, longtime intimate and campaign chairman, as a "committee of one" to oversee a process quite similar to the one Carter had used. As he had remarked several weeks earlier, "The way Carter did it worked out pretty well."

Brountas had already prepared a list of about twenty-five names "that had come up" in one way or another—meaning all the usual suspects. And, a few days after the final primary, the Boston lawyer went to Washington to begin a screening process he and Dukakis had decided should be as "nonpublic as possible." He called on about forty members of the Senate and House, meeting each without any staff members in the room. To make them as forthcoming as possible, Brountas took no notes and promised, he said later, "I would report only to Dukakis" on what they had to say. "Most of them were willing to confide in me because they thought it was important."

Brountas sought reactions to the names on his list, other suggestions, and in ten or twelve cases, he asked the senators and congressmen if they were willing to be considered themselves. Those interviews completed, he flew back to Boston and began calling governors and mayors. Meanwhile Bob Farmer, the campaign's chief fund-raiser, polled leading contributors, and Susan Estrich consulted the senior staff of the campaign. Dukakis himself made about a dozen calls. Brountas also had brought together cadres of lawyers and accountants, all volunteering their services, to go through the financial and personal data submitted by those being seriously considered. It was, all in all, the kind of investigative and consultative process that seemed to offer the best chance for finding the right candidate—and avoiding some serious gaffe.

Although Dukakis made a point of refusing to prepare either long or short lists of possibilities, the Democrats who in the end received serious consideration were almost entirely those that nearly everyone in politics would have predicted. A possible exception was Representative Lee Hamilton of Indiana, who had impressed Dukakis by his performance in the Iran-contra investigation and by the counsel he had been giving him on foreign-policy questions. Two of the most obvious possibilities, Senators Bill Bradley of New Jersey and Sam Nunn of Georgia, asked not to be considered.

Four years after Mondale had picked Geraldine Ferraro, there was no woman on the list of genuine possibilities. Although Ferraro had shown herself to be a top-drawer campaigner and unshakable in the white-hot controversy over her husband's financial affairs, the opinion polls suggested a woman on the ticket could be trouble. And neither Dukakis nor his party wanted to risk such trouble when they had a rich opportunity to win the White House. Besides, there was no woman with the obvious political or governmental experience to fill Dukakis' needs.

Dukakis himself had been making it clear privately, at least as far back as the New York primary campaign in April, that he recognized the need for a state governor like himself to choose someone, probably from Congress, with credentials as a Washington insider and on foreign-policy issues. During a small supper at the apartment of NBC News commentator John Chancellor two nights before the primary, Dukakis spelled out these priorities explicitly. "That didn't rule out others," Brountas said, "but it became pretty clear to me where he was headed." There were also the obvious considerations of political balance. Other things being equal, Dukakis would profit most from a moderate to conservative Democrat from a big state, preferably in the South. Liberal orthodoxy on issues was not required. "I'm not looking for a clone of Michael Dukakis," Dukakis said.

In a matter of days, the lists of those being speculated upon in the press and political community—and somewhat more seriously inside the Dukakis campaign—all had the same names: Senators Lloyd Bentsen of Texas, John H. Glenn of Ohio, Dale Bumpers of Arkansas, Bob Graham of Florida and Albert Gore of Tennessee; Representatives Hamilton, Tom Foley of Washington, the House minority leader, and Dick Gephardt of Missouri, like Gore one of the rivals vanquished in the primaries.

The quadrennial exercise of speculating about vice presidential possibilities is one of the fascinating rites of American politics. At least since 1952, vice presidents had been, or had become, men of stature and prominence—Richard Nixon, Lyndon Johnson, Hubert Humphrey, Spiro Agnew, Gerald Ford, Nelson Rockefeller, Walter Mondale, George Bush. But once in office, they had been largely downgraded or even ignored unless a crisis of real or potential succession pressed them into public consciousness. Still, the process of choosing a vice presidential nominee became a consuming issue in the press and political community for a few weeks every four years. In Washington during this period the topic didn't have to be spelled out when one political player asked another, "Whaddaya hear?" Moreover, the intensity of the gossip and the speed with which rumors made the rounds bore no relationship to the amount of hard information anyone had about what was really going on.

Dukakis himself, despite his insistence on a dignified process that would embarrass no one, stirred the pot from time to time. Appearing with Glenn before a labor union audience in Ohio, he asked: "What do you think of John Glenn?" And when that produced the predictable raised hands and cheers, Dukakis added: "It's unanimous, isn't it?" A few days later he turned the gossip in a new direction, albeit only momentarily, by appearing with Bentsen at a rally in Texarkana, Texas.

Based on the slightest evidence, the stock of a particular candidate could shoot up or down with lightning speed. One day the story was that Glenn was badly handicapped because he still had $2.4 million in debt left over from his own presidential campaign in 1984. The next it was that Glenn was a likely winner if Governor Richard Celeste of Ohio would agree in advance to appoint a black congressman from Cleveland, Louis Stokes, to fill his Senate seat.

The only real wild card in the game, however, was Jesse Jackson, still campaigning even after the final primary results and the predictable flood of commitments had assured Dukakis the nomination.

The fact is that Jackson had never figured in Dukakis' calculations until it was no longer possible to ignore him. Dukakis was as aware as everyone else in politics of opinion polls that showed Jackson on the ticket would be a disaster in November; the electorate was still not ready for a black nominee— or, at least, this black nominee. And beyond the race question, Jackson clearly had none of the Washington credentials Dukakis needed most of all.

The inability of Dukakis to say just those things was the ultimate proof, if any were needed, of the special insulation Jesse Jackson enjoyed as a black candidate in the Democratic Party. No one complained seriously that Jimmy Carter should choose Morris Udall because he finished second in 1976 or argued that Fritz Mondale was under any obligation to accept Gary Hart in 1984. Not since 1960, in fact, when John Kennedy chose Lyndon Johnson as his running mate, had a Democratic presidential nominee selected the individual who had been his principal challenger for the nomination. And that choice created an uproar at the Democratic National Convention in Los Angeles. But there was a double standard in dealing with black politicians in the Democratic Party that put real restraints on Dukakis' freedom of action.

Some professionals were counseling Dukakis to tell Jackson right from the start that he wouldn't be the vice presidential candidate, for lack of governmental experience, thus nipping in the bud extravagant hopes among Jackson's followers. But by the time Brountas began seriously examining the question, there seemed no way to avoid keeping the civil rights leader off the lists.

"How in the hell can you do that?" Brountas asked rhetorically after the fact. "You have seven candidates, he came in second. You have seven million votes, over a thousand delegates. He's the only black in the field and before you consider anyone else, you eliminate him? There's no way Dukakis would do that. As a result of his performance in the election, he had to be considered and he was considered. He earned the right to that consideration."

Jackson had been sending signals of varying degrees of ambiguity and subtlety as far back as the day after the New York primary in April, when he told reporters: "I need his support base to win. He needs my support base to win. Together we can win." That remark was taken as evidence Jackson definitely was interested. But, as already noted, he was furious at Jerry Austin, his campaign manager then, and at Willie Brown, the speaker of the Assembly in California and his campaign chairman, for suggesting publicly that he should be considered for vice president when he was still running a presidential campaign.

Moreover, in continuing his now academic campaign for the nomination, Jackson was rubbing a few sore spots. Early in May he had revived old complaints about the fairness of the delegate-selection process and demanded a share of the superdelegates corresponding to his popular vote. He also had begun talking about "specific pledges" he wanted in the Democratic platform. And he had once again begun complaining that Dukakis had not come forward with a detailed plan for a federal budget. But at the same time he often seemed conciliatory toward Dukakis, as if that posture might help his chances to be on the ticket. "A lot of what we stand for has already been absorbed by the other campaign," he said in Los Angeles near the end of that primary campaign.

A week before the California primary, Jackson once again insisted he had "earned" the right to be considered. "If I were to win the nomination, with the kind of campaign that Dukakis has run, he would deserve consideration and he would get it," he said. "If he wins, I deserve consideration."

Dukakis was not having an easy time dealing with the pressure. Asked one day if Jackson's second-place showing in the contest for the presidential nomination gave him a special call on the vice presidential nomination, Dukakis replied: "I don't think that that gives you a leg up"—suggesting he might be ready to stiff his rival. But then on the eve of the California primary, Dukakis went to Jackson's suite at the Hyatt Wilshire Hotel in Los Angeles—a gesture that appeared more than conciliatory. Asked again if Jackson "deserved" the nomination, Dukakis said: "No, I don't think Jesse agrees with that. He himself has said it's up to the nominee to make that decision."

The following day, however, Jackson turned up the heat at a postprimary press conference. "If the issue is that he wants someone from the South," said Jackson, "I'm from the South. If [it's] someone who has had an impact on southern politics, I've done that. If it's someone who can mobilize a mass of Democrats, I've done that. If it's someone who is not limited to regional appeal but has national appeal, I've won primaries from Vermont to Puerto Rico, from Mississippi to Michigan, from Texas to Alaska."

Just how serious Jackson was about the vice presidency at different stages of these final weeks was impossible to determine. Ronald H. Brown, the Washington lawyer who had taken over convention arrangements for his campaign not long after the New York primary, put it this way: "At first Jesse was . . . titillated by it. But the more he thought about it, the more sense it began to make. And also, if he was going to do this, he clearly was going to be the centerpiece from the primaries to convention—'What's Jesse gonna do?' and all that stuff." And Jackson was never one to avoid being a centerpiece.

In a brief working vacation at the LaCosta resort in southern California at which Brown surfaced as Austin's replacement in the vanguard of the campaign, Jackson and Brown discussed the question. They decided that the candidate should say only that "I deserve serious consideration"—a resolve that Jackson sometimes kept, sometimes violated over the next month.

The problem was that once the possibility was raised, there was no way to control the heady feeling that developed among Jackson's supporters that he had earned second place on the ticket by finishing second in the primaries and caucuses. Although there was no precedent for that rationale being decisive in choosing a running mate, its apparent logic carried more weight with Jackson's followers than opinion polls showing him to be a drag on the ticket. Jackson's base, Brown said later, "felt very strongly about it." But the sentiment was not limited to the politically unsophisticated. A week after California, the Congressional Black Caucus passed a resolution endorsing Jackson for vice president.

"He got to the point where he thought it was possible," Ron Brown recalled. "It started to escalate, and we knew there were some dangers there. People were getting worked up about this thing. He thought he had earned the right to take it as far as it could go—that is, if there was a shot at there being a black on the ticket, we ought to do everything we could to make it happen."

Moreover, again because of his special insulation, Jackson could follow this course of pursuing the vice presidency while keeping his presidential campaign alive without fear of public criticism from fellow Democrats. If he had been white, he could have expected some demand that he get behind Dukakis in the interest of party unity. But few in the party were prepared to risk being accused of racism by making such a demand of Jackson.

The public ritual dance continued through June. One day Dukakis said Jackson was still being given "very serious consideration" for the nomination. The next day Jackson raised the ante by saying he had made a decision in his own mind about whether he wanted it but would not reveal it yet, then added that Dukakis "must remove any remaining barriers" of race or sex in choosing his nominee. A couple of days later, Dukakis assured everyone that the selection was "still a very open process" and that there was still no "short list" of choices.

The personal relationship between Jackson and Dukakis had never been an easy one. Jackson viewed Dukakis somewhat disparagingly as a manager rather than a political leader. And although Dukakis had dealt, usually successfully, with black leaders in Boston politics, he was never comfortable with Jackson's flamboyant, press-driven personality.

Jackson was struck by the differences between their cultural and personal backgrounds. "History gives Dukakis a tailwind and gives me a headwind," he said after the campaign. "How we relate to those who came on immigrant ships and those who came on slave ships is quite different. . . . Dukakis speaks of coming to Ellis Island and dropping his chains. My people came to Charleston, South Carolina, and picked up their chains."

Their private meetings, Jackson complained frequently, were "like two ships passing in the night" in which neither candidate got down to cases. Others who had attended Dukakis-Jackson meetings over the previous fifteen months agreed that their conversations were largely expressions of goodwill and general concerns, rarely focusing on particular complaints they might have had with one another.

Given that background, the Dukakis managers were delighted when their candidate and Kitty invited Jackson and his wife, Jackie, to join them for a July 4 dinner at their Brookline home, and then to accompany them to the banks of the Charles River for fireworks and the traditional concert by the Boston Pops orchestra. The message Dukakis was sending with this gesture was that Jackson, as the last survivor among his rivals, was entitled to special recognition and treatment.

Publicly the dinner seemed to be a public relations ten-strike. Although the Jacksons arrived an hour and a half late, the initial reports were all glowing. Jackson emerged from dinner, rubbing his stomach and telling reporters it had been "a balanced meal, well cooked." And he limited himself to one cryptic pronouncement to the press on the state of their relations, saying: "In some sense, Michael Dukakis and I have the challenge of forging a new equation, a new coalition, to take our nation to another level of moral consideration." After dinner the two couples went on to the fireworks and concert, where they were photographed sitting in a row smiling broadly.

Ron Brown thought the whole evening "really raised the stakes" by projecting the picture of a political summit. "I was there," he said later. "It looked like the ticket. The crowds were screaming, you know, firecrackers are going off, the flags are waving, the Boston Pops is playing. The president and the vice president and their wives are there together. It really did have the effect of raising the stakes."

Jackson, more importantly, had used the occasion to make it clear to Dukakis that he definitely wanted the vice presidency, not just "serious consideration." And he had expected, Jackson said later, that Dukakis "was going to say you can't win" because he had been looking at the polling data and needed someone "to fill that gap." And he had expected the familiar argument from Dukakis, he said, that "when I win, you win." But it didn't happen. "The fact is," Jackson recalled, "is that night we didn't discuss that." Instead, the evening was spent on "mostly family talk" until "when he finally asked me would I like to be considered, I said yes." But just at that point, he said, one of Dukakis' daughters came into the room offering ice cream, and the discussion was never pursued.

Nonetheless, as Brown recalled it, "Jesse was up after the meeting" when he came to his campaign manager's hotel room at the end of the evening.

"He popped the question," Jackson told Brown—meaning that Dukakis had asked him if he wished to be considered.

"What did you tell him?" Brown asked.

"I told him yes," Jackson replied. "I told him why I should be."

Later Jackson had some private complaints. The dinner had been traditional New England July 4 fare—clam chowder, poached salmon in a white sauce and peas, a chocolate torte and ice cream for dessert. But Jackson is lactose-intolerant and thus allergic to the milk that was the base of the chowder and to ice cream. Jackson's staff had not mentioned this problem to the Dukakis staff when plans for the dinner were being made. And accounts written by reporters traveling with him indicated that Jackson was annoyed because he had not had the opportunity to discuss the vice presidency further.

If the July 4 meeting cleared the air in the sense that Dukakis learned Jackson was serious about the vice presidency, it did nothing to slow the pace of Jackson's public campaigning for the nomination. Two days later in Memphis, he said: "They say they want balance. Governor Dukakis' father was a doctor, his mother a teacher. My mother was a maid, my father a janitor. That's balance."

Jackson also was continuing to heighten the pressure by dropping hints of floor fights over the platform and perhaps the convention rules. In fact, most of the disagreements about the platform, all minor, had been settled several weeks earlier in meetings on Mackinac Island in Michigan and in Denver. In one key concession, Dukakis agreed to Jackson's demand that the platform should say South Africa should be categorized officially by the United States as a "terrorist state."

But Jackson's continued hints of floor fights over rules or platform questions began to irk Dukakis. "Jesse Jackson can do anything he wants to do," the nominee-presumptive said a week before the convention was to open. "I'm going to the convention and I'm going to win it."

Jackson also turned up the heat by announcing that there would be a "Rainbow Express" bus caravan to take him and his supporters to Atlanta. The buses would leave Chicago and make stops at Indianapolis, Louisville, Nashville and Chattanooga to pick more adherents along the way—finally reaching Atlanta on Saturday, two days before the official opening of the convention.

Meanwhile, the Paul Brountas "committee of one" process of narrowing Dukakis' choices for a vice presidential nominee had reached the point at which the lawyers and accountants in Boston were examining the financial and personal data submitted by those willing to be considered.

Although Dukakis kept his own counsel, there was no mystery about the political equities involved in various options. John Glenn seemed the most obvious favorite. His popularity at home probably could assure the Democrats of Ohio's twenty-three electoral votes, a critical prize always hotly contested and one the Republicans were relying heavily on winning. And although Glenn had failed as a candidate for the 1984 presidential nomination, he was a respected and authentic American hero, as well as a senior member of the Senate with strong credentials on national-defense questions.

There were strong political or personal arguments that could be made for several of the others. The choice of Lloyd Bentsen, the conventional wisdom had it, would make Dukakis competitive for the twenty-nine electoral votes of Texas. At a minimum, George Bush and the Republicans would be forced to spend time and resources defending a state they counted as part of their base. Selecting Bob Graham might do the same in Florida, although astute Democrats recognized that Florida would be the single most elusive target among the large Sun Belt states.

The other prospects seemed to present more serious problems. Dukakis admired Lee Hamilton, but Indiana was relatively small (twelve electoral votes) and congenitally Republican. The choice of either Gore or Gephardt was obviously risky because both finished far behind Jackson in competing for the presidential nomination. To pass over Jackson for either Gore or Gephardt would be to invite serious trouble at Atlanta.

The one thing Dukakis had decided was that he would make the choice in advance of the convention. Such an early decision, his strategists recognized, would avoid the convention being dominated by speculation over the choice and continuing campaigning for home-state favorites by delegates certain to be disappointed. Most important, such a preemptive strike could prevent the building sentiment for Jackson among black delegates and supporters from reaching critical mass. Democratic convention veterans had visions of demonstrations in the convention hall and in the streets getting out of hand—and dominating the television coverage, which was after all the main reason for having a convention whose presidential nominee was already determined.

Just a week before the gavel was to fall in Atlanta, Brountas and John French, a lawyer from Minneapolis who also had been a Dukakis classmate at Harvard Law, flew to Washington for a final meeting with Jackson. The session had been delayed until late in the process, Brountas said, because it had taken Jackson longer to submit the personal and financial data French and others were reviewing.

Brountas and French met with Jackson for two and a half hours in a room at the J. W. Marriott Hotel. Jackson brought along John White, the former Democratic national chairman who had arranged his meeting with Clark Clifford and the party wise men, and Ron Walters, a Howard University professor and political adviser. They sat in a bedroom, with Brountas, Jackson and French in chairs and White and Walters perched on the edge of a bed. As White later recalled the meat of the conversation, it went like this:

Jackson: "Mr. Bronson, are you telling me I'm seriously being considered for vice president by Governor Dukakis?"*

Brountas: "I would not be here, I would not participate in anything that wasn't honest."

According to White, French proceeded to interrogate Jackson, "like a deposition," about all his financial matters, including allegations of fiscal irregularities regarding his Chicago-based organization, PUSH. Jackson answered them all, White recalled, noting that he drew no salary from PUSH and was willing to settle any legitimate financial claims against PUSH. Asked why he had failed to fill out some questions about his health in the questionnaire submitted to him, White said, Jackson replied that unless Dukakis was releasing his own, he didn't see why he should.

---

*Over the course of the campaign the occasions when Jackson was annoyed with Brountas could be signaled by him referring to him as "Attorney Brountas" or, sometimes, "Attorney Bronson"—a mistake that never seemed quite inadvertent.

Brountas then asked, according to White, whether Jackson had any family problems or "outside romantic interests," and Jackson said, "No." These personal questions, White said, were worded "uncomfortably" by Brountas but in a cool and professional manner. As the interrogation proceeded, White said, Brountas suddenly got a phone call. He took it in another room and when he returned he said he had to get back to Boston. Jackson insisted that first they go out and meet the awaiting press. Brountas didn't want to, and finally the group went down to a lower floor to avoid the reporters. As they walked out, White recalled, a group of young white women, some of them holding babies, spied Jackson and rushed over to him and he took some of the babies in his arms. Brountas, observing the scene, grinned and said: "Gee, that never happens on our campaign."

Later, after Brountas and French had left, White recalled, Jackson referred to the meeting as "a charade."

Brountas, recounting the meeting himself after the campaign, remembered that Jackson "wanted to be consulted about the final candidate" if he himself was not the one chosen. "I told him that probably would not happen," Brountas said. "I didn't think it was right if Dukakis picked X, to have to clear it with Jesse Jackson. Why not clear it with John Glenn or other candidates?"

But Brountas did tell Jackson that "Dukakis would make up his mind" within forty-eight hours and that Jackson would be notified. He recalled saying, "Reverend Jackson, you're not going to read about it in the newspapers."

Brountas went to National Airport and telephoned Dukakis to tell him of the Jackson meeting and make plans for a final conference that night to take one last look at the choices. "When I left that morning," he recalled, "he had not made up his mind." And Dukakis had spent part of the day conferring with senior advisers—Susan Estrich, Jack Corrigan and Kirk O'Donnell—on the question. Brountas wanted everyone to take one more look at a meeting that night, but there were electrical storms in the area and flights were delayed. Dukakis, who was cutting his grass when Brountas called, seemed prepared to go ahead without another review. But Brountas objected, and through a freak circumstance his complaint made its way into the next morning's editions of the *Boston Globe*.

Brountas was using a pay telephone and, although there were reporters at the airport, believed he could not be overheard, only to find out otherwise. "There was a young kid [nearby] that looked like she was in high school," he said, "but she was an intern for the *Globe*. She didn't know who the hell I was, but she heard me say to Kitty, 'Put Michael on the phone. This is the biggest decision that he's got to make during this campaign, and I don't want it made this way.' "

The weather finally lifted, and Brountas flew back to Boston for one final meeting at 10:30 P.M. around the Dukakis kitchen table—the candidate, his wife, Brountas, Estrich and Corrigan. The possibilities were still the same— Bentsen, Glenn, Jackson, Gore, Gephardt, Hamilton, Graham—and the pros and cons were run through once again. After an hour and a half, Brountas said, "we went around the table and all of us were in favor of Bentsen." The other "finalist," unsurprisingly, was Glenn.

The decision having been made, Dukakis decided there was no point in delaying action on it. It was now close to midnight, but he decided to call Bentsen immediately, confirm his willingness, then begin telephoning the others on the list in the morning. One of the aides tried the call three times but Bentsen had gone to bed at 11 P.M. and turned off his telephone. So Dukakis and his inner circle decided they would start the process early the next morning.

Sometime around 6:30 A.M., Dukakis phoned Bentsen. He had turned the bell on his phone back on. "I was using an electric razor and I damn near didn't get the call then," Bentsen said later. "I visited with Mike on the phone. I told him I'd do it, and then I went in to wake up [his wife] B.A. She was asleep. I awakened her and said, 'B.A., we're on the ticket.' She said, 'We're on what?' I said, 'We're on the ticket.' " Whereupon, Bentsen said, she groaned "and put her head back in the pillow."

About 6:45 A.M. Dukakis called Brountas. Inasmuch as he had reached Bentsen, it was time to put the wheels in motion. Brountas had a charter on standby at Logan and would fly to Washington to pick up the Bentsens and bring them back to Boston for a noon announcement rally at Faneuil Hall. Estrich convened the senior staff about 7 A.M., began planning the rally and then joined Dukakis at the State House to begin calling the candidates not chosen.

Brountas had compiled telephone numbers for all the prospective candidates, including the one for the hotel in Cincinnati where Jackson was staying that night, before leaving for Washington about 8 A.M. But he had forgotten to give Estrich that number the previous night, and by the time she got it, Jackson was on the way to the airport to catch his flight. "There was," Brountas said later, "absolutely no intention to delay reaching him at all. There was no reason for it."

But Jackson arrived at Washington National still in the dark. As he came through his gate, reporters swarmed around him, asking his reaction to the choice of Bentsen. Jackson was obviously stunned and furious as he was ushered tight-lipped through the crowd into his car for the drive downtown. His ire spilled out later in the day at a press conference. Asked if he was angry, he replied bitingly: "No, I'm too controlled. I'm too clear. I'm too mature to be angry. I am focused on what we must do to keep hope alive."

After the fact, Jackson pictured himself as having been particularly restrained. "I could have taken the position," he said, "that . . . we'll resolve this matter Thursday night"—meaning at the session of the national convention set aside for balloting on the vice presidential nomination. But even without the explicit threat, the message of Jackson's anger came through.

Bentsen, meantime, had been calling some of his Texas friends with the news. Among them was John White, who had shared Brountas' interrogation of Jackson just before the decision was made. White knew Jackson hadn't been told. "Call Jesse right now," he told Bentsen. Bentsen tried but didn't get the call through until the next day. However, White said later, "as a result of Bentsen's call, he and Jesse hit it off." Later on, White said, Jesse had more conversations with Bentsen and told him: "I like this guy. I can talk to him."

The missed phone call, Ron Brown said, was a Dukakis mistake rather than a deliberate offense, but nonetheless "infuriated a lot of people." And that reaction was apparent that same night when Jackson appeared at a convention of the National Association for the Advancement of Colored People and shouted: "I may not be on the ticket but I'm qualified." His tone was defiant. "I am expected to register, motivate and deliver more votes than any congressman alive," he said, "and for that work, there must be partnership, equity and shared responsibility."

The next morning, Dukakis also addressed the NAACP convention amid a coolness that bordered on hostility. Dukakis met with the organization's leaders in advance of his speech but offered them no explanation of his choice of Bentsen over Jackson. Neither did he even mention it in his speech to an overflow audience whose prime interest clearly was "Why not Jesse?" The NAACP's executive director, Benjamin Hooks, felt obliged to call on some delegates to remove handmade signs posing various versions of that question before Dukakis entered the hall. Dukakis' attitude seemed to be that the decision was his to make and he had made it. Period.

The missed telephone call was a blunder that largely reflected Dukakis' own political insensitivity and lack of understanding of Jesse Jackson's obsession with "respect." Dukakis himself had not been offended four years earlier when he was in a similar position and heard on the radio that Mondale had chosen Ferraro. The Massachusetts governor was not given to rudeness, but he had never been a man who worried very much about the forms and protocols of politics. On the contrary, he seemed to consider them largely nonsense; he was too busy with the substance. But Dukakis and Jackson were very different personalities, and the Dukakis advisers should have realized at the moment the decision was made that the first priority was to notify Jackson. Now their failure to do so had created an incident that was clearly more than a distraction.

The next day Jackson, now back in Chicago, ratcheted up the pressure a notch, calling the Dukakis choice of Bentsen "a recommendation" and hinting after all that it might be contested on the floor of the convention. "If such a floor contest were to take place," he said, "there's room for it in the rules. . . . The floor is wide open on Thursday. At this point, based upon the projected scenario of Governor Dukakis, I'm not part of the equation." Other signs of distance also emanated from the Jackson camp. Brown disclosed he had suspended talks with Susan Estrich on platforms and rules issues. And Assemblywoman Maxine Waters of California, a militant Jackson supporter, said the snub had been deliberate. "They weren't simply careless," she told a national television audience.

Over the next two days the signals were more mixed. Ron Brown said that "good open lines of communication" had been restored between the two campaigns. But Jackson, leaving Chicago on the Rainbow Express, was still testy. "Mr. Bentsen represents one wing of the party, I represent the other wing," he said. "It takes two wings to fly, and so far our wing is not connected." He suggested that former President Jimmy Carter be asked to mediate, a notion quickly shot down by the Dukakis strategists who didn't want to give the dispute such cosmic proportions. Then, arriving at Louisville the following day, Jackson sounded more conciliatory after a telephone conversation with Dukakis. "Leaders must build, leaders must heal," he said. "Our challenge is to communicate across misunderstandings to unify our party and to challenge our nation."

The so-called caravan from Chicago had become seven buses, six of them full of reporters, photographers and television crews. The trip that had originally been seen as a vehicle for a mass movement to Atlanta had instead become—perhaps inevitably with Jesse Jackson—essentially a rolling press conference.

Dukakis and his advisers had been monitoring the Jackson activity closely as the convention approached. "It was now over," Brountas said later. "Mathematically Jesse Jackson couldn't win . . . but he continued to campaign. He felt it was an obligation to his people and he told me this. They had worked hard and he felt it was just something that he personally couldn't turn off. He had to continue to do this because when he went to Atlanta his supporters had to be recognized. We had to listen to 'em and we had to hear what they were saying. . . . There are all kinds of ways you can go to Atlanta for a convention and the bus is least likely. So there was a statement there in the Chicago bus trip. It kept the momentum and the tension growing."

The same could be said of the missed telephone call. Jackson could have simply brushed it off as the kind of mechanical mistake that any campaign could make. He was, after all, a candidate who had failed to show up in time for his own live television show ending the California primary campaign just a few weeks earlier. But it was clear he was looking for fuel to keep his crusade alive for a few more days, and the missed phone call was a gift from the heavens. As Ron Brown said later, "it increased our leverage."

Jackson aside, the reaction to Bentsen had been almost universally favorable. Even the liberal activists who were no fans of the Texas Democrat were muted, perhaps because they recognized the political hazards in the Jackson alternative. And the pragmatic professionals were generally approving because they thought the choice reflected a hardheaded political judgment that made sense and a self-assurance on Dukakis' part. He was a candidate who could handle a vice presidential nominee who disagreed with him on some major issues.

Dukakis' decision apparently was, to a large degree, a matter of personal chemistry. He had met Bentsen twice in the Capitol, as well as on that stop in Texarkana, and he was impressed by the expertise of the chairman of the Senate Finance Committee. "He liked the idea that Bentsen was a strong figure in the

Senate," Brountas said, and an insider who would help Dukakis "bridge the gap" in his own experience.

The political equities were considered but apparently not paramount. "I think the fact he was from the South was helpful," Brountas said. "Texas was not the overriding consideration. It was never that 'we're going to pick Bentsen because it's Texas' or 'we're going to pick Bentsen because it's a parallel to the Kennedy-Johnson thing.' "

Bentsen, then sixty-seven, had all the requisite credentials. He had served in the House of Representatives from a South Texas district from 1949 to 1955, then left to build a fortune in a private investment business before defeating a liberal Democratic senator, Ralph Yarborough, in a 1970 primary and a Republican congressman, George Bush, in the general election. He had never been accused of being a charismatic politician. But by 1982, he had been reelected with 60 percent of the vote, putting together the financing and staff for a sophisticated get-out-the-vote campaign that was widely credited with electing the entire Democratic state ticket.

The Texas Democrat was clearly more conservative than Dukakis on some issues. He had supported the MX missile, the B-1 bomber and aid to the contras. And he had excellent credentials on civil rights issues, extending as far back as a vote against the poll tax in 1949. As Dukakis pointed out in introducing him as his choice, Bentsen had scored "the proverbial legislative grand slam" as chairman of the Finance Committee by steering through in 1987 a trade bill, welfare reform and the plant-closing notification bill. Dukakis kept repeating that he didn't require a clone. "I wanted somebody," he told a meeting of editors and reporters at the *Washington Post*, "who is strong, a doer, who in general terms shared my values and goals and aspirations."

Bentsen had stubbed his toe only on one or two occasions. In 1976 he made a brief and monumentally unsuccessful run for the Democratic presidential nomination. And in 1987 he had been embarrassed by disclosure of a "breakfast club"—sessions with him over breakfast—for lobbyists who produced $10,000 or more for his reelection campaign in 1988. When reporter Tom Edsall described the plan in the *Washington Post*, Bentsen quickly scuttled it.

In retrospect, the arguments for Glenn seemed more compelling. For one thing, he was clearly a lot better bet to assure Ohio than Bentsen was to assure Texas. Beyond that, his stature as a national hero offered instant insulation to Dukakis against suggestions of weakness or a lack of patriotism. Perhaps most important, Glenn the all-American boy from the small town in Ohio would have been the ideal complement to the son of Greek immigrants in a campaign based on "the American dream" theme.

But at this stage of the campaign, not all of the Dukakis political calculations were based on realistic assessments of the outlook in the fall. Dukakis strategists considered Texas a definite possibility, and they even believed they had enough of a chance in Florida to send Steve Rosenfeld and Paul Pezzella back there for the general election. When the opposition was going to be George Bush, anything seemed possible.

But, as the Democrats began gathering in Atlanta the week before the convention, they were far less concerned with the nuances of the fall electoral-vote strategy than with the immediate problem of dealing with Jesse Jackson early and effectively enough to assure a successful convention. As Ron Brown, with only modest hyperbole, put it, "This party was hanging by a thread in Atlanta."

Within the Dukakis campaign, the concern was more specific: The nominee had to avoid a repetition of the scarring experience Fritz Mondale had been through with Jackson in 1984.

In that campaign Jackson had finished third, behind Gary Hart as well as Mondale, rather than second. But he was offended when Mondale did not include him among those interviewed in St. Paul as possible vice presidential candidates. And Jackson spent the entire summer, even after Mondale's nomination, without delivering a public endorsement. Mondale finally convened a meeting of black Democratic leaders, including Jackson, in St. Paul on Labor Day weekend to resolve the problem. And before that session in the St. Paul Hotel downtown, Mondale met privately with Jackson at his home.

The two erstwhile rivals were then driven to a schoolyard for a press conference at which Jackson was expected to resolve the remaining doubts about his support. But, with Mondale standing at his side trying to avoid looking either uncomfortable or angry, Jackson refused to use the word "endorse," instead making a point of his continuing right to disagree if the occasion arose. The result was a political disaster—television film of the Democratic nominee being jerked around publicly by Jackson, and appearing to accept it.

Later that night, after a stormy meeting at the hotel, Jackson finally went the last mile—but only after more than two hours of wrangling set off by Jackson supporters trying to force Mondale into a politically suicidal commitment to a huge public-jobs program. If the story from the schoolyard was a bummer, the denouement was no better in political terms. In fact, Mondale had made no concessions to Jackson, but the pictures conveyed from St. Paul that night seemed to confirm the pictures the Republicans had been drawing of him as a captive of Democratic constituency groups.

This time the issues to be settled were trivial compared to the jobs program Jackson had demanded in 1984. On Friday Ron Brown had flown to Nashville, stopping point for the Rainbow Express, where he met in an all-night session with Jackson and key supporters—former Gary Mayor Richard Hatcher, writer and teacher Roger Wilkins, Representative Charles Rangel, former Manhattan Borough President Percy Sutton—to settle on their demands. The platform issues were mostly ones on which Dukakis had already agreed—planks calling for the designation of South Africa as a "terrorist" state, same-day voter registration, statehood for the District of Columbia, increased set-asides for minorities in federal contracts. And the same was true of the other changes Jackson sought—an expansion of the Democratic National Committee to accommodate more of his supporters, revisions in the delegate-selection rules.

The one specific on which the Jackson campaign could gain no satisfaction was the immediate replacement of Paul Kirk as the Democratic national chairman. Kirk was widely credited with having been a remarkably successful party leader, but Jackson believed he had tilted against him during the nominating process and wanted him out. On this one, however, the Dukakis camp never budged.

Brown flew back to Atlanta early the next morning and began a series of meetings over the weekend, first with Brountas alone, then with larger groups of advisers from both campaigns. According to several participants, the meetings were cordial enough, but what Brown called "a kind of impasse" was reached Sunday that made it clear the two principals had to be brought together.

Meanwhile, the political atmosphere grew increasingly heated. Jackson arrived late Saturday and delivered a ninety-minute speech in oppressive heat at Piedmont Park, repeating his insistence on describing the situation as one of "shared victory and shared responsibility." When he made that speech, Brountas recalled, "I thought, 'We've got problems, some real problems.' " Sunday, speaking to more than three thousand supporters at the Fox Theatre, Jackson was at his most militant. "I will not give up," he boomed. "I have one gear. It's forward ever, backward never. I will never surrender. You must never surrender."

Jackson said later that he began to fear the situation would get out of hand. "We got to Atlanta," he said, "and I sensed that our momentum was continuing to build . . . that they had dropped the ball and I had picked it up and they didn't know how to get the ball back." If he had remained "out in front," he said, it might have caused "complications" so he "took the initiative" in arranging a meeting with Dukakis in the latter's suite at the Hyatt Regency Monday morning.

Dukakis, arriving Sunday to claim his prize, was publicly placatory. "Every team has to have a quarterback—that's the nominee," he said. "You can't have two quarterbacks. On the other hand, every team has to have terrific players in the backfield and up in the line. That's the way you win." But there was no indication this labored metaphor was hitting home with Jesse Jackson, master of the labored metaphor.

The hazard in the lack of an agreement between Dukakis and Jackson was increased significantly by the fact that all this was happening on the eve of the convention. The atmosphere in convention cities is quite unlike anything else. The entire city becomes a political hothouse in which the acorn of a rumor can become a full-grown oak in a matter of hours as thousands of delegates, reporters and hangers-on mill around the hotel lobbies, all asking the ultimate question of politics: "Whaddaya hear?"

The sticking point for Dukakis was Jackson's apparent demand for a greater role than the candidate was willing to give him. "The concerns were words like 'partnership,' 'shared power' and 'shared responsibility,' " Brountas said. "Many people interpreted that as a co-presidency of some sort." At the Monday breakfast meeting, which included only the two candidates, Brountas and

Brown, the Dukakis chairman spelled out their concern. "I explained to him
. . . why I had problems with those terms," he said. But Jackson countered
that Brountas was viewing them "too legalistically" and chided him, as he
often did, for being too much the lawyer. Jackson said, for example, that when
he referred to "partnership" he was thinking of it as only an expression of
greeting to a friend, as in "Hey, partner, how you doing?"

This explanation was obviously disingenuous. Jackson was pushing for a
role not only in the campaign but also, assuming the election of Dukakis, in
the transition and the new administration. On this point, as with Kirk, Dukakis
was not prepared to budge. Jackson would be assured of a part in the campaign,
with a plane and funding from the party, and some of his operatives would be
folded into the Dukakis organization. Just how much of a voice Jackson would
have later would be determined by how things worked out in each phase—
meaning they would worry about the campaign now without making any commitments on what was to come in the transition or thereafter.

The key to the meeting, however, seemed to be that, at long last, the two
candidates aired some of the complaints they had with each other. "Each of
them," Brown said, "got a chance to tell the other what had pissed them off
during the campaign, in terms of what the other had said." Predictably, Jackson
complained about the missed telephone call. Dukakis said he had been annoyed
by Jackson's use of metaphors suggesting that Dukakis might be evincing racist
attitudes toward him.

Once the air had cleared, at least for the moment, Brown produced his list
of specifics, the four men ran through them and Brown and Brountas began
drafting statements for both principals to use at a press conference. Lloyd
Bentsen was summoned to join the group and the press conference. "That's
the picture we wanted," Brown said later, "The ticket and Jesse Jackson."

Both Brountas and Brown recalled the meeting having been essentially
over before Bentsen arrived. But Jackson insisted that Bentsen was very helpful
in easing the concerns of Dukakis and Brountas about the need to talk of putting
together "constituencies" of Democrats to win the election. "Being a Texas
senator," Jackson said, "he understands coalitions and constituencies." Bentsen "knew instinctively," he said, that "if you go and campaign among Hispanics, talk Spanish and eat tacos," or "go over to the black side of town and
do a soul shake or some cultural expression, eat a biscuit," these things could
be done without losing support elsewhere in the electorate. Jackson described
Bentsen's special talent as a conciliator this way: "He can go from biscuits to
tacos to caviar real fast, knowing that's just the cultural diversity that makes
up America."

Bentsen said later that when he was called in, Dukakis and Jackson "had
not resolved their differences. I made the point that it was like a three-legged
stool. All of us had a part to play, a role to play, and it was going to be a very
tough election and a difficult one to win. Each of us brought something to the
party. That Jesse very definitely did, with his constituency, and I thought I did

with my constituency, and that Mike obviously did. That winning would be a close one, and it would take the concerted efforts of all three of us to do it. I remember afterward someone asked Jesse about it [the meeting], and he said, 'Lloyd Bentsen speaks grits.' '' And John White recalled later that Jackson had told him Bentsen had ''saved the meeting.''

Shortly before noon, in a jam-packed press conference in the hotel basement, the differences were publicly resolved—or, at least, papered over.

''We have had a very, very good talk this morning about this campaign, about our convention and about what we're going to do together,'' Dukakis said. Jackson, he added, would ''play a major role in this campaign'' and his supporters would be ''an essential part of the coalition we build coming out of this convention to win a Democratic victory in November, and to provide this nation with strong, new, hopeful, confident and optimistic leadership in January.'' Jackson described the meeting as ''very thoughtful and thorough'' and added: ''We're now on a track that will lead to expanded involvement, more excitement and great motivation to build a team that will carry us to victory and will spare the people of the agony, abandonment and neglect they felt these last seven years.''

Jackson reiterated that his name would be placed in nomination for the presidency—joking that ''I'm still looking for a Chicago miracle,'' a reference to his home city's reputation for producing majorities from thin air. But Jackson's name would not be put forward for vice president. And only three of the thirteen platform planks Jackson was supporting would be brought to the floor. The touchiest, calling for statehood for Palestine, would be advanced only for discussion purposes; a potentially awkward vote would not be held.

Asked the terms of the agreement that had ended the impasse, Dukakis replied: ''There's no deal and there's no fine print. That's not the way you win elections. It's a matter of respect.''

The bottom line was that, in the end, Michael Dukakis had stared down Jesse Jackson. The man who finished second would be given the ''respect'' that was always his first priority, but no assurances of a voice in a Dukakis transition or administration.

Now the rest of the week could be devoted to celebrating the ticket that revived the ''Boston-Austin axis'' of 1960—Michael Dukakis and Lloyd Bentsen.

23

A Wasted Opportunity

News of the rapprochement between Michael Dukakis and Jesse Jackson sent a wave of relief through the convention city, transforming the atmosphere in a single afternoon. Anxiety became euphoria. Dukakis had held firm; Jackson had gone along. Everything was on track for a Democratic convention that—unlike so many in the past—might send the delegates home with some genuine basis for optimism about winning the White House in November.

There were, however, some unanswered questions. Some insightful southern Democrats wondered whether, even given the eventual result, Jackson had been accorded so much prominence that it would be harder to reclaim white Democrats who had supported Ronald Reagan so avidly four years earlier. Longtime Jackson-watchers realized there still might be trouble from that quarter. Jackson had not achieved what he really wanted—to be "in the room," as politicians say, when the door was closed and the powers made the final decisions. And Dukakis himself had yet to resolve doubts about whether he had a coherent message to bring to the general election campaign other than the fact that he was not George Bush. "Good jobs at good wages" was not going to be enough.

The delegates were ambivalent about Dukakis. They were impressed by his political accomplishments over the previous sixteen months. They were confident he had the ability to occupy the presidency. But few of them knew him very well, and many of them felt it difficult to warm to him—or to draw any warmth from him. Fritz Mondale might have been a doomed candidate in 1984, but he was a man with a long history in the political trenches who had established his bona fides as a quintessential Democrat for all seasons.

At the moment, however, those doubts were quibbles in the heady optimism that the delegates carried into the first convention session in the cramped Omni arena that night. They had been promised a keynote speech by Ann Richards, the determinedly down-home state treasurer of Texas, that would tell the country, as she put it, "how the cow ate the cabbage" in eight years of Republican rule. And they were prepared to cheer her on.

The delegates were not disappointed as Richards introduced herself by saying: "After listening to George Bush all these years, I figured you needed to know what a real Texas accent sounds like." Then, in the most memorable passage, she added: "For eight straight years George Bush hasn't displayed the slightest interest in anything we care about. And now that he's after a job he can't get appointed to, he's like Christopher Columbus discovering America. He's found child care. He's found education. Poor George, he can't help it. He was born with a silver foot in his mouth."

The delegates roared their approval. If some of them had some lingering doubts about Michael Dukakis, there were few who questioned the proposition that George Herbert Walker Bush made a perfect target for a united Democratic campaign. Indeed, Bush was seen as such a figure of ridicule that even former President Jimmy Carter had suggested in an interview with a suburban Atlanta newspaper that he had "a very serious problem of silliness."

The following night there was even more ridicule. Ted Kennedy delighted the delegates jammed into the too-small hall by ticking off a list of Reagan administration failures and asking, in a booming shout that grew louder with each repetition: "Where was George?"

"We all know the answer to all these questions," Kennedy declared. "George Bush is the man who is never there."

Watching on television, Bush's media expert, Roger Ailes, was more interested in what the ridicule might say about the campaign ahead. As he said later:

"I honestly sat there and watched it and thought, oh, well, that's the theme of one ad, 'Where was George?' Oh, well, there's the theme of another ad. I mean I saw it in terms of advertising and I thought they must have had ads. *I* would have. . . . So I thought every time they hit him, I said, well they're going to do a gaffe ad, silver foot in the mouth, they'll play off of that. They'll go back and take six of his gaffes, string them together, get people laughing at him and have her tie it off with that line. That's a great ad. I was sitting there watching the Democratic convention writing their ads. That's when I decided, oh, boy, we got trouble here."

For the Democrats at the convention, however, the focus of all eyes the second night was Jesse Jackson. His speech was such a drawing card that the Omni overflowed to the point that several hundred Democrats and reporters were denied admission by fire department officials. Jackson's fifty-minute speech was largely a compilation of all the things he had been saying on the campaign trail over the previous year or more. But the critical paragraph—and the one that the delegates were listening to hear—was the one that seemed to define his commitment to the man who had defeated him.

"Tonight I salute Michael Dukakis," Jackson said. "I have watched a good mind fast at work, with steel nerves, guiding his campaign out of the crowded field without appealing to the worst in us. I have watched his perspective grow as his environment has expanded. I have seen his toughness and tenacity close up, and I know his commitment to public service." Jackson's assessment was by no means an affectionate embrace, but it seemed positive enough to put to rest any lingering fears that he would go off the reservation.

Earlier—before prime-time television viewing—the last business with any potential for causing discord had been handled expeditiously. The Jackson forces had proposed two changes in the platform, which the Dukakis majority quickly rejected. One was a plank calling for tax increases on wealthy individuals and corporations, defeated 2,499 to 1,091. The second was a declaration against "first use" of nuclear weapons, defeated 2,474 to 1,022. Dukakis was not about to walk into the trap of being a "tax increaser" or "soft" on national security. As Jackson had agreed, his proposal for a plank endorsing a Palestinian state was debated, principally off camera, then withdrawn without a vote that could have exacerbated black-Jewish tensions that had been so apparent in the New York primary. The 5,200-word platform, a compendium of innocuous generalities the Republicans would find hard to exploit on grounds other than its brevity, was adopted unanimously.

The following night the delegates nominated Michael Stanley Dukakis on the first ballot, 2,876 votes to 1,218 for Jesse Louis Jackson. Then Willie Brown, Jackson's chairman, came to the podium to call for Dukakis' nomination by acclamation. In his suite Dukakis and his family watched on television while other cameras watched them. Dukakis smiled broadly and, after demurring momentarily, even accepted a glass of celebratory champagne.

The only off-key note of the evening had been the nominating speech of Bill Clinton, the forty-one-year-old governor of Arkansas who went on for thirty-two minutes and lost his audience. Clinton was a politician of solid accomplishment and bright promise, an intelligent man who made a misjudgment that spoiled his first moment in the brightest of political suns. Two of the television networks found it all too much for their delicate sensibilities and cut away from the podium, ABC to show some documentary film on Dukakis, NBC to floor reporters who interviewed delegates criticizing Clinton on the length of his speech. To television, the ultimate sin was to be boring.

Dukakis' achievement had been a remarkable one. In a decade he had risen from the wreckage of his defeat at the hands of Ed King in that Massachusetts primary to the pinnacle of American politics. In just sixteen months he had brought himself from the relative obscurity of Beacon Hill through the primaries and caucuses of fifty states, winning from Florida to Washington, from Hawaii to Maine, over seven determined rivals. And he had done so with a campaign that was as distinguished by its decency as by its doggedness.

What Dukakis had not accomplished up to that point, nonetheless, was the making of an emotional connection with either the delegates in the Omni or the millions of voters watching on their home screens. And it was a failure that the best Democratic professionals recognized, discussed endlessly in the lobbies and bars of the convention hotels—and hoped against hope that he might correct when he made his acceptance speech the following night.

Democratic conventions are often perilous exercises that leave the party with bleeding political wounds. Twenty years earlier, the convention in Chicago that nominated Hubert Horatio Humphrey turned, literally, into a riot in the streets that left the party hopelessly divided over the war in Vietnam and the viewers appalled. In 1972, the convention at Miami Beach was so unruly and disorganized that the nominee, George McGovern, could not deliver his acceptance speech before 2 A.M. In 1980, the "high point" of the New York convention was the scene of President Jimmy Carter pursuing his vanquished opponent, Ted Kennedy, around the platform trying to get him to pose for the traditional closing unity tableau. And four years later, Walter F. Mondale compounded his problems by using his acceptance speech to announce that if elected, he would raise taxes.

But on closing night in Atlanta, the delegates were exultant. All the pitfalls had been avoided. It remained only for Dukakis to sound the battle cry to send the Democrats into the general election campaign with genuine reasons to believe the White House was within their reach.

Dukakis, as he had done often in his march to the nomination, rose to the occasion.

Much of the speech was well-crafted but conventionally inspirational political rhetoric. "If anyone tells you," he said, "that the American dream belongs to the privileged few and not to all of us, you tell them that the Reagan era is over and a new era is about to begin. . . . Because it is time to raise our sights, to look beyond the cramped ideals and limited ambitions of the past eight years, to recapture the spirit of energy and confidence and of idealism that John Kennedy and Lyndon Johnson inspired a generation ago."

"This election," he said at another point, "is not about ideology, it's about competence."

But the passages that reached the delegates most obviously were those in which Dukakis seemed to reveal a little more of himself than he had exposed in his campaign for the nomination. "We're going to win," he said, "because we are the party that believes in the American dream, a dream so powerful that no distance of ground, no expanse of ocean, no barrier of language, no distinction of race or creed or color can weaken its hold on the human heart. And I know because, my friends, I'm a product of that dream and I'm proud of it, a dream that brought my father to this country seventy-six years ago, that brought my mother and her family here one year later; poor, unable to speak English, but with a burning desire to succeed in their new land of opportunity.

"And tonight, in the presence of that marvelous woman who is my mother and who came here seventy-five years ago, with the memory in my heart of the young man who arrived at Ellis Island with only twenty-five dollars in his pocket but with a deep and abiding faith in the promise of America—and how I wish he was here tonight. He'd be very proud of his adopted country, I can assure you."

In the end, however, the most striking feature of the Dukakis speech was the use, by this ostensibly unemotional technocrat, of a series of grace notes.

He kidded about his own well-earned reputation for frugality, assuring his audience he still owned the ancient snowblower displayed in a television film shown as his cousin Olympia introduced him. And he paid tribute in English and his fluent Spanish to Willie Velasquez, the leader of the Southwest Voter Education Project who had died only a month earlier. He singled out Jesse Jackson's daughter Jackie, watching from a box with her father and mother, as a "remarkable young woman who goes to school in my state." And he recalled Ann Richards' pride in her "almost perfect" granddaughter.

"And my thoughts tonight and my dreams for America are about Ann Richards' granddaughter Lily, about young Jackie Jackson and about the baby that's going to be born to our son John and his wife, Lisa, in January. . . . God willing, our first grandchild will reach the age that Jackie Jackson is now at the beginning of a new century. And we pray that he or she will reach that age with eyes as filled with the sparkle of life and of pride and of optimism as that young woman that we watched together two nights ago. Yes, my friends, it's time for wonderful new beginnings: a little baby, a new administration, a new era of greatness for America."

Finally, Dukakis returned to his Greek heritage, repeating a pledge the people of Athens would take on ceremonial occasions: "We will never bring disgrace to this, our country, by any act of dishonesty or cowardice. We will fight for the ideals of this, our country. We will revere and obey the law. We will strive to quicken our sense of civic duty. Thus, in all these ways, we will transmit this country greater, stronger, prouder and more beautiful than it was transmitted to us."

When Dukakis finished, the delegates erupted in a prolonged demonstration. The band played and the platform filled with the Dukakis family and those of Lloyd Bentsen and Jesse Jackson—all borne along on the same tide of optimism that carried the delegates and Democratic leaders out of the Omni and Atlanta. They had enjoyed a successful convention. They were running against George Bush. Surely, happy days were here again.

Once the shouting died down, however, Dukakis and his strategists were faced with the reality that there was work to be done. The candidate needed to settle on themes that would express the essence of his claim on the presidency, and the campaign needed to seize the offensive and set the agenda for the debate with Bush.

Some of the professionals within the operation had become uneasy about the way Dukakis seemed to be temporizing in the six weeks between the California primary and the convention. He had spent twenty-seven of the forty-one days in Massachusetts, principally working on state business.

Dukakis' devotion to his responsibilities in the State House had been a problem all along—and would continue to be—for his political operatives. He had promised himself at the outset that he could run for president without neglecting the state's business and he was determined to meet that obligation. He had found, he said, that the long plane rides on campaign trips gave him excellent opportunities to work uninterrupted on state matters. And it was work that he relished.

What some of those political operatives failed to understand was that Dukakis had always been more interested in government than in politics—even when, after his comeback in Massachusetts in 1982, he had become a more practiced politician. In his eyes, politics was first of all a necessity if you were to be in a position to use government to improve the lives of your constituents. And Dukakis was persuaded that he could combine the two in this campaign. As Nick Mitropoulos saw it, Dukakis wanted to point to success stories in Massachusetts but he also "wanted to do his job."

Dukakis had been what the politicians called, often derisively, a government junkie for his entire adult life, and perhaps even before he reached adulthood. Richard Dolins, a psychiatrist in Scarsdale, New York, remembered a story that told volumes about Dukakis.

As a senior at Barnstable High School in Hyannis in 1951, Dolins was chosen as a delegate to "Good Government Day"—an annual mock state government run by students much like those called "Boys' State" or "Girls' State" in other jurisdictions. The young Dolins came up from Cape Cod to Boston full of high hopes. The government assignments would be determined by lot, and Dolins had visions of being governor or maybe at least a member of the state Senate. "But when I opened my envelope," he recalled thirty-seven years later, "I'm on the sewerage commission." He felt disappointed and demeaned, wondering "how in the hell I'm going to go back" to Barnstable High and explain to a school assembly that their representative ended up on the sewerage commission.

When the "commission" met, however, Dolins found a different viewpoint. He was seated next to this bright kid from Brookline High named Michael Dukakis. "He knew everything about sewerage," Dolins recalled. "He knew everything about government." The two delegates went to lunch together and the young Dukakis lectured his new pupil about how wonderful government could be and what an opportunity had been offered by their appointment to the mock sewerage commission. It was the essential Michael Dukakis, and in 1988 he was no different.*

Moreover, when Dukakis had gone out campaigning during this preconvention period, he seemed singularly lacking in a coherent message—often simply reacting to the latest troubles of the Reagan administration, sometimes assailing Bush on drugs or Noriega, Ed Meese or Iran-contra. Asked one day in Oregon if his campaigning had not become "too reactive," he shrugged and replied: "My message has always been economic."

There were reasons alarm bells could not be easily heard. There were many days during this period when the political news was Jesse Jackson's latest twist

*We asked Dukakis about this incident in June of 1988 and he remembered Richard Dolins and even that he had become a doctor. He couldn't recall the sewerage commission assignment or his enthusiasm for it, but he smiled and said: "I gotta admit it. It does sound like me."

or turn on the vice presidential question, or fresh "inside" stuff on the ups and downs of John Glenn or Lee Hamilton. And, anyway, the opinion polls were continuing to give the Dukakis campaign nothing but good news. A *Wall Street Journal*–NBC survey taken June 9–12 showed Dukakis with 49 percent, Bush with only 34. A Gallup poll of June 10–12 had it 52 to 38. After the fact, everyone around Dukakis insisted that they had never "believed" the polls and had always understood his standing had been inflated by his weekly primary successes over Jackson. But they would not have been human if they were not lulled into some complacency by such repeated "evidence" that things were going well.

By convention time, however, as the glow of California faded, the margin had begun to narrow. An ABC–*Washington Post* poll conducted a week before Atlanta put Dukakis ahead only 48 to 42, and a *New York Times*–CBS poll two days later found it 48 to 44, almost within the statistical margin of polling error.

Some of the professionals were clearly concerned that the decline was more than the distance from California. Kirk O'Donnell, just joining the campaign, recalled Tom Kiley, a polling expert from Boston who was overseeing the Dukakis media strategy, telling him: "We're losing on the evening news all the time." O'Donnell, who had been brought in to produce competitive "sound bites" for Dukakis, agreed. "What you had was Bush's attacks in June were very effective," he said later.

The problem seemed to be differing assessments within the campaign on how serious a problem the Bush offensive was, and how to respond to it. Tubby Harrison recalled that the first national poll he conducted for the campaign in June had shown Dukakis' "vulnerability" on the crime issues. "We picked up the furlough thing very early," he said. "We knew it was a real problem. It didn't come as any surprise. You wouldn't have had to poll to know the furlough thing could be very dangerous, but it showed up very early. We knew that crime and capital punishment and all of that were going to be the issues."

On the other hand, although the private polling showed the soft-on-crime message as dangerous in May and June, the campaign's experience with the voters in the late primaries and the public polls didn't seem to reflect any damage. Susan Estrich wanted to run some early commercials dealing with the furlough issue. And there were intense discussions of the possibility Dukakis might simply "do a mea culpa"—say that the Willie Horton episode had been a tragedy and that he was sorry it happened, but also point out that prison-furlough programs were used almost everywhere, including in California under Ronald Reagan.

Jack Corrigan recognized that the facts of the Horton case were, as he put it, "troubling for people who didn't know Michael Dukakis" and that the racial element—Willie Horton was black—went "right to the heart of people's fears." Commercials financed by a Republican group ostensibly independent of the Bush campaign showing a picture of Horton were already running in June. But Corrigan and Estrich both recognized that the first imperative for the campaign was, as Corrigan put it, "to shift the campaign to our agenda." And, he said, "every time you respond [to the opposition], you lose that opportunity."

Although all of his advisers minimized it after the fact, there was another important element in the failure to respond early—the reluctance of the candidate himself. Dukakis simply found it impossible to believe that such "issues" as prison furloughs, his veto of the bill to require the pledge of allegiance in the schools and, later, his membership in the American Civil Liberties Union would be taken seriously as legitimate concerns by the American people. These were clearly not presidential issues. "In retrospect," Nick Mitropolous said, "I don't think he took them seriously enough."

Beyond that, Dukakis still held to the textbook view of how a campaign should be operated. He wanted to run on his record and his ideas, and he was convinced that once the voters understood that record and those ideas, they would recognize he should be the president of the United States. Snapping back at Bush on the furlough question, he feared, would be seen as negative campaigning. And, said Mitropoulos, "the reluctance to be negative was something he felt all along."

In any case, such a diversion would interfere with the strategic plan for the campaign then in force. It had three phases. The first would be an effort to lay out the case that, as Estrich put it, "Michael Dukakis cares about people like you" by citing his record of accomplishments and specific proposals on "basic economic working-people issues" such as housing, health care and education. The second would be to make the case for change, and the third would be to contrast Dukakis with Bush in terms of leadership and character.

"It was not true that we had no strategy," Estrich said later. "But it is true we faced a strategic decision and we made one which most people will say was not correct. The strategic decision was to try to build the case for Michael Dukakis, build a foundation under a guy who's ethnic, never been around this track, who's running for the first time, to try to build a foundation for him on issues, on an affirmative agenda, on character and leadership and on change. Or do you adopt the Ailes-Atwater approach, which is you've got an opponent in a somewhat weakened position, never let them off the mat? The other way of translating it was: Who's going to be the issue in this campaign, you or George Bush?"

In the weeks before the convention Dukakis had tried to implement the strategy with swings through the South, the Midwest and the Far West. In the South in particular he emphasized drugs and his own record on crime, trying to build a layer of insulation against the efforts of Bush and his managers to depict Dukakis as just another "soft" liberal lineal descendant of George McGovern and Fritz Mondale. There was no indication in the polling data that the voters were listening, but it was easy to put off any further assessments of the strategy until the convention.

The first result of the convention was another lurch upward in the polling figures. An ABC-*Washington Post* survey the day after the convention had Dukakis leading Bush by twelve percentage points. Then an NBC poll three days later showed a margin of seventeen—Dukakis 51, Bush 34. Once again, the Dukakis managers kept assuring everyone that they recognized the figures were probably inflated and probably driven more by reactions to Bush than hard support for Dukakis. But, even discounted, the figures were impressive enough that they lessened the pressures within the campaign—and within Dukakis himself—to do things a great deal differently.

In the time between the two conventions Dukakis once again embraced his duties as governor with gusto, spending all or part of sixteen of the twenty-five days in Massachusetts. And when he did go on the road, often to set-piece events such as the conventions of the Urban League and the National Governors' Association, there was still no central theme expressed in terms that could be easily understood. While Dukakis was touring Texas with Bentsen at his side, Bush was continuing to hammer away at the pledge of allegiance, gun control, the death penalty and the ACLU.

Dukakis did have those somewhat legalistic answers on both the pledge to the flag and the prison-furlough questions, and he planned to slap back at Bush with them in the first debate. But at that point a debate was a month or more away, and the charges against Dukakis were being given wider distribution every day.

"It was a mistake made," Estrich said later of the decision not to fight back immediately, "in thinking that somehow the American people would somehow dismiss these as trivial issues by comparison to the larger issues that we were addressing. . . . It didn't recognize that there were value questions underlying them that needed to be addressed. And it didn't recognize . . . that this campaign was essentially issueless in a [time] of peace and prosperity. The road not followed was to run the same kind of campaign against them that they ran against us."

The Dukakis advisers understood, she recalled, that "we were never going to win on the furlough question. . . . What we might have done is admit a mistake, then find a way to change the subject to something else."

When Dukakis did capture broader attention from the television networks, and presumably the voters, it was not always necessarily to his advantage. Campaigning in Louisville, Dukakis assailed the Reagan administration's record on official corruption by observing: "There's an old Greek saying: A fish rots from the head first." The point Dukakis was trying to make was a valid one—that Ronald Reagan's own "contempt for public service" would inevitably attract people to his administration with a similar attitude and a consequent lack of concern with questions of ethics. But Dukakis' brief foray into colorful language was quickly translated by a sanctimonious George Bush into "a cheap shot" that equated the sainted Reagan with a rotten fish. Dukakis was talking about the administration rather than the president, but that is precisely the kind of distinction that never seemed to come through on the television news.

The most damaging episode, however, was one that developed ten days after the Democratic convention—and demonstrated in the starkest possible terms the willingness of the news media, including some highly respected newspapers, to traffic in rumors in the name of keeping up with the competition.

At the convention in Atlanta some supporters of Lyndon H. LaRouche, the widely discredited political cultist, had distributed fliers saying that Dukakis had required psychiatric treatment for emotional depression on two occasions. The first, the fliers charged, was after the death of his brother Stelian in an automobile accident in 1973, and the second after Dukakis' defeat by Ed King in 1978. The notion that anything the LaRouche forces might purvey would have any validity was mind-boggling. These people, after all, were the ones who kept telling the world that Queen Elizabeth was a dope pusher. But the rumor buzzed through the political community, along with another that the *Detroit News* was about to "break a story" confirming this accusation. Some Bush operatives quietly encouraged reporters to look into the whole thing. And some organs of the press, justifying their actions on the basis of competitive pressures, did just that.

At this point, there was no way any legitimate news organization could justify publishing this gossip. But when a reporter for the *Boston Herald* asked Dukakis at a press conference whether he had ever received such treatment, the *Boston Globe* reported the question—along with an assertion that there was no evidence to support the rumor. Dukakis had brushed aside the question, but the campaign was concerned enough to decide a denial was in order. Dayton Duncan, the campaign press secretary, issued a statement that Dukakis "has never been treated for mental depression or mental illness of any kind at any time." Dukakis decided that would be enough; he would not release his personal medical records.

The result was a story in the *Washington Times* with a headline reading: "Dukakis Psychiatric Rumor Denied" and, the following day, a modest story on an inside page of the *New York Times* under the heading: "Candidates' Health Discussed." Many other newspapers, including the *Washington Post* and the *Baltimore Sun*, had published nothing about the rumor on the very sensible ground that there wasn't a single fact that had been established to support it.

But then Ronald Reagan—perhaps inadvertently, perhaps not—made it impossible for anyone in the press to ignore the "story" any longer. Asked as he left the White House pressroom about Dukakis' refusal to release his medical records, Reagan delivered one of his patented and sometimes mischievous one-liners. "I'm not going to pick on an invalid," he said.

Dukakis was now obliged to produce Dr. Gerald R. Plotkin, his personal physician since 1971, to issue a three-page statement and answer reporters' questions. Dukakis, said Plotkin, was "in excellent health" and had had "no psychological symptoms, complaints or treatment."

Reagan apologized, saying, "I don't think I should have said what I said," and Dukakis replied that no apology had been necessary. The fact was that the whole affair had been a farce. But that didn't prevent it from being a damaging one. "We dropped eight points in a week," Tubby Harrison said.

About the same time, with the Republican convention approaching, there were new reports of complaints about "Boston"—the Dukakis high command in the headquarters at 105 Chauncy Street. The "message team" was reported to be in disarray—an army of high-priced consultants producing commercials that either Dukakis himself or Estrich and Corrigan were rejecting. State operations were having trouble getting either money or decisions fast enough. Operatives for Jesse Jackson were not being brought into the organization as fully or as quickly as the agreement at the convention between the two men had required. Estrich and Corrigan were jealous of their prerogatives and thus resisting bringing into the campaign other Democratic professionals who might have been helpful.

The significant thing about these complaints was probably less their validity—some were valid, some were not—than the fact they were so widespread. The pattern was a common one to campaigns in trouble, and for the first time the notion began to take hold that Michael Dukakis might not have the boat ride to the White House promised by those opinion polls in July showing him seventeen percentage points ahead of George Bush.

But the complaints missed the central point about the state of the Dukakis campaign as the Republican convention and then the general election approached. The hard fact now was that money and organization were far less important than they had been in the primaries and caucuses. Those factors were still important, but they could make a difference principally at the margins, in a close race. Good commercials could help but the imperative now was for Dukakis himself to perform well on "the free media"—principally the television network news programs every night. Money—and the Dukakis campaign had plenty—would help staff field operations to identify, register and turn out supporters. But it was Dukakis himself who had to give those voters reasons to be supporters.

As Jack Corrigan observed one day in Boston: "You reach the point where the candidate has to do it for himself."

And Dukakis was not doing it. He was going through the motions of campaigning. But he was not presenting a coherent rationale for his candidacy—or, at least, not one that was understandable to the electorate. And he was not rebutting the continued assault from Bush on the pledge of allegiance and the prison-furlough programs.

"Part of it was the other side," pollster Harrison said later. "Part of it was our failure to attempt to set the campaign or the election on our terms rather than theirs.''

The Boston command at one point set up what one insider called ''the response team'' to deal with Bush's charges. ''Why wasn't there an offense team?'' this insider asked in frustration after the campaign. ''We were just getting the ball back over. How about us serving?''

By the time the Republicans began to gather in New Orleans for their own convention, the success of their strategy—and the price of Dukakis' approach—were there for all to see. Opinion polls showed the race essentially dead even. The seventeen-point lead of July had gone up in smoke. It was now George Bush's turn to capitalize on his party's national convention—if he had the stuff to do so. And on that point, the jury was still out.

PART VI

New Orleans: The Republican Convention

24

Still in Reagan's Shadow

All through George Bush's successful drive for the Republican presidential nomination, he had been under pressure to be his "own man." His impressive résumé was filled with jobs, with the exception of his election to Congress long before, that had been given to him. As a result, he had developed the image of a political courtesan, always subject to somebody else's bidding, carrying somebody else's mail. That perception was greatly reinforced by the manner in which he became Ronald Reagan's running mate in 1980, and how he then toed the line so unwaveringly for nearly eight years as his genuflecting vice president.

Back in 1980, when it was clear that Reagan would be nominated but while Bush remained in the race, there was inevitable speculation about Bush as the No. 2 man on the Republican ticket. On the campaign trail, reporters took to asking him from time to time about his interest in the second spot. He always responded—with obvious and increasing irritation—that he was running for president, not vice president, and would not consider the latter. Pressed on the matter, he finally replied at one press conference that reporters should "take Sherman and cube it."

The remark, while it might have thrown the casual listener, did not need explaining to his audience of political junkies. He was referring to the statement of General William Tecumseh Sherman of the Union Army after the Civil War when similarly pressed on the notion of a draft for the presidency: "I will not accept if nominated and will not serve if elected." "Cubing" that remark seemed to be about as categorical as Bush could get in expressing his unavailability for the vice presidential nomination.

At the Republican convention in Detroit, however, Bush behaved in the fashion of an ardent suitor for the job. He endured in silence the negotiations between Reagan and former President Gerald Ford over the possibility of Ford accepting the second slot on the ticket. And by the time that ludicrous exercise had run its course and Reagan finally called Bush to offer it to him, General

Sherman had long since been forgotten. Bush grabbed the chance gleefully. Asked at a postselection press conference about "take Sherman and cube it," he sloughed the question off. He couldn't very well have indicated he would take the No. 2 job, he explained, while he was still officially in the race for the presidential nomination. The notion that he could simply have declined to comment on the inquiries about his availability apparently did not occur to him. Instead he felt that to knock down the speculation he had to gush that particularly memorable bit of hyperbole. Just repeating the Sherman statement wasn't enough, but one might have thought "squaring" Sherman would have done the trick.

That, though, was George Bush—the man who seemed to overdo everything, whether it was denying he would accept the runner-up spot when he was dying for it, or being not simply 100 percent for Ronald Reagan once he was aboard, but 200 percent or more. In the vice presidency, the same reputation for excessive zeal was sustained by his all-out, unwavering support of his benefactor. That behavior in turn fed the nagging "wimp factor," as did his personal awkwardness as a candidate when he set out on his quest to be Reagan's successor. Reagan's own physical presence and self-confidence made Bush in contrast seem even weaker, and Bush's penchant for the prissy remark at times cast him as the Little Lord Fauntleroy of the campaign trail. Typical was his response to criticism in the spring of 1988 that he was running a negative campaign. He wasn't going to let the Democrats get away with it, he said at one point, when they started pulling "the naughty stuff" on him.

The wimp label so irritated Bush that when *Newsweek* magazine put him on its cover with the caption "Fighting the Wimp Factor," key aides were ordered to cut off a team of *Newsweek* reporters researching a postelection book on the 1988 campaign. Once Bush had nailed down the nomination, mention of "the wimp factor" tapered off generally in the news media, but it remained the subject of inside jokes in the press corps and among the late-night television comics. And as long as George Bush continued to be seen with that crooked grin of his as the Charlie McCarthy sitting on old ventriloquist Edgar Bergen's knee, it was hard for many to picture him as the next president of the United States.

Bush, though, firmly believed or convinced himself that the only way one could honorably function in the vice presidency was to stand foursquare behind the president. He grew up, he liked to say, to believe that "loyalty is not a character flaw." If some of his political aides wanted him to put distance between himself and Reagan to give himself a clearer identity with the voters, he was having none of it. He might dance around the edges of independence, but never, ever plunge into it with a categorical disagreement with the president.

In the midst of pressure on beleaguered Attorney General Edwin Meese to resign in the face of conflict-of-interest charges, Bush strategists publicly expressed the fear that Meese would saddle him with the so-called sleaze issue. But Bush himself, while allowing that he was "concerned," quickly added: "I don't think it's my role as vice president to try to go out there and suggest Mr. Meese ought to go or stay.'' An investigation was going on and he wasn't going to prejudge it, he said. That, too, was George Bush.

While he would not plunge into open independence, he would dip his toe in occasionally, with mild proposals to cut the capital-gains tax, boost incentives for oil drilling or move more quickly against acid rain. He would also allow himself some slight implied criticism of Reagan, as he did in Los Angeles in late May in declaring that as president he would not "bargain with terrorists, and I won't bargain with drug dealers either, whether they're on U.S. or foreign soil.'' This last came as the Reagan administration continued its negotiations with Panama's General Noriega, accused of drug dealing.

Two days before the California primary in which he ran unopposed, Bush—obviously looking toward the general election in a state where environmental issues had particular salience—called for a delay in the administration's plan to permit oil drilling off the Northern California coast. The statement came only a month after Bush, following the lead of Governor George Deukmejian, his state campaign chairman, had said he favored offshore drilling under certain environmental safeguards. But Republican Senator Pete Wilson, running for reelection in opposition to further drilling, had urged him to shift gears. So Bush, rather than breaking flatly with the Reagan administration, proposed only that the drilling be held up until he became president, at which time he would take a fresh look. For Bush, that was going ankle-deep in independence, but no more. And the next day, at an Ontario fund-raiser, he was back on dry land, saying that while protecting the environment was important, "we've got to grow, we've got to have a strong energy base.''

In an appearance before an ABC News panel in Los Angeles on primary day, Bush allowed himself another ankle-deep difference, saying he couldn't agree with the president's suggestion at his Moscow summit meeting a few days earlier that the Soviet Union had experienced "a profound change of policy.'' He didn't think, Bush said, "we know enough to say that there is that kind of fundamental change, a turning inward a la China, on the part of the Soviet Union.'' But this, too, was a mild separation from Reagan, and one that would reassure Americans that he would not be a pushover for the Russians as president.

Appearing before the annual convention of the National Association for the Advancement of Colored People in Washington in mid-July, on the eve of the Democratic National Convention, Bush uttered another implied criticism of his boss, saying there would be "a new day" for civil rights under his own administration and he would be "personally involved in protecting the civil rights of all Americans.'' He specifically reiterated his support for the concept of affirmative action, which some others in the Reagan administration had tried to roll back. But again he was careful not to give offense to Reagan.

Within the Bush campaign, his strategists had come to accept that their candidate was not going to break in any notable way with the president, and at least to rationalize that it wasn't necessary. With voters not having a clear impression of Bush himself, as those focus groups in New Jersey had strongly suggested, it was more important that he say and do things that demonstrated his own strength and his own ideas, unrelated to Reagan. But still he resisted urgings, telling his closest aides that the time to step out on his own was at the Republican convention, after the mantle of party leadership had formally been passed to him.

At the same time, according to campaign insiders, Bush was in the doldrums as he continued to read how he trailed Dukakis in the polls, and how the polls continued to register strong negatives toward him among the voters. After the election, one key strategist described Bush's mood at this juncture as "resignation" that he might be going down to defeat, but coupled with determination to persevere.

In mid-July, as the Democrats at their convention in Atlanta pummeled Bush with their Ted Kennedy-led "Where was George?" and Ann Richards' "born with a silver foot in his mouth," the object of their derision went off trout fishing near Cody, Wyoming, with his buddy Secretary of Treasury Jim Baker. The trip was not conceived, as widely assumed at the time, as a specific means for Bush and Baker to take stock of the campaign and jointly plan for the fall. Baker earlier had made plans to go fishing with Congressman Dick Cheney of Wyoming, Gerald Ford's White House chief of staff, but Cheney had a heart-bypass operation and couldn't go. Baker, aware that Bush was dispirited by what he was reading in the polls, urged him to take Cheney's place, and he agreed. So while all the Bush-bashing was going on in Atlanta, Bush and Baker were off matching wits with trout. (One of the better wisecracks at the convention, from House Majority Whip Tony Coelho, played on the Bush-Baker fishing trip, and on Bush's lingering "wimp" image. Bush, Coelho said, "wears cowboy boots over argyle socks" and Baker had gone along "in case George is too squeamish to bait his own hook.")

Although Lee Atwater was running the campaign, he was told early by Bush that eventually Baker would be coming over to take charge, and that was fine with Atwater, who had worked admiringly under Baker in the 1980 and 1984 campaigns. Baker took pains all through 1987 up to this point not to look over Atwater's shoulder. But he did take an interest in how things were going and did from time to time talk to Atwater and to Bob Teeter about overall strategy. And he did take some shots offstage, referring once to the campaign team, when things were going badly, as "the sophomores." While some inside the campaign fretted about Bush's failure to step out more on his own, Baker counseled patience. It would be a mistake, some recalled him saying as the summer started, "to use the bullets too early," because the campaign only had so many to expend and the whole fall campaign lay ahead.

Baker himself was not eager to leave Treasury and get into the campaign. After his four years as Reagan's White House chief of staff, he clearly relished running his own department at Treasury. And he was, beyond that, very concerned about how he was perceived in policy as opposed to political circles. He never regarded himself primarily as a political operative and didn't want the public generally to see him as such. One day early in 1987 when one of us went over to see him at Treasury on a matter not related to the Bush campaign, he inquired about how the campaign appeared from the outside to be going. The talk got around to whether and when he would be joining it, and he said he was in no rush. At one point he asked how he was likely to be perceived if he took over the campaign. He did not use the word, but it was clear he did not want to leave his very influential policy post and risk being regarded simply as a political hack. There was no mention of his rumored ambition to become secretary of state in a Bush administration, but it did not take a mind reader to fathom what he seemed to be thinking.

In any event, Baker's formal entry into the campaign was agreed upon by now but not announced, and Bush returned to the campaign trail refreshed and rededicated. Campaigning in Michigan, he insisted he had not watched or heard any of the Democratic convention and all the Bush-bashing. "That's the beauty about the wilderness," he said. "You don't have to listen to Teddy Kennedy." He did suggest, though, that the Democratic antics "might show desperation" and that "maybe it will backfire on them. Maybe people won't like just tearing down the other guy," he said. "I have a feeling, I always have, that if you just go nasty, go ugly, it isn't an effective way to do business." That was a judgment, though, that his own campaign had already been testing before the Democratic convention with his bashing of Dukakis on the flag and furlough "issues."

Now that the Democratic convention was over, there were two major pieces of business for Bush to attend to. One could be handled largely by his staff, but the other required the prospective nominee's personal decision. The first was the writing of a party platform; that one would be easy. The second would be the selection of a vice presidential nominee, and that would be Bush's own call presumably with a great deal of input from his politically savvy strategists.

Concerning the first item, Republicans, unlike the Democrats, were much more together as a party and had come to realize that a national convention best served the party and the nominee by displaying unity, not disarray. Whereas the Democrats, anticipating considerable internal conflict, had held their platform and rules committee deliberations well in advance of their convention, the Republicans would gather in the convention city a few days before the opening of the convention, work out a few mild platform disagreements and get on with the celebrating.

As for the second item, Bush had let it be known early that he wasn't going to be in any rush to select and make known his running mate. Although he had nailed down the nomination for all practical purposes in March, he said he wanted to wait to see who the Democratic vice presidential nominee was before making up his mind on his own. Dukakis' selection of Lloyd Bentsen, the man who had beaten him in his earlier bid for a Senate seat, offered some interesting angles. That choice was, among other things, an obvious effort to tie Bush down to more campaigning in his own state of Texas, presumably safe for Bush before Dukakis picked Bentsen. Bush could counter that move, or even trump it, tying Dukakis down in his own backyard by picking a running mate from the Northeast, such as Republican Governor Tom Kean of New Jersey or former Governor Richard Thornburgh of Pennsylvania, recently appointed attorney general by Reagan. Having this option was ample justification for Bush waiting until Dukakis made his pick before addressing his own.

Of all men, George Bush had to know the critical importance of the decision on a vice presidential nominee. He himself was the vice president little more than a month when he came within a bullet's width of being elevated to the presidency in the assassination attempt on President Reagan. Bush had to know what a great responsibility this choice was, not only in terms of his own chances for reelection but also, and more important, in terms of national stability and the continuity of governing, if something untoward should befall him once elected president.

There were, to be sure, plenty of stories and gags about vice presidents and their insignificance. Harry Truman's vice president, Alben Barkley, liked to tell audiences: "Once upon a time there was a farmer with two sons. One of them ran off to sea. The other was elected vice president of the United States. Nothing more was ever heard of either of them." When Dwight D. Eisenhower was in the Oval Office, the popular gag was that Richard Nixon's favorite pastime was challenging the president each morning to a race up and down the Capitol steps. FDR's petulant vice president, John Nance Garner, was reported as describing the vice presidency as "not worth a bucket of warm spit"—and there were those who heard him who said the reporter had gotten the last word wrong. Peter Finley Dunne's Mr. Dooley insisted that the chief function of the vice president was "to inquire after th' hilth of th' president" and that "th' prisidincy is th' highest office in the gift iv th people. Th' vice-prisidincy is the next highest an' th' lowest. It isn't a crime exactly. Ye can't be sint to jail f'r it, but it's a kind iv disgrace. It's like writin' anonymous letters.' "

Even in a serious vein, the job had the reputation of being a fifth wheel. Woodrow Wilson in his doctoral thesis said of the vice president: "His position is one of anomalous insignificance and curious uncertainty. . . . The chief embarrassment in discussing his office is that in explaining how little there is to be said about it, one has evidently said all there is to say." That may have been so about the office itself, but what it could lead to was another matter altogether. John Adams summed it up succinctly when, as vice president to George Washington, he said: "In this, I am nothing. But I could be everything."

Indeed, it was the intention of the founding fathers, in originally having the runner-up in the presidential election become vice president, to have an individual of high esteem waiting in the wings. Those who held the job in those earliest years—Adams, Jefferson, Aaron Burr—were so regarded. But when an electoral college tie between Jefferson and Burr in 1800 led to the election of president and vice president as a team, the quality of the No. 2 man in general declined, as geographic ticket-balancing came increasingly into play.

Yet the frequency with which vice presidents ascended to the Oval Office—five times in this century—and the steady upgrading of their assigned responsibilities by the presidents under whom they served, gradually made the office less of a joke and more of a sought-after stepping-stone for ambitious political figures. Bush's impending nomination would mark the seventh time in the last eight elections that one or more of the presidential nominees had first been vice president. And of the twenty-two individuals nominated for or holding the office since World War II, the overwhelming number were individuals who had credible credentials for the presidency, if it came to that. They included Republicans Nixon, Henry Cabot Lodge, Nelson Rockefeller, Bob Dole and Bush himself, and Democrats Barkley, John Sparkman, Estes Kefauver, Lyndon Johnson, Hubert Humphrey, Sargent Shriver and Walter Mondale. In all that time, it could be argued, there were only three vice presidential nominees whose qualifications could be seriously questioned in terms of preparedness to take over the presidency in crisis—Republicans William E. Miller in 1964 and Spiro T. Agnew in 1968 and Democrat Geraldine Ferraro in 1984.

One thing could be said for George Bush—he had been around a long time, and he knew who the most outstanding people in his party were. He said as soon as he had the nomination sewed up that his first yardstick in picking his running mate was whether that individual was qualified to take over as president. Then he wanted someone, he said, who would be philosophically compatible with him and would be as loyal to him as vice president as he had been to Reagan.

As early as March, as soon as it was clear he would be the nominee, Bush had been getting advice on how to go about choosing his running mate. One who volunteered his two cents was a man who had been on both ends of the choice—Nixon. One night he "slipped into town"—that was how our source described the arrival of a former president of the United States—and had dinner with the Bushes and Atwater in the vice president's residence at the old Naval Observatory. After dining, Bush and Nixon repaired to another room, where for about an hour Nixon gave Bush the benefit of his thinking. He told him, our source informed us later, (1) not to ignore or underestimate the right wing on the choice, because it had hurt him; (2) to be very hard-line on crime and on relations with the Soviet Union because that would help him with the right; (3) to develop an independent identity, but only after the convention; (4) to get Reagan to do as much campaigning as he could. In 1960, Nixon told Bush, Eisenhower didn't campaign much for him because, Mamie Eisenhower told him later, Eisenhower's doctors said he was not up to it. But the president himself, Nixon said, was aggravated at Nixon for not asking him. Ike, he said, thought he hadn't asked because Nixon felt he needed—like Bush now—to be seen as his own man.

Another source indicated that Nixon had advised Bush to float a large number of prospective nominees as a way to ingratiate himself among party leaders who could thenceforth boast that they had nearly become vice president. That, indeed, was precisely the scam Nixon himself had pulled off in both 1960 and 1968, when he intentionally created the impression that he was considering a large number of prospects. On both occasions he also asked a much larger group of Republicans for their advice on the choice, to massage them. In the end, in each case, Nixon then picked the man he wanted—Henry Cabot Lodge in 1960 and Spiro T. Agnew in 1968.

But Bush did not want to make a circus out of the selection, as it was in 1980 when Reagan seemed merely to settle for him after the much-ballyhooed vice presidential negotiations with Ford had collapsed. He was going to make his selection through a dignified process that would not demean either the choice or those bypassed. He assigned Bob Teeter to work out such a process and then had Teeter get memos from his principal advisers, from which a first list of about twenty names was culled. That list was then culled to about a dozen by Bush, including what Teeter acknowledged later were "a few decoys." That list in turn was pared to about seven or eight. And if qualification to be president was the first measurement, there were several obvious candidates.

One of the Republicans most clearly in that category was Dole. When Ford chose him as his running mate in 1976, there were no questions raised about his qualifications to sit in the Oval Office. He was an experienced and serious legislator and politician, and strong in the Farm Belt, if somewhat too acerbic for the tastes of some. His wit always amused the press, but many fellow Republicans didn't think he was all that funny. This was especially so when he turned his humor on them.

Nixon, in the depth of his Watergate woes and afterward, was a special Dole target. When, running for reelection, he was asked whether he wanted Nixon to campaign for him in Kansas, Dole replied that as far as he was concerned "I'd settle for a flyover in *Air Force One*." And, after Nixon's resignation, when Reagan invited the three living former presidents—Carter, Ford and Nixon—to represent him at the funeral of Egypt's Anwar Sadat, Dole described the trio as "See no evil, speak no evil—and evil."

Dole also was, like the Bush of the 1988 campaign, a conservative. But he had tarnished his reputation in 1976 with his slashing attacks at the opposition, especially his rantings about "Democrat wars" in his debate against vice presidential nominee Fritz Mondale. Although he had mellowed a great deal since then, the "Bad Bob" Dole had surfaced again, under considerable prodding from Bush's agents, in the 1988 primary campaign. Bush did not forget that encounter via television on the night of the New Hampshire primary when Dole instructed Tom Brokaw, also interviewing Bush on a remote hookup, to tell him to "stop lying about my record."

Dole, however, was first and foremost a pragmatic Republican. Once he was eliminated from the race, he pledged his support to Bush and returned to the hustings to campaign and raise money for the party and the prospective nominee at a number of party state conventions. "Nobody could ask the man to do more than he's done for me," Bush said at one point. He put his name on a fund-raising letter to eradicate Dole's 1988 campaign debt, telling recipients that "Bob Dole waged a valiant and spirited contest for president" and he counted him as a friend. Whether, given Dole's temperament, he could function loyally in Bush's shadow for four years was, however, the big question.

The second obvious prospect was Jack Kemp. He, too, was an experienced legislator and a conservative, and his selection would be seen as a reaching out by Bush to the party's right wing, to whom Kemp was the true ideological heir to Reagan—or at least to the Reagan they thought they had helped elect but who had often disappointed them. But Kemp like Dole had an independent streak, and his criticisms of the Reagan White House on economic and monetary matters, and his pressures for greater gestures to black America, grated on many in the administration. Beyond that, Kemp could talk your ear off—and did, at the drop of a discussion on matters dear to his heart.

"Kemp used to drive Bush nuts at leadership meetings with Reagan," a Bush insider told us. "He'd go on about taxes and SDI and never stop. He [Bush] would look at him like a guy looks at a nagging wife. You know Jack. He's rah-rah; Christ, he's all over you, and Bush likes a little flight distance." Another insider recalled Bush saying about Kemp: "He's such a pain in the ass. He's always pushing me."

But for all that, Kemp was an energetic and forceful politician, and he did have the right wing strongly in his corner. For that reason, when Kemp was trounced in Iowa and New Hampshire, Bush hoped the New Yorker would get out of the race and endorse him. Some House colleagues, however, pressed Kemp to stay in, and after more than two years of nonstop campaigning he insisted on going on. But when he was buried in South Carolina and then on Super Tuesday, Kemp agreed to quit. Before endorsing Bush, however, he wanted assurances of where Bush stood on the issues most important to him, including SDI, the Strategic Defense Initiative. "With Kemp, everything is issues," one of his strategists said, somewhat derisively.

In any event, Bush and Kemp met for breakfast, and Kemp came away, a Kemp insider told us, not sensing "any real commitment." Kemp told him, he said, that Bush "just kept asking me about a bunch of procedural type things—how was I going to do the endorsement." Bush and Kemp had another dinner meeting and the result was the same. Afterward, this Kemp insider told his candidate on the vice presidential nomination: "Jack, he's not going to pick you. You're just oil and water. It's not going to happen. And you have not proven in the campaign that you've got anybody out there—there's no great force of folks that are going to automatically jump on the ticket."

Another account of the Bush-Kemp breakfast suggests that Kemp wasn't the only one present unhappy with it. "It was cordial," this source told us, "but Kemp ended up lecturing Bush on SDI. He found out that Bush knew nothing about it. He urged Bush to get a decent briefing. The conversation aggravated Bush but he did get briefed. Three weeks later he came out for [deployment of] it. Kemp may have lost his chance of being vice president in the process but he didn't care. He got his ideas across." But at this juncture, Kemp was still on the list of obvious vice-presidential prospects.

Kemp himself said after the election that he thought the significance of his breakfast meeting with Bush in terms of the vice presidential selection had been greatly overblown. All he did at that meeting, he said, was suggest to Bush that he ought to look at the latest developments in SDI technology and consider trying the "Team A–Team B" concept that was used at the CIA when he was director to determine Soviet military capabilities and debate the pros and cons. Later on, Kemp said, "I heard I had overpushed on SDI." At the same time, he said, he recognized how his intensity affected some people. "You know me," he remarked, grinning. "Looking back, I can imagine at a [cabinet] meeting [someone saying] 'Goodness gracious, can you imagine having Kemp in this room?'"*

After Dole and Kemp, however, there was a big gap in the vice presidential list. The first step in Bush's review was the requesting of financial and bio-graphical information from Dole, Kemp and at least eight other prominent Republicans: Dole's wife, Elizabeth, Senators Alan Simpson of Wyoming, Pete Domenici of New Mexico, John Danforth of Missouri and Dan Quayle of Indiana, Governors John Sununu of New Hampshire and Carroll Campbell of South Carolina and former Governor Lamar Alexander of Tennessee. Two other big-state governors—George Deukmejian of California and James Thompson of Illinois—and new Attorney General Thornburgh were also said to be under consideration, although Deukmejian had said flatly he wasn't interested. Bush decided against Thornburgh because he had just been named to Reagan's Cab-inet, but one Bush strategist said later that Thornburgh would have been the best choice because with him Bush "could have put Pennsylvania in his pocket [and] it would have been all over."

Of all these, in spite of Bush's insistence that he was looking first for qualified individuals, some were clearly included for political window dressing. Sununu and Campbell were getting payoffs for helping him get the nomination; Elizabeth Dole was a sop to women and, maybe, her husband as well. Bush was known to like Simpson a great deal, and Domenici, Danforth and Alexander were all highly regarded on their records. As for Quayle, his name on the list was a mystery. He was regarded generally as a pedestrian legislator, and what Republican candidate needed help carrying Indiana? Bush knew Quayle mostly as this young senator who would often drop by at Bush's Capitol Hill office for the president of the Senate just to talk. Bush, said one insider later, was always "susceptible to Quayle's ass-kissing." But surely that wasn't any rec-ommendation to be a heartbeat away from the presidency.

*Kemp made this remark in an interview in his Capitol Hill office on the last day of his House service—before Bush asked him to join the Cabinet as his secretary of housing and urban development.

As the Republican convention prepared to open in New Orleans in mid-August, the speculation continued to center on Dole and Kemp. But because Bush was holding his cards extremely close to his vest, that's all it was—speculation. And there was still the old problem. On the eve of his nomination, Bush remained the subject of criticism that he had not yet stepped out from the shadow of Ronald Reagan. Perhaps in his selection of a running mate he might find a way to do so, and demonstrate at last that he was his own man.

A month earlier at a campaign stop in Greenville, South Carolina, told by reporters that many Republicans were waiting impatiently for his vice presidential pick, Bush had replied: "Tell them to cool their jets. I'll be out at the appropriate time to make that announcement, and it will be laden with suspense . . . and everybody will say, 'What a fantastic choice!'" Bush could not have known as he said those words how right he would be—but for the wrong reason.

25

Dan Quayle for What?

Ten days before the official opening of the Republican National Convention in New Orleans, the steady hand of Jim Baker finally took the reins of George Bush's presidential campaign. With Bush still trailing in the polls and talk about a lack of direction in the campaign, Bush with obvious pleasure introduced his new campaign chief at the Bush headquarters, just a block east of Baker's old office at the Treasury Building. The vice president announced at the same time that he would start working regularly out of the campaign headquarters, instead of in the West Wing of the White House two long blocks to the west. The two moves obviously sought to convey the same message: It was time to get down to serious business.*

Lee Atwater, as previously arranged, would continue to be the day-to-day manager of the campaign. His deft construction of the southern "firewall" that stopped all Republican challengers in their tracks in the South Carolina primary and then on Super Tuesday had secured his position against carpings about his youth and, some said, uncouth. The one valid criticism still heard was that so

---

*Bush actually worked out of a small office at the vice president's residence most of the time in the fall when he was not campaigning on the road.

much money was spent so early that Bush was unable to do the breadth of campaigning in the late spring and summer that might have kept Dukakis from building such a wide lead by June.

But Baker after the election came to Atwater's defense, telling us that the "front-loading" of heavy spending had been planned all along as part of the strategy to blow away the opposition early in the South. "That was a conscious decision to front-load," Baker said, "that this year it was different because of Super Tuesday." There were early discussions, he recalled, to make sure there was enough money left to run in Illinois and Wisconsin, and that was done, though as matters turned out Bush was in the clear by then. "It was consciously planned," he said, "that they were going to go for the quick kill and the early knockout because of the front-loading aspect of Super Tuesday."

In retrospect, Baker said, "it might have been a bit more judicious to say, 'Okay, let's go for the early kill, but let's at least save enough money so we can travel and we can be visible going into our convention, because there's going to be a long flat period.' " The front-loading, Baker conceded, did dry up the campaign's resources and consequently it was difficult maintaining any sort of momentum and managing to dominate the news after Dukakis himself had locked up the Democratic nomination. At the same time, he said, "I don't think there was anything that the campaign could have done to avoid the natural advantage that Dukakis had by running against Jesse Jackson every Tuesday after Bush had locked the [Republican] nomination up . . . and appear very moderate and appear like a winner."

With the Dukakis vulnerabilities as identified in the New Jersey focus group in hand, however, Bush had made the most of what travel money he had, and the controversy that was developing in the news media from their use kept those matters—principally the flag pledge and the prisoner furlough—before the voters. Now, as the convention platform committee met in New Orleans, Bush moved to put his early stamp on it with an unusual appearance. Taking note of the Democrats' decision to write a short platform setting forth general objectives, Bush called the result "a document of deceit" and Dukakis a deceitful candidate for ducking ideological differences with him and failing to spell out concrete proposals—a rather ironic charge coming from Bush. "He's the stealth candidate," Bush said. "For while he can't decide about the Stealth bomber, he favors instead stealth policies that can be neither seen nor heard. His campaign jets from place to place, but no issues show up on the radar screen."

Dukakis for his part refused again to rise to the bait. "George Bush has some of the highest negatives ever recorded in the history of American politics," he said, "and I think one of the reasons for it is people have seen his campaign as an essentially negative campaign."

The Republican platform committee, with Bush supporter John Tower keeping his menacing eyes riveted on what was going on, John Sununu as Bush's platform spokesman and Charlie Black behind the scenes deftly navigating the shoals, produced a longer document but one that did not box Bush in. It joined in the Dukakis-bashing with a vow that "we must never allow the presidency and the Department of Justice to fall in the hands of those who coddle hardened criminals and turn killers and rapists loose on the public." No names were mentioned, but readers were free to guess to whom it referred.

The platform turned out not to be essentially different from the 1984 version, with minor skirmishes on issues such as abortion, affirmative action and the Equal Rights Amendment, all of which the relatively few moderates on the committee lost, assuring a conflict-free convention week—or so the Bush strategists thought.

At the same time, Bush continued going after Dukakis, this time in Pennsylvania on the issue of crime. In Erie, he told the state chapter of the Fraternal Order of Police that his "first concerns are the protection of law-abiding citizens and the abuse of our system of constitutional protection by thugs who can hire smart lawyers and find the right judges to set them free." Without mentioning Dukakis by name he warned that "there are those like the ACLU [the American Civil Liberties Union of which Dukakis was, Bush repeatedly proclaimed, "a card-carrying member"] whose first concerns are the protection of criminals' rights and the potential abuse of power by the police." Thus was another "proof" of his opponent's softness on crime spotlighted in the campaign. And, he went on, again without mentioning Dukakis, "I think about the face that angers us all—the arrogant face of a criminal, back on the street once more because of a permissive plea bargain or some furlough."

In a press conference in Pittsburgh, though, Bush insisted that he was going to "be positive" at the Republican convention about to open. "But I can't guarantee that somebody is not going to take a swipe at Michael Dukakis," he added. "I have a lot of friends out there, and they didn't like the vicious, personal attacks [against Bush in Atlanta]. I did not react to them, but I can't control everybody."

Public-opinion polls taken in advance of the Republican convention were now indicating that Bush's negative campaigning was, indeed, paying off. The Gallup poll showed Dukakis' lead had slipped to only 49 percent to 42, and an NBC News-*Wall Street Journal* survey had it down to ten points. The Gallup poll also found that Dukakis' unfavorable ratings had risen from the teens to 30. It was still lower than the 41 percent unfavorable for Bush, but the trend line clearly was going in the direction the Bush strategists—and their willing candidate on the stump—had been working so diligently toward.

In the week before the convention officially opened in the Superdome, many of the Bush strategists arrived in New Orleans for the platform deliberations, to help with convention arrangements or just to keep their ears to the ground. Among them was Jim Lake, Reagan's 1984 campaign press secretary and a man with a lot of friends and a lot of credibility in the press corps. As soon as he arrived on Wednesday in his capacity as the Bush director of communications, he started to hear speculation about Quayle.

On the Friday night before the opening of the convention, Lake and his wife had dinner at Le Ruth's, a swank restaurant across the Mississippi in Gretna, with four reporters—Susan Page of *Newsday*, her husband, Carl Leubsdorf, of the *Dallas Morning News*, John Mashek, then of the *Atlanta Constitution* and now of the *Boston Globe*, and Tom Ottenad of the *St. Louis Post-Dispatch*. In the course of conversation they started to review the names of those being mentioned as Bush's running mate. "Come on now, Lake," he later recalled one of the reporters saying, "you can't be really serious about Quayle." Lake replied that he knew Quayle was on the list "like everybody else, but I don't know whether he's serious about him or not. I don't have any particular inside knowledge."

The notion of Quayle seemed preposterous to the reporters around the table. "God, if you do that," Lake remembered one of them saying, "there are going to be all these stories about Paula Parkinson and what a lightweight [Quayle was]." Parkinson was the female lobbyist who once posed nude for *Playboy* magazine and was part of a party that also included Quayle at a Florida golfing resort one weekend in 1980. Quayle said later he had played golf and left the day after she arrived. He was not accused of having been involved with her and the story did not hinder his overwhelming Senate reelection. As for the "lightweight" reference, Quayle's reputation in the Washington press corps was that, as Lyndon Johnson once said of Gerald Ford, he couldn't walk and chew gum at the same time.

These matters were speculated on around the table and the conversation made an impression on Lake. "Those were the very thoughts I'd had on the three other days of the week that I'd been hearing these stories," Lake said, "and I got to thinking—'They [the Bush insiders] can't be really serious about this.' To make sure, on Saturday morning I called Craig Fuller. He was stuck in the White House." Lake told Fuller: "Look, it's none of my business, nobody asked me about vice president, but I feel compelled to offer an opinion. . . . You know, the last couple of days there've been a lot of stories about Quayle." Lake repeated the dinner conversation and told Fuller that these were reporters he respected and "they were exactly right" about the storm that a Quayle selection would kick up. Fuller thanked him for passing the conversation on, Lake said, and then told him, "I think we're beyond that." But Fuller suggested Lake tell Teeter what he had heard.

Lake called Bob Teeter, heavily involved in the selection process, at the Jefferson Hotel in Washington and, Lake said, "I got from him feedback that sounded very much like he agreed. In fact, I had no doubt he agreed." Teeter asked him whether he had passed the story on to Roger Ailes. Lake said no. Had he told Bush? Lake again said no but would if Teeter thought he ought to. Teeter said he'd let Lake know "if I think it's necessary." That reply, Lake said later, gave him "the distinct impression that Quayle was not his candidate, although he got a lot of credit for him being his candidate."

The next morning, Sunday, Lake attended a meeting on convention matters at which Ailes was present. When Ailes got up and walked out at one point, Lake followed him out, stopped him in the hall and gave him the same report. Ailes said he had had Quayle as a client, thought he'd be a good choice but said he wasn't pushing for him and had no idea he had any more of a chance than any of the others. Lake replied: "Quayle's a fine guy, but we'll face two or three weeks of Paula Parkinson and lightweight. Do we want to come out of the convention with that? I don't think so." And that's where Lake left it. He figured he'd done what he could.

Another who was hearing Quayle's name bandied about and was incredulous that he could be under serious consideration was Ed Rollins, the 1984 Reagan-Bush campaign manager who had been in Kemp's corner this time around. On Friday, Rollins got word from an Indiana source that Bush's friend and onetime, short-time New Jersey Senator Nick Brady had been in to see Quayle and to check on him with other senators. "You don't send Nick Brady, who had been a part-time senator, up to say, 'Gee, what do you think of Dan Quayle?'" Rollins said later. "Guys just don't know Brady that well. It's not like they're going to say, 'The guy's a fuckin' lightweight, what are you doing?' It wasn't like if it had been a Laxalt or somebody who had been around there twenty years who really had their confidence. . . . The problem was you could take any group of political reporters or any group of political people in this town, put them down and just say, 'Hey, what do you think of Dan Quayle? I'm really serious about putting him on the ticket.' In thirty five seconds you'd have it all out there. There wouldn't have been a person in the room stand up [for his selection]."

The fact was, however, that Bush did hold just such a meeting of political people that Friday afternoon in his office in the Executive Office Building. Attending were Atwater, Teeter, Ailes, Fuller, Brady and Sheila Tate, Bush's campaign press secretary. It lasted for two and a half hours and the subject was the vice presidential selection. Bush, according to one who attended, asked each of those in the room to list his or her top three choices and say why, and then sat with "a poker face" listening intently. Seven prospective candidates were prominently mentioned: Bob and Elizabeth Dole, Jack Kemp, Pete Domenici, John Danforth, Alan Simpson and Dan Quayle. And while there was no sweeping consensus for any one of them, the one most often proposed by this knowledgeable circle of political pros was Quayle. He was first on Fuller's and Ailes' lists, and lower on Atwater's and Teeter's. If any of them was concerned about the Paula Parkinson story or Quayle's military service, it didn't come up in any memorable way.

In New Orleans, the convention opened in festive spirit. Banjo strummers, trumpet players and strutters waving open umbrellas greeted conventioneers as they poured off their planes into the airport. Downtown, paddle-wheel boats cruised up and down the Mississippi packed with revelers. The lobbies of the city's new and old hotels overflowed with exuberant Republicans looking forward to a week of extravagant eating in some of the country's best restaurants and drinking in some of its most colorful saloons. Everything seemed in place for a smooth celebration, from an inoffensive platform to an inoffensive candidate, and if neither promised to set the convention ablaze, it would at least be harmonious, with few distractions from the temptations of the nation's capital of Epicureanism.

As often happens at such events, one temporarily jarring note was sounded in an exclusive story in the *New York Post*. The turret gunner of a plane involved in the 1944 mission in which Bush's own plane was shot down claimed that Bush, who bailed out and later was picked up by an American submarine, could have averted the crash and saved the lives of his crew by ditching the plane in the Pacific. The man, Chester Mierzejewski, said he saw no fire in the plane from a Japanese attack, as Bush claimed, but only "a puff of smoke." The story created a furor at the Hyatt Regency Hotel across from the Superdome, the press headquarters where hundreds of reporters milled in search of a story that would ignite the convention.

The Bush campaign promptly released an intelligence report of the mission stating that "after releasing his bombs, Lt. (jg) Bush turned sharply to the east to clear the island [Chichi Jima, his target, 600 miles southwest of Japan], smoke and flames enveloping his engine and spreading aft as he did so and his plane losing altitude. . . ." The report said Bush and another crew member had bailed out but the other's parachute failed to open. Reporters at the convention who contacted the former gunner were told by him that Bush later had told him he had tried to contact his two crew members before bailing out but they didn't reply and he was sure they were dead. "I have to give him the benefit of the doubt," Mierzejewski said. "I can't prove otherwise."

Dukakis promptly said it was "unfortunate" that such a story had surfaced and he commended Bush for "enormous courage and tremendous patriotism" as a combat pilot in World War II. "I don't think that kind of thing has any place in the campaign," he said. "This is a man who flew fifty-eight missions and did so with great valor and great courage."

By the next day, the story was lost in the convention fever, raised to a boiling point by the arrival Sunday of the man who had brought the Republican Party back to political prosperity, Ronald Reagan. How effectively Reagan in less than eight years had sent packing the few liberals and moderates in the party was seen in the platform. And his personal popularity within the party, and among the public, seemed as high as ever as a mob packed the New Orleans Convention Center to hear him on his arrival. He got the Democratic-bashing going by calling the opposition's convention in Atlanta "the biggest masquerade since last year's Mardi Gras" and warned that although the Democrats had "started using our words and slogans" they remained "a party still marked by "strident liberalism and negativism." The country, he said, "needs the strength, vision and true grit of George Bush." The convention, meanwhile, waited to see all three demonstrated in Bush's acceptance speech, which now approached as his one opportunity, after months of trying, to establish himself as his "own man."

As Reagan worked his charm on New Orleans, Bush stayed back in Washington honing his acceptance speech and weighing the matter of his vice presidential selection. Jim Baker and Bob Teeter conferred with him, but he alone, from all reports, pored over the financial and biographical information on prospective running mates gathered for him by Robert Kimmitt, the Washington lawyer and Baker associate assigned to the task. That isolation in making this very critical decision later drew much criticism, especially in light of Bush's eventual choice. But he had no apologies after the election for how he had gone about it. He said, however, that protecting the feelings of those passed over was an important factor to him in keeping the selection procedure close to his vest. "I am confident the process worked well," Bush said. "Bob Kimmitt did a thorough job and the process did not result in humiliating semi-public interview sessions that, in my view, damage those who are not selected. I had several meetings with top advisers in which I kept my own notes, so I could go back as things unfolded, to check on the pros and cons of each suggested potential nominee."

On Sunday morning, three of the hopefuls on the list—Dole and Kemp, who were thought to have the inside track, and Quayle, dismissed by many as a long shot took to the television talk shows to make their cases. Kemp sought to portray Bush as an enthusiastic supporter of SDI while privately harboring doubts; Dole played down his personal differences with the nominee, painting himself as a team player; Quayle demonstrated some talent as an attack dog, castigating the Democrats as "a party of gloom and doom" that under Dukakis would "send this nation into retreat." The appearances of the three intensified talk of their chances. Another senator being mentioned, Alan Simpson, took himself out of contention on another Sunday talk show, saying his pro-choice position on abortion would make him a liability.

Reagan's farewell speech on Monday night in the Superdome was the emotional magnet the convention planners knew it would be. One of their concerns in planning the convention, in fact, was that the retiring president would so outshine the nominee that Bush might leave New Orleans still in Reagan's shadow. But Reagan did his part to signal the change of the guard, declaring that he would be "a foot soldier" in the campaign to elect Bush, and he implored the delegates and the nation watching on television—one more time—to "go out there and win one for the Gipper." In obvious retort to the taunt at the Democratic convention of "Where was George?" Reagan told the assembled Republicans that "George played a major role in everything we've accomplished. . . . George was there." Without Bush succeeding him, he said, "everything we have achieved will be at risk." And for all that speculation about what Bush did or didn't tell him in their private weekly White House meetings, Reagan said: "The George Bush I've seen up close, when the staff and cabinet members have closed the door and when the two of us are alone, [is] someone who's not afraid to speak his mind and who can cut to the core of an issue." This was not the occasion, though, to disclose what Bush had said to him, so that little mystery remained safe.

Bush was back in Washington at the vice president's residence that night, dining with friends and watching the festivities on television. At one point a reporter from Topeka was shown asking Bob Dole at a Kansas delegation reception whether he didn't think the vice presidential selection process was a bit "demeaning," being stretched out as it was. Dole acknowledged he had reservations about the whole thing. Pete Teeley, one of Bush's dinner guests, watched the vice president as Dole's exchange with the reporter played on the screen. Bush, who several times had said publicly he wanted the process to be dignified for those under consideration, said nothing. But Teeley as a longtime Bush-watcher got the picture. "I thought to myself," he said later, "that really ends it for Dole." Kemp on the other hand gave a good speech that night and Teeley thought Bush was impressed, although he said nothing about that either. On the way home, Teeley's wife asked him: "What do you think?" Teeley answered: "I think it's Kemp." He said later: "I thought Dole had taken himself out of it and it would go to Kemp."

Roger Ailes, who was also there that night, agreed about the Dole part. When his response about the "demeaning" process came on over television at Bush's house, Ailes said, "I saw him [Bush] look at the set. . . . His body language said everything he needed to say."

Dole indeed was less than enthusiastic about the whole vice presidential selection process. When Bush called him originally to ask him to fill out the financial questionnaire, Dole told us after the election, "I said, 'I'll fill them out if they don't cost any money.' Because you had to go to these accountants, and that's about five hundred bucks an hour." Dole had it done anyway and answered some additional questions from Kimmitt, but when he hadn't heard anything as the convention approached, he said, "I tried to send word to Bush through Jim Baker about two and half weeks before New Orleans that I'd be very happy just to issue a one-line statement that I had no interest in the number two spot, and I was willing to help Bush in any way he wants as Republican leader or whatever. But I don't want to go down to New Orleans and grovel around down there for the second spot. I assume that message was conveyed, and the fact I never heard from Bush led me to believe he must have had someone else in mind."

As for his response to the question from the Kansas reporter about whether he thought the process was "demeaning," Dole recalled, "that hit the fan" in the convention hall. One of the networks in short order was reporting that Dole had taken himself out of consideration. Jim Lake and Charlie Black rushed up to his sky box at the convention hall, where he had gone after the Kansas reception, to calm him down. After the election, Dole reflected on the episode. "You have to watch these state reporters going after a big story," he said. "It might have cost me the second spot." And he laughed. But apparently it was no laughing matter to George Bush.

The incident, however, may have played a role in accelerating the announcement process. According to Bush insiders, he began to balk at the previously agreed timetable worked out to generate maximum television coverage.

That plan was for Bush to withhold his choice until the final day of the convention, Thursday, break the news at a breakfast meeting of the Texas delegation and then hold a full-fledged press conference. But maybe Dole was right; maybe the process was demeaning. It began to eat at him.

Meanwhile, in New Orleans, the concern that Reagan would outshine Bush so nagged at the convention organizers that for a time the plan was for Reagan to get in and out of New Orleans before Bush arrived on Tuesday morning, so that the contrast would not be measured by the news media. Finally, though, the strategists decided that not having them meet and appear together would be more embarrassing, and draw more negative press reaction, than if they met and Bush was eclipsed one more time. As a middle ground, it was decided that with *Air Force Two* bearing Bush coming into New Orleans at Belle Chasse Naval Air Station and Reagan on *Air Force One* leaving from there, the simplest solution was for the two men to meet briefly there and then Reagan would depart. Bush would then have the stage all to himself to play out the planned vice presidential scenario at his leisure.

On the flight down to New Orleans, however, Bush continued to champ at the timetable. He told Baker, Teeter and Fuller he had made up his mind before he got on the plane—but he didn't tell them who it was. They told him if that was the case, he ought to tell the press pool accompanying him, and so he walked up and did so. The reporters thereupon reminded him of Dole's remark about a "demeaning" process. Bush said he didn't think it was, but obviously he worried about it. He returned to the front of the plane and again told his chief aides he wanted to speed up the process. He had made up his mind to make the announcement that day, on arrival, and end the suspense for all concerned.

At one point, Baker, Teeter, Fuller and Ailes had a betting pool on the choice, putting their guesses in slips of paper that Teeter collected and held. Nobody, Teeter said later, had the winner.

When the plane landed, Bush talked to Reagan briefly on the tarmac, whispering his choice to him. Reagan played the straight man, telling reporters as he was leaving: "I just tried to make a deal with George—that I'd tell him where to find the best blackened redfish if he'd tell me who's going to be vice president." He didn't let on that he now knew.

When Reagan finished his remarks, Bush inadvertently gave the convention press corps something to chew on for the next several hours that had nothing to do with his choice of a running mate. He and his wife called over three of their grandchildren, the children of their son Jeb and his Hispanic-American wife, Columba, to meet the Reagans. In telling them of the approaching children, Bush was heard to refer to them as "the little brown ones." The remark set off a temporary flurry over Bush's well-documented penchant for putting his foot in his mouth, and he later reacted in anger to any suggestions that he meant the comment in any derogatory way. "Those grandchildren are my pride and joy and when I say pride I mean it," he declared.

When the Reagans left, Bush adjourned to an admiral's house at the

naval station with Baker, Teeter, Fuller, Atwater, Ailes and Margaret Tutwiler, Baker's deputy. Bush had told Baker of his choice, but none of the
others in the party. At Bush's instruction, Fuller started placing calls to the
losers, and Bush got on the phone himself to break the news—but only that
the individual being called was not being selected. Fuller told others later that
he had placed half the calls before he himself knew who the choice was. It
was, apparently, like the countdown at the Miss America pageant—"and the
fourth runner-up is——"

When Dole got his call from Bush, he recalled later, Bush told him only
that "it's really been a tough decision. I've thought about it a lot. I've just
decided to go another way." Bush, Dole said, "indicated it was between me
and this other way." Bush didn't say who "the other way" was, but Dole
assumed it was Pete Domenici and after Bush hung up Dole tried to reach
Domenici. When he found out later the choice was Quayle, he said, "I must
say it was a stunner."

After Bush told him he wasn't been tapped, Dole said, "he asked for
Elizabeth—so I think he wanted to save a dime. I said, 'No, I'll have her call
you back.' " His wife called Bush and also was told she had been passed by.
"I don't think she ever thought it would be her," Dole said, "but you always
kind of wonder if it's a big game. You get a woman in there, you get your
chief adversary and then you throw in a few others and you let Ailes make the
decision." Dole said he had heard that Ailes had threatened to quit if Bush
picked him, and also that after Bush had surveyed Senate and House Republicans
and they were all heavily for Dole, Quayle was not on the original list "and
Ailes penciled his name in."

Why did Dole want to be the vice presidential nominee, after all? It was
no secret that he didn't hold Bush in very high regard and was still bitter about
Ailes' "straddle" ad on taxes in New Hampshire that he believed had done
him in.* And he was Republican leader in the Senate, where he had an independent voice. It was hard to picture him as anybody's yes-man, let alone
George Bush's. But an even stronger Senate leader, Lyndon Johnson, had agreed
to run for vice president; there was always that possibility that lightning would
strike.

"You get to be my age," Dole said later, "you sort of look at it maybe
as the last chance you're ever gonna get the other." But, he added, "I never
worried about it, I wasn't losing any sleep over it. I felt from the standpoint
of being effective, you're going to be better in the leader's office." Still, he
said, he could have helped the ticket in the Midwest and, once elected, could
have helped Bush deal with the "tough guys" in both parties in the Senate who
respected him and who were his friends.

---

*After the election, Dole was talking to us about President-elect Bush's deficit-reduction dilemma.
"He's got to come to me on a tax increase," he said. "He beat me up enough on that in New Hampshire."
He was referring obviously to Ailes' television commercial aired over the last weekend. "I didn't care
much for his 'straddle' ad," he said.

Back at the admiral's house at the naval air station, Bush made the final call—to Senator J. Danforth Quayle of Indiana. Bush told him, according to Baker, he was "the first choice and my only choice" and Quayle didn't need any time to reply. He, like the rest of the political world when the news got out, was stunned, but beside himself with joy.

Later, some Bush insiders speculated that Quayle made the final cut more out of the process of elimination than as a positive Bush selection, especially if the two most orthodox choices, Dole and Kemp, were bypassed. Ailes had written Bush a memo at one point urging him, in Ailes' words later, to "throw a few long balls" to inject some excitement into the convention. And picking Dan Quayle certainly qualified.

Quayle was instructed to meet the paddle-wheel *Natchez* that was bringing Bush down the Mississippi to Spanish Plaza at the foot of downtown New Orleans, where Bush would announce the decision.

Among those waiting with considerable interest in that decision were two old Republican battle horses who had signed up to handle the campaign of the vice president, whoever he or she turned out to be. One was Stuart Spencer, the veteran California political consultant who was far and away the party's best troubleshooter. He had traveled in 1976 with Gerald Ford and in 1980 and 1984 with Ronald Reagan, applying the best political antenna in the business to spot trouble as soon as or even before it happened. He was brash but good-natured and he didn't hesitate to tell a candidate, even if that candidate was the president of the United States, that he had screwed up.

Spencer was tired, however, of the job of muzzling presidential candidates who spoke before they thought. Back in May, he and Atwater took a long walk in Beverly Hills one day and then sat on a park bench and discussed what role Spencer might play in the fall campaign. Spencer said he wanted to manage the vice presidential campaign because in his mind it had never been done right. "No matter how simple it looks or how easy it looks," Atwater recalled Spencer telling him then, "the shit always hits the fan." Atwater didn't think much about the observation at the time, but he readily agreed to Spencer's offer, though saddling him with the vice presidential candidate seemed to some others like a waste of Spencer's talent.

The other old veteran awaiting the decision was Joe Canzeri, a longtime political and campaign aide to Nelson Rockefeller who had worked often with Spencer in past national campaigns and had been in the Reagan White House for a time before starting a lucrative public-relations firm in Washington. A week or so earlier, Spencer had called Canzeri and told him: "We're gonna do a different job this time—the vice president." Canzeri asked: "Who's the candidate?" Spencer replied: "Hell, I don't know."

On the morning of Bush's arrival in New Orleans, Spencer and Canzeri were in Spencer's suite at the Marriott awaiting word. Spencer, according to Canzeri, was pushing Domenici, like himself a westerner. The two designated vice presidential handlers were watching out their hotel window as Bush's riverboat was docking when the word came over television that the choice was Quayle. Spencer turned to Canzeri. "Do you know anything about this guy?" he asked. Canzeri said he had met him a couple of times and that "he's a senator from Indiana." As they talked, watching Bush's arrival on the television screen, Canzeri recalled, "all of a sudden he [Quayle] came up on the platform and the first thing he did was grab Bush. And Stu says, 'Well, we gotta correct that.' " Spencer said later he was "surprised but not shocked" at the choice because he knew Quayle was on the list of eight finalists. Of Quayle's manner of greeting Bush, he said, "I thought he was pretty hyper."

On the dock, the heat of the day was oppressive. Both men stood in their shirt sleeves, Bush without a tie as he announced his surprise choice—"a young man born in the middle of this century and from the middle of this country . . . a leader in matters of national security . . . a man of the future." Quayle was absolutely giddy with happiness, grabbing his benefactor by the shoulder and repeatedly hugging his arm, gamboling around the platform like the jackpot winner on a television game show.

The bizarre scene was reminiscent of the memorable moment at the 1972 Republican National Convention in Miami when entertainer Sammy Davis, Jr., came up behind President Richard Nixon and gave him a full-blown bear hug. Quayle wasted no time jumping into the role of cheerleader, extolling the virtues of the man who had just propelled him squarely onto the political stage and exhorting the crowd to leap into the fray against the Democrats. "Let's go get 'em!" he yelled. "All right? You got it?"

Bush himself looked on a bit thunderstruck at the display of juvenile enthusiasm he had unleashed. His reaction, too, was reminiscent of another scene between a presidential nominee and his running mate, maybe the most bizarre we have ever covered over the course of eight presidential campaigns. It took place in a Pittsburgh hotel ballroom in 1968 when independent candidate George Wallace introduced his vice presidential choice—retired Air Force Chief of Staff Curtis LeMay. LeMay was a former head of the Strategic Air Command, the American airborne nuclear attack arm, whose hard-line attitude inspired the motto "Bombs Away with Curt LeMay," and his first remarks indicated why.

"We seem to have a phobia about nuclear weapons," he said as Wallace stood by, proud of his acquisition. "I think most military men think it's just another weapon in the arsenal," LeMay went on. "The smart thing to do when you're in a war—hopefully you prevent it. Stay out of it if you can. But when you get in it, get in it with both feet and get it over with." Wallace had no trouble with that. He felt the same and had said so many times.

But LeMay wasn't through. He proceeded to debunk as "propaganda" all those reports that nuclear explosions caused permanent and hereditary damage to human and plant life. He cited tests at the Bikini atoll in the Pacific, telling of movies taken after the blasts. "The fish are all back in the lagoons," he said, "the coconut trees are growing coconuts, the guava bushes have fruit on them, the birds are back. As a matter of fact, everything is about the same except the land crabs. They get minerals from the soil, I guess, through their shells, and the land crabs were a little bit hot, and there's a little question about whether you should eat a land crab or not." Wallace began to squirm, but LeMay pressed on.

The rats on the atoll, he reported with the straightest and sternest of faces, were also "bigger, fatter and healthier than they ever were." Now, while it was true that a nuclear war would be "horrible," the general conceded, there really wasn't any difference between getting killed by a nuclear bomb or by a "rusty knife" in Vietnam. "As a matter of fact," he proclaimed, crowning his remarks, "if I had a choice I'd rather be killed by a nuclear weapon."

A thoroughly appalled and shell-shocked Wallace finally stepped in to try to salvage the disaster. He told the guffawing reporters that LeMay wasn't advocating the use of nuclear weapons at all. But LeMay stepped in again to say that was true, but "if I found it necessary I would use anything we could dream up. . . ." For the rest of the campaign, Wallace spent a fair amount of time trying to explain away old "Bombs Away LeMay." Compared to that scene, young Danny Quayle's joyous cavorting around the platform in New Orleans was nothing for George Bush to worry about.

Nevertheless, the convention city was immediately abuzz with criticism of Bush's choice and speculation on what had possessed him to make it. He had promised to pick the man best qualified, or at least qualified, to become president if anything happened to him. And that man was "Danny" Quayle? Even the most loyal professional hacks had trouble keeping a straight face on that one. Bush himself indicated he wanted to reach out to the younger generation. When we asked him after the election for the one deciding factor in his choice, he said Quayle "represents the next generation and the future. I felt that his experience in defense matters and his sponsorship of the Job Training Partnership Act would be strong pluses. I liked the fact that he had served in both the House and Senate." But others said Ailes and Teeter, both of whom had had Quayle as a client in his Senate campaigns, had talked Bush into it; each denied it. Still others speculated that Bush above all wanted a vice president who would serve in the mold of unswerving loyalty that his own performance in the job had set—that he wanted a George Bush's George Bush. If that was the case, he seemed to have picked unerringly in Dan Quayle.

Up in Spencer's suite, he and Canzeri had reason to think they had signed on to the wrong part of the campaign. Spencer said later: "I realized he was jumping from 'A' ball to the major leagues in baseball terms, but he had run good races in Indiana." Shortly after the announcement scene on television, Spencer got a call to go to Jim Baker's suite in the same hotel. And shortly after that, Spencer called Canzeri. "Joey," he said, "get up and get your candidate." Canzeri took Quayle and his newly assigned Secret Service contingent, drove over to Quayle's hotel, packed him up and moved him to the Westin Hotel, which had better campaign communications facilities. "He seemed to be a decent guy," Canzeri said. "There was a little fear in his eyes, I saw that."

That night, Spencer and Canzeri, and former White House political director

Mitch Daniels, who was from Indiana, had dinner with Quayle at the hotel. "We filled him in on what to expect and what was going to happen and so forth," Canzeri said. "He didn't really know what he was going to do, but he liked the idea that he had a bunch of keepers or handlers." Not being clairvoyants, though, they weren't really able to prepare Quayle for what was about to come crashing down on him, and them.

Although the new team of Bush and Quayle was not anything like the old one of Wallace and LeMay, the first Bush-Quayle joint press conference the next morning at the Marriott Hotel nevertheless had its unfortunate moments. Bush and Quayle encountered questions—and Quayle provided answers—that gave both of them considerable cause for concern, and sent the Bush strategists into a full-fledged exercise in damage control.

One of the first issues raised was the Paula Parkinson weekend, and Quayle did not handle it well at all. Asked whether it was accurate that he had met her only once and played golf the rest of the time—the official line his office had put out—Quayle haughtily and inexplicably replied: "No." Well, then, what was accurate? "That has been covered and there's nothing to it," he shot back. Had he ever seen the woman on another occasion? "No," he snapped.

Quayle got on his high horse as well when questioned about reports that contra resupply meetings were held by associates of Oliver North in his Senate office and whether he had ever discussed contra resupply with Bush. "No," he replied indignantly, "and the question is off base as far as those meetings going on."

The major stumbling block in the press conference, however, came when a reporter told Quayle that Democrats were already pointing out that although he was "someone who says he's tough on defense" he "didn't fight in the Vietnam War." Did he think that was a low blow? In the same lofty vein, Quayle called the comment "a cheap shot," adding: "I have a deep affection for those men and women who sacrificed their lives in Vietnam, and for anybody to imply anything different is just simply wrong." The question, however, was not Quayle's affection for those who went to Vietnam, but why he himself, of service age, hadn't gone with them.

Pressed on why he had chosen to go into the National Guard in 1969, which then was widely regarded as a haven for those who didn't want to go to Vietnam, Quayle proceeded to paint himself as a small-town boy who grew up thinking about his future—getting married, going to law school, raising a family—and trying to fulfill those plans. "I did not know in 1969 that I would be in this room today," he said, in the most revealing—and damaging—remark of the press conference. The clear implication was that had Quayle known his actions would be of potential damage to a future political career, he would have acted differently. Compounding the apparent callousness was the fact that Quayle in the House and Senate was a hawk on the Vietnam War and on military affairs generally. As if to temper the curse somewhat, Quayle gratuitously threw in that his brother did go into the Marine Corps during the Vietnam War.

At another point, Quayle was asked whether he was going to be the Republican ticket's "pit bull," going after the Democrats in the customary attack role of a vice presidential nominee. Quayle denied it, but Bush stepped in. "We're going to tell the truth," he said, "and it's going to seem like they've engaged a couple of pit bulls." That was a promise that in due time would be kept with a vengeance.

The Bush strategists, watching the Quayle performance, knew at once that they had an Indiana monkey on their backs. And they knew at the same time that after all the questions raised about Bush's judgment in selecting him, they couldn't simply toss him off; they at least had to teach him how to ride side-saddle. In the whole campaign year, this was a moment that separated the men from the boys. From all signs, the presidential nominee had royally screwed up. The one basic axiom in the selection of a running mate was that if he could bring something positive to the ticket, fine, but it probably wouldn't be much. The main thing was that he not do anything to hurt the ticket. And here in the very first hours of the Bush-Quayle ticket it was thrown back on the seat of its pants, on the defensive. The rhubarb threatened to detract from Bush's nomination that night and his acceptance speech the following night, the speech that was already being billed and depended upon—as the vehicle by which George Bush would at last step out of Ronald Reagan's shadow.

Spencer later sized up the situation as a huge press corps at the convention without a story and with a candidate they knew little about. "The first question was 'Who he?' " Spencer said, "and then the fifteen thousand-plus animals down there started asking 'What he?'—trying to win a Pulitzer Prize. There were charges flying everywhere."

All afternoon the Bush strategists dealt with the press inquiries about Quayle's National Guard service. In the course of Kimmitt's review of his record, Quayle had been asked about his military service and had said exactly what it was. When he was asked whether there was anything in his background that could be politically damaging, he said no. The matter of his military record had come up in his successful challenge of Democratic Senator Birch Bayh but he won and six years later was overwhelmingly reelected. It was understandable that he would believe that the issue was behind him. "He wasn't holding back," Spencer said later. "It was so long ago. He forgot."

But still the questions came, and criticisms from Vietnam veterans' groups charging that Quayle had joined the Indiana Guard to stay out of Vietnam and further his education. And coming from a rich and influential Indiana family that owned the *Indianapolis Star* and *News*, the state's most powerful newspapers, questions were being asked about how he got into the Guard in the first place. Was he given special treatment?

In the hope of nipping the problem in the bud, it was decided to have Quayle appear on each of the four networks that night before the roll call of the states that would officially make Bush the party's presidential nominee. After some coaching, Quayle made the rounds of NBC, CBS, ABC and CNN with Jim Lake as his handler. "I felt sorry for the guy to a degree," Spencer said. "He didn't know anybody around him. There were all these strange faces, but he was very cooperative." In the first of the interviews, Tom Brokaw in the NBC sky booth asked whether he had received any help getting into the Guard. Quayle said it was twenty years earlier but maybe "phone calls were made." That response opened the door. When Quayle and Lake left the booth Lake told him: "You know, if you know calls were made, you ought to say what they were. But if you don't know they were, you shouldn't go speculating."

In the next interview, in the CBS sky booth, Dan Rather asked Quayle what his worst fear was. "Paula Parkinson," he replied, as Lake's eyes rolled to the ceiling. When they came out, Quayle said to his keeper: "I know, I know, I shouldn't have volunteered Paula Parkinson." Lake suggested to him that he might have thought of some other "worst fear." The next two interviews, with CNN's Bernard Shaw and ABC's Peter Jennings, went fine, Lake said later, but after the round of the network booths "he had two more lumps . . . by the time the convention was over that night, we were in deep soup, not so much on Paula Parkinson but because maybe some calls were made."

Almost lost in the shuffle was the convention roll call that at the end gave Bush the presidential nomination by acclamation. To the political pros, one of the worst sins that could be committed by a campaign was to "step on your own story"—to permit something to happen that overshadowed an event that otherwise would cast the candidate in a very favorable light. It was happening, in spades, and it could happen again, at much greater cost to the candidate, on the next night when Bush was scheduled to give his acceptance speech.

Now was the time to see what the candidate, and his campaign, were made of. Unlike the Dukakis hierarchy, which was essentially Boston-grown, a collection of political jockeys essentially in the race to boot one horse, Michael Dukakis, home, the Bush brain trust was the all-star team of the Republican Party. By Atwater's count, some twenty-eight members of the staff had been in three or more presidential campaigns, and those at the top were battle-hardened. According to Lake, who was involved in most of the damage-control meetings, no one was critical of Quayle or of Bush for picking him, in spite of the obvious danger signals. Lake expressed the mood as the Bush strategists gathered after the press conference to deal with the trouble:

"What any one or two people may have said to each other privately, I don't know about. In fact it was amazing—very damn little second-guessing that I heard. The fact is, when you're in this, you're in it. If you're professionals [you say] 'How do we get out of here?' You don't get into recriminations and pissing and moaning. That night it was, 'We're in deep shit. How do we get out? We gotta run down all the tracks.' "

Immediately after the final gavel that night, the top hierarchy of the Bush campaign gathered in the Marriott Hotel suite of Jim Baker. Among those present with Baker were Atwater, Spencer, Dick Darman, Baker's old White

House and Treasury sidekick; Kimmitt, Lake, Charlie Black, Paul Manafort and Margaret Tutwiler, Baker's deputy. Baker had already called Quayle and told him the campaign needed answers from him because they were all facing "a fire storm" the next day over what he had said to the networks. Darman and Kimmitt were dispatched to Quayle's suite. The others exchanged reports of what they had heard being talked about and asked about on the convention floor and by reporters. "We had to talk through the things we knew, the things we didn't know, what our options were," Lake recalled. "Everybody agreed, we had to find out the answers; we didn't know the answers."

When Darman and Kimmitt finally returned, Lake said, "they didn't know much more. But they felt better. They felt he wasn't lying about anything or hadn't lied, and they felt that he probably hadn't done anything out of the ordinary or improper." Quayle's father was awakened and interrogated about what actions he had taken. To get more answers, assignments were given to those in Baker's suite to make various phone calls around. The meeting went on until about 3:30 A.M. when the participants broke for a little sleep. Baker appeared on early morning network television to express confidence in Quayle and to say a full explanation of his military service was being prepared. Others of the hierarchy reconvened in Atwater's suite at 6 A.M. and stayed there all day getting and sifting information until it was time to go to the Superdome for the next session. The Quayle fire brigade knew it had to throw enough cold water on the Guard flap so that the flames would not consume Bush's acceptance speech that night.

The most serious rumor was that Quayle would be dropped from the ticket. The orders, according to Rich Bond, were: "Squash it. Squash that one like a bug. That's unthinkable." The Bush handlers well remembered the chaos George McGovern created in 1972 when he bounced Thomas Eagleton as his Democratic running mate after disclosure of Eagleton's shock treatments for depression.

By about six o'clock that night it was decided enough rebuttal was in hand. The question now was how best to make use of television's consuming interest in the Quayle flap to dampen the furor down and clear the way for Bush. Much debate ensued about whether the "spin doctors" should simply go down onto the convention floor, where the resultant mob scene would make it very difficult for reporters to ask probing follow-up questions, or go to the anchor booths and risk extended interrogation. Lake urged the latter course on Baker, arguing that his special credibility would be the campaign's best weapon in throttling down the Quayle story. In characteristic synchronization, Baker, Fuller and Teeter each showed up on one of the three major networks right at 8 P.M. as the final session of the convention opened, and each spouted the previously agreed-to line. Baker confirmed that Quayle's father had sought help in getting him into the Guard but insisted that he had not received any undue special treatment. And Teeter reported that "we haven't found anything at all . . . that was inconsistent with what Senator Quayle has said." At the same time, Bond was rehearsed and then sent out to deliver the spin to the local network television affiliates.

Right afterward, a small press pool was ushered in to see Quayle in a mobile home behind the podium in the Superdome. Again, Lake, the communications director, was at his side to make sure he didn't overcommunicate. As instructed, Quayle told the reporters that he knew they had a lot of questions, but this night belonged to George Bush and he would be happy to answer all their inquiries the next day at a press conference. The reporters tried to press him, but to no avail. "You could see his jaws tighten," Lake recalled. "He wanted to answer those questions. I just pushed him aside." Quayle then walked out and on up to the convention podium to give the brief speech written for him by the Bush operatives accepting the vice presidential nomination.

Now that the Bush strategists were stuck with Quayle—and insiders insist there was never any talk about kicking him off the ticket—they were not giving him the slightest room to free-lance. In advance of the speech, according to Canzeri, he had wanted to deliver it off notes on a card, but he was told he had to use a TelePrompTer. Because he said he had never used one before, Canzeri set one up in his suite at the Westin and guided him through a rehearsal beforehand. The speech went off well, and the convention cheered him when he said at one point that "as a young man, I served six years in the National Guard and, like the millions of Americans who have served in the Guard and serve today . . . I am proud of it."

The Guard story was not, by any means, dead. The questions kept coming that night and for days and weeks afterward, especially with the reports that members of his influential Indiana family had made inquiries about his enlistment in his behalf. But for this night at least, the fire brigade had kept it sufficiently under control to enable Bush to have the spotlight squarely on him for his big moment, his one big chance to put his stamp indelibly on the convention and on the Republican Party.

Much later, we asked Lake what he thought of Quayle, seeing him up so close during those frenzied first days as the vice presidential nominee. "Here's a guy, a forty-one-year-old senator from Indiana," Lake said. "He was absolutely thrilled, walking on air to be the nominee of his party for the vice presidency. . . . He was absolutely out of it. And he thought he was a pretty good guy, a pretty able fellow, had dealt with the press in three or four elections, and he felt that he knew all this stuff. So I think he felt shell-shocked at the intensity of the attention, the aggressiveness of the press. . . . I think he would have been dazed even if he didn't have the National Guard [controversy]. . . . He'd died and gone to heaven, and all these people were shooting at [him]. . . . He was very pleasant, he was very easy to deal with. . . . I like him. I felt sorry for him, not to realize what he'd stepped into. Kind of like a kid who had been playing sandlot ball, a pretty good sandlot ball player. Somebody says, 'You ought to be playing in the World Series.' He says, 'Oh, shit, I know the game. Pretty good hitter.' He didn't realize it wasn't even the same game."

With Quayle on the back burner, for the time being anyway, Bush stepped up squarely to the prime opportunity of his career to tell the millions of Americans watching the convention on television who he was in his own right. In a strong and even voice, he gave the speech of his life. The message in itself was unspectacular. For all the advance billing about how the speech would establish Bush as his "own man," this politician who for nearly seven years had faithfully subordinated himself to the views and policies of Ronald Reagan, declared that essentially he intended to continue to follow in Reagan's footsteps, to carry on the Reagan Revolution. Taking note of Franklin D. Roosevelt's admonition to the voters in 1940, when he was seeking an unprecedented third term, not to change horses in midstream, Bush observed: "Now, after two great terms, a switch will be made. But when you have to change horses in midstream, doesn't it make sense to switch to the one who's going the same way?"

It was the tone that struck the audience. Crisply and confidently delivered, the speech conveyed a greater sense of compassion and a greater willingness to bare personal feelings than Bush had shown in the past. He called the presidency "an incomparable opportunity for gentle persuasion," particularly in the area of race relations. "I hope to stand for a new harmony, a greater tolerance," he said. "We've come far, but I think we need a new harmony among the races in our country. We're on a journey to a new century, and we've got to leave the tired old baggage of bigotry behind."

Bush talked, too, about the need to channel the nation's prosperity "to pursue 'the better angels,' " what he called "prosperity with a purpose." It meant, he said, "teaching troubled children through your presence that there's such a thing as reliable love. Some would say it's soft and insufficiently tough to care about these things. But where is it written that we must act as if we do not care, as if we are not moved? Well, I am moved. I want a kinder, gentler nation." All this was a far cry from the uncertain man who seemed always striving so awkwardly to demonstrate a personal toughness that might counter "the wimp image." Here at last was a seemingly different George Bush confidently stepping out on his own. The audience in the Superdome cheered and applauded loud and long, and even in the network anchor booths, the hardened news oracles of the television era spoke in laudatory terms of his performance.

The aura of the acceptance speech might have suggested to those who heard it that George Bush would henceforth be a candidate of warmth, goodwill and compassion on the stump. But his managers, still keeping an eye on the polls, had other ideas. The assault on Dukakis was toned down somewhat for the evening, but most of the elements of the hardball approach were mentioned, including the pledge to the flag and the death penalty for drug dealers. And as another reminder, Bush asked the audience to rise and join him in the pledge of allegiance. The message on this night, though, was that of a "gentler, kinder" George Bush leaving his party's convention clearly in charge, and leaving the conventioneers in an upbeat mood.

An ABC News–*Washington Post* poll reported in the next morning's paper, of 1,119 likely voters over a seven-day period, had Bush closing the gap with Dukakis, 49 percent to 46, basically a tie given the poll's declared margin of error. This was better news than the Bush strategists had hoped for, coming before the full weight of the convention had been felt. The Bush strategists had counted on a lift from the convention to put them squarely into contention with Dukakis, and these figures suggested that such a "bump" could send their candidate past the Democratic nominee. That is, unless the Quayle flap undid all the positive events of the convention, including Bush's commanding acceptance speech.

In a further effort to make sure it didn't happen, Bush and Quayle flew from New Orleans the next day to Huntington, Indiana, Quayle's hometown, where he once was an executive at the family-owned *Huntington Press-Herald*. It was a festive homecoming, but it turned into a circus and a bizarre exercise in press-bashing. Quayle, after speaking from a platform in front of the courthouse, took off his suit jacket and strode over to the jam-packed press section. Reporters traveling with his party who had been unable to question him at length until then began to bombard him with inquiries about the circumstances of his National Guard enlistment. He answered over the public-address system, which allowed the thousands of hometown supporters to hear, and the crowd began to boo and jeer each questioner. The freewheeling nature of the format suggested that the Quayle handlers had intentionally rigged it to make the press corps appear to be an unruly mob, and some reporters flatly charged as much. But Spencer insisted later that the public-address microphones were used because "fifty or sixty reporters in the back couldn't hear."

For about half an hour, Quayle fielded the questions, as the crowd got more and more intemperate toward the reporters, booing them and shouting "Boring, boring" as the questions continued to focus on Quayle's National Guard service. "Where did *you* serve?" some in the crowd demanded of the interrogators. All that Quayle would allow was that he had done "what any normal person at that age would do—call home. You call home to Mother and Father and say, 'I'd like to get into the National Guard,' " he explained. "Is there anything wrong with asking your mother and father's friends for advice?" He acknowledged that an executive in one of his family's newspapers, retired Major General Wendell Phillipi of the Indiana National Guard, had helped him get in, but he denied any impropriety.

The staging of the press conference, intentionally or not, helped shape the pattern of Quayle's defense—that he was being martyred by the sniping, insensitive news media. The press corps, for its part, played right into the campaign's hands, Spencer said later, by being so "surly . . . I'd never seen anything like it," and the crowd reacted. "The question turned from 'What's he?' to 'Who the hell are these guys going after him?' "

The carping at accompanying reporters continued the next day as Bush and Quayle traveled into neighboring Ohio, and Bush himself likened the media focus on Quayle to a "feeding flurry" of bluefish. Quayle was scheduled to go on to the Illinois State Fair with Bush the next day but instead was flown back to Washington for a few days of "preparations" before being sent out on his own. Aides insisted he was not being coached, but it was obvious that Stu Spencer, the campaign-hardened troubleshooter, was being given a task worthy of his talent. "It became 'Dan Quayle Goes to Candidate School,' " Bond said later. And Canzeri observed: "You take a guy out of the Golden Gloves and throw him in the ring with Joe Louis. He took a few big hits. They weren't knockout punches but they were close to it. Then we had to take him back and do the roadwork and teach him how to box."

When Spencer first volunteered for the job of running the vice presidential campaign, he had a new approach—"sandwiching" the Democratic presidential nominee. The Republican vice presidential nominee would be sent to places in advance of him to criticize him and hence try to affect the agenda of his visit. Then he would return after the Democratic candidate had left and take pokes at what he had said. But Spencer's scheme hadn't figured on Dan Quayle. That plan obviously would have to be scrapped now. "We knew we were going to have to script him," Canzeri said.

There obviously would be some more days and perhaps even weeks of Quayle being on the griddle, and hence in the public spotlight. But a way had to be found to put him and his problems in the proper perspective of things. This was a race for the White House between George Bush and Michael Dukakis; as Labor Day and the traditional start of the general election campaign approached, the Bush strategists addressed themselves to returning the country's attention to them.

PART VII

The General Election

26

The Air War

From the very start of the direct battle between George Bush and Michael Dukakis, it was clear that the war would be fought through the fall on two fronts—on the ground and in the air. The ground war would take place in the traditional political trenches of campaign stumping across the country. At the same time, the air war would be waged over the television networks that had by now become the primary means by which the candidates and their campaigns were brought every night directly into the living rooms of the great American electorate.

Even before the Republican convention in New Orleans, Dukakis' ability to wage both wars had suffered a serious blow from a presumably neutral quarter The judge in the Iran-contra conspiracy case, U.S. District Court Judge Gerhard A. Gesell, in early August, decided to postpone the start of the trial of indicted Oliver North, scheduled for mid-September, until after the election. Gesell ruled that the prosecutors and North's lawyers needed more time to resolve the sticky question of dealing with thousands of classified documents sought as evidence on both sides.

Bush, asked about the delay, said he had "no reaction," but his strategists obviously were relieved—and Dukakis' chagrined. They were hoping that the North trial would bring new revelations about Bush's role in the Iran-contra affair that would rekindle the whole issue in the general-election campaign. Only after the election would they realize what Gesell's decision may have cost their candidate, when such revelations did indeed indicate a much deeper Bush involvement in funneling aid to the contras than he ever acknowledged in the campaign.

Dukakis, with hope gone that the trial would pry open damaging information to Bush, resumed the attack on the Iran-contra issue on his own. In Boston on the last day of August, he demanded: "The American people would like to know the answer to an important question. Mr. Bush, you sat through five meetings on this subject. How can you say now that you did not know this was a straight arms-for-hostages deal?'' All through September, Dukakis asked the question in speeches across the country. But Bush ignored him—and reporters covering him who attempted to keep the issue afloat. The vice president instead continued on the attack himself against the Dukakis vulnerabilities that the Bush researchers had identified months earlier.

While the war on the ground was essential, the dominant element became the competition over the nation's airwaves. Network television became the eyes and ears that enabled the voter to witness what was said and done on the stump—and in the television studios and advertising agencies that had become critical adjuncts to each campaign. To a far greater degree in 1988 than in the past, the networks found themselves deftly manipulated by the campaigns—and far more by the veteran Bush strategists, working with a pliable candidate, than by the Dukakis team, hampered by a balky one.

In this framework, a case can be made that Michael Dukakis' fate in the presidential election was settled in the air war that now flared in the five-week period from the Republican National Convention at New Orleans and his first debate with George Bush at Winston-Salem, North Carolina, on September 25.

The three major television networks—NBC, CBS and ABC—contributed to Dukakis' lot by allowing their coverage, day after day, to be dictated by an agenda carefully prepared by the professionals managing the Bush campaign. Taken together over that period, the reports television news presented to more than 40 million Americans every night exceeded even the dizziest expectations of the Bush strategists.

The networks were not totally at fault for Dukakis' fate, by any means. The Democratic candidate and his strategists were hopelessly unprepared and ineffectual in dealing with the real world of a general election campaign. By contrast, the principal advisers to Bush—Jim Baker, Lee Atwater, Bob Teeter, Roger Ailes—devised and carried out a campaign plan that took the initiative from the outset and never allowed Dukakis off the defensive during the entire period.

Even before the Republican convention, Teeter said later, he and his associates realized the importance of laying the general election groundwork early. The period between the conventions, he said, was one ''where you had to accomplish some things'' because ''the public was really going to pay attention to this campaign over a relatively short period of time, and that it would be won and lost after Labor Day.'' It wasn't that what was done early would be immediately critical, Teeter said, but rather that ''the perceptions you were setting would be very important to you in the fall . . . you set a theme or an issue or subject, and you stick with it for a while.'' And the central theme, established early, was that George Bush represented ''mainstream America'' and Mike Dukakis did not.

It was critical to achieve four objectives going into the general election campaign, he said. The first was that Bush had to set a perception of himself as an independent figure beyond being Reagan's vice president. This Bush had done "far beyond our expectations" in his acceptance speech, Teeter said. Then, he said, "we had to control the agenda. We wanted to maximize the difference between the two candidates, make Bush and Dukakis as different as possible, as far apart. And raise Dukakis' negatives."

The campaign preferred to call the negative attacks "contrasts," and Teeter insisted afterward that was exactly what they were and were intended to be.* "It became kind of a joke that what used to be attack speeches became contrast speeches," he said, "but the fact really was, we didn't want to just slam him; we did want to contrast him and say, 'Here are two guys who are very different on A and B and C. Bush is here and Dukakis is here.' And certainly we wanted to nail him, but at the same time it was very important to us to make sure people saw them as very different choices. . . . If you took George Bush out and kind of stood him up with all the bark off and said, 'Here's who this guy is. Here are his values, his priorities, his record. And did the same thing to Dukakis. Bush was a whole lot closer to where the majority of Americans were."

That may or may not have been so. The problem for Dukakis in that particular show-and-tell was that Bush and his strategists would be doing the showing and the telling about both candidates, and the Mike Dukakis the voters would see was not by a long shot the one the Dukakis camp would have accepted as a valid presentation of the man.

The Republican campaign was quintessentially shallow but dramatically effective. The vice president raced around the country from one camera-ready setting to another, attacking, attacking, attacking. And if the attacks were centered on issues that had little relevance to the presidency—most notably the pledge of allegiance and the prison-furlough program—it was also true that they provided excellent videotape to enliven the evening news broadcasts.

Dukakis, by contrast, clearly didn't know how to play the game. He spent almost the entire time on the defensive, forever explaining, explaining, explaining. And—with one or two exceptions—when the Democratic candidate did try to play the good-videotape, sound-bite game, he made a hash out of it.

The failures of the networks could not be blamed first on the reporters and producers assigned to the coverage of the campaign. Many of them were knowledgeable political reporters, skilled and serious professionals who recognized when they were being made patsies by the Bush campaign. Instead, the failure could be traced to the inherent peculiarities of the medium.

Television had a built-in bias toward the "story" that could be told with film or videotape showing people in action or an interesting scene—a "good visual," as the political consultants called it. There was a premium on a story that could be summed up in the shortest possible time because time was so precious. There was a resistance to complexity and nuance. There was an

*In the semantic game that political consultants played to make what they were doing seem less offensive, they also called negative attacks "comparative."

absolute abhorrence of anything that viewers might find boring. A politician talking—if he simply could not be ignored—was always more acceptable to television news if he was doing so in a visually interesting setting, rather than simply standing at a podium before a blue curtain.

The Bush campaign managers understood all these criteria and were working for a candidate who was willing to do whatever they suggested. The Dukakis managers clearly understood them less well and were working for a candidate who resisted the knowledge and seemed most at home standing at a podium before a blue curtain.

Considering the heat of the controversy over Dan Quayle, it might have been expected that Bush would be the one suffering on television in those first days after the convention. But whatever damage to Bush was reflected in opinion polls showing widespread doubts about Quayle seemed to be ameliorated somewhat by the pictures of Bush "standing by" his much-abused running mate, as ABC put it—as if there were much else he could have done at that point. Politicians had known since the Richard Nixon "Checkers" speech in 1952 that you didn't go wrong defending yourself against what was perceived as an assault by the press. Beyond that, however, the discipline of the Bush campaign meant the candidate made certain to deliver his own message as well, in sound bites that didn't tax either the networks' or the viewers' powers of discernment. Two of the networks, for example, showed him telling a rally audience in Dayton: "We are the United States of America. Let's keep the progress going. We do not want to go the other way."

A couple of days later Bush even seemed to be making an asset of his choice. All three networks showed the Republican candidate assuring a convention of the Veterans of Foreign Wars that Quayle "did not go to Canada, he did not burn his draft card and he damn sure didn't burn the American flag"—a standard that could have been met by millions of Americans not chosen for vice president.

The timing of the remark about the flag seemed suggestive when the next day Senator Steve Symms of Idaho, a chest-thumping conservative, claimed he had been told there was a photograph of the young Kitty Dukakis burning an American flag at a demonstration in 1970 against the war in Vietnam. The candidate's wife denied the accusation categorically and heatedly, telling reporters: "It's outrageous. It did not happen." And Symms never produced either the photograph or whoever had told him that it existed. But the charge hung in the air for several days—one more rap against Dukakis as the liberal whose patriotism was suspect.

Dukakis and some of his strategists argued in retrospect that the Quayle flap might have made it more difficult for them in setting out an agenda of their own early in the campaign. But Dukakis, waiting for the more or less "official" opening of the general election campaign on Labor Day, wasn't ready to do any such thing. Instead, he spent most of the last two weeks of August on "regional days"—tours to different parts of Massachusetts that he made annually to talk and listen to his constituents. Asked if he was worried about wasting time, he replied on one occasion: "It's only August." On another: "I am a sitting governor."

The days spent in his home state were politically counterproductive. Dukakis tried to use them to show the national press accompanying him some of the success stories that had been achieved during his stewardship as governor. But the reporters were interested in only two stories. The first was why he was wasting all this time while Bush campaigned full tilt for the presidency. The second was his response to whatever charge Bush had made against him that day.

On August 22, Dukakis was in Andover, Massachusetts, defending his own record of military service. The next day, in Beverly, he was defending his veto of the pledge-of-allegiance bill. In Springfield a couple of days later, he was complaining that it was "difficult to get through" all the noise about Quayle. The picture of Dukakis doing no more than roaming apparently aimlessly around his home state, pausing only to defend himself each day, became so obvious that Kirk O'Donnell announced that daily press conferences would no longer be held. The theory was that reporters then would be obliged to use whatever Dukakis was saying in his speech of the day. But the edict itself was quickly turned into another story about the campaign on the defensive and in disarray —and was quickly smothered in its cradle.

Meanwhile, Bush was providing the networks with high-class visuals, refusing to hold press conferences and getting away with it famously. One reason was the ability to produce the one-liners that were catnip to television. In Texas on August 25, Bush said Dukakis "sometimes gives me the impression he is opposed to every new weapons system since the slingshot"—a line that NBC used immediately, ABC and CBS when he repeated it a few days later at a defense plant in St. Louis. A few days later the line of the day was: "I wouldn't be surprised if he thought that a naval exercise was something you find in Jane Fonda's workbook."

The Dukakis campaign's attempts to seize the attention seemed to backfire regularly. When Lloyd Bentsen went to the VFW convention and, as ABC put it, "lashed back" at the Republicans on the defense issue, the coverage focused no more on the good reception he received than on the booing at the mention of Dukakis' name. But the fact was that, the booing aside, the picture was one of the Dukakis campaign once again on the defensive, this time through its vice presidential nominee.

The treatment of a brief Bush offensive on the environment illustrated the value of proper settings. On August 31, Bush went to the shore of Lake Erie south of Detroit to be photographed with the water in the background while he outlined his plans for the environment. CBS showed Representative John Dingell, a Michigan Democrat, countering that the Reagan administration had "done absolutely nothing" on clean water, and NBC's reporter, Lisa Myers, observed that the speech was "sharply at odds with the record of the Reagan administration.'' Dukakis himself, campaigning in California, was shown by all three networks replying in incredulous tones: "Talk about an election-year conversion." But the memorable moment that night was George Bush with that nice clean, blue lake in the background.

The following day the Bush campaign was even more successful. The candidate flew into Logan Airport and then sailed around Boston Harbor while giving a running commentary on Dukakis' failure to clean up the filth. "My opponent's solution—delay, fight, anything but cleanup," he said. "Well, I don't call that leadership and I certainly don't even call that competence.'' The Dukakis campaign had been alerted and three small boats of counterdemonstrators waving anti-Bush signs trailed the vice president's boat. But John Sununu, the New Hampshire governor who displayed such enmity to Dukakis all year, was ever vigilant, lining up other Republicans on the Bush boat in an attempt to block the cameras' view of the demonstrators.

ABC showed videotape of trash in the water and the foamy wake behind the Bush boat. CBS called it "floating political theater" and NBC informed its viewers Bush had "staged a raid" in his opponent's home territory. Only ABC made any serious attempt to sort out the complex story of who was responsible for not cleaning up Boston Harbor.

In fact, Dukakis had some vulnerability on this question. On two occasions he had sought waivers from provisions of the Clean Water Act to delay construction of sewage-treatment plants after the program had become involved in fiscal and jurisdictional snarls. But it was also true—and overlooked—that the administration in which Bush claimed to have been an influential player had a wretched record on enforcing the Clean Water Act. And it was also true, as the court-appointed Special Master who handled litigation over the pollution pointed out, that Dukakis was the official who finally came up with a plan for cleaning up the harbor. Dukakis' record on environmental questions was so superior to Bush's that he had the endorsements of most of the leading environmental groups.

Jack Corrigan, the Dukakis campaign director of operations, marveled after the election at the "unbelievable chutzpah" Bush had shown in attacking on that particular issue. "He should have been ridiculed for that," he said. Instead, the Bush campaign was praised for a successful "hit" in enemy territory.

All of the "visuals" arranged by the Bush campaign did not involve bodies of water, however. Another favorite was an appearance before a phalanx of uniformed policemen as their union endorsed the Republican candidate. That little drama was played out in several states, most notably with the Boston police, whose spokesman announced for the networks that "we feel Governor Dukakis is soft on crime" and complained that he did not support the death penalty. Dukakis tried to counter that one with a rally of other Massachusetts policemen and a passionate defense from Mario Cuomo. But the man-bites-dog story here was hometown cops turning on their governor. ABC noted that the Boston union had twice endorsed Ronald Reagan, and CBS pointed out that crime was down under Dukakis' administration. But, once again, the picture overwhelmed the disclaimers.

Dukakis' own attempts to use the same techniques often backfired. A few days before Bush's Boston event, Dukakis went to the Los Angeles Police Academy, a visit that ABC anchor Peter Jennings introduced by saying the candidate "spent today responding to another Republican charge, that he's soft on crime." ABC also showed the police chief and Republican Bush supporter, Daryl Gates, advising Dukakis that he should "burn that ACLU card so fast" if he wanted to be credible on the crime issue.

The rebuff was all the more striking in its contrast with George Bush's next visual—videotape on all the networks of him watching the destruction of a Pershing missile as part of the implementation of the INF treaty. ABC did report that an acre of trees had been bulldozed on the military base to give the cameras the best possible angle. But the important thing was the tape of the vice president being so clearly identified with a dramatic and laudatory event.

The critical dynamic, however, was that the campaign war was being fought on issues raised by Bush while Dukakis was almost always on the defensive, even if not always explicitly. Two days after the Boston Harbor event, Dukakis seemed to have scored with a visual of his own—an appearance on Ellis Island with his mother, Euterpe, and a visit to the Statue of Liberty with Mario Cuomo, where he was shown before a bank of flags leading the pledge of allegiance. The "story" made all three networks but the message was clearly that Michael Dukakis was in so much trouble on this issue that he had to use such a ploy. The same night CBS and ABC showed a brief "press availability" of Bush pitching horseshoes at the vice presidential residence in Washington.

Although the opinion polls at this point were showing the contest essentially even, Dukakis was the one who had been sliding. And every story seemed to be put into that context. When Dukakis announced that John Sasso was returning to his campaign, a move he had been wanting to make for months, CBS called it "a sign their [the Bush campaign] hardball tactics are working." ABC cited Dukakis' "troubled campaign," and NBC described the step as "risky but necessary" because the campaign was "in serious trouble."

The success of the Bush campaign in setting the agenda was also apparent in the relatively rare cases when the networks strayed from the daily coverage to do separate reports on issues. During this period, all three networks did pieces on the pledge of allegiance or the use of the flag in the campaign, and one or the other of them did such stories on the furlough question, Boston Harbor and the Dukakis nay-sayers in his home state. But there were none on such Dukakis-raised issues as housing, child care or the problem of financing a college education.

The latter case offered an instructive example. On September 7, Dukakis visited Kean Community College in New Jersey to outline an innovative, perhaps even radical, program that would have made college loans universally available to young Americans who would repay them through payroll deductions after they had completed their education. ABC and CBS coverage at least provided brief listings of the main points of the plan, but NBC limited itself to a three-sentence summary by anchor Tom Brokaw. The college-loan program was newsworthy enough to the *Washington Post* to merit a report by Edward Walsh that ran a full column of type. But none of the networks stood back and took even a television-level look at the whole question of public policy on the opportunity for higher education. (One of the reasons the networks may not have had time for such a report was that the same day they had another dandy visual—Bush telling an audience of veterans: "Today is Pearl Harbor Day, forty-seven years ago to this very day." He was widely ridiculed for this date mix-up, but even so he got the coverage, and "getting on the six o'clock news" one way or another was the name of the game.)

After the election Susan Estrich cited the college-loan issue as one with which the Dukakis campaign had tried to change the subject away from the Bush agenda, and had fallen short. "An education proposal doesn't really change the subject, not in the environment in which we live," she said, "because attack-response makes the evening news. An education proposal doesn't. The best you get out of that one is a one-day story."

In fact, in this case, the proposal did seem to have some resonance despite the passing treatment it received from the networks. As the campaign went on, reporters covering Dukakis and Bentsen noticed that one of the surefire applause lines in their speeches would be any reference to the plan for college loans. That response suggested that the plan did have some appeal to the middle class, as the Dukakis strategists had hoped, and that the news had gotten through to at least some voters directly faced with sending their kids to college.

Perhaps the day that best summed up Dukakis' problems with television coverage—and with his own campaign—was September 13. That morning Dukakis went to Chicago and delivered what the campaign considered a major speech on the relationship between the United States and the Soviet Union. But that afternoon he made the classic mistake of "stepping on" his own story by taking a ride, wearing a helmet, in an M-1 tank at a General Dynamics plant in Sterling Heights, Michigan. The stunt buried the speech on television, where the tape showed Dukakis looking very much like Alfred E. Neuman in that tank while the sound track recorded reporters in the press stand hooting with laughter.

The *Washington Post* published a picture but treated the speech on relations with the Soviets seriously for more than a column, mentioning the tank trip only twelve paragraphs into the account. But in terms of agenda-setting and political impact, a sober story even in the *Washington Post* was small-caliber stuff compared to network tape of Dukakis in that tank.

Among those who immediately understood the potential mileage in the tank episode were the Bush managers watching the television news in their Fifteenth Street headquarters in Washington—and enjoying it immensely. "I thought it was a bonanza," Lee Atwater said later. "I thought it was the biggest bonanza I had seen in the whole campaign. I could immediately think of three analogies that everybody could relate to and laugh their ass off at—Rocky the Squirrel, Beetle Bailey and Alfred E. Neuman. . . . It was a gold mine.'' Dukakis had broken an axiom of politics—that presidential candidates don't wear funny hats—and was paying heavily for it.

Nor was that the only occasion on which Dukakis stepped on his own story. At another point he delivered a speech to an American Legion convention that was well received—good news for a candidate in trouble on the defense issue. But then he trumped his own ace by holding a press conference at which he seemed to be watering down his opposition to the Strategic Defense Initiative. Unsurprisingly and justifiably, the SDI angle was the story that day.

The Democratic candidate did not always come out the loser in this battle of the sound bites, however, even if it seemed that way at the time. Sometimes he managed a draw. Bush wandered into trouble one day when he visited a Portland, Oregon, shipyard and was rudely heckled by the workers there. Even his ostensibly peerless campaign staff apparently wasn't aware that Dukakis had visited the same shipyard earlier in the summer and received a warm welcome. But the value to Dukakis was mitigated by the fact that on the same day, campaigning in Niles, Illinois, he was interrupted by a fist-swinging brawl between his supporters and antiabortion protesters that made exciting fodder for the networks. It was no secret in American politics that voters were not comfortable with candidates whose appearances provoked violence.

Dukakis himself scored on occasion. The networks gave extensive coverage to a visit on September 9 to Commerce, Texas, in the home district of Speaker Sam Rayburn, where Dukakis called the use of the pledge of allegiance issue an attack on his patriotism and likened it to McCarthyism. Recalling a Rayburnism, he declared: ''The American people and the people of Texas can smell the garbage.'' Then he added: ''I'm not questioning Mr. Bush's patriotism . . . but I do question his judgment.''

It should not be overlooked, however, that Dukakis' success with that event may have had something to do with its Bush-like quality. There was a good visual, a huge outdoor rally crowd as a backdrop and inflammatory language that could be capsulized easily.

The best moment for the Democratic nominee came on September 20, when all three networks turned on Bush for at least one news cycle. On this day, Dukakis outlined his plan for providing health insurance for most, although not all, of the 37 million Americans not already covered. The CBS coverage was particularly thorough. The network showed Dukakis first at a Houston hospital, meeting with families without insurance, then at Western Kentucky University describing his own plan, which was spelled out on the screen. Next the network's medical reporter, Susan Spencer, provided a background piece on the health insurance issue. It included, among other things, a moment from a *Meet the Press* appearance earlier in which Bush had been nonplussed by a question from David Broder of the *Washington Post* on how many Americans lacked health insurance. "I don't know the answer to that, no," Bush was shown replying. The piece went on to discuss pros and cons, mostly pros, of the plan, including a Democratic congressman, Fortney ("Pete") Stark of California, observing that the "George Bush la-de-da BMW set" always had health insurance coverage. NBC and ABC also gave the plan full coverage, the former showing the same moment from *Meet the Press* that CBS had used.

But what made the story was the fact that Bush had chosen that day for a second visit to a flag factory in New Jersey, where he was shown delivering this economic news: "Flag sales are doing well and America is doing well and we should understand that and we should appreciate that." All three networks showed that scene juxtaposed against Dukakis asking derisively, "Where is George Bush? He's visiting a flag factory," and Dukakis asking Bush: "Don't you think it's about time you came out from behind the flag and told us what you intend to do to provide basic health insurance for thirty-seven million Americans?"

George Bush had finally gone so far that even the television networks were rebelling. "That," Lee Atwater conceded later, "was one flag factory too many." Or, as another Bush campaign operative put it the following day, "We rode that horse one day too long."

The episode also scotched an ad Roger Ailes, the Bush campaign's media consultant, had prepared showing schoolchildren reciting the pledge of allegiance while a voice-over told how Dukakis had vetoed a bill requiring teachers to see that they did so every day. "As it turned out, that issue passed us," Ailes said later, then added: "Frankly, we held it in reserve to the end."

But the flag overkill was the exception. The Bush campaign had set out with two essential elements to its strategy—"to stay on the offensive and keep control of the agenda," in Atwater's formulation. Within that strategy, Bob Teeter devised the themes the campaign would follow for the next few days or the next week and Atwater found the tactical opportunities for expressing those themes. This approach required flexibility. When the Bush managers learned that Dukakis planned to spend the third week in September talking about national-defense issues, they put aside their own plan to talk about the economy and switched to defense—convinced this was the one subject on which they were certain to come out ahead. "If national defense is the number one topic of the week," Atwater said, "that's a loser for him."

But the successful use of these tactics also required the successful use of network television because that was the source of the basic meat-and-potatoes diet of political news in American presidential campaigns. Asked later if he thought the networks had "rolled over" for the Bush campaign, Ailes preferred to put it differently.

"We felt that we were doing reasonably well in the evening news," he said, "but we thought it was because we were giving the networks what they wanted. . . . They either want mistakes, pictures or attacks and we were giving them pretty good pictures and pretty good lead stories and we were sticking to our theme of the day, whatever that was. . . . We were disciplined, giving them the sound bites and the feed that they wanted. It wasn't that they were rolling over for us. It was that we were basically programming something that they would air, and therefore we were basically doing our job at that time.''

The satisfaction within the Bush campaign was obvious. "I don't remember," Ailes said, "going to a staff meeting during that time in which we felt we got our brains kicked out on the evening news. . . . And there were many other nights during the campaign we did have that discussion the next morning. . . . We felt it was because he [Dukakis] was in a little bit of disarray. They expected, after our convention, they expected us to go on our ass . . . and we didn't go on our ass.''

The Dukakis managers also were aware that some serious damage had been done in the first weeks after the Republican convention. Perhaps most important, the issues Bush was using—the pledge of allegiance, the furlough program, the death penalty, gun control—to make the case that Dukakis was unpatriotic and "soft on crime" were doing more than that. "I always believed," said Ailes, "that the cluster of those negatives painted a picture of Michael Dukakis the public needed to have. In other words, any one of those alone would not have been enough to do much damage.'' The picture that these particulars were allowing voters to draw, with some help from Bush, was the inference that the Democratic nominee was not only unpatriotic and soft on crime but also soft or weak on national defense.

Tubby Harrison, Dukakis' polling consultant, put it this way: "The liberal-conservative ideology became a very important factor, perceived ideology became a very important factor and that's what you're basically talking about. You're talking about pledge, you're talking about furloughs, you're talking about defense. . . . That whole thing is 'The Liberal' and the liberal who is soft on crime, soft on defense.''

One of the ways the Dukakis campaign might have snapped back would have been with television advertising either rebutting the Bush line or trying to take the offensive for itself. When you are under attack, Lloyd Bentsen said after the campaign, "you've got to come back with TV commercials right away. . . . Politics is a contact sport." But Dukakis was reluctant. When Bentsen suggested ads that might take some sting out of the gun-control issue in Texas, he said, Dukakis "personally changed them" to tone them down. Moreover, the candidate was still not convinced these wild accusations would matter in the end. "He just didn't believe those charges would stick," Bentsen said.

The Bush campaign could not believe its good fortune in Dukakis' unwillingness to defend himself against such attacks. "In fairness to Lee and those guys," Ed Rollins of the Kemp campaign said later, "I don't think they ever expected to run a whole negative campaign. I think what they thought was they would get about a two-week, three-week run of these commercials and Dukakis would come right back at 'em, and then they'd have to basically shift their strategy. It's sort of like running off-tackle. You assume sooner or later they'll put a man over there and they're gonna stop it. But if you can run off-tackle all day, run-off tackle. They may have planned to take it to a higher road, [but] this thing was working. They weren't going to take any chance of changing the chemistry of this thing.'' Indeed, the relentlessness of the Bush attack was reminiscent of the Washington Redskins' pile-driving fullback John Riggins, who would pound the same hole in the opposing line for play after play until he finally got stopped.

Quite aside from the candidate's reluctance, the campaign's media advertising operations were in a state of continuing flux and disarray. New advertising experts were being brought into the campaign, proposing and producing spots that would be approved, revised, perhaps approved again, then rejected—either by Dukakis himself or one of those in the campaign high command. In some cases later in the campaign, some of Dukakis' state campaign directors even produced spots of their own, flew them into Boston for approval, then rushed them back to get them on the air to deal with particular situations. That was what happened with Tony Podesta, who was running the California operations. Dukakis was being killed in the state by two Bush ads—one on Boston Harbor, the other on crime and the furlough issue—and failing to react until Podesta forced the issue. Similarly, in other states, ads tailored to local concerns—gun control in East Texas, for instance—had to be pushed through the Boston bureaucracy before it was too late.

But the fault was with the candidate as well as the bureaucracy. In a post-election article in *New York* magazine, one of those who was in charge for a time, New York advertising man Ed McCabe, seemed to catch the candidate's attitude with remarkable accuracy.

''Like so many people,'' McCabe wrote, ''Michael Dukakis, I think, felt advertising was a necessary evil. Something other people could take care of. And, sure, George Bush could use it to sling mud, but *he* wouldn't stoop to that sort of thing. I don't think he ever understood the importance of advertising in this particular election. And I don't think he ever realized that there's one thing the American people dislike more than someone who fights dirty. That's someone who climbs into the ring and won't fight. That's what really happened here. He threw the fight.''

McCabe, understandably, may have overstated the role advertising might have played for Dukakis. Although Bob Teeter always argued that the advertising helped the Bush campaign ''control the agenda'' to some degree, commercials could not compare in impact to the day-after-day impact of ''losing'' on the evening news. As Dukakis himself said after the election, ''The six o'clock news has become almost the be-all and end-all.''

There were, nonetheless, some memorable spots used by both sides, to mixed results, later in the campaign. The single most effective, by the estimates of most professionals, and one whose impact probably could not be overstated, was the thirty-second spot called ''Revolving Door'' produced by Ailes to exploit the furlough issue. That was the ad, as already noted, that showed a prison guard and a long line of convicts walking through a steel revolving gate, while on the screen the legend told him how Dukakis' "revolving-door prison policy gave weekend furloughs to first-degree murderers not eligible for parole." It bore the crushing close: "Now Michael Dukakis says he wants to do for America what he has done for Massachusetts. America can't afford that risk."

When the Democrats complained that the exploitation of the Willie Horton case was racist, Ailes could reply that he had never used Horton in an ad. But the fact was he didn't need to do so. Other "independent" Republican advertising, and news media coverage, made it clear he was black.

The spot on which the Bush campaign took the most heat, legitimately, was one based on Dukakis' ill-starred ride in that tank. It showed Dukakis riding around, smiling and waving at the camera, while an announcer and the legend on the screen said: "Michael Dukakis has opposed virtually every defense system we developed. He opposed new aircraft carriers. He opposed antisatellite weapons. He opposed four missile systems, including the Pershing Two Missile deployment. Dukakis opposed the Stealth bomber and a ground emergency warning system against nuclear attack. He even criticized our rescue mission to Grenada and our strike against Libya. And now he wants to be our Commander-in-Chief. America can't afford that risk." The summary of Dukakis' position on defense priorities was, unsurprisingly, a clever distortion and misrepresentation. But the operative element was that devastating picture of Alfred E. Neuman in the tank.

The Dukakis campaign finally produced some ads, but the evidence of them having much impact was scant. The most noteworthy were a series of ads—essentially defensive in nature—depicting political handlers sitting around a table talking about packaging candidates. One of the actors, not coincidentally, looked somewhat like Roger Ailes. The message at the end of each was: "They'd like to sell you a package. Wouldn't you rather choose a president?" The problem with the spots was that they were too much "inside baseball" for casual viewer-voters to grasp.

One of the most puzzling aspects of the Dukakis media campaign—and the candidate's own campaigning, for that matter—was the decision against exploiting the "American dream" thesis: the candidate as the son of immigrants. The evidence during the primaries had suggested a strong positive reaction to this perception, particularly among Roman Catholic ethnic Americans with similar family histories—many of them the Reagan Democrats who were a special target of the fall campaign. Ed McCabe did produce a spot using this theme but it was scuttled after it tested poorly with a focus group.

The Dukakis campaign also took one final, devastating blow from a television network on the night before the second and final presidential debate. ABC's *World News Tonight* devoted almost thirteen minutes, including one commercial, to a bizarre summary of where the campaign stood at that moment. It was introduced by Peter Jennings as "something that has not been done before" and as "the most comprehensive poll of the entire campaign for the

White House" covering "each of the fifty states" and a sample of "almost ten thousand likely voters." ABC News and the *Washington Post*, Jennings announced portentously, "have just conducted" the poll and it had found Bush an "overwhelming favorite" for the White House.

These introductory remarks were misleading on several counts. The polling had not "just" been completed; some of it went back as long as three weeks —far too dated to be trusted. And the suggestion that it could be used as a valid indicator of the situation in "each of the fifty states" was grossly misleading. Even ten thousand interviews would equate to only two hundred voters per state, too small a sample for statistical reliability. In fact, the number of interviews per state ranged from only one hundred to five hundred, which meant the margin of error in some of those states was plus or minus ten percentage points. As a matter of fact, there probably wasn't any reason to be polling in such states as Mississippi, South Carolina or Alabama; anyone in either campaign would concede they were solid for Bush. But ABC News presented this story as a report based on polling data, not just seat-of-the-pants estimates. And, as it turned out, not all of the data was accurate. Bush was shown with a lead in Iowa when all other surveys from other sources suggested Dukakis would win there, as he subsequently did.

But ABC News was not to be denied its right to define the campaign. Bush was shown with a "firm" hold on twenty-one states with 220 electoral votes, Dukakis "firm" in only three states and the District of Columbia with only 30 electoral votes. Another fifteen states with 180 votes were "leaning" to Bush, only four with 59 votes to Dukakis. The Democrat, said Jennings, would have to win all seven toss-up states, hold all his own and win 73 percent of the electoral votes from those leaning to Bush. Jennings kept cautioning viewers that all these calculations were based on what would happen "if the election were held tomorrow." But the effect was no less overwhelming.

Nor was Jennings the whole story. His summary was followed in quick succession by reports analyzing the "internals" and showing more bad news for Dukakis, the situation in the South and "the national picture." Finally, ABC offered reactions from the two campaigns. "It's interesting and encouraging," said Bush. "This survey is very, very encouraging," said Bush campaign manager James Baker. Dukakis would not respond, and Jennings reported rather petulantly that his campaign had "gone out of its way to discredit the poll," then showed Paul Brountas saying the overall figures showed the contest "a very close one." In fact, the popular-vote margin in the latest ABC-*Post* poll was only 51 percent for Bush to 46 for Dukakis, not necessarily the stuff of landslides.

The ABC News poll was so far out of bounds that even Lee Atwater was taken aback. As he put it later, "I thought the most devastating thing of the whole campaign—I found myself for the first and only time ever feeling sorry for Dukakis—was the ABC coverage of the poll results announced the night [before] that debate. It had to be unnerving."

By contrast with ABC, its polling partner the *Washington Post* treated the same material with more caution. The *Post* pointed out that some of the polling dated back to September 21 and had been "supplemented with recent surveys conducted in individual states as well as with reports from the field by *Washington Post* political reporters." The *Post* also noted that although the larger states had been surveyed after the first presidential debate, "most interviews were done before the vice presidential debate." The burden of the story was the same—that is, that Bush held an imposing lead in the contest for electoral votes—but the treatment was far more responsible.

The networks were not always the sole villains, however. Although the newspapers did a better job separating issues from visuals for their readers, they were also too often timid in telling those readers, with the bark off, what was happening in the campaign of 1988. One trend particularly obvious as the campaign wore on was an inclination of newspapers to deal with the negativism of the campaign in what they considered to be an evenhanded manner. There were countless stories about how "both candidates" were "going negative." But the example cited to make that case against Dukakis was usually the same one—his contention that Bush had voted to cut Social Security benefits. In fact, there was an element of exaggeration in that charge; Bush had voted only to freeze a cost-of-living increase.

By contrast, the plain fact was that from the outset George Bush ran a campaign distinguished by a degree of negativism and intensity that had never been seen in presidential politics in the television age—a campaign that appealed to the lowest common denominator in the electorate. Bush himself always blithely brazened it out—denying while appearing in Findlay, Ohio, or "Flag City," that his assault on Dukakis' veto of the pledge of allegiance bill suggested that "somehow that's questioning somebody else's patriotism." That was precisely what Bush was doing to Dukakis, and it worked like a charm.

By September 16, little more than a week before the first debate, the almost-even race of Labor Day had begun to open up to an eleven-point Bush lead in the Hotline/KRC tracking polls that provided a three-day rolling average of a sample of 1,002 respondents.* More to the point, by the time of that debate, the share of the electorate disapproving of Bush—his "negatives"—had dropped from more than 40 percent to about 30 percent while those for Dukakis had risen from less than 30 to more than 40 percent.

Looking back, Susan Estrich said: "I think the critical time was the last two weeks of August, but it may be that there was nothing we could have done." She may have been right about the critical period, but there were many things Dukakis and his campaign failed to do that might have minimized the damage.

Instead, the high hopes of early summer in Boston had been transformed

*The Hotline was a computerized campaign information service that operated all through the 1988 campaign. It called itself "the daily briefing on American politics" and became a staple source of information on what was happening across the country for both news and political organizations. Beginning Labor Day, Hotline and KRC Communications Research of Cambridge, Massachusetts, tracked the progress of the campaign right up until Election Day.

to high anxiety as the September polls told the story of Dukakis' slide, and as his campaign looked more closely at the dimensions of the task ahead, state by state—the ground war in the trenches.

27

The Ground War

In the heady days after Michael Dukakis locked up the Democratic nomination in the California primary, and as late as the convention in Atlanta, all things had seemed possible. If the talk in Atlanta of a "fifty-state strategy"—competing in every state—was always somewhat exaggerated, it was nonetheless true that even several southern states seemed realistic targets in the quest for the 270 electoral votes needed to win. By the campaign strategists' estimates, and those of some other Democratic professionals, Dukakis enjoyed a good chance of winning in Arkansas, Tennessee, Kentucky and quite possibly Louisiana, where the depressed economy argued for change. North Carolina and Georgia also appeared to be within reach; both were states with fast-growing suburban areas, and North Carolina in particular had a substantial population of workers in high-tech industries for whom Dukakis might have appeal.

Moreover, the early indications were that most white politicians in the region were prepared to stick with the ticket, if only because they could point to the choice of Lloyd Bentsen as evidence that Dukakis was not another Mondale. So Dukakis had reason, or so he thought, to look with some optimism toward the South.

Every four years, in fact, Democratic strategists became beguiled by Dixie. They looked at the large populations of black voters who could be expected to vote nine to one or better for their candidate, and they would say to themselves: This time it must be possible to put this thing together.

On paper, the proposition looked reasonable. In states in which blacks would cast 25 percent of the total vote, the Democratic candidate needed to win only about 35 percent of the white vote to make a majority. In some southern states with the heaviest concentration of blacks—Louisiana, South Carolina and Mississippi—it might take as little as 31 to 32 percent of the white vote.

Yet it was in just such states that a Democratic nominee—or at least a liberal Democratic nominee like Michael Dukakis—found it most difficult to get enough white votes to win. In 1984, Walter Mondale's share of the white vote dropped to less than 20 percent in several southern states. And in states where the black population was so small that a Democrat needed 42 or 43 percent of the white vote—such as Arkansas and Kentucky—a liberal Democrat had a better chance of achieving that figure. In other words, the turnout of blacks for a Democratic nominee came at the cost of sharply diminished white turnout.

To some extent, this phenomenon may simply have been a product of racism. Or, more accurately, it may have been resurgent racial resentment during the Reagan administration, much of it focused on affirmative action programs and federal requirements for fixed percentages of government contracts to be set aside for minority business. Black and white Democratic politicians had learned to coexist and even cooperate in local and state elections. But that symbiosis didn't seem to apply to presidential elections, and sometimes not to other federal elections.

The inclination of white Democratic leaders to give less than their full support to the party's national candidates had given rise to resentment among some black leaders, for whom the presidential campaigns had the most relevance. Late in the 1984 campaign, Mayor Richard Arrington of Birmingham complained that the same white Democrats who were taking a walk in the Mondale campaign earlier had been telling blacks that "party unity" required them to accept state candidates they found hard to swallow—most notably then Governor George C. Wallace.

At the same time, many southern whites saw the Democratic Party as "the black party" and they were reluctant to identify themselves with it, particularly if the presidential nominee was a liberal from the Midwest or Northeast. Michael Dukakis certainly fit that description, and by mid-September, the real world of southern politics had intruded on his campaign's optimism.

Although Dukakis and his managers were still unwilling to say so publicly, they had essentially abandoned twenty-four states with 180 electoral votes. They still nourished hopes of winning Louisiana, Arkansas and possibly North Carolina. But they were now writing off as prime targets the entire South except Texas and the Mountain West except Colorado and possibly Montana, plus such congenitally Republican redoubts as Indiana, Kansas, Nebraska and New Hampshire.

The Dukakis campaign, in short, had come to grips with the "electoral college lock" the Republicans had been building steadily since the days of Richard Nixon. With 180 votes apparently beyond reach, Dukakis had to win his 270 electoral votes from the remaining 358, an imposing assignment by any standard. Or, put another way, the Republicans needed only 90 of those 358 to put George Bush in the White House.

The numbers the Republicans were using were only slightly different. They began with that southern and western base, including Texas, and added Ohio and New Jersey, the two industrial states with the greatest proclivity to vote their way, to reach 273 votes. Even with a "worst-case scenario" of a poor performance by Bush in the debates, Lee Atwater said, they would still be able to win if they held New Jersey and Ohio.

In fact, the Republican "lock" was never quite that immutable. Four years earlier, with Ronald Reagan running for reelection, the party's ostensible base had included California, Washington and Oregon. But this time some of the dynamics were different. California was closely contested. And Dukakis seemed likely to win both Washington, which had not voted for a Democrat since Hubert Humphrey in 1968, and Oregon, which had not gone Democratic since Lyndon Johnson's race in 1964. These two states in the Pacific Northwest were part of a group the Dukakis campaign had labeled "the clean states" during the primaries—states with recent traditions of relatively clean politics and governors who, like Dukakis himself, were progressive and effective—Neil Goldschmidt in Oregon, Booth Gardner in Washington.

But, quibbles about individual states aside, the managers of both campaigns recognized that the real playing field for the 1988 campaign would be a handful of large and medium-sized states in which Bush's success in painting Dukakis as a soft-on-crime liberal had not effectively ended the argument by Labor Day or shortly thereafter.

Thus, over the final six weeks of his campaign Dukakis would spend fully three fourths of his time in eight states—California, Illinois, Michigan, Texas, New York, Ohio, Pennsylvania and Missouri. And Bush would spend more than half of his time in only six—California, Illinois, Michigan, Missouri and, of course, Ohio and New Jersey. In short, the battle was being waged largely on ground Dukakis needed to sweep if he was to have a chance. Said Atwater, "Literally, in those last weeks of the campaign, there wasn't a single state that he was in that he didn't have to have, to win the whole election."

The best measure of the dimensions of Dukakis' task was that he felt obliged to campaign frequently in those final weeks in New York and Pennsylvania, both states that by that point should have been put way beyond the reach of the Republicans.

Dukakis did not have to be in that dire situation. If he had not allowed himself to be thrown so completely on the defensive on the issues that made him appear soft on crime, there was no fundamental reason he could not have been competitive in New Jersey, a state with a heavy population of ethnic voters to whom he could have appealed. His particular problem there was an especially pervasive concern about crime in the suburban communities in the northern part of the state.

The Democratic nominee also was paying a price now for his decision to choose Lloyd Bentsen rather than John Glenn for the vice presidential nomination. No one knew it better than Atwater. "If they had taken John Glenn and you'd have had a relatively close election," he said later, "that would have stymied our whole campaign because I doubt that we would have seriously tried to compete in Ohio. . . . It was a totally irrational political decision."

By this point in the campaign, it also was becoming clear that Glenn, one of the few authentic American heroes, would have offered Dukakis some insulation against the perception of him as less patriotic than Bush. At a union hall in Philadelphia one morning in September we saw Glenn, traveling with Dukakis, volunteer an angry red-faced "how dare they" denunciation of Bush on the pledge-of-allegiance issue. The outburst evoked roars of approval from the blue-collar audience, suggesting that Glenn's ire might have made a compelling commercial. But the Dukakis campaign, predictably, did not film Glenn's protest or re-create it for a spot later.

Despite the dimensions of the problem, Dukakis was not exactly barefoot in competing in his eight prime target states. The 1988 campaign was the first in a generation or longer in which the Democrats were able to compete with the Republicans on even or perhaps better-than-even terms in money.

The federal public financing system provided each candidate with $46 million for the general election. But a special provision of the 1974 act, written in after the 1976 election, also allowed them to raise essentially unlimited amounts—known as "soft money"—to be used ostensibly for party-building activities such as voter registration and turnout programs for the entire party ticket. As a practical matter, this money was controlled by each party's presidential campaign and used to free up the limited public money for television advertising specifically promoting the national ticket.

Predictably, the Republicans had been the first to tumble to the virtues of "soft money," raising several million dollars in several big states during the 1980 Reagan-Carter campaign. In 1984, the Republicans extended the system, and the Democrats began to catch on—but only to the extent of raising relatively small amounts in a handful of states.

But 1988 was to be a different story. Bob Farmer, the peerless fund-raiser who had made it possible for Dukakis to spend right up to the $23-million limit in the primaries, announced that he now intended to raise $50 million for the general election. The figure looked extravagant but Farmer was not to be taken lightly. In the primary campaign he had found nine hundred people who raised $10,000 or more, a not inconsiderable task when the contribution limit was $1,000. Included were three hundred who raised $20,000, seventy-five who raised $50,000 and twenty-three who raised $100,000.

In pursuing the "soft money," Farmer's principal tool was a "trustees" program under which 130 people wrote their own checks for $100,000, the limit imposed by the campaign, and another 150 individuals either contributed or raised $100,000. "While $100,000 isn't what it once was, it's still very significant," Farmer said later. That money, combined with the proceeds of the usual fund-raising galas and dinners and a direct-mail program that produced $18 million, finally totaled $68 million, putting the Democrats in a competitive position with the Republicans, an unprecedented situation for recent years.

The money was dispensed through "committees" established in party headquarters—"Victory '88" for the Republicans, "Campaign '88" for the

Democrats. The Democratic operation was particularly noteworthy because it accomplished something never before managed by the party—the distribution of national money to state party committees. Some of the state politicians, unsurprisingly, complained that the amounts were inadequate, but the truth was they far exceeded anything they had ever received in the past. And some of the state operations used some of the money for such things as computerizing voter lists that would stand them in good stead in future elections.

It was no surprise when after the election Bob Farmer easily won his own election to become treasurer of the Democratic National Committee.

The soft money was particularly important to the Dukakis campaign because a decision had been made early in the game to rely heavily on field operations, especially in the major industrial states, to identify, register and turn out Democratic voters. Charlie Baker, the young professional who had run the New Hampshire primary campaign and who had earned his stripes doing field work for Dukakis in Massachusetts, was assigned to direct the operation. Eventually "field," as it is called inside a campaign operation, had more than three thousand people on the Dukakis payroll, more than five hundred in California alone.

The notion of trying to win a presidential campaign with young operatives canvassing precincts seemed anachronistic in the television age. But for the Dukakis campaign, doing so made a lot of sense, particularly when there was already adequate public money for television. As a general rule, professionals in both parties agreed, it took more effort to see that Democratic-leaning potential voters, generally of lower education levels, actually registered and then got to the polls than it did with Republicans. And it was axiomatic in presidential elections that a high turnout favored the majority-party Democrats.

The result of this strategy was that in most major states, Dukakis had armies of field operatives and Bush only troops. But the Republicans could expect their voters to be more reliable about turning out, and in many of these states they had volunteer bases the Democrats could not match. As a result, the Bush campaign tended to put more of its soft money into targeted direct-mail appeals, telephone canvassing and, in some key states, sophisticated and extensive absentee-ballot programs.

The thesis of the Dukakis campaign was that if the race were close in these big states, the field operations could make the difference. In California, the campaign eventually identified 780,000 "low propensity" Democrats—individuals who could be counted upon to vote right if they could be gotten to the polling places. That approach might very well have worked in a tight contest. But, as the old story goes, if you're going to make rabbit stew, the first thing you have to do is steal the rabbit—have a tight contest.

In other areas, the Dukakis campaign had far more complex and continuing problems than did the Bush operation. John Sasso's return on Labor Day seemed to lift Dukakis out of a funk into which he had been falling along with the poll numbers. But the tension between Sasso and Susan Estrich, whom Sasso had now superseded as the de facto campaign manager, was reflected throughout the operation, particularly among staff members who felt a primary loyalty to one or the other of them. Sasso felt the campaign had not expanded as it should have in the year he had been in exile in the advertising business, and he began to make changes. New advertising people were enlisted, as well as such established professionals as Mike Berman, an old Mondale hand; Tom Donilon; Ed Reilly and Bob Shrum from the Gephardt campaign; media consultant Bob Squier and Mike DelGuidice from the Mario Cuomo operation in New York.

There were problems in state operations as well. Some of them had been entrusted to old Dukakis associates from Boston with limited political experience, and some of the professionals without that history questioned their credentials. The inevitable bad blood developed between some of the operatives in the field and "Boston"—just as it always did in any campaign where things were not going well. In Washington old Democratic hands were beefing because they had volunteered their help and been turned aside—a syndrome equally common in such situations.

Jesse Jackson clearly was not happy with what was going on. In his convention meeting with Dukakis, Jackson had recommended that two of his principal advisers, former Mayor Richard Hatcher of Gary and former Governor Toney Anaya of New Mexico, be brought into the upper levels of the Dukakis operation. But the Dukakis advisers had ignored the suggestion. Hatcher and Anaya were considered too difficult and politically aggressive to bring inside the operation. Nor were the Jackson state operatives being brought into the tent at a pace to satisfy him.

"Rather than accept our structure," Jackson said later, "they decided to circumvent our structure and they created their own. It created resentment [among blacks] all over the country." In some states, the clashes were conspicuous. In Michigan, the Dukakis coordinator, John Eade of Boston, and Joel Ferguson, the architect of Jackson's solid caucus victory over Dukakis there, were involved in a running, semi-public argument and competition over who would run the voter registration and turnout operations, especially in the cities with heavy concentrations of black voters.

Sasso made a point of calling on Jackson and holding several long conversations with him that seemed on the surface to ease the tension. But it never entirely dissipated. "There never was a comfort level that I would consider to be normal," Jackson said after the election. There was always the sense among the Dukakis people, he said, that he was a frightening figure to white voters in a way that could not be overcome.

Nevertheless, Jackson did campaign North and South for the Dukakis ticket, before white and black audiences alike, mocking that concern as he went. One frigid night, arriving at an airport hangar in Vermont that was jammed with five thousand people waiting to hear him speak, he turned to an aide and said: "Look at all these scared white people!"

On another occasion, Jackson went to Chattanooga—TVA country—to speak to three thousand workers, most of them white conservatives, facing job losses as a result of management policies of subcontracting work abroad. Jackson got up and started by telling the crowd he was brought up not far from there in Greenville, South Carolina. Then, as he remembered, it went like this:

"I listened to Tennessee Ernie Ford and Ernest Tubb and Red Foley just like I listened to Ray Charles and B.B. King."

"Yeah, yeah, yeah."

"I listened to Minnie Pearl and Grandpa Jones, too."

"Right, right."

"Let me ask y'all something. I think that we should raise the minimum wage."

"Right."

"I think that if women are willing to work they should get paid."

"Right."

"And we need a national health plan based on sickness, and not just based on wealth."

"Right."

"All of our children should have a chance to go to college and teachers to get paid."

"Right."

"We need to protect our social security."

"Right."

Then, Jackson recalled, "I say, 'All of those are liberal programs.' And they say, 'Aw, shit, Jesse!'

"Then I say, 'Y'all down here are getting sidetracked by liberal and conservative as a label. You're too poor to be talking about conservative. You act as if you and Reagan got something in common. What you and Reagan got in common?' " And the crowd roared: "Nothing!"

Jackson argued after the election: "These were the people who were supposed to be afraid of me and couldn't relate to me. The reality is America is changing faster than the leadership is. To dismiss all those people as unredeemable racists is a mistake. Their exposure has been limited. . . . It's a matter of more and more exposure." But the Dukakis campaign did not seem quite ready to run the risk.

Ron Brown, for his part, expressed disappointment later in the manner in which Jackson was utilized. The Dukakis strategists, he said, made a decision that "the key to winning" was recapturing the allegiance of Reagan Democrats and that to accomplish this end, "they had to keep Jesse at a distance."

The core of the problem for Dukakis with black leaders was their inability or unwillingness to generate optimum turnout for him. The Massachusetts governor had never had the kind of relationship with black leaders that Fritz Mondale had enjoyed. He had never been in the trenches in the struggles for civil rights, either in the South or in Congress. And, like his fellow white candidates, he had devoted little attention to the black community during the primaries, obviously fearing a backlash from Jackson if he seemed to be intruding on his constituency. As a result, Dukakis had made no emotional connection to rank-and-file black voters or to the local black ministers and politicians, whose enthusiasm was essential to a high turnout in cities like Chicago, Philadelphia and Detroit.

Sasso felt the campaign was behind the curve but by no means hopeless. "I can't say it was winnable for sure," he said later. "Bush had a lot going for him—peace, prosperity, Reagan and all of that. But there were some big openings there."

The principal problem, however, was that Dukakis had still not found a formula for countermanding the Bush campaign's disciplined and intense attack on him as another weak liberal who could not be trusted to fight crime and preserve the national security. "We were trying to get our message out and we had to deal with all the junk that was out there," Sasso said.

From the outset, at the meeting with Dukakis at which he agreed to return, Sasso had been urging his candidate to strike back. In a conversation in Dukakis' kitchen in Brookline, he told him: "You know, Mike, that the two things people most look for in a president are strength and commitment. They gotta believe you're strong and they gotta believe you're committed to a set of values." Then he recalled how Dukakis had struck back at Richard Gephardt in Iowa in 1987 when the Missouri congressman depicted him as being afraid to stand up to the Japanese on the trade question.

"When Gephardt started attacking you as weak last August . . . what did you do?" he recalled asking Dukakis. "You put it right in his face. You said, Richie, let's debate face-to-face. You knocked him on his ass and you never heard from him again. That's the model. You know that, for Christ's sake. What are you doing? You knocked the guy right on his ass and that was the end of him. You didn't hesitate twenty-four hours. You were right in his face. People didn't think you were negative."

But Dukakis was never persuaded that a harsh counterattack was wise. And he clearly was not comfortable with the way the campaign had to be conducted. As Kirk O'Donnell put it: "The structure of the general election was a structure he did not like. It was not a structure he had ever been in in public life, in a campaign, before. The whole life on the plane, the motorcade, do the speech, then go off to the next event, when he didn't have contact with voters, contact with the press, strictly living off a speech. A speech-driven campaign, a photo opportunity, sound-bite competition was an environment that he didn't like and it showed."

Dukakis himself said after the election: "One of the things that makes the final [election] difference is that you're walled off. I get my kicks out of this by being with people." In the primaries, he recalled, it was possible to meet informally with reporters and potential supporters and simply interested voters. In the general election, he added, "that just disappears."

Even when Dukakis tried to play the symbolic game, it sometimes didn't work out well. One day in early October, he visited an auto parts plant in Wellstown, Missouri, to give a speech decrying foreign ownership of assets in the United States. As it turned out, the plant was owned by an Italian holding company—an embarrassment for the candidate that drowned out his message for another news cycle.

George Bush, meanwhile, was continuing to pound Dukakis day after day. His campaign advisers had decided that backlash on the exploitation of the flag required playing down the pledge-of-allegiance issue for a while, although Roger Ailes did hold that commercial in reserve. But there were no restraints on the exploitation of the Willie Horton case and the prisoner-furlough question as the final proof that Michael Dukakis was soft on crime and criminals. Bush was clearly enjoying himself, spinning off one-liners. In Texas, he told some delighted supporters that while Clint Eastwood challenged villains with "Go ahead, make my day," Dukakis told them: "Go ahead, have a nice weekend." In Arkansas, he confided that Dukakis had given prisoners "a Club Med vacation."

Bush never appeared restrained by good taste in his relentless campaign to exploit the crime issue and Dukakis' opposition to the death penalty. One of the low points came in mid-October at Christ the King High School in Queens, where Bush had arrived to claim the endorsement of the Police Benevolent Association. It was another well-staged media event—the PBA endorsement had actually been voted earlier in the campaign. Several hundred uniformed cops lined up behind Bush while he addressed hundreds of high school students equipped by the campaign with signs and flags to wave for the television cameras.

Then Matthew Byrne, the father of a young policeman slain in the line of duty, presented his son's shield to Bush and told him that he had established a foundation in his son's name. To which Bush responded with a world-class cheap shot: "If the liberal governor of Massachusetts doesn't understand it when a Matt Byrne stands up and creates a foundation for his son, I do and so do the American people." If winning the election required a suggestion that his opponent would not sympathize with the father of a slain policeman, so be it.

Most striking about Bush's use of such tactics was his success in getting away with it. "We were surprised," Dukakis adviser Jack Corrigan said later, "that they paid no penalty for running this kind of campaign." On the contrary, Bush's negatives were declining rapidly while disapproval of Dukakis rose at a similar pace.

Bush's campaign on the prison-furlough issue also was being helped along by Republican organizations ostensibly not connected directly to his campaign. In California, an independent expenditure committee was running television commercials and press conferences featuring the Maryland couple victimized by Willie Horton. In Illinois, the Republican state committee distributed a flier telling voters: "All the murderers and rapists and drug pushers and child molesters in Massachusetts vote for Michael Dukakis. We in Illinois can vote against him.'' In Maryland, a Republican fund-raising letter featured pictures of Dukakis and Horton and asked: ''Is this your pro-family team for 1988?'' In Pennsylvania, a writer who had written extensively about the Willie Horton case was being brought in to speak to Republican audiences.

The response from the Bush campaign chairman, James Baker, was that, deplorable as they might be, these were independent efforts over which the campaign had no control—a denial that raised eyebrows considering how completely the Bush campaign controlled everything else the Republican Party was doing in 1988.

Occasionally, when there seemed to be signs of a backlash, the Bush campaign would venture into other issues. Shortly after the first debate, Bush suddenly produced a plan to help young Americans save for their education or a home or to start a business. It would defer the taxes on the interest on $1,000 a year deposited in IRA-like accounts—a plan that some accountants quickly figured would amount to a saving of $15.14 a year. Dukakis, waving a twenty-dollar bill to represent the savings, ridiculed the proposal as ''a new definition of trickle-down economics.''

The tax-deferral proposal, a child-care plan and his call for lowering the capital-gains tax were among the few specifics Bush ever presented during the campaign about his intentions in the White House. Baker and Bob Teeter insisted after the fact that he had taken firm stances on many issues, and the campaign produced a guide to his issues positions. But most of it was amorphous boilerplate, and there was never any question that the issues to which the campaign was giving prime visibility were those that questioned Dukakis' strength and patriotism.

Bush also was supported by what Atwater called the ''tactical flexibility'' of his campaign. One day, the candidate was scheduled to visit a Hispanic-American food-packaging business in Union City, New Jersey, to discuss the potential for minority enterprises when his campaign managers learned that Dukakis was speaking elsewhere about national-security policy. At a brief rally before the visit to the plant, Bush posed rhetorical questions to Dukakis about whether, on second thought, the Democratic candidate was still a critic of the invasion of Grenada and the bombing of Libya by the Reagan administration.

When the crowd reacted favorably, Craig Fuller, traveling with Bush, telephoned the response to the Fifteenth Street headquarters. The campaign strategists there then produced several other questions, which were relayed back to Fuller in time for him to put them on cards for Bush. When the vice president raised them at the food plant, the questions made far better material for television sound bites and newspaper stories alike than a discussion of minority enterprises. What's more, they competed for valuable airtime with what Dukakis was saying that day to counter the Bush rap that he was soft on defense.

Bush also followed a deft strategy in striking at Dukakis' claim to competence. The forays into his opponent's home territory—to sail Boston Harbor and accept the police endorsement—raised questions about whether the Massachusetts governor's stewardship had been as effective as he was claiming. And elsewhere Bush was telling audiences repeatedly that "the Massachusetts miracle" would better be described as "the Massachusetts mirage"—particularly in light of a discovery that the state was facing a budget deficit of several hundred million dollars, clearly requiring new taxes and spending reductions.

In fact, similar shortfalls were happening in many of the industrial states, including some with Republican governors such as California and New Jersey, because their tax systems were keyed to the federal tax code. The changes that had taken effect in 1987 as a result of the Tax Reform Act had cut state revenues sharply—and put Dukakis on the defensive. His situation was no worse than that in several other states, but he was the one running for president, not George Deukmejian or Tom Kean.

The hard truth, however, was that no issues other than those Bush had kept on the agenda all through the late summer and early fall were getting any significant attention. And all of them were working against Dukakis, steadily driving his "negatives" upward.

Dukakis' support for gun control was proving particularly threatening in some key areas. In Pennsylvania, Dukakis' state campaign coordinator, Lanny Johnson, was appalled to discover that fully 60 percent of Pennsylvania adults held hunting licenses and thus were prime targets for heavy mailings not only from the Bush campaign but also from the National Rifle Association. In parts of Texas, Dukakis coordinator Tom Cosgrove also found, the gun-control issue had so much volatility it clearly required tailored advertising to make clear this liberal from Massachusetts was not threatening Texans' hunting rifles. Lloyd Bentsen, campaigning intensively in his home state for both the vice presidency and reelection to his Senate seat, kept reassuring his constituents that, as a hunter himself, he knew there was no reason for concern.

By late September or early October, however, it was becoming increasingly apparent that the gamble on Bentsen in Texas was not paying off and that Bush was likely to capture the state's twenty-nine electoral votes. And Dukakis was being forced to devote so much time to states supposedly part of his base, including Pennsylvania, that Texas could no longer be given the kind of priority originally planned. Although the polls still showed Dukakis with a lead in New York, not even that state was totally safe for him anymore.

As the presidential debates approached, Dukakis was in serious trouble— running six to eight points behind Bush in some national opinion polls, and as much as twelve points behind in others. His negatives had reached 40 percent or higher and, for the first time, were exceeding his favorable ratings. Strategically, Dukakis had been backed into a corner. Most of the South, including Florida, now seemed out of reach. The imperative of debating George Bush face-to-face now assumed enormous proportions, far greater than Dukakis and his advisers had imagined in those balmy days of summer.

28

The Not So Great Debates

The basic question that governed a candidate's decision on whether he would debate his opponent, and under what terms, was a simple one: Who was ahead and who was behind? If you were ahead, and especially if you were the incumbent, you could take debates or leave them, and many incumbents left them. If you were behind, you extolled them as an essential element in the exercise of a free society and insisted the voters were entitled to them. Translation: You might not be able to catch up to your opponent without them.

And so it was in late August when the managers of George Bush and Michael Dukakis sat down to negotiate on debates between the two nominees and their running mates. Eighteen months earlier, when Republican National Chairman Frank Fahrenkopf and his Democratic counterpart, Paul Kirk, had agreed that the two parties would run three debates between the presidential nominees and one between their running mates, it had not been possible to answer that basic question. But by late August it was; the public-opinion polls showed that Bush had overcome Dukakis' early summer lead of up to seventeen percentage points and was edging ahead. So it was not surprising that as an opening gambit the Bush campaign announced that the vice president, the incumbent of sorts as defender of the Reagan administration, would not be taking part in any early debates. Two of them, one scheduled by the League of Women Voters in Birmingham, Alabama, on September 8 and another in Annapolis, Maryland, on September 14 sponsored by the Fahrenkopf-Kirk bipartisan Commission on Presidential Debates, would have to be canceled.

Jim Baker, who had skillfully handled the debate negotiations in 1980 and 1984 for Ronald Reagan, said the Bush campaign had never said it would be bound by the recommendations of Fahrenkopf and Kirk and that the details of any debates would have to be negotiated by the rival campaigns. But under no circumstances, Baker stipulated, would the vice president be debating before September 20. Indeed, as early as the Republican convention in New Orleans, the Bush media consultant, Roger Ailes, was saying he wasn't sure there ought to be any debates, but that if there were, one ought to be enough.

The Dukakis campaign chairman and chief debate negotiator, the candidate's Boston friend, lawyer Paul Brountas, was predictably irate, calling Bush's refusal to debate until the third week in September "shocking" and "inexcusable." The Dukakis campaign said it wanted four debates, but that obviously was an opening gambit both sides knew would be negotiated down.

The reasons for the Bush camp to behave as it did were equally obvious. Beyond the fact that he was moving ahead in the polls and represented the incumbent administration, he had a reputation as a weak debater, in spite of some passable performances in the Republican exchanges in the preconvention period. Not forgotten in political circles were his dismal debate with Reagan in Nashua during the 1980 primary (in which his memorable failure was not in the debate itself but in the argument beforehand over who should participate), and his 1984 encounter against Democratic vice presidential nominee Geraldine Ferraro. In the latter one, Bush came off as patronizing and even a bit gun-shy against the first woman on a major-party national ticket.

The Dukakis camp, for its part, had reasons to want several debates beyond the fact that he was slipping behind in the polls and was the challenger. He had considerable experience with the television debate format as moderator for two years on the public television forum, *The Advocates*, for which he had gotten very high marks. And in the Democratic debates during the primaries, he always acquitted himself well, and sometimes more than that. He was a bulldog for facts with a debating style and personality to match. The more debates there were, his people figured, the better his chances of being elected.

As far as the debate negotiations were concerned, however, it was no match. The smooth-talking Baker, with Ailes as his gruff bully-boy, treated Brountas and Susan Estrich, Dukakis' campaign manager, to a classic performance of the good-cop, bad-cop routine. Baker would say that in his opinion debates had the effect of "freezing" the campaign for days before they occurred, and Bush really didn't want more than one. Then Ailes would say he didn't see why there should be any debates at all, especially when Dukakis was "a professional debater." Whenever the discussions got intense, Ailes recalled later, Baker would get up and announce that he had to go to another meeting. "I'll leave you here with Ailes," he would say, at which, Ailes said, the Democrats would become more pliable. "They were easy," he said. Brountas, for his part, said he wasn't taken in for a moment by the caper. "Save it for the press," Brountas said later he told Ailes. But the fact was Baker got most of what he wanted.

From the Bush camp's point of view, the Dukakis side outfoxed itself from the start by making impossible demands. In addition to calling for four debates, three between Bush and Dukakis and one between Dan Quayle and Lloyd Bentsen, the Dukakis negotiators said they wanted direct exchanges between the candidates, rather than panelists asking questions. And they wanted debates exclusively devoted to foreign policy and domestic policy, and earlier dates. These were conditions beyond what had prevailed in the 1980 and 1984 debates, and Baker felt they enabled him to offer what had been done in those years as eminently reasonable. Baker was so confident of what the public reaction would be that he made clear to Brountas he was willing to walk away from the table and have no debates.

The discussions reached a point, Brountas said later, "where I wanted to make sure I wasn't going to be bluffed." Baker said he would agree only to two presidential and one vice presidential debate between September 25 and October 15. "Are you telling me it's a take-it-or-leave-it proposition?" Brountas remembers asking. When Baker responded that it was, he said, he complained that the proposition was unfair because the television networks on most of the nights in that period would be airing the Olympics and major-league baseball playoffs, and the largest possible audience should be the objective. "That's not my problem," Brountas says Baker told him. "I didn't schedule the World Series. I didn't schedule the Olympics."

Brountas asked Baker: "If I say, 'Take it and shove it,' what's your position going to be?" Baker replied, he recalled, "I can risk that position. I think I'll come out all right on that, Paul. I'll go to the American people and say, 'Look, last time we only had three debates, two presidential and one vice presidential debate. I'm giving Brountas the same number of debates they had last time. I'm giving him a choice of twenty-five days. He can pick the nights—any nights he wants. Are you going to tell me you're going to say no to that? I think I'm going to win that battle.' " Hearing that, Brountas told us, "I made the judgment that he was right." If it had been a high-stakes poker game, in other words, Brountas might have walked out of the room in a barrel.

At one point in the negotiations, as Brountas pushed for three presidential debates, Baker suggested tongue in cheek that maybe his side would agree if the Dukakis side was willing to drop the vice presidential debate. According to Bob Goodwin, an Ailes aide in the talks, Brountas and Estrich quickly declined. In a subsequent meeting, though, Brountas said he was willing, figuring that with the expectations of a decent performance by Quayle so low, it would be easy for him to exceed them and hard for Bentsen to come out a winner. But Baker told Brountas: "Our vice presidential candidate wants to debate. The vice president wants him to debate."

The one thing that Brountas did win on, Baker said later, was agreement to have the candidates stand instead of sit, and to let Dukakis stand on a riser behind his podium to compensate somewhat for the candidates' difference in height. Tom Donilon, the former Joe Biden consultant who joined the Dukakis negotiating team, said later that Dukakis won other concessions that were to his advantage. The Bush side agreed to ninety-minute debates instead of sixty minutes and in having mostly television journalists who Donilon contended would handle follow-up questions better because they were used to the medium. Print journalists, he said, would be more likely to read their questions and be less comfortable before the cameras.

Donilon's role in the negotiations, and then in preparing Dukakis and Lloyd Bentsen for their debates, provided an interesting study in how the news media, television particularly, have increasingly winked at conflicts of interest and at journalism's traditional responsibility to be impartial toward political candidates. Donilon was a key figure in the Walter Mondale campaign of 1984 and participated in Mondale's preparations to debate Ronald Reagan. He joined Biden's campaign for the 1988 Democratic nomination and, after it collapsed in the fall of 1987, while practicing law in Washington signed on with CBS News as a consultant. In that capacity, Donilon sat in on the briefing of anchorman Dan Rather in preparation for his stormy interview with George Bush during the Iowa caucuses. Donilon continued to be a CBS News consultant thereafter and in September joined the Dukakis team, this time to help negotiate the conditions of the presidential debates. In that role, he recommended that the network anchormen, which included Rather at CBS, be selected as panelists or moderators. (Rather was selected for the second presidential debate but declined.) After that, Donilon headed the team that prepared Dukakis for his debates with Bush, and Bentsen for his debate with Quayle.

Such arrangements have become more common as enterprising political operatives trade on their insider experience or reputations with pliable television and newspaper executives to work both sides of the street. Another prime example in 1988 was Robert Beckel, the manager of the losing Mondale campaign in 1984 who, while continuing to function in 1988 as a political adviser to candidates, including Dukakis, did television commentary for a large number of local stations around the country and for network news shows. Beckel managed to obtain press credentials that enabled him, for example, to witness campaign debates from a seat in the press section and then, immediately afterward, offer himself to "other" reporters there for expert comment on the debates, in some cases involving Democratic candidates with whom he had counseled in the 1988 campaign. In this manner was journalism's integrity protected against the host of critics who question it. But after columnist George Will felt free to help prepare Ronald Reagan to debate Jimmy Carter in 1980, and then went on the air after the debate and praised Reagan's performance, anything seemed acceptable to some television and press employers.

An irony in all this business about conflict of interest surrounding the debate negotiation was an objection from the Bush camp about the inclusion of another Dukakis adviser, former Mondale lieutenant Richard Moe, on the Dukakis negotiating team. Moe should not be involved, the Bush operatives insisted, because he was a member of the bipartisan Commission on Presidential Debates that was going to sponsor two of the agreed-to debates. Moe was dropped.

The final memorandum of understanding set out the terms—two presidential debates and one vice presidential debate within the time frame the Bush side demanded, with panelists from the news media, open-ended in subject matter and the candidates standing—Dukakis on a soap box if he so decided. The first debate, sponsored by the Commission, was set for Wake Forest University in Winston-Salem, North Carolina, on Sunday, September 25. The procedure agreed to for selecting the panelists provided that each side submit ten names and the Commission submit ten more. The campaigns in collaboration then picked two names from each of the three lists, for a pool of six, from which the Commission then selected the final three, including one from each of the candidates' lists. Baker was largely responsible for this approach, to assure relative neutrality and reduce haggling. Four years earlier, about a hundred names were kicked around for the first Reagan-Mondale debate before agreement was reached on the panelists. This time, Lee Atwater picked up the phone and called the tall, stocky Donilon. "All right, Big Daddy," he asked, "you want to make a deal?" Within a few minutes the panel was set: Jim Lehrer of the *MacNeil/Lehrer News Hour* as moderator and John Mashek of the *Atlanta Constitution*, Anne Groer of the *Orlando* (Fla.) *Sentinel* and Peter Jennings of ABC News as the questioners.

As had now become routine, both candidates were trained for the encounter as if they were fighters getting ready for a championship bout. Elaborate issues books were compiled to bring them up to speed on all manner of subjects likely to be raised. Sparring partners armed with responses the opponent could be expected to make engaged in mock debates with each candidate, with political aides playing the roles of the questioning reporters. The rehearsals were videotaped for reviewing by the candidate, and Ailes also, in his phrase, "wargamed" the exercise with panelist stand-ins and without Bush.

Playing Dukakis for the Bush drills was Dick Darman, a Harvard-bred man of Massachusetts known for suffering fools reluctantly. "Darman was very good, too," Ailes said. "Appropriately arrogant and humorless." Bob Goodwin played the moderator and campaign aides Debby Steelman, Margaret Tutwiler and Jim Pinkerton were the panelists. The mock debates took place in Bush's dining room in the Washington residence with exact replicas of the podiums set up. Darman gave answers written by Pinkerton, the research chief, and Baker, Ailes, Teeter, Atwater, Fuller, Tate, Dennis Ross and onetime Bush aide Vic Gold observed and coached the candidate from time to time. Darman would give his closing statement in a heavy Boston accent, and at one point showed up on the set wearing a tank helmet.

For Dukakis, Bob Barnett, a Washington lawyer who impersonated Bush in Geraldine Ferraro's preparations to debate him in 1984, played the same role again. Barnett in the ensuing four years had updated his issues book on Bush and was ready. He looked and sounded the part. (After the 1984 campaign, Bush, in talking to us about having Ferraro and Barnett in for lunch, couldn't remember his name. "The guy who played me," he said. "The preppy guy.") Dukakis, according to Donilon, at first resisted heavy preparation, but once he understood the necessity and thoroughness of the drill, he threw himself into it.

Donilon had an explicit game plan for Dukakis. He had to show he could slug it out with the vice president of the United States, but he also had to show it in a way that did not reinforce his troublesome image as cold and aloof. He told Dukakis that the candidate who was "the appropriate aggressor" usually won. He coached him to put the debate on his own terms and "point out Bush's inconsistencies." At the same time, Donilon remembered, Dukakis was reminded that it was important "that it needed to be done in a confident fashion and not look prosecutorial; not whining, not pointing." But, Donilon observed, "he was the challenger. . . . He had to demonstrate that he was able to stand up to Bush, move Bush around the stage, cross that invisible threshold that challengers have to cross to be in charge in presidential debates." Other goals were to hit at Bush's vulnerabilities and lack of judgment, and then make the case for economic change.

Part of the Bush strategy in advance of the first debate was to try, as incongruous as it seemed, to have the news media see the contest as a kind of reverse David against Goliath, but with the taller and more experienced Bush cast as David and the shorter and less-experienced Dukakis—whom Ailes always referred to as "Shorty"—as Goliath. Aides continued to circulate Ailes' spin about Dukakis being a "professional debater" with broad television experience and Bush being a poor one, obviously trying to lower expectations for Bush in the debate and hence make it easier for him to get good grades afterward. "We capitalized on that, frankly," Baker said later, "and the vice president was perfectly willing for us to do that. It wasn't an insult to his manhood for us to go out and say, 'Hey, wait a minute. Our guy's not that good a debater.' He basically let us go out and trash his debating ability, but it paid off."

Not only was Bush willing to go along, but he joined the spin, too, and then some. In a pre-debate press conference, after laying the party line on the assembled reporters, Bush explained that he was "lowering expectations"! Ailes couldn't believe his ears. "The guy does that," he said later, laughing. "You never tell him what the drill is because he just blurts it out."

The question of voters' perceptions of whether one or the other candidate had "done well" in a debate was not, however, a laughing matter. For all the hours of preparation and rehearsal, the campaign strategists on both sides knew that what millions of voters took away with them from a presidential debate was not the specific answers on complex national questions, but rather an overall impression of the debaters. Would Bush or Dukakis be the more "sincere" candidate? Which of them would be more "likable" to the viewers? Such judgments over the ninety-minute course of a debate—or however long a voter stayed tuned in—could determine the vote of millions of Americans too busy, too lazy or too uninterested to follow the campaign on a day-by-day basis. The debates therefore became a handy crutch on which voters could lean in making a decision. And, considering that debate answers as often as not were mere regurgitations of boilerplate responses given repeatedly on the stump, such debates were not satisfactory in themselves for making voting decisions, and deciding the outcome of an election. Yet because they were the single most sustained dose of candidate exposure most voters were likely to get, they took on immense importance in the eyes of the candidates, their managers, the news media and the electorate.

In the first debate, Dukakis, in the fashion of Nick Mitropoulos' "mongoose," pounced early and often. The opening question from Lehrer—"What is it about these times that drives or draws so many Americans to use drugs?"—went to Bush. He answered it with a mushy monologue about "a deterioration of values" including "talk of legalizing or decriminalizing marijuana and other drugs" that required better education and a tougher attitude toward crime. Dukakis struck. Conceding that "it's important that our leaders demonstrate those values from the top," he blasted "a government that's been dealing with a drug-running Panamanian dictator" who had been "dealing drugs to our kids." He concluded sharply: "Values begin at the top, in the White House." Score round one for Dukakis.

Dukakis got the second question from John Mashek, on deficit reduction, and he went after Bush with his answer to that one, too. After noting that as governor he had balanced ten straight budgets (Massachusetts law required it), he said he would cut "certain weapons systems," invest in economic growth, reduce interest rates, collect "billions" in uncollected taxes and reduce farm subsidies. Bush, he said, wanted "to give the wealthiest taxpayers in this country a five-year, $40-billion tax break"—apparently Bush's capital-gains tax reduction plan—and still "spend a lot of money on additional programs. If he keeps this up," Dukakis said as the audience laughed, "he's going to be the Joe Isuzu of American politics."

Bush seemed rattled. "Is this the time to unleash our one-liners?" he asked, again blurting out his strategy. And then he unleashed one: "That answer was about as clear as Boston Harbor." He went on to a rather thin defense of his proposal to cut the capital-gains tax as job-producing and hence revenue-producing, mentioned his "flexible freeze" approach to deficit reduction and reiterated his insistence that the economy would "continue to grow because I will not raise taxes." Round two to Dukakis.

On a question about national health insurance, Bush said he wanted more "flexibility in Medicaid," to which Dukakis replied familiarly, "But George, that's no answer." Bush came back lamely, "You don't like the answer, but it's an answer." Dukakis the mongoose struck again: "Well, no, it's no answer to those 37 million people, most of them members of working families who don't have a dime of health insurance and don't know how to pay the bill if their kids get sick at night. . . ." Round three to Dukakis.

It went on like that, with Dukakis boring in at every opportunity. When Bush dragged out Dukakis' statement that "I am a card-carrying member of the ACLU" and dusted off the flag-pledge issue and denied he was questioning his opponent's patriotism, Dukakis scored his best blow of the night. It was here that he bristled, charged Bush with "questioning my patriotism" and scowled: "I resent it. I resent it." He went on in a lecturing tone: "My parents came to this country as immigrants. They taught me that this was the greatest country in the world. I'm in public service because I love this country. I believe in it. And nobody's going to question my patriotism as the vice president has now, repeatedly. The fact of the matter is if the pledge of allegiance was the acid test of one's patriotism, the vice president's been the presiding officer in the United States Senate for the past seven and a half years. To the best of my knowledge he's never once suggested that a session of the Senate begin with the pledge of allegiance.'' He noted that he had been quick to defend Bush when his military record was attacked just before the Republican convention and said it was time to get on to real issues. ''Those are the concerns of the people that are watching us tonight,'' he said. ''Not labels that we attach to each other's questions about each other's patriotism and loyalty.'' Bush stood silently, looking somewhat sheepish. Round four to Dukakis.

Bush continued to give himself away as the scripted debater. On a question about the homeless, he trotted out his acceptance-speech reference to ''a thousand points of light''—meaning, he said, ''the enormous numbers of shelters and organizations to help.'' After he had used the expression twice more, and talked again about how he was ''haunted'' by the tribulations of deprived inner-city children, an exasperated Dukakis blurted: ''Being haunted, a thousand points of light—I don't know what that means. I know what strong leadership is. I know what's happened over the course of the past eight years. These programs have been cut and slashed and butchered and they've hurt kids all over this country.'' Round five to Dukakis.

Bush was not entirely out of it, however. When Dukakis was asked how he squared his opposition to the death penalty with his support of abortion on demand, he said the issues had to be dealt with separately. He took the occasion of the death penalty part of the question to bring up Bush's demand for the death penalty against drug dealers, noting that ''his administration has a federal furlough program which is one of the most permissive in the country, which gave last year seven thousand furloughs to drug traffickers and drug pushers, the same people that he says he now wants to execute.'' Bush hopped on the answer to inject the Massachusetts prison-furlough program and the infamous Willie Horton into the debate. ''When a narcotics wrapped-up guy goes in and murders a police officer, I think they ought to pay with their life,'' he said. ''. . . So I am not going to furlough men like Willie Horton, and I would meet with their, the victims of his last escapade, the rape and the brutalization of the family down there in Maryland.'' Finally, score a round for Bush.

Dukakis recovered quickly, however. Bush was asked whether, if the Supreme Court were to make abortions illegal again, ''do you think the women who defy the law and have them anyway, as they did before it was okayed by the Supreme Court, and the doctors who perform them, should go to jail?'' Bush replied: ''I haven't sorted out the penalties, but I do know, I do know that I oppose abortion. And I favor adoption. . . . I'm for the sanctity of life, and once that illegality is established, then we can come to grips with the penalty side, and of course there's got to be some penalties to enforce the law, whatever they may be.''

The mongoose pounced again. ''Well,'' Dukakis snapped, ''I think what the vice president is saying is that he's prepared to brand a woman a criminal for making this decision. It's as simple as that. I don't think it's enough to come before the American people who are watching us tonight and say, 'Well, I haven't sorted it out.' This is a very, very difficult and fundamental decision that all of us have to make. And what he is saying, if I understand him correctly, is that he's prepared to brand a woman a criminal for making this choice.'' When Bush tried to explain, Dukakis cut him off with a curt "Let me finish," and he went on in the same slashing vein. Another round for Dukakis.

Bush seemed to be reeling. He stumbled through a defense of why he had once toasted deposed Philippines dictator Ferdinand Marcos for his devotion to democratic principles. And he got mixed up on a defense question, saying: "We are going to make some changes and some tough choices before we go to the deployment on the Midgetman missile, or on the Minuteman, whatever it is. We're going to have to—the MX. We're going to have to do that." And then he added inexplicably: "It's Christmas." He apparently had been coached to make a joke about his earlier confusion of Pearl Harbor Day. After he had said in a speech on September 7 that it was the anniversary, gags circulated widely that he didn't want to debate on this night, September 25, because it was Christmas. Rattled, it just tumbled out, to laughter from the perplexed audience. Trying to recover, Bush seemed to use another scripted line, the apparent reference to Dukakis as a cool, unflappable operator: "Wouldn't it be nice to be the iceman so you never make a mistake?" And Dukakis, indeed, was behaving on this night as if ice water were coursing through his veins.

Bush did have one very good moment later, ironically in trying to defend himself on the arms-for-hostages deal. Jennings asked him whether he would ask President Reagan "for permission to tell the American people what advice you did give him" on the matter. Dodging the question and still stumbling over his words, Bush tried to turn the question onto Dukakis, questioning his positions on the American presence in the Persian Gulf and policies toward Afghanistan and Angola. He brought forth this garble: "You judge on the record. Are the Soviets coming out of Afghanistan? How does it look in a program he called or some one of these marvelous Boston adjectives up there and—about Angola—now we have a chance—several Bostonians don't like it, but the rest of the country will understand."

Many in the audience, apparently responding to the Boston-bashing since the sentence made no sense, applauded. Bush went on, mentioning how Dukakis "goes around ranting about Noriega," and then he finally got something out right. "He can talk about Iran-contra and also," he said, a light bulb going on at last, "I'll make a deal with you. I will take the blame for those two incidents if you give me half the credit for all the good things that have happened in world peace since Ronald Reagan and I took over from the Carter administration." Heavy applause, and another round for Bush.

When he attempted to continue, Lehrer cut him off, leading Bush to protest that his warning light was only on yellow. Lehrer apologized and asked him to proceed, adding, "You said nobody's perfect." Bush replied: "I said I wasn't perfect. Where was I?'' Dukakis jumped in, grinning: ''Twenty-fifth of December, Mr. Vice President.''

The rest of the debate was routine, with Bush making certain not to waste another prepared one-liner. In a discussion of the relative qualifications of their running mates, Bush observed: ''We'll have an opportunity to see the two of them in action in a friendly forum . . . wonderful friendly fashion like this.'' Then he added: ''I had hoped this had been a little friendlier evening. I wanted to hitchhike a ride home in his tank with him.''

The verdict at ringside was that Dukakis had won, but not by a knockout. There was no major gaffe of the sort that had severely damaged earlier presidential candidates, such as Gerald Ford's insistence in 1976 that Eastern Europe was not under Soviet domination. Nevertheless, the Dukakis strategists were buoyed by their candidate's aggressive performance. The Bush team sent its ''spin patrol'' with the coordinated ''talking point'' that Dukakis had proved that he was a flaming liberal. Some, like Darman, expressed ''amazement'' that he hadn't ''tried to move to the center,'' as any deft politician so far out on the left would have attempted to do. Or, as Jim Lake put it, reading from the same sheet music, Bush had ''put Dukakis in the left-wing radical fringe'' of his party. (Lake told us later that Darman, after watching the debate and noting that Dukakis was holding to some liberal positions, hit upon a remarkable strategy in the anything-goes era of the spin. ''You know what?'' he told Lake. ''The best thing for us to use is the truth.'' Dukakis had sounded like a liberal, so why not hammer at that?) Ailes said the two objectives for Bush going in were to have voters liking him when it was over and to have them see Dukakis as a liberal, and both were achieved.

Behind this facade, however, Bush himself told Baker he hadn't done as well as he could have. ''I'm going to do a heck of a lot better the next time,'' Baker remembered him saying that night. Ailes said later that Bush did not get a full night's rest the night before because he was out in his backyard looking with his Secret Service agents for ''Spikey,'' a stuffed animal of one of his granddaughters. ''I can take this guy,'' Ailes said Bush told him after coming off the stage.

The day after debates, the first order of business is always damage control, and which side labors to dig itself out is usually a fair indication of the true reading inside the campaign of who won and lost. Dukakis had scored effectively with his charge that Bush in his vague answer on penalties for women who would have abortions under a Supreme Court prohibition. In a press conference the next morning to ''clarify'' Bush's position, Baker reported that his candidate ''thinks a woman in a situation like that would more properly be considered an additional victim'' and that the performers of abortions were the ones who should face criminal prosecution.

But Dukakis was doing some damage control of his own. He put out a statement listing six instances in which he disagreed with ACLU positions. He said he was against ending tax-exempt status for Catholic schools, against opposing child pornography laws and did not want the words "under God" stricken from the pledge of allegiance.

In the next days, the campaign dialogue returned to the old themes, with Bush interspersing selected issue positions with Dukakis-bashing. With the flag-pledge controversy having been cooled off by, as Ailes put it, going "a flag too far" with the flag-factory extravaganza in New Jersey, the Bush campaign put even greater emphasis on the prisoner-furlough story.

In an apparent effort to temper criticism, Bush made one notable speech to the Ohio Republican Party convention in Columbus in which he toned down his slashing at Dukakis, saying on defense that his opponent "tends to be more skeptical of American power than trusting of it," and on prison furloughs that "I have, frankly, more sympathy for the victims of crime than the criminals who commit them. I believe in 'the forgiveness of sin and the redemption of ignorance.' But I also believe society has the right and duty to permanently protect itself from those who are so far incorrigible." At the same time, however, the prison-furlough television ad continued to run, and in unscripted speeches Bush returned time and again to that scene of convicted murderers and rapists being loosed by the governor of Massachusetts to rape and pillage. Dukakis started airing his "Packaging of George Bush" television commercials featuring actors impersonating Bush's media consultants planning to exploit the flag-pledge and prison-furlough controversies.

The focus of the campaign meanwhile shifted to the vice presidential nominees as their October 5 debate in Omaha approached. Since the close of the Republican convention, Dan Quayle had continued to shadowbox with his past, first as the controversy about his National Guard service stretched on and then as he campaigned in a manner that looked suspiciously as though he had been assigned to the minor leagues. In fact, although Stu Spencer's plan of having the vice presidential nominee "sandwich" Dukakis had been abandoned because of lack of confidence in Quayle, a second, safer part of Spencer's approach was carried out. Quayle was scheduled into secondary media markets, mostly in Republican areas, to anchor that base and free up Bush to challenge Dukakis in the industrial belt and other areas he needed to win.

After completing what Rich Bond called "Candidate's School" under the wing of Spencer, Joe Canzeri, Mitch Daniels and their associates, and while questions still had to be dealt with over who helped Quayle get into the National Guard and how, he was sent out to help himself. On the theory that the best defense was a good offense, the Bush campaign picked the news media and those ever-serviceable "left-wing liberals" to wrap Quayle in the martyr's cloak.

The first week after the close of the convention, when Bush went to Chicago and told a cheering Veterans of Foreign Wars convention that his running mate had been put "under shrill, partisan attack," he declared: "Let his attackers cast the first stone. Let them cast it. He served honorably." Quayle then was rushed out to Chicago to thank the VFW members and to soak up more favorable publicity at a time he badly needed it. He drew a roar of approval when, after acknowledging that his Guard unit was never called up to active duty, he said: "After these last seventy-two hours, no one can say I've never faced combat." He assured the convention delegates that no improper influence was used to get him into the Guard and none was needed because the Guard had openings at the time he applied. That claim, too, underwent sharp press scrutiny, with conflicting reports. Indiana Guard records indicated that in June 1969 it was above authorized strength, permitting recruiting only on a limited basis.

The Paula Parkinson story wouldn't die either. *Playboy* magazine released quotes from her from an advance copy of the November issue in which she alleged that Quayle had "flirted" and danced "extremely" closely with her and "wanted to make love" with her during the Florida weekend. Parkinson said she rebuffed Quayle. Former Congressman Tom Evans of Delaware, who had brought her to the resort, accused her of making up the story to boost the sales of the magazine, which had paid her for the interview. Quayle denounced the charges as "outrageous lies" and cautioned reporters to "be a little bit careful about this because it's totally untrue." He reminded them he had a wife and three small children.

The Bush campaign, ever vigilant for easy targets of opportunity, next whisked Quayle off to a National Guard convention in St. Louis, where he sought to shift the focus from himself with a blistering attack not only on Dukakis but on his predecessor Democratic candidates. Dukakis' defense policies, he charged, were a "replay of the McGovern-Carter-Mondale dogma that has shoved the Democratic Party over to the far left." On these trips, Quayle spoke briefly from scripts and his handlers kept the press away from him so that he wouldn't have to field the pesky questions that haunted his candidacy. And the questions kept coming—about his college and law school grades, which he wouldn't release, and about how he got into law school in the first place, amid reports from some faculty members that he was at best a mediocre student who was more interested in his golf game than in his studies.

Occasionally Quayle would champ at the bit placed in his mouth by the handlers. In early September, speaking to the City Club of Chicago on national defense, he chucked his text and winged it, with disastrous results. He rambled, misquoted people and generally botched the effort. Afterward, Canzeri, in Washington, talked by phone with Spencer, traveling with the candidate. "Why did you let him?" Canzeri asked. Spencer replied: "I want him to step on his dick, and then we'll own him again."

It was clear the handlers would have to hold the reins a bit tighter; the colt was getting a little frisky. Opening a local Bush campaign headquarters in a suburb of Milwaukee, Quayle quipped: "Want to hear a sad story about the Dukakis campaign, another sad story? The governor of Massachusetts, he lost his top naval adviser last week. The rubber duck drowned in his bathtub."

The remark was rather juvenile coming from a vice presidential candidate, but it could be forgiven because Quayle after only a few weeks out on the stump was still riding his campaign bicycle with the training wheels on. His handlers had little confidence in his ability to pedal without them, and much concern that if they took them off, in his immaturity he'd go careening into a telephone pole. "We were continually putting out fires," Canzeri said later. "There was a sense we couldn't turn him loose on your group [the press]." In internal discussions, he said, Quayle had a short attention span. "He didn't want anything on paper. His eyes would glaze over. He'd go away from us. There was an immaturity," he said, but also a cockiness that he could deal with anything.

Quayle's observations could be downright mind-boggling at times. At a press conference in Moore, Oklahoma, in mid-September, he referred to the Holocaust against Jews in World War II as "an obscene period in our nation's history." When reporters pointed out that this tragic event was a part of Nazi Germany's history, he observed that "our nation was on the side of justice" in the war. "I mean we, we all lived in this century," he went on. "I didn't live in this century, but in this century's history."

For these reasons, the Bush campaign approached Quayle's debate with the smooth-talking, unflappable Lloyd Bentsen with considerable trepidation. This time, unlike the case in the first presidential debate, the strategists didn't have to con the news media to lower expectations about their candidate; they couldn't get much lower. Quayle was put through a mock debating session with Senator Bob Packwood of Oregon, a similarly mild-mannered gent, playing an aggressive Bentsen. But afterward, Packwood walked over to Quayle and, Bob Goodwin recalled later, told him: "I know Lloyd Bentsen. He won't attack you the way I did today. He's a gentleman. You don't have to be worried about being attacked." In the rehearsal, Margaret Tutwiler sat in as moderator and coaches included Spencer, Daniels, Ailes, speechwriter Ken Kachigian and, on occasion, Baker. The session was taped and played back to Quayle.

By this time he had taken to noting to audiences, in the context of his own youth and experience, that John F. Kennedy had served less time in Congress than he had when Kennedy ran for and was elected president in 1960. During the debate preparations, according to Canzeri, Quayle was specifically told not to make the Kennedy comparison in the debate.

Bentsen, meanwhile, prepared as if he were taking his college entrance exam. "He was very nervous about the debate," Donilon said, "because his expectations were through the ceiling." He worked harder, Donilon said, than any other politician he had ever worked with. Congressman Dennis Eckart of Ohio, a young look-alike, played Quayle in the mock sessions.

The vice presidential debate took place in Omaha's Civic Auditorium. Judy Woodruff of the *MacNeil/Lehrer News Hour* was the moderator and the panelists were Tom Brokaw of NBC News, Brit Hume of ABC News and Jon Margolis of the *Chicago Tribune*. Even before the questioning started, Woodruff in her introduction captured what was on the voters' minds—or should have been. "Based on the history since World War II," she said, "there is almost a fifty-fifty chance that one of the two men here tonight will become president of the United States." Then, in her opening question to Quayle, she bored in. Taking note of general criticism about "your decision to stay out of the Vietnam war [and] for your poor academic record," Woodruff pointed out that other prominent Republicans had joined in. She said that Alexander Haig had "said that your pick was the dumbest call George Bush could have made" and that Bob Dole had said "that a better-qualified person could have been chosen." What about it?

Quayle defended his qualifications, which he said, "are not age alone," noting that "I have more experience than others that have sought the office of vice president." In the area of national security and arms control, jobs and education and the budget deficit, he said, "I have more experience than does the governor of Massachusetts." Then, to prove his point, he began to throw around missile and arms-control lingo: "You have to understand the difference between a ballistic missile, a warhead, what throw-weight, what megatonnage is. You better understand about telemetry and encryption. And you better understand that you have to negotiate from a position of strength." He talked about his authorship of the Job Training Partnership Act that he said had trained "over 3 million economically disadvantaged youth and adults in this country" and called for the line-item veto to deal with the deficit.

Bentsen in response drove home Woodruff's point. "The debate tonight is not about the qualifications for the vice presidency," he said. "The debate is whether or not Dan Quayle and Lloyd Bentsen are qualified to be president of the United States. Because Judy, just as you have said, that has happened too often in the past. And if that tragedy should occur, we have to step in there without any margin for error, without time for preparation, to take over the responsibility for the biggest job in the world, that of running this great country of ours; to take over the awesome responsibility for commanding the nuclear weaponry that this country has. No, the debate tonight is a debate about the presidency itself, and a presidential decision that has to be made by you. The stakes could not be higher."

In the course of the ninety-minute debate, other issues came up—differences between Bentsen and Dukakis, approaches to social security, the environment, aid to the disadvantaged at home and the contras in Nicaragua, campaign contributions, occupational safety, farm subsidies, the war on drugs, arms sales to Iran. Whenever possible, Quayle would use the question to attack Dukakis, obviously according to the game plan. But again and again the questioners returned to the "heartbeat away" matter—what Quayle in particular would do if lightning struck. And each time he was asked he would respond merely by repeating a defense of his qualifications.

Brit Hume asked him: "Let us assume, if we can for the sake of this question, that you have become vice president and the president is incapacitated for one reason or another, and you have to take the reins of power. When that moment came, what would be the first steps that you'd take, and why?" Surely, with the army of handlers hovering protectively over Quayle, he was prepared to knock this obvious question out of the box.

"First," Quayle replied haltingly, "first, I'd say a prayer for myself and for the country I'm about to lead." So far, so good. "And then I would assemble his people and talk." And that essentially was it. Quayle then went back to the matter of qualifications. "And as I have said, age alone, although I can tell you, after the experiences of these last few weeks in the campaign, I've added ten years to my age, age alone is not the only qualification," he repeated. He talked again of his twelve years in Congress and the three areas of experience mentioned earlier. And his eight years on the Senate Armed Services Committee, he concluded, "has given me the experience to deal with the Soviet Union and how we can move forward. That is just one of the troubling issues that's going to be facing this nation, and I'm prepared."

But Hume obviously wasn't prepared to accept that answer. When his turn came around again, he went back to his first question. "You said you would say a prayer and you said something about a meeting," he said. "What would you do next?"

Quayle was defensive. "I don't believe that it's proper for me to get into the specifics of a hypothetical situation like that," he said. "The situation is that if I was called upon to serve as the president of this country, or the responsibilities of the president of this country, would I be capable and qualified to do that?" And he proceeded once again to reiterate his qualifications, adding that "I have traveled a number of times. I've been to Geneva many times to meet with our negotiators as we were hammering out the INF treaty. I've met with the Western political leaders—Margaret Thatcher, Chancellor Kohl; I know them, they know me. I know what it takes to lead this country forward. And if that situation arises, yes, I will be prepared, and I will be prepared to lead this country if that happens."

Three questions later, Tom Brokaw tried. Maybe Hume's question was hypothetical, he said, but "it is, sir, after all, the reason that we're here tonight, because you are running not just for vice president, and if you cite the experience that you had in Congress, surely you must have some plan in mind about what you would do if it fell to you to become president of the United States, as it has to so many vice presidents just in the last twenty-five years or so."

One would have thought that Quayle would be happy to have another crack at the question he had so ineffectively answered on the first two occasions. Instead, he showed exasperation. "Let me try to answer the question one more time," he said. "I think this is the fourth time that I've had this question." Brokaw corrected him: "The third time." Quayle went on. "Three times that I've had this question, and I will try to answer it again for you as clearly as I can, because the question you are asking is what kind of qualifications does Dan Quayle have to be president, what kind of qualifications do I have and what would I do in this kind of a situation." He was only half right. He wasn't being asked again about his qualifications.

Quayle continued: "And what would I do in this situation? I would make sure that the people in the Cabinet and the people that are advisers to the president are called in, and I would talk to them, and I will work with them. And I will know them on a firsthand basis, because as vice president I will sit on the National Security Council. And I will know them on a firsthand basis because I'm going to be coordinating the drug effort. I will know them on a firsthand basis because Vice President George Bush is going to re-create the Space Council, and I will be in charge of that. I will have day-to-day activities with all the people in government. And then, if that unfortunate situation happens —if that situation, which would be very tragic, happens, I will be prepared to carry out the responsibilities of the presidency of the United States of America.''

And then, still another time, Quayle started talking about his qualifications. ''It is not just age; it's accomplishments, it's experience,'' he repeated. ''I have far more experience than many others that sought the office of vice president of this country. I have as much experience in the Congress as Jack Kennedy did when he sought the presidency. . . .''

Bentsen stiffened at this last. Invited by Woodruff to respond, he glared across the stage at his opponent. ''Senator,'' Bentsen intoned, ''I served with Jack Kennedy. I knew Jack Kennedy. Jack Kennedy was a friend of mine. Senator, you are no Jack Kennedy.''

The audience erupted in cheers, whoops and applause. This time the mongoose was mild-mannered Lloyd Bentsen. Quayle had not directly compared himself with Kennedy, only—accurately—with his length of congressional service. But Bentsen's reply hit him between the eyes nonetheless, and he seemed stunned. ''I saw his Adam's apple going up and down,'' Bentsen told us later. ''I saw the shocked look on his face.''

Amid the shouting and handclapping, Quayle finally spoke up. ''That was really uncalled for, Senator,'' he said forlornly. Bentsen gave no ground. ''You are the one that was making the comparison, Senator,'' he said, ''and I'm the one who knew him well. And frankly I think you are so far apart in the objectives you choose for our country that I didn't think the comparison was well taken.''

In the battle of sound bites that had come to be the yardstick of winning and losing debates in the television era, it was a clean knockout. Quayle kept standing at his podium, but he clearly was rocked by Bentsen's lightning punch, and he figuratively staggered through the rest of the debate. There was no question that the ''you're no Jack Kennedy'' line would dominate all coverage of the debate that night and for days to come. The retort was so devastating that the impression broadly held was that Bentsen had been programmed to make it, since Quayle had used the Kennedy comparison on the stump. But Bentsen told us afterward that the only time the matter had come up was during one mock debate with Dennis Eckart in Austin. Bentsen said he had remarked casually to Eckart that ''you're no Jack Kennedy and George Bush is no Ronald Reagan.'' The comment passed without any plan of working it into the actual debate, Bentsen said, and he used it in Omaha only because when Quayle made the Kennedy reference again ''it just finally galled me.''

In the Quayle holding room where his handlers watched, Canzeri remembers Mitch Daniels' reaction when Quayle made the Kennedy reference. "God damn it!" Daniels groaned. "We told him not to get into that." But one of the problems with Quayle, Canzeri said, was "an impatience of youth. . . . He's a fairly quick study, but [about] what he wants to hear. If he's interested he's interested, if he's not he's not. It's that immaturity and lack of attention. If he doesn't like it he goes away from it. . . . He was like a kid. Ask him to turn off a light, and by the time he gets to the switch, he's forgotten what he went for."

The Kennedy comparison had its genesis, Canzeri said, in the staff's quest for ways to deal with Quayle's youth as a point of criticism. "I even called up [Mount] Rushmore to check the ages of the presidents who were on the mountain," he said, "because I thought that would be a great backdrop for him to stand in front if those guys were all in their forties." Such was the lively imagination of the hired gun, circa 1988. "Then we were going to go to Independence Hall one time on the youth thing," he said, "because the framers of the Constitution, I think, averaged forty-two years of age, and they would have averaged thirty-something if it hadn't been one of them who was seventy-five at the time. . . . Then somebody came up with the fact, 'Hey, this guy's spent as much time in the Congress as Kennedy.' That's where that started."

Beyond that, Canzeri recalled, Ailes and Teeter were very big on the notion that Quayle could be a major draw with the eighteen-to-forty-five generation, in much the way that Kennedy was, and Marilyn Quayle also pushed the idea. "Ailes at one point wanted me to set up a deal where he'd be in a convertible and girls would tear off his cuff links," Canzeri said. "They really thought he was going to have this Kennedy feeling and charisma. . . . It might have sounded good in a meeting, but when you really thought of it, those things don't work, because the guy unfortunately does not have a lot of charisma. But the camera makes love to the guy. I never saw a guy take better pictures than this guy. But he looks twelve. He got his hair cut one day and we all died. He looked ten. But hers [Marilyn Quayle's] was the Kennedy thing."

After Bentsen's retort, though, "the Kennedy thing" was quickly deep-sixed, though it continued for weeks to be the brunt of jokes. ("What did Marilyn Quayle say to Dan Quayle after making love? 'Senator, you're no Jack Kennedy.' ") It didn't take long, either, for the Bush fire brigade to slide down the firehouse pole and get to the scene of the blaze. The morning after the debate, Rich Bond was on the Quayle press plane as we flew into Missouri to resume the vice presidential campaign, geared to secondary markets. Reporters gathered around him as he gave us the benefit of his insight as to what the campaign was really all about. "The way Dukakis wants to push the dialogue," Bond said, "is, 'Dan Quayle is running for president.' He's not running for president. He's running for vice president." That was literally true, but it dodged the "heartbeat away" factor.

Bond labored mightily that day, on the plane and in impromptu press conferences on airport tarmacs between flights to the next Podunk, to make the case that a vice presidential nominee should be viewed in terms of how qualified he was to hold a president's coat rather than fill his shoes. In 1980, he pointed out, Bush as Reagan's running mate never faced the kind of scrutiny that Quayle was enduring. But Bush clearly had the résumé and experience to satisfy the "heartbeat away" factor. At one stop, Bond commented in talking of Quayle's potential that he thought he'd be qualified to be president "someday." Only when he was reminded that Bush had said in looking for a running mate that his prime yardstick would be the ability to take over the presidency, and only when specifically asked whether Quayle was qualified to do so "today," did Bond—after an eloquent pause—say yes.

But did it matter? A poll taken in Cuyahoga County (Cleveland), Ohio, by Republican County Chairman Bob Hughes after the debate found that of one thousand registered voters surveyed, those who picked a winner named Bentsen by four to one. But when asked whether the debate would influence their vote, more than four out of five said it would not. So Quayle continued on his merry way.

On route to a rally that first post-debate morning at Missouri Southern State College in Joplin, Bond continued as designated spin doctor to operate on the press. Although Quayle didn't say so the night before, Bond confided, it was implicit in his answers that if tragedy struck he would carry out the policies of President George Bush. Sure enough, at the rally, Quayle explained that what he meant to say was that "the core of my thinking is this: There is no question that I would maintain and build on the excellent policies of George Bush."

Cornered by the awareness that he had not done well in the debate, Quayle revealed an intensified tendency to go on the attack. He charged that Bentsen, who had not been asked about his own qualifications in the debate, "waffled, shuffled, ducked and dodged." And, after largely ignoring Bentsen for weeks, he included him in his Dukakis-bashing. In the debate, he said, "the senator from Texas hid the fact that, if he continued the policies of the Massachusetts liberal, murderers would be let out on the streets and drug kingpins would not suffer capital punishment." Nor did Bentsen say, Quayle pointed out, although the question had not come up, "whether or not he would enforce a law which requires teachers to lead students in the pledge of allegiance to the flag." He sounded like a young Dick Nixon, Joe McCarthy or—in the great Hoosier tradition—former Senator William Jenner of Indiana, who with McCarthy majored in smearing liberal Democrats as unpatriotic and communists in the early 1950s when Quayle was still in knee pants.

Later, at a high school in suburban Atlanta, Quayle called the question about what he would do if he suddenly became president "inappropriate" but that he was "delighted to be able to take the heat for the campaign . . . to be the lightning rod." But still he struggled, and three days later, in response to a written question at the Economic Club of Detroit, he finally was more specific. "If it is an assassination," he said with visible irritation, "the first thing to do is you get on the phone and call the head of the CIA and see what he thinks it was. You don't convene a cabinet meeting right away. You call him. You get your secretary of defense, your national security adviser, your secretary of state, and you meet with them immediately.'' There would be contingency plans to meet various situations, he said, but "I'll tell you what. I'm not going to go out and hold a news conference about it. I'm going to put it in a safe and keep it there."

While Quayle was thus continuing to control the damage he had inflicted upon himself—and Bentsen had compounded with his deft performance—Bentsen blossomed overnight into the star of the Democratic ticket. Earlier, the Dukakis campaign had looked to him chiefly for help in Texas, but after the debate Democratic leaders around the country clamored for him. Typical was an appearance at Glaziers Union Local 252 in northeast Philadelphia. As the band thumped out the theme from *Rocky*, Representative Bob Borski introduced Bentsen as not only "a class gentleman" but the man "who taught young Dan Quayle a few lessons." The crowd erupted in cheers when Borski asked: "Didn't it feel especially good as Democrats when he protected Jack Kennedy's name?''

Bentsen himself, a man notably reserved and mild-mannered in conversation, did not hesitate to press his new advantage and celebrity. Quayle, he told postdebate audiences, "left Omaha with no forwarding address." And, promising that "we're going to open the Quayle season a little early this year," he asked: "Why do Republicans fear debates? For the same reason bologna fears a slicer." Perhaps Bentsen's debate success would not be critical in moving votes, but there was little doubt that his performance, and his energetic follow-up on the stump, was energizing many Democratic activists in important states across the northern industrial belt. And psychologically, after the long period of doldrums in which Dukakis had seen his lead in the polls vanish and turn into a deficit, Bentsen finally was giving the Democrats something to cheer about.*

Quayle and his wife, Marilyn, meanwhile, were growing increasingly annoyed at how they were being treated. They were resentful not only at the recurring press questions but also at stories that the Bush campaign had so little confidence in Quayle's ability to stay out of trouble that everything he said and did was orchestrated by his handlers, who were keeping him on a short leash. Finally, campaigning in Ohio, he issued a personal declaration of independence. "There's not going to be any more handler stories," he proclaimed to the traveling press corps, "because I'm the handler." He said he had just "got tired of all that bad publicity, so I figured it couldn't get any worse and I was going to take over." He admitted that "that so-called handlers' story, part of

*Two polls taken after the election suggested that Bentsen's presence on the ticket did make a difference, if not a decisive one, in the vote for the Democratic ticket. One for the American Medical Political Action Committee by Hamilton and Staff found that 43 percent of Dukakis voters surveyed said his choice of Bentsen as his running mate was a reason for their vote, and 41 percent said Bush's choice of Quayle was a factor. Exit polls by CBS News found that 10.9 percent of all voters interviewed gave the identity of the vice presidential candidates as a reason for voting for Dukakis, to only 4.3 percent who had that reason for voting for Bush.

it is true. But more than should be," he said, and he was assuming charge of his own campaign. "I'm Doctor Spin," he declared. If reporters had questions from then on, he said, "I don't want you to ask some aides. You ask me and I'll give you the answer."

Quayle, it turned out, had complained to Jim Baker not only about being excessively handled but about reports that staff aides were making critical, anonymous statements about him to the press. Baker said Quayle was "justified in being steamed" and said that "if I could find out who it was who criticized him they would be fired." But the notion that the Bush strategists, who knew Quayle was a problem child, would let him free-lance his way through the rest of the campaign was preposterous, and they did not. As for suspicions that Quayle's "declaration of independence" was a Spencer Special—that is, an intentional caper to combat all the stories painting Quayle as a puppet on a string—Canzeri would only say, with a wry grin: "I was told not to respond to that question."

A continuing problem for the handlers, though, was Marilyn Quayle. She always wanted to be consulted on everything, and wanted to go everywhere with her husband. She was put off when he was given a private tour of a super-secret Air Force installation buried in Cheyenne Mountain and she was excluded. The handlers were greatly relieved when they found that she was excellent in interviews and agreed to leave the campaign plane and go off on her own. Quayle's Senate staff aides were an irritant, too, because, Canzeri said, they kept encouraging their boss to campaign as if he were still in Indiana. Attitudinally, he said, "they never left Indiana in the whole campaign." There were those in the Bush campaign, indeed, who felt it might have been better had Quayle, too, never done so—literally. As a measure of the enthusiasm for the No. 2 man, according to Canzeri, the Bush campaign "never spent thirty cents of advertising on this guy" after his nomination.

For most of the eight days after the vice presidential debate until the second and final debate between Bush and Dukakis, the latest installments of *The Trials and Tribulations of Dan Quayle* kept much of the press spotlight on him. That focus gave the Dukakis camp hope that the "heartbeat away" issue would at last start cutting deeply, positioning Dukakis to make a dramatic comeback in his second encounter with Bush. Polling data, however, provided little encouragement for the hope. While voters seemed to have concluded that Quayle was a second-rater and Bentsen clearly preferable, they didn't make the connection that this judgment was relevant to their choice for president.

Bush in fact widened his lead over Dukakis in most public polls, and on the night before the second Bush-Dukakis debate, ABC News released its fifty-state survey suggesting that Bush had just about locked up the election. The Dukakis camp was irate at the poll—with, as already noted, ample reason. Donilon, Dukakis' chief debate coach and sometime CBS consultant, later called its release by his rival network "the most irresponsible journalistic act in American history, maybe." It helped create the impression that Dukakis would need a near knockout blow against Bush in the debate to scramble back into the race. In fact, according to John Sasso later, Dukakis had reduced a twelve-point deficit in the campaign's own polls to about five or six. "With all our problems we were still within striking distance going into that second debate," he said. "We had fought back. We were behind the eight ball, no question about it. We were fighting a rearguard action." But if Dukakis could put Bush on the defensive, he argued, he could still win the election.

The Bush-Dukakis rematch was supposed to be sponsored by the League of Women Voters, but two days before the Bentsen-Quayle debate it had pulled out, charging "campaign manipulations." As far as the campaigns and much of the press corps were concerned, it was good riddance, because the League in past sponsorships had been officious and irritatingly self-important. The bipartisan commission that had run the other two debates was asked by the candidates to take over and did, but not until after the League denied it the use of the hall in Los Angeles, the Shrine Auditorium, it had leased for the debate. The League wanted the commission to pay it not only a $40,000 retainer put down for the Shrine auditorium but an additional $50,000 in incurred expenses. The commission refused and instead obtained use of Pauley Pavilion on the UCLA campus. Commission officials speculated that the real reason the League pulled out was that it had been unable to raise the money needed to stage the debate. One thing was certain: the League, which coveted the debate sponsorship as a mark of its integrity and importance, by its action guaranteed that it would be out of the presidential debate business for the foreseeable future.

For this second debate, the tone and scope of preparations for each candidate were markedly different from the first. Bush came in off the campaign trail, Lake recalled, tired and a bit agitated about having to go through the mock debate drill again. The heavy issues briefing of the first debate was dispensed with. The candidate stood at his podium without jacket and tie and disposed of the jabs thrown at him by Darman, again playing Dukakis, and the panel of Pinkerton, Tutwiler and Teeter aide Craig Smith, with Lake as moderator. In two sessions, his coaches were amazed at his improvement over the first debate, and especially his toughness with Darman. The only special drill rehearsed was what to say and do if Dukakis demanded a third debate or tried to change the format by eliminating the panel.

Dukakis' preparation was also curtailed, but not so much out of confidence—although after the first debate he was sure he could handle Bush again—as out of the way he felt. The staff did not disclose the fact at the time, but said later that Dukakis was ill the night before and was running a fever the morning of the debate. A three-hour debate preparation session was canceled and instead he received only a briefing on the previous day's news developments before going to the hall for the usual light and sound checks. Then he returned to his hotel room and slept most of the afternoon.

But there were no complaints in the Dukakis hierarchy that he was not prepared; he was a bear for facts and one more briefing wasn't going to make a difference. He was particularly ready for a question on crime, aides said, because he had reviewed the answer thirteen times about his father being mugged and his brother killed by a hit-and-run driver on drugs or drinking, and because the issue was hotter now. "Bush had really raised the level of that issue since the first debate," Donilon said. "He had a lot more cop 'sea of blue' speeches. He had directly attacked Dukakis as not being sensitive to the victims of crime." And, Donilon noted, "they had trotted out the Barneses [the Maryland couple victimized by Willie Horton] in press conferences and raised the issue of apology, so that it was an even more salient and hot political issue at that point."

Donilon drilled Dukakis to think in terms of clusters of questions. No matter what the specific question was, Donilon told him—prison furlough, death penalty, victims of violence—"what he's saying to you is, 'You're soft on crime.' " And whatever the question, then, the answer should be the one carefully prepared and rehearsed.

Yet when that question came from CNN anchorman Bernard Shaw opening the debate in Pauley Pavilion that night—"Governor, if Kitty Dukakis were raped and murdered, would you favor an irrevocable death penalty for the killer?"—he inexplicably did not use the answer that could have squelched Shaw and showed Dukakis to be tough, passionate and compassionate all at the same time. Instead, his bland reply that "I've opposed the death penalty during all of my life," then citing how crime was reduced in his state without it and finally going into a short monologue on the need to fight drug traffic, left the audience, and Dukakis' strategists, aghast and baffled. The aides around him were at a loss to explain why he didn't use the ready reply, but not one of them deigned to criticize him. Donilon voluteered that he shared part of the blame for not getting "closure" on the issue with Dukakis—that is, not making absolutely sure that the candidate grasped the concept in recognizing "the crime cluster" and countering it as planned.

Dukakis never seemed to recover from that first question and disappointing answer. In the Dukakis holding room, his strategists watched disheartened but still hoping he would recover. As one of them said later, there were "eighty-eight minutes left and you only need thirty seconds to win a debate," but Dukakis didn't seem to have the right thirty seconds in him. John Sasso speculated later that Dukakis' first answer so "gnawed on him" the rest of the way that he couldn't really get back on track.*

The opening question to Bush from Shaw was also designed to be a shocker. "Now to you, Vice President Bush," he said. "I quote to you this from Article Three of the Twentieth Amendment to the Constitution: 'If, at the time fixed for the beginning of the term of the President, the President elect shall have died, the Vice President elect shall become President,' meaning, if you are elected and die before inauguration day—"

---

*After the election, Sasso said of presidential debates: "The premium not to make a mistake is too high in this business. The spontaneity is out of this thing. And we're all susceptible to it because the minute you make a mistake the networks lead with it. You can make the most brilliant policy speech, if you trip on the way up, that's it. So we all say, 'Whatever happens, just play it safe.' "

Bush broke in. "Bernie!" he cried in mock offense, drawing laughter from the audience and deftly taking the edge off the question.

Shaw continued: "—automatically, automatically, Dan Quayle would become the forty-first president of the United States. What have you to say about that possibility?" Bush replied that "I'd have confidence in him" and proceeded to spin off the same old qualifications Quayle had mentioned in his debate with Bentsen.* The rest of the way was all downhill for Bush. He easily handled questions on his no-new-taxes pledge while hitting Dukakis as a tax-raiser in Massachusetts, and he spun out his boilerplate answers on defense cuts, the deficit, defending Social Security, abortion and judicial appointments. He defended the tone of his campaign while in the same breath pinning the liberal label on Dukakis yet again. And he pointedly rejected as planned the idea— from panelist Margaret Warner of *Newsweek*, not Dukakis—of a third debate.

"No, I will not agree to another debate," he said firmly. "The American people are up to here with debates." He said he was "going to carry this election debate all across this country" in the remaining weeks, "and the answer is no, I am not going to have any more debates. We don't need any more debates." Dukakis rather weakly replied that "I can understand, after the vice presidential debate, why Mr. Bush would want no more debates." But he didn't bother to press the issue.

At the same time, Dukakis had to defend himself against a questioner's suggestion that "the American public admired your performance [in the first debate], but didn't seem to like you much." Citing his victorious campaign for the Democratic nomination, Dukakis offered that "I'm a reasonably likable guy" and said he hoped and expected the people would like him as president. But "I'm also a serious guy" who addressed issues "in a very serious way," he added. So much for lightening up.

Dukakis, as Sasso testified later, "knew immediately" after the debate that he had lost. And when he told Sasso coming off the stage that "I blew it," he was expressing the clear consensus of the audience in Pauley Pavilion, in the press area, in the candidates' holding rooms and in the living rooms of America. The Dukakis "spin doctors" circulated among the reporters afterward prescribing the customary dose of feel-good medicine about their candidate, but few were swallowing. The prognosis on Mike Dukakis' political health was now bleaker than ever, with only three and half weeks of campaigning to go.

---

*After the election, when we asked Bush what his personal reaction had been to Shaw's startling question to Dukakis, he replied: "Bernie asked me in that same debate how I'd feel if I died before taking office. Some questions are tougher than others. Some questions are more morbid than others. That's politics."

29

The Dukakis "Surge"

Michael Dukakis' disastrous performance in the second debate with George Bush took the heart out of the Democratic campaign. "What we needed was a five-to-seven-point swing," Susan Estrich said later. "We got it. It just went against us. We saw the floor fall in that weekend."

The Dukakis campaign was now threatened with political hemorrhage. New opinion surveys measured the damage daily. The candidate's "negatives" moved above the 45 percent mark, headed for 50 percent and electoral disaster—as television news programs screened over and over his failure to deal effectively with Bernie Shaw's stunning question. In the headquarters in Boston, there were well-grounded fears that leading Democrats across the country would begin publicly abandoning the ticket with three weeks to go.

On Saturday, after hours of meetings to agonize over alternatives, the Dukakis strategists took an extraordinary step. They described to reporters from the *Washington Post* what quickly became known as "the eighteen-state strategy" for pulling the election out of the fire.

The states, the Dukakis line went, were all ones in which the Democratic nominee was either leading or within close enough striking distance to be realistic possibilities in those final three weeks. Along with the District of Columbia, they represented 272 electoral votes, just 2 more than needed. The states were California, New York, Pennsylvania, Illinois, Ohio, Michigan, Massachusetts, Wisconsin, Washington, Minnesota, Maryland, Iowa, Connecticut, Oregon, West Virginia, Hawaii, Rhode Island and Vermont.

To that core group, the Dukakis managers added seven others, with 43 electoral votes, in which they considered the campaign still competitive. The seven were Missouri, Kentucky, Colorado, New Mexico, Montana, North Dakota and South Dakota.

The Dukakis camp's assessment of the situation was very much the same as that within the Bush campaign. Even during the last two weeks, the Bush managers ran commercials in Colorado, New Mexico, South Dakota and Montana because they believed those electoral votes had not been finally nailed down. But the Dukakis tactic was extraordinary in several respects. By identifying prime targets that could provide only the bare minimum to win, the Dukakis managers were confirming Lee Atwater's formulation that the Democrats needed to fill an inside straight—including Ohio. And they were conceding that the campaign was down the drain in some major states in which they had been claiming to be competitive—most notably Texas, the home state of their vice presidential nominee, and New Jersey.

But politics is perceptions and atmospherics, and the Dukakis operatives were convinced they had to give other Democrats a rationale for standing firm, and the press some reason to believe the election was not already history. As Charlie Baker, the field director, put it: "We felt we had to float the fact that there was a credible scenario." The "eighteen-state strategy" accomplished that much, if just barely.

Dukakis was called on to try to restore morale within the campaign itself. A rally made up largely of campaign workers was thrown together at Faneuil Hall in Boston for a pep talk from the candidate. His parents, he said, "taught me always to keep fighting for what I believe and to fight harder than ever when the going gets tough."

Bush, meanwhile, was trying to avoid either appearing overconfident or making the kind of mistake that would change the equation. Pressed by reporters in Denver for specifics on how he would deal with the deficit and the contra question as president, he made it clear that the last thing he wanted to do was talk about issues. "Now I'm having trouble with these questions," he said, "because they are putting me beyond where I want to be. And so, if I don't answer some of them from here on in, it is because I am focusing on November 8 and I don't want to be dragged beyond that because things seem to be going well now." Dukakis' efforts to rekindle the Iran-contra issue himself after postponement of the Oliver North trial had been so unsuccessful that the matter had not even came up in the second presidential debate. Bush was nearly home free, and he knew it.

Over the weekend John Sasso reached decisions on tactical and strategic changes in the campaign for the final three weeks. First, Dukakis would begin accepting, even aggressively seeking, more opportunities to appear live on national television. Quick appearances were scheduled on the *Larry King Live* program on CNN and *Nightline* with Ted Koppel on ABC. New advertising time also was put in the works—at least two five-minute network appearances, half-hour broadcasts if they could be arranged. Dukakis would be available for the *Today* show and live interviews with Brokaw, Rather and Jennings.

The more significant decision, however, was for Dukakis to move immediately to a frankly populist message—"I'm on your side"—to cast himself as the champion of average Americans doing battle against the candidate of privilege and wealth. "George Bush cares about the people on Easy Street," he said in Saginaw, Michigan. "I care about the people on Main Street. I'm on your side."

The campaign had been holding the populist argument in reserve for months, hoping to lay a groundwork of positions on specific issues—housing, health insurance, education, child care—that would give credibility to Dukakis' case for the presidency. "There was," Jack Corrigan said later, "always the plan to close with an 'on your side' argument." Sasso recalled discussions of the theme at the time he returned to the campaign on Labor Day. "We decided at that point, after the second debate, that we had to move. We couldn't wait any longer. . . . We were going to use it the last two weeks as a closing argument. We accelerated that a week because of the second debate."

But the Bush campaign was not sitting idly in the grandstand. On the same day Dukakis began using the "on your side" message, the Republicans began running their controversial but obviously stunningly effective commercial showing Dukakis in the M-1 tank. The ad proved to be singularly effective because it crystallized, if misleadingly, the picture of the Democratic nominee as a man too weak to be trusted with the national security.

Meanwhile, the Dukakis assault on "free media" was playing to decidedly mixed reviews. The appearance with Ted Koppel, intended to help repair the damage from the second debate, was, if anything, even less impressive. The candidate seemed to be listless, vague and legalistic. His own managers drew comfort from the rationalization that it was a late-night show with a following among insiders, not the mass audience of the evening news broadcasts.

Dukakis was doing marginally better, however, on the network news programs—in part because he had simplified his message, in part because he had been handed some targets of opportunity. Six days after the debate debacle, he scored strongly in Illinois, waving the vicious Willie Horton brochures distributed by Republicans there and telling a cheering crowd: "Friends, this is garbage. This is political garbage. This isn't worthy of a presidential campaign." That same night a new ABC News–*Washington Post* poll showed he had cut the Bush lead back to 52 to 45, nothing to crow about but at least a sign his campaign had not thoroughly hemorrhaged. A few days earlier other surveys had shown Bush's lead in double digits.

In New York on October 20, Bush and Dukakis attended the annual Al Smith dinner sponsored by the Catholic archdiocese to raise money for church charities and usually considered a command performance. Dukakis was in fine form, making the kind of self-deprecating jokes so prized at that traditional event. "Now, I've been told that I lack passion, but that doesn't affect me one way or the other," he said. "Some people say that I'm arrogant, but I know better than that. And there are even those who say I'm a technocrat, but it's less than 15 percent." The white-tied crowd packed into the Waldorf-Astoria ballroom rocked with surprised laughter. Maybe this guy Dukakis wasn't such a total stiff, after all. Bush's speech also made a hit. Gesturing to the audience in its formal finery, he called the dinner the equivalent of "a come-as-you-are party in Kennebunkport."

But Dukakis seemed snake-bit, even his best moments tarnished by problems. While he spoke in the ballroom, dozens of reporters in the galleries and pressroom buzzed with the latest: Donna Brazile, a bright young black woman holding a middle-level post in the Dukakis campaign, had been fired after accusing the Bush campaign of using "every code word and racial symbol to package their little racist campaign," and demanding that Bush "fess up" to rumors circulating about his personal life—rumors that proved to be unfounded.

As the campaign entered its final two weeks Dukakis continued to ride the "on your side" slogan that had now become the campaign's dominant theme. He used it repeatedly in every speech, adapting it to one specific after another. Campaign researchers had calculated, for example, that the reduction in capital-gains taxes Bush was proposing would have saved him $22,000 in taxes over the previous three years. "George Bush wants to give George Bush a tax break," Dukakis shouted to perhaps ten thousand people who packed a downtown plaza in San Diego. "He's on their side. I'm on your side."

At about this point the crowds turning out to hear Dukakis seemed larger and more enthusiastic in their response to him. The candidate and his advisers became caught up in what they saw as evidence of a "surge" in support that might carry him to an upset. Obviously buoyed by that crowd in Broadway Circle in San Diego, Dukakis proclaimed: "Either you're all crazy or we're going to win on the eighth of November."

The hard truth was that even candidates heading for political oblivion often draw huge crowds late in a campaign. Four years earlier Walter Mondale was greeted by cheering throngs through most of the final ten days of his campaign, and then was drowned in a tidal wave of votes for Ronald Reagan. And twenty-four years before that, even Barry Goldwater—facing a landslide defeat at the hands of Lyndon Johnson—attracted large and boisterous audiences late in the campaign. As an election drew near, more supporters seemed ready to participate in what they saw as a moment in political history uniquely accessible to them. But the size of crowds was a notoriously inaccurate barometer of what was happening in the electorate at large—particularly in an age when only the smallest fraction of the voters saw anything beyond what was on television.

Dukakis, however, was no less energized. "The final push was always planned," Estrich said, "but the emotion he found came from the crowds, the moment, the sense that [he could win]."

Dukakis also was convinced that there was a backlash growing against the tactics Bush had used, especially in exploiting the Willie Horton tragedy. Citing the Illinois brochures, he would demand that Bush take steps to remedy the situation. "When you throw garbage in the street," he said, "you've got a responsibility to go out there and clean it up." Moreover, he believed those tactics were a Bush smoke-screen he could blow away to expose the real differences between himself and the Republican vice president. "There's something going on. It's not just the sleaze, it's the reason for it," he told us in an interview at the San Diego Airport. "We've got to expose the sleaze for what it is. Second, we've got to address these issues."

The belief in the surge theory seemed to grow every day in the Dukakis camp, fed by the conviction that the harsh campaign run by Bush could be turned against the Republican nominee. Although Dukakis avoided accusing Bush directly of racism in the exploitation of the Willie Horton matter, others—including Bentsen and Jesse Jackson—were less hesitant. For one of the few times in the entire campaign, Bush found himself on the defensive, telling reporters on *Air Force Two*: "There isn't any racism. It's absolutely ridiculous, and everybody sees this as some kind of desperation move. . . . "

Dukakis was increasing ebullient, at least as he presented himself to the electorate. He preached the gospel of "on your side" in one rally after another as the bands pounded out Neil Diamond's "Coming to America." Holding a "town meeting" at Independence, Missouri, he was asked by John Truman, a high school sophomore, how he was like "my great, great-uncle" Harry. "We're a little behind," Dukakis replied, with Truman's uphill 1948 battle over Thomas E. Dewey obviously in mind, "but we're going to win."

Dukakis then went on to make another, most curious comparison between himself and the former Democratic president that suggested he didn't really understand why Harry Truman did upset Dewey that year. "People say to me every once in a while, 'You're not passionate,' Dukakis told Truman's descendant. "My memory of President Truman was that he demonstrated his passion by the things he did in public service. Once in a while, he used to get mad—at music critics of the *Washington Post*.* But he demonstrated his commitment and his passion by what he did."

That description of Harry Truman hardly squared with the picture of the tough little man from Independence who regularly railed at his political foes, often in salty language—and who engineered his victory over Dewey by excoriating a "Do-Nothing Congress" from the rear of his whistle-stop train across the country. It was the passion he unleashed openly that inspired listeners to shout "Give 'em hell, Harry!" and Truman to snap back:" I just give 'em the truth and they think it's hell!" Forty years later, Mike Dukakis may have been giving George Bush his version of Hades, but it never reached the hot intensity of Harry Truman's fiery blasts at his opposition that won the 1948 election.

Dukakis did have a considerable capacity, however, for righteous indignation. He showed it when President Reagan, campaigning for Bush elsewhere in Missouri, claimed that if Truman were alive in 1988, he would have been a Republican. That contention, Dukakis declared, was "one of the more incredible statements of all time."

The "new" Dukakis may have been mostly a product of the change in what he was doing every day—holding "town meetings," talking more often to the press, submitting to interviews with the networks. "It transformed him as a candidate," Kirk O'Donnell said. "As a candidate who's viewed as emotionally distant, he needed that contact with the press and the voters. He became a much better candidate. . . . What is he best at? Retail politics."

---

*This was a reference to a scathing letter Truman wrote to critic Paul Hume in response to a less-than-enthusiastic review of a singing recital of the president's daughter, Margaret.

Dukakis also found one more chance to answer, in only a marginally more effective way, that infamous question—this time in an interview with the man who had asked it, Bernard Shaw of Cable News Network. In a motel room in Youngstown, Ohio, Shaw opened the interview but before he could get started, Dukakis interrupted and brought up the matter himself. The exchange went this way:

Dukakis: "Lots of people have asked me about that question you asked me at the debate, and let me say that I thought it was a fair question, a reasonable one. I think it took me aback a little bit. And in thinking about it, had I had a chance to answer it again, let me just say this: Kitty is probably the most—is the most precious thing, she and my family, that I have in this world. And obviously if what happened to her was the kind of thing you described, I would have the same feelings as any loving husband and father."

Shaw: "Would you kill him?"

Dukakis: "I think I would have that, that kind of emotion. On the other hand, this is not a country where we glorify vengeance. We're a country that believes in the law and I believe very strongly in the law. But I'm a member of a family that has been victimized by crime and knows what it's like to feel the pain of crime. My dad practiced medicine for fifty-two years and was practicing when he was seventy-seven, when he was bound and gagged and beaten by an intruder who was looking for drugs in his office. My only brother lost his life in a hit-and-run accident where we've always assumed that the person who hit him was either drunk or on drugs. It's one of the reasons why I've worked so hard as governor of my state, not only to get crime down, and we have, by more than any other industrial state in this country, but to reach out to victims. And I guess, had I had to do it over again, that's the kind of answer I would have given."

That response was the one that had been so thoroughly rehearsed in Dukakis' debate preparations. He got it right this time, but much too late—and without the mass audience that had seen and heard his inadequate reply at UCLA earlier.

Going into the final ten days there was still no hard evidence that Dukakis was making a great deal of progress. Bush's negatives were rising marginally, but he still held a lead in various polls of between eight and fourteen percentage points. Bob Teeter saw some signs of movement toward Dukakis in his overall matchup numbers on the popular vote, but there was nothing to indicate it would translate into Dukakis winning all those states whose electoral votes he needed. Within the Dukakis campaign, the hope was that the candidate could pull close enough in those final days so that organizational superiority would pay off in such states as California, Illinois and Pennsylvania. And that again was a case of, first steal the rabbit.

There was, however, one subjective indicator that suggested some Dukakis progress. Bush was now clearly on the defensive and, on one or two occasions, Sasso thought, a little "rattled" by the building tension. In Illinois, the vice president lashed back at the "on your side" attempt to paint him as the candidate of the privileged. Dukakis was trying "to divide America by class," he said in a particularly cogent piece of political analysis. "I'm not going to let that liberal governor divide this nation."

Inside the Bush campaign there was some uneasiness. "We were clearly on the defensive the last two weeks and out of steam," Jim Baker confessed later. "We'd run national defense, we'd done what we could do on the environment, we'd done the social stuff in terms of law and order, we'd done economic growth and taxes."

The uncertainty in the Bush entourage became apparent a little more than a week before the election. Dukakis, riding a whistle-stop train called the *Surge Express* through California's Central Valley, decided to stop dodging the "L word" that had become a staple of the Republican repertoire of derision. "Yes," Dukakis said, "I am a liberal in the tradition of Franklin Roosevelt and Harry Truman and John Kennedy." Dukakis' managers were startled because such a declaration had not been part of the plan for the final days and some feared it might detract from the "on your side" message. But, several advisers said later, Dukakis had become angered by Reagan's claim to Truman and felt this was the proper way to express that anger.

At first, Bush brushed off questions about his reaction to the Dukakis concession that he was indeed a liberal. He was willing now to let his opponent define himself. But Bush's handlers, delighted at the opening, changed his mind. In St. Louis, Bush suddenly told a campaign crowd: "Miracle of miracles; headlines, read all about it. My opponent has finally—after knocking me in the debate—called himself the big 'L word,' called himself a liberal."

Going into the final week Sasso was flying by the seat of his pants, trying to reinforce the perception of optimism and keep his own troops energized. At one point, he suddenly changed the schedule and flew Dukakis into Newark Airport for a rally of campaign workers, confiding to the press that tracking polls now showed Bush's lead in New Jersey had been cut from sixteen to six points in ten days. It was a classic case of blue smoke and mirrors. When another Dukakis adviser said, "If we're only behind six points in New Jersey, we got a shot," Sasso shrugged and confessed: "I made that up."

In fact, the Bush managers had become a little nervous about New Jersey themselves—enough to schedule the candidate into the state for one last visit two days after Dukakis' stop. Atwater said the slump for Bush they recorded was partly a product of not having campaigned there recently, and partly a result of a sudden decline in the fortunes of Pete Dawkins, the Republican challenging Senator Frank Lautenberg. "There was a suction created when the bottom dropped out of the Senate race," Atwater recalled. "All of a sudden we started dropping." But the movement in New Jersey was less than a trend and the state quickly firmed up for Bush.

By the final weekend, all the data pointed to a Bush victory. California and Illinois appeared too close to call, and Michigan and Missouri were still not out of sight for Dukakis. But Bush had effectively nailed down Texas, Ohio and New Jersey and was at least competitive in Pennsylvania.

Lacking a miracle, Dukakis tried to substitute frenzy. He campaigned at a demonic pace, his chartered Boeing 737—dubbed the "Sky Pig" by less-than-admiring reporters—flying back and forth across the country. His itinerary on Saturday took him from Chicago to Detroit to Denver, then back to Rock Island, Illinois, Lansing, Michigan, and—finally—McAllen, Texas. Bush was "slipping and sliding," Dukakis insisted. "We're rocking and rolling."

Bush campaigned at a grueling but slightly more measured pace. And he continued to exhibit defensiveness about the Democratic attacks on the harshness of his campaign. "I'm getting sick and tired of my opponent's complaining about the rough and tumble of this campaign," he said in Los Angeles. "He seems to forget those personal attacks, night after night on me, on my character at that idiotic Democratic convention. Those twenty negative commercials that he produced and ran until he found out the American people weren't buying any of that. And all the last-minute attacks his squad are heaping on us. The American people are fair. They see through this last-minute smoke screen and so now all that's left is this daily whining about a negative campaign."

But Dukakis was not to be deterred. In the final forty-eight hours of the campaign he flew 8,500 miles, made campaign stops in eleven cities in nine states. In the last thirty-six hours alone, he crossed all four time zones three times—ending up by making his way back to Boston from the West Coast with stops in Des Moines at 4 A.M. and Detroit at 7 A.M. Arriving home in the early morning of Election Day, he voted and then took part in a series of radio call-in shows around the country in one last bid for votes.

Whether the "surge" was real or illusory was never entirely clear. Lee Atwater was convinced the notion was "bogus," largely something the press accepted too uncritically. "I never once saw any evidence in the data," he said later. "I couldn't find a real surge. . . . I didn't think this dirty-campaign stuff was cutting at all with the voters." Bob Teeter saw the popular vote getting "closer" but never threatening Bush's electoral-vote base. Tracking polls, published and private, showed a slight but measurable tick upward in Bush's negatives and a corresponding rise in Dukakis' favorable ratings. The final Hotline/KRC tracking had the margin at six points, two or three points less than a week earlier, six or seven points less than it had been two weeks earlier. Most of the final published polls put Bush's lead at about ten points, a slight drop in some of them over the final two weeks.

On election night, November 8, the returns that made George Bush the nation's forty-first president gave him 53.9 percent of the popular vote to 46.1 for Dukakis. The margin of 7.8 percent indicated there had been a slight tightening at the end, but Bush also had won forty states, Dukakis only ten plus the District of Columbia. Bush won 426 electoral votes, Dukakis only 112.*

The Dukakis "surge" had proved to be a ripple. But perhaps the ultimate irony was that Dukakis had managed to convey at least the impression of

---

*Dukakis ended up with 111 in the final electoral college count when one elector from West Virginia cast his ballot for Bentsen for president, Dukakis for vice president.

movement, and to win the battle for attention on television in those last two or three weeks, by stealing a page from Bush's strategy book. Dukakis had used a basic ingredient of the formula that Bush had employed to put the election out of reach weeks earlier—a simplistic message that tugged at voters' emotions and did not tax their intellect. Bush's was that Dukakis was not in "the mainstream of America" and Bush was. Dukakis' was that "I'm on your side." It was an appropriate end to the presidential campaign of 1988—a shallow appeal, tailored for the television sound bite, to an electorate that would not insist on something better.

At the World Trade Center in Boston, with wife Kitty at his side, Dukakis outwardly took the defeat in the matter-of-fact, no-nonsense manner that had marked—and often plagued—his long and finally unsuccessful bid for the White House. He congratulated Bush, saying: "He will be our president. We will work with him."

At the Brown Convention Center in Houston, with his wife, Barbara, along with a host of children and grandchildren, Bush celebrated his victory by observing: "A campaign is a disagreement, and disagreements divide. But an election is a decision, and decisions clear the way for harmony and peace." In other words, now that the battle had been fought and won, it was time to put the bitter past behind.

30

Anything Goes

Almost from the moment candidate George Bush became President-elect George Bush, he underwent a remarkable transformation. There were no more references to liberals from Massachusetts who opposed recitation of the pledge of allegiance in classrooms. There were no more references to Willie Horton and murderers being turned loose to rape and pillage. Nor did he have anything to say about card-carrying members of the ACLU.

The reason was all too obvious: President-elect Bush recognized as his first priority the need to cleanse the air of division and partisanship that had poisoned the political atmosphere throughout the presidential campaign of 1988. Only then could the act of governing responsibly in a system of divided partisan responsibility and power go forward.

The war for the White House against Michael Dukakis was over, and had been won handily. In the contest over which of the candidates could display the most American flags at his rally and hence was the more patriotic, the tug-of-war for the broad stripes and bright stars clearly went to Bush. Now it was time to put aside the weapons and the rhetoric of that war, and to dismiss or, in some cases, reassign the mercenaries who planned and carried it on. On the day after his election victory, Bush announced his first cabinet appointment. As widely expected, the commander-in-chief of his campaign army, James A. Baker III, would be his secretary of state. But the move was not regarded as narrowly political because Baker had been Ronald Reagan's secretary of treasury and as such had achieved a reputation well beyond the image of a political hack.

Two members of the original Gang of Six—the general staff of the campaign army—were also appointed to the Bush Cabinet. Nicholas Brady would stay on as carryover secretary of treasury from the Reagan administration and Robert Mosbacher would become secretary of commerce. Lee Atwater, the career political warrior, appropriately was put in charge of the peacetime army as chairman of the Republican National Committee. Bob Teeter was offered but eventually declined the post of White House deputy chief of staff and Craig Fuller, hoping to be made White House chief of staff, packed his bags and went into the private sector when Bush passed him over in favor of Governor John Sununu, who had performed so effectively under fire in the battle of New Hampshire. As for Roger Ailes, the other career political mercenary, he went back to being the most formidably tough Green Beret in the business, with bayonet fixed as always.

Others in the Bush campaign army were given lower-level posts or "warehoused" for the next presidential or other Republican campaign in the government, at the Republican National Committee, the GOP House and Senate campaign committees, in Republican congressional offices on Capitol Hill and in the offices of friendly political consulting, lobbying and law firms in Washington and elsewhere. By this means were the best and most experienced veterans of political combat kept available for the next war—a sort of political National Guard of the Republican Party that would facilitate rapid mobilization when the troops were needed again.

The election of George Bush had confirmed the importance and value of having such a standing political army, complete with a phalanx of combat-experienced veterans in command positions. Atwater's calculation that he had twenty-eight individuals in his campaign who had worked in three or more presidential campaigns underscored the point. At the same time, Bush's election was confirmation that the era of the campaign professional had reached maturation. The hired guns of the Bush campaign had taken an uninspiring, uncharismatic political figure long on résumé but short on vision, a man held in very low regard by the voters at the outset. And without the benefit of a national crisis or any rallying positive issue of his own, they had turned him into a near-landslide winner, at least in the electoral college.

Not since Harry Truman, widely pilloried in 1948, made a whipping boy of the "Do-Nothing Congress" and upset Thomas E. Dewey had that formula worked. In 1952, 1956 and 1960, personally popular candidates Dwight D. Eisenhower and John F. Kennedy won; in 1964 Lyndon B. Johnson was elected by voters scared to death of Barry Goldwater; in 1968 and 1972 Richard Nixon won in the stormy atmosphere of the Vietnam War and protest at home; in 1976 Watergate and the Nixon pardon delivered the White House to Jimmy Carter; in 1980 the hostage crisis and economic chaos did the same for Ronald Reagan, and in 1984 his popularity wafted him in for a second term.

The political mercenaries were in the field in most of these elections, to be sure, but they never achieved the dominance or the visibility that they had in 1988. They enlisted in both the Bush and Dukakis armies, and in those of all or most of the candidates for the nomination in each party. But the Democratic recruits were neither as well coordinated nor as experienced and effective as those who signed up for the Bush drive to the presidency. The best of the professionals who had worked for Bush's Republican opponents almost at once joined the Bush campaign when it became clear that he would be the party's nominee.

On the Democratic side, by contrast, the troops who had slogged along with Dukakis to the nomination circled their wagons defensively in a Boston fortress mentality that shut out or resisted offered or available transfusions of political talent, experience and energy. John Sasso, Dukakis' chief strategist, conceded in a speech before the World Trade Center Club in Boston after the election that "Democrats, with a long reputation for scrapping and then making up, in reality do not reach out well." He commended the Bush approach, observing that "a successful campaign is always reaching out—past hard feelings, even to defeated and bitter opponents."

Many of the best Republican hired guns of 1988 had earlier worked in the presidential campaigns of Richard Nixon, Gerald Ford and Ronald Reagan. But in those campaigns the conditions in the country, as just noted, were never as conducive to the political magic the professionals offered as they were in 1988. The issueless, charisma-barren campaign between George Bush and Michael Dukakis was ideal for the practice of their special art of public-opinion manipulation, and they had a field day.

It is important to note that the same campaign technocrats who gave the country the feel-good, "Morning Again in America" optimistic and positive campaign that reelected Ronald Reagan in 1984 just four years later gave it perhaps the most mean-spirited and negative campaign in modern-day American political history. Like the old out-of-work geography teacher who assured the school superintendent that, concerning the shape of the world, he could "teach it round or flat," these strategists-for-hire could "go positive" or "go negative," whichever was required to win.

In 1984, the Republican political general staff had an easy task. It had an incumbent president of immense personal popularity who with his own innate optimism had no trouble at all anesthetizing the American electorate. The happy circumstance of having the Summer Olympics in Los Angeles that year gave the Reagan strategists a convenient handle; they borrowed the popular chant at the games, "U.S.A.! U.S.A!" for the president's rallies and he told the dozing faithful that "America is back" and "going for the gold." The effort was made all the easier by a self-immolating Democratic candidate in Walter Mondale, who sealed his own defeat in his convention speech accepting his party's nomination, by forthrightly declaring that an income tax increase was needed, and if elected he would seek one.

In 1988, the same Republican campaign professionals faced a harder job. Their candidate through most of his primary-state victories and almost up to his nomination was a bland figure given to gaffes and subject to wide ridicule as a "wimp," blindly following in the shadow of the man who had pulled him from the waters of political oblivion and made him his manservant. He was regarded unfavorably by as much as or more than 40 percent of voters surveyed in various polls and nothing seemed to work to diminish that rating. The "feel-good" of 1984 obviously wouldn't do the trick this time around. Since their own candidate's "positives" couldn't be raised significantly, his managers had to "drive up the negatives" of his opponent. That would be a simple task against a man so little known by the voters. These skilled artisans of derogation, with a little research and a lot of imagination and ruthlessness, would have no trouble defining him as unpatriotic, soft on criminals and a risk to the very security of the nation.

One of the ironies was that the Republican candidate had a very strong positive case to make on the usually surefire issue combination of peace and prosperity. But so little confidence did his managers have in his ability to ride these legitimate issues to victory that they opted to construct a campaign of distortion, character assassination and division that would be a more dependable vehicle in which to ride over the prostrate form of his opponent to the White House. That campaign at the same time enabled Bush to finesse the truly serious issues facing the country, setting up a smoke screen behind which he was able to speak in vacuous generalities about "values" and avoid programmatic specifics that voters had a right to expect in a presidential campaign.

In "going negative" against Dukakis, Bush was also able to divert press and public attention from his role in the Iran-contra affair, making it easier for him to stonewall on it throughout 1988. Only after the election did the significance of this tactic become clear. Under court order in connection with the Oliver North trial, the government in early April, 1989 acknowledged that the Reagan administration had continued military aid to the contras through Central American countries in 1985 and 1986, in the face of a congressional ban. The 42-page government admission of facts, provided in lieu of the disclosure of classified documents, indicated strongly that Bush had taken part in efforts to funnel aid to the contras through Honduras under a quid pro quo of continued U.S. assistance to that country.

in a news conference, was asked three times about the matter and
̶ ̶ refused to answer on grounds he did not want to "prejudice" the
̶ ̶ ̶ ̶ ̶ ̶ ̶ ̶ . He said he would entertain no more questions on the matter. At
the trial's end he would say only—and defiantly—that there was "no quid pro
quo." End of discussion. The ability of candidate Bush to tap-dance his way
through the campaign on the matter, and then slam the door closed on it as
president, underscored the imperative of relentless questioning of a candidate
by the news media before the insulation of the Oval Office engulfs him. To be
sure, no amount of pressure from reporters was likely to force Bush to say
more than he wanted on his Iran-contra role. It probably would have taken
release of the government admissions during the campaign to force his hand.

The press in 1988, as in the past, took criticism for being too tough on
the candidates and not tough enough. In Bush's complaints about the news
media, and in his avoidance of reporters' specific Iran-contra questions, he took
a leaf from the book of Richard Nixon in the 1968 presidential campaign. Then,
candidate Nixon said he had a plan to end the war in Vietnam—but couldn't
and wouldn't reveal it lest the plan be jeopardized. He was peppered with
questions about it for months but refused to answer, until the reporters grew
weary of the exercise. In the end, Nixon was able to get through the whole
campaign without telling voters what he intended to do about the single most
critical issue facing the country that year. Similarly, Bush wore down the press
by stonewalling on his role in the biggest foreign-policy fiasco of the administration in which he served, and like Nixon made it to the White House with
his lip still buttoned, on that issue anyway.

At the same time, he was able to make Dukakis' patriotism a centerpiece
issue, with the American flag as its prop. When Bush talked about the pledge
to the flag and prisoner furloughs, he did so in terms of "values" as well as
judgment, implying a moral superiority over Dukakis. And in the process of
challenging the opposing candidate's patriotism, Bush and his handlers also
went about methodically poisoning the public mind toward the Democratic
Party's patriotism as well, in a fashion that had been going on at least since
the Vietnam War.

Protest against the American involvement in that war was equated with
lack of patriotism, and even disloyalty. The attack on Dukakis over the pledge-
of-allegiance veto played deftly on the public attitude fostered by Republican
candidates since Vietnam that Democrats, liberal Democrats especially, were
less patriotic than they. The insinuation inherent in the criticism of the veto
caught the incredulous Dukakis by surprise; he could not bring himself to believe
that the controversy over the pledge of allegiance in his state could be built
into a credible national issue to challenge his patriotism. But he was very wrong.

There was, accordingly, a certain irony, too, in Bush's reference to Vietnam in his inaugural address. "We need compromise," he said then, "we've
had dissension. We need harmony; we've had a chorus of discordant voices.
For Congress, too, has changed in our time. There's grown a certain divisive-

ness. We've seen the hard looks and heard the statements in which not each other's ideas are challenged but each other's motives. And our great parties have too often been far apart and untrusting of each other. It's been this way since Vietnam. That war cleaves us still. But, friends, that war began in earnest a quarter of a century ago, and surely the statute of limitations has been reached. This is a fact: The final lesson on Vietnam is that no great nation can long afford to be sundered by a memory.''

Bush seemed to be speaking here about the lingering ''Vietnam syndrome''—the continuing argument over the merits and quality of the American involvement in the war, and the reluctance thereafter to engage in further foreign adventures. The argument did divide many Republicans and Democrats, but it was the Republicans who ever since that involvement ended had used the liberal protest against the Vietnam War as evidence of disloyalty to flag and country. And in yet another irony, it was the Republican vice presidential candidate in 1988 whose enlistment in the National Guard in 1969 had raised a much more serious issue of patriotism—and hypocrisy—than did Dukakis' veto of the flag-pledge bill.

Bush himself dealt with the Dan Quayle problem by charging his critics with disloyalty, again using the flag as his symbol. In his speech before the VFW convention in Chicago, Bush proclaimed that while Quayle hadn't gone to Vietnam, ''he did not go to Canada, he did not burn his draft card and he damn sure didn't burn the American flag.'' Who did? Although the Bush campaign disavowed any connection with Senator Steve Symm's totally uncorroborated charge that Kitty Dukakis had once been photographed burning the flag, Bush's harangue carried the same basic implication of disloyalty.

After he was settled in the Oval Office, we asked Bush why, considering that he had the winning issues of peace and prosperity on his side, it was necessary to raise such issues against Dukakis as his positions on the pledge of allegiance, prisoner furloughs and the ACLU. He replied: ''Peace and prosperity were the winning issues. The issues of the pledge and furloughs were brought up because they are symbolic; symbolic of an approach to government that does not track with common sense. The governor said ideology does not count, only competence. I think ideology does count, and it was essential that the governor's very liberal record be put into focus. In the Democratic primary he ran as a liberal; then he tried to mask it. So we had to bring out his record—accurately but forcefully.

''A lot of issues come up in a campaign. Each candidate brings up some; the media raise others; still others rise up from the grass roots. I always believed I would win because I stood for peace and prosperity, for a kinder, gentler nation that set its sights on the coming century, a nation of limited government with emphasis on education and a more internationally competitive economy. The American people evidently agreed with me.''

After the divisive rhetoric in which Bush engaged on the stump in 1988, however, it was going to take more than a conciliatory inaugural address to make the Democrats forget the kind of campaign Bush ran against Dukakis, and against the whole Democratic Party. In the composition of Congress, with the Democrats' improving their margins slightly in both the House and Senate, Bush faced a constant reminder of one failure of his campaign, in spite of its obvious success. The Reagan Revolution, and Bush's election, had cemented the Republican Party's hold on the executive branch—winning the White House in five of the last six elections—but had not wrested control of the legislative, holding the Senate for only six years of the last thirty-two and never the House in that time. It was to this failure that Lee Atwater said he would address his efforts as Republican national chairman. Until the GOP held both houses of Congress and the presidency, and a majority of governorships and state legislatures, it could not lay claim to status as the majority party.

The split control of national power after the 1988 election—the Republicans holding the executive branch, the Democrats the legislative as well as a majority of elected offices at the state and local levels—guaranteed that the war would go on. There had been no true party realignment, yet the outcome of the presidential contest forced the Democrats once again to look at themselves and ask why it was they could not break what now seemed to be an iron Republican grip on the White House. For a long time they had convinced themselves that the problem was money. But in 1988 their fund-raising for the general election—more than $50 million generated by Bostonian Bob Farmer for use mostly in the states for grass-roots organizing for all party candidates—matched and possibly surpassed the amount raised and spent by the Republicans.

One reason clearly was that the Democrats had permitted the Republicans to paint them in caricature—too liberal, too free-spending, soft on crime and patriotism, dominated by eastern "elitists," still a tool of organized labor and—importantly, especially in the South—too black. And it was not just the Republicans. A fight continued to be waged through the 1988 campaign between the party's liberals and its moderates and conservatives over the best face the party should show to the country. The fight, conducted during the 1988 primary period through the candidacies of the party's presidential hopefuls, was not resolved with the nomination of Dukakis, a northerner too liberal for southern conservatives and not liberal enough for blacks and other liberals attracted to Jesse Jackson. The fiasco of Super Tuesday, rather than producing a candidate more acceptable to the South as intended, lifted Dukakis and Jackson and buried the chances of the one candidate, Richard Gephardt, who, had he been nominated, might have been acceptable to the region.

After the election, a fight for control of the Democratic National Committee involving the same factions produced more soul-searching and the first black, Washington lawyer Ron Brown, to become either party's national chairman. Southern white Democrats, all too aware of the party's steady slide in their region, greeted Brown's election with all the enthusiasm of a small boy confronting a plate of spinach. And at the same time, blacks dispirited by Jackson's failure to gain the vice presidential nomination and by a sense of being taken for granted continued to grouse. It was not the stuff of which a party comeback was likely to be made. In the South particularly, a way had to be found to appeal to culturally conservative voters without sacrificing the party's traditional commitment to social justice, and to activist government to pursue it.

The Super Tuesday experiment was not the only 1988 innovation that turned out unsatisfactorily. In Michigan, the Republican Party was so torn apart in the wake of its decision to move its delegate selection to the front of the political calendar that it moved swiftly, in conjunction with the Democrats, to restore the presidential primary for 1992. Other states that had advanced the dates of their primaries or caucuses were having second thoughts. And once again there was talk about regional primaries and of finding a way to deny Iowa and New Hampshire roles in the selection of the nominees disproportionate to their size and normal political influence.

Not surprisingly, Bush after the election saw nothing wrong with the process, the early start and—especially—Super Tuesday, which he said "has some merit." American campaigns, said the man who survived and won on generalities and negative attacks on his Democratic opponent, "allow voters to really get to know the candidates—to know what they believe and where they stand on issues. . . . As tough and as grueling as it is, I think our campaign process tests the mettle of any individual aspiring to the office of the presidency. And the test is taken in front of the voters. . . . Some say the campaigns are too long. But it's the people who will decide how long a campaign should be. They know when to pay attention and for how long. . . . Early start or late start, the system rewards the candidates with the strongest message. Candidates without a message are weeded out. . . ."

But money as much as message narrowed the field in 1988. The nominations of Bush and Dukakis added new weight to arguments that the candidate who raised the most money could win by waging a political war of attrition. Bush's foes had spent themselves out of the race by Super Tuesday and Dukakis' opponents fell one by one as their money dried up, until only Jackson, who had his own support system and was not dependent on television advertising or on winning to stay in the race, remained to challenge him. Dukakis' campaign treasury enabled him to suffer major back-to-back defeats in two large states, in the Illinois primary and the Michigan caucuses, and remain a front-runner.

And in all this, in both parties, the emphasis in 1988 was on the mechanics of politics rather than in the airing of substantive issues on which the voters would make a judgment on the direction of the country. Mechanics—and personalities. The rise and fall of Gary Hart, and then of Joe Biden, also crowded out serious issue discussion and centered much of the 1988 campaign on the candidates' "character." That focus in turn generated an increasingly intensive debate over the role of the news media in ferreting out details of the personal lives of candidates, and the relationship between the press and politicians. After a period in which fears of an era of journalistic witch-hunting were widely aired, those fears subsided, but political figures were newly alerted to the interest of press and public in their private lives.

Still another irony in this "year of the character issue" was the fact that

464 ☆ THE GENERAL ELECTION

very little was said or written about the character of a candidate who gave his hired guns a free hand to plot and implement a no-holds-barred campaign of negativism and distortion against his opponent—and then acquiesced in being the personal implementer of that campaign on the stump.

Of the role of the hired guns in presidential campaigns, Bush after the election allowed that "it can be overdone," but he insisted that the "ability of the American people to judge candidates on the issues and not, as many cynics claim, on the basis of imagery" was "consistently underrated." Campaigns, he argued, "are ultimately about ideas and leadership" and "no consultant can make up for a candidate who is deficient in these vital areas." Bush's own consultant-orchestrated smoke-screen campaign, however, convincingly refuted that notion.

Bush also expressed concern about "undue focus on personalities in place of the issues, and the importance of maintaining a civil public discourse," but he added: "Close scrutiny comes with the territory and anyone who runs for the presidency knows that. However, all too often innocent people—family members, for example—are caught up in the frenzy and that is a shame."

Magnifying the increased attention to the mechanics and personalities of politics, and the decreased attention to substantive issues, was the continuing dominance of the television medium over the entire election process. From the reporting of candidate activities and behavior in public and in private to the reporting of election results that substituted network exit polls for actual voting, television became the arbiter of what was important, and what was worth putting before the voters. As a result, the candidates and their handlers played as never before to the television cameras, devising their schedules and events with the objective not as much to make a thoughtful, persuasive case on an issue as to win airtime with an irresistible "sound bite." Gary Hart had a theory that a successful candidate had to reduce his message as his target audience got larger, until in a general election covered by network television he lamentably had to "get it down to bumper-sticker language."

On the occasions when a candidate did make a substantive speech, it could usually be topped in the competition for time on the evening news by an attack from the opposition—or a gaffe by the candidate himself. Dukakis recalled after the election how the one time he stumbled walking down the stairs from his plane in Chicago the picture made all the networks. "I really started feeling sorry for Jerry Ford," he said. "What was important was the picture at six o'clock."

Bob Teeter, in claiming that Bush had made a large number of very substantive speeches in the campaign, acknowledged that they seldom got much play, and that the Bush campaign learned that what he called "contrast" remarks—attacks on Dukakis—invariably were the way to get the candidate on the evening news. Teeter said also that a major reason Bush made speeches laying out his positions on issues rather than simply attacking his opponent was that Bush wanted to feel he was being a positive campaigner—while also going on the attack daily. Moreover, Teeter said, having the positive-issue speeches compiled in a book gave the campaign ammunition to use with reporters who constantly charged that Bush was running one of the most negative campaigns in memory.

That tactic was trotted out by none other than Jim Baker in a speech before the National Press Club on the Thursday before the election. He boasted of "a 347-page book entitled 'Leadership on the Issues' " that contained "over two hundred separate policy proposals" Bush had made during the campaign. "We issued that book for a reason," Baker said, "a reason which goes beyond the simple fact that we believe the public has a right to know what the candidates stand for." The reason, he said, was to make the point that "we *have* issued detailed proposals—on child care, on cleaning up the environment, on college savings bonds. . . ." But, Baker complained, "the plain fact is that these proposals do not always make the news. They have not been the major focus of news coverage of the campaign, which . . . has been dominated by the latest polling information, the most clever 'sound bites' and the sharpest barbs aimed at the other candidate."

Baker told of a television network producer after one Bush speech informing a Bush traveling aide: "We're not putting a story on tonight. You had no new sound bites. And you didn't attack Dukakis." If the press and public were frustrated "with respect to the candidates not talking substance," Baker said, that frustration was "matched in equal measure by the frustration of the candidates that the substance they do put forward is often lost in the noise." But who was generating the noise with all that stuff about flags, furloughs and the ACLU? Baker did not say. It was not the Bush campaign's fault, he suggested, that the sound bite had come into vogue.

"If summing up our case in thirty seconds or less . . . is what it takes to get on the evening news, then a winning strategy simply requires that we do so," Baker said. "It is simply a fact of life—not of our making—that the American people get most of their news from television's evening news programs." Besides, he said, Dukakis would not lose because of negative campaigning against him, but because he was "outside the mainstream" of majority thinking in the country. Why then not simply present the man and his positions straightforwardly, without the distortions? The reason, in the view of Bush's hired guns, was that doing so would not assure Dukakis' defeat. The thinking involved here was not fundamentally different from the notion that five presidential campaigns earlier had dictated the Watergate break-in—that whatever it took to win, and win decisively, should be done; nothing was to be left to chance.

Dukakis, who made a more diligent attempt to campaign on substantive issues, resisted pressures from campaign aides to go on the attack sooner and more often, and to defend himself against Bush's assaults on his patriotism. He told us after the campaign: "It might be argued I should have fired back immediately, but there would have been less voter participation"—suggesting voters would have been even more turned off by the bickering.

John Sasso, his chief strategist, acknowledged in a speech to the World

Trade Center Club in Boston after the election that Dukakis had erred in not answering Bush's charges "more quickly." But he conceded also that "our own lack of a central sustained theme created . . . a playing field . . . that allowed flags and furloughs to dominate." And it was likewise a mistake, he said, "to take for granted that voters will automatically assume the Democratic candidate holds dear the country's basic values: God, patriotism, family and freedom." Especially when Bush on the stump and in his television ads was insinuating the opposite. "Who would have dreamed," Sasso asked, "that Mike Dukakis, whose own father used to cry in his love for America, would be judged as short on patriotism? It's crazy." Crazy, but it worked.

Nevertheless, Dukakis suffered from a largely successful effort by Bush's strategists to suggest the two campaigns were equally negative. In one of the most transparent fictions of the year, Roger Ailes and Bush himself repeatedly suggested that their own attacks on Dukakis on the flag, furlough and other issues were merely answers to a negative campaign launched by the Democrats at their convention in Atlanta. They pointed to the "Where was George?" taunts by Ted Kennedy and others and Ann Richards' oft-quoted line that Bush was "born with a silver foot in his mouth" as the first shots fired. In fact, Bush had used the pledge-of-allegiance issue against Dukakis at least six weeks earlier, on the night of the last primary election of the season in California.

In a year in which there was a great deal of demand for "balanced" reporting of the election and criticism of the press for not striking that balance, it would have been inaccurate to report that the two campaigns were equally responsible for the tone of the campaign. The Bush campaign, as we have seen, made a conscious and critical strategic decision to define Dukakis in the most negative way possible as the most effective means to combat the voters' very negative view of Bush. Only when Dukakis' "negatives" began to soar as a result of this deliberate Bush campaign tactic was Bush able to cut into his lead in the polls and eventually pass him.

Dukakis, out of either conviction or naïveté, looked upon the fall campaign as an educational exercise. If he told the voters what he had done as governor, what needed to be done in Washington and what he intended to do when he got there in contrast to what the Reagan administration had done, he believed, the people would certainly elect him. George Bush did, as Baker noted, make proposals along the way. But at the same time his strategists threw up a smoke screen of attacks on Dukakis that drove those proposals from view, along with Dukakis' own positive ideas for a new administration. In the hands of Bush's hired guns, the concept of campaign as educational exercise crumbled before the concept of campaign as warfare, and Dukakis was gunned down in the process.

Dukakis for one refused after the election to blame the professionals. "The candidate always has control," he said; the question was "whether he exercises it or not. There's no such thing as a candidate not knowing what's going on. I don't see how you can argue that hired guns have taken over." Clearly, he was not letting Bush off the hook for the campaign he ran against him. Bush, for his part, continued to insist after the election that he had not run a negative campaign. "Ultimately campaigns are about ideas and leadership," he told us. "I enjoy the rough and tumble and vigorous debate as much as anyone and believe they can contribute to greater public understanding. Yet I am strongly opposed to campaigns that bring up a man or woman's race, religion, family or background, or campaigns indulging in innuendo or gossip. I do think it is proper to bring out issues that properly position a candidate on his record." And that, Bush's answer implied, was all that he had done.

Some Dukakis aides, such as Jack Corrigan, contended that after all was said and done, the election came down to a referendum on continuing the policies of Ronald Reagan, and that Dukakis could never win a contest so framed. But a post-election Gallup poll of 2,325 voters for the Times Mirror Company, publisher of the *Los Angeles Times* and other newspapers, concluded that the assault on Dukakis had been responsible for Bush's victory. "We find the success of the Bush campaign was based on making liberalism, the pledge of allegiance and the prison-furlough controversy salient, while at the same time making Bush vulnerabilities of less relative importance," the Gallup Organization reported.

When George Bush took the oath of the presidency at the Capitol on January 20, 1989, and repeated his vision, first expressed in his acceptance speech in New Orleans, of a "kinder, gentler nation," he was in effect asking for the American electorate to understand that getting elected required one George Bush, and governing the country effectively required another. He was telling the voters that the campaign could be discounted as a dependable guide to what his behavior would be in the White House.

But if a campaign for the presidency is supposed to provide the voters with the material with which to make an informed decision on the individual they want to lead their country, they should see the same one on the campaign trail as the one who eventually is sworn in and addresses them on Inauguration Day. That did not happen, and it is not likely to happen, as long as "Anything Goes" continues to be the marching song of the political mercenaries who, in Roger Ailes' phrase, "war-gamed" the presidential campaign of George Bush in 1988—and stand ready to do the same in the campaigns of the future.

Index

Abortion, 432
Abraham, E. Spencer, 87, 91, 93, 94, 95, 96
Adams, John, 370
Adultery, 205, 213
AFL-CIO, 296, 297, 299, 306
Agnew, Spiro T., 58, 67, 372
Ailes, Roger, 7, 9, 11, 14, 15, 74, 79, 112, 119–125 *passim*, 141–143, 155, 158, 159, 352, 378–379, 385, 408–411 *passim*, 422, 425, 426, 429, 430, 434, 441, 457, 466
Alabama, 42, 47
Alexander, Lamar, 374
Amdar, Sheila, 251
American flag. *See* Flag, American; Pledge of Allegiance
Anaya, Toney, 419
Anuzis, Andy, 95, 96
Anuzis, Saul, 92, 95, 96
Arafat, Yasser, 312
Arkansas, 42
Armandt, Lynn, 185, 196, 197–198, 201, 212
Arrington, Richard, 39, 281, 415
Askew, Reubin, 54
Atlanta (Ga.), 47
Atwater, Lee, 12, 15, 43, 69–74, 78–80, 88, 95, 103–104, 109, 111, 117–165 *passim*, 368, 375–376, 379, 385, 390, 406, 408, 416, 423, 429, 449, 454, 455, 457, 462
Austin, Jerry, 287–289, 294, 307, 308, 314–315, 319–324, 328–329, 336

Babbitt, Bruce, 220, 224–225, 227, 229, 246, 249, 254, 257, 265, 266, 270–271
Baker, Charlie, 12, 272, 275, 294, 418, 449
Baker, Howard, 31, 34, 69, 74, 78, 104
Baker, James A., III (Jim), 9, 25–31, 67, 74, 84, 368–369, 375–376, 381, 383–384, 390–391, 412, 423–430 *passim*, 434, 444, 454, 457, 465
Bakker, Jim, 72
Barkley, Alben, 370
Barnes, Angela and Clifford, 12, 15, 446
Barnett, Bob, 429
Barrett, Laurence, 178
Bayh, Birch, 389

Beatty, Warren, 195, 211
Beckel, Robert, 428
Bentsen, Lloyd
  advocacy of TV ads, 409
  debate, 437–443
  and gun control issue, 424
  selection as vice presidential candidate, 340, 343–350, 369–370, 416
  Senate election of 1970, 65, 71, 346
  as star campaigner, 443
Bergen-Belsen, 29
Berman, Mike, 419
Bettag, Tom, 118, 120, 122, 123, 124
Biden, Joe, 43–45, 115, 119, 137, 147, 175, 216–217, 230–254 *passim*, 463
Bieber, Owen, 299
Big government, 24–25
Bisignano, Tom, 252
Bitburg cememtery, 29, 30
Black, Charlie, 51, 69, 83, 100, 376, 382
Blacks, 462
  and Dukakis, 419–421
  and Jackson, 44–45, 318–319
  and Jews, 312–313, 316–317
  in Louisiana, 46
  in Michigan, 299
  in Milwaukee, 305
  and politics of South, 38–39, 414–415
Blanchard, James, 296
Bode, Ken, 182
Bond, Rich, 88, 91, 94, 95, 98, 99, 101, 106, 109, 125, 128, 129, 391, 435, 441–442
Bork, Robert, 34, 225, 230, 235–236, 242
Borosage, Bob, 288, 321, 322
Borski, Bob, 443
Boston (Mass.), 275
Boston Globe, 342, 360
Boston Herald, 275
Bottaro, Tim, 250–251
Bradlee, Ben, 209
Bradley, Bill, 222, 334
Brady, Nicholas, 74, 130, 379, 457
Branstad, Terry, 102
Brazile, Donna, 451
Breaux, John, 46
Broadhurst, Bill, 174, 176, 181, 188, 192–193, 196–198, 204, 212
Brock, Bill, 105, 129, 140, 143, 146–148, 150
Broder, David, 76, 407